Desktop KornShell Graphical Programming

Addison-Wesley Professional Computing Series

Brian W. Kernighan, Consulting Editor

Desktop KornShell Graphical Programming

J. Stephen Pendergrast, Jr.

ADDISON-WESLEY PUBLISHING COMPANY

Reading, Massachusetts   Menlo Park, California   New York
Don Mills, Ontario   Wokingham, England   Amsterdam   Bonn
Sydney   Singapore   Tokyo   Madrid   San Juan
Paris   Seoul   Milan   Mexico City   Taipei

Many of the designations used by manufacturers and sellers to distinguish their products are claimed as trademarks. Where those designations appear in this book and Addison-Wesley was aware of a trademark claim, the designations have been printed in initial caps or all caps.

The programs and applications presented in this book have been included for their instructional value. They have been tested with care, but are not guaranteed for any particular purpose. The publisher does not offer any warranties or representations, nor does it accept any liablities with respect to the programs or applications.

The publisher offers discounts on this book when ordered in quantity for special sales. For more information please contact:

Corporate & Professional Publishing Group
Addison-Wesley Publishing Company
One Jacob Way
Reading, Massachusetts 01867

Library of Congress Cataloging-in-Publication Data

Pendergrast, J. Stephen
    Desktop Kornshell Graphical Programming / J. Stephen Pendergrast.
        p.   cm. — (Addison-Wesley professional computing series)
    Includes bibliographical references and index.
    ISBN 0-201-63375-2   (paper : alk. paper)
    1. Kornshell (Computer program language)   2. Computer graphics.
    I. Title.   II. Series.
    QA76.73.K67P46 1995
    005.13'3– –dc20   95-387
                                                                          CIP

ISBN 0-201-63375-2

Text printed on recycled and acid-free paper.

1 2 3 4 5 6 7 8 9 CRW 98979695
First Printing, August 1995

To my wife, Victoria, and my son, Stephen.

Contents

Figures

Tables

xxiii

Program Listings

Preface

In early 1991, I wrote the first prototypes of a tool that would eventually evolve into the Desktop KornShell (dtksh for short). After a year or so I thought I was finished, having written a couple of versions of the tool itself, some manual page entries, and seven example programs. Then people started using the tool, and I learned a harsh reality: writing the tool itself is only a small fraction of the work. Writing manual page entries for every language feature is not enough either—that limits your audience to people who like reading manual pages, a dying breed. Writing a short tutorial gets you a little farther—now there will be a handful of people who can muddle through, but they won't be very happy.

What one has to do is write examples that cover virtually every feature in the language and also write a comprehensive tutorial. Undertaking such a project requires that one talk to many dtksh users to find out what they had trouble learning, and for what purposes they are using dtksh, and understanding the most common problems they are likely to encounter. Well, here it is!

Book Organization

Chapter 1 provides an introduction to Desktop KornShell, explaining typical uses, comparing it with other tools, and providing a glimpse into how the language works. Chapters 2 through 34 are organized into four major parts:

- Part I: X Programming Tutorial

  This part assumes you know nothing about X programming; it teaches you to use dtksh with a simplified set of programming utilities that is available free on the Internet (details are given later in this preface). This part of the book is meant to be read in chapter order; concepts build on each other in tutorial fashion.

- Part II: Advanced Programming

  This part goes deeper into X programming with dtksh. It uses the traditional X interfaces instead of the simplified utilities of Part I. Some chapters in this part assume you are a C language programmer, some chapters assume you are an expert X programmer. The presumed knowledge level is stated in the introduction to each chapter. You can skip around in this section; the ordering of most chapters is unimportant.

- Part III: Utilities and Applications

  Several larger programs are presented in this part of the book. Each chapter begins with an overview of the requirements of the application. Strategies to implement the requirements are discussed. Finally, the complete dtksh code that implements the application is presented.

- Part IV: Reference

  This part of the book contains chapters that are meant mainly as reference materials. Many of the chapters in this part are not meant to be read page for page; they contain alphabetical summaries of commands and are meant to be used as a reference during program development. The first two chapters are an exception: Chapter 28, *KornShell Language Review*, and Chapter 29, *KornShell Style Guide*. Those two chapters are tutorial in nature and contain information about the base KornShell language used for dtksh.

How to Use This Book

There are two main audiences for this book: experienced shell programmers who want to learn X graphics programming, and experienced C (or C++) language X programmers. The following sections outline the needs of these different types of readers and suggest ways to use this book to meet those needs.

Notice that I didn't mention people who know neither shell programming nor X. That was deliberate. No book can be all things to all people, and this one is no exception. Teaching shell programming from scratch is out of bounds for this book. That subject really requires a book of its own, and there are several excellent ones already out there (see the Bibliography). So, if you know absolutely nothing about shell programming, I advise you to start with a more basic tutorial before continuing here.

Experienced Shell Programmers

These people can write shell scripts in their sleep, but they may know little or nothing about X Window and Motif programming. They're often system administrators, integrators, or even sophisticated end users. They may need to learn KornShell features if they are primarily Bourne shell or csh programmers. Even if they are already familiar with KornShell, they probably need to learn the new KornShell-93 features since those are the latest innovations. They usually need a lot of tutorial information on graphics programming. Finally, they want examples—lots of examples.

Readers who are knowledgeable in some shell other than KornShell should carefully study Chapter 28, *KornShell Language Review*. KornShell is syntactically different from csh, and has many extensions beyond Bourne shell.

Readers who are KornShell programmers should still scan Chapter 28, *KornShell Language Review*, looking for the KornShell-93 New Feature symbol shown here. It denotes parts of the KornShell language that are new with the latest version (on which dtksh is based). Some of these features are highly useful for graphics programming. Chapter 31, *KornShell Command Reference*, also uses this icon to highlight commands that are new or changed in KornShell-93.

> KSH93

The shell-knowledgeable reader should then read the X and Motif tutorial chapters (in Part I). These chapters do not assume any prior X experience and should be absorbed carefully. If possible, a system with dtksh installed should be nearby so the reader can experiment with the example programs. Nothing can substitute for hands-on experience when learning graphics programming. The example programs can be obtained over the Internet, so you don't have to type them in (see later section on *Obtaining the Example Programs*).

A first-time X programmer can skip Part II on first reading. These chapters contain advanced material and sometimes assume the reader is X and C literate.

Experienced X Programmers

These people usually know how to write shell scripts too, but they may not be used to thinking of the shell language as a powerful graphical programming language. They might need some refresher material on shell programming. They don't need tutorials on basic X terminology or concepts, but they do need to know how X Window functions were mapped into the dtksh language from the C language, and they need to know what features in X are not currently supported by dtksh. And they too want examples—lots of examples.

These readers should study Chapter 28, *KornShell Language Review*, especially if they are not experts in shell programming or use a shell other than KornShell. If they are very fond of the traditional X function names and arguments, such readers should probably skip right over Part I of this book (which presents a simplified interface) and proceed to Part II. Part II begins with Chapter 17, *Traditional X Commands*, which is a summary of how the X functions are provided by dtksh.

Typeface Conventions

This book follows these typeface conventions:

- A `computer typeface` font is used in the programming examples. In the main body of text, this font is also used to denote dtksh functions, built-in commands, and other programming elements.

- A `computer typeface italic` font is used to denote parts of a command that the programmer can choose. Words using this font are merely place-holders; the programmer would not type them in literally. For example, the following specification

  ```
  typeset [options] variable[=value]
  ```

  indicates that `typeset` and `=` are literal strings, whereas `options, variable`, and `value` are symbolic and could vary. Also note the usual use of brackets to indicate optional items in syntax summaries.

Other Conventions

References to books in the Bibliography are presented in brackets, and give the last names of each author and the year. The Bibliography at the end of the book lists entries alphabetically by first author. For example:

See [Bolsky and Korn 1995] for more details on KornShell programming.

Technical and historical notes, parenthetical remarks, and anecdotes are presented using an indented paragraph in a small typeface. For example:

> The main body of the text presents tutorial material; there are times, however, when technical fine points need to be presented for completeness. Instead of using footnotes, this book uses an indented, small–font paragraph for these items. You can skip them if you are not interested in such details.

Obtaining the Example Programs

Most readers want examples because that's the easiest way to learn. This book has literally hundreds of examples to satisfy this need. Some examples are short—perhaps only one or two lines—and some span several pages. But whether short or long, each one is included to illustrate directly and concretely a point made nearby in the main text.

The tutorial chapters (Part I) illustrate every Motif graphical object with one or more example programs. The chapters in Part III contain several longer examples that show commonly used techniques for combining several graphical objects.

You can obtain the source code for all these examples without cost if you have access to the Internet. Just use the `ftp` program to contact the Addison-Wesley anonymous file server as follows:

- `ftp` to the machine `aw.com`
- Log in as `anonymous`. Give your email address as the password.
- Change to the directory containing information about this book:
  ```
  cd /aw.prof.computing.series/pend.dtksh
  ```

- Prepare for binary transmission:

  ```
  binary
  ```
- Execute the command:

  ```
  mget examples.tar.Z
  ```
- Use `quit` to exit `ftp`. You are now back at the UNIX shell prompt.
- Use the UNIX `uncompress` command on the file:

  ```
  uncompress examples.tar.Z
  ```
- Use the UNIX `tar` command to unpack the directory:

  ```
  tar xfv examples.tar
  ```

After following this procedure, you will have a directory called `dtksh.examples`. See the `README` file in that directory for further instructions.

If you do not understand how to use the `ftp` program or the other programs mentioned, ask your system administrator for help or consult UNIX documentation.

A Note on Examples

Every figure and program listing in this book that references an example program contains the name of that program; in this way you can easily figure out which program to run as you follow the text. Before running examples in Part I of this book, you need to set and export the environment variable `XUTILDIR` to be a full path to the `dtksh.examples` directory you unpacked. For example, if you unpacked the `tar` file in your `$HOME` directory, then you would do the following:

```
XUTILDIR=$HOME/dtksh.examples
export XUTILDIR
```

Acknowledgments

This book was a massive effort, requiring the same amount of time to write as the gestational period of the woolly mammoth. Coincidentally, the weight of a newborn woolly mammoth is approximately the same as the weight of the paper used to print the dozens of drafts of this book, which were tirelessly and thoroughly reviewed by many dedicated professionals. Without their help, this project would long since have become extinct.

Foremost, I must give credit to my wife Victoria. Besides having to put up with a husband who set up an entire computer center in the kitchen for 17 months (including two computers, a laser printer, and a dozen thick reference manuals strewn on every available horizontal surface), she provided me with constant support and encouragement.

David Korn, inventor of the KornShell, was instrumental in making dtksh a reality. He was amazingly responsive to requests for features and changes to the KornShell-93 architecture, many of which were directly for the benefit of dtksh. In addition, he answered many questions about KornShell architecture and provided me with valuable comments on this book, as well as prerelease versions of his own book on KornShell-93 [Bolsky and Korn 1995]. David also introduced me to John Wait at Addison-Wesley, who, it turns out, was the ideal editor for this work.

Betty Dall, lead engineer of the Common Desktop Environment Motif toolkit subsystem, provided insightful comments on the early versions of this manuscript and invaluable technical advice. In addition, she wrote and formatted most of Chapter 34, *Motif Widget Reference*, when my wrists (and wits!) started to give out near the end of this project.

David L. Beckedorf, of DLB Research, Inc., was one of the most thorough reviewers I have ever come across. His suggestions ranged from pure grammatical corrections, to fine points of word usage, to highly technical suggestions about X Window System programming. David is a multitalented individual, to be sure.

Bill Baker, of Novell, Inc., tested every single one of the more than 100 example programs to make sure they did what I claimed they did.

Other very useful comments were provided by Louis Iacona, Hok Chun Lee, Terri Laird, Steve Humphrey, Steve Zwaska, Joe Veach, Donald McMinds, Hao Wei Liu, Eric Wallengren, and Ming Gao.

The people at Addison-Wesley were terrific. John Wait took a chance on a new author and patiently answered my frequent questions about how to go about producing this book. His assistant, Kathleen Duff, was quick to offer assistance and support when I needed a fax, overnight delivery, or a contact for advice. Mike Hendrickson kept me on schedule and approved my weird production requests (Bookmark ribbons in the spine? Michelangelo cover art? No problem!). Marty Rabinowitz and the other folks in the production department offered sage advice on formatting. Lorretta Palagi and Hope Steele did a great job copy editing, and W. Richard Stevens provided advice culled from his vast writing experience. Finally, the index was prepared by the folks at Northwind Editorial.

I was fortunate indeed to find this group of talented people willing to spend so much time helping me produce this work. Any errors are, of course, solely my responsibility.

Readers are encouraged to send any suggestions or comments for future revisions of this work to me using electronic mail at the address shown below.

J. Stephen Pendergrast, Jr.
stevepe@aw.com   May 1995

1 *Introduction*

1.1 What Is the Desktop KornShell?

The Desktop KornShell (dtksh) is an extended version of the popular KornShell programming language. It contains new built-in commands that allow you to create and manage Motif graphical objects and to create friendly, graphical shell scripts. Because dtksh is a powerful interpreted language you can create programs in a fraction of the time it would take to create them in a compiled language such as C.

```
Desktop KornShell = KornShell-93 + X Graphics
```

The dtksh interpreter is a standard part of the Common Desktop Environment (CDE) specification. This specification has been adopted by every major UNIX system vendor, so you can be sure dtksh will be widely available, allowing you to write scripts that will run unchanged on a variety of UNIX systems and different vendors' hardware.

In addition to Motif graphical extensions, dtksh contains a number of new commands that allow it to access other aspects of the Common Desktop Environment. For example, there are new built-in commands that bring up CDE help system screens, communicate to other applications using the CDE ToolTalk communication service, and access internationalized message catalogs. There are also commands that allow you to attach compiled C code to the dtksh process and create your own custom extensions.

Dtksh is based on the latest version of KornShell, and it contains new programming constructs such as floating-point math, associative arrays, a C style `for` loop, and other additions. These features make dtksh a rich language you can use to write industrial-strength applications with confidence.

Figure 1-1. Output of loan.sh. The same output is also produced by
`xuloan.sh`. This simple program illustrates a typical use of dtksh: providing a
friendly front end that prompts the user for a few pieces of information and then
performs some action.

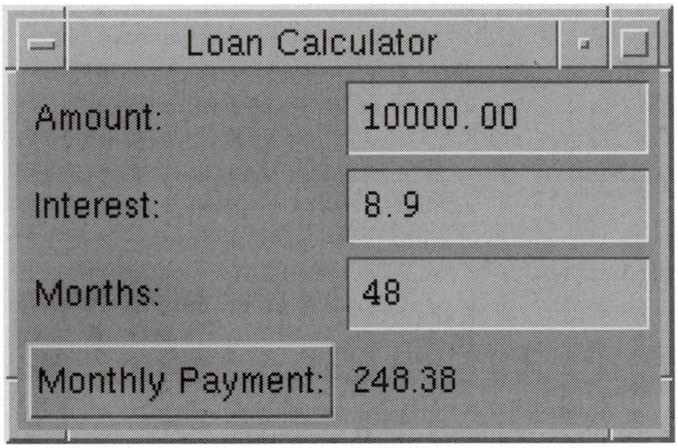

What Does a Graphical Shell Script Look Like?

As shipped by the CDE vendors, dtksh provides new built-in commands that
directly correspond to the raw X Window and Motif graphics functions. For an
experienced X programmer, this is wonderful—such experts can use the same commands they are familiar with from writing C language Motif programs. For the traditional shell programmer, however, these interfaces tend to be too low level and
can be daunting. To meet the needs of the novice graphics programmer, this book
contains a complete set of simple, consistent utilities that are suitable for a wide
range of programming tasks. These utilities are written as shell functions, the text
of which is provided in the Cookbook section. You needn't type them from scratch,
they are provided for free on the Internet. For details, see *Obtaining the Example
Programs* on page xxxii.

Part I of this book is devoted to this simplified interface and assumes the reader
knows nothing about X or Motif. Part II is geared toward experienced X program-

mers or programmers who want to learn the "raw" X interfaces for advanced programming tasks after they have mastered Part I.

Listings 1-1 and 1-2 provide an example of the difference between the two programming interfaces. You don't need to understand what every line of code does at this point. These programs are merely presented to give you a feel for how X programs look, the next chapter gets into the details. Both listings implement a simple program that prompts the user for a few pieces of loan information and then calculates and displays the monthly payment amount. The running program is shown in Figure 1-1.

Listing 1-1. Simplified X Functions (xuloan.sh). The simplified utilities were used to produce this program. Note the consistent XU (X Utilities) prefix on all function names. All the chapters in Part I of this book uses this simplified interface exclusively.

```
. $XUTILDIR/xutil.sh          # Load utility functions

function CalculateCB {
    float amount interest
    float result
    integer months

    # calculate and display the monthly payment

    XUget $AMOUNT value:amount
    XUget $INTEREST value:interest
    XUget $MONTHS value:months
    (( interest = interest/1200 ))   # monthly percentage
    (( result = (interest / \
        (1-(exp(log(1+interest)*(0-months)))))*amount ))
    XUset $PAYMENT \
        labelString:"$(printf "%.2f" result)"
}

XUinitialize TOPLEVEL LoanCalc "$@" \
    -title "Loan Calculator"

XUcolumn COL $TOPLEVEL  # A column stacking parent

# Create the fields for prompting and showing results

XUaddmoneyfields $COL AMOUNT "Amount:" 12
XUaddfloatfields $COL INTEREST "Interest:" 12
XUaddintegerfields $COL MONTHS "Months:" 12

# Create a button to calculate the result

XUaddbuttons $COL CALCULATE "Monthly Payment:" "CalculateCB"
```

```
XUlabel PAYMENT $COL labelString:" "

XUalign2col $COL      # align fields in 2 columns

XUrealize $TOPLEVEL
XUmainloop       # go into a loop processing input
```

Listing 1-1 uses the simplified interface to create the application, whereas Listing 1-2 shows how the program is written using traditional X function calls.

One thing that should be made perfectly clear is that you can use both the simplified X utility interface and the traditional X function calls in the same program. Think of the simplified interface as merely a layer of sugar coating on top of the traditional X interfaces. Also, while designing this set of utilities I tried to be consistent with the traditional X functions and terminology so those of you who go on to learn the traditional calls won't have to unlearn any material.

Listing 1-2. Traditional X Functions (loan.sh). By contrast, this version of the same program uses the traditional X functions. This style of programming is used in Part II of this book, and is more suitable for X experts or programmers who want to create advanced graphics programs. Note the more complex function calls, with more arguments. This version also has less functionality than the version written with the XU library; it performs less error checking, for example.

```
function CalculateCB {
    float amount interest
    float result
    integer months

    XtGetValues $AMOUNT value:amount
    XtGetValues $INTEREST value:interest
    XtGetValues $MONTHS value:months
    (( interest = interest/1200 ))  # monthly percentage
    (( result = (interest/ \
        (1-(exp(log(1+interest)*(0-months)))))*amount ))
    XtSetValues $PAYMENT \
        labelString:"$(printf "%.2f" result)"
}

XtInitialize TOPLEVEL loancalc LoanCalc "$@" \
    -title "Loan Calculator"

# A row stacking parent with two columns (note: we
# must set numColumns to 4, not 2, to achieve this)
XtCreateManagedWidget COL COL XmRowColumn $TOPLEVEL \
    orientation:horizontal numColumns:4 packing:PACK_COLUMN

# Create the fields for prompting and showing results
```

```
XtCreateManagedWidget AMOUNTLABEL AMOUNTLABEL XmLabel $COL \
    labelString:"Amount:"
XtCreateManagedWidget AMOUNT AMOUNT XmTextField $COL

XtCreateManagedWidget INTLAB INTLAB XmLabel $COL \
    labelString:"Interest Rate:"
XtCreateManagedWidget INTEREST INTEREST XmTextField $COL

XtCreateManagedWidget MONTHLAB MONTHLAB XmLabel $COL \
    labelString:"Months:"
XtCreateManagedWidget MONTHS MONTHS XmTextField $COL

# Create a button to calculate and display the result

XtCreateManagedWidget CALCULATE CALCULATE XmPushButton $COL \
    labelString:"Monthly Payment:" mnemonic:C
XtAddCallback $CALCULATE activateCallback "CalculateCB"
XtCreateManagedWidget PAYMENT PAYMENT XmLabel $COL labelString:" "

XtRealizeWidget $TOPLEVEL
XtMainLoop       # go into a loop processing input
```

1.2 Applications Suitable for DTKSH

Traditionally, shell languages have been used for administration, installation, and simple application programming. Shell scripts are suited to these tasks for several reasons. The shell is very good at spawning other UNIX processes, connecting one process to another, and capturing and filtering output. Shell languages also contain programming constructs for prompting, printing output, manipulating variables, looping, and conditional execution. Also, because the shell is interpreted and not overly concerned about variable types, writing simple programs is fast—far faster than writing in C or other compiled languages.

Before dtksh, UNIX shell languages were strictly line oriented, so in the new world of friendly graphical UNIX the usefulness of the shell for tasks like simple user applications and administration was fading. Dtksh restores the ability of an interpreted shell to handle these kinds of applications.

Here's a simple rule of thumb for those of you old enough to remember line-oriented UNIX:

> *Use dtksh for the same kinds of programs in the new graphical world for which you might have used line-oriented shell in the old line-oriented world.*

This includes administrative scripts, simple end-user applications, and automating tasks you need to perform day to day. If you use existing line-oriented shell scripts now, you might even be able to convert them into graphical applications by adding some code and running them under dtksh. This is possible because dtksh is a superset of the standard KornShell. Such a conversion might be hard or easy depending on how the existing script is organized, but it is unlikely to require a complete rewrite.

The program illustrated in Figure 1-1 is just one small piece of a larger application that will be developed throughout Part I—it implements a checkbook handling application. Each piece is built up from scratch to illustrate some aspect of the dtksh programming interface. Figure 1-2 shows some other screens from that and other programs developed in this book.

Rapid Development

Dtksh is also useful for some kinds of programs, such as demonstration software, for which line-oriented shells weren't suited. A line-oriented demonstration isn't going to be useful if your aim is to excite a potential customer. Dtksh is great for this kind of application, because of the rapid development cycle and the ability to customize such demonstrations in the field in a short time.

For example, I once wrote a distributed database front end using dtksh; the demonstration was directed toward the retail industry. A few weeks later, I needed a similar demonstration but wanted to target the banking industry. The changes to my dtksh scripts only took about half an hour, which would have been impossible if that demonstration had been written in the C language. In C there would have been about four times as much code to change, time wasted compiling the code, and cryptic core dumps instead of useful error messages—all of which would have added up to much lower programmer productivity.

Application Size

While there is no particular limit to the size of a dtksh application, dtksh is usually used for applications with between 100 and 1000 lines of code. If you plan to write an application much larger than a few hundred lines of code, you would be well advised to follow consistent coding standards. Even if you are writing short programs, getting in the habit of following a consistent style will aid your efforts. See Chapter 29, *KornShell Style Guide*, for some recommended practices.

1.3 Relationship to Other Tools

There are several other tools available as freeware or shareware that bear some resemblance to dtksh. The most popular of these as of this writing are TCL/TK and WCL. Both of these are interpreted languages that can be used to write X programs. Both of them are freely available over the Internet (which is not the case for dtksh, although dtksh is expected to become a standard part of most UNIX systems).

Besides these freely available tools, dtksh bears a great resemblance to its predecessor, wksh, which is mainly shipped with the Novell UnixWare version of UNIX.

Figure 1-2. Some Example Screens.   All of the screens below are taken from examples that are explained later in this book. As you can see, dtksh can be used for many different purposes.

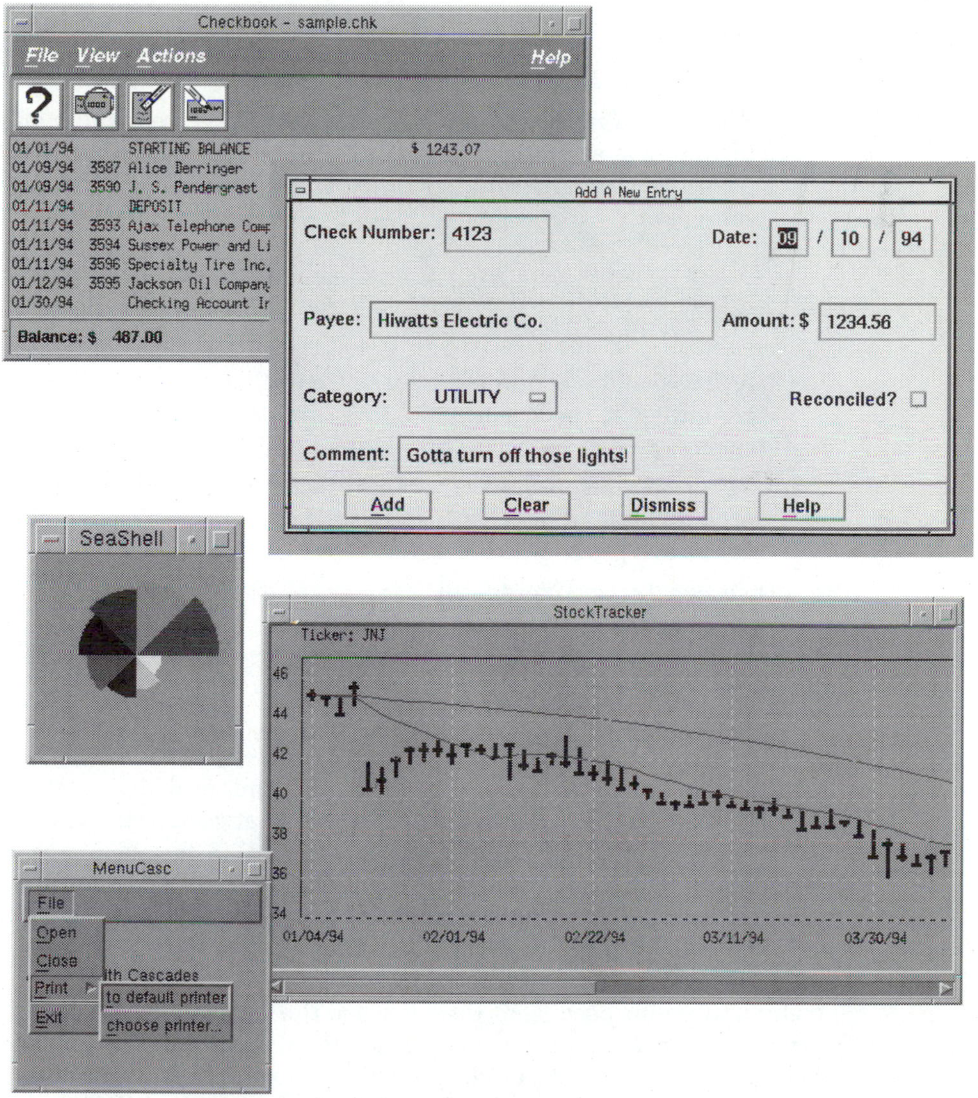

WKSH

Dtksh is based on a tool called wksh. The main differences between dtksh and wksh are as follows:

- Wksh is based on the older KornShell-88, whereas dtksh is based on Korn-Shell-93. KornShell-93 has many additional features over KornShell-88, such as associative arrays, floating-point math, POSIX compliance, and others. Thus, dtksh has all those feature advantages over wksh.

- Dtksh has far better coverage of Motif functions than wksh, and has extensive coverage of CDE interfaces such as the help system and ToolTalk that wksh lacks. Dtksh also has superior internationalization features.

- Wksh has a facility to call C functions directly from shell without first registering them as built-in commands. Dtksh does not have this feature, but it does allow the programmer to register a C function as a new built-in command.

    > A C function must have `argc`, `argv` style arguments to be registered as a new built-in command. There are some other restrictions as well, which are discussed in Chapter 23, *Attaching C Code*.

- A few commands differ in syntax from wksh to dtksh. Also, dtksh takes advantage of the KornShell-93 hierarchical variable name space for passing certain kinds of data to user-defined functions.

- Wksh contains a set of very terse aliases for all X commands. Dtksh does not provide these aliases, although it is trivial to create such aliases in order to port wksh programs to dtksh.

So, dtksh can be considered the next generation of the wksh tool. Dtksh is not strictly a superset of wksh, so an existing wksh script will not necessarily work when run under dtksh. In practice, relatively few changes must be made to "port" a wksh script to dtksh.

TCL/TK

TCL/TK was written by John Ousterhout and provides a shell-like language, although there are many syntactic differences between it and the POSIX shell standard. It does not use the Motif widget set and, in fact, does not even use the Xt Intrinsics layer of X. The widget set provided by TCL/TK is in many ways more elegant and simpler than the Motif widget set, and it provides a Motif-like look and feel. The main reason people use TCL/TK is this simplicity, and because the source code is of high quality and freely available.

Unfortunately, because it does not use the worldwide standard Motif widget set or the Xt Intrinsics, some problems arise when using TCL/TK for industrial-strength programming in the CDE environment. For example, it is not possible to use any of the many commercially available or free widgets with TCL/TK because it does not use Xt. Also, because it does not use Motif widgets, it may not work well in the CDE environment.

TCL/Motif

In addition to TCL with the TK toolkit, there is also a TCL binding to Motif freely available on the Internet. This version does not have the problems just mentioned, but neither does it have the advantage of TCL/TK's simple widget set. In addition, as of this writing, it does not provide anything close to the level of coverage of Motif, Xt, and CDE functionality that dtksh does. For someone who already knows shell programming, dtksh is the obvious choice since such a person would have to learn an unfamiliar language to use TCL with Motif bindings.

WCL

WCL (widget creation library) provides an enhanced resource file notation that allows X resource files to create widgets. Unlike TCL/TK, it provides the real Motif widget set. However, the WCL interpreter provides a very limited set of Motif and Xt commands, and in practice one must attach a lot of C code to get any real application working. The interpreter is sufficient only to put together prototypes of screen layouts, and it lacks the extensive interfaces to other CDE features that dtksh provides (such as access to the CDE help system and ToolTalk).

1.4 Graphical Builder Tools

As of this writing, there are a few simple tools available for graphically creating dtksh scripts. More sophisticated tools are likely to become available in the near future. Because the purpose of this book is to teach you all aspects of dtksh programming, I will assume that all screen layouts are created by hand. Even if a builder tool is used to create screen layouts, any real program always contains code to alter the screen dynamically: there's no getting around knowing the dtksh language, and any programmer who uses such a tool would be well advised to understand how screens are laid out by hand, using the programmatic interfaces.

Let the Builder Buyer Beware

Builder tools can be a great aid in the creation of some static screen designs, but there are some disadvantages to such tools that novice X programmers usually don't think about.

A relatively small amount of a graphical application is involved with screen layout and setup; usually only about 25 percent of a typical dtksh program is so employed. This means that the builder tool is only automating a small fraction of the programming effort; the programmer still needs a firm foundation in fundamental graphics programming for the rest. The prospect of using a builder tool sometimes lulls people into thinking they won't have to learn much about graphics. This is never the case.

A programmer who is familiar with the graphical objects and their proper use knows that screen layout is largely a matter of choosing the right combination of manager objects, after which the screen typically lays itself out in a reasonable way. There are many cases when laying out the screen programmatically is far easier than using a builder tool. A dramatic example of this is a calculator program, in which there are 25 or more buttons laid out in neat rows and columns. The programmer using a builder tool will have to painstakingly create each button individually; the dtksh programmer will use a `for` loop to create buttons inside a RowColumn manager widget that will automatically place the buttons in a pleasing layout. The dtksh programmer will finish the task of laying out the screen in about 12 lines of code, long before the builder program user has clicked enough mouse buttons to finish the task.

Project-Specific Considerations

Many builder tools do not give the programmer sufficient support to handle proper resizing of the application. They often encourage the programmer to hard code x and y coordinates of objects laid out on the screen. This becomes a nightmare in the case of an internationalized program in which labels and other strings will change size when the program is run using a different language catalog. At this writing, only the high-end builder tools provide good support for internationalization. In today's global economy, the programmer would do well to write programs using message catalogs (see Chapter 22, *Message Catalogs*) from the start if there is even the slightest chance that the program could be used in other countries.

Some tools write out the generated program in a proprietary format. This makes it difficult for you as a programmer to do some things: how do you compare two different versions of your graphical program in such a case to see what changed? How do you print the code out for review?

Finally, builder programs tend to be expensive. As of this writing, such programs for C language graphics programming cost between a few hundred and a few thousand dollars.

It is well worth learning the dtksh language thoroughly before evaluating whether such a builder tool is worth the cost. If you do evaluate a builder tool, keep in mind the issues just raised, and ask the tool vendor whether those kinds of issues are handled by their tool in a way that meets the needs of your project.

1.5 Desktop KornShell History

Here we review a little UNIX history. In the beginning, there was the Bourne shell: an interpreted language that allowed line-oriented scripts that controlled other UNIX commands to be written. The Bourne shell was the scripting language of choice on UNIX systems, because it was the only shell guaranteed to be installed on every different vendor's version of UNIX. Soon other shells were developed that had feature advantages over the Bourne shell. Among these was the KornShell, invented at AT&T Bell Laboratories by researcher David Korn.

KornShell eventually became the most popular alternative to the Bourne shell, in large part because it was compatible with the Bourne shell, so it could run the many thousands of Bourne shell scripts that had been written over the years. KornShell contained numerous extensions over the Bourne shell that made it a better programming language as well. These extensions included arrays, built-in mathematical functions, and string operators. However, some programmers were reluctant to take advantage of these added features for fear they would have to move their scripts to variants of UNIX that did not have KornShell available.

KornShell continued to evolve over a period of years, and major releases of it were named using the year in which that release first became available as a suffix. For example, the release in 1988 was named KornShell-88.

> Bug fix releases to each major release are denoted by affixing a letter to the end of the name, such as ksh-88a, ksh-88b, ksh-88c, etc.

The 1988 version became a standard part of many major UNIX variants, such as the Hewlett-Packard HP/UX system, the IBM AIX/6000, Novell's UnixWare, and others. Several years after its introduction, KornShell-88 was almost as prevalent as the Bourne shell.

The Roots of X

Meanwhile, a consortium was forming to promote distributed graphical programming systems. This consortium included the Massachusetts Institute of Technology, Digital Equipment Corporation (DEC), International Business Machines Incorporated (IBM), Hewlett-Packard Incorporated (HP), and many other companies and academic institutions. This was the X Consortium, and in 1983 they fielded the first public release of the X Window System. This system quickly grew in popularity, but it lacked a powerful set of standard graphical objects.

In 1988, another consortium called the Open Software Foundation (OSF) was formed. Many of the companies in the X Consortium were also members of the OSF, including IBM, HP, and DEC. Soon after its formation, the OSF released version 1.0 of the OSF/Motif graphical toolkit, a set of graphical objects defined to be used with the X programming system. By 1990, Motif had become one of the major standard graphical object packages.

When Worlds Collide

Around this same time, these two technologies—X and KornShell—were merged. Extensions to the KornShell were added that allowed it to create X graphical objects. This version was called the Windowing KornShell (wksh). Because UNIX had gone graphical on most platforms, this was a welcome addition to the shell language. Wksh was not widely available, however.

In 1993 a new major release of KornShell became available, aptly named Korn-Shell-93. KornShell-93 contained significant enhancements such as associative arrays, floating-point math, new string operators, and other features.

The CDE Connection

Now, these two developments—KornShell-93 and the Windowing KornShell—exhibited the same problem that the original KornShell had: some programmers were wary of using their new extended features because these shells had not propagated to all major UNIX versions. It might have taken years for these extended versions of the KornShell to become widely available. Luckily, at precisely the same time, a new initiative swept across the UNIX industry—the Common Open Software Environment (COSE). This was a set of specifications agreed on by the major UNIX vendors and formalized by existing standards bodies in a dramatically shorter time than usual. Part of this set of specifications covers the graphical user interface and tools associated with UNIX, and is called the Common Desktop Environment (CDE). KornShell-93 and the X Window features of the Windowing Korn-Shell were combined during this initiative and renamed "Desktop KornShell" (dtksh). Desktop KornShell was specified in the CDE as the scripting language to use for writing X Window System applications. Dtksh is guaranteed to be installed on any CDE compliant system.

1.6 Summary

The Desktop KornShell, or dtksh, is an extended version of the popular KornShell programming language. It is based on the latest version of KornShell from AT&T Bell Laboratories, and it includes many useful extensions such as associative arrays, floating-point math, and a hierarchical variable name space.

Dtksh is a part of the Common Desktop Environment specification, and as such it will be a standard tool shipped with every major version of UNIX in the near future.

Dtksh provides access to X and Motif functions by adding new built-in commands. The first part of this book uses a convenience layer called the XU library, which teaches you X programming in a simpler way. The second part of this book explains the "raw" X interfaces and other advanced features of dtksh, such as the ability to extend the dtksh language by attaching C code compiled into shared libraries.

Other interpreted scripting languages exist for X, but they generally do not provide the tight integration with the CDE environment and adherence to international standards that dtksh does.

Builder tools that generate dtksh are already becoming available, but this book will stick to the raw dtksh programming language. You should be cautious when deciding whether to use a builder tool: there are some potential difficulties such as comparing versions of software, internationalization, etc. Tools should be evaluated carefully according to the needs of your project.

PART I *X Programming Tutorial*

This part of the book contains a complete tutorial on X programming; it assumes you know nothing about X but are a competent shell programmer.

It explains how to use a simplified X programming interface built out of aliases and functions defined in the cookbook section of this book. These aliases and functions map directly to the standard C language interface for X, but are far simpler for the novice X programmer to use. In fact, they are simpler for expert X programmers as well!

The second part of this book goes into depth on the standard X calls, and if you are an experienced X programmer and don't care to use the shortcuts presented in this chapter, you might just skim this part of the book or proceed directly to Part II.

2   *X Window Basics*

2.1 Introduction

In this chapter you will learn how to write X programs using dtksh. The material is intended for programmers who know basic shell programming techniques, but not necessarily X programming concepts. If you know some kind of shell language other than KornShell, you might first want to read Chapter 28, *KornShell Language Review*.

As you read, you should have access to a graphical workstation with CDE installed so you can try out the programs presented here. For information on obtaining the example programs using anonymous ftp on the Internet, see *Obtaining the Example Programs* on page xxxii. It is important that you obtain these example programs, because they contain a file called `xutil.sh` that is essential for running these examples. That file provides a set of dtksh functions and aliases that implements a simplified interface to the X functions. In addition to being free on the Internet, the full text of that file is included in this book with complete explanations (see Chapter 27, *The X Utilities*).

To aid readers without previous X programming experience, new terms are highlighted by presenting their definitions set off from the main text, so that if you forget what a term means, you can easily flip back a few pages and find the definition without searching for it in the index.

2.2 The Nature of X

The X Window System (or simply X) is a distributed, client–server system for creating and running graphical applications. It is based on a layered, object-oriented set of software libraries.

That might sound like just a lot of buzzwords, but X really does meet this definition in every way. In an industry filled with hype, X is a good example of well-architected technology that provides concrete benefits to the users. The next few sections explore each piece of this definition, explaining the terminology and ideas that will be used throughout the rest of this book.

X as a Distributed Client–Server System

X provides a distributed architecture based on the client–server model. This means that different pieces of the system can run on different machines over the network. The programs you write using Desktop KornShell might be running on one machine, but the graphics rendering, mouse handling, and keyboard processing might be running on another. This is entirely transparent to your program; you get this feature automatically by using X.

The Roles of X Processes

At least three different processes are typically involved in an X session:

- The display server
- The window manager
- One or more client programs.

These processes can all be on the same physical machine, or all on different machines, or any other combination. When these processes are distributed across more than one machine, they communicate using a special protocol over a network.

The display server (also known as the X server) usually runs on the machine closest to the user, the desktop (see Figure 2-1). This is the process that actually paints pixels on the screen, detects mouse movements, intercepts key presses from the keyboard, etc. You should be aware that in X the terms "server" and "client" are the opposites of the way most people think of them; the X display server typically runs on the desktop hardware (client machines), and the X client programs often run on the larger (server) machines in the network. The way to keep this straight is to think in terms of what the X display server does: it provides display services for the X client applications.

The window manager is a special process that coordinates actions that the user wants to perform on the client programs. For example, if the user wants to resize a certain client, or bring one client window on top of another, the window manager gets involved. Frequently the dtksh programs you write don't need to know anything about these kinds of interactions—the graphical objects you use will respond appropriately to resizing.

The programs you will write using Desktop KornShell are the client processes. These are applications that users employ to get work done. The client process sends messages to the X server to display graphical objects on the screen, and receives messages from the X server when there is keyboard or mouse action.

Figure 2-1. Distributed X Architecture.   Because of the distributed nature of X, it is possible to run the display server, window manager, and various client application programs on different machines connected by the network.

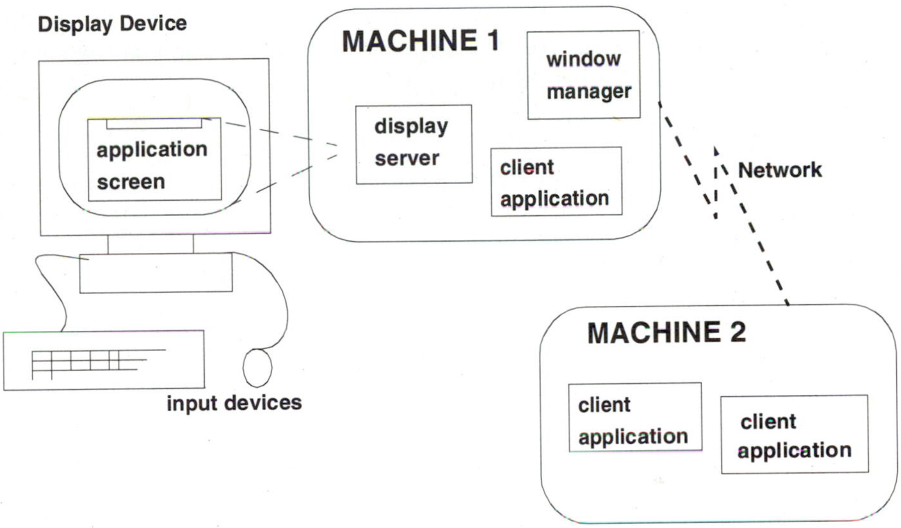

X as a Layered Software System

The C language X application programmer uses a layered set of libraries to write programs. Dtksh uses those same libraries to get its work done, and it maps the C language functions contained in those libraries into new dtksh built-in commands. So although the dtksh programmer does not program in C or use the X libraries directly, it is still important to understand the relationship between the different layers of software.

The X software is divided into three distinct layers (Figure 2-2):

- **Motif**

   This layer includes many predefined graphical objects and convenience functions that, when combined, form graphical programs. It is the highest layer.

   The X Window System allows other sets of graphical objects besides Motif. Some others that you may have heard of include OPEN LOOK, MOOLIT, and the Athena widget set. However, Motif is now recognized as the worldwide standard on UNIX systems and in the CDE environment.

- ### X Toolkit Intrinsics

  Also known as the "Xt Intrinsics," or simply "Xt," this layer includes basic commands for creating and manipulating graphical objects. It must be used together with a set of graphical objects, such as those provided by Motif.

- ### Xlib

  This layer is more primitive, and includes commands for low-level drawing, color allocation, mouse and keyboard handling, and other basic functions. The Xt layer and Motif widget layer use the Xlib layer to display graphical objects. Sophisticated applications might also use the commands in this layer to perform arbitrary drawing.

Figure 2-2. X Software Layers. The application programmer can use any or all of the layers of X software, but most calls are to the two highest layers, Motif and the Xt Intrinsics. In Part I, this book will use a simplified set of functions and aliases called the XU library to make things easier for X novices.

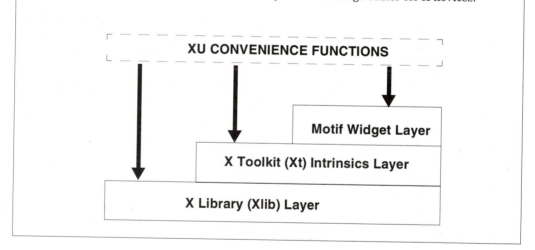

An X program often uses all of these layers of software to get the job done. This can be very confusing to the novice X programmer, since the functions provided by these layers are not consistent.

> I do not mean to disparage the designers of X when I say this. The fact is that the different layers of the X system were developed over a period of years by many different organizations; it is not surprising that inconsistencies crept in over time. X is like a 50-carat diamond—very valuable and beautiful but inevitably containing some flaws.

For this reason, Part I of this book will use a simplified interface, called the X Utilities (henceforth XU) instead of directly calling the Motif, Xt, or Xlib functions.

X as an Object-Oriented System

The X Window System was designed with an object-oriented philosophy. All this really means is that the system encourages programming by combining reusable pieces of code (objects) whose internal operations are hidden. A programmer communicates with the objects by modifying their publicly accessible parts. Objects can receive notification of events, and they know how to process those events. The programmer can sometimes direct the object how to handle certain kinds of events.

Although many KornShell programmers might not be accustomed to writing object-oriented programs, you'll find that it only takes a little practice to get used to this way of thinking, and it is the most natural way to create graphical programs. This is because graphical programs by their nature are event driven: The user might choose to interact with any piece of the screen at any time—usually by moving the mouse pointer over a graphical object and selecting it. The old line-oriented notion of performing one task at a time in a strict sequence simply won't do: the user wants to be able to move around in the application at will, choosing to interact with any graphical object at any time.

2.3 The Ingredients of an X Program

In X terminology graphical objects are called *widgets*. If you have ever taken an economics course you will understand the reason for this term. When economics professors want to hypothesize about a factory that produces some kind of product but it doesn't matter precisely what kind—they say "Suppose we have a factory that produces widgets." Similarly, X uses the term *widget* to refer to any kind of generic graphical object.

> ***Widget:*** A graphical object such as a PushButton or ScrollBar, or a graphical object that manages the layout of other graphical objects.

Examples of widgets include PushButtons that can be "pushed" by moving the mouse pointer over them and clicking a button; TextFields into which the user can type or edit text; and ScrollBars that the user can use to scroll through a window on the screen. In the chapters following this one, you will learn about the entire menagerie of widgets available in Motif. There are many different kinds of widgets, each with specific uses in different situations.

Each widget belongs to a certain *class*. A PushButton is one widget class, a Scroll-Bar is another.

> ***Widget class:*** A type of widget.

Some kinds of widgets look and behave in similar, but not identical, ways. For example, a ToggleButton widget is similar to a PushButton widget, but it looks a little different because it displays a darkened rectangle when it is "on" and an empty

rectangle when it is "off." This is carried out in X by *subclassing* both of these widget classes from another widget class (in this case the Label widget). In other
words, internally both the PushButton and the ToggleButton widget share much of
the same behavior because they were derived from another, simpler widget.

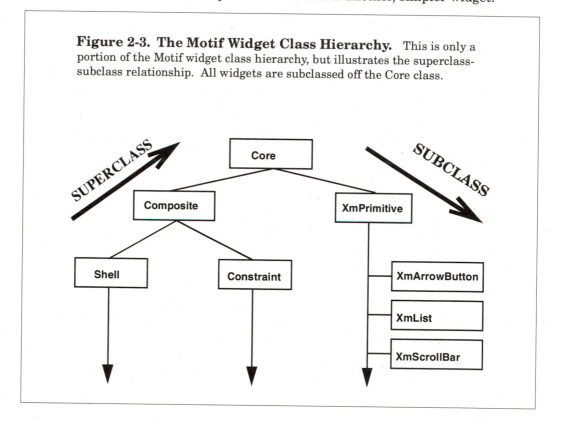

Figure 2-3. The Motif Widget Class Hierarchy. This is only a
portion of the Motif widget class hierarchy, but illustrates the superclass-
subclass relationship. All widgets are subclassed off the Core class.

When one widget class is derived from another, it is termed a *subclass* of the parent class. The parent is called the *superclass* of the derived class.

   Subclass: A class derived from another (parent) class.

   Superclass: A class from which a subclass has been derived.

All widget classes are ultimately derived from a base class called *Core*. The relationship between classes and subclasses forms a tree-like structure called the *widget class hierarchy.*

   Widget class hierarchy: The tree-like structure formed from the
   paths of inheritance from class to subclass.

Figure 2-3 shows part of the Motif widget class hierarchy. In this portion of the hierarchy, the core class appears at the top, and its subclasses branch off below.

A graphical program might contain several different *instances* of a particular widget class. For example, there might be two PushButtons on a particular screen, one that confirms an action and one that cancels an action. Even though these are both PushButtons, they are distinguishable from one another because they are different instances of the class PushButton.

Newly created widget instances are attached to a parent widget. Each widget can have at most one parent. There is one special widget in the application that has no parent; it is called the top level or *root* widget of the application. This parent-child relationship between widgets forms a tree-like structure called the *widget instance hierarchy*.

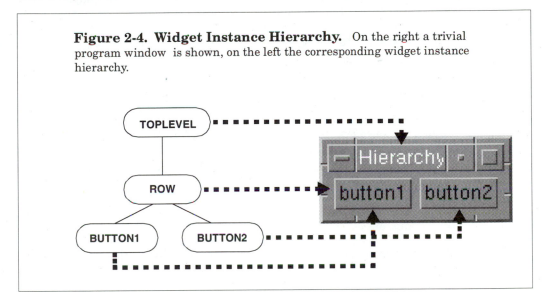

Figure 2-4. Widget Instance Hierarchy. On the right a trivial program window is shown, on the left the corresponding widget instance hierarchy.

Figure 2-4 shows a simple X program along with its corresponding widget instance hierarchy; the program that produced this output is shown in Listing 2-1. You will learn shortly how to read this code.

Listing 2-1. Simple Instance Hierarchy (hierarch.sh). This program creates four widgets: the TOPLEVEL widget created by the XUinitialize call, a widget named ROW that can stack child widgets in rows, two children of ROW called BUTTON1 and BUTTON2. By the end of this chapter you'll understand the particulars of this code.

```
. $XUTILDIR/xutil.sh

XUinitialize TOPLEVEL Hierarchy "$@"
XUrow ROW $TOPLEVEL
```

```
XUaddbuttons $ROW \
    B1 "button1" 1 'print button1 pushed' \
    B2 "button2" 2 'print button2 pushed'
XUrealize $TOPLEVEL
XUmainloop
```

Pieces of data are stored with the widgets that control how they look or respond to the outside world. These pieces of data are called *resources*; each resource has a name. The name can be used to set or retrieve resource data values. For example, the piece of text that appears on a PushButton or ToggleButton is the `label-String` resource. You can initialize resources when a widget is created, or change them later. Some resources are used to report back data that the user has stored in the widget. For example, the TextField widget, which displays some editable text, stores the current text it holds in a resource called `value`.

> **Resource:** A named piece of data stored with a widget instance that controls some aspect of how the widget looks or behaves.

2.4 Your First X Program

I've been hitting you with a lot of theory for the last few pages, and I'm sure you're anxious to see how this actually works. So, let's write an X program! Listing 2-2 implements the graphical dtksh equivalent of the all time classic example program, *hello world*. This program will pop up a window that contains the text: hello, world. To execute this program, simply call dtksh and give `hello.sh` as its argument:

```
dtksh hello.sh
```

Alternatively, you can add a shell specification line to the beginning of the file:

```
#!/usr/dt/bin/dtksh
```

This must be the very first line of the file. The `#!` construct tells the operating system to use the given path as the shell instead of the default `/bin/sh`. You must then make the file executable by using:

```
chmod +x hello.sh
```

Figure 2-5 shows the resulting output. If you've already got X programming experience, this should look very familiar to you; dtksh commands map directly to their C language counterparts. One thing that might surprise you is the brevity of this program compared to an equivalent C language Motif program, which is about 20 to 25 lines long compared to the four commands required in dtksh. The C language equivalent to this program requires four `#include` directives alone; the dtksh programmer is almost finished by the time the C programmer has written any executable code!

Listing 2-2. Hello World (hello.sh).

```
. $XUTILDIR/xutil.sh

XUinitialize TOPLEVEL Hello "$@"
XUlabel LABEL $TOPLEVEL labelString:"hello, world"
XUrealize $TOPLEVEL
XUmainloop
```

Figure 2-5. Output of hello.sh.

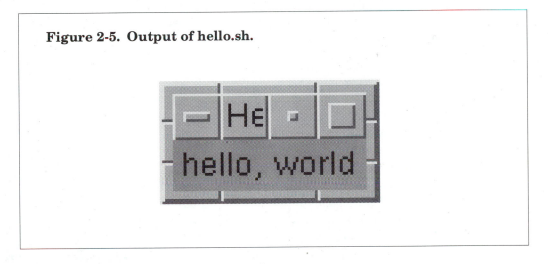

The next sections will dissect the hello.sh program line by line and show you how it works, and along the way you will learn more about X programming.

2.5 Steps of an X Program

Every X program goes through four steps:

1. Initialize the X Toolkit
2. Create widgets
3. Realize widgets
4. Go into a loop to process events.

The nice thing about the hello.sh example is that it contains exactly one command for each step; it is in some sense the smallest possible X program. In detail these steps perform the following actions:

- Step 1 starts the X Window system, sets up a communication path to the X server, and performs all the other actions necessary to initialize an X program. It also creates the first widget of your application; all other widgets will be descendants of this "root" widget.

- In step 2, widgets are created; usually this also involves setting up initial resources for each widget.

- Step 3 usually only requires one line of code, a call to the XUrealize command. Here, the widgets created in step 2 are *realized*. This is a confusing term for beginning X programmers, but you can think of this step as making the widgets "come to life." This step causes the X server to allocate data structures for each widget so they can appear on the display.

  ### *Realize:* Before a widget can appear on the display, it must be realized. Realizing a widget makes it "come to life" by allocating data structures for it on the X server.

- Step 4 also requires only a single command and that command doesn't even require any arguments! The command is XUmainloop, and it causes the X program to begin processing events.

Initializing the Toolkit

The first line of hello.sh brings in the XU convenience functions using the "dot" command of KornShell:

```
. $XUTILDIR/xutil.sh
```

As mentioned before, this is a set of utilities that provides a simplified interface to X. The text of these utilities is provided in Chapter 27. For information on how to obtain this file using the Internet see *Obtaining the Example Programs* on page xxxii. This program assumes you have installed xutil.sh in a directory pointed to by the variable $XUTILDIR.

The second line in hello.sh is a call to XUinitialize; it performs actions necessary to set up the Xt Intrinsics layer of the X system (Figure 2-6). The first argument, TOPLEVEL, is the name of a variable. This can be any legal KornShell variable name, but by convention I always use the string TOPLEVEL for my programs. This variable will be set by the XUinitialize command to the *widget identifie*r of the topmost, or root, widget of this application. The widget identifier, or *handle* as it is sometimes called, can be used to attach other widgets to the root widget. The root widget provides a rectangular area, or window, for the rest of the application.

> It is possible to create applications with more than one independent window. The widgets that control these separate windows will be discussed in future chapters. Still, only the widget created by XUinitialize is the root widget.

The second argument to XUinitialize, Hello, is the *application class*. By default, this string will appear in the title bar of the window that contains this application. The application's class is also used to determine defaults for the application (this will be fully explained in Chapter 8, *Resources and Resource Files*). By convention, this argument should begin with an uppercase letter, and should contain no whitespace or special characters.

Any other arguments on the XUinitialize command are used to set options on this application. As you can see, I've used the shell notation "$@" here, which means "expand all the arguments given to this shell script, properly quoted." Thus, you can execute this script with options that will be passed to the Xt Intrinsics via the XUinitialize command. For example, there is a standard option that causes the application to come up as an icon rather than an expanded window, -iconic. As written, you could execute hello.sh like this to start it up as an icon:

```
dtksh hello.sh -iconic
```

See Appendix B for a complete list of standard X options accepted by XUinitialize.

Creating Widgets

The third line of hello.sh creates the widget used to display the "hello, world" text (Figure 2-7). Here, I've chosen a Label widget; it is a Motif widget that can display lines of read-only text.

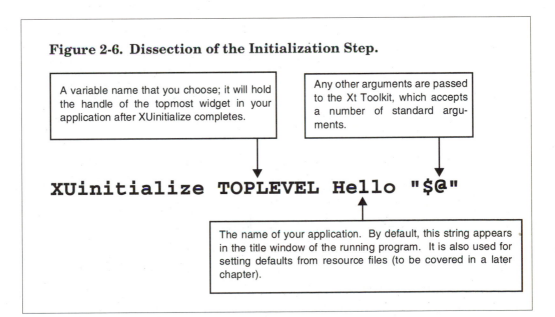

Figure 2-6. Dissection of the Initialization Step.

A variable name that you choose; it will hold the handle of the topmost widget in your application after XUinitialize completes.

Any other arguments are passed to the Xt Toolkit, which accepts a number of standard arguments.

```
XUinitialize TOPLEVEL Hello "$@"
```

The name of your application. By default, this string appears in the title window of the running program. It is also used for setting defaults from resource files (to be covered in a later chapter).

The function XUlabel creates this Label widget instance. The first argument, LABEL, is the name of a variable that will be set to the handle of the newly created Label widget. After XUlabel executes, you can use this handle to change the appearance of the Label widget.

The second argument is the parent to which the label should be attached, in this case $TOPLEVEL. That variable was set in the XUinitialize command, and is the root widget of this application.

Any other arguments to this command are resource settings. Recall that a resource is a named piece of data that controls some aspect of how a widget behaves or appears. In this case, the program sets one resource of the Label widget, the label-String resource. This resource is the piece of text displayed by the Label widget. Notice that the notation requires a colon (:) between the resource name and its value setting. There can be any number of these *resource:value* pairs, each a separate argument to the command. Note that if the *value* contains whitespace it must be quoted.

The XU library contains a function for each widget in Motif that will create an instance of the widget. For example, to create a PushButton widget you would use a command called XUpushbutton, to create a Text widget you would use XUtext. All of these commands take identical arguments as the XUlabel command illustrated earlier. Some of these functions actually create whole groups of widgets in commonly needed configurations; these are discussed in more detail in the next few chapters.

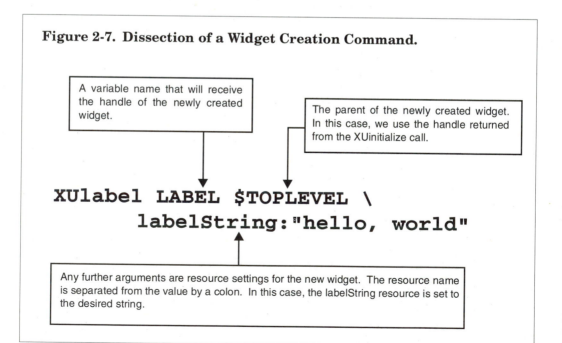

Figure 2-7. Dissection of a Widget Creation Command.

A variable name that will receive the handle of the newly created widget.

The parent of the newly created widget. In this case, we use the handle returned from the XUinitialize call.

```
XUlabel LABEL $TOPLEVEL \
        labelString:"hello, world"
```

Any further arguments are resource settings for the new widget. The resource name is separated from the value by a colon. In this case, the labelString resource is set to the desired string.

Realizing the Widget Hierarchy

The fourth line of `hello.sh` realizes the widget hierarchy using the `XUrealize` command. As I mentioned before, this step is necessary to get the widgets to appear on the display. The term *realize* here is used in the sense of "to make real"; what this command actually does is inform the display server that this widget should become a real graphical object. This command takes as its arguments the identifiers of the widgets you wish to realize. In this program, the `$TOPLEVEL` argument again refers to the root widget of this application. All children of that widget will also be realized (and their children recursively); in this example the only child is the Label widget whose identifier is `$LABEL`.

Event Processing Loop

The final line of the program is a simple call to `XUmainloop`, with no options. This causes the script to go into a loop to process events. Unlike line-oriented programs, graphical X programs don't follow a linear flow of control. This is because the user of a graphical interface could choose to interact with any part of the screen at any time. Because of this, the entire X program works by responding to events generated by the user or the system. For example, when the user pushes a button on the screen, that action sends an event to the PushButton widget instance that the user has selected.

> ***Event:*** Some occurrence in a graphical program that may require action by the application. Example: the user selects a PushButton widget by moving the mouse pointer over it and pressing a mouse button.

The `XUmainloop` command never returns: it waits for an event to occur, then triggers pieces of code in the appropriate widget to process the event. Some of this event handling code is built into the widgets themselves and some might be provided by the application programmer. Because it never returns, `XUmainloop` should be the last statement of any graphical program; any statement following it will never be executed. In contrast, if you forget to put the command `XUmainloop` in your application, it will exit silently without ever displaying any graphics at all. That's because no events will be processed—including events that tell widgets to paint themselves on the display!

In the `hello.sh` program, all events are handled automatically by the widgets, there are no programmer-specified event handling functions. For example, if the user resizes the window, the shell widget will take care of resizing the borders of the window, and the Label widget will automatically center the text string based on the new size. Another event that is automatically handled by this application is the Exit event. The user may select Exit from the window manager menu, which causes this program to shut down and disappear from the screen. Thus, `XUmainloop` does not cause an infinite loop, even if it might appear so at first glance; the user can cause the program to exit by causing XUmainloop to trigger an application termination event.

The next section shows how a programmer can specify actions invoked when certain events are triggered on a widget.

Callbacks

In the simple hello.sh program we've been discussing, all the events were handled by the widgets and the X Window System automatically. In a real program, at least some events are handled by programmer-defined event handler functions. By far the most common way of specifying such a function is by using a widget's CallbackList resources. A callback is a function that is stored in a special resource of type CallbackList. Most widgets have one or more of these callback resources.

> ***Callback:*** A function provided by the X programmer that is stored in one of a widget's CallbackList resources and is triggered by a widget-defined event.

For example, the PushButton widget is used to display a "button" that the user can "push" by putting the mouse cursor over the button and pressing a mouse button. The PushButton widget has a resource of type CallbackList whose name is activateCallback. This callback is triggered when the user activates (pushes) the button.

The next example, Listing 2-3, shows how a PushButton's activateCallback resource is used. It is a simple program that displays a PushButton labeled "goodbye, world" (Figure 2-8). When this button is pushed, the application exits.

Listing 2-3. A Simple Callback Example (goodbye.sh).

```
. $XUTILDIR/xutil.sh

XUinitialize TOPLEVEL goodbye Goodbye "$@"
XUpushbutton PUSH $TOPLEVEL labelString:"goodbye, world"
XUaddcallback $PUSH activateCallback "exit 0"
XUrealize $TOPLEVEL
XUmainloop
```

This program looks a lot like the previous one, except it creates a PushButton widget instead of a Label widget. In addition, there is another line of code: a call to the XUaddcallback command. This command associates the dtksh command string exit 0 with the PushButton's activateCallback resource (Figure 2-9). That's the callback that is executed when the user selects the button widget.

You might be wondering why the program didn't simply set the activateCallback resource directly on the XUpushbutton command line the same way as any other resource (like labelString). This is because a CallbackList resource can

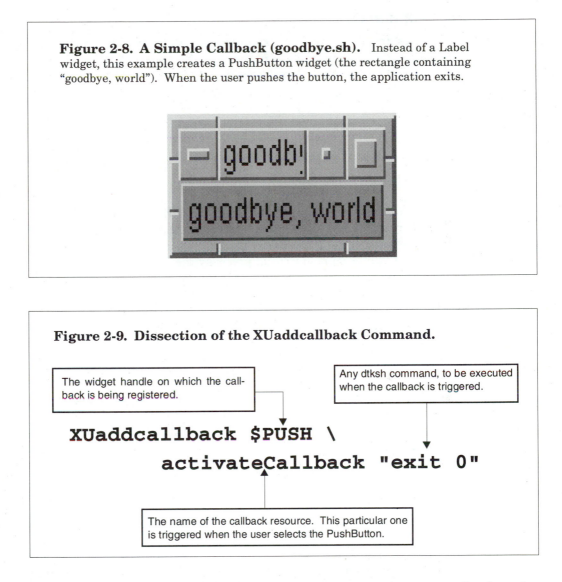

Figure 2-8. A Simple Callback (goodbye.sh). Instead of a Label widget, this example creates a PushButton widget (the rectangle containing "goodbye, world"). When the user pushes the button, the application exits.

Figure 2-9. Dissection of the XUaddcallback Command.

The widget handle on which the callback is being registered.

Any dtksh command, to be executed when the callback is triggered.

```
XUaddcallback $PUSH \
        activateCallback "exit 0"
```

The name of the callback resource. This particular one is triggered when the user selects the PushButton.

hold more than one command to be executed when the event occurs. So, there is a special function provided by the Xt Intrinsics for associating a command with a re-source of type CallbackList.

It would work just fine if a program directly set the activateCallback resource on the XUpushbutton command line, and in fact some Motif widgets even require the programmer to set some callbacks that way under certain circumstances. How-ever, as a matter of style I generally prefer to use XUaddcallback; that makes the special nature of the callback resource explicit.

2.6 Resource Commands

As you saw from the previous examples, the programmer can specify resource values when widgets are created. However, you're not stuck with those initial resource settings—X lets you change resources at any time or find out what the current values are.

Changing Resources

Resources can be changed any time after a widget has been created by using the command:

```
XUset $widget resource:value ...
```

This command's first argument specifies the widget to be changed (it's the handle that's returned in the variable that appears as the first argument to the widget creation command). After that, there can be any number of *resource:value* arguments to set values on resources in precisely the same way as they can be set during widget creation.

Getting Resource Values

Resource values can be retrieved any time after widget creation by using the command:

```
XUget $widget resource:variable ...
```

Again, the first argument is used to specify the widget whose resource value is being retrieved. The rest of the arguments are of the form *resource:variable*. This is a very similar notation to that used in the XUset command, but instead of a value following the colon the name of a *variable* appears. That variable will be set to the value of the corresponding resource.

2.7 More About Callbacks

There are a few additional features of the callback mechanism that are important to know. As you have seen, you can specify any piece of dtksh code as the value of a callback resource, and a widget-defined event will trigger that code to be executed.

Some information gets passed into your callback routine at the time it executes. This information is passed to your callback in the form of variables that are local to your callback. In other words, these variables exist only while your callback function is executing.

- CB_WIDGET

    This variable is set to the identifier of the widget on whose behalf this callback is executing. This is useful in cases for which you are using a common function to handle callbacks for more than one widget.

- CB_CALL_DATA

   Some widgets will pass some callback-specific data to your callback routine. In X terminology, this is termed *call data*. These pieces of data will be passed to your callback in this variable. Actually, this is a hierarchical variable, and subfields of it will be set to specific portions of the call data.

   > Hierarchical variables are new in KornShell-93; previous versions of KornShell had a flat name space. To learn about this and other new features in KornShell-93, see *KornShell Language Review* on page 543.

Listing 2-4 shows both of these features of callbacks. In this example, two Scale widgets are displayed. Whenever one Scale is moved by a user, the other one is forced to move such that the sum of the values of the two Scales is always 10. The same function is used for two different Scale widget callbacks: the dragCallback (which is called whenever the Scale is moved), and the valueChangedCallback (which is called only when the user releases the mouse button). In this case the CB_CALL_DATA variable contains two subfields: VALUE (which contains the new Scale value), and REASON (which contains a string indicating why the callback is being called).

> ***Call data:*** Data values passed by a widget to a callback routine. These values differ depending on the widget and the specific callback name. Each data value is passed as a field of a hierarchical variable whose base is CB_CALL_DATA. For example, the string indicating the reason that the callback was triggered is available in: ${CB_CALL_DATA.REASON}.

When the user is in the process of dragging either Scale, the other Scale will change (using the dragCallback). When the user releases the Scale, the label at the bottom will be updated to show the new sum (using the valueChangedCallback). See Figure 2-10.

Listing 2-4. Variables In Callbacks (scales.sh). This program illustrates the use of the CB_WIDGET and CB_CALL_DATA variables that are set during the execution of a callback. The function MoveScaleCB uses $CB_WIDGET to get the current value of the Scale that the user is moving. Later in the same function, ${CB_CALL_DATA.REASON} is checked to see whether the function is being called as a result of a valueChangedCallback (as opposed to a dragCallback).

```
. $XUTILDIR/xutil.sh

function MoveScaleCB {
        widget other=$1
        integer v v1 v2
```

```
                  XUget $CB_WIDGET value:v
                  XUset $other value:"$((10-v))"

                  if [[ ${CB_CALL_DATA.REASON} == CR_VALUE_CHANGED ]]
                  then
                          XUget $SCALE1 value:v1
                          XUget $SCALE2 value:v2
                          XUset $LABEL labelString:"$v1 + $v2 = 10"
                  fi
}

XUinitialize TOPLEVEL Scales "$@"
XUcolumn COL $TOPLEVEL
XUscale SCALE1 $COL \
          maximum:10 \
          orientation:horizontal \
          showValue:true
XUaddcallback $SCALE1 valueChangedCallback 'MoveScaleCB $SCALE2'
XUaddcallback $SCALE1 dragCallback 'MoveScaleCB $SCALE2'
XUscale SCALE2 $COL \
          maximum:10 \
          value:10 \
          orientation:horizontal \
          showValue:true
XUaddcallback $SCALE2 valueChangedCallback 'MoveScaleCB $SCALE1'
XUaddcallback $SCALE2 dragCallback 'MoveScaleCB $SCALE1'
XUlabel LABEL $COL labelString:"0 + 10 = 10"
XUrealize $TOPLEVEL
XUmainloop
```

Figure 2-10. Output of the Summed Scales Program (scales.sh).

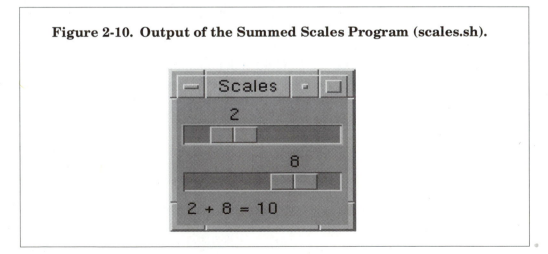

2.8 Widget States

Several states are associated with each widget; these states can be used to achieve certain display effects that are commonly needed in programs. The states are:

- **Realized vs. Unrealized**. You might recall that when a widget is realized the graphics server is made aware of it. If a widget is not realized, it cannot be displayed on the screen, its manager parent does not take it into account when laying out space for its children, and the widget cannot receive events. Effectively, it does not exist in a usable fashion. By default, when a widget's parent is realized the child widget becomes realized as well.

- **Managed vs. Unmanaged.** If a widget is managed, then its parent takes it into account. The parent will arrange the layout of its managed children, and will allocate space for them on the screen. By default, the widget creation commands in the XU library manage the widgets automatically, but an option is available (-u) that causes the widget to be initially unmanaged.

- **Mapped vs. Unmapped.** The mapped state determines whether the widget will actually paint itself on the screen. A widget must be both realized and managed in order to be mapped. If a widget is realized and managed but not mapped, then its parent will allocate space for it on the screen, but nothing will appear. There will be nothing but a blank area where the widget would have appeared. This is useful in situations in which you want a widget to appear only under certain circumstances, but you don't want the screen to resize or change depending on whether the widget is displayed or not. By default, widgets are mapped automatically when they are managed. This default can be changed on many widgets by setting the `mappedWhenManaged` resource to false.

- **Sensitive vs. Insensitive.** Widgets that can take user input, such as TextFields, Scales, or Buttons, can be either sensitive or insensitive. When such a widget is insensitive it will not respond to keyboard or mouse input. Some widgets will have a different appearance when they are insensitive; for example, an insensitive PushButton widget will appear "grayed out." Manager widgets can also be set to the insensitive state, in which case all the children they manage will be made insensitive to input. Sensitivity changes should be used when under some conditions it does not make sense for the user to interact with a widget; its most common use is to disable menu items that do not apply at a given time in the application.

Figure 2-11 illustrates the effects of these states using a simple example program that has three pushbutton widgets. The program used to produce this illustration is explained in Listing 2-5.

Figure 2-11. Widget States.   From left to right: Button 2 is unmapped, Button 2 is unmanaged, Button 2 is unrealized, Button 2 is insensitive. Note that
when unmapped, space is left for the button; when unmanaged or unrealized, the
space is removed; and when insensitive, the button has a stippled appearance.

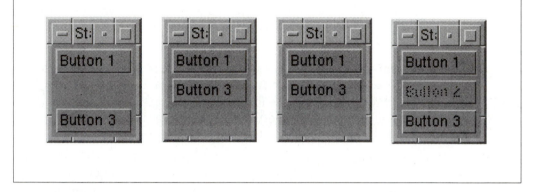

Listing 2-5. Widget State Demonstration (states.sh). After a simple set of three
button widgets is realized, the program changes the state of the second button depending on
the value of its first argument.

```
. $XUTILDIR/xutil.sh

XUinitialize TOPLEVEL States "$@"
XUcolumn COL $TOPLEVEL
XUaddbuttons $COL \
        B1 "Button 1" 1 'print button 1 pushed' \
        B2 "Button 2" 2 'print button 2 pushed' \
        B3 "Button 3" 3 'print button 3 pushed'
XUrealize $TOPLEVEL

case "${DTKSH_ARGV[1]}" in
unmap)              XUunmap $B2 ;;
unmanage)           XUunmanage $B2 ;;
unrealize)          XUunrealize $B2 ;;
insensitive)        XUinsensitive $B2 ;;
esac
XUmainloop
```

There are commands to change these state components of widgets, and other commands to test what the current state of a widget is:

`XUrealize` *widget* `XUunrealize` *widget*	Change widgets to the realized or unrealized state. When unrealized, a widget does not exist from the point of view of the graphics server. As such, it cannot be managed.
`XUmanage` *widget* ... `XUunmanage` *widget* ...	Change widgets to the managed or unmanaged state. When unmanaged, the widget's parent does not display it or leave space for it.
`XUmap` *widget* ... `XUunmap` *widget* ...	Change widgets to the mapped or unmapped state. A widget must be realized, mapped, and managed to appear on the screen. If a widget is managed but not mapped, its parent will leave an empty space for it.
`XUsensitive` *widget* ... `XUinsensitive` *widget* ...	Change widgets to the sensitive or insensitive state. An insensitive widget cannot accept user input.
`XUisrealized` *widget* `XUismanaged` *widget* `XUissensitive` *widget*	These commands can be used to test whether a widget is realized, managed, or sensitive. They return success (zero) if the widget is in the state being tested, or failure (nonzero) otherwise. Thus, these commands can be used conveniently with the `if` and `while` statements of KornShell. Note that there is no command to test the mapped state.

2.9 Summary

In this chapter you learned how to use the XU simplified programming interface to create X applications using dtksh. You also learned basic X terminology and a little about the X Window System.

X Terminology

X is a distributed, object-oriented system. It contains several layers of software, the topmost of which is the Motif widget programming level.

X programs are composed of graphical objects called widgets. Widgets contain pieces of data called resources that determine how they look or behave. Widgets respond to events by triggering pieces of code that are either provided by the widget itself or by the programmer. Callbacks are pieces of code provided by the programmer that can handle some kinds of events.

The Steps of an X Program

Every X program goes through four steps:

- initialize the toolkit
- create widgets
- realize the widget hierarchy
- loop processing events.

Getting and Setting Resources

Resources can be set when a widget is created by placing *resource*:*value* pairs at the end of the creation command. Resources can be set later using the XUset command, and the current value of a resource may be retrieved at any time using the XUget command. The XUget command takes *resource*:*variable* arguments and places the *values* of the desired resources in the *variables*.

Callbacks

The programmer registers pieces of code to perform actions when specific events occur on a widget. These are called callback functions or simply callbacks. Two variables are passed in to every callback function:

- CB_WIDGET holds the handle of the widget on whose behalf the callback was executed.
- CB_CALL_DATA is the base of a hierarchical variable that contains other values that are specific to this widget and this callback resource. Subfields of this variable will hold various useful kinds of data. For example, when the Scale widget's valueChangedCallback is triggered, the new value of the Scale is passed to the callback function in ${CB_CALL_DATA.VALUE}.

3 *Motif Widget Taxonomy*

3.1 Introduction

As you saw in Chapter 2, *X Window Basics*, widgets are very important to X programming. They provide the vehicle for interacting with the user, laying out the screen design, and routing events to callback code. To be an effective X programmer, you need to become familiar with the different widgets and how they are used. This chapter acquaints you with the Motif widgets and the circumstances under which you might use one widget or another. This chapter does not provide detailed programming information on the widgets: it's meant only to give you a broad view of the kind of widgets available. This broad view will lay the foundation for later chapters in which every Motif widget will be explained in more detail, along with comprehensive programming examples.

3.2 Primitive Widgets

Some widgets cannot serve as parents; they are the *primitive widgets* (derived from the class XmPrimitive).

> **Primitive widget:**   A widget that cannot serve as a parent.

You should not interpret the term primitive to mean that these widgets are simplistic or trivial. Some of them are relatively simple, such as the Separator widget, which does nothing other than provide a horizontal or vertical line on the application's window for decoration purposes. However, some of the primitive widgets are quite sophisticated, such as the Text widget, which can display a multiline field of text and allows the user to perform complex editing tasks.

You've already seen two primitive widgets in the examples in the last chapter: the Label and the PushButton. The Label widget displays a noneditable line of text, and the PushButton widget gives the user a way to execute a command by selecting the button with the mouse. Besides these, there is the List widget, which can display a list of selectable text items; the ScrollBar widget, which allows the user to scroll a region of the application; and several other variations on buttons that have specific uses. A list of all the primitive widgets is given in Table 3-1.

Table 3-1. The Primitive Widgets

Widget	Description and Typical Uses	Appearance
ArrowButton	A button that displays an arrow pointing up, down, left, or right. Useful for indicating an action that will increment (up arrow) or decrement (down arrow) a value, or an action that will move data from one place to another.	
CascadeButton	Similar to a PushButton, but useful for cascading menus. When the button is selected, a menu containing other buttons appears to the right or under an arrow. This is used to create multi-level menu systems.	
DrawnButton	A button on which arbitrary graphics can be drawn using low-level Xlib layer commands. This is used when the programmer needs to create a highly customized kind of button.	Varies in appearance; the programmer specifies the appearance.
Label	A noneditable text item or icon. Used to provide labels or decorations on the application window.	

Table 3-1. The Primitive Widgets (continued)

Widget	Description and Typical Uses	Appearance
List	Displays a list of text items or icons. Callbacks are available to perform an action when an item is selected (or double-clicked). Multiple items may be selected by dragging the mouse through the list with a button depressed.	
PushButton	A button that can contain text or an icon. When pushed, a callback is executed.	
ScrollBar	Displays a bar with a slider area (also called a *thumb*). The user can move the slider by dragging the mouse. Callbacks report when the Scrollbar is moved. Typically used to scroll another widget that does not entirely fit on the screen.	
Separator	Provides a horizontal or vertical line. This is used to provide visual separation between other widgets.	
Text	Provides a multiline text area that can be edited by the user. Useful in any situation where the user must be prompted for multiline text. Provides callbacks for intercepting text insertion, deletion, cursor motion, and other editing functions.	

Table 3-1. The Primitive Widgets (continued)

Widget	Description and Typical Uses	Appearance
TextField	Provides a single-line text area that can be edited by the user. Useful when the user must be prompted for a single line of text. Same kinds of callbacks are provided as the Text widget.	I think that I shall never see
ToggleButton	Similar to the PushButton, but also provides a small area that shows the current state of the button. This area gets filled with a dark color when the button is *on*. Pressing the button toggles the state. Useful for situations when the user must choose one of two alternatives.	✔ Married toggle state indicator label

3.3 Gadgets

Gadgets were originally created as a performance enhancement to the Motif widget set. They look identical to widgets, and behave the same as well, but they differ in that they save memory by sharing certain data structures with their parent. There are gadget counterparts to many of the primitive widgets just explained (see Table 3-2).

Table 3-2. Gadgets

Gadget Name
ArrowButtonGadget
CascadeButtonGadget
LabelGadget
PushButtonGadget
SeparatorGadget
ToggleButtonGadget

Listing 3-1 illustrates the interchangeability of widgets and gadgets in the case of a PushButton. In this program, two buttons are created inside a column-stacking RowColumn widget. The topmost one is a PushButton widget, and the second is a PushButton gadget. From the programmer's point of view, the only difference is using the `XUpushbuttongadget` command instead of the `XUpushbutton` command to

create the widget. From the end user's point of view, there is no visible difference
in either appearance or behavior. The running program is shown in Figure 3-1.

Listing 3-1. Widgets and Gadgets (widgad.sh). To the programmer, there is little
difference between using a widget or a gadget. As shown below, simply using XUpushbuttongadget instead of XUpushbutton does the trick.

```
. $XUTILDIR/xutil.sh

XUinitialize TOPLEVEL Widgadget "$@"
XUcolumn col $TOPLEVEL
XUpushbutton push $col labelString:"I'm A Widget"
XUpushbuttongadget pushg $col labelString:"I'm A Gadget"
XUrealize $TOPLEVEL
XUmainloop
```

Figure 3-1. Widgets and Gadgets (widgad.sh). On the top, a Push-
Button widget, on the bottom, a PushButton gadget. There is no visible difference.

In general, you should use the Gadget form of any primitive widget whenever you
don't need access to the widget-specific resources.

> Actually, there is some controversy on this point, with some people arguing that
> under certain circumstances gadget performance is worse than widget
> performance. In particular, gadgets cause more network traffic than widgets do
> because the parent of the gadget must closely track the movements of the mouse
> pointer. However, many of the Motif widgets create gadget subcomponents
> automatically, so the network traffic problem is not necessarily solved if the
> programmer avoids using gadgets. Also, gadgets do save memory and definitely
> decrease startup time. In addition, the Motif toolkit continues to be improved in
> this area. My recommendation is to use gadgets in most cases.

Chapter 34, *Motif Widget Reference* contains complete resource listings and indicates those that are not available to Gadgets.

3.4 Composite Widgets

Widgets that can serve as parents are called *composite widgets* (they are derived from the Composite superclass). Composite widgets often don't even show up on the screen (or perhaps they have a border but no other visual components). They are used to arrange the layout of their children on the display or to provide a view into a large child. You can put composite widgets inside of composite widgets to any level of nesting.

> **Composite widget:** A widget that can serve as a parent. It can contain one or more child widgets. It may or may not appear on the screen itself.

There are two main branches under the composite widget part of the hierarchy, the Constraint widgets and the Shell widgets.

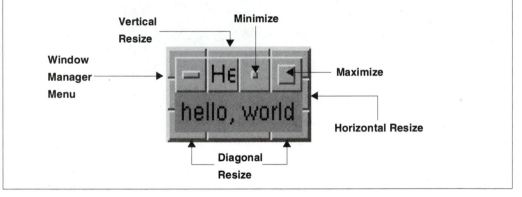

Figure 3-2. Window Manager Decorations.   On the outside edges of the shell widget a number of "decorations" appear. They are created and used by the window manager, not the application itself.

Shell Widgets

> ***ALERT! MAJOR TERMINOLOGY COLLISION AHEAD!***

I hope I got your attention, because this confuses a lot of people learning Desktop KornShell programming. The Shell widget class has nothing to do with shell in the sense of KornShell. It's called the *Shell* widget class because such widgets provide a separate window for their children. Such a window can be moved independently from the application's primary window (the window created by XUinitialize) and it looks to the end user like a separate application.

> ***Shell widget:*** A subclass of Composite that provides a separate
> window for its children. This has nothing to do with shell in the sense of
> KornShell. This separate window can interact with the window man-
> ager.

Shell widgets interact with the window manager. Recall that the window manager
is a process that is responsible for resizing, moving, and dismissing application windows. The window manager can put "decorations" around the border of the Shell
widget. These decorations allow the user to resize, move, iconify, and perform other
operations on the shell widget (and its children).

Figure 3-2 points out the window manager decorations that Shell widgets receive
by default. Some Shell class widgets display only a subset of these standard decorations, and some (such as the MenuShell widget) do not interact with the window
manager at all.

Listing 3-2 shows how to create and display a Shell widget. The resulting output
is shown in Figure 3-3.

Listing 3-2. Shell Widget Example (popup.sh). A TopLevelShell widget is created,
but will not appear on the screen until the PushButton ($PUSH) is selected. This is accom-
plished by calling XUpopup on the TopLevelShell's handle. The TopLevelShell widget contains
another PushButton that, when selected, causes the TopLevelShell to be removed from the
screen using XUpopdown.

```
. $XUTILDIR/xutil.sh

XUinitialize TOPLEVEL Popup "$@"
XUpushbutton PUSH $TOPLEVEL labelString:"popup window"
XUaddcallback $PUSH activateCallback 'XUpopup $POPUPSHELL'

XUtoplevelshell POPUPSHELL $TOPLEVEL title:"Popup Shell Example"
XUpushbutton POPPUSH $POP labelString:"Pop Me Down"
XUaddcallback $POPPUSH_activateCallback "XUpopdown $POPUPSHELL"

XUrealize $TOPLEVEL
XUmainloop
```

After the toolkit is initialized, a PushButton widget is created as a child of
$TOPLEVEL. This PushButton widget receives a callback function—a call to XUpop-
up. That command will cause the widget named by its argument (which must be a
Shell-class widget) to appear. You will note that the call to XUpopup is inside single
quotes—that's because the variable POPUPSHELL has not yet been initialized, so we
must delay its expansion until the callback is actually invoked.

> Another alternative would have been to move this XUaddcallback command past
> the call to XUtoplevelshell so the $POPUPSHELL variable would be initialized;
> in that case double quotes would work.

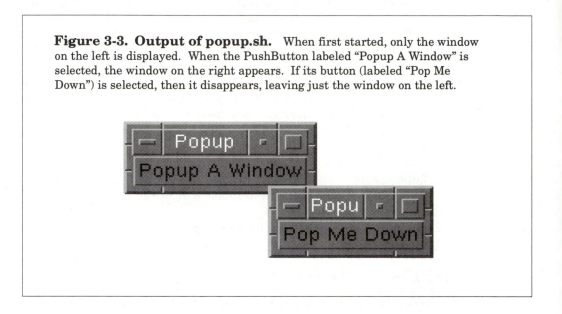

Figure 3-3. Output of popup.sh.   When first started, only the window on the left is displayed. When the PushButton labeled "Popup A Window" is selected, the window on the right appears. If its button (labeled "Pop Me Down") is selected, then it disappears, leaving just the window on the left.

Next, a TopLevelShell widget is created using the command XUtoplevelshell. It takes the same arguments as all the other widget creation commands: the name of a variable to receive the widget handle (POPUPSHELL), the parent of the new widget ($TOPLEVEL), and resource settings. Notice that I set the title resource to the string "Popup Shell Example." The title resource specifies a string that will appear at the top of the shell widget window. This new Shell-class widget will not appear on the screen until it is explicitly displayed using XUpopup.

After POPUPSHELL is created, a PushButton widget (POPPUSH) is added as its child, and is set up so when it is pushed XUpopdown is executed. The XUpopdown command will remove the shell widget POPUPSHELL (and all its children) from view, but it still exists and could be brought back by another call to XUpopup.

Table 3-3 lists all the Shell widgets that programmers use, along with information on their most common uses and differences.

Table 3-3. Shell Class Widgets

Shell Widget	Typical Uses in X Application Programming
ApplicationShell	Created by XUinitialize for the main application window. Usually not used by the programmer.
DialogShell	Motif convenience functions use this as the parent for various dialog widgets.

Table 3-3. Shell Class Widgets (continued)

Shell Widget	Typical Uses in X Application Programming
MenuShell	Does not communicate with the window manager. Used for creating the window that contains different kinds of menus.
TopLevelShell	Similar to ApplicationShell. Should be used by the programmer for additional top-level windows in the application. To the end user, such windows will look just like other application windows.
TransientShell	Should be used for additional top-level windows that do not need to be independently iconified. The minimize window decoration will not appear (nor will it appear in the window manager menu).

3.5 Manager Widgets

The Manager-class widgets also provide services for their children, mainly in layout and geometry management. However, they have one interesting feature that no other class of widgets can boast: many of them have the ability to add new resources to their children. These are called *constraint* resources because they are often used to constrain how the child is placed in a window. When a child widget is created with a Manager widget as its parent, it can gain new resources that it otherwise would not be able to.

> ***Manager widget:*** A subclass of Composite that manages the layout or geometry of its children.

> ***Constraint resource:*** A resource added to a child by its parent. Such a resource is usually used to manage ("constrain") the child's geometry in some way.

For example, a BulletinBoard widget is a Manager widget that can arbitrarily position its children by x, y coordinates. Each child of a BulletinBoard widget will get two new resources, x and y, which can be used to specify its position relative to the upper left corner of the BulletinBoard's window. Other types of constraint resources are also provided by other Manager widgets, such as the Form widget.

Table 3-4 shows all the Manager-class widgets, with information on when you might use them in a program.

Table 3-4. Manager Class Widgets

Manager Widget	Typical Uses	Appearance
Command	A standard dialog to prompt the user for a textual command string. Contains a command history list. Used when it is desirable to give the user a line-oriented method of executing commands as a short cut.	history area command entry area
DrawingArea	Provides an area on which Xlib commands can be used to draw arbitrary graphics. Children can be placed anywhere in the drawing area. Typically used to create customized pseudo-widgets.	Appearance varies; the programmer can draw arbitrary graphics in the rectangular area provided by the DrawingArea widget.
FileSelectionBox	A standard dialog for prompting for a filename. Allows the user to browse through files and directories, and shows a list of available files and standard buttons. Used to prompt for a filename.	filter Filter /home/pend/DEMOS/dtk/PROGS/* Directories / Files file and directory lists DEMOS/dtk/PROGS/. DEMOS/dtk/PROGS/.. DEMOS/dtk/PROGS/DONE DEMOS/dtk/PROGS/TIF DEMOS/dtk/PROGS/WIDGETS cascb fsb gadget goodbywi hello2 lab list mainwin selected file Selection /home/pend/DEMOS/dtk/PROGS/ buttons OK Filter Cancel Help

Table 3-4. Manager Class Widgets (continued)

Manager Widget	Typical Uses	Appearance
Form	Allows complex interchild relationships to be represented, such as: *place child A to the left of child B*. Children can also be placed relative to edges of the form itself. Such relationships are maintained after resizing the window.	**label children placed in complex relationships to each other** label0 label1 label2 label3
Frame	Places a border around its child. Used to set some widgets apart from others visually.	label0 **frame border** — label1 label2 label3
MainWindow	Creates a number of children in a common format used by many applications (menu bar at top, work area with optional scrollbars, message area at the bottom). Often used for the top-level structure of an application.	**menu bar** **command area** MainWindow File View Options Help 1989 1990 1991 1992 **application area** **scroll bars**

Table 3-4. Manager Class Widgets (continued)

Manager Widget	Typical Uses	Appearance
MessageBox	A standard message box format with a message area at the top and several standard buttons at the bottom. Used for various kinds of messages: errors, warnings, information, etc.	
PanedWindow	Allows several children to be stacked vertically in a way that allows the end user to determine how much vertical area each child receives. Used when there are several major display areas in a program and the user might want to have control over how much screen real estate is allotted to each.	
RowColumn	Stacks children in regularly spaced rows and columns. Used when children need to be stacked horizontally or vertically.	
Scale	Provides a slider area (or *thumb*) that the user can move by dragging the mouse. Often used to prompt the user for a numeric value.	

Table 3-4. Manager Class Widgets (continued)

Manager Widget	Typical Uses	Appearance
ScrolledWindow	Provides a view into a larger child. ScrollBars appear if the child is too large horizontally or vertically. Used when a large widget or set of widgets must be displayed in a limited space.	 **object being viewed** **scroll bars**
SelectionBox	Provides a standard dialog that prompts the user to select one of several items. Contains a scrolled list, a text area containing the selection, and several standard buttons. Used to prompt the user for one of numerous choices.	**list of items** **selected item** **standard buttons**

3.6 Summary

This chapter has presented a brief overview of all the Motif widgets, showing you how they look and indicating when you might use one or another. There are several broad categories of widget:

- **Primitive widgets**. These widgets are used for basic user input or decoration purposes. Some primitive widgets are quite sophisticated, like the Text widget that provides complex editing capability, but others are very simple.

- **Gadgets**. These widgets are objects similar to widgets, but they are optimized for performance. There are gadget counterparts to most of the primitive widgets. To the user and programmer they appear the same.

- **Shell widgets**. These widgets are used when a program needs a separate independent window. They are displayed using the XUpopup command, and can be hidden using XUpopdown.

- **Manager widgets**. These widgets are used to arrange other widgets on the screen, or provide a scrolled window into a larger widget. Sometimes they do not even appear on the screen themselves.

4   *The Standard Main Window*

4.1 Introduction

A great many applications are similar in appearance and have some common elements:

- A *MenuBar* at the top of the window that provides menu buttons. The user can perform actions using these menus.

- A *work area* in the center of the window provides application-specific information. Often, this work area uses ScrollBars to allow viewing work area items that do not fit on the screen.

- A *message area* near the bottom of the window provides feedback to the user on the state of the application, or whether the last action the user attempted was successful.

See Figure 4-1 for an example of this kind of application. Now, not every application requires all of these elements; some applications require none of them. But a wide range of applications fits this mold: everything from spreadsheet programs to word processors to database front ends. Because this is such a common application paradigm, users are comfortable with it—they've seen it a thousand times. So it's a good idea to design your applications with these standard elements unless there is some fundamental reason not to.

Because of this common "look and feel" for many kinds of applications, Motif provides a widget, the MainWindow widget, to implement it. The MainWindow widget is really a set of widgets put together in a standard way. The programmer must create each of the other standard elements—MenuBar, work area, ScrollBars, and message area—separately. The programmer then sets some resources of the

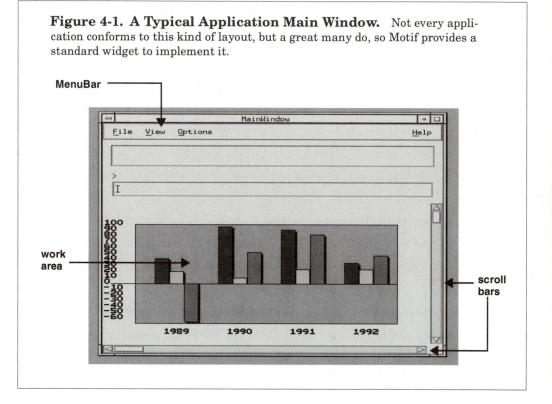

Figure 4-1. A Typical Application Main Window. Not every application conforms to this kind of layout, but a great many do, so Motif provides a standard widget to implement it.

MainWindow widget to identify these components, and the MainWindow widget then lays them out in the standard arrangement.

> The Motif MainWindow widget also provides another component called the Command area in which the user of the application can type line-oriented commands and can select previous commands from a history window. Personally, I think this is rather useless and is a throwback to line-oriented application days. I have also seen virtually no commercial applications actually use this feature. So, I'm not going to discuss it further here. However, there is another use of this area that will be discussed in a future chapter—providing a button bar.

Chapter Strategy

In this chapter, I show you how to use the MainWindow widget by creating the scaffolding for a checkbook handling program. At first, this scaffolding will create a window with all the desired graphical elements without creating any of the callbacks that actually do the work. Thus, running the script will just show the visual elements of the application. Later chapters will continue to build on this example, until by the end of this book all the callbacks will be defined and the application will be complete.

Because a number of different widgets are required to build this scaffolding, this chapter also shows you the rudiments of how to create Pulldown menu systems, TextField widgets, and List widgets. However, I'm not going to attempt to explain every nuance of how those widgets work here. They are discussed further in the following chapters:

- Menus: Chapter 13, *Menu, Please*
- Lists: Chapter 15, *The List Widget*
- TextFields: Chapter 16, *Text and TextField Widgets*, also some sections of Chapter 6, *Prompting Using Custom Dialogs*.

If you get the urge to learn more about the details of one of these widgets as you read this chapter, go right ahead.

4.2 Checkbook Application Requirements

Applications should be designed with the requirements of the user in mind. The application in this case will be a checkbook management program. It will provide all the elements necessary to track and manage a personal checking account.

> Perhaps my lawyers and I should point out here that this and other applications in this book are presented as examples only in "as-is" condition. They are not warranteed for any particular purpose, and the author and publisher of this book are not liable for any damages caused by the personal or commercial use of these applications. In other words, if you actually use this program to balance your checkbook and some bug causes a check to bounce on you, I'm not paying the bank penalty. Comprende?

You should always take some time—for simple applications perhaps only a few minutes—to write down the requirements of your application. This will help you design the interface. The preliminary requirements for this application are as follows:

- The application will display a listing of all checks, deposits, etc.
- The current balance of the checking account will be displayed at all times.
- There will be a standard MenuBar containing at least these menu buttons:
    1. `File` contains items to Open, Close, Save, and Print the checkbook.
    2. `View` contains items to change how the check items are displayed, such as the amount of Detail shown.
    3. `Actions` contains items that allow the user to add, modify, or delete entries from the checkbook.
    4. `Help` contains items to provide the user of the application with various kinds of information.

Now that we have defined the basic requirements, you can see immediately that this application fits in well with the standard main window paradigm discussed earlier. In this case, we will use a Motif List widget as the work area, and the application will display the current balance of the checkbook in the message area, which will be a Motif TextField widget.

The next few sections will discuss how to create the MainWindow and its subcomponents using the XU library functions.

4.3 Creating the MainWindow Widget

The MainWindow widget is created using the command `XUmainwindow`, which takes the same arguments as any of the other widget creation commands you've come across so far. A number of resources are supported by the MainWindow widget, but the most commonly used ones are:

- `menuBar`, `messageWindow`, and `workWindow` are the widget handles of the subcomponents we have discussed. The programmer must create these components as children of the MainWindow widget, then set these resources of the MainWindow widget afterward (so it knows which child corresponds to each component).

- `showSeparator` is a boolean resource. If set to `true`, then a Separator widget will appear between the MenuBar area and the work area.

- `scrollingPolicy` can take the values `STATIC` or `AS_NEEDED`. If set to `STATIC`, then ScrollBars always appear around the work area; when set to `AS_NEEDED` they only appear if the work area is too large to fit in the Main-Window. The default is `AS_NEEDED`.

- `scrollBarDisplayPolicy` can take the values `AUTOMATIC` or `APPLICATION_DEFINED`. If set to `AUTOMATIC`, then all scrolling is carried out on your behalf by the MainWindow widget. Otherwise, you have to handle the scrolling yourself by registering callbacks on the ScrollBars. The default is `APPLICATION_DEFINED`.

As you can see in Listing 4-1, I didn't set any resources of the MainWindow. The default `scrollBarDisplayPolicy` is `APPLICATION_DEFINED`. That turns out to be acceptable for this example because I happen to be using a List widget for the work area, and the List widget handles scrolling automatically. However, in most cases you will probably need to set this resource to `AUTOMATIC`. In general, leaving this at the default of `APPLICATION_DEFINED` is only for sophisticated applications that need to fine-tune their scrolling behavior.

Listing 4-1. Creating the MainWindow (chkbook1.sh).

```
. $UXTILDIR/xutil.sh

XUinitialize TOPLEVEL Checkbook "$@"

XUmainwindow MAINWIN $TOPLEVEL
```

4.4 Creating the MenuBar and Pulldown Menus

Now that we've got our MainWindow, we need to create each of its components. First, we'll make the MenuBar and the Pulldown menu system. Normally this is a tedious process in Motif, but the XU convenience commands come to the rescue by providing a simple way to make Pulldown menu systems (even complex ones).

Take a look at Listing 4-2. The first line, a call to the XUmenubar command, creates a MenuBar and stores its handle in the variable MB.

> Actually, a MenuBar is nothing more than a RowColumn widget with its resources configured in a certain way. When you think about it this is quite logical, since a MenuBar is nothing more than a horizontal stack of buttons, and the RowColumn widget is quite capable of stacking widgets horizontally. From now on I will use the term MenuBar as if it is a kind of widget.

Note that this widget is created as a child of the MainWindow widget—that's very important. All the subcomponents will be direct children of the MainWindow.

Listing 4-2. CheckBook Pulldown Menus (chkbook1.sh). After creating a MenuBar using the XUmenubar command, four separate calls to XUmenusystem are used to create the Pulldown menu system. Note the use of compound variable names with the MB variable used as a base—this keeps related object variables organized. After all the menus are created, the menuHelpWidget resource of the MenuBar widget is set to the handle of the Help menu button, which causes that menu button to be right aligned.

```
XUmenubar MB $MAINWIN

XUmenusystem $MB \
    MB.FILE "File" F { \
        MB.FILE.OPEN    "Open" O openCB \
        MB.FILE.SAVE    "Save" S saveCB \
        MB.FILE.SAVEAS "Save As..." A saveasCB \
        - - - - \
        MB.FILE.PRINT   "Print ..." P printCB \
        - - - - \
        MB.FILE.EXIT    "Exit" E exitCB \
    }

XUmenusystem $MB \
    MB.VIEW "View" V { \
        MB.VIEW.CHECK   "Sort by Category" C sortcategCB \
        MB.VIEW.CHECK   "Sort by Date and Check" D sortdateCB \
        - - - - \
        MB.VIEW.DETAILS "Show Details" e showdetailsCB \
    }

XUmenusystem $MB \
    MB.ACTIONS "Actions" A { \
```

```
            MB.ACTIONS.ADD    "Add Entry"              A addCB \
            MB.ACTIONS.EDIT   "Edit Selected Entry"    E editCB \
            - - - - \
            MB.ACTIONS.DELETE "Delete Selected Entry" D deleteCB \
        }

    XUmenusystem $MB \
        MB.HELP "Help" H { \
            MB.HELP.CONTEXT "On Context ..." C helpcontextCB \
            MB.HELP.VERSION "On Version ..." V helpversionCB \
        }

    XUset $MB menuHelpWidget:${MB.HELP}
```

The XUmenusystem Command

After creating the MenuBar, we need to create Pulldown menus—the kind that appear when the user selects a button in the MenuBar. This is accomplished using the XUmenusystem command.

The first argument to XUmenusystem is the handle of a MenuBar. Further arguments are in the following format:

> *variable label mnemonic action*

1. The name of a *variable* that will be set to the handle of an element of the Pulldown menu.

2. The *label* that should appear on this element of the Pulldown menu.

3. The *mnemonic* that should be used on the label. A mnemonic is a single letter that can be used to select the menu item without using the mouse. On most keyboards, you press a special key (such as ALT) plus the mnemonic in order to trigger the menu you wish to appear. Once the menu is showing, simply pressing the mnemonic letter for an item selects that item (no ALT is needed once the menu is displayed).

4. An *action* to perform when the item is selected. This can be either a dtksh command string, or an open curly brace. If it is an open curly brace, then another level of menu will be created, and there should be further sets of four arguments up to a matching close curly brace that define the items in the list. This nesting can occur to any level, and cascades of menus will be created automatically.

Another feature is that a set of four dashes (- - - -) can be used instead of the usual set of four arguments, and in that case a Separator is created at that point in the menu. Separators are useful in menus to keep groups of related commands visually distinct from one another. Figure 4-2 breaks down the function of each argument in a simple call to XUmenusystem.

There are other more advanced features of this versatile command, and they are
discussed in Chapter 13, *Menu, Please*.

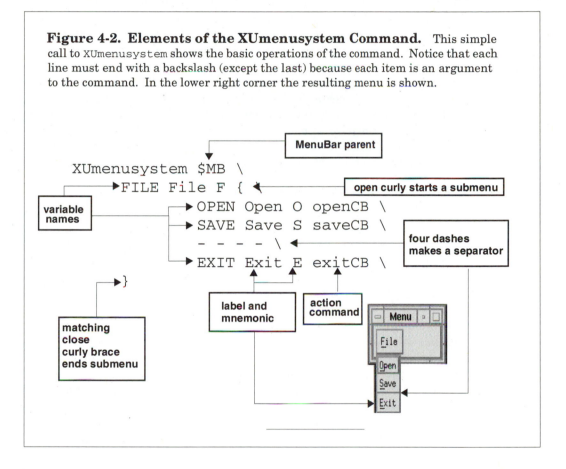

Figure 4-2. Elements of the XUmenusystem Command. This simple
call to XUmenusystem shows the basic operations of the command. Notice that each
line must end with a backslash (except the last) because each item is an argument
to the command. In the lower right corner the resulting menu is shown.

The menuHelpWidget Resource

The MenuBar has one special resource that you need to be aware of: menuHelp-
Widget. By convention, every MenuBar should have a Help button, and the widget
handle of that button should be stored in the menuHelpWidget resource of the
MenuBar widget. This is because the Motif style guide requires that the Help button come last and be right aligned in the MenuBar; this is done on your behalf by
the MenuBar after you set this resource. You can see an example of this at the very
end of Listing 4-2.

Organizing the XUmenusystem Arguments

To keep all these arguments organized, I like to indent each of the sets of four arguments according to the level of menu being created, keeping the curly braces matched. Of course, you must put a backslash on the end of each line, because this is a single long set of arguments to one command.

As you can see from the examples, a great many variable names are required—one for each element of the Pulldown menu. These variables are necessary because a good program should set the sensitivity state of each menu item depending on the current state of the program, and so you need a way to reference each item. For example, when the program first comes up, there is no checkbook file open, so the Print and Save items in the File menu don't make sense. A well-written program will set those to be insensitive so that the user can't select them. To keep the variables organized, I like to follow the convention of naming Pulldown menu item variables hierarchically, using the MenuBar parent variable name as the base of the hierarchy.

4.5 Adding the Work and Message Areas

Next we need to create the work and message areas. These can be any widget or combination of widgets; it's entirely up to the application programmer.

In this application the Motif List widget fits the needs of the work area perfectly. The List widget can be used to display entries from the checkbook. It has all the features we'll need: the ability to highlight items, the ability to register a callback that will be triggered when the user double-clicks on an item, and the ability to arbitrarily add, delete, and modify items.

For the message area, this application just needs to be able to display the current balance of the checkbook, and a simple TextField widget will do the job nicely.

Listing 4-3 shows how both are created. As with the MenuBar, both of these areas are created as children of the MainWindow widget.

The List widget is created using `XUlist`, which stores its handle in the variable `WORK`. I set only two resources: `visibleItemCount`, which will set the initial number of lines of text the widget will display; and `listSizePolicy` which determines how the List will respond to user resize requests. The `RESIZE_IF_POSSIBLE` option is used, which will cause the list to attempt to grow large enough to show all its entries; Scrollbars will appear in both horizontal and vertical dimensions if growth is not possible. This is almost always the way you want the List widget to behave.

Listing 4-3. Work and Message Areas (chkbook1.sh).

```
XUlist WORK $MAINWIN \
    visibleItemCount:8 \
    listSizePolicy:RESIZE_IF_POSSIBLE \
    fontList:fixed
XUtextfield MESSAGE $MAINWIN \
    editable:false \
  cursorPositionVisible:false
```

The TextField widget displays a single line of text, which is what we need for the message area, but by default it allows the user to edit the text. In this case that's not desirable, so I set the `editable` resource to the value `false`, which disallows editing. In addition, a single line of read-only text does not need a cursor, so I disable display of the cursor by setting the resource `cursorPositionVisible` to `false`.

4.6 Setting the MainWindow Areas

Once all the widgets are created, it is necessary to tell the MainWindow which of its children will serve in each of the roles. This is done by setting resources of the MainWindow widget. The resources are:

- `workWindow`, the handle of the work area widget
- `menuBar`, the handle of the MenuBar widget
- `messageWindow`, the handle of the message widget

Listing 4-4 shows the `XUset` command required in the case of our example application.

> Motif provides a "convenience" function for setting these resources called `XmMainWindowSetAreas`, but with dtksh it's simpler to just set the resources directly. The Motif convenience function is easier to use in C where more work is involved in setting resources.

As you can see, you simply provide the values of the widget variables as the values of these resources. Listing 4-4 also finishes up the script by realizing the widget hierarchy and calling `XUmainloop` to process events.

Listing 4-4. Setting the MainWindow Areas (chkbook1.sh). After the areas are set, the widget hierarchy is realized, some fake entries are added to the List widget using a function called `fakeitems`, and the usual `XUmainloop` function is called.

```
XUset $MAINWIN \
    menuBar:$MB \
    workWindow:$WORK \
    messageWindow:$MESSAGE

fakeitems   # create some fake data

XUrealize $TOPLEVEL
XUmainloop
```

4.7 Scaffolding

To get a feel for how the full application will look, a "stub routine" is called that creates some fake entries in the list widget and puts an appropriate string in the message area. This technique is very common: create a sample screen with no callbacks to actually do the work, just fill in some sample values to see if it looks ok. It is often helpful to bring your program's potential users in to give you comments on these mocked-up screens.

> I used an early prototype of dtksh to create programs for my wife's business (you think *your* users are tough!) She was somewhat skeptical until I showed her some of my initial mock up screens, at which point her jaw dropped and she said, "wow, that looks just like a professional program!" At that point I gently reminded her that "I *am* a professional programmer."

In this example, the scaffolding simply creates a few fake checkbook entries in the List widget using the XUlistappend command. That command's first argument is the handle of the List widget to which you wish to add items; any further arguments are the text items to be added. After that, a fake balance is placed in the message area by using XUset to change the value resource of the TextField widget. This is shown in Listing 4-5.

Listing 4-5. Filling In Fake Values (chkbook1.sh).

```
function fakeitems {
    XUlistadd $WORK 0 \
        '10/15/94 1025   Ms. Alice Swenson              $299.37' \
        '10/22/94 ----   DEPOSIT ********             $1042.92' \
        '10/30/94 1026   The Phone Co.                  $99.87' \
        '11/01/94 1027   Electric Co. Inc.              $87.22'
    XUset $MESSAGE value:'Checkbook Balance: $2099.43'
}
```

Taking a Test Drive

Now we have a complete screen; it won't do anything, mind you, since I have not yet defined any of the callback functions. But it will run, and thanks to the temporary scaffolding it will even appear to be a real application. At this point, we can take it for a test drive, to see how things look and behave. The complete application is in a file called chkbook1.sh, and you can execute it by running the command:

```
dtksh chkbook1.sh
```

Figure 4-3 shows the application as it appears when it first comes up. A few things you might notice:

- No ScrollBars are showing because all the items fit in the allotted space.
- As expected, the Help menu button is right aligned (because we set the menuHelpWidget resource of the MenuBar).
- The mnemonic letters that were chosen for the menu items are underlined.

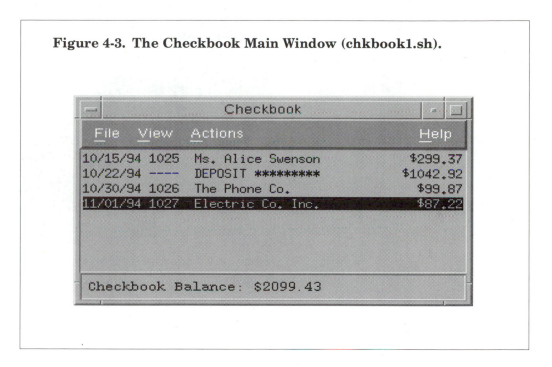

Figure 4-3. The Checkbook Main Window (chkbook1.sh).

Testing the Menus

Even though I have not defined the callback functions that are registered for the menu items, it is still possible to select menu buttons to see if all the Pulldown menus are set up as intended. This is always a good idea—it's easy to give the wrong order of arguments to the XUmenusystem command. A common mistake is to leave out the mnemonic for one or more items; that throws off all the other arguments and your menu items will look like garbage after the point of the error. Another common error is to forget the backslash at the end of one or more lines, or to accidentally put whitespace after a backslash. In these cases you will probably get warnings from the shell when you try to execute the script.

Figure 4-3 shows the File menu. It is set up as intended. Notice the use of Separator widgets to group commands in the menu. Also notice that every item has a mnemonic, and the mnemonics are the ones we intended. It's important to check all the items for mnemonics because you can sometimes accidentally use the same letter twice within a menu; in that case Motif will simply ignore the second mnemonic resulting in an item with no mnemonic.

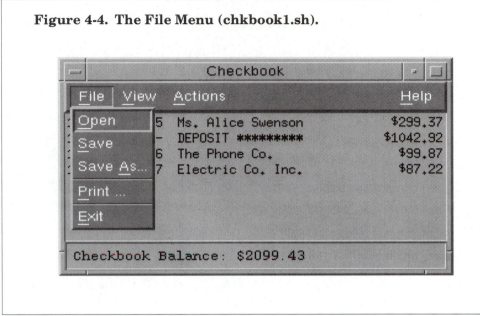

Figure 4-4. The File Menu (chkbook1.sh).

Checking Resize Behavior and ScrollBars

It's important for an application to respond correctly to resize requests by the user. The user can resize the application by grabbing one of the corner areas of the window with the mouse and dragging it to a new size, or by using the window manager menu.

What is proper resize behavior? Well, users normally resize an application because they want to see more (or sometimes less) of the work area. So, the desired result is that the work area changes size, getting more space or giving up space, while the other areas remain a constant size (as much as possible anyway).

Using the MainWindow widget usually results in proper resize behavior, but it's a good idea to put it to the test. Figure 4-3 shows how this application responds to a resize request to a smaller size in the vertical dimension and to a slightly larger size in the horizontal dimension. All of the vertical space was taken from the work area (the List widget), which is correct. As you can see, a ScrollBar has now appeared on the right! This is because the entries no longer all fit on the display. Grabbing the ScrollBar will confirm that it is functional (it's a good idea to check, sometimes ScrollBars fail to work because the `scrollingPolicy` resource is not set correctly).

The Help button is still positioned at the right side of the MenuBar, even though the window is now wider.

Figure 4-5. The MainWindow After Resizing (chkbook1.sh).

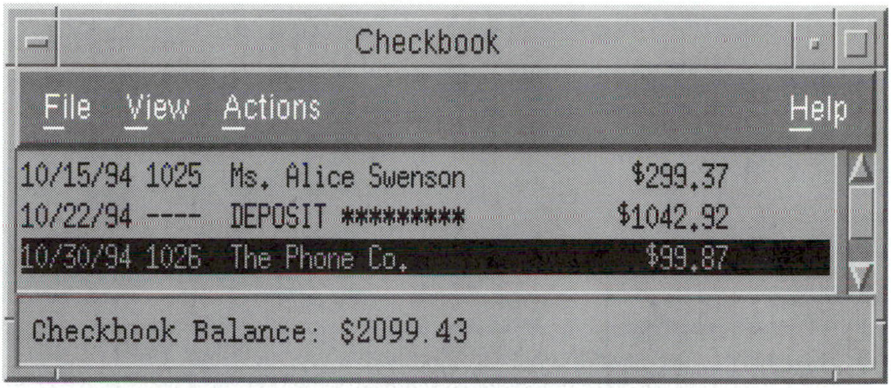

4.8 The Real Thing

At this point we have a pleasing screen layout that has been lightly tested. It uses some scaffolding routines to provide simulated data, but none of the callback functions are defined. If you were to select a menu item, a warning message would appear on the terminal from which you ran the program: "function <fill in the blank> not found."

In a real project, you might even bring in a potential user at this point to see what they think about the program. The danger is, of course, that you'll have a conversation that goes something like this:

User: Gee, those screens look terrific!

You: (blushing) Thanks. I am a professional Graphical Interface programmer, you know.

User: I can see now why you get the big bucks. Well, I guess we can ramp up production and install this puppy next Tuesday, right?

You: Uh, er, well, you see it's just a, I mean, well...

So, make sure your user knows that there's plenty more work to be done once the screens are mocked up.

It's time to make some of this application real by replacing the scaffolding with functions that do work (hopefully by next Tuesday). Before doing that, though, we need to make some design decisions:

- What will be the format of our check book data file?
- How will we represent the data file internally?
- How will the user modify the data?

These design decisions are discussed in the next few sections.

The Flat File Database

It is reasonable to represent the checkbook data file as a "flat file database," Which is a simple ASCII file in which each line is a single record. Fields within each record are delimited by some character that will never appear in the data.

> What is this discussion doing in a book on graphical programming? Well, there are many applications that need some kind of small database. Consider programs like "to do" list trackers, telephone number lookup, etc. All can profitably use flat file databases.

This kind of database is fine for tasks involving up to a few thousand records. Since the intent of this example is to provide a checkbook handling program for personal use, that should be sufficient—most people don't use more than a few hundred checks per year. The user could always break up the checkbook files by year if performance became an issue.

What fields do we need in each record? The following seems like a good first cut:

- MM, DD, YY. These three fields will hold the month, day, and year of the record. They are all integers.
- PAYEE. This will hold a string indicating who received the check.
- CHECKNUM. An integer indicating the check number. If this record does not have a check number, the field is left blank (a single space).
- AMOUNT. The amount of the transaction, a floating-point number with two decimal digits.
- CATEGORY. A string indicating the nature of the check. Values are user defined and should be short. For example, TELEPHONE, AUTO, UTILITY, CHARITY, MORTGAGE, or PERSONAL. Useful for tax purposes or obtaining breakdowns of expenses by category. One special system-defined value, CREDIT, is used for all entries that add money to the checking account.
- RECON. An integer, either 1 or 0, indicating whether this check has been reconciled (come back from the bank). Zero means it has not come back.

- COMMENT. A string in which the user puts any commentary information desired on this record.

I like to use the pipe symbol (|) as the field separator. It's highly unlikely to be needed anywhere in the string fields of the checkbook (PAYEE, CATEGORY, COMMENT). In any case, we'll write the program to make sure the user can never put that character in any field. Listing 4-6 shows a sample file whose fields match this format.

Listing 4-6. A Checkbook Flat File Database (sample.chk). Fields are delimited by the pipe symbol, and are (in order): MM, DD, YY, PAYEE, CHECKNUM, AMOUNT, CATEG, RECON, and COMMENT. The checkbook application will be enhanced to read, write, and modify files in this format.

```
1|1|94|STARTING BALANCE| |1243.07|CREDIT|1|
1|9|94|Alice Derringer|3587|90.13|CLEANING|0|
1|9|94|J. S. Pendergrast|3590|100.00|PERSONAL|1|spending loot
1|11|94|Ajax Telephone Company|3593|69.15|TELEPHONE|0|
1|11|94|DEPOSIT| |1.98|CREDIT|1|book royalty
1|11|94|Sussex Power and Light|3594|89.27|UTILITY|0|
1|12|94|Jackson Oil Company|3595|235.99|FUEL|1|Service charge
1|11|94|Specialty Tire Inc.|3596|187.50|AUTO|0|New Tires
1|30|94|Checking Account Interest| |18.83|CREDIT|1|
```

The XU Database Functions

How should we read the database file in to our program? How should it be represented internally?

The simplest answer is simply to read in each line of the file and then store them in an array. When fields need to be broken out, we can use the common trick of redefining the IFS (internal field separator) variable and using the read built-in to break up the line.

> For more information on this technique, see Chapter 28, *KornShell Language Review*, which has an example called *Parsing Files Using Read* on page 580.

However, there's no need to reinvent the wheel. A simple set of functions to manipulate flat file databases is included in the XU library.

Without going into excessive detail (it's all explained in Chapter 33, *XU Library Reference*), here are the database functions provided by xutil.sh that we will be using in this chapter (other functions are explained as needed in future chapters):

- XUdbopen *variable path delimiter*

  Opens the *path* as a flat file database. *Delimiter* is a single character used to delimit fields in the record. A database handle is returned in *variable*. It will be used with other XU commands. The records are stored in the array ${*variable*.record[*]} for easy linear access. The *path* is

stored in ${*variable*.file}. The number of records is of course:
${#*variable*.record[@]}.

> If you are not familiar with this notation for finding the number of elements of an
> array, you might want to review how KornShell arrays work. See *Indexed Array
> Variables* on page 555, and also *Other Kinds of Variable Expansion* on page 558

- XUdbsplit *variable index array-variable*

  Split up record number *index* by the database's delimiter, storing each field
  in successive entries of the given *array-variable*. Here, the *variable* is
  the same variable name that was used on the XUdbopen call. Note that this
  is a variable name, not an expanded variable, you do not put the dollar sign
  ($) in front.

These database functions are written entirely as shell functions, but provide reasonable performance for small to moderate size databases. For example, on an Intel
486 class machine XUdbopen takes under 1 second to open and read in a 500-record
file. XUdbsplit can process about 250 records per second (including looping overhead) on the same hardware. Of course, by the time this book is published that's
likely to be considered a slow machine!

> You should be aware of one other limitation; KornShell-93 arrays may have at most
> 4096 entries. Thus, the XU database functions described here are limited to
> databases with that number of records. However, you would probably want to use a
> real database of some kind if that many records were expected to be present in an
> application.

Replacing the Scaffolding

Now we're ready to replace the scaffolding used previously with a command that
really reads and formats records from a flat file database. First I define some variables that will make the use of the XU commands more readable. We will be using
XUdbsplit to parse records into individual fields; it puts each field in an element of
an array passed in as an argument. So, we will be indexing into an array to access
individual fields. For this reason, it is convenient to define variables whose names
correspond to field names and whose values are the numbers corresponding to the
array indexes. These variables are defined as readonly because they are constants that we never wish to change. Once defined using readonly, the variable
cannot be changed again in the program; attempts to do so will cause a run-time
error. These definitions are shown in Listing 4-7.

We also need a variable to hold some global state information about the application. For example, it makes sense to define a variable that holds the current View
menu settings (sort order, detailed viewing mode, etc.). For that reason, a variable
called STATE is defined, and it will be used as the base for hierarchical variables that
will contain this kind of information. It's a good idea to put related information like

this in hierarchical variables—that keeps the information organized and reduces the number of separate globals. These variables are defined in Listing 4-7.

Listing 4-7. Database Field Variables (chkbook2.sh). One `readonly` variable is defined for each field record, and they are initialized to the field order index. They can be used as indexes to arrays of parsed fields as produced by `XUdbsplit`. In addition, some global state variables are defined for the application.

```
. $XUTILDIR/xutil.sh

# Database Field definitions

readonly MM=0 DD=1 YY=2 PAYEE=3 CHECKNUM=4 AMOUNT=5 \
    CATEG=6 RECON=7 COMMENT=8

typeset STATE=""
integer STATE.DETAILS=0
integer STATE.SORTORDER=CHECKNUM
```

Next we need a function that actually reads records from the database, calculates the checkbook balance, and adds formatted entries to the List widget for viewing. This is implemented as a function called `update_display` that is shown in Listing 4-8. After declaring some local variables, the function starts by deleting all the previous List items using the function `XUlistdeleteall`. This is necessary to make the function general purpose—it can be called at any time to update the display. The function assumes the database has already been opened using `XUdbopen`, with the database handle stored in the variable `DB`. The next step is to cycle through all the records totaling up the checkbook balance and displaying the records. A C-style `for` loop is used, and it takes advantage of the fact that `XUdbopen` stores the records in an array (in this case `${DB.record[*]}`). Note the use of the KornShell notation `${#DB.record[@]}`, which expands to the number of elements of the array `DB.record` that are set.

Within the `for` loop, the `XUdbsplit` function is used to parse individual fields into an array named `f`. To keep track of the running checkbook balance, it is necessary to check whether the `CATEG` (category) field is the special value `CREDIT`, indicating a deposit, interest payment, etc. If the category is `CREDIT`, then the `AMOUNT` field is added to the running total, otherwise it is subtracted. You can see how this code's readability benefits from using the read-only variables defined before to access fields in the array.

After the running total is updated, the record is formatted and added to the List widget for display to the user. The formatting task is necessary to make the output more palatable—the raw database record isn't very legible. I've split the formatting task into a separate function called `format_record` because the exact method of formatting depends on what viewing mode the user has chosen, so it isn't trivial. Formatting is discussed in the next section.

The final step, which occurs after the `for` loop completes, is to update the message area to include the checkbook balance. This amounts to a simple formatting task, which is carried out by the KornShell built-in command `printf`; the result is displayed by using `XUset` on the message widget's `value` resource.

Listing 4-8. Reading and Displaying Data (chkbook2.sh). This function assumes the database has already been opened via `XUdbopen`. It runs through the record array keeping track of the running balance, and adds formatted records to the List widget as it goes. After all records are scanned the balance is displayed in the message area.

```
function update_display {
    integer running
    typeset f line

    XUlistdeleteall $WORK

    for (( i = 0; i < ${#DB.record[@]}; i++ ))
    do
        XUdbsplit DB $i f
        if [[ ${f[CATEG]} == CREDIT ]]
        then
            (( running += f[AMOUNT] ))
        else
            (( running -= f[AMOUNT] ))
        fi
        XUlistappend $WORK "$(format_record "${f[@]}")"
    done
    XUset $MESSAGE \
        value:"$(printf "Balance: \$%9.2f" $running)"
}
```

Formatting the Display List

The `update_display` function calls the function `format_record` to create a nice-looking output string for display in the List widget. This formatting function is shown in Listing 4-9. It displays different levels of information depending on the setting of `STATE.DETAILS`. If `STATE.DETAILS` is zero, then only summary information is displayed:

```
MM/DD/YY CHECKNUM PAYEE AMOUNT
```

The `AMOUNT` field will be shifted over into its own column if the record is of category `CREDIT`. This helps visually separate the deposits from the withdrawals.

If `STATE.DETAILS` is set to 1, then a higher level of detail is displayed:

```
[+] MM/DD/YY CHECKNUM PAYEE AMOUNT CATEG COMMENTS
```

As before, AMOUNT goes in a different column for CREDIT records. If the line begins with a plus (+) then that record has been reconciled (i.e., a plus appears in column 1 if the RECON field is nonzero).

This formatting task is straightforward, being basically an exercise in using the printf built-in command. The arguments to this KornShell built-in are identical to those of the C function with the same name.

Listing 4-9. Formatting Records for Display. Credits are put in a different column from debits by using a different formatting string held in the variable fmt. The function supports displaying in either a short form or a detailed form depending on the flag STATE.DETAILS.

```
function format_record {  # args are fields
    typeset f
    set -A f "$@"

    if [[ ${f[CATEG]} == CREDIT ]]
    then fmt="            %8.2f"
    else fmt="%8.2f            "
    fi
    if (( STATE.DETAILS ))  # Show all details
    then
        if (( f[RECON] ))
        then recon="+"
        else recon=" "
        fi
        printf "%s %2.2d/%2.2d/%2.2d %5.5s %-25.25s $fmt %-9.9s %-20.20s" \
                "$recon" ${f[MM]} ${f[DD]} ${f[YY]} \
                "${f[CHECKNUM]}" "${f[PAYEE]}" \
                ${f[AMOUNT]} "${f[CATEG]}" "${f[COMMENT]}"
    else
        printf "%2.2d/%2.2d/%2.2d %5.5s %-25.25s $fmt" \
                ${f[MM]} ${f[DD]} ${f[YY]} "${f[CHECKNUM]}" \
                "${f[PAYEE]}" ${f[AMOUNT]}
    fi
}
```

Replacing the Fakeitems Function

To test these formatting and display functions, we can replace the call to fakeitems with a function that will open a sample checkbook file using XUdbopen followed by a call to update_display. Such a function, called open_checkbook, is shown in Listing 4-10.

A sample checkbook data file called sample.chk is provided with the example programs in the Data subdirectory. Replace the previous call to fakeitems with this code:

```
if [[ -r ${DTKSH_ARGV[1]} ]]
then
    open_checkbook ${DTKSH_ARGV[1]}
else
    print "Usage: $0 file"
    exit
fi
```

The XUinitialize command leaves any unparsed standard X arguments (such as
-iconic) in the array DTKSH_ARGV. So, this code checks to see whether a file was
given on the command line, and if so it calls open_checkbook, a function shown in
Listing 4-10 that simply calls XUdbopen and then updates the display. The resulting output is shown in Figure 4-6.

Figure 4-6. Checkbook Using Real Data (chkbook2.sh). This is
"no details" mode, which is the default for the application.

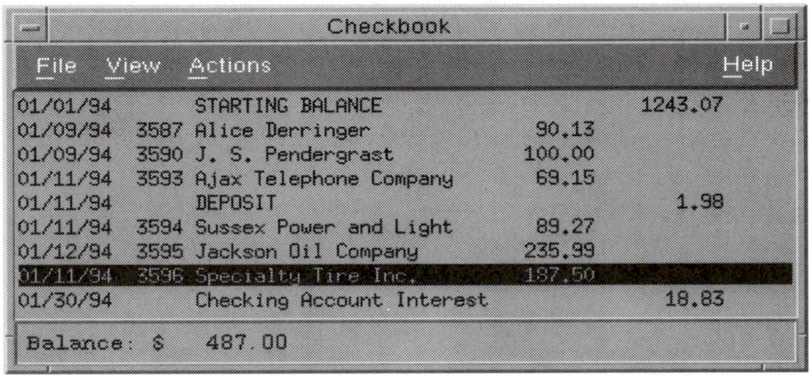

Listing 4-10. Opening the Database (chkbook2.sh).

```
function open_checkbook {    # path
    typeset path=$1

    XUdbopen DB "$path" "|"

    update_display
}
```

Note that this application is still not "real" because it is not possible to open a different file using the File menu, etc. The file must be provided on the command line at the moment. The next chapter will show you how to prompt for file paths and perform other operations that require prompting the user with a dialog box.

Adding the Show Details Callback

Now, we can create one of our missing callback functions: `showdetailsCB`. That's the function we registered as the action for the `View` menu's `Show Details` menu item. (This was defined way back in Listing 4-2 on page 55).

Listing 4-11. Toggling Details View (chkbook2.sh). This function toggles the STATE.DETAILS variable using the logical *not* math operator, then resets the menu item's label appropriately.

```
function showdetailsCB {
    STATE.DETAILS=!STATE.DETAILS      # logical not
    # change the menu label appropriately
    if (( STATE.DETAILS ))
    then
        XUset ${MB.VIEW.DETAILS} labelString:"Don't Show Details"
    else
        XUset ${MB.VIEW.DETAILS} labelString:"Show Details"
    fi
    update_display
}
```

Figure 4-7. Selecting Show Details (chkbook2.sh). The checkbook window after selecting "Show Details." Note that the user has resized the application to be wider after selecting Show Details mode (so you can see the whole screen).

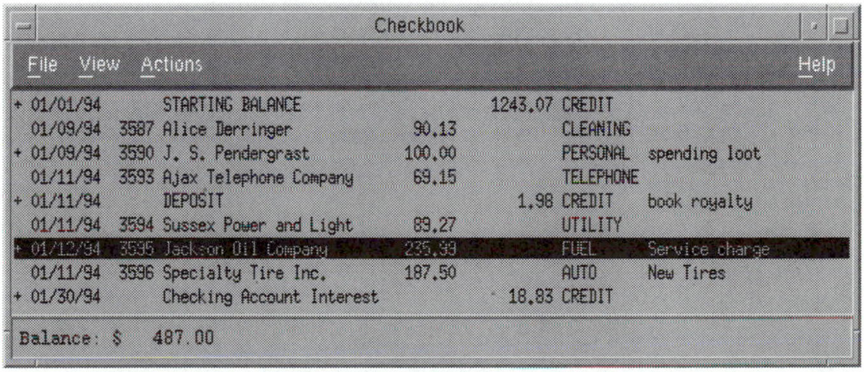

This callback function will switch the display to the detailed viewing mode, then call `update_display` to show the changes. In addition, the function will change the label in the `View` menu from "Show Details" to "Don't Show Details," and should act as a toggle. So, selecting the same menu item again would bring the display back to the lower level of detail. An appropriate function for accomplishing this is shown in Listing 4-11.

Once this function is included in the application, the `Show Details` menu item becomes operational. Figure 4-7 shows the results of selecting the menu item.

Onward and Upward

As you can imagine, more and more of the undefined callback commands can now be created until you have a fully functional application. In fact, that's just what the next few chapters are going to do. Most of the remaining menu items require techniques that have not been discussed yet, such as popping up prompt dialogs or help dialogs.

This checkbook application will continue to be refined throughout the rest of this book, until a fully functioning application is created. Each new feature added to the program will teach you more about dtksh programming. The final version of the checkbook program is presented in its entirety in Chapter 25, *Checkbook Application*.

4.9 Summary

This chapter has shown how to use the MainWindow widget to create a top-level screen for an application. It also covered creating simple systems of Pulldown menus. The example used throughout this chapter is a preliminary version of a checkbook handling program. This same program will continue to be enhanced throughout the rest of this book.

Steps for Using the MainWindow Widget

- Initialize the toolkit, as usual.
- Create a MainWindow widget as a child of the top-level widget using `XUmainwindow`.
- Create a MenuBar as a child of the MainWindow using `XUmenubar`.
- Create any Pulldown menus you need as children of the MenuBar using `XUmenusystem`.
- Create your work area widget—it can be anything your application needs. It should also be a child of the MainWindow widget.
- Create a message area widget—it can be anything but is often a TextField widget with the `editable` resource set to `true`.
- Set the `menuBar`, `workWindow`, and `messageWindow` resources of the Main-Window widget to the appropriate widget handles of its children.

Test Driving Your MainWindow

Even though you may have defined no callbacks, there are important things to check in your application after the MainWindow is set up. It may be necessary to put some small scaffold routines in your code temporarily to populate data before you can check some things. Important items to check include the following:

- Make sure resizing works as a user would expect.
- Make sure all the Pulldown menus look ok and all have mnemonics defined. Problems are likely to be caused by bad arguments to the XUmenusystem command.
- Make sure ScrollBars work as expected. Problems are likely to be caused by incorrect settings of the scrollingPolicy resource.

Using XU Database Functions

Many applications have a need for a simple database of some sort. For this reason, the XU database convenience functions are provided in this book. These functions are used in this chapter to read records from a flat file and parse the records into fields.

- XUdbopen is used to open a file and define its *delimiter*. It reads the records into an array.
- XUdbsplit is used to split a record into individual fields.

5 *The Standard Dialogs*

5.1 Introduction

In the last chapter you learned how to create a MainWindow widget which defines a standard layout for an application. By the end of that chapter, we had built a screen complete with menus and data display, but most of the callbacks were not defined. For example, it was not possible to open a new file using the File menu, add a new record, or delete an old record. All of those tasks have one thing in common—they need to prompt the user with a *dialog*.

> **Dialog:** A separate window that appears in order to prompt the user for some information, inform the user of some problem, ask the user to confirm a dangerous action, give the user help, etc.

Motif provides some predefined dialogs that are useful in many situations. This chapter shows you how to use all these predefined dialogs, by continuing to expand the checkbook program we worked on in the last chapter. You will learn how to do the following:

- Use WarningDialogs and ErrorDialogs to inform the user of problems.
- Use a FileSelectionDialog to implement the Open and Save callbacks.
- Use a QuestionDialog to confirm a delete request.
- Use an InformationDialog to show the user a list of missing checks.
- Use a PromptDialog to get a single piece of information from the user.
- Use a SelectionDialog to prompt the user for a check category to calculate the total amount of money spent in that category.

- Use a CommandDialog to allow the user to execute UNIX commands.
- Customize the predefined dialogs by changing labels or unmanaging children.

Other Dialog Chapters

Dialogs are a big subject; this chapter focuses on the simple, predefined Motif dialogs. Chapter 6, *Prompting Using Custom Dialogs*, shows you how to define your own dialogs to prompt for arbitrary pieces of information. Chapter 7, *Help Me!*, shows you how to use the CDE Help system dialogs. The Help dialogs technically fall in the category of "predefined dialogs," but the subject of Help is a rich one and deserves an individual chapter.

5.2 General Dialog Concepts

As I said before, dialogs are separate windows that pop up (usually in response to a user request) to prompt the user for some data or display information. Before we dive into writing more code (I know you just can't wait—neither can I), let's review a few concepts that apply to all dialogs.

Areas of the Dialog Window

Just as there is a standard look to the MainWindow of most applications, there is also a standard look to dialogs. Consistency helps users move from one application to another and helps them to avoid errors. Motif defines a certain look and feel that all dialogs are supposed to follow; it goes without saying that the standard dialogs provided by Motif adhere to these recommendations.

Besides the usual window manager supplied areas such as the title area, resize borders, and window manager menu, dialogs have the following standard areas:

- **Work Area**: this area contains informational labels, and sometimes areas for data entry. This area is at the top of the window. It can be simple, consisting of only one or two widgets, or quite complex with many different parts.
- **Command Area**: this area contains one or more buttons to perform actions. It is at the bottom of the window, and there is usually a Separator between it and the work area. Often one button is set up as the *default button*. The default button has a wider border and is executed if the user types the ENTER key.

Figure 5-1 illustrates the standard dialog areas. Consistency in the use of button names in the command area is very important. Here are the standard button labels (in the order they should appear from left to right) and the actions that should occur when they are selected:

OK   For dialogs that only display a message, this button dismisses the
              dialog (pops it down). For dialogs that prompt for information,
              pressing this button indicates the user is satisfied with the data
              entered; the dialog is dismissed in this case as well.

Apply   This button only appears on Selection-type dialogs (to be discussed
              in a moment). It is the same as OK, but leaves the dialog up instead
              of dismissing it.

Cancel   The user has decided not to follow through with the action that ini-
              tiated the dialog; the dialog is dismissed without effect.

Help   The user wants more information about the workings of the dialog.
              Another screen should pop up to provide this information, and the
              original dialog should remain active.

The programmer can determine which of these buttons appears by managing or
unmanaging them. The programmer is also allowed to define new buttons that will
appear in the command area of the standard Motif dialogs, a MenuBar that will
appear at the top of the dialog, or one other widget that will be used to add more
display or control items to the dialog.

Figure 5-1. The Standard Dialog Areas. Two different standard
Motif dialogs are show. On the left a WarningDialog, on the right a SelectionDialog. Even though they are different, they share a common layout: a work area
at the top of the window, which can be simple or complex, and a command area
at the bottom of the window containing one or more action buttons. Note the
wider border on the default button, and the Separator widget between the two
areas.

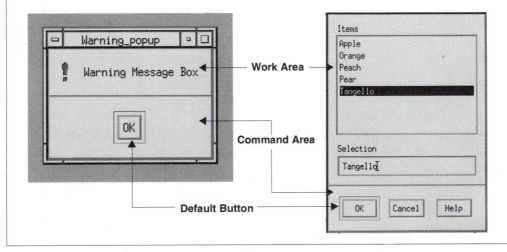

Types of Standard Dialog

There are two flavors of predefined dialogs: message dialogs and selection dialogs. The work area of a message dialog displays a static piece of text (the message), and one of several predefined icons indicating the nature of the message. The work area of a selection dialog contains a label, a user writable text area, and optionally a selection list area. The user may type in a response, or choose a response from the list of items. Figure 5-1 shows a message-type dialog on the left and a selection-type dialog on the right.

Message Dialogs

Here is a list of all the predefined message dialogs, with an indication of when you might use them:

ErrorDialog
: Use this to inform the user of some error in the application that may require immediate attention.

InformationDialog
: Use this to give the user a short informational message. It should be limited to no more than 10 or 15 lines of text, because no ScrollBars are available.

QuestionDialog
: Use this to ask the user a yes/no question. For example, you can use this to tell the user a destructive operation is about to occur and ask for confirmation.

WarningDialog
: This is similar in nature to the ErrorDialog, but should be used in situations where the user does not need take any immediate action. It indicates that a minor problem has occurred in the application.

WorkingDialog
: You can use this to tell the user that a time consuming operation is going on. It should be used when an operation is going to take between 10 and 30 seconds so the user doesn't think the application has locked up. For a discussion of what to do for other amounts of time, see Chapter 10, *Providing Feedback During Long Callbacks*.

Selection Dialogs

Here is a discussion of the selection style dialogs, with information on when you might use each one:

SelectionDialog
: This is the archetypal selection type dialog, providing a list area and a text entry area. It is used when there is a list of typical choices that a user can make, but it also makes sense for the user to type in an arbitrary string.

For example, if you were prompting the user for a fruit name, you could provide a list of five or six common fruits in the list area, but they would be free to type in "mango" instead of selecting one of the choices offered.

CommandDialog

This is very similar to a SelectionDialog, but each entry the user makes is retained in the List area. In other words, this dialog has a history mechanism. This dialog is useful in situations where the user might want to repeatedly execute some selections that they have input. For example, a CommandDialog would be useful if you want to give the user a way to execute UNIX commands.

FileSelectionDialog

This is the most complex of the dialogs. It provides a complete mechanism that allows the user to browse for a file. It displays directories and files and allows displayed files to be filtered by a pattern (for example, it could show only files ending in .c). You should use this in situations where the user must provide a filename.

PromptDialog

This is nothing more than a SelectionDialog with the List area unmanaged. It is used as a simple way to prompt the user for a single string when there are no particular choices. For example, prompting the user for a name is a good use of this simple dialog.

Modal Dialogs

Ah, *modal dialog*, now there's an impressive phrase. What a marvelous term! It sounds so abstract and so tediously technical; you can simultaneously put people to sleep and convince them you are a graphics whiz simply by saying things like "Unfortunately, I was forced to use a modal dialog."

> *Modal dialog:* A dialog that demands immediate attention because it puts the application into a "mode" in which only the dialog window accepts user input. The user can do nothing until the dialog is dismissed by selecting one of its action buttons.

But there's nothing really mysterious about it once you know that "modal" is just the adjectival form of the word "mode". Graphical programs are normally *modeless*; the user can choose to interact with any object on the screen at any time simply by clicking on the object with the mouse. This is in contrast to most old fashioned line-oriented programs that typically were modal. In those applications, the user had to follow a strict flow of control, they did Task A, then Task B, in that order (and only in that order, thank you very much). Users hate that, because that's not the way the human mind works (unless the mind happens to belong to a FORTRAN programmer).

This is precisely why most users prefer graphical programs—they are free to do what they want, when they want, in any order. They can change their mind right in the middle of filling out a form, go back and change a field to another value, even cancel the whole form with one swift click of the mouse.

Unfortunately, I Was Forced to Use a ...

But occasionally modality is required even in graphical programs. Sometimes ordering tasks is essential, sometimes it just makes good sense. For example, let's say the user just tried to save a file, but the disk is out of space and the save fails. A well-written application must inform the user of this—loss of data could occur otherwise. Loss of data is the one unforgivable sin an application can commit. Not only must the application inform the user, it must be certain that the user received the message. In this case it makes sense to inform the user with a modal ErrorDialog. The user will not be allowed to continue interacting with the application until they acknowledge the error message by clicking on the OK button in the ErrorDialog message area.

Other errors that are less critical may not require modal dialogs. For this reason, dialogs can be brought up in either modal or modeless form. You choose this as an option when you create the dialog widget.

Avoiding the "M" Word

The ability to create modal dialogs is commonly abused by novice X programmers. In many cases, they are used to writing line oriented programs, and it's easier to think in terms of "first Task A then Task B in that order."

Resist this urge! Learning to write modeless programs takes a little practice, but your users will thank you in the long run. To steel yourself, Table 5-1 presents a set of common situations with some commentary on whether modal dialogs are appropriate as a solution. If you are considering using a modal dialog, take a look at this table before succumbing to the "M" word.

Table 5-1. To Mode or Not to Mode

Situation	OK to Use a Modal Dialog?
A critical error has occurred, and it is essential for the user to know about the error before continuing to use the application.	Go ahead and use a modal dialog with a clear conscience.
A minor error has occurred. The user should know about it, but they could continue using the application.	Probably should not be modal, but you need to use judgment based on the severity of the error.

Table 5-1. To Mode or Not to Mode (continued)

Situation	OK to Use a Modal Dialog?
There are several questions you wish to ask the user, and you are considering popping up several modal dialogs in sequence, one for each question.	No, No, No! This is not how graphical programs are written. You should write a custom dialog that asks all the questions on one screen (to be discussed in the next chapter).
The user has initiated a destructive operation (such as deleting a record or file) that cannot be undone. You are considering creating a modal QuestionDialog to inform them that the operation is destructive and ask if they wish to continue.	Yes, this is a job for modal dialogs.
You have so many fields in one form that you can't fit them all on the screen. You are considering creating several modal dialogs with different subsets of the fields you want to prompt for, which will be presented in sequence.	Cringe. This is a poor way to write a graphical program. The correct way to handle this is with a single form that can toggle among several different screens of information. An example of how to implement such a form is presented under the heading *Multiple Screen Dialogs* on page 214.

Shades of Modality

The modality of a dialog is controlled by its `dialogStyle` resource. It takes one of the following values:

`DIALOG_MODELESS`   The dialog will be modeless.

`DIALOG_PRIMARY_APPLICATION_MODAL`   The dialog will be modal across only the main window of this application. If there are other windows, they may continue to operate.

`DIALOG_FULL_APPLICATION_MODAL`   The dialog will be modal across all windows of this application.

`DIALOG_SYSTEM_MODAL`   The dialog is modal across all applications running on the display. The user may not interact with any application until the dialog is dismissed.

As you can see, there's modal and then there's modal. There are shades of modality, and the preceding list is in order from the lowest level (modeless) in which any window on the display may take input, all the way to the highest level (system modal) in which no other window—not even ones in different applications—can take input until the dialog is dismissed.

Whether your dialog should be `PRIMARY_APPLICATION_MODAL` or `FULL_APPLICATION_MODAL` depends on the nature of your application and the nature of the dialog. If your application only has a single main window, there's not much difference. If your application has windows that act very independently of each other and the modal dialog only applies to the top-level window, then `PRIMARY_APPLICATION_MODAL` is indicated. More common is `FULL_APPLICATION_MODAL`.

Needless to say (but I'll say it anyway) `SYSTEM_MODAL` should be reserved for very special circumstances. It's hard to imagine an error condition so bad that you'd actually want to lock out every application running on the display device to get the user's attention. In fact, by locking the user out of all the other windows, you may make it more difficult for them to correct the problem! For example, they might want to keep your error dialog on the screen (so they don't forget the exact error message) while they look around the file system using a terminal emulator or file browser. They will likely be quite annoyed to find they cannot do anything but quit the dialog.

> Some legitimate uses of `SYSTEM_MODEL` include screen lock programs or dialogs used to confirm if the user wants to log out of the desktop or shut down the whole system.

5.3 The Message Dialogs

The simplest kinds of dialogs are those of the message type: the WarningDialog, InformationDialog, QuestionDialog, WorkingDialog and ErrorDialog. These dialogs are used to display informational messages to the user. As shown in Figure 5-1 on page 77, these dialogs contain a message area, message icon, and buttons in the action area. Often there is only an OK button, or just an OK and Help button in the action area. Occasionally, when there is some operation in progress that the user could decide to terminate, a Cancel button is also displayed.

Creating Message Dialogs

You can create these dialogs using XU functions, which take arguments identical to all other XU widget creation commands:

```
XUwarningdialog [-u] variable parent [resource:value ...]
XUinformationdialog [-u] variable parent [resource:value ...]
XUerrordialog [-u] variable parent [resource:value ...]
XUquestiondialog [-u] variable parent [resource:value ...]
XUworkingdialog [-u] variable parent [resource:value ...]
```

> As is often the case in Motif, these functions actually create several widgets to get the job done, with the resulting collection of widgets acting like a single widget. Thus, these dialogs are actually built out of a DialogShell widget with a BulletinBoard widget child managing a MessageBox, SeparatorGadget, and several PushButtonGadgets.

With the -u option, the dialog is initially unmanaged, which is usually the way you want to call these functions. These functions return the handle of a MessageBox widget in *variable* whose parent is a DialogShell widget. As a convenience, Motif allows you to pop up the dialog by managing the widget handle returned in the *variable* (using XUmanage). The alternative of using XUpopup to display the dialog is less convenient because you'd have to obtain the handle of the parent of the MessageBox first (using XUparent).

The most commonly needed resources for these widgets are:

messageString

: The string that appears in the message area.

cancelLabelString,
helpLabelString,
okLabelString

: The strings that appear on the Cancel, Help, and OK buttons. The defaults are: "Cancel," "Help," and "OK."

defaultButtonType

: Indicates which of the three buttons should be the default button. The default will get a wider border and will be executed when the user presses the ENTER key. The allowed values are DIALOG_OK_BUTTON, DIALOG_HELP_BUTTON, and DIALOG_CANCEL_BUTTON. The default is DIALOG_OK_BUTTON.

cancelCallback,
helpCallback,
okCallback

: The callbacks for the three action area buttons. If any of these callbacks is undefined, the corresponding button does not appear.

dialogTitle

: The string that appears in the title of the dialog.

dialogStyle

: Used to set the modality of the dialog. The default is DIALOG_MODELESS; other values are: DIALOG_FULL_APPLICATION_MODAL, DIALOG_PRIMARY_APPLICATION_MODAL, and DIALOG_SYSTEM_MODAL as explained under *Shades of Modality* on page 81.

So, to create a WarningDialog identical to the one shown on the left in Figure 5-1, one could use this command:

```
XUwarningdialog WARNING $TOPLEVEL \
        dialogTitle:"Warning Popup" \
        messageString:"Warning Message Box" \
        okCallback:'XUunmanage $CB_WIDGET'
```

Notice that the `okCallback` is defined directly on the widget creation command instead of using `XUaddcallback`. It is a common programming practice for this kind of widget to set button callbacks directly on the widget creation line, although it is also possible to use `XUaddcallback` after creation for these resources.

In this case, the `okCallback` simply pops down the dialog using `XUunmanage`—that's typical in this kind of dialog.

> Motif returns the handle of a MessageBox widget in the variable passed to the creation function. The MessageBox widget's parent is a DialogShell widget. When the child of the DialogShell is managed or unmanaged, the dialog is popped up or down. It is also possible to use `XUpopup` and `XUpopdown` on the parent of the MessageBox; in this case you would have to retrieve the parent's widget handle using: `XUparent variable $child`.

Also note the use of single quotes to enclose the callback command; that's necessary because `$CB_WIDGET` won't hold the widget handle until this command executes. If I had used double quotes then `$CB_WIDGET` would be expanded immediately (most likely to the empty string) whereas by using single quotes the expansion is delayed until callback execution time. This is something you must watch out for. The safest solution is to use single quotes when registering callbacks if there's any question about when a variable's value is available.

Reusing Dialogs

As you might imagine, any real application is likely to have many situations in which warnings, errors, or general information needs to be presented to the user using these dialogs. In many cases it doesn't make sense to create a separate instance of such dialogs for every message required—it's more efficient to keep reusing the same WarningDialog by redefining the `messageString` resource and then popping the dialog back up.

This is such a common technique that the XU functions provide conveniences for managing message dialogs this way. They all take the same kinds of argument:

```
XUwarning [-m] [labeloptions] title message okcb cancelcb errorcb
XUerror [-m][labeloptions] title message okcb cancelcb errorcb
XUinformation [-m][labeloptions] title message okcb cancelcb errorcb
XUquestion [-m][labeloptions] title message okcb cancelcb errorcb
XUworking [-m][labeloptions] title message okcb cancelcb errorcb
```

The *title* argument sets the `dialogTitle` resource, the *message* argument sets the `messageString` resource, and the *okcb*, *cancelcb*, and *errorcb* arguments set the various button callback resources (if set to the empty string the corresponding button does not appear). The -m option, if present, makes the dialog full application modal (this is the most common type of modality required). By default, the dialogs are modeless. The *labeloptions* can be used to change the default button labels and can be one or more of

```
-ok oklabel
-cancel cancellabel
-help helplabel
```

Notice there is no variable argument to return the widget handle—that's because these functions reuse the same dialog widgets over and over, just changing resources as needed. If you need them, the handles are available in the global variables: `_XU.warningdialog`, `_XU.errordialog`, and `_XU.informationdialog`. Also, there's no parent argument as in the widget creation command, these routines always use the root window of your application as the parent. So, the previous example could be rendered like this:

```
XUwarning "Warning Popup" \
        "Warning Message Box" \
        'XUunmanage $CB_WIDGET'
```

Notice that this is a lot less typing than the previous example, a definite plus! Also notice that I simply left out the *cancelcb* and *helpcb* arguments—by leaving them out they will default to the empty string, which will cause those buttons not to appear. If I wanted a help button to appear but no cancel button, I could use something like this:

```
XUwarning "Warning Popup" \
        "Warning Message Box" \
        'XUunmanage $CB_WIDGET' '' `myhelpCB'
```

In other words, just use an empty string for the callback argument of any button you don't want to appear.

Use of Message Dialogs in the Checkbook Program

For a more extensive example of the use of these dialogs, I will upgrade the checkbook program introduced in the last chapter to check for bad records. It will display a WarningDialog immediately after starting if any bad records are detected.

Listing 5-1 gives the text of a function called `check_record` that uses several XU convenience functions to make sure a check database record is in the proper format. If the record is correct, the function simply returns success (zero); if the record is corrupt, it appends an error message to the variable named by its first argument and returns failure (nonzero).

> This function makes use of `nameref` variables, which allow a variable to be called by reference. If you are not familiar with `nameref` variables, see *Name Reference Variables* on page 555.

The `check_record` function uses several XU commands: `XUisinteger`, `XUisfloat`, and `XUisdate`, which check to make sure their arguments are integers, floating-point numbers, and valid dates, respectively. They all return success (zero) if their arguments are in the expected format.

> The command `set -A f "${@:3}"` that appears near the beginning of `check_record` creates an array named `f` that holds the arguments to the function starting at the third argument and continuing for all arguments. In other words, `f[0]` will be set to `"$3"`, `f[1]` will be `"$4"`, etc. If you are not familiar with this notation, you should probably review *Other Kinds of Variable Expansion* on page 558.

Listing 5-1. Checking for Corrupt Records (chkbook3.sh). This function takes a variable name, line number, and data fields as its arguments. It checks to make sure the fields are in the proper format using various XU routines to validate data. If an error is detected, a message is appended to the variable and a failure code is returned.

```
function check_record {
    # usage: check_record variable line-number field1 field2 ...
    nameref e=$1
    typeset line=$2
    typeset f
    set -A f "${@:3}"   # set array f to all args past third

    if (( ${#f[@]} < NUMRECORDS ))
    then
        e=$(print "$e\nLine $line: too few fields")
        return 1
    fi
    if ! XUisinteger "${f[RECON]}"
    then
        e=$(print "$e\nLine $line: bad reconciled field")
        return 1
    fi
    if ! XUisdate "${f[MM]}" "${f[DD]}" "${f[YY]}"
    then
        e=$(print "$e\nLine $line: bad date")
        return 1
    fi
    if ! XUisfloat "${f[AMOUNT]}"
    then
        e=$(print "$e\nLine $line: bad amount")
        return 1
    fi
    return 0
}
```

Once we have this function, it is possible to enhance the previously defined `update_display` function. Recall from the previous chapter that this function takes the database records and formats them for display in the List widget of the checkbook program. It makes sense to do validation checks of this kind in this function—we are running through the records anyway. Listing 5-2 shows an enhanced version of `update_display` that makes use of the `check_record` function (right after the call to `XUdbsplit`). Any error messages are appended to a local variable called `errors`.

Once the `for` loop is finished, this variable is checked to see if there were any messages (i.e., if it is not zero length then some errors occurred). If errors did occur, then a WarningDialog is displayed using the `XUwarning` function. Furthermore, I decided not to bother the user with the details of the error unless they specifically request them by pressing the Help button. So, the Help button is set up so that it displays an InformationDialog using the `XUinformation` function. That InformationDialog contains the detailed error strings contained in the `errors` variable.

Listing 5-2. Using Warning and Information Dialogs (chkbook3.sh). This modified version of `update_display` uses the `check_record` function to validate each line; error messages are appended to the `errors` variable. Following the `for` loop, if the `errors` variable is not empty the `XUwarning` function is used to create and display a warning message.

```
function update_display {
    integer running
    typeset f line errors=""

    XUlistdeleteall $WORK

    for (( i = 0; i < ${#DB.record[@]}; i++ ))
    do
        XUdbsplit DB $i f
        if ! check_record errors $((i+1)) "${f[@]}"
        then continue
        fi
        if [[ ${f[CATEG]} == CREDIT ]]
        then
            (( running += f[AMOUNT] ))
        else
            (( running -= f[AMOUNT] ))
        fi
        XUlistappend $WORK "$(format_record "${f[@]}")"
    done
    if [[ "$errors" ]]
    then
        XUwarning "Warning" \
            "Some records appear to be bad.
            They have been skipped.
            For more information, press Help" \
            : "" "show_error '$errors'"
    fi
```

```
XUset $MESSAGE \
    value:"$(printf "Balance: \$%9.2f" $running)"
XUset $TOPLEVEL title:"Checkbook - ${DB.file}"
}
```

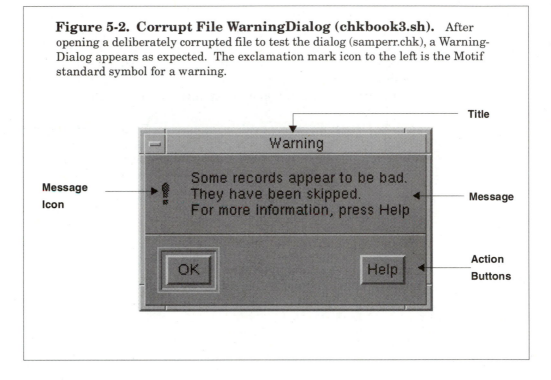

Figure 5-2. Corrupt File WarningDialog (chkbook3.sh). After
opening a deliberately corrupted file to test the dialog (samperr.chk), a Warning-
Dialog appears as expected. The exclamation mark icon to the left is the Motif
standard symbol for a warning.

A sample file, `samperr.chk`, which deliberately contains corrupt database records
is included with the example programs in the `Data` subdirectory. The checkbook
program was run using this file as input, and it produced the output shown in Figure 5-2. The results of then pressing the Help button of that WarningDialog are
shown in Figure 5-3.

You might notice that in both cases, I did not use modal dialogs. Admittedly, the
initial dialog that warns of the corrupt records is a borderline case. I decided to make
that dialog modeless because the problem doesn't stop the user from effectively continuing to use the application. If I had decided otherwise and made that dialog modal, I would have upgraded it from a WarningDialog to an outright ErrorDialog. The
InformationDialog used to report further details of the problem should definitely not
be modal.

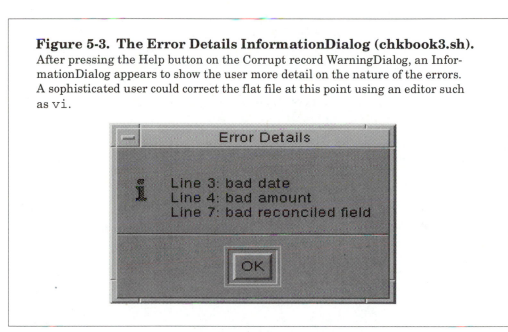

Figure 5-3. The Error Details InformationDialog (chkbook3.sh).
After pressing the Help button on the Corrupt record WarningDialog, an InformationDialog appears to show the user more detail on the nature of the errors. A sophisticated user could correct the flat file at this point using an editor such as vi.

Using the QuestionDialog for Confirming Deletion

Like the InformationDialog, ErrorDialog, and WarningDialog, the QuestionDialog is also based on the MessageBox widget. It is used in slightly different situations—those that require the user to answer a yes/no type question. As explained earlier, you can create a QuestionDialog using the XUquestiondialog command, which takes the same kind of arguments as any other widget creation command. You can also create a reusable QuestionDialog using the XUquestion convenience function.

In the checkbook program, it is reasonable to use a QuestionDialog to confirm a record deletion request. So, I'll implement another one of the menu items, the "Delete Selected Record" item in the Actions menu. To do this, I need to define a function called deleteCB that implements the desired action; it appears in Listing 5-3.

Listing 5-3. Using a QuestionDialog.

```
function deleteCB {
    integer index f

    XUlistgetselectedpos index $WORK
    let index--

    XUdbsplit DB $index f
```

```
      XUquestion -m "Confirm Delete" \
         "Really delete check:
         $(format_record "${f[@]}")" \
         "_delete $index" : "helpCB delete-confirm"
}

function _delete {   # index
    integer index=$1

    XUdbdelete DB $index
    update_display
}
```

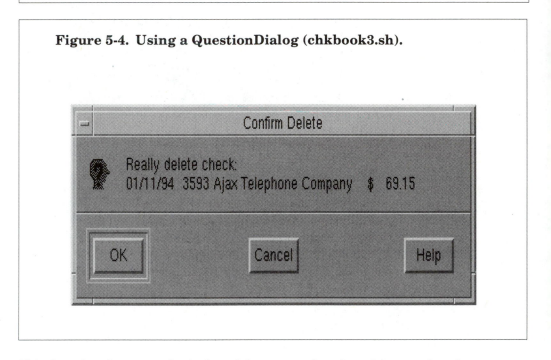

Figure 5-4. Using a QuestionDialog (chkbook3.sh).

This function first gets the index of the currently selected item using the XUlistgetselectedpos command. That command stores the index of the selected item
in the variable named by its first argument (its second argument is the handle of
the List widget). If no item is selected, then zero is stored in the index, and in that
case our function pops up a reusable warning message and returns.

Because the array of checkbook records starts at 0 and the index returned from
XUlistgetselectedpos starts at 1, the returned index must be decremented before proceeding. Next, the function uses XUquestion to ask the user to confirm that
they really want to delete the item. The XUsplitdb and format_record functions

are used to format the message. If the user hits the OK button, the function `_delete` is invoked and does the real work; it removes the item from the database using `XUdbdelete` (another one of those nifty utility functions), then updates the display.

The help callback is set to a function call to `helpCB`, which will invoke the CDE help system. I won't be defining that function until Chapter 7, *Help Me!*. The QuestionDialog created by the call to `XUquestion` is shown in Figure 5-4.

The technique of splitting the actual deletion code into two parts is a common one. In this case, the main callback function (`deleteCB`) simply sets up the QuestionDialog and returns. The real work of deleting the record is carried out using a secondary function named `_delete`. I like to use the convention that such secondary routines—the ones that really do the work—begin with an underscore. This immediately shows the person reading the code that this function's purpose is to finish a task started by some other function.

Customizing Message Dialogs

Message dialogs can be customized in several ways. You can add child widgets to the MessageDialog, and it will act as a manager for those children. The children will be positioned in the dialog depending on what type of widget they are:

- A MenuBar widget will be placed at the top of the dialog.
- A PushButton widget or gadget will be placed in the action area after the OK button.
- Any other kind of widget will be placed below the message string.

These customizations can be used to make the MessageDialog more functional.

5.4 The SelectionDialog

SelectionDialogs are used to give the user a choice of several items in a list, while simultaneously allowing them to type in a selection. It is composed of a List area, a TextField area for typing, and the usual dialog action area containing buttons.

You create a SelectionDialog using

```
XUselectiondialog variable parent [resource:value ...]
```

The most commonly used resources of the SelectionDialog are

`cancelCallback,` `helpCallback,` `okCallback`	The callbacks for the three action area buttons. If any of these callbacks is undefined, the corresponding button does not appear.
`dialogTitle`	The string that appears in the title of the dialog.

Within the context of the `okCallback`, the variable `${CB_CALL_DATA.VALUE}` holds the selected text.

Once the SelectionDialog widget is created, it is possible to gain access to the widget handles of its subparts by using this command:

```
XUselectionchildren variable
```

Here, `variable` is the name of the variable that was used to create the Selection-Dialog. Note well: pass the name of the variable, don't expand it by putting a dollar sign in front! The reason is that this command will create hierarchical children attached to the variable passed in; these hierarchical children hold the handles of the SelectionDialog's children. The child variables are

- `OK_BUTTON`
- `APPLY_BUTTON`
- `CANCEL_BUTTON`
- `HELP_BUTTON`
- `LIST`
- `TEXT`
- `LIST_LABEL`
- `SELECTION_LABEL`

The most commonly needed is of course `LIST`, because you need to fill in the list with the desired selections. For example, the following code will create a Selection-Dialog with several fruitful choices in the list:

```
XUselectiondialog SELDIAG $TOPLEVEL
XUselectionchildren SELDIAG      # NOTE! No $ in front of SELDIAG
XUlistappend ${SELDIAG.LIST} \
        Apple Pear Peach Banana
```

As you can see, the `XUselectionchildren` routine created a hierarchical variable called `SELDIAG.LIST` that holds the handle of the dialog's List widget. More examples of how you can use these child handles in *Customizing the SelectionDialog* on page 94.

Using a SelectionDialog to Display Category Totals

The next example uses a SelectionDialog to implement a new checkbook function that will prompt the user for a check category and display all checks in that category. This new function will be added to the View menu.

The function `showcategCB`, shown in Listing 5-4, implements this feature. It first runs through all the records in the checkbook, using an associative array to keep a list of indexes for each category. In effect, the associative array is being used in this case to compute a list of unique category names.

> If you are unfamiliar with the associative array feature of dtksh, you might want to read *Associative Array Variables* on page 556 before continuing.

Next, a SelectionDialog is created. Notice that the code first checks to see if the variable we have chosen to hold the handle is empty. This strategy avoids accidentally creating a second dialog if one is already on the screen. Note that the XU widget creation functions arrange for the handle variable to be unset if the user destroys the widget using the window manager—so whenever the variable SELCATEG is blank that means the widget does not exist.

Next, we retrieve the SelectionDialog's children's handles using XUselection-children. The category names are sorted using a trick—first the positional parameter list is replaced by the list of associative array indexes (the category names, expanded using the notation: "${!array[@]}") with the set command. Next, the positional parameters are sorted using set -s. Finally, the positional parameters are expanded on the end of a call to XUlistappend. Note that this trick is possible because the positional parameter list is not used in this function.

Listing 5-4. The Category List Feature (chkbook3.sh).

```
function showcategCB {
    integer i
    typeset f

    if [[ ! $SELCATEG ]]
    then
        XUselectiondialog SELCATEG $TOPLEVEL \
            dialogTitle:"Select a Category for Display" \
            okCallback:'showcateg_okCB' \
            applyCallback:'showcateg_applyCB' \
            cancelCallback:'XUdestroy $SELCATEG' \
            helpCallback:'helpCB category-selection'
        XUselectionchildren SELCATEG
    fi

    XUset ${SELCATEG.LIST_LABEL} \
        labelString:"Choose a Category:"

    XUlistdeleteall ${SELCATEG.LIST}

    # sort the categories by cleverly using set -s
    set "${!CATEGORIES[@]}"
    set -s
    XUlistappend ${SELCATEG.LIST} "${@}"
```

```
      XUmanage $SELCATEG
}

function showcateg_okCB {
    showcateg_applyCB
    XUdestroy $CB_WIDGET
}
```

The LIST_LABEL handle is used to change the labelString that appears above the List to a more appropriate string. The resulting SelectionDialog is shown in Figure 5-5. The next section will show you how a customized SelectionDialog is used to display the results.

Figure 5-5. SelectionDialog Used to Choose a Category.

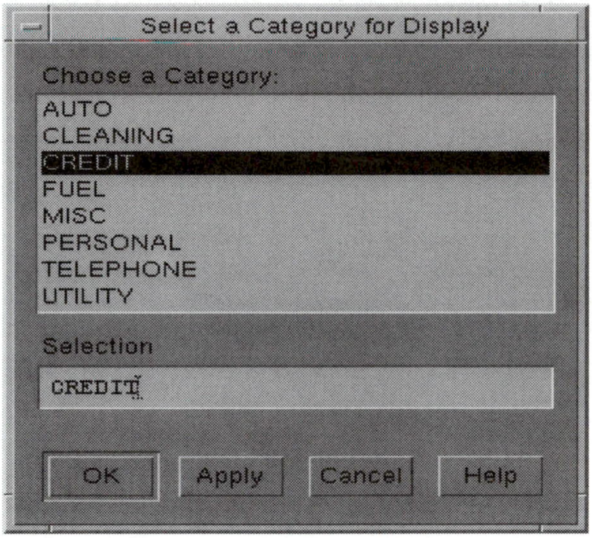

Customizing the SelectionDialog

When the user selects a category to view, the application should show a list of all the checks in that category, along with the total amount for that category. I want to pop this up as another dialog window, but what kind of dialog is the right one?

You might think this is a job for the InformationDialog, but that isn't satisfying because there could be many records of a particular type—certainly there could be too many to fit on the screen. We need a List widget with ScrollBars to hold the displayed entries. But wait—a SelectionDialog does provide a List widget with Scroll-Bars, so it's almost what we need. Unfortunately, it has things we don't need like that pesky Text area and an Apply button. Also, it's not immediately obvious where we can display the sum total for the category in a SelectionDialog.

It turns out these problems can all be overcome very easily because of our friendly XUselectionchild function. The strategy will be to get the handles of all the sub-components using that function, then manipulate those components until we get what we want. For example, if we don't need a particular piece of the dialog, we can simply use XUunmanage to make it disappear!

Listing 5-5 shows this strategy by implementing showcateg_applyCB. A Selection-Dialog whose handle is stored in the variable SHOWCATEG is created (if it does not already exist), followed by a call to XUselectionchildren to retrieve the subcomponent handles. The unnecessary Text area, Apply button and OK buttons are unmanaged.

Following this, the database records are scanned looking for items in the desired category. As they are found, they are added to SHOWCATEG.LIST. A running total for the category is also maintained. Finally, the SELECTION_LABEL is used to display the result of the calculation. It doesn't much matter that this is an unusual use of this particular part of the dialog—it happens to be in the right spot, so why not use it! The resulting dialog is shown in Figure 5-6.

Listing 5-5. A Customized SelectionDialog (chkbook3.sh).

```
function showcateg_applyCB {
    integer i
    float total

    if [[ ! $SHOWCATEG ]]
    then
        XUselectiondialog SHOWCATEG $TOPLEVEL \
            dialogTitle:"Records in Selected Category:" \
            cancelCallback:'XUdestroy $SHOWCATEG' \
            cancelLabelString:"Dismiss"

        XUselectionchildren SHOWCATEG
        XUunmanage ${SHOWCATEG.TEXT} ${SHOWCATEG.APPLY_BUTTON} \
            ${SHOWCATEG.OK_BUTTON}
    fi

    XUlistdeleteall ${SHOWCATEG.LIST}
    for (( i = 0; i < ${#DB.record[@]}; i++ ))
    do
        XUdbsplit DB $i f
        if [[ ${f[CATEG]} == ${CB_CALL_DATA.VALUE} ]]
        then
```

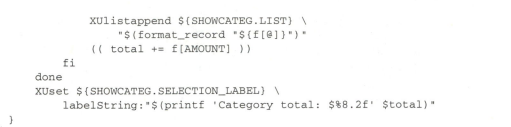

```
          XUlistappend ${SHOWCATEG.LIST} \
              "$(format_record "${f[@]}")"
          (( total += f[AMOUNT] ))
      fi
  done
  XUset ${SHOWCATEG.SELECTION_LABEL} \
      labelString:"$(printf 'Category total: $%8.2f' $total)"
}
```

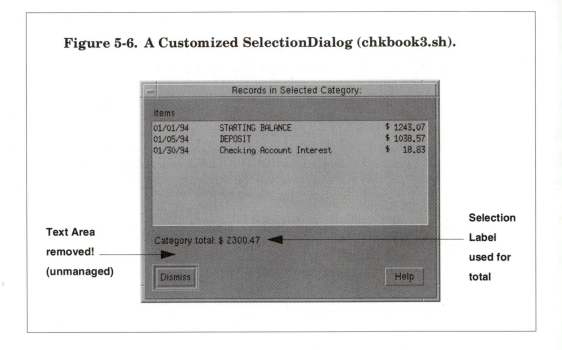

Figure 5-6. A Customized SelectionDialog (chkbook3.sh).

5.5 The FileSelectionDialog

Allowing the user to browse for a file to open is one of the most common features that graphical interfaces need to provide; it's not surprising that Motif provides a ready-made dialog for this task—the FileSelectionDialog.

The FileSelectionDialog is one of the most complex predefined Motif widgets. It contains the following areas (see Figure 5-7):

Filter   A TextField widget that displays the current directory being browsed. The last component of this TextField is a UNIX style pattern that can be used to filter which files are displayed.

File List	A List widget displaying all the files that match the pattern in the current directory.
Directory List	A list of all directories immediately below the current directory. The user may double-click on one of these directories to enter it and display its files.
Current Selection	A TextField that displays the current selection. The user may fill this in by either typing directly in the TextField or by selecting an item from the File List.
Action Buttons	The Action Button area contains:

- OK, which indicates the user is satisfied with the current selection.
- Filter, which reapplies the pattern to the files in the current directory. The user selects this after changing the pattern.
- Cancel, which indicates the user does not wish to proceed
- Help, which indicates the user wants more information.

You can create a FileSelectionDialog using the usual kind of widget creation command:

```
XUfileselectiondialog variable parent [resource:value ...]
```

Several resources are commonly used when creating this widget:

pattern	A UNIX style pattern that is used to filter which files are displayed in the file list. It is displayed to the user as the last component of the Filter area. The default is *, which matches all files.
directory	The initial directory displayed in the directory list. The default is the current working directory.
cancelCallback, helpCallback, okCallback	The callbacks for the three action area buttons. If any of these callbacks is undefined, the corresponding button does not appear.

dialogTitle   The string that appears in the title of the dialog.

There are many other resources, they just aren't needed very often. For example, it is possible to change all the Labels that appear on buttons and above the Lists. As with all the widgets, complete resource specifications are included in Chapter 34, *Motif Widget Reference*.

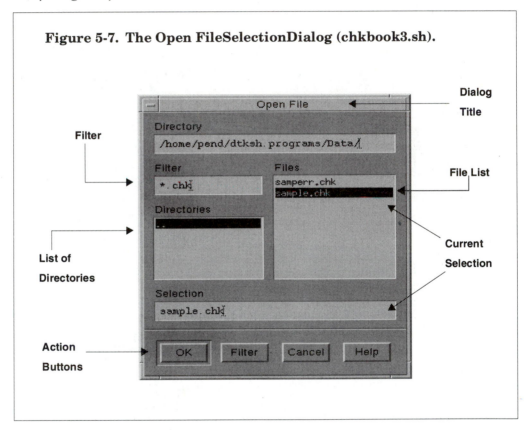

Figure 5-7. The Open FileSelectionDialog (chkbook3.sh).

Using a FileSelectionBox for the Open Command

Now we have the tool for one of the most important callbacks in the checkbook program—openCB. It allows the user to open a new checkbook file. Listing 5-6 shows the text of this function. The openCB function creates the FileSelectionDialog and sets up all the callbacks. Notice that it sets the pattern resource to the string "*.chk". That's because I chose the file extension ".chk" as this application's default for its data files. There is no particular need to choose such a default, but using a standard extension can help users find files that are used for your application more easily. The user can change the filter if they don't like the default convention by simply typing a new value in the Filter area.

Listing 5-6. The Open File Callbacks. It is interesting to note the simplicity with which the feature-rich FileSelectionDialog can be created. In just a few lines of code, the complete dialog is defined and all the necessary callbacks are set up. This code uses the technique of destroying the dialog when it is no longer needed.

```
function openCB {
    if [[ ! $OPENDIALOG ]]
    then
        XUfileselectiondialog OPENDIALOG $TOPLEVEL \
            dialogTitle:"Open File" \
            pattern:"*.chk" \
            defaultPosition:true \
            okCallback:open_okCB \
            cancelCallback:'XUdestroy $OPENDIALOG' \
            helpCallback:"helpCB file-menu"
    else
        XUmanage $OPENDIALOG
    fi
}

function open_okCB {
    typeset path=${CB_CALL_DATA.VALUE}

    cd ${path%/*}
    open_checkbook "${path##*/}"
    XUdestroy $CB_WIDGET
}
```

Notice that I set the cancelCallback to a command that will destroy the entire dialog. That means it will cease to exist if the user hits the cancel button. I like this method of handling this particular dialog because it's simple and clean. The FileSelectionDialog comes up quickly when called on so there's no particular need to keep it hanging around dormant. Also, you have to be prepared to recreate it at any time anyway because the user could explicitly destroy it using the window manager menu's Close item.

Just as we did with the SelectionDialog in the last section, we first check to see if the variable OPENDIALOG is empty before creating a new one.

The okCallback is set to another function called open_okCB. That function starts by getting the selection value from the CB_CALL_DATA.VALUE variable. That variable is set by dtksh automatically when the callback is invoked, and contains the text of the selection area (i.e., the name of the file).

Details of Opening the File

I decided that this application should actually change directory to that of the selected file. This is a choice you need to make for your application; I could just as easily have allowed the application to remain in its original directory by opening the file using a full path.

Here, I used a little known KornShell feature to divide the full path up into its directory and filename components. The notation

```
${variable%/*}
```

will strip a trailing suffix that matches the pattern `/*` off the named `variable`. The notation

```
${variable##*/}
```

will strip a maximal match of the pattern `*/` off the beginning of the named variable. For more information on this nifty feature, see *Other Kinds of Variable Expansion* on page 558. So, `open_okCB` changes the current directory to the selected directory, then calls `open_checkbook` on the filename. It then cleans up by destroying the FileSelectionDialog.

As before, I set the `helpCallback` to an as-yet-unwritten function called `helpCB`, which is explained in Chapter 7, *Help Me!*. The FileSelectionDialog created by this code is shown in Figure 5-7 on page 98.

5.6 The PromptDialog

The PromptDialog is really just a stripped-down version of the SelectionDialog; it's a SelectionDialog with no List area. Figure 5-9 shows a PromptDialog. It's useful for prompting the user for a single line of text. You create it with the usual kind of widget creation command:

```
XUpromptdialog [-u] variable parent [resource:value ...]
```

The most commonly used resources of the PromptDialog are:

`textString`	The string displayed in the selection area. This is often used at creation time to set a default value.
`selectionLabelString`	The Label above the selection area. This is used to indicate to the user the nature of the information they are expected to provide.

`cancelCallback,`
`helpCallback,`
`okCallback`
	The callbacks for the three action area buttons. If any of these callbacks is left undefined, the corresponding button does not appear.

`dialogTitle`	The string that appears in the title of the dialog.

Within the context of the okCallback, the variable CB_CALL_DATA.VALUE will contain the value stored in the selection area.

Implementing Save As With a PromptDialog

I'll use a PromptDialog to implement a simple version of the "Save As" menu item in the File menu of the checkbook application. Note that a more complete version of "Save As" should really allow the user to browse the file system for a suitable directory.

The File menu calls the function saveasCB to implement this feature (see Listing 5-7), which allows the user to save the current checkbook in a different file name. This function is shown in Figure 5-9.

Listing 5-7. A PromptDialog for "Save As" (chkbook3.sh). The saveasCB function merely brings up a PromptDialog, initializing the textString resource to the current filename.

```
function saveasCB {
    if [[ ! $SAVEDIALOG ]]
    then
        XUpromptdialog SAVEDIALOG $TOPLEVEL \
            dialogTitle:"Save File" \
            selectionLabelString:"Save Checkbook To:" \
            textString:"${DB.file}" \
            okCallback:saveas_okCB \
            cancelCallback:'XUdestroy $SAVEDIALOG' \
            helpCallback:"helpCB save-as"
    fi
    XUset $SAVEDIALOG textString:"${DB.file}"
    XUmanage $SAVEDIALOG
}

function saveas_okCB {
    typeset path=${CB_CALL_DATA.VALUE}

    if [[ -f $path && $path != ${DB.file} ]]
    then
        XUquestion -m "File Exists" \
            "Overwrite existing file $path?" \
            "_saveas '$path'" \
            : \
            "helpCB overwrite-warning"
        return
    fi
    _saveas "$path"
}

function _saveas {   # path
    DB.file=$path
```

```
        XUdbwrite DB > ${DB.file}
        XUset $TOPLEVEL title:"Checkbook - $path"
    }
```

This function does nothing more than create the PromptDialog using `XUprompt-dialog`. The `textString` in the selection area is initialized to the current name of the checkbook file. As before with the FileSelectionDialog, I use the strategy of destroying the dialog when it is no longer needed.

The `okCallback` is set to a function called `saveas_okCB`, also show in Figure 5-9. That function checks to see if the file name (stored in `CB_CALL_DATA.VALUE` by dtksh) already exists. If it does exist, then the user is asked whether they wish to overwrite it using a QuestionDialog (Figure 5-8). If the user selects the `okCallback` of the QuestionDialog, then the actual save is performed by a function called `_saveas`.

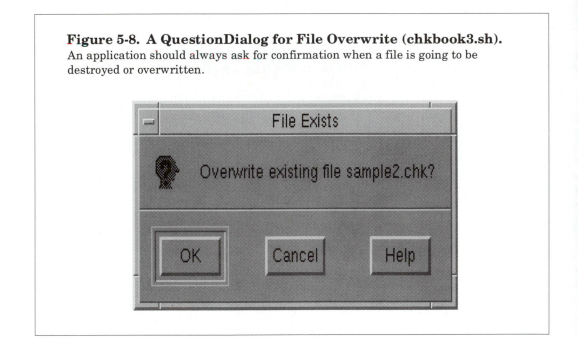

Figure 5-8. A QuestionDialog for File Overwrite (chkbook3.sh).
An application should always ask for confirmation when a file is going to be destroyed or overwritten.

If the file did not exist in the first place, then `_saveas` is called directly, without going through a QuestionDialog. This technique of calling a subroutine from a QuestionDialog for confirmation in one program path and calling it directly in another is quite common in graphical programs.

The PromptDialog created by these commands is shown in Figure 5-9.

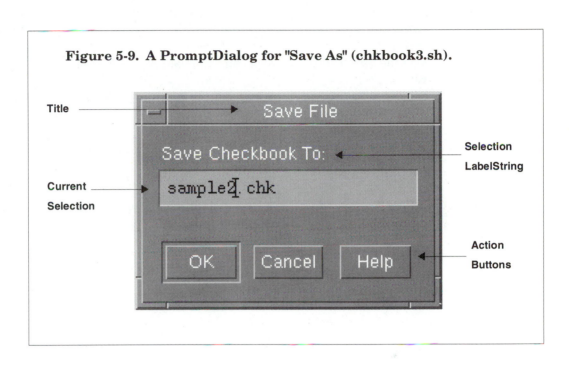

Figure 5-9. A PromptDialog for "Save As" (chkbook3.sh).

5.7 Next Steps

The checkbook application now has quite a bit of functionality. It is possible to open new files, save files, delete records, display records matching a certain category, and choose either a short or detailed listing format. The parts of this program that have been explained so far total under 300 lines of code! Next, you will learn how to piece together your own custom dialogs, and by the end of the next chapter the program will be able to create new records and edit existing records. More functionality will be added in future chapters, and the final checkbook program (called simply chk-book) is presented in its entirety in Part III.

5.8 Summary

This chapter has presented information on using the predefined Motif dialogs. Examples of each kind of dialog were presented by building on the checkbook example program begun in the last chapter. You learned how to do the following:

- Use InformationDialogs, WarningDialogs, and ErrorDialogs to give the user simple messages.
- Use the QuestionDialog to ask the user to confirm a checkbook record deletion.

- Use the `XUinformation`, `XUwarning`, `XUerror`, `XUquestion`, and `XUworking` conveniences to automatically reuse the same dialog for messages in different parts of the program.
- Use the SelectionDialog to prompt the user for a selection from a list of items.
- Use the FileSelectionDialog to prompt the user for a filename to open a checkbook data file.
- Use the PromptDialog to ask the user for a filename for saving a checkbook data file.

6 *Prompting Using Custom Dialogs*

6.1 Introduction

In the last chapter you learned how to use the predefined Motif dialogs to perform some common tasks. Even though the predefined dialogs can be customized to some degree by unmanaging children, modifying labels, or adding a work area, they are still fairly limited. For example, you can't add new buttons to the action area.

In most situations, custom dialogs must be created to prompt for information. This chapter covers the following topics:

- Shows you how to create a simple two-column dialog to prompt for multiple data fields.

- Discusses which widgets should be used to prompt for different kinds of information.

- Shows you how to validate the information entered in a dialog.

This chapter stresses the operational aspects of dialog programming, and does not get into advanced topics such as arbitrary layout of children. All the layouts will be of a simple two-column variety (these are useful in many situations).

6.2 The Two-Column Dialog

The Motif toolkit does not provide a single flexible predefined dialog that is useful for multiple value prompting. Creating a customized dialog can be a frustrating exercise if you are new to X, because it generally requires that you know how to use numerous management and control widgets, sometimes to an excruciating level of detail.

Although it may be true that a deep knowledge of Motif is required to create some very fancy kinds of dialog, it should be easy to create what I call a *two-column dialog*,

which is a simple dialog with an action area at the bottom with command buttons
and a two-column area at the top. The left column holds labels describing what kind
of data is expected in each field, and the right column holds corresponding controls
that allow the user to fill in the desired value. Figure 6-1 shows a typical two-column
dialog.

> ***Control:*** A widget (usually primitive) used to prompt the user for a
> piece of information, such as a TextField, Scale, or ToggleButton.

The XU convenience library contains a comprehensive set of functions that allows
you to put together dialogs of this kind with surprisingly few lines of code. The
remainder of this chapter shows you how to use these functions, and explains some
general guidelines for effective prompting.

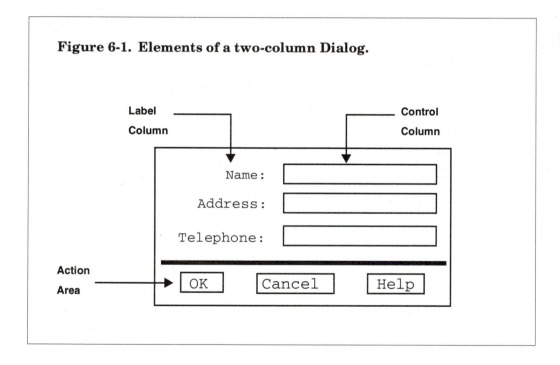

Figure 6-1. Elements of a two-column Dialog.

Creating a Simple Dialog Widget

The first step is to create a SimpleDialog widget. That's not really a single Motif
widget, but an abstraction created by the XU library function:

```
XUsimpledialog variable parent [resource:value ...]
```

This function creates a dialog with a RowColumn widget as its work area and an
empty action area. The handles of these components are stored in *variable*.WORK

and *variable*.ACTION, respectively. The handle of the DialogShell parent widget is returned in *variable*. This convenience function creates numerous widgets to get the job done, and sets things up so there is reasonable resize behavior.

Note that this function does not automatically manage the simple dialog. That's never what you as the programmer want to happen, because there are no buttons or prompting widgets defined yet. It would look silly for the dialog to pop up empty and then fill up with buttons and controls later! Instead, you must bring up the dialog using XUmanage $*variable* when all its children are defined. This is illustrated later.

Adding the Action Area Buttons

Once such a dialog is created, the action area can be populated using:

```
XUactionbuttons parent [ [option] variable label command ...]
```

This function creates multiple PushButton widgets in an action area *parent* widget. After the first argument, further arguments are in sets of three, each set of four arguments defines one button:

option   This is either -d, meaning that the following button defini-
                tion is the default button, or -c, meaning that the following
                button definition is the Cancel button.

variable   The name of a variable that will receive the handle of the
                newly created button. If you do not need the handle returned
                in a variable, you may substitute a dash (-) character for this
                argument.

label   The initial label that appears on the button.

command   A dtksh command string that will be executed when the but-
                ton is selected.

It is important to inform the simple dialog widget which button is the default button and which is the Cancel button using the -d and -c options. This is because the Motif style guide requires that when the user presses the ENTER key the default button action is executed, and when the user presses the ESCAPE key then the Cancel button action is executed.

The following XUactionbuttons command creates a standard set of buttons:

```
XUactionbuttons ${DIALOG.ACTION} \
        -d DIALOG.OK       "OK"     O okCB \
        -c DIALOG.CANCEL "Cancel" C cancelCB \
           DIALOG.HELP     "Help"   H helpCB
```

Adding Labels and Controls

You can create any kind of widgets you want in the work area of the SimpleDialog, but XU provides a set of very convenient routines to speed your task. These routines first add a label to the work area, then a control widget (or widgets) that provide the input area and validation. For example,

```
XUaddfields ${DIALOG.WORK} \
        DIALOG.NAME "Name:"    val_name 20 \
        DIALOG.ADDR "Address:" val_addr 20
```

creates two TextField widgets 20 columns wide and associated labels. It also installs validation functions on the TextField widgets (in this case the functions are `val_name` and `val_addr`, respectively). I'll be going into the details of using all these commands in the remainder of this chapter. For now, it's enough to know that these functions automate the task of adding commonly needed kinds of controls to your dialog, and they all have arguments in the same order to make it easy to remember how to use them. The first argument is always the handle of the work area of your dialog. Arguments following that are in sets, each set defines one control. The first argument of each set is a variable name that will receive the handle of the control widget, the second argument is the text of the label, the third argument is used for validation of the data, and the next argument specifies the size or some other visual aspect of the control.

If none of the XU-provided functions suits your task, you can create controls in the work area by hand. Simply create a label widget first, followed by any widget of your choice.

Displaying the Dialog

When you've finished creating action area buttons and controls, you complete the dialog and display it using two simple lines of code:

```
XUalign2col ${dialog.WORK}
XUmanage $dialog
```

The `XUalign2col` command aligns the SimpleDialog's work area into a two-column format. The `XUmanage` command manages and pops up the dialog.

Listing 6-1 uses the XU functions to create a complete dialog that prompts for three pieces of information. The running program is shown in Figure 6-2.

Listing 6-1. Creating a Two-Column Dialog (twocol.sh). This short program defines a complete dialog that adheres to the Motif style guide and prompts the user for three Text strings. The dialog is displayed when the user presses the button labeled "Show Dialog."

```
. $XUTILDIR/xutil.sh

XUinitialize TOPLEVEL Twocol "$@"
```

```
XUpushbutton PUSH $TOPLEVEL \
    labelString:"Show Dialog" \
    activateCallback:'XUmanage $DIALOG'

XUsimpledialog DIALOG $TOPLEVEL \
    title:"Personal Information"

XUactionbuttons ${DIALOG.ACTION} \
    -d DIALOG.OK         OK   okCB \
    -c DIALOG.CANCEL     Cancel   cancelCB \
       DIALOG.HELP       Help     helpCB

XUaddtextfields ${DIALOG.WORK} \
    DIALOG.NAME     Name:        ver_name    16 \
    DIALOG.ADDR     Address:     ver_addr    16 \
    DIALOG.PHONE    Telephone:   ver_phone   16

XUalign2col ${DIALOG.WORK}

XUrealize $TOPLEVEL
XUmainloop}
```

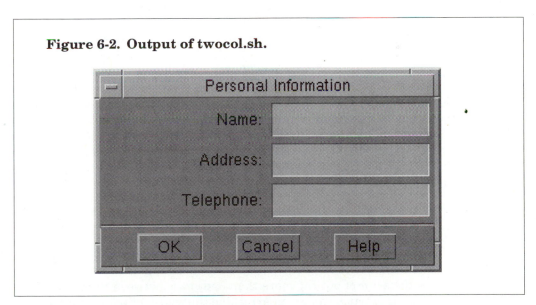

Figure 6-2. Output of twocol.sh.

The remainder of this chapter details how to prompt for different kinds of information using the XU functions; it also discusses related issues such as validating fields and changing the order of field traversal.

6.3 Prompting for Text

When an application needs to prompt for arbitrary sets of characters such as names or addresses, the control of choice is the TextField widget. This widget provides numerous keyboard and mouse editing functions. It is created using this command:

```
XUaddtextfields $parent [variable label validation columns ...]
```

This command can be used to create any number of TextField widgets as children of a single *parent* widget. Each TextField is defined by four arguments. The handle of the new TextField is stored in *variable*. A caption is created that displays the *label*. The *validation* command can be any dtksh command string; it is called when the user presses ENTER or TAB while in the field. When this command executes, you can access the current text by retrieving the `value` resource of `$CB_WIDGET`, and then you can do any kind of validation desired. If an incorrect value is entered, you might want to pop up a WarningDialog or ErrorDialog as described in the previous chapter.

> In cases where the text can truly be any string you can simply use the colon command (:) of the shell (which does nothing) as the validation function.

The TextField that is created will be large enough to display *columns* characters. Note that this does not limit how many characters the user may type; if the user types beyond the visible limit of the TextField it will scroll to accommodate more text.

Common Types of Validation

For TextField controls, common types of validation include disallowing certain characters, only allowing a fixed set of values, or only allowing values that match some pattern. In addition, it is often convenient to automatically select the text of a field when it is entered so the user can just type in a replacement value, and sometimes it is useful for fixed width fields to automatically traverse to the next field when the user types in the last position.

> When text is selected, it appears in reverse video and the user may replace the contents of the selected text by typing.

It may also be desirable to fix errors automatically for the user by setting the `value` resource. For example, if a field should contain a full name, the user might make the error of putting more than one space between the first and last name; the validation function can fix an error like that without bothering the user by resetting the value before it exits. Listing 6-2 shows a function that validates a name in this way. It disallows punctuation characters embedded in the name (except for a period, which could be used after a middle initial or in a title such as Ms. or Dr.). It condenses multiple spaces to a single space automatically.

Listing 6-2. Validating a TextField. This function is appropriate for use as a validation function for a Text or TextField widget. After getting the current value of the TextField,
the function immediately resets the value by substituting a single space for any multiple
spaces. The field is also checked for illegal punctuation characters using pattern matching.
Note that period (.) characters are removed from the string before doing the pattern match
looking for punctuation.

```
function val_name {
        typeset text

        Xuget $CB_WIDGET value:text

        XUset $CB_WIDGET value:"${text/ +( )/ }"
        if [[ ${text/./} == *[::punct::]* ]]
        then
                XUwarn "Bad Name" \
                        "Name contains punctuation"
        fi
}
```

Disallowing Certain Characters

You might want to disallow characters from even being typed into the Text or Text-
Field widget in the first place. This can be accomplished using the convenience
function:

```
XUtextallowchars [ $widget pattern ] ...
```

where $widget is the handle of a Text or TextField widget, and pattern is any
valid KornShell pattern string. Any number of pairs of arguments can be specified.
If the user attempts to type any character that is not matched by pattern, then the
terminal bell rings and the offending character does not appear in the widget. Note
that you should call this command immediately after creating the Text or TextField
widget. For example, the following code creates a TextField that will not accept
digits:

```
XUaddtextfield ${DIALOG.WORK} \
        DIALOG.NAME "Name:" : 32
XUtextallowchars ${DIALOG.NAME} '[!0-9]'
```

Notice that this example uses the colon command (:) as the validation function.
The colon command does nothing; it is the KornShell equivalent of no operation.

Forcing Uppercase or Lowercase

Similarly, there are times when you don't wish to allow lowercase (or perhaps
uppercase) letters in a TextField. Instead of using XUallowchars to disable one

case or another, it is better to simply convert the case on the user's behalf. This can be accomplished using:

```
XUtextforcecase [-u|-l] $widget ...
```

This command automatically changes text typed by the user to uppercase (with the -u option) or lowercase (with the -l option).

Other Text Convenience Functions

The following two functions are also useful in some situations:

```
XUtextautoselect $widget ...
XUtextautotraverse [ $widget length]...
```

The XUtextautoselect command arranges for the named text *widgets* to be selected automatically when they gain focus. In this way, anything the user types will replace the contents of the text field. If the user wants simply to edit the field, they can click on it with the mouse to cancel the selection. This should only be used in fields where the most common action by a user is to replace the entire contents rather than making surgical edits to the field.

The XUtextautotraverse command takes pairs of arguments. The first item in the pair is a widget handle, and the second is an integer specifying a length in characters. If the user types in the field until the cursor gets to position *length*, then focus is passed to the next widget automatically. This is useful in situations where there is a fixed length field (like Social Security number or a product code). It saves the user the trouble of hitting ENTER or TAB to go to the next field.

6.4 Prompting for Integers

There are several different ways to prompt for an integer, depending on the situation:

- Any integer can be represented by a TextField widget set up with appropriate validation functions.

- Integers in a small fixed range (where the range spans no more than about 100) can be represented by a Scale widget.

These kinds of integer controls can be created using:

```
XUaddintegerfields $parent  [variable label columns ]...
```

This creates a TextField widget that only allows integer values. The widget is created the specified number of *columns* wide. The handle of the widget is stored in *variable*. A *label* caption is created as well. The TextField is set up so it only accepts digits, any other character causes the terminal bell to ring. Each triplet of arguments (*variable, label, columns*) defines a TextField.

To retrieve values from the TextField widget, simply use `XUget` to retrieve the `value` resource.

6.5 Prompting for Real Numbers and Money

The XU library provides these functions to prompt for floating-point numbers and monetary values:

```
XUaddfloatfields $parent [variable label columns]
XUaddmoneyfields $parent [variable label columns]
```

In each case, a TextField is created with a validation function that only allows a floating-point number. The arguments are similar to those for the `XUaddinteger` function explained earlier.

The `XUaddmoneyfields` command is quite similar to `XUaddfloatfields`, but its validation function only allows two decimal places.

6.6 Prompting for Dates

The XU library can create a series of widgets appropriate for prompting for date values:

```
XUadddatefields $workarea [variable label  ]...
```

This function creates three TextField widgets separated by Label widgets containing the slash (/) character. The first TextField holds the month, the second the day, and the third holds the year.

The *variable* receives the handle of the RowColumn widget that stacks the various subcomponents. It is also used as a base for hierarchical variables that will receive the handles of the TextFields: *variable*.MM, *variable*.DD, and *variable*.YY.

Validation functions are added to the TextFields to ensure they hold a valid date. The validation functions know about leap years, etc., when making this calculation.

> Actually, the whole month, day, year combination is only validated when the user presses TAB or ENTER on the year field. This allows the user to change the date without getting an error message before they are finished.

(Listing 6-3 uses this function to create a date field. The first field in the dialog displayed later in Figure 6-5 shows how it looks.)

6.7 Prompting for Yes/No Values

The ToggleButton widget displays a label and a small square. The square is filled in with a check mark if the value indicated by the label is "on" or "true." If the user selects the button with the mouse, the state of the button changes to the opposite of its current state (see Figure 6-3).

Figure 6-3. A ToggleButton.   Because the square contains a check mark, the state of the button is true. If selected with the mouse, the square would empty signifying false. A second selection would change the state back to true.

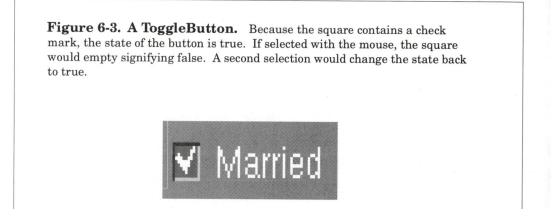

The XU library provides a convenience for creating one or more ToggleButtons prefixed by a Label:

```
XUaddtogglefields $parent [variable label  buttonlabel  ] ...
```

As with other functions of this type, `variable` receives the widget handle of the newly created ToggleButton. `Label` appears in the label column of the two-column widget, and `buttonlabel` is the string that actually appears on the button itself. To access the value of the ToggleButton, use `XUget` to retrieve the `set` resource, which will hold either the string `true` or `false`.

6.8 Prompting for Multiple Choices

When there is a fixed set of choices for a field, but more than two or three, using ToggleButtons becomes cumbersome. They take too much space in the window. The best choice in a case like this is an OptionMenu. The OptionMenu looks like a button, and its label shows the current value of the field. However, when the button is "pushed," a menu appears that contains all the choices (see Figure 6-4).
To create an OptionMenu, you can use the XU function:

```
XUaddptionmenu variable $parent label [item ...]
```

Note that this command has a different order of arguments than the other commands you've seen so far. Also note that this command creates only a single Option-Menu, whereas the other commands you've seen so far could create one or more controls.

Figure 6-4. An OptionMenu.   To the left, an OptionMenu displays its current value. On the right, the menu that appears when the OptionMenu is selected. The menu appears such that the current selection is still in the same place. The user can drag the mouse pointer up and down and make a selection by releasing the mouse button.

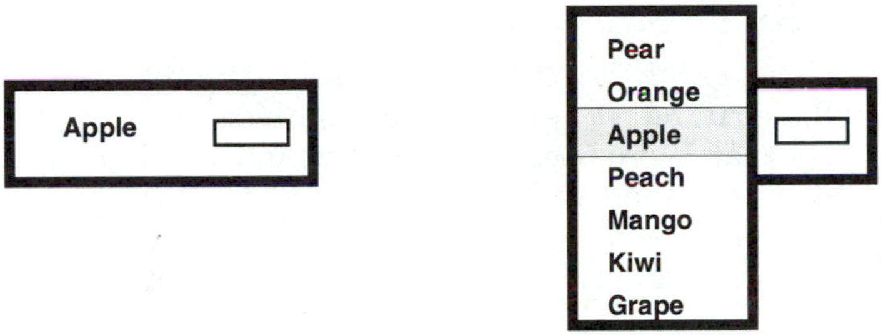

This command creates a *label* and one OptionMenu and stores its handle in *variable*. The parent is $workarea. One or more *item* arguments can be used to specify the contents of the OptionMenu. By default, the first item in the menu is displayed. You can display another value using

```
XUsetoption $optionmenu item
```

where *item* is the actual string label that appears on the desired value.

The XU library arranges for the current value of the option menu to always be available in *variable*.VALUE.

6.9 The ENTER Key in TextFields

By default, pressing the ENTER key within a dialog invokes the default button, whereas pressing the TAB key changes the focus to the next field. This can be frustrating to many users when the focus is in a TextField widget. Most users expect that when they press ENTER in a TextField the focus will change to the next field.

Technically, you (the dialog programmer) are not supposed to change this behavior. However, if your users are providing you with your living, you might consider whether the people who wrote the Motif style guide will be willing to pay your mortgage! Users often have strong opinions about these kinds of things.

The XU library provides a simple way to change this behavior:

```
XUsettraversalorder $dialog $default $textfield1 $textfield2 ...
```

The first argument is the dialog handle, the second is the handle of the default button, and all further arguments are the handles of TextField widgets in the dialog.

Pressing ENTER will go from the TextField to the next widget, and after the last TextField the default button will be executed.

Note that you are not setting the order of TextField traversal here, you are simply specifying that the ENTER key should not execute the default action for all Text-Fields given in the argument list, but rather should go to whatever widget follows the TextField. Motif sets up the order of widget traversal such that it is the same as the creation order (by default).

6.10 A Complete Example

Now we'll extend the checkbook example to allow the user to enter new checks (the lack of this feature has been a glaring omission until now). Listing 6-3 presents the code. As usual, I first check to see if the "Add Check" dialog already exists by testing whether its handle variable is empty. If it does not exist, it is created. A simple dialog is created using XUsimpledialog. Following that, the action buttons are created using XUactionbuttons.

Listing 6-3. The New Check Dialog (chkbook3.sh).

```
function addCB {
    if [[ ! "$ADDPOP" ]]
    then
        XUsimpledialog ADDPOP $TOPLEVEL \
            title:"Add A New Entry"
        XUadddatefields ${ADDPOP.WORK} \
            ADDPOP.DATE Date:
        XUaddtextfields ${ADDPOP.WORK} \
            ADDPOP.CHECKNUM "Check Number:" : 20 \
            ADDPOP.PAYEE Payee: : 20
        XUaddmoneyfields ${ADDPOP.WORK} \
            ADDPOP.AMOUNT    Amount:    9
        XUaddtextfields ${ADDPOP.WORK} \
            ADDPOP.COMMENT Comment: : 20

        # Sort categories using set -s
        set "${!CATEGORIES[@]}"
        set -s
        XUaddoptionmenu ADDPOP.CATEG ${ADDPOP.WORK} Category: \
            "${@}"

        XUaddtogglefields ${ADDPOP.WORK} \
            ADDPOP.RECON "Reconciled?" " "

        # Don't allow the pipe symbol in Payee or Comment

        XUtextallowchars \
            ${ADDPOP.PAYEE} "[!|]" \
            ${ADDPOP.COMMENT} "[!|]"
```

```
        XUalign2col ${ADDPOP.WORK}

        # Add the action buttons at the bottom of the dialog
        XUactionbuttons ${ADDPOP.ACTION} \
            -d ADDPOP.ADD        Add      add_addCB \
               ADDPOP.CLEAR      Clear    add_clearCB \
            -c ADDPOP.DISMISS  Dismiss  add_dismissCB \
               ADDPOP.HELP        Help    'helpCB _context ${ADDPOP.WORK}'

        # Set up fields so that Enter does not execute
        # the default action unless the user is on the
        # last field

        XUsettraversalorder ${ADDPOP} ${ADDPOP.ADD} \
            ${ADDPOP.DATE.MM} ${ADDPOP.DATE.DD} \
            ${ADDPOP.DATE.YY} ${ADDPOP.CHECKNUM} ${ADDPOP.PAYEE} \
            ${ADDPOP.AMOUNT} ${ADDPOP.COMMENT}
        addhelp \
            $ADDPOP                    add-entry \
            ${ADDPOP.DATE}             date-field \
            ${ADDPOP.DATE.LABEL}       date-field \
            ${ADDPOP.CHECKNUM}         number-field \
            ${ADDPOP.CHECKNUM.LABEL}    number-field \
            ${ADDPOP.PAYEE}            payee-field \
            ${ADDPOP.PAYEE.LABEL}      payee-field \
            ${ADDPOP.AMOUNT}           amount-field \
            ${ADDPOP.AMOUNT.LABEL}     amount-field \
            ${ADDPOP.CATEG}            category-field \
            ${ADDPOP.CATEG.LABEL}      category-field
    fi
    add_clearCB  # initialize fields
    XUmanage $ADDPOP
    XUsetfocus ${ADDPOP.DATE.MM}
}
```

A series of commands is then employed to create the controls, including calls to XUadddatefields, XUaddmoney, XUaddtogglebuttons, etc. The XUtextallowchars command is used to prevent the user from typing the pipe symbol in either the PAYEE or COMMENT fields. That would be bad since I am using the pipe symbol to delimit the database records.

The XUsettraversalorder command is used to enable the ENTER key on the text widgets, and then the dialog is completed by calling XUalign2col.

Next, a function called add_clearCB is invoked to clear out the fields. It also initializes the date fields to the current day using the UNIX date command, which is a reasonable default in this case. The CATEGORY is also defaulted to MISC. The dialog is then popped up using XUmanage.

The resulting dialog is shown in Figures 6-5 and 6-6.

Figure 6-5. The New Check Dialog Screen (chkbook4.sh). The screen as it first appears. The current date is automatically filled in. Because the date fields are in autoselect mode, the 11 appears in reverse video. The date fields are also set up to autotraverse when two digits are entered.

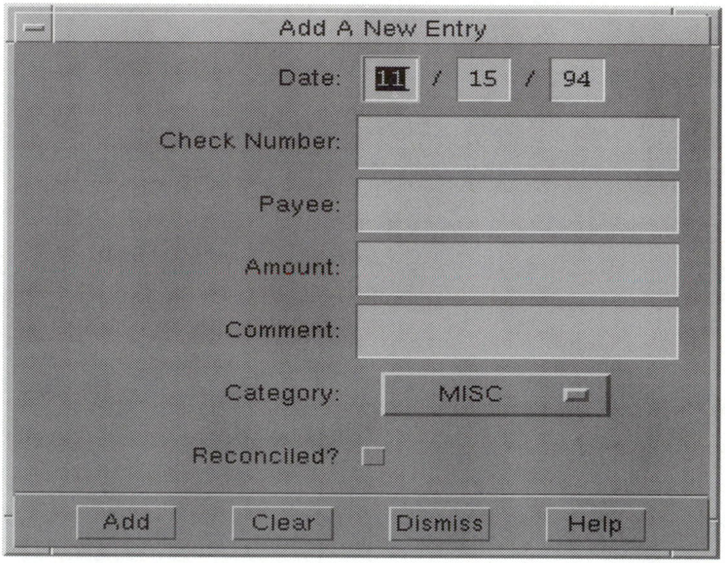

The Add Action Button

Listing 6-4 shows the add_addCB function, which is invoked when the user presses the Add button. It retrieves all the dialog field values into an array called f. It uses the read-only constants previously defined for field indexes. A for loop is used to run through the fields in the order defined for the database, building the record. The XUdbappend command is used to append the new record to the internal database data structures.

Note that as the function gathers the data fields, it must in some cases coerce the value as held in the widget with the value as desired in the database. For example, the RECON field is represented as a ToggleButton, and its set resource is either the string true or false, whereas the RECON field in the database file should be either a zero or one. So, an if statement is used to convert it.

Figure 6-6. Adding a New Check.   The same screen, but now some
data have been entered by the user.

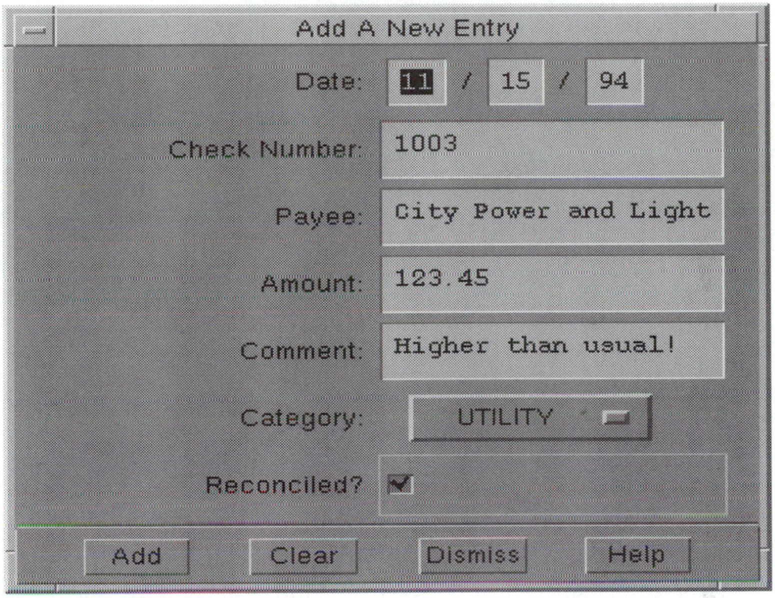

Listing 6-4. Adding the Record (chkbook3.sh).

```
function add_addCB {
    typeset f record
    integer i

    f[KEY]=$(newkey)
    XUget ${ADDPOP.CHECKNUM} value:f[CHECKNUM]
    XUget ${ADDPOP.DATE.MM} value:f[MM]
    XUget ${ADDPOP.DATE.DD} value:f[DD]
    XUget ${ADDPOP.DATE.YY} value:f[YY]
    XUget ${ADDPOP.PAYEE} value:f[PAYEE]
    XUget ${ADDPOP.AMOUNT} value:f[AMOUNT]
    XUget ${ADDPOP.COMMENT} value:f[COMMENT]
    f[CATEG]="${ADDPOP.CATEG.VALUE}"
    XUget ${ADDPOP.RECON} set:f[RECON]
```

```
    if [[ ${f[RECON]} == true ]]
    then f[RECON]=1
    else f[RECON]=0
    fi

    record=
    for (( i = 0; i < NUMFIELDS; i++ ))
    do
        record="$record|${f[i]}"
    done
    record=${record:1}

    XUdbappend DB "$record"
    update_display
    add_clearCB KEEPDATE
}
```

6.11 Validation

When the user presses the Add button (or OK, or Apply, or whatever your dialog
uses) fields must in general be revalidated. This is easy to see from our example,
because the current `add_addCB` function would allow the user to enter a check with
no AMOUNT, PAYEE, etc.

Whenever practical, you should set up fields so it isn't possible to create a bad
record in the first place by using character-by-character validation. The XU convenience functions strive to do this. However, sometimes it is not possible to detect a
bad value immediately when it is entered; sometimes bad values cannot be detected
until other fields are filled out. For example, if a user is entering a date and enters
February 29, it isn't possible to figure out if that's valid until after the year is entered.

Because users can hit that OK button at any time, it is certainly possible for them
to leave required fields empty. In most cases, empty includes fields entirely composed of whitespace. The XU library provides a command to help you detect empty
fields:

```
    XUisempty string ...
```

This command returns success if all of its string arguments are composed entirely
of white space, or are truly empty. It can be used in conjunction with dtksh conditional commands:

```
    if XUisempty "$value"
    then ...
```

You must potentially do a great deal of validation work within your OK button callback. In the case of TextFields, you often need to do precisely the same validation

that you specified in a validation function on the `XUtextfield` command. That's because those validation functions only get called when the user leaves the field using TAB or ENTER—they may have decided to hit the OK button without leaving a field.

This type of validation is performed in the final checkbook application (`chk-book.sh`).

Programmatically Invoking a Validation Callback

You can programmatically trigger a widget's callbacks using:

```
XUcallcallbacks $widget callbackname
```

This executes all the callbacks of type `callbackname` for the `widget`. For Text-Field widgets, the `XUaddtextfields` function uses the `activateCallback` for verification. So, if you created a TextField like this:

```
XUaddtextfields $workarea NAME Name my_verify 16
```

then you can invoke the verification function, `my_verify`, by using:

```
XUcallcallbacks $NAME activateCallback
```

The advantage to doing this instead of simply calling `my_verify` directly is that there may be multiple verification functions registered for the widget. For example, the `XUaddfloat` function registers an `activateCallback` for the TextField widgets it creates. You might also decide to add other validation functions yourself by using `XUaddcallback`. In that case, one simple call to `XUcallcallbacks` will invoke both validation functions.

6.12 The User Is Always Right

Time for a bit of philosophy. When you design dialogs, you need to make them easy to use. This means sending the focus to a logical place to lead the user through a set of actions; it means validating every possible error; it means providing concise and informative error and warning messages.

Some programmers have the attitude that graphical programs are inherently easy to use just because the user has a mouse and can move anywhere at any time. If the user makes a mistake, it must be the user's fault. If a bug is reported, the programmer tries to blame the user for the mistake. This is a bad attitude.

A True Story

I once installed a dtksh application for a user who had no previous computer experience. She was worried about using it; there had never been a computer in her office before. She was worried she'd make a mistake and lose important records. I told her this: "If you make a mistake, it's not your fault. It's my fault. If my program allows you to make a mistake, I'm to blame. If it doesn't provide you with enough information to get the job done, that's my fault too. By definition, you will never be blamed for any error." She had complete confidence after that, and was successfully using the most complex features of the program within hours.

This is a healthy attitude for any programmer. Don't ever blame the users for anything—it should not be possible for them to make a mistake. It is your job to make their job easy, to make it difficult or impossible for them to err.

6.13 Summary

This chapter showed how to create a relatively simple but quite useful kind of dialog that contains labels on the left and control widgets on the right, with action buttons at the bottom. To create such a dialog you must follow these steps:

- Create a dialog using XUsimpledialog.
- Add action area buttons using XUactionbuttons.
- Create one or more prompting fields using any of the prompting functions shown in this chapter.
- Align the labels using XUalign2column.
- Display the dialog by calling XUmanage on its handle.

The XU library provides a number of predefined functions for creating useful controls:

- XUaddtextfields can create one or more TextFields to prompt for string values.
- XUaddinteger can create fields useful for prompting for integer values.
- XUaddreal and XUaddmoney create controls that can prompt for floating-point or monetary values.
- XUadddates creates several TextField widgets and provides validation functions for date fields.
- XUaddtogglebuttons creates one or more ToggleButton widgets to prompt for yes/no values.
- XUaddoptionmenu creates one OptionMenu widget that can be used to prompt for one of several fixed choices.

7 *Help Me!*

7.1 Introduction

This chapter will help you help your users. In it, you learn these techniques:

- Display a help browser by registering `helpCallbacks`.
- Provide context-sensitive help when the user presses the F1 function key.
- Provide context-sensitive help by allowing the user to select a widget with the mouse pointer.
- Create help files with hypertext links and compile them into a help volume.

This chapter concentrates on the programming aspects of creating an effective help system. Authoring help is a subject unto itself, and I will do no more than offer some general pointers in that area.

The CDE help system can display SGML (Standard Generalized Markup Language) files. That's an ASCII file with embedded structure that allows links to other help topics, formatted text such as italic, bold, bullet lists, etc., embedded graphics, and many other features. The CDE help system defines a set of SGML constructs called the HelpTag Document Type Definition (DTD). I will be showing you how to use the most common HelpTag DTD constructs, but a full discussion of SGML and HelpTag is beyond the scope of this book. See [CDE Help, 1994] for complete details.

7.2 On Being Helpful

The subject of help systems always reminds of the pathos-laden final scene from the Science fiction classic *The Fly* (I'm referring to the 1958 original starring Vincent Price). A scientist who became half-man half-fly in an experiment gone horribly wrong is stuck in a spider web. He cries out "Help me! Help me!" in a terrified voice at least eight octaves above soprano. A nearby friend hears him, but it is too late—the spider is already munching on our tragic hero. The friend crushes both man–fly and spider with a stone to end the ordeal.

The point is (you weren't entirely sure there was going to be a point, were you?), users have certain expectations when they ask for help—it is the programmer's responsibility not to crush them with a stone when they ask. The next few sections offer some guidelines.

Just the Facts

When users ask for help, they want a *short* explanation of what they need to do *now*. They don't want an encyclopedic explanation of the entire application. Thus, help should be *context-sensitive* whenever possible, and should be worded crisply and concisely to get the user back to work as quickly as possible.

> ***Context-sensitive help:*** Help that is tailored to the actions the user is currently attempting to perform.

My rule of thumb is that the user should not have to read for more than 10 seconds to figure out what they need to know. Because people typically read at speeds between 200 and 400 words per minute, this means an average help screen should contain no more than about 50 words. Sometimes this ideal length cannot be attained, but it's a good general goal.

Digging Deeper

Even though users want terse explanations on the main help screen, they want to be able to get more in-depth information easily if the short description was not sufficient. For this reason, *hypertext* links should be provided throughout most help screens.

> ***Hypertext:*** Highlighted text in a help screen that can be selected by the user using the mouse to bring up more detailed information on the highlighted term.

I will show you how to create hypertext links in your help screens later in this chapter.

Help is Nice, But...

Users do not want to *depend* on help for day-to-day use of the application. Asking for help should be the exception rather than the rule, especially after the first few uses of an application. Applications should be designed clearly so users don't need help in the first place.

Some users feel stupid when they ask for help. They subconsciously fear their boss will walk in and "catch" them reading help instead of doing work. For this reason, they tend to skim help screens that are too long and detailed; this can lead to errors since they might miss important information. If users have to constantly ask for help long after learning how to use an application, the application is at fault, not the user.

Figure 7-1. Elements of the CDE Help System.   Product families are made up of volumes, which in turn are made up of topics. There is always a home topic, and usually a copyright topic. There may also be an index and glossary.

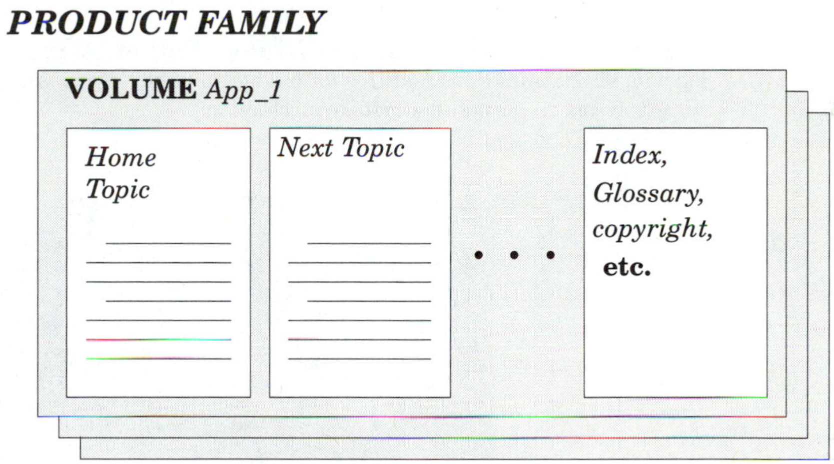

PRODUCT FAMILY

VOLUME *App_1*

Home Topic	*Next Topic*	• • •	*Index, Glossary, copyright,* **etc.**

7.3 Help File Structure

In CDE, help files are organized into *volumes* and *topics*. A volume is a set of help information that describes an application. A topic is a description of a single feature or function in the application. It is also possible to group several related volumes into a *product family*, which makes it easier for the user of a large system of applications to find related information.

Every volume has a *home topic*; that's the first topic shown if the user asks for general information about the application. Volumes also usually have a *copyright topic* that describes copyright and version information about the application.

In addition, the CDE help system directly supports the notion of a help *index*; like the index of a book it contains a list of phrases and keywords sorted alphabetically. The help system has the notion of a *glossary* as well; again, analogous to the glossary of a book, it contains phrases along with their definitions. These elements are shown in Figure 7-1.

I'll be describing precisely how you define these different help file components a little later; for now it is sufficient for you to have a general feel for these phrases.

7.4 The CDE Help Widgets

Help volumes are displayed by using special widgets. There are two widgets provided by CDE for help: the HelpDialog and the QuickHelpDialog. The HelpDialog provides many features such as a list of topics and several navigation commands. A HelpDialog is shown in Figure 7-2. QuickHelpDialog is a stripped down version that has fewer features but takes up less screen space (see Figure 7-3).

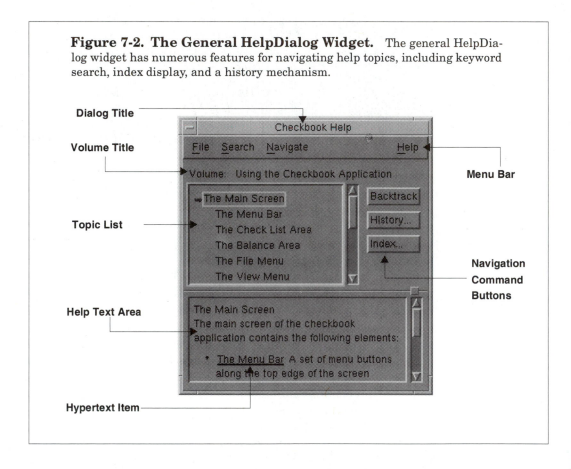

Figure 7-2. The General HelpDialog Widget. The general HelpDialog widget has numerous features for navigating help topics, including keyword search, index display, and a history mechanism.

You create these dialogs using the commands:

```
XUhelpdialog [-u] variable $parent [resource:value ...]
XUquickhelpdialog [-u] variable $parent [resource:value ...]
```

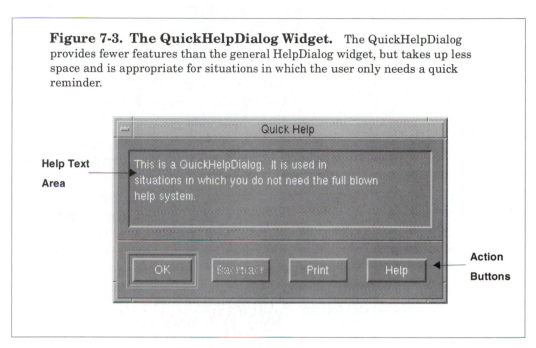

Figure 7-3. The QuickHelpDialog Widget. The QuickHelpDialog
provides fewer features than the general HelpDialog widget, but takes up less
space and is appropriate for situations in which the user only needs a quick
reminder.

These commands take the usual widget creation command arguments, and store
the handle of the newly created dialog in *variable*. As with most dialogs, you
should normally use the -u option to cause them to be created initially unmanaged.
You cause them to be popped up by managing this returned handle using
XUmanage.
    The following resources are the most commonly used for both these dialogs:

dialogTitle	The string that appears in the title area.
rows, columns	The number of rows and columns of characters displayed in the help text area.
helpType	One of: HELP_TYPE_FILE, HELP_TYPE_STRING, HELP_TYPE_DYNAMIC_STRING, HELP_TYPE_MAN_PAGE, or HELP_TYPE_TOPIC. These are explained in more detail later.
helpFile	If helpType is HELP_TYPE_FILE, this string is the path to a file that should be displayed in the help area.
helpVolume	This is a string indicating the volume of help being accessed. Help volumes are explained later.

stringData   If helpType is HELP_TYPE_STRING or HELP_TYPE_DYNAMIC_STRING, this should be set to the string to be displayed in the help text area.

manPage   If helpType is HELP_MAN_PAGE, this is a string naming the manual page entry, such as "sed". If a particular section of the manual is desired, the section number should precede the page entry, such as "3 crypt."

locationId   If helpType is HELP_TYPE_TOPIC, this string names the location identifier within the help volume. Help volumes are explained later.

Listing 7-1 shows a complete program that creates the QuickHelpDialog shown in Figure 7-3. The program shows the simplest kind of help, which displays a fixed string of text embedded directly in the script. The main window of the application is a simple PushButton that creates and manages the QuickHelpDialog when pressed.

Listing 7-1. Creating a QuickHelpDialog (qhelp.sh). This example shows how to create a simple QuickHelpDialog widget with a fixed string help message.

```
. $XUTILDIR/xutil.sh

function helpCB {
        XUquickhelpdialog HELP $TOPLEVEL \
            dialogTitle:"Quick Help" \
            helpType:HELP_TYPE_STRING \
            rows:5 \
            stringData:'This is a QuickHelpDialog.  It is used in
situations in which you don't need the full blown
help system.'
        XUmanage $HELP

}


XUinitialize TOPLEVEL Quick "$@"
XUpushbutton BUTTON $TOPLEVEL labelString:"Help Me! Help Me!"
XUaddcallback $BUTTON activateCallback helpCB
XUrealize $TOPLEVEL
XUmainloop
```

To create a general HelpDialog widget, you would only have to change the widget creation command from XUquickhelpdialog to XUhelpdialog. However, the general HelpDialog widget is not really suited to displaying the kind of fixed string data shown in Listing 7-1; it is more useful for displaying a full volume of hypertext help as is described in a moment.

Types of Help

There are several different ways of displaying help text with these help widgets:

- Display a particular volume and topic.
- Display a plain text file.
- Display a fixed string.
- Display a fixed string but allow the help widget to determine where to break the lines. This is called a *dynamic string*.
- Display a UNIX manual page entry.

For each method of display, you need to set the `helpType` resource to indicate the desired type of help, and one or more other resources to indicate the location of the help text. The rules are summarized in Table 7-1.

Table 7-1. Setting HelpDialog Resources

helpType Resource Setting	Other Resources
HELP_TYPE_TOPIC	Set `helpVolume` to the volume name and `locationId` to the topic identifier string.
HELP_TYPE_STRING	Set `stringData` to the desired string. Newlines will be honored literally when displaying help.
HELP_TYPE_DYNAMIC_STRING	Set `stringData` to the desired string. The help widget is allowed to break lines on word boundaries as it sees fit.
HELP_TYPE_FILE	Set `helpFile` to the full path of a file containing ASCII text.
HELP_TYPE_MANUAL_PAGE	Set `manPage` to a string in the same format as accepted by the UNIX man command.

Listing 7-2 is a complete program that illustrates all of these options. Its main window is composed of a set of PushButtons, one for each of the preceding options. When one of the buttons is pressed, the corresponding type of help is displayed. The main workhorse of this program is a function called `helpCB`, which takes different options depending on the desired type of help. This function creates a Quick-HelpDialog, then sets the appropriate resources to display the desired help type.

Figure 7-4. Different Types of Help Display (help.sh).   Three of
the different button press options allowed by help.sh are displayed below. On
top, a fixed string is displayed. In the middle a dynamic string is displayed.
Note that the help system chooses line breaks based on word boundaries. At the
bottom, a file is displayed.

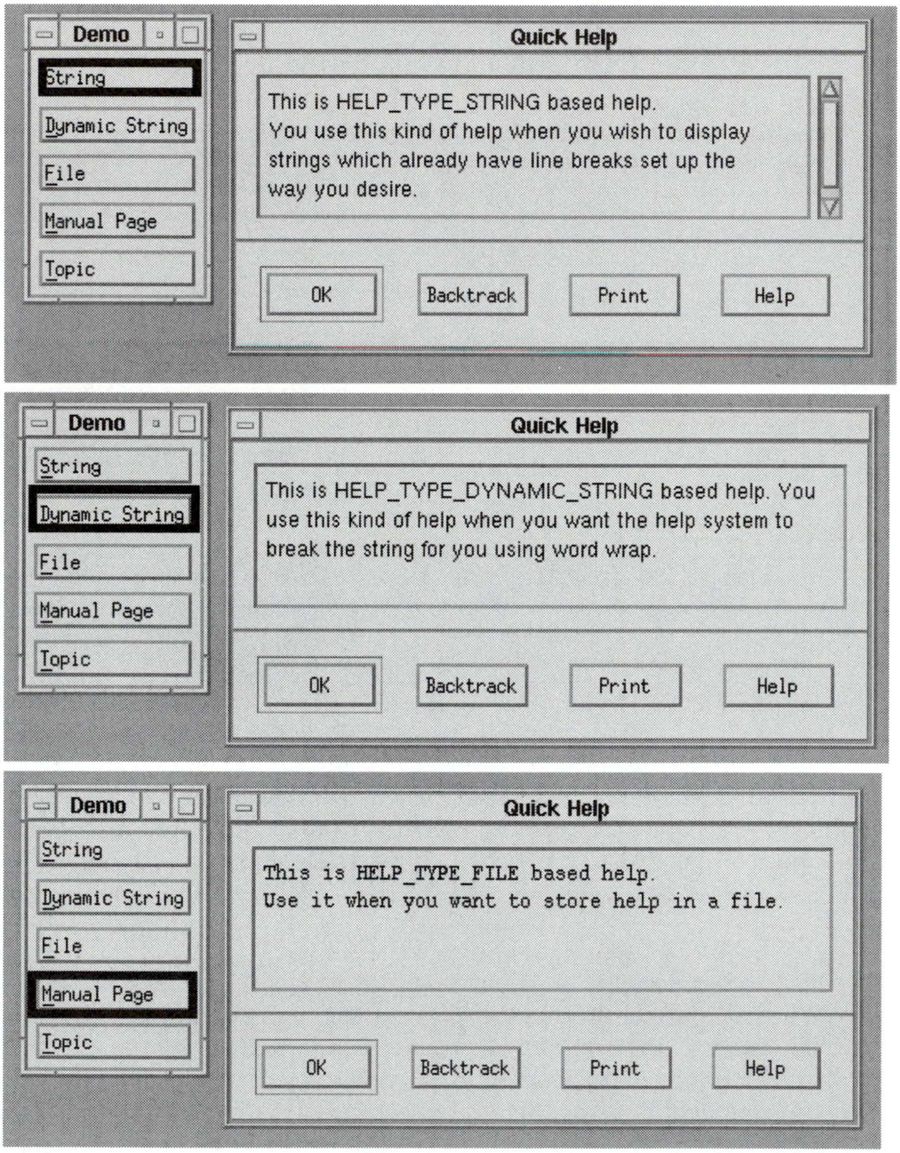

Some of the resulting output screens generated by running this program are shown in Figure 7-4.

Listing 7-2. Help Display Options (help.sh). This program illustrates all five methods of displaying help using the QuickHelpDialog widget. The general HelpDialog widget is almost always used only with the HELP_TYPE_TOPIC method, although the other methods work for it as well.

```
. $XUTILDIR/xutil.sh

HELPSTRING="This is HELP_TYPE_STRING based help.
You use this kind of help when you wish to display
strings which already have line breaks set up the
way you desire."

DHELPSTRING="This is HELP_TYPE_DYNAMIC_STRING based help. \
You use this kind of help when you want the help system to \
break the string for you using word wrap."

print "This is HELP_TYPE_FILE based help.
Use it when you want to store help in a file." > Helpfile.hlp

function helpCB {
    if [[ ! $HELP ]]
    then
        XUquickhelpdialog HELP $TOPLEVEL \
            dialogTitle:"Quick Help" \
            rows:5
    fi

    case "$1" in
    STRING)
        XUset $HELP \
            helpType:HELP_TYPE_STRING \
            stringData:"$HELPSTRING"
        ;;
    DSTRING)
        XUset $HELP \
            helpType:HELP_TYPE_DYNAMIC_STRING \
            stringData:"$DHELPSTRING"
        ;;
    FILE)
        XUset $HELP \
            helpType:HELP_TYPE_FILE \
            helpFile:Helpfile.hlp
        ;;
    MANPAGE)
        XUset $HELP \
            helpType:HELP_TYPE_MAN_PAGE \
```

```
                    manPage:"cat"
            ;;
        TOPIC)
            XUset $HELP \
                helpType:HELP_TYPE_TOPIC \
                helpVolume:AppVolume \
                locationId:providing-help
            ;;
        esac
        XUmanage $HELP
}

XUinitialize TOPLEVEL Demo "$@"
XUcolumn COL $TOPLEVEL
XUaddbuttons $COL \
    COL.STRING     "String"          "helpCB STRING" \
    COL.DSTRING    "Dynamic String"  "helpCB DSTRING" \
    COL.FILE       "File"            "helpCB FILE" \
    COL.MANPAGE    "Manual Page"     "helpCB MANPAGE" \
    COL.TOPIC      "Topic"           "helpCB TOPIC"

XUrealize $TOPLEVEL
XUmainloop
```

7.5 Creating Help Volumes and Topics

If you want to take full advantage of the HelpDialog widget, it's necessary to create help volumes with tagged topics, hypertext phrases, an index, copyright screen, and glossary. This section describes how to create each of these elements.

Several steps are required to create this kind of help:

1. Create a HelpTag format file containing the help text. This is an ASCII file that contains annotations indicating where topics begin, index entries, etc. It also supports many formatting constructs such as bullet lists and font changes.

2. Use the CDE command dthelptag to generate a volume file from the HelpTag file. This command also does syntax checking on your HelpTag file.

3. Test your help volume using the CDE command dthelpview.

4. Use the HelpDialog to display the help using HELP_TYPE_TOPIC mode.

HelpTag File General Concepts

A HelpTag format file is a simple ASCII file that contains SGML (Standard Generalized Markup Language) annotations to indicate structures within the text.

> SGML is an internationally recognized standard for creating structured text. HelpTag is a set of SGML structure definitions that is appropriate for use with the CDE help system.

These structures consist of a *tag* surrounded by angle brackets, followed by some text, followed by an end marker. The end marker is also enclosed in angle brackets, and is the same tag word preceded by a backslash (\) character. For example, the following HelpTag notation specifies that the word "always" should appear emphasized (in italics):

```
You should <emph> always <\emph> write clear help screens.
```

Tagged elements can span multiple lines. The help system will format your annotated file appropriately for the size of the HelpDialog screen. As a help author, you are responsible for defining the *structure* of the help text, not the *format* of the text. So, in the preceding example, you specify that the word "always" should be emphasized; the fact that this is represented by italics is determined by the help system.

Short Form Tags

Because this notation can be verbose at times, HelpTag defines a set of shorthand notations for commonly used structures. For example, surrounding text by double exclamation marks (!!) is equivalent to using the <emph> tag:

```
You should !!always!! write clear help screens.
```

Another (more general) shorthand notation is to use the pipe symbol (|) following the keyword as a delimiter. In this case there is no closing brace and another pipe symbol denotes the end of the structure. For example:

```
You should <emph|always| write clear help screens.
```

Defining a Volume

There are several standard parts to a help volume:

- **Home Topic**. The first topic in the help volume. It is marked by the <home-topic> tag, and can be displayed by the HelpDialog by setting the locationId resource to the string _hometopic.

- **Other Topics**. There can be any number of other topics. Different levels of topic are allowed; there are main topics and subtopics. The first level of topic may be tagged <chapter> or <s1> interchangeably. Further levels may be tagged <s2>, <s3>, etc. I prefer to simply skip the <chapter> tag (less typing!) and start at the <s1> level. You may place identifying tags on these topics by placing the notation id=*identifier* before the closing angle bracket, i.e.:

    <s1 id=general-info>

  Identifiers must begin with an alphabetic character and can be composed of alphabetic characters, the digits 0 to 9, or the characters + or -. In this example, you would display this topic by setting the locationId resource of the HelpDialog to the string general-info.

- **Entities**. It is possible to include multiple files in a help volume by declaring the external files as *entities*. It is also possible to import graphic files (such as TIFF format files or X pixmap files) into a help volume in this way. In addition, an entity can simply be a piece of text referenced by a symbolic name (similar to using a variable in your text). Entity tags are explained below.

- **Meta Info**. This is a set of general information about your help volume. There are several standard pieces of meta information, such as the title of your help volume (using `<title>`), an abstract for your volume (using `<abstract>`), and a copyright notice (using `<copyright>`). To display these standard items, you would set the `locationId` resource to `_title`, `_abstract` or `_copyright`, respectively.

  It is also possible to put topics in the meta information sections that should not be displayed in the HelpDialog topic hierarchy.

- **Glossary**. This is an alphabetical list of definitions of terms that appear throughout the volume. It is marked with the `<glossary>` tag. In the topic text you may mark glossary items using the `<term>` tag (shorthand: surround the word by ++), in which case the user can bring up the definition simply by clicking on the item.

  Within the glossary definition, you define terms using the `<dterm>` tag; the term consists of anything on the same line as the `<dterm>` tag, its definition is anything on following lines up to the next `<dterm>` tag.

Listing 7-3 summarizes the structure of tags required to define a help volume. A complete example including all of these basic elements is presented later in Section 7.6, *A Complete Volume Example*.

Listing 7-3. High-Level View of a Help Volume.

```
Entity declarations (must come first)
<helpvolume>
        <metainfo>
                <title>  title text
                <copyright>
                        copyright text
                <abstract>
                        abstract text
                other topics may be defined here that
                should not appear in the HelpDialog topic tree.
        <\metainfo>

        <hometopic> title text goes to end of line
                body text of home topic
        <s1 id=identifier> title of the subtopic goes to end of line
                body of the subtopic
```

```
               More subtopics can go here.

        <glossary>
                  <dterm> term to be defined goes to end of line
                           definition of term

                  More term definitions can go here
    <\helpvolume>
```

Defining and Using Entities

As mentioned earlier, it is possible to include external files using an entity declaration.

> There are several other reasons for declaring an entity, such as defining a named string to be referenced throughout your help topics, or for including graphics in your help system screens. Refer to [CDE Help Guide, 1994] for more information about these uses.

The format of this construct is

```
    <!entity identifier FILE "path">
```

where identifier is a string (no whitespace allowed) that will be used to reference the entity later, and the file's name is *path*. Entity declarations must come first in your help volume file, before any other structure tags. For example, this entity declaration associates the identifier `myfile` with a file named `./mydir/file`:

```
    <!entity myfile FILE "./mydir/file">
```

Later, at the point at which you want the entity to be included, use the *entity reference* notation:

```
    &identifier;
```

In the example above you would use:

```
    &myfile;
```

Some Other HelpTag Constructs

There are dozens of very useful HelpTag markup tags you can use to format text. I can't cover them all in this book. You should read [CDE Help Guide 1995] for complete details. However, I present a few of the most useful constructs in Table 7-2 to give you a taste of what's available, and so you can follow the examples presented later.

Table 7-2. Some Useful HelpTag Constructs

`<!-- any text -->`	This is a comment; it will not appear in the help text display.
`<xref identifier>`	Creates a cross reference to a topic. The `identifier` should refer to a topic ID (for example, as specified by `<s1 id=identifier>`. The title of the referenced topic is displayed, and if the user clicks on it then that topic replaces the help screen. An example of this is shown in the next section.

`<list type>`
`* list item #1 text`
`* list item #2 text`
`...`
`<\list>`
	This construct creates a list. The asterisks (*) are literal—they delimit each list item. The `type` specifies the kind of list desired, and may be one of `bullet` (for a bullet list), `order` (for a numbered list), or `plain` (for a list with no leading marker).
	
	A number of other features are available with this construct, see [CDE Help Guide 1995].

`<idx|term|`	(Note: this is shorthand notation, which is almost always used with this particular tag). This tag creates a new `term` for the help index. If the user views the index, they will see this term, and clicking on the term will bring them to whatever topic this tag has defined.

`<caution>`
`text of caution`
`<\caution>`
	This inserts a caution. It should be used when there is a danger of loss of data or some other undesirable result. There are also tags that work the same way for warnings and notes: `<warning>` and `<note>`.

7.6 A Complete Volume Example

Now we'll create a help volume for the checkbook application. Instead of creating one large file for the help volume, I'll divide it into logical pieces and use the entity declaration feature to tie them together. I'll divide the volume into the following files:

- `Chkbook.htg` will be the main help volume file. By convention, help volume files should end in the extension `.htg`. This file will only contain entity declarations and references for the other files.
- `MetaInfo` will hold the meta information section.
- `MainScreen` will hold the home topic and topics relating to the checkbook program's main screen.

- `AddScreen` will hold topics relating to the "Add New Check" screen.
- `Glossary` will hold glossary term definitions.

The Volume File

Listing 7-4 shows the contents of the checkbook volume file, `Chkbook.htg`. As stated earlier, I have chosen to use this file solely to include other files. This is not strictly necessary; I could have intermixed any HelpTag constructs in this file, or I could have simply put all the help constructs in one large file. This method is preferred, however, because it organizes each piece of the help in its own file.

Listing 7-4. The Checkbook Volume (Chkbook.htg). All files included in the volume must be declared using the `!entity` construct. Following that, the files are included in order using the `&entityname;` notation.

```
<!entity MetaInformation FILE "MetaInfo">
<!entity MainScreen FILE "MainScreen">
<!entity AddScreen FILE "AddScreen">
<!entity Glossary FILE "Glossary">

&MetaInformation;
&MainScreen;
&AddScreen;
&Glossary;
```

The Meta Information File

Listing 7-5 shows the meta information file, MetaInfo. It contains the three standard pieces of information: the title, copyright, and abstract. Note the use of the string:

```
&copy;
```

in the copyright section. That is a predefined string entity that expands to the standard copyright symbol: ©. A number of these predefined string entities exist, see [CDE Help Guide 1995] for a complete list.

Besides the title, copyright, and abstract, you may put regular topic definitions within the meta information section using the `<s1>`, `<s2>`, etc., tags. Such topics will not appear in the HelpDialog's topic listing. In the case of the checkbook application, there was no need to use this feature.

From your dtksh application, you can jump to the title, copyright, and abstract sections by setting the `locationId` resource of the HelpDialog to the strings `_title`, `_copyright`, and `_abstract`, respectively.

Listing 7-5. MetaInformation Example (MetaInfo).

```
<metainfo>
            <title> Using the Checkbook Application
            <copyright> &copy; 1994 Addison-Wesley Publishing Company.
            This example program may be freely copied and distributed
            as long as its origin is disclosed.
            <abstract> Help for using the Checkbook example program.
<\metainfo>
```

The Help Topic Files

By far the largest section of the volume is the topics that actually provide help text.
I have split up topics into two files—one for each of the checkbook program's
screens.

To keep this example short, the first of these topic files doesn't define every topic
completely.   As you can see in Listing 7-6, the home topic and the menu bar topic
are fully defined, but the rest of the referenced topics are just "stubbed in" by including nothing more than a title. This technique is often used in the early stages of help
design; it's similar to stubbing in callback routines while designing screens. I used
a common technique in designing these screens: a bullet list is used in conjunction
with the <xref> tag as a launch point to other topics. The <xref> tag will be replaced by the referenced topic's title when the screen is displayed to the user.

The home topic can be displayed from your program by setting the `locationId`
resource of the HelpDialog widget to the string _hometopic. Other topics are referenced by setting `locationId` to the identifier you define in the `<s1 id=identi-
fier>` tags.

This listing also illustrates the use of the `<idx>` tag to mark index entries. It's a
good idea to have at least one index entry per topic, and even more for complex topics.
A good rule of thumb is to include an index entry for every major concept discussed
in the help topic text.

Listing 7-6. Main Screen Help Topics (MainScreen). The home topic and the
menu bar topic are completely shown, while other topic references are simply stubbed in for
this version of the Main Screen help file. Note the use of bullet lists as kickoff points for other
topics—the <xref> tag is used immediately after the bullet (asterisk) and will be replaced by
the referenced topic's title.

```
<hometopic> The Main Screen
<idx|main screen, the|

The main screen of the checkbook application
contains the following elements:

<list bullet>
* <xref menu-bar> A set of menu buttons along the top edge
```

```
of the screen
* <xref check-list> A scrollable list of checkbook entries
* <xref balance-area> A line at the bottom of the screen shows you
the current checkbook balance.
<\list>

<s1 id=menu-bar>  The Menu Bar
<idx|menu bar, the|

The menu bar contains pull down menus that allow
you to do different operations to check entries:

<list bullet>
* <xref file-menu> contains items to open new checkbook
files, save changes, and print checkbook entries.
* <xref view-menu> contains items to change how checkbook
entries are displayed, search for entries, etc.
* <xref actions-menu> contains items to allow you to add new entries,
delete entries, and modify existing entries.
* <xref help-menu> contains items to give you help about
the checkbook program.
<\list>

<!-- The following topics are simply stubs to be defined later -->

<s1 id=check-list> The Check List Area

<s1 id=balance-area> The Balance Area

<s1 id=file-menu> The File Menu

<s1 id=view-menu> The View Menu

<s1 id=actions-menu> The Actions Menu

<s1 id=help-menu> The Help Menu
```

Listing 7-7 shows the help topics for the Add Entry screen of the checkbook application. It includes glossary references surrounded by ++ (I'll discuss this further in the next section). It also illustrates the use of ! ! around text for emphasis. Such text will appear in italics when the help screen is displayed.

Listing 7-7. The Add Entry Topic (AddScreen). Topics for the checkbook program's Add Entry screen. Note the use of ++ around terms to denote glossary references, the use of ! ! surrounding text for emphasis. Here again bullet lists are used as kickoff points to other topics by using the <xref> tag.

```
<s1 id=add-entry> The Add Entry Screen
<idx|add entry screen, the|
```

```
The Add Entry Screen allows you to create new checkbook
entries.  Each checkbook ++entry++ contains the following
information:

<list bullet>
* <xref date-field> the date of the entry
* <xref payee-field> the name of the "payee".
For deposits, this is the word DEPOSIT.
* <xref amount-field> the amount of the entry.
* <xref category-field> the ++category++ of the item.
For deposits or other credits, this should be CREDIT.
<\list>

<s1 id=date-field>  The Date Field
The date field contains three areas: month, day, and year.
Each area is a text field that should be set to a number.  If
you type exactly two characters, you automatically move to the
next field.

<s1 id=payee-field> The Payee Field
This can be any string, and indicates who the check was paid
to.  For example, !!Sussex Power and Light!!.  In the case of
deposits use the word DEPOSIT and set the ++category++ to CREDIT.

<s1 id=amount-field> The Amount Field
This is the amount of the entry, in dollars.  It may be 0.00 for
entries whose ++category++ is VOID.

<s1 id=category-field> The Category Field
This field holds the ++category++ of the check.  Select a new
category by selecting it with the mouse.  Any entry that should be
a credit to the account (such as a deposit, interest payment, etc.)
should have a category of CREDIT.
```

The Glossary

A glossary is a list of terms with their definitions. As you saw earlier, your help topics can mark text as glossary terms using the ++*term*++ notation. Text marked like that can be clicked by the user to show the term definition.

The glossary section defines the terms using the <dterm> tag. Any text following the <dterm> tag to the end of the line is the term being defined, and any text from the next line to the following <dterm> tag is the definition (see Listing 7-8).

Listing 7-8. The Glossary (Glossary).

```
<glossary>
   <dterm>entry
```

```
A single checkbook record is called an entry.  An entry could
be a deposit, interest payment, void check, or a regular check.


<dterm>category
Each check entry has a category associated with it which indicates
the nature of the entry.  All entries that add money to the account
have a category of CREDIT.  Other categories are user definable.
For example, you could create categories for TELEPHONE, AUTO,
UTILITY, or CHARITY to denote different check purposes.
```

7.7 Compiling the Help Volume

Now that we've got all the elements of the help volume defined, we need to "compile" it using the `dthelptag` utility. This is relatively straightforward:

1. Create a directory and copy all the help volume files there (Chkbook.htg, MetaInfo, MainScreen, AddScreen, and Glossary).

2. Create a file called `dthelptag.opt` to hold default options for the `dthelptag` utility. Put these lines in that file:

    ```
    memo
    onerror=go
    search=./
    search=../
    ```

3. Run the `dthelptag` utility as follows:

    ```
    dthelptag -verbose ./Chkbook.htg
    ```

4. If there are any syntax errors or undefined cross references, fix them and go back to step 3 and rerun `dthelptag`. Errors are stored in a file called Chkbook.err.

5. Otherwise, you should find a file called `Chkbook.sdl` in your directory. This is your run-time help file.

7.8 Testing the Help Volume

Once you have successfully created the run-time help file, you can immediately test it using the CDE `dthelpview` utility. In our example, use the following command:

```
dthelpview -helpTopic ./Chkbook.sdl
```

This command brings up a HelpDialog widget and displays your home topic. You can use the features of the HelpDialog widget to test the hyperlinks, index, glossary terms, etc. You can also make sure the help topics look the way you intended.

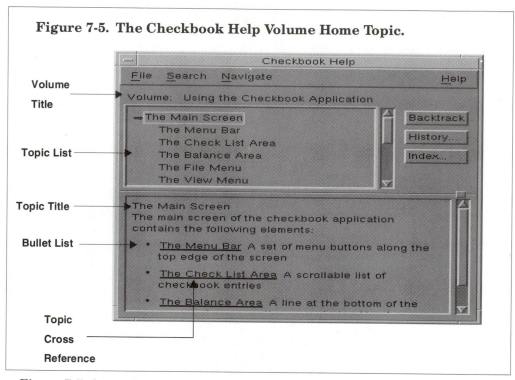

Figure 7-5 shows the initial screen displayed by dthelpview from our example. Notice the appearance of the bulleted list—the cross-referenced topic titles appear underlined. That indicates to the user that more information on that term can be obtained by clicking on it with the mouse.

Figure 7-6 shows the results of selecting "The Add Entry Screen" from the Help-Dialog topic list. Note the glossary term marking for the word entry. In this case, a dashed underline is used to denote a term that is contained in the glossary. This figure also shows the result of selecting the glossary term entry. A separate window is created to display the word's definition.

7.9 Tying Help into the Application

Users can request help in several ways:

- The MainWindow of the application usually contains a MenuBar with an item called Help. That menu should contain standard items to launch several different kinds of help about the application.

- Dialogs usually have a command button labeled Help. Usually this should bring up a help topic that explains the purpose of the dialog and provides hypertext launch points to get more information on each field in the dialog.

Figure 7-6. The "Add Entry" Topic and Glossary.   On top, the "Add Entry Screen" topic has been selected by the user. Note that it is preceded by a dash in the topic list. This screen contains a glossary definition for the word "entry". It is denoted by a broken underscore. If the user selects this word, then a separate glossary screen appears with the definition of "entry" displayed.

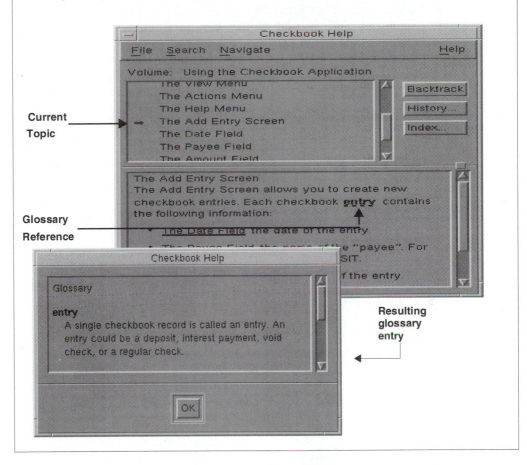

- It is also common to provide a context-sensitive facility when the user presses a dialog's `Help` button by allowing the user to select one of the widgets in the dialog using a special "question mark cursor". This action should bring up help specific to the selected widget.

- With the focus on a particular widget (such as a TextField), the F1 function key should provide help specific to that widget.

   Some keyboards actually have a key labeled HELP for this purpose, but F1 has become a widespread standard for requesting help.

The following sections implement each of these kinds of help for the checkbook application.

The helpCB Callback Revealed

You may have noticed that all along in the checkbook script when I defined menus, screens, and buttons I sometimes registered an as-yet-undefined callback function named helpCB. That function was always given one mysterious argument, a string like add-entry or _copyright. You have probably realized by now that these strings are actually help topic identifiers.

The complete usage specification of the checkbook application's helpCB is:

```
helpCB [-v volume] [context|topic-identifier]
```

The helpCB function uses the Chkbook.sdl file as the help volume unless the -v option is provided and specifies a different volume.

If its argument is the literal string context, then helpCB turns the mouse pointer to a question mark cursor, allowing the user to select a widget. The selected widget's helpCallback is executed. If the selected widget does not have a helpCallback registered, then its parent is searched for a helpCallback. This process continues until either an ancestor of the selected widget is found that has a helpCallback or the root widget is encountered, in which case an InformationDialog is displayed indicating that there is no help available for that widget.

If the argument is not the literal string context, then it is assumed to be a help topic that is to be displayed using a HelpDialog widget.

Listing 7-9 shows the definition of helpCB. As you can see, it's quite simple. It starts by decoding arguments, then creates a HelpDialog widget whose handle is stored in the variable HELPPOP (if it does not already exist).

Listing 7-9. The helpCB Function (chkbook3.sh).

```
function helpCB {
    if [[ ! "$HELPPOP" ]]
    then
            XUhelpdialog -u HELPPOP $TOPLEVEL \
                dialogTitle:"Checkbook Help" \
                rows:5 \
                columns:40
    fi
    case "$1" in
    _context)
            XUwidgethelp $2
            return
            ;;
    _onhelp)
            XUset $HELPPOP \
                helpType:HELP_TYPE_TOPIC \
```

```
                    helpVolume:Help4Help \
                    locationId:_hometopic
            ;;
    *)
            XUset $HELPPOP \
                helpType:HELP_TYPE_TOPIC \
                helpVolume:$XUTILDIR/Help/Chkbook.sdl \
                locationId:"$1"
            ;;
    esac
    XUmanage $HELPPOP
}
```

Locating the Help Volume

Notice that in `helpCB` the `helpVolume` resource is set to `$XUTILDIR/Help/Chk-book.sdl`. Using a full path to the `.sdl` file is one method of locating the help volume. There are other ways of locating the run-time help volume, however. Instead of specifying a full path, you can also just give the volume name (which is the run-time file name without the .sdl extension, in this case just `Chkbook`). If you use this method, then the `Chkbook.sdl` file must be installed in one of the paths specified by the variable `DTHELPSEARCHPATH`. By default, that variable includes the directory `$HOME/.dt/help`, followed by several standard CDE system help directories. A program is provided with CDE called `dtappintegrate` which can register your application's help volume in one of these system-wide areas. See [CDE Help Guide 1995] for more details.

User-Selected Context-Sensitive Help

When called with the `context` argument, the `helpCB` function provides help on a user-selected widget. This is entirely handled on the programmer's behalf by the XU function:

```
    XUwidgethelp $widget
```

where `$widget` specifies the handle of a widget whose children are candidates for selection by the user. In the case of a dialog, you would provide the handle of the dialog itself, for example. This single function call takes care of the whole process of changing the mouse pointer to a question mark cursor, determining which widget (if any) is selected, and finding the appropriate `helpCallback` to invoke. It could be the helpCallback of the exact widget the user selected, but if none exists then the widget hierarchy is searched for any ancestor of the selected widget that has a `helpCallback`.

When you create your dialog, make sure to register `helpCallbacks` for any widgets that you want to have context-sensitive help. In the case of the checkbook program, `helpCallbacks` are provided for every field using `helpCB` with the appropriate topic argument.

It's also a good idea to register a `helpCallback` for the dialog itself because it can serve as a default help screen in case you fail to register a `helpCallback` for some widgets in the dialog.

7.10 Providing Help Using the F1 Key

The Motif toolkit provides direct support for F1 key help. The default key handler for F1 will figure out which widget has focus and will call its `helpCallback` function, or the `helpCallback` function of its nearest ancestor if it has no `helpCallback` of its own. So, assuming you have set up your `helpCallback` functions as recommended, there is literally nothing else to do to get this feature.

7.11 Providing Pointer Location Help

It is common in graphics applications to provide a single line of help that changes depending on where the mouse pointer is located. Such help reminds the user of the function of a particular field, button, or icon. It is possible to provide help like this using dtksh, but the mechanisms for doing this are rather advanced. For a complete example of how to provide help like this, see the listing for see Listing 19-1., *Checkbook Icon Help (chkbook.sh)* on page 409.

7.12 The MainWindow Help Menu

The `Help` MenuButton that appears in the MainWindow can be used as a general launching point for several different categories of help. The CDE Style Guide specifies a standard list of menu items that this menu should provide:

- `Help on Application` should provide a general introduction to your application. The _hometopic of your help volume is an appropriate choice for this.

- `Help On Context` should provided context-sensitive help, like that provided by `helpCB` with the `context` argument.

- `Help On Version` should provide copyright and version information (as provided by the _copyright topic).

- `Help On Help` should display help on the help facility itself. CDE provides a default volume, `Help4Help` that is guaranteed to be installed. You can simply display the _hometopic topic of that volume to provide this.

Listing 7-10 shows an updated `XUmenusystem` command that creates a menu with these standard elements and uses the previously defined `helpCB` to display appropriate help items.

Listing 7-10. Checkbook Help Menu (chkbook3.sh).

```
XUmenusystem $MB \
    MB.HELP "Help" H { \
            MB.HELP.CS   "Context-Sensitive Help" C \
                                "helpCB _context $TOPLEVEL" \
            MB.HELP.OV   "Overview"       O "helpCB _hometopic" \
            MB.HELP.KB   "Keyboard"       K "helpCB keyboard" \
            MB.HELP.UH   "Using Help"     H "helpCB _onhelp" \
            MB.HELP.PI   "Product Information"   P "helpCB _copyright" \
    }
```

7.13 Summary

- CDE provides a rich help system that supports hypertext, glossary entries, indexing, and sophisticated navigation.

- The HelpDialog and QuickHelpDialog widgets provide several methods of displaying help: fixed strings, dynamic strings that allow the help system to choose word breaks, ASCII files, manual page entries, and HelpTag format help volume topics.

- To provide hypertext capabilities you must create a help volume. The format of a help volume is an ASCII file that includes HelpTag structure markers. These markers define the volume title, copyright message, glossary, topics, and other structures in the text such as bulleted lists or emphasized text.

- Once the HelpTag format file is defined, it is compiled into a run-time help file using the dthelptag utility.

- You can view and test your run-time help file using the dthelpview utility.

- Help is hooked into your application by defining menu items that launch certain help topics implicitly, or by adding helpCallbacks to individual widgets.

- If the user presses the F1 function key, the current widget's helpCallback will be executed.

- In addition, you can allow the user to select a widget using the pointer by using the XUwidgethelp command. That command turns the mouse pointer into a special question mark cursor. Then if the user selects a widget it executes that widget's helpCallback. If the selected widget has no helpCallback, ancestors of the widget are searched to see if they have a helpCallback registered—the first one found is executed.

8 *Resources and Resource Files*

8.1 Introduction

Up to this point, the examples presented have all been self-contained. Any resources we wished to change were set directly in the program script, either at widget creation time or afterward by using XUset. However, for some kinds of resources this is not a good solution—the user may want to configure some aspects of the application differently and you don't want them to have to edit your dtksh script. Also, some resource types like colors and fonts are hardware or installation dependent and should not be hard-coded into your application.

For this reason, X provides the concept of a *resource file*. That is a file external to your application script that can be used to set defaults for resources. This chapter discusses these topics:

- How to write a resource file
- How to change resource defaults using command line options
- Appropriate uses for different kinds of resource defaults
- The order of resource default sources in an X program
- How to set legal values for colors, fonts, and other kinds of resources.

A resource file for the checkbook application is developed using the techniques discussed.

8.2 Using Resource Files

Default values for widget resources may be specified in special types of files called *resource files*.

> ***Resource file:*** A file containing specifications that become default values for resources that are not set programmatically.

Resource files are composed of lines with the following format:

```
widgetspec.resource:   value
```

Breaking this format down into its constituent pieces:

widgetspec   A specification of which widget's resource is being referenced. This is composed of a list of widget *names* (see below) separated by periods. An asterisk (*) can be used as a wildcard to match any sequence of widget names. Also, widget classes can be used in place of specific widget names to set resource defaults globally for a class of widgets.

resource   A resource name, such as labelString.

value   The new default value for the resource.

In addition, blank lines in a resource file are ignored, and lines beginning with an exclamation mark (!) are treated as comments.

8.3 A Simple Example

Listing 8-1 shows a resource file specification that might be used with the hello.sh program (the hello.sh program listing appears on page 23). It redefines the foreground color of all widgets named LABEL to white and the background to black, specifies that all widgets of class XmLabel should be aligned to the end of the space they are given, and specifies that all widgets named LABEL1 should use the font 12x24 (a relatively large font).

> In the text of this book, I always leave off the "Xm" prefix on widget class names; this is the usual X convention. However, in a resource file the full widget class name, including the prefix, is required. So, even though in the text of this book I refer to "the PushButton widget", in a resource file you must specify XmPushButton to match the Motif PushButton widget class.

In addition, the initial size of the application window is set to be 100 pixels wide and 50 pixels high using the geometry resource (this is explained under *Geometry* on page 162).

The effects of these resource settings on the appearance of hello.sh are shown in Figure 8-1.

The simplest way of trying this yourself is to copy this resource specification file to your $HOME before executing hello.sh. The resource file name (Hello) matches the second argument to XUinitialize, which is the application class.

Listing 8-1. A Resource Specification for hello.sh (Hello). By starting the resource specifications with an asterisk, all widgets at any level in the application are matched. In some cases, I used the widget's name, LABEL, and in some cases I used the widget's class, XmLabel. Since there is only one Label widget in this application, the effects are the same.

```
*LABEL.foreground:white
*LABEL.background:black
*LABEL.fontList:12x24
*XmLabel.alignment:ALIGNMENT_END
*geometry:  100x50.
```

Figure 8-1. Result of Using a Resource File (hello.sh, Hello).
On the left, the hello.sh program with no resource file. On the right, the same program is run, but this time with the Hello resource file copied to $HOME.

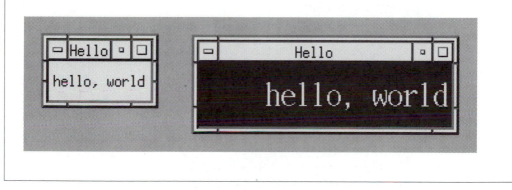

What's in a (Widget) Name?

Let's take a moment to discuss names. Every widget has a name; virtually the only use of a widget's name is for reference in a resource file. The XU convenience library functions that create widgets (like XUlabel, XUpushbutton, etc.) make the widget name the same as the last component of the variable that will receive the handle (it could be hierarchical). So, if you create a widget like this:

```
XUlabel var.label1 $parent
```

then the name of the newly created widget would be label1, which is the last component of the hierarchical name var.label1. If you use a regular variable rather than a hierarchical variable, the widget's name is the same as the variable name.

Recall that widgets have a parent/child relationship forming the widget instance hierarchy in a running program. In similar fashion, you can construct the *full name* of a widget by stringing together the names of all its ancestors with periods in between each one. You start with the application class name, which is the same as the second argument to XUinitialize, then add each widget's name with periods in between. For example, consider this simple program:

```
XUinitialize TOPLEVEL Myapp "$@"
XUrowcolumn ROW $TOPLEVEL
XUpushbutton PUSH $ROW
```

This creates a RowColumn manager widget with a PushButton inside. The full name of the PushButton is:

```
Myapp.ROW.PUSH
```

One trap you must avoid is confusing this widget naming scheme with the Korn-Shell hierarchical naming scheme. The notation is the same: names separated by periods; but this is purely a coincidence. If you use a hierarchical variable to hold a widget handle, that is entirely different from the widget's full name. To change our previous example slightly:

```
XUinitialize TOPLEVEL Myapp "$@"
XUrowcolumn MYAPP.ROW $TOPLEVEL
XUpushbutton BUTTONS.PUSH $ROW
```

The widget's name is the same as it was in the previous example: Myapp.ROW.PUSH.

The XUinfo Command

Figuring out the names of the widgets in a program can be difficult, especially if there are many levels in the instance hierarchy. The XUinfo command can be used to print a list of widgets in your program, along with information about them (including their full names):

```
XUinfo [$widget ...]
```

With no arguments, this command prints a list of all widgets in your application, along with their class names, flags indicating whether they are realized, managed, or sensitive, and the full widget name. If supplied with arguments consisting of widget handles, XUinfo prints information just on those widgets.

So, if you're having trouble figuring out the name of a widget, a simple solution is to insert a call to XUinfo in your script temporarily; the call should be placed immediately following the spot where you create the widget in question. It is also sometimes helpful to insert a call to XUinfo (with no arguments) right before the XUmainloop command—that will print a list of all widgets.

A Widget by Any Other Name

A pitfall that traps many novice X programmers is that *widget names need not be unique*. It's perfectly all right for two or more widgets to have the same name, or even the same full name. For proof, consider another variation on our example:

```
XUinitialize TOPLEVEL Myapp "$@"
XUrowcolumn ROW $TOPLEVEL
XUpushbutton VAR1.PUSH $ROW
XUpushbutton VAR2.PUSH $ROW
```

Both PushButtons have the same name, PUSH, and the same full name, myapp.ROW.PUSH. Far from being a problem, the fact that multiple widgets can have the same name can be taken advantage of when constructing resource files. For example, let's say you design a set of forms that uses Label widgets as titles over certain sets of fields. You could name all these title-type resources TITLE, then in a resource file you could specify that all widgets named TITLE should use a large font and appear in the color green, for example.

8.4 More Complex Specifications

The following table shows some other examples of resource specifications that might be used in an application. These examples show the use of pattern matching and the use of widget names vs. widget classes in resource specifications.

Table 8-1. Examples of Resource Specifications

Resource File Specification Line	Resulting Program Appearance
`*borderWidth:    2`	All borderWidth resources of all widgets in the entire application are defaulted to 2.
`*XmLabel.borderWidth:    2`	The borderWidth resources of all Label class widgets in the application are defaulted to 2.
`*mywidget*borderWidth:    2`	The borderWidth resources of all widgets which have an ancestor widget named mywidget any number of levels in the widget hierarchy above them are defaulted to 2.
`*mywidget.borderWidth:    2`	The borderWidth resources of all widgets named mywidget are defaulted to 2.

Table 8-1. Examples of Resource Specifications (continued)

Resource File Specification Line	Resulting Program Appearance
`*mywidget*myotherwidget*borderWidth:    2`	The widget hierarchy is searched for a path that contains a widget named `mywidget`. The subhierarchy below that is searched for widgets named `myother-widget`. All `borderWidth` resources of all widgets below such a subtree will be defaulted to 2.
`*XmForm*mywidget*XmLabel.borderwidth:    2`	All Label class widgets which have an ancestor named `mywidget` which in turn has an ancestor which is a Form class widget will have their `borderWidth` resources defaulted to 2.
`MyApp.form.pane.search.borderWidth:    2`	All widgets whose fully qualified hierarchical names exactly match the path `MyApp.form.pane.search` will have `borderWidth` resources defaulted to 2.

There are many ways to specify resource files for a dtksh program. First of all, every user has a file in his or her $HOME directory called .Xdefaults. Resource settings may be placed in this file, which has precedence over any other resource file. Next, there can be an application specific resource file. By default, this file is named:

        $XHOME/app-defaults/*app-class*

where $XHOME is a system defined environment variable that depends on your installation. The *app-class* portion of this path is the same as the application class argument on the XUinitialize call (the second argument).

It is possible to override this default path by specifying one of the following variables:

- XFILESEARCHPATH or XUSERFILESEARCHPATH

    These variables can be set to a full path name of a file, and the special string %N can be included in the path to specify the application class name.

- XAPPLRESDIR

    This variable can be set to a path to a directory. If this variable is not set, the user's $HOME is searched instead. This directory should contain a file with the same name as the application class.

8.5 Setting Resources Via Command Line Options

As mentioned earlier, X automatically recognizes certain command line options passed to the `XUinitialize` command. For that reason, all the example programs in this book place the notation `"$@"` at the end of the `XUinitialize` command. In that way, a user of the dtksh script could pass in any of the standard commands (see Appendix B for a complete list). Many of these standard options will set new defaults for resources. For example, the standard option

        `-background` *colorname*

will set the default background of many widgets to the named color (such as "red"). There is another command line option that will actually set an arbitrary default resource of an arbitrary widget to a value:

        `-xrm "`*widgetspec.resource:value*`"`

Here, `xrm` stands for "X Resource Manager." The resource manager is a subsystem of X that can manage resources and their values. You will note that the *widgetspec.resource* specification is separated from the value with a colon, in a similar notation to that used in the `XUset` command. The one difference is the *widgetspec* portion, which supports the same notations as explained earlier for resource files. For example, you could change the `hello.sh` string to be right justified instead of centered by executing it like this:

        `dtksh hello.sh -xrm "*LABEL.alignment:ALIGNMENT_END"`

8.6 Order of Resource Defaults

As you've seen, there are numerous ways to set a resource. Table 8-2 summarizes this information and also specifies the order of precedence used to determine the value of a resource. In addition, it presents some guidelines on when you might use one method over another to set a resource.

Resource Value Types

Each resource takes a specific type of value; some are integers, some hold arbitrary strings, etc. You've seen examples of several different types of resource throughout this book. Some resources take values that are more complex, such as the `fontList` resource, which takes a font name, or resources like `foreground` or `background`, which take color names. The next few sections discuss these more complex resource types.

Colors

Resources such as `foreground` and `background` are available for most widgets to set the foreground and background color.

> In C language X documentation, resources of this kind are listed as being of type `Pixel`.

Table 8-2. The Order of Resource Defaults

Order	Method of Setting Resource	When to Use This Method
1	Programmatic resource settings using `XUset` or during widget creation using `XUlabel`, `XUpush-button`, etc.	Use this for values that must be under strict programmatic control and don't make sense for the user to change under any circumstances.
		For example, you should not fix colors or fonts programmatically, because different users have different color and font preferences, different hardware renders colors slightly differently, and some fonts may not always be installed on every system.

2	Command line options such as:
	
	    `-background`
	
	    `-xrm`
	
	etc.
		The end user of your application may wish to employ these options at run time. They will only be able to change those resources that were not set programmatically (as above).

3	The `.Xdefaults` resource file.	The end user of the application may wish to set defaults based on their preferences in this file.
4	Files specified by the environment variables `XFILESEARCHPATH`, `XUSERFILESEARCHPATH` or `XAPPLRESDIR`/*app-class*	Again, the end user would specify one of these resource file mechanisms to make local customizations.
5	The application resource file: `$XHOME`/*app-defaults*/*app-class*	The application programmer should create this file, and resources that could differ depending on hardware or installation site specifics should be set here. For example, colors, fonts, hard-coded sizes of main windows, etc.
6	The widget's own default for each resource.	If none of the above resource setting methods has been used, the widget itself provides a default. These defaults are listed for each widget and resource in Chapter 34, *Motif Widget Reference*. When the default is what you need, don't specify a value!

These types of resources should never be hard coded in any serious application. The reason is simple: you don't know if the end-user has a color monitor!

Resources of this kind can be set to either a color name or a hexadecimal color value. The available color names are stored in a file called `/usr/lib/X11/rgb.txt`.

On some systems the rgb.txt file may be stored elsewhere. Most notably, on SunOs systems it is usually stored under /usr/openwin/lib. If you have trouble locating this file, ask your system administrator where the X configuration files are stored on your system.

Most standard colors have names, like red, green, blue, brown, and yellow. There are also some more exotic color names, such as Corn Flower Blue, plum, and Snow.

It's helpful to peruse the rgb.txt file to find out what's available. Listing 8-2 is a simple program that allows you to select a color name from a list; the resulting color is displayed by changing the background of a Label widget. The rgb.txt file is parsed using a loop. The file is composed of lines with four fields: the level of red, green, and blue used to create the color, and the name of the color. The output from this example program is shown in Figure 8-2.

Listing 8-2. A Simple Color Name Browser (color.sh). This program creates a Label widget and a List widget. The List widget is set to contain all the color names in the rgb.txt file. The color name is the last of four fields in each line of the file. When an item is selected from the list, the function showcolor is called, which gets the color name selected and sets the background color of the Label widget.

```
. $XUTILDIR/xutil.sh

function showcolor {
    typeset color

    XUget $LIST selectedItems:color
    XUset $LABEL background:"$color"
}

XUinitialize TOPLEVEL Color "$@"
XUcolumn COL $TOPLEVEL
XUlabel LABEL $COL \
    labelString:"Select a Color Name"
XUscrolledlist LIST $COL \
    visibleItemCount:10
XUaddcallback $LIST \
    browseSelectionCallback showcolor

while read red green blue name
do
    XUlistappend $LIST "$name"
done < /usr/lib/X11/rgb.txt

XUrealize $TOPLEVEL
XUmainloop
```

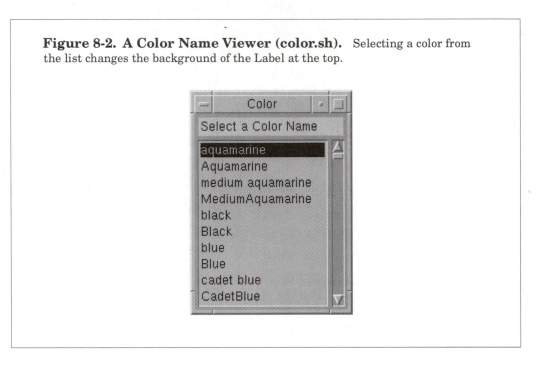

Figure 8-2. A Color Name Viewer (color.sh).   Selecting a color from
the list changes the background of the Label at the top.

The hexadecimal format of a color allows you to individually select the red, green,
and blue color levels.

> Recall from your grade school science classes that all colors can be created by
> mixing various levels of red, green, and blue.

This format always starts with the number sign (#), then there are three sets of
hexadecimal digits (one set for red, one for green, one for blue). The sets may be one,
two, or four hexadecimal digits (but all three sets must have the same number of
digits).

For example, this is a legal color composed of three sets of single hexadecimal digits, with a red value of "f" (15), a green value of 0, and a blue value of 1:

    #f01

Here is an example with three sets of four hexadecimal digits, where the red value
is `ffff`, the green is `0000`, and the blue is `1111`:

    #ffff00001111

Black is composed of the lowest levels of all colors: `#000`. White is composed of
maximum intensity of all colors: `#fff` (or `#ffffff`, or `#ffffffffffff`). Vari-

ous shades of gray are composed of roughly equal amounts of all three components; for example a medium gray might be #505050. A gray with slight blue tendencies might be: #5050a0.

One important point to keep in mind is that the same hexadecimal value may look different on different monitors. Also, color monitors have a limit on the number of colors they can display, sometimes as few as 16. If you choose a value that cannot be displayed because all colors are in use, the closest matching color available will be selected by the display server.

A program demonstrating the use of hexadecimal color formats is presented in Listing 8-3. It allows the user to select red, green, blue (RGB for short) values using Scale widgets and displays the resulting color. The running program is shown in Figure 8-3.

It's usually better to stick with the named colors rather than composing your own because the resource file will be more readable and hardware dependencies will be avoided.

Listing 8-3. Setting Color by RGB (color2.sh).

```
.  $XUTILDIR/xutil.sh

function showcolor {
    typeset red green blue color

    XUget $RED value:red
    XUget $GREEN value:green
    XUget $BLUE value:blue
    color=$(printf "#%2.2x%2.2x%2.2x" $red $green $blue)
    XUset $LABEL background:"$color"
}

XUinitialize TOPLEVEL Color "$@"
XUcolumn COL $TOPLEVEL
XUlabel LABEL $COL \
    labelString:"Select Red, Green, and Blue Values"

XUscale RED $COL \
    maximum:255 \
    orientation:horizontal \
    showValue:true \
    value:255
XUaddcallback $RED dragCallback showcolor
XUlabel tmp $RED labelString:"Red"

XUscale GREEN $COL \
    maximum:255 \
    orientation:horizontal \
    showValue:true \
```

```
      value:255
XUaddcallback $GREEN dragCallback showcolor
XUlabel tmp $GREEN labelString:"Green"

XUscale BLUE $COL \
    maximum:255 \
    orientation:horizontal \
    showValue:true \
    value:255
XUaddcallback $BLUE dragCallback showcolor
XUlabel tmp $BLUE labelString:"Blue"

XUrealize $TOPLEVEL
XUmainloop
```

Figure 8-3. Red, Green, Blue Color Selection (color2.sh).

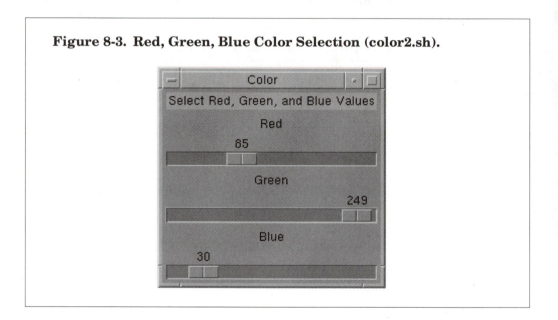

Fonts

Widgets that can display text, such as the List, Label, and PushButton or TextField widgets have a resource named `fontList`. This resource can be set to a font name.

Actually, Motif allows this resource to be set to a list of font names (hence, the resource is named `fontList`), and widgets such as Text and Label can contain multiple fonts. However, in the first release of the Common Desktop Environment, dtksh does not allow these widgets to display multiple fonts, so only the first font in the `fontList` resource will be used. Future releases of dtksh are likely to allow multiple fonts in these widgets.

A complete list of fonts available on your system can be obtained by running the command xlsfonts. There are usually many fonts installed on a system.

There are two general types of font: fixed width and proportional. In a fixed-width font, all characters are the same width. Every system has a default fixed-width font named fixed, and a default proportional font named variable.

It is often desirable to use fixed-width fonts in the Text, TextField, or List widgets when you need text to "line up." For example, in the checkbook example program it is important for the List widget that displays check entries to use a fixed font—otherwise the formatted fields would not align and it would look messy.

Most systems have a set of traditional X Window System fonts with names such as 8x13, 9x15, or 12x24. Those are fixed-width fonts, and the name of the font gives the width and height (in pixels). Some of these font names have a "b" suffix, such as 8x13b, which denotes a bold typeface.

Figure 8-4. Elements of a Font Name. Fully qualified font names contain a number of descriptive fields that can be used to specify a font. Any of these fields may be replaced by an asterisk in order to allow the system to choose a font. In this example, only the first seven fields are specified, the asterisk at the end allows the system to choose further fields (the remaining fields are resolution dependent and should normally not be specified).

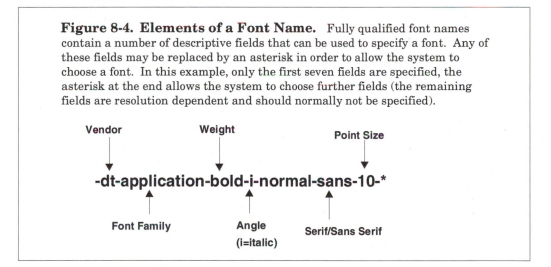

Besides these simple fonts, there are others (sometimes hundreds) installed on a given system that use a *fully qualified font name*. This name describes characteristics of the font, such as the *typeface family* (Courier, Palatino, Helvetica, New Century Schoolbook, etc.), the *weight* (normal, bold, etc.), the *angle* (normal, italic), and the point size. There are also a number of machine- or resolution-dependent fields at the end of the specification. The fields of such a full font name are separated by dash (-) characters. It is possible to specify an asterisk for any fields in the name, which allows any match at that point. It is a good idea to use the asterisk feature for the last few fields which are dependent on the resolution of the monitor being used as the display device. Figure 8-4 explains the elements of a font name that are most often specified, and shows the use of an asterisk for the resolution-dependent fields.

The CDE Preferences folder contains an application that allows you to browse fonts on your system and see how they look. A much simpler font browser program (very similar to `color.sh`) is presented in Listing 8-4. It uses the `xlsfonts` utility to print a list of all the fonts on the system. The font names are stored in a List widget, and when the user selects one, some sample text is displayed in the chosen font. The output of this browser is shown in Figure 8-5.

Listing 8-4. A Simple Font Browser (font.sh). The code here is almost identical to the `color.sh` example, but this program reads the list of fonts by spawning a call to `xlsfonts` and sets the `fontList` resource of the label instead of `background`.

```
. $XUTILDIR/xutil.sh

function showfont {
    typeset font

    XUget $LIST selectedItems:font
    XUset $LABEL fontList:"$font"
}

XUinitialize TOPLEVEL Font "$@"
XUcolumn COL $TOPLEVEL
XUlabel LABEL $COL \
    labelString:"Select a Font Name"

XUscrolledlist LIST $COL \
        visibleItemCount:10
XUaddcallback $LIST \
    browseSelectionCallback showfont

xlsfonts |
    while read name
    do
        XUlistappend $LIST "$name"
    done

XUrealize $TOPLEVEL
XUmainloop
```

Geometry

Shell class widgets have a resource called `geometry` that can be used to set an initial size and position on the screen. The `geometry` resource takes the following format:

```
[width x height][[+|-] x-coord [+|-] y-coord]
```

Figure 8-5. Output of the Font Browser (font.sh).

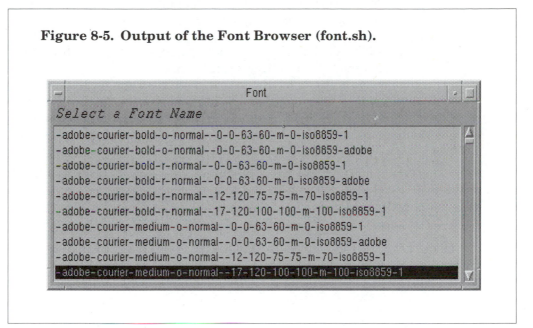

where *width* and *height* specify a desired size in pixels, and a positive or negative *x-coord* and *y-coord* specify the placement of the corner of the window. Positive coordinate values place the upper-left hand corner of the window relative to the left or top of the display, whereas negative values place the bottom right-hand corner of the Shell window relative to the bottom or right of the display. For example,

```
400x300+0-0
```

specifies that the Shell window should be 400 pixels wide, 300 pixels high, and should be placed in the lower left-hand corner of the display. On the other hand,

```
+300+200
```

leaves the size of the Shell widget unspecified while placing the left side of the Shell window 300 pixels from the left edge of the screen and the bottom of the Shell window 200 pixels from the bottom of the screen.

Either (or both) of the two parts of the specification (size or placement) can be present.

Pixmaps and Bitmaps

Some widgets allow graphical data to be displayed. For example, the Label widget can be made to display a graphic by setting a resource called `labelPixmap` to the name of a file in X11 bitmap or pixmap file. A bitmap file contains an image that uses only two colors, whereas a pixmap file may have multiple colors. Bitmap and pixmap format files may be created by using the CDE `dticon` utility. Traditionally, bitmap files use the extension `.bmp` and pixmap files use the extension `.xpm`. For example, a file called `apple.bmp` might be a two-color rendition of an apple, while `apple.xpm` would be a multicolor rendition.

Some widgets also allow the user to decorate them by setting a graphic on their background; this is accomplished by setting the `backgroundPixmap` resource.

When you set any of these pixmap resources, you may either specify a full path to a bitmap or pixmap file, or a relative path that will be searched for in a set of directories specified by the `XBMLANGPATH` variable. That variable contains a colon-separated list of directory names, similar to `PATH`. For example, if `XBMLANGPATH` was set like this:

```
XBMLANGPATH=$XHOME/bitmaps:$HOME/bitmaps
```

and you created a bitmap file named `mybitmap` and stored it in `$HOME/bitmaps`, then in your dtksh script you could create a Label that displays this bitmap image using

```
XUlabel BITLABEL $PARENT \
     labelType:PIXMAP \
     labelPixmap:mybitmap.xbm
```

Like any other resource, these can be set from resource files in identical fashion. Examples of using bitmaps on labels are shown in Listing 12-1, *Creating PushButtons (pushbut.sh)* on page 260.

8.7 The Dtksh Standard Resource File

CDE includes a standard resource file for dtksh programs named `Dtksh`. It is placed in the standard `app-defaults` directory when CDE is installed. Thus, if you use the string `Dtksh` as the name of your application (i.e., the second argument to `XUinitialize`), you will pick up this standard set of defaults.

Even if you want to customize certain aspects of how your application looks, it is a good idea to include this standard resource file in your resource file. This is because the standard resource file sets up colors and accelerators for the CDE help system widgets and contains other defaults that are important to maintain a standard appearance across applications. You can include the standard dtksh resource file by inserting this line in your resource file:

```
#include "Dtksh"
```

This should usually be the first line of your resource file.

8.8 A Resource File for the Checkbook Program

To make the checkbook example program look a bit spicier, we can use the resource file shown in Listing 8-5. One thing to note is that more specific resource specifications come first. In this case, the font specification for the XmList class widgets appears before the *fontList specification, which will set the font for all widgets.

The geometry resource setting is a practical consideration. If the checkbook program is run with no argument, it will come up displaying an empty List. But, because the List is empty, it will not request any extra space and will come out too small—later when the user opens a file or adds a check entry ScrollBars will appear. By setting geometry up front, we ensure that the application starts out big enough to accommodate a full check entry without horizontal ScrollBars.

Finally, to make the application more pleasing to look at, I set the background color of all XmList widgets to a light gray color. This will help to distinguish visually the check entry List from other elements of the MainWindow.

Listing 8-5. Checkbook Resource File (Checkbook). This resource file sets the geometry to a fixed size to prevent the program from coming up too small on blank files. It sets all XmList class widget's background color to a light gray to set them off from other screen elements. The XmList font is set to the default fixed-width font on the system, and all other fonts are set to a large (14-point) bold sans serif font.

```
#include "Dtksh"

Checkbook.geometry:450x250
*XmList.fontList: fixed
*XmList.background: lightgrey
*fontList: -dt-application-bold-r-normal-sans-14-*
```

8.9 Summary

- Resource files should be used to set resources that the user might want to customize, or that might vary based on hardware (color, size) or system installation (fonts). There are multiple levels of resource defaults, including those set directly in the application, those set as command line options, and those set in the user's .Xdefaults file.

- Colors may be specified as either names (from $XHOME/lib/rgb.txt) or as hexadecimal values with two hex digits for each of the red, green, and blue intensity values.

- Font names can be found by running the program xlsfonts. The font name indicates several important aspects of its appearance.

- Geometry specifications can be used on Shell-class widgets to set their initial size and placement.

Figure 8-6. The Checkbook Program with a Resource File.
Above, the checkbook program without any resource file. Below, the program using the Checkbook resource file.

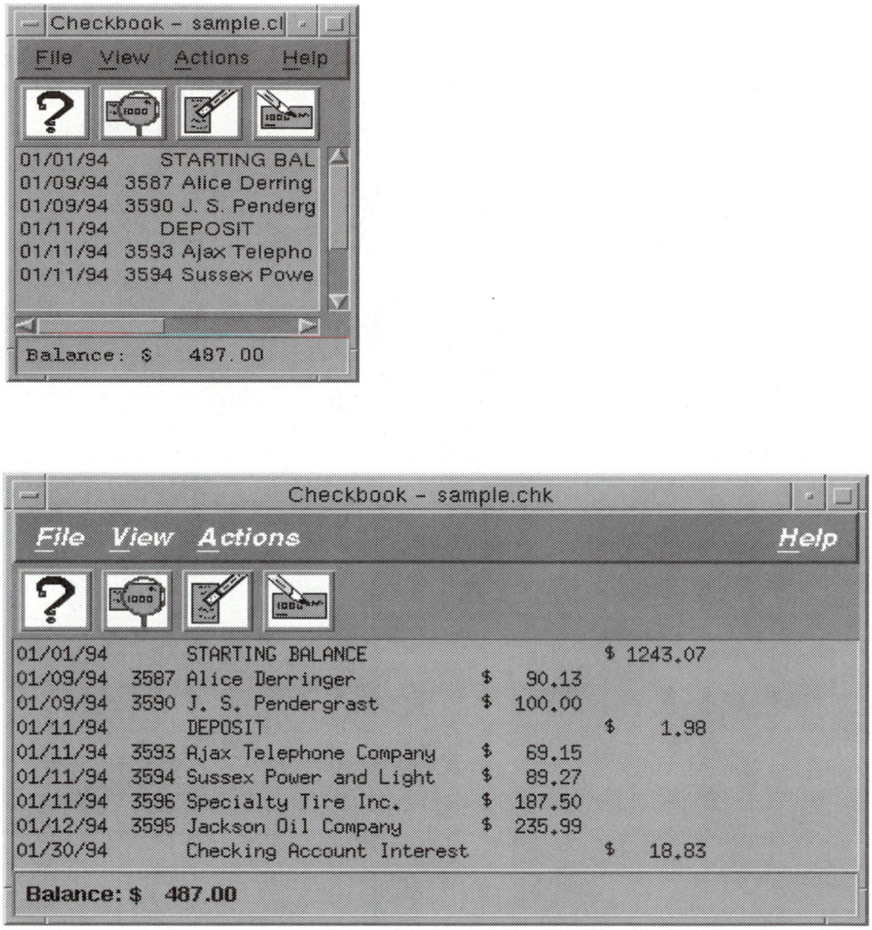

9 *Widget Layout Using Managers*

9.1 Introduction

In previous chapters we've only used simple arrangements of widgets to get our work done, usually just stacking them in simple rows or columns. Although such arrangements are commonly used and are easy to program, there are times when you need more control over widget placement. Motif provides several manager widgets that can arrange children in useful ways. In this chapter, you will learn:

- The most common mistakes and pitfalls when using manager widgets and how to avoid them
- How to use the RowColumn widget to stack widgets
- How to arbitrarily place widgets in a BulletinBoard using x, y coordinates
- How to use a Form widget to specify relative placement of children
- How to use the PanedWindow widget to provide user-resizable areas in your application
- How to use the ScrolledWindow widget to provide a view into a larger child widget
- How to use manager widgets to create multiscreen dialogs.

Near the end of this chapter, our old friend the checkbook program will get a face-lift. The dialog that allows the user to create a new check entry will be rewritten so it simulates the look of a real check.

9.2 Manager Widget General Concepts

Before proceeding to the details of the individual manager widgets, let me explain a few concepts about them. It is important for you to be familiar with these concepts so you can understand some of the examples and recommendations that will follow.

Geometry Negotiation

When a child is created and managed, it negotiates a size with its manager widget parent. This process can be quite complex, because the child's parent might in turn have to negotiate a size with its manager parent (managers can manage other managers and so on). In addition, whenever a child is created and managed, the manager parent must decide where to position the child relative to other children. This whole process of choosing size and placement is called *geometry negotiation*.

> ***Geometry:*** The height, width, and placement of a widget.

> ***Geometry negotiation:*** The process of choosing a geometry involves a negotiation between the parent and child. The child requests a certain height and width, the parent may either accept, deny, or modify the requested dimensions. The parent may in turn have to ask for more or less space from its parent, so the negotiation process can be quite complex.

This negotiation process happens when the child and its parent are managed, and can happen again if the child changes size and requests more (or less) space.

Different manager widgets follow different rules when deciding where to place children (and how big the children are allowed to be). For example, the RowColumn widget stacks children in rows and columns. Sometimes resource settings of the manager influence the placement strategy. For example, the RowColumn widget has a resource called `numColumns` that determines how many columns or rows to use when placing children.

Using Constraint Resources in Layout

In some cases *constraint resources* are added to the child by the manager parent, and settings of these resources are used by the manager parent to determine how to lay out the child or choose its size. For example, the Form widget gives a constraint resource called `resizable` to each child. If this resource is set to `false`, then the form will not allow the child to change size after its initial placement.

Creating Children of Manager Widgets

Whenever a new child is created and managed, the negotiation process must be carried out to choose its geometry. As just stated, this process can cause a chain reaction of negotiations if there are several nested levels of manager widget.

If you were to create several children in such a nested hierarchy of managers, this process would be repeated for each child and could become quite slow and inefficient, because many negotiations and renegotiations would have to take place up and down the widget hierarchy. Worse yet, you can get unexpected layout results if several children are added to a manager widget in such a way that geometry negotiation must be carried out separately for each child. It is difficult to explain why this is so without getting into a very technical discussion of geometry negotiation, so take my word for it.

The solution to these problems is simple if you follow this rule of thumb:

> *Don't manage a parent widget that will receive more than one child until all its children are created and managed. In this way, all the negotiation happens once—when the parent is managed.*

In other words, create an unmanaged parent widget, then create all its children, then manage the parent (using XUmanage). To create any widget unmanaged, simply give the -u option to the XU widget creation command. For example:

```
XUform -u FORM $parent
# create children of $FORM here...
XUmanage $FORM
```

This sequence delays all child layout and negotiation until the XUmanage command is called. Thus, all children are laid out simultaneously, and there is only one negotiation with any ancestors of the manager widget.

> Note that any widgets you create before calling XUrealize on the root widget will not perform any geometry negotiation until they are realized. The rule of leaving managers unmanaged until all children are added is meant for situations in which you create widgets after the initial XUrealize, such as when creating a popup dialog or adding widgets to a particular screen after it is already visible.

Taking this tactic to its logical conclusion, you should also not manage any ancestor managers that will receive more than one child. The general strategy is to create all the parents that will take more than one child unmanaged, then create all the children, then manage each parent in the reverse order in which they were created. For example:

```
XUform -u FORM1 $parent
XUrowcolumn -u RC1 $FORM
# create children of $RC1 here ...
XUrowcolumn -u RC2 $FORM
# create children of $RC2 here ...
XUmanage $RC2      # walk back up the tree, managing
XUmanage $RC1      # parents in the reverse order
XUmanage $FORM     # in which they were created
```

9.3 Common Manager Widget Problems

There are several problems that almost every Motif programmer stumbles over when they first try to use managers to lay out widgets. In this section, I'll describe the problems so you'll be aware of them and the terminology associated with them.

Specific recommendations to avoid these problems are discussed in individual widget sections.

The Resize Behavior Problem

Using manager widgets to enforce a desired resize behavior is not easy for new Motif programmers. Actually, it's not very easy for experienced Motif programmers either. When struggling with a Motif resize problem, one gets a good idea of the frustrations Alice felt while talking to the Caterpillar:

> *"Explain Yourself!"*
> *"I can't explain myself, I'm afraid, Sir," said Alice, "because I'm not myself, you see."*
> *"I don't see," said the Caterpillar.*
> *"I'm afraid I can't put it more clearly," Alice replied, very politely, "for I can't understand it myself, to begin with; and being so many different sizes in one day is very confusing."*
> *"It isn't," said the Caterpillar.*

—From "Alice's Adventures in Wonderland," by Lewis Carroll

Changing size can be very confusing, the Caterpiller's opinion notwithstanding. In the following pages I'll give you some rules of thumb that work in most cases, and will point out the most common resizing pitfalls so your adventures will be at least a bit less confusing.

In general, you will avoid many resizing problems if you start with a clear idea of what behavior you want for your application. Usually, when the user resizes a window they expect certain areas of the screen to remain a fixed size (such as the MenuBar or a single line message area at the bottom of the window), and one other area (the work area) should grow or shrink as needed to fill the rest of the space.

However, there are exceptions to this general rule. It is appropriate in some cases to make certain dialogs fixed in size—disallowing resizing altogether. Some very sophisticated programs may want to "divvy up" extra available space proportionately among two or more areas of the screen.

The "Screen Dance" Problem

If a widget needs to grow or shrink while it is visible, or if a child is managed or unmanaged causing its manager parent to grow or shrink, the application will sometimes experience a problem known as the *screen dance*. This is a disconcerting "flipping" or "flashing" effect that occurs because managers are in a state of flux as they negotiate and renegotiate geometry. Eventually the screen does settle down, and this problem does not cause any loss of functionality in the application; it just looks bad.

Several ways are available to avoid or reduce the screen dance effect:

- Instead of unmanaging a widget that should no longer appear on the screen, consider unmapping it instead. Unmapping a widget leaves the space for the widget intact but empty, thus no geometry negotiation occurs. In some situations unmap is not desirable, but appropriate use of unmap instead of unmanage is one simple way to avoid screen dance.

  > One pitfall of this method is that you cannot unmap a widget that is not yet realized, so you may need to test whether a widget is realized using `XUisrealized` before calling `XUunmap`.

- If you need to unmanage a group of widgets while a screen is being displayed, try to put them all in one common manager parent, and unmanage this parent instead of each individual child. This avoids multiple geometry renegotiations.

- Some managers have resources to help you avoid screen dance. For example, the BulletinBoard and Form widgets have a resource called `resizePolicy` that can be very helpful in this regard. These resources are discussed in later sections for each individual widget.

9.4 The RowColumn Widget

The RowColumn widget is the Swiss Army knife of Motif programming—it has many features that are used only in specialized situations. For example, when a RowColumn widget is being used as a MenuBar, the `menuHelp` resource can be set to the handle of one of its MenuButton children, which forces that child to be right-aligned. The RowColumn has a lot of resources like that—they are used only in one specific situation. All of these specialized resources make this widget seem very complicated to a person who reads about it in a manual page. In reality, this is not a difficult widget to master, and it is one of the most commonly used managers.

The rowColumnType Resource

Much of the Jack-of-all-trades behavior of the RowColumn is controlled by the `rowColumnType` resource. It takes different values depending on whether the RowColumn is being used as a MenuBar, OptionMenu, or as a general-purpose manager widget. In this chapter, we are only interested in the general-purpose mode, which is accessed by setting this resource to `WORK_AREA`—this is the default for `rowColumnType`, so there is no need to set it explicitly.

Single Rows and Columns

The RowColumn widget is one of the most useful manager widgets because stacking child widgets in simple rows and columns is desirable in many situations.

One of the simplest uses of the RowColumn is to create a single row (horizontal stack) or a single column (vertical stack) of children. To accomplish this, simply set the `orientation` resource to either `VERTICAL` or `HORIZONTAL`. For example:

```
XUrowcolumn ROW $parent orientation:HORIZONTAL
```

This resource also affects how children are placed in the RowColumn. If orientation is HORIZONTAL, then each new child is added to the end (the right) of a row. If it is VERTICAL, then each child is added to the end (bottom) of a column. The direction and order in which children are placed is called the *major dimension*.

Because programmers very commonly need to create children stacked in a single row (horizontal stack) or column (vertical stack), the XU library provides the following convenience functions, which create RowColumn widgets and automatically set the orientation:

```
XUrow variable $parent [resource:value ...]
XUcolumn variable $parent [resource:value ...]
```

The XUrow command creates a RowColumn widget with orientation set to HORI-ZONTAL, and XUcolumn creates a VERTICAL RowColumn. Listing 9-1 shows a complete program that uses XUcolumn to stack some Label widget children. Another (very similar) example program is provided in the example directory that shows the use of XUrow; it is called rcrow.sh. The output of both of these example programs is shown in Figure 9-1.

Figure 9-1. Single Rows and Columns.   On the left, a stack of labels created using XUrow, on the right the same stack using XUcolumn.

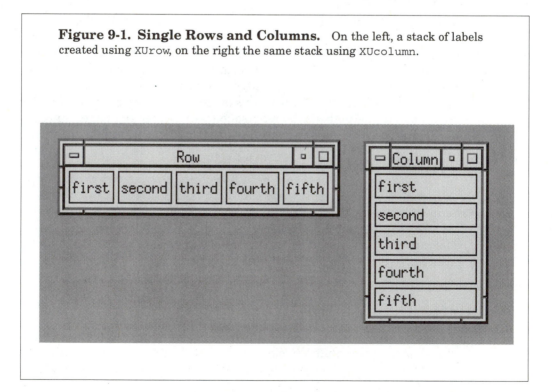

Listing 9-1. Creating a Single Column (rccol.sh). This program uses `XUcolumn` to create a RowColumn widget that stacks its children vertically, and then creates several Label children.

```
. $XUTILDIR/xutil.sh

XUinitialize TOPLEVEL Column "$@"
XUcolumn COL $TOPLEVEL

for label in first second third fourth fifth
do
    # we don't need to access the labels later,
    # so just use a temporary variable
    XUlabel tmp $COL \
        labelString:"$label" \
        borderWidth:1
done

XUrealize $TOPLEVEL
XUmainloop
```

These simple example programs will be used throughout this section to demonstrate other features of the RowColumn widget. I will to use the -xrm standard X option to redefine some resources of the RowColumn widget and explore how this affects child management.

Stacking children in single-file fashion is useful in a wide variety of situations, including:

- **Captions**. When designing screens, you often want to put a Label widget next to a control widget to "caption" the control (explain what it is used for). You saw simple examples of captioning in Chapter 6, *Prompting Using Custom Dialogs*. Caption Labels are usually either placed to the left of or over the captioned control widget. The RowColumn widget can be used to caption widgets by creating the Label and control as its children.

- **Stacking Like Controls**. Sometimes screens need to stack several like controls in a row or column. The `XUadddate` convenience function uses a RowColumn to create a horizontal stack of TextField widgets to hold the month, day, and year.

- **Dividing Screen Areas**. Sometimes applications need to create several independent screen areas stacked vertically, for example, a Label that will hold some status information stacked on top of a List widget that displays choices, with a row of action buttons later. RowColumn widgets can be used for this kind of purpose as long as specialized resize behavior is not necessary. If special resize behavior is needed (such as giving all new space to the List) then the Form widget discussed below is preferable to the RowColumn for this use, at least at the topmost management level; RowColumn widgets can often be used for the parts that do not require resizing.

Spacing and Margins

Several resources affect how the RowColumn spaces its children:

marginWidth   The amount of space between the left and right edges of the RowColumn and its children. The default is 3 pixels for WORK_AREA RowColumn widgets (the kind we're discussing in this chapter).

marginHeight   The amount of space between the top and bottom of the Row-Column and its children. The default is 3 pixels for WORK_AREA RowColumns.

spacing   The amount of space to leave between children in both horizontal and vertical directions. For WORK_AREA RowColumns, the default is 0 pixels.

It is sometimes necessary to set these for aesthetic reasons, preferably in a resource file. When a RowColumn is being used to closely stack children, you sometimes need to set marginWidth and marginHeight to zero to avoid too much whitespace.

The Packing Resource

The RowColumn widget's packing resource affects how children are sized and placed. There are three possible values for this resource:

PACK_COLUMN   Each child will be forced to the same size. The widest child's width will be used as the width for every child, the tallest child's height will be used as the height of every child. Children are placed in a number of columns equal to the setting of the numColumns resource (default is 1). The use of numColumns is discussed more fully later.

PACK_TIGHT   Each child takes up exactly as much room as it needs. Children are stacked in the major dimension, and wrap to the next row or column when there is no more room.

PACK_NONE   Children remain their preferred size and are not stacked; it is up to the application to explicitly set the x, y coordinates of each child (otherwise they will all pile up at x=0, y=0). Normally, you won't use this setting, because it makes the RowColumn widget virtually equivalent to a BulletinBoard widget.

The default is PACK_TIGHT for RowColumns being used in WORK_AREA mode.

We can use the `rcrow.sh` program to see these effects by using the `-xrm` standard X option to set the packing resource. For example,

```
dtksh rcrow.sh -xrm "*packing:PACK_COLUMN"
```

can be used to change the default packing to `PACK_COLUMN`. The effects of setting the packing resource to all three of its legal values is shown in Figure 9-2.

The setting you should use in your application depends on the particular situation. If you are using the RowColumn widget to simply provide a caption for another widget, you will usually use `PACK_TIGHT`. If you are arranging many widgets of a similar type, the regularly spaced visual effect of `PACK_COLUMN` is often more desirable. There are exceptions to both of these recommendations, and you must use your aesthetic judgement.

Figure 9-2. The Effect of the packing Resource.   On top, a row stacking RowColumn in `PACK_TIGHT` mode. All the widgets are given just enough space to fit. In the middle, `PACK_COLUMN` mode is used to force all widgets to the same size (both width and height). At the bottom, `PACK_NONE` performs no layout, the programmer is responsible for setting x, y coordinates. Because we did not set x, y, they default to zero and the widgets overlap each other.

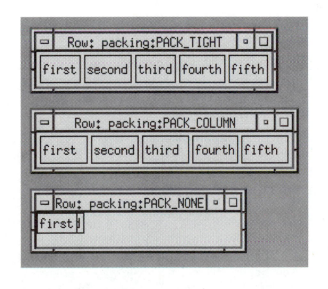

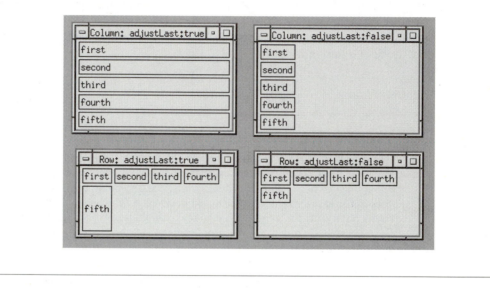

Figure 9-3. The Effect of the adjustLast Resource.   On top, a column stacking RowColumn widget manages children with `adjustLast` set to `true` (left) and false (right). On bottom, the same results for a row stacking RowColumn. If `adjustLast` is set to `true`, then the last column or row of children is forced to fill the remaining available space. Note that you need to resize the applications to see the effect in the case of the row stacking examples.

Adjusting the End Items

The `adjustLast` resource of the RowColumn determines whether items in the last row (for horizontal RowColumns) or column (for vertical RowColumns) are sized to fill all available space. This is a boolean resource that can be set to the values `true` or `false`. If `true`, then the row or column is sized to fill all available space. The default is `true`. The easiest way to explain this is to show an example. Using the `rccol.sh` and `rcrow.sh` example programs in conjunction with the handy `-xrm` option to set `adjustLast` like this:

```
dtksh rccol.sh -xrm "*adjustLast:false"
```

I produced the output shown in Figure 9-3. As you can see, setting `adjustLast` to true causes the last row or column of widgets to be "stretched" to fill the space. There are two typical uses of this stretching effect:

- **Aesthetics**. This is a simple way to ensure that widgets inside a column stacking RowColumn fill all available space and look balanced.

- **Dividing Screen Areas**. When a RowColumn is being used to divide several areas of a screen and the bottom-most area should always receive any extra space due to resizing, a setting of `adjustLast:true` can sometimes be used to get the desired resize behavior.

Multiple Columns

When packing is set to `PACK_COLUMN`, it is possible to set the preferred number of columns the RowColumn widget creates. This is controlled by the `numColumns` resource, which has a default of 1. The `numColumns` resource is ignored if `packing` is not set to `PACK_COLUMN`, a fact that causes much gnashing of teeth for novice Motif programmers.

The `numColumns` resource works as you might expect for vertical RowColumn widgets, but it is highly confusing in the case of horizontal RowColumns. This is because in horizontal RowColumn widgets the `numColumns` resource actually sets the number of *rows*, not the number of columns. This is clearly a very poorly named resource, and this is a further cause of frustration for new Motif programmers. Using the `rccol.sh` and `rcrow.sh` example programs, again in conjunction with the `-xrm` option, you can see the effect of this resource is illustrated in Figure 9-4.

Figure 9-4. The Confusing numColumns Resource. The sense of the ill-named `numColumns` resource changes in row-stacking RowColumn widgets (i.e., when orientation is `HORIZONTAL`); it becomes the number of *rows* in that case. On the left, a row-stacking RowColumn with `numColumns` set to 2 actually has two rows, not two columns. On the right, a column stacking RowColumn does have two columns when `numColumns` is set to 2, as expected.

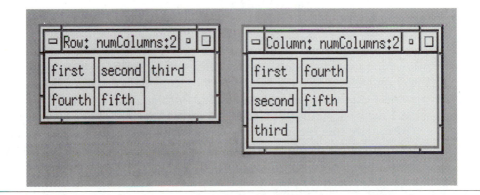

One final source of frustration should be noted: occasionally you would like to have a certain number of columns, say, two, and you would like to add children to the RowColumn widget in row-wise fashion (i.e., first the upper left child, then the upper right, then wrap to the next row, etc.). However, the only way to specify two columns would be to create a vertical (column-wise) RowColumn with `numColumns` set to 2. But in that case, the children will be added from top to bottom instead of from left to right.

The solution to this problem is to create a horizontal RowColumn widget with the `numColumns` resource set to the total number of children divided by two! For convenience, instead of counting up the number of widgets you can simply create all the children first, then use `XUget` on the `numChildren` resource of the RowColumn to find out how many children there are, then use `XUset` to set `numColumns` to that divided by two. Listing 9-2 illustrates this technique.

Listing 9-2. Adjusting numColumns (rcnumcol.sh).

```
. $XUTILDIR/xutil.sh

XUinitialize TOPLEVEL Column "$@"

XUrow RC $TOPLEVEL \
    packing:PACK_COLUMN

XUlabel tmp $RC labelString:"left1"
XUlabel tmp $RC labelString:"right1"
XUlabel tmp $RC labelString:"left2"
XUlabel tmp $RC labelString:"right2"
XUlabel tmp $RC labelString:"left3"
XUlabel tmp $RC labelString:"right3"

XUget $RC numChildren:n
XUset $RC numColumns:$((n/2))

XUrealize $TOPLEVEL
XUmainloop
```

The output produced by running `rcnumcol.sh` is shown in Figure 9-5. This program produces the desired number of columns and allows the programmer to create the child widgets in a logical order. The `XUalign2col` convenience function, which you were exposed to in Chapter 6, *Prompting Using Custom Dialogs*, actually does what I have shown here—retrieves `numChildren`, divides by two, etc.

Of course, this technique can be generalized to any desired number of columns: simply divide the number of children by the number of desired columns (instead of two as in this example).

Other Generally Useful RowColumn Resources

The RowColumn widget has several other resources that are useful for general child layout. Some are given here, others are not because they're usually only used when the RowColumn is in a mode other than `WORK_AREA`. For a complete list of RowColumn resources, see *The RowColumn Widget* on page 763.

Figure 9-5. Output of rcnumcol.sh.

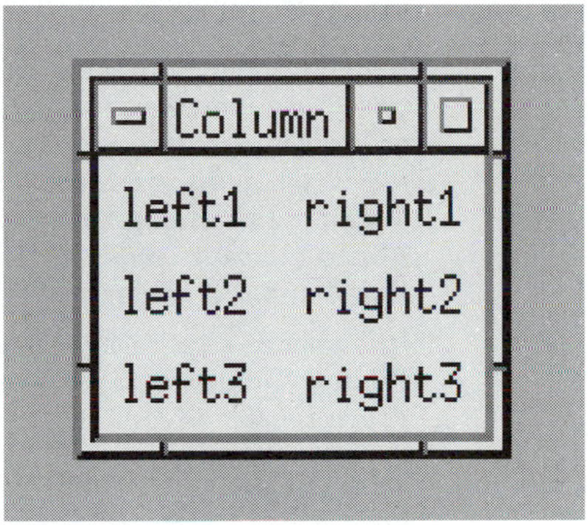

adjustMargin   If set to true (the default), then any Label widgets created as
                      children of the RowColumn will align. The RowColumn wid-
                      get will actually modify resources of the Label children to
                      accomplish this. For horizontal RowColumn widgets, the top
                      and bottom margins of the Label children are aligned,
                      whereas for vertical RowColumns the left and right margins
                      are aligned. If you don't want the margins aligned, set this
                      resource to false.

entryAlignment,   The entryAlignment resource takes one of the values:
isAligned   ALIGNMENT_BEGINNNING (the default), ALIGNMENT_CENTER,
                      or ALIGNMENT_END. It specifies how Label children should be
                      aligned. This resource will override the alignment resource
                      of each Label child of the RowColumn.

                      This is a source of much confusion to novice Motif program-
                      mers, who often attempt to set the alignment of the children
                      instead of setting the entryAlignment of the RowColumn
                      parent. They are surprised to find that the Labels ignore the
                      alignment resource setting.

The `entryAlignment` resource does not take effect unless the `isAligned` resource is set to `true` (which is the default). If you need to have Labels with different alignment settings in a single RowColumn, you must set `entryAlignment` to false and set each individual widget's `alignment` resource.

`resizeHeight,`
`resizeWidth`

If `true` (the default for both) then the RowColumn is allowed to request more or less space in the vertical (`resizeHeight`) or horizontal (`resizeWidth`) dimensions after it is initially managed. Setting one or both of these resources to `false` will disallow size changes after the RowColumn is first managed. This could cause requests for size changes by children of the RowColumn to be denied.

It is useful to set these resources in some cases to make sure the RowColumn does not "dance" (rapidly change size) while your program is running.

`entryCallback`

This callback is executed when any button in the RowColumn is activated. This callback must be set before the button children are added to the RowColumn. It is occasionally useful to define a single function that will trigger when any button in the RowColumn is pressed, rather than adding individual callback functions to each child. The variable `CB_CALL_DATA.WIDGET` is set to the widget handle of the child that was activated.

RowColumn Widget Constraint Resources

The RowColumn widget gives only one constraint resource to its children: `positionIndex`. This resource determines the place this child should occupy in relation to its siblings; it is an integer between 0 and the number of children in the RowColumn.

Normally, when you add a child to the RowColumn widget, it is placed at the end of the list of children. By setting this resource, you can insert a new child anywhere in the child order, thus changing where it (and all children following it) will appear. If you set this resource, the `positionIndex` resources of all children following the child on which you set it are renumbered appropriately.

You can set this resource either during widget creation time or later (using `XUset`). It is occasionally useful to be able to change the placement of a child in a RowColumn. For example, if you have a vertical stack of Label widgets that you wish to keep in alphabetical order, this constraint resource would allow you to add a new Label to the stack in the proper place.

RowColumn Widget Pitfalls

The most common mistakes people make with the RowColumn widget include the following:

- Set `numColumns` without setting `packing` to `PACK_COLUMN`. The symptom of this problem is that your `numColumns` setting is ignored.

- Forget that `numColumns` really means "numRows" for horizontal RowColumn widgets. To really set the number of columns for horizontal RowColumn widgets you set `numColumns` to the number of children divided by the desired number of columns.

- Try to set the `alignment` resource of Label widget children of the RowColumn. Instead, you must either set the `entryAlignment` resource of the RowColumn (to change all labels to the same alignment), or disable the RowColumn's `entryAlignment` feature by setting its `isAligned` resource to `false`.

9.5 The BulletinBoard Widget

The BulletinBoard widget has a very nonchalant management philosophy, as if it's saying: "You tell me where you want the child, and I'll put it there." It's just that simple; you specify an x and y coordinate for each child using constraint resources, and they'll be unceremoniously deposited there by the BulletinBoard.

This very simplicity lulls novice X programmers into using this widget. Of course, two or three days after starting to use the BulletinBoard for every management task imaginable, these same programmers will demand that their boss approve a purchase order for a $5000 builder tool because they're tired of figuring out the x, y coordinates by trial and error. Predictably, once they have purchased the builder tool, they use it to create even more BulletinBoard widget instances with lots of hard coded x, y children—making any kind of sensible resize behavior impossible and forcing them to lay out dialogs over again every time a `labelString` resource or font changes!

The Zero Option

The solution to this problem is simple: don't use the BulletinBoard widget! It's almost never the right widget to use. Actually, I've never found any use for it whatever other than as a superclass for other more functional widgets or in complex applications that need to do custom geometry management. Sometimes I go years at a time without even thinking about BulletinBoard widgets; and I suspect you'll do likewise.

The Coordinate System

The coordinates are set on each child using the `x` and `y` resources. The `x` resource goes from zero on the left of the BulletinBoard, with positive numbers increasing toward the right. The y resource starts at zero from the *top* of the widget, and positive numbers go down—this is the opposite of the usual y axis numbering scheme you may have learned in school. Numbers represent pixels in this case. See Figure 9-6.

Figure 9-6. The Coordinate System. The origin of the coordinate system is the upper left corner of the BulletinBoard widget, with positive x values going to the right and positive y positions going down.

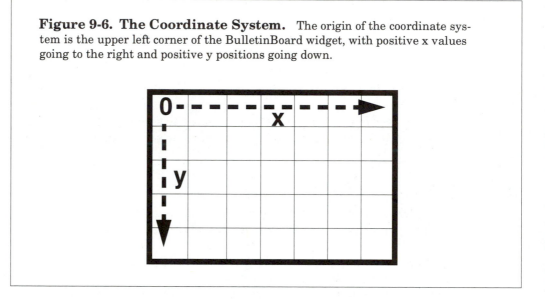

A simple illustration of the coordinate system is shown in Listing 9-3. Here, Label widgets are created in a diagonal line. After the BulletinBoard widget is created, children are added to it using a `for` loop. The coordinates of each child are calculated by multiplying the child's index by 12. The first child will be at position $x=12$, $y=12$, the next at $x=24$, $y=24$, etc. The BulletinBoard widget sizes itself so it can fit all its children.

Listing 9-3. A Simple BulletinBoard Widget (bb.sh). This program creates a BulletinBoard widget and adds 10 Label widget children to it. The children's x, y coordinates are chosen by multiplying the child number by 12, thus the children form a diagonal line from upper left to lower right of the application window.

```
. $XUTILDIR/xutil.sh

XUinitialize TOPLEVEL BulletinBoard "$@"
XUbulletinboard BB $TOPLEVEL
for (( i = 1; i <= 10; i++ ))
do
    XUlabel tmp $BB \
        labelString:"$i" \
        x:"$((i * 12))" \
```

```
            y:"$((i * 12))"
done


XUrealize $TOPLEVEL
XUmainloop
```

A somewhat more complex use of the coordinate system is shown in Listing 9-4. In this program, high school level trigonometry is used to position Label widgets in a circular pattern similar to a clock face. We start by calculating the angle (in radians) of the traditional placement of "1" on the clock. Because a full circle is 2π radians and the angle for 0 radians is the 3 o'clock position, we need to subtract two twelfths of a full circle from zero to get the starting angle. The x coordinate of the number is the cosine of the angle, and the y coordinate is the sine of the angle. The for loop steps through one-twelfth of a full circle on each iteration, creating Label widgets with the proper coordinates. I think you'll agree this is easy as pi (sorry about that).

The output of these two programs is presented in Figure 9-7.

Listing 9-4. The bbclock.sh Program. Here, the coordinate system is used in a slightly more complex fashion to create children in a circle. The variable angstep is set to one-twelfth of a full circle (in radians). The for loop steps through the numbers 1 through 12, incrementing the current angle as it goes. The x and y coordinates are calculated using the sin() and cos() trig functions to trace out a circle centered at position 60,60 going out a radius of 50 pixels.

```
. $XUTILDIR/xutil.sh
XUinitialize TOPLEVEL BBclock "$@"
XUbulletinboard BB $TOPLEVEL

float PI=3.1415926535979
float angstep=2*PI/12    # full circle is 2*PI radians
float angle=0-angstep*2 # start at 1 O'clock position
integer x y

for (( i = 1; i <= 12; i++, angle+=angstep ))
do
    # find x, y coordinates 50 pixels out from
    # the center of the circle, which is at
    # the bulletinboard position 60,60.
    (( x = 50*cos(angle) + 60 ))
    (( y = 50*sin(angle) + 60 ))
    XUlabel tmp $BB \
        labelString:"$i" \
        x:$x \
        y:$y
done
```

```
XUrealize $TOPLEVEL
XUmainloop
```

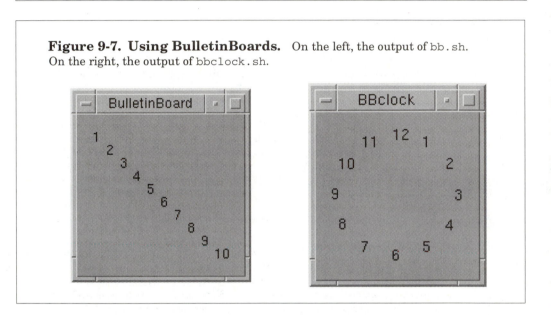

Figure 9-7. Using BulletinBoards. On the left, the output of bb.sh. On the right, the output of bbclock.sh.

Child Placement Resources

The marginHeight and marginWidth resources can be used to place a minimum distance between a child and the edges of the BulletinBoard. The default for both these resources is 10 pixels. The marginHeight resource determines how close the child can come to the top and bottom edges, and the marginWidth resource affects the left and right edges. If you attempt to put a child too close to the top or left edges of the BulletinBoard, it will be moved so as to meet these margin requirements. If you attempt to put a child too close to the right or bottom, then the BulletinBoard will resize itself (if possible) so the desired margin is maintained.

The allowOverlap resource determines whether the BulletinBoard will allow its children to overlap each other. If set to true (the default) then overlaps are allowed.

> As of this writing, this resource does not appear to be working. I was able to write a program with allowOverlap set to false that showed no difference in behavior when children overlapped or not. By the time this book is published, this might be corrected.

Resizing the BulletinBoard

The resizePolicy resource can be used to control how the BulletinBoard widget can resize itself. The BulletinBoard will normally resize only when one or more of its children requests more or less space. This resource may take one of the following values:

- RESIZE_ANY (the default). The BulletinBoard is allowed to grow or shrink as it sees fit.

- RESIZE_NONE. This setting disallows any resizing once the BulletinBoard is managed. It should be used when you want to make sure the BulletinBoard always remains a fixed size (for example, to avoid "screen dance").

- RESIZE_GROW.   This value allows the BulletinBoard to get bigger, but not smaller. You should use this setting when some child of the BulletinBoard might grow or shrink, and you want to allow for growth so children don't get truncated but you don't want the screen to dance every time a child gets smaller.

Other General BulletinBoard Resources

Several other BulletinBoard resources are useful in general layout situations:

buttonFontList,

textFontList

These resources provide default fonts for any button (buttonFontList) or Text (textFontList) children of the BulletinBoard widget.

borderWidth,

shadowType

The borderWidth resources specifies the thickness (in pixels) of the BulletinBoard's border.

If the BulletinBoard has a nonzero width border, then shadowType specifies how it appears. This resource can take one of the following values:

SHADOW_ETCHED_IN, a double-width border is used to make the border appear to be inset into the window.

SHADOW_ETCHED_OUT, like SHADOW_ETCHED_IN, but the widget is made to appear to be raised out of the window.

SHADOW_IN, the widget appears to be inset into the window.

SHADOW_OUT, the widget appears to be raised out of the window.

BulletinBoard DialogShell Related Resources

The BulletinBoard has special resources that come into play when it is used to create dialogs. Most of these resources are only useful when the following conditions are met:

- The immediate parent of the BulletinBoard is a DialogShell widget. Bulletin-Boards are used by many of the Motif compound widgets such as the FileSelectionDialog, WarningDialog, etc., by making them the children of a DialogShell.
- The `dialogStyle` resource is not set to `WORK_AREA`. The default for `dialogStyle` is `WORK_AREA` unless the BulletinBoard is a child of a DialogShell, in which case the default is `DIALOG_MODELESS`. For a complete description of the other settings for `dialogStyle`, see *Shades of Modality* on page 81.

Resources used in this manner include:

`autoUnmanage`	When `true` (the default), the BulletinBoard is automatically unmanaged when any button contained in it is pressed. There are two exceptions: the Help and Apply buttons.
`cancelButton,` `defaultButton`	These resources can be set to the widget handles of the Cancel and OK (`defaultButton`) buttons. The default button gets a different appearance, and is executed if the user types `Enter` while any child of the dialog has focus.
`defaultPosition`	If `true` (which is the default), then the BulletinBoard will be centered within its DialogShell parent. There is rarely any reason to change this default.
`noResize`	If `true` (the default is `false`) then the window manager will not include resize handles on the DialogShell window containing the BulletinBoard. Also, the resize item in the window manager window will not appear. You should use this if you want to prevent the user from resizing the dialog.

Do not confuse this resource with the `resizePolicy` resource which is used to determine how the BulletinBoard responds to its own children's requests for more or less space. |

BulletinBoard Widget Pitfalls

The most common pitfall when using the BulletinBoard widget is (to put it bluntly) *using the BulletinBoard widget in the first place!* As I mentioned in the introduction of this section, this is rarely the correct widget to use since it forces you to hardcode x, y coordinates of its children. Usually, the Form widget (discussed later) is a better choice if you need fancy layout. If you just need simple stacks of children, the RowColumn widget is the obvious choice.

9.6 The PanedWindow Widget

The PanedWindow widget allows the programmer to stack several child widgets vertically in independently resizable *panes*. The user can change the size of each pane by dragging a *sash* with the mouse. The sash is a small rectangular area. The PanedWindow widget usually displays a Separator between each child's pane, although it can be suppressed using resource settings if desired. See Figure 9-8.

Figure 9-8. Paned Widgets (paned.sh). On the left, the bottom pane has been given more space than the top. On the right, after the user resizes using the sash, the full text is displayed.

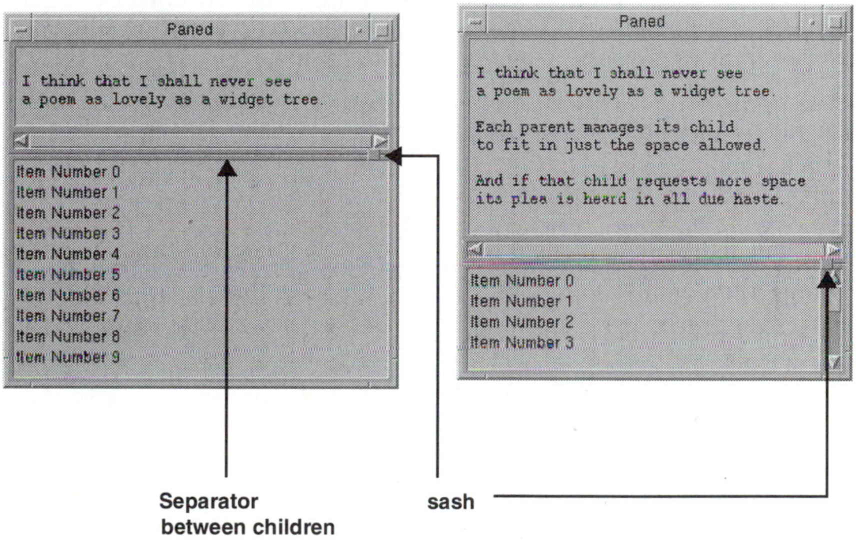

Separator between children

sash

The PanedWindow widget is usually used when you need to display several different areas on the same screen and each area could be too large to fit in the allotted space. It is up to the user to decide how much space each area should be allotted; the user can change the amount of space given to each area at any time depending on the needs at the moment.

You can create a PanedWindow widget using the usual kind of XU library widget creation command:

```
XUpanedwindow [-u] variable $parent [resource:value ...]
```

As usual, *variable* will receive the widget handle of the newly created PanedWindow widget. The -u option creates the PanedWindow initially unmanaged, which is suggested if the PanedWindow will be created following the call to XUrealize (see the previous discussion, *Creating Children of Manager Widgets*, on page 168).

Each child of the newly created PanedWindow gets its own pane, and one sash appears between each pair of children. The PanedWindow sizes itself to be the width of the widest child. The PanedWindow will try to grow high enough to encompass all of its children's full heights. In normal use, each child should support scrolling in at least the vertical dimension.

A simple example of a PanedWindow is shown in Listing 9-5. In this example, two children are created: a ScrolledText widget and a ScrolledList widget.

> The ScrolledText widget is really a composite made up of a Text widget inside a ScrolledWindow widget. The ScrolledList widget is composed similarly of a List widget inside a ScrolledWindow widget.

Both of these widgets support scrolling. The example program adds some data to both of these children so we can better see how the PanedWindow works. The resulting output is shown in Figure 9-8.

Listing 9-5. Using a PanedWindow Widget (paned.sh).

```
. $XUTILDIR/xutil.sh

XUinitialize TOPLEVEL Paned "$@"
XUpanedwindow PANE $TOPLEVEL

XUscrolledtext TEXT $PANE \
    rows:4 columns:40

XUset $TEXT value:"
I think that I shall never see
a poem lovely as a widget tree.

Each parent manages its child
to fit in just the space allowed.

And if that child requests more space
its plea is heard in all due haste."

XUscrolledlist LIST $PANE \
    visibleItemCount:5

for (( i = 0; i < 10; i++ ))
do
        XUlistappend $LIST "Item Number $i"
done
```

```
XUrealize $TOPLEVEL
XUmainloop
```

Constraining Child Size

The children of the PanedWindow widget receive several constraint resources that can be used to control how they are sized:

allowResize   If `true` (the default) then the child is allowed to resize itself, otherwise the PanedWindow will refuse all resize requests for the child.

paneMinimum,   The minimum and maximum sizes (respectively) that the
paneMaximum   child is allowed to be. If these two resources are both set to the same number, then no sash will appear (it would be pointless since the size of the child is fixed).

The `paneMinimum` resource can be used to ensure that at least some minimum amount of the child is visible at all times. In some cases, it's perfectly all right to allow the user to resize a pane all the way down to nothing, in other cases you might want some part of the pane to always show. It is best not to hard-code `paneMinimum` in a script, but rather to set it in a resource file. That's because the size of a child depends on factors such as fonts in use or the resolution of the display device.

The `paneMaximum` resource is useful for limiting the size that can be taken up by a pane. I rarely set this resource (except to use it to create a fixed pane by setting it equal to `paneMinimum`). If you do decide to set this resource, it is again wise to use a resource file.

Fixed Size Panes

The special case of setting `paneMinimum` equal to `paneMaximum` deserves some attention. Let us say you are creating a screen with two resizable panes, and you need a third area—a Label at the bottom of the screen to display a message. A logical choice would be to use the PanedWindow for all three of these sections of the screen, but make the Label child a fixed size by setting `paneMinimum` equal to `paneMaximum` on that child. The question is: to what size should you set them? Clearly the size of the Label widget is hardware and font dependent. It would be nice to calculate the size programmatically to avoid having to put it in a resource file.

The way to do this is to create the Label widget first, then ask the Label how big it is by using `XUget` to retrieve its height resource. Then you can set the `paneMinimum` and `paneMaximum` resources to the proper size. For example:

```
XUpanedwindow -u PANE $parent
... create two resizable children here...
XUlabel MESSAGE $PANE labelString:"Initial Message"
XUget $MESSAGE height:h
XUset $MESSAGE paneMinimum:$h paneMaximum:$h
XUmanage $PANE
```

It is important to note here that this trick of retrieving the size of the child only works for Primitive widgets. Manager-class widgets will not report their actual width or height until after they are managed. X does contain a function call, XQueryGeometry, that can get the preferred width and height of a Manager-class widget, but that function is not available directly in dtksh.

Other PanedWindow Resources

Here are some other PanedWindow resources that are occasionally useful:

marginHeight, marginWidth	Specifies the distance between the top and bottom edges (marginHeight) or left and right edges (marginWidth) of the PanedWidget's children. The default for both is 3 pixels.
sashHeight, sashWidth	The height and width of the sash. The default for both is 10 pixels.
sashIndent	Specifies the placement of the sash. Positive values specify an offset from the left edge, negative from the right edge (as in a geometry specification).
sashShadowThickness	The thickness of the sash shadows.
separatorOn	If true (the default) then a Separator is drawn between each child.
spacing	The distance between child panes.

PanedWindow Pitfalls

The PanedWindow is relatively easy to use, and there are few pitfalls. The most common error I have seen is a stylistic one: creating too many resizable panes. The human factors of the PanedWindow deteriorate if there are more than two resizable panes (fixed panes in which paneMinimum is equal to paneMaximum pose no problem). This is because the question of which pane will gain or lose size is no longer intuitive when there are more than two resizable panes.

My advice is not to create more than two resizable panes. If your application requires more than two resizable areas, consider allowing the user to pop up a separate window for some of the data; in that way the user can resize the whole window in any way they desire.

9.7 The Form Widget

The Form widget is the most feature rich of the Motif manager widgets. It allows the programmer to specify sophisticated child layout relationships in several different ways, and it provides excellent control over resize behavior. This flexibility is both blessing and bane. The Form widget has features that allow almost any kind of layout—if you can figure out how to use the features in the correct way! There are a dizzying array of resources, constraint resources, and rules for using them, and all the choices available can overwhelm the novice Motif programmer.

My strategy in this chapter is not to teach you every possible feature of the Form widget, but rather to show you a few common ways of using it to solve the layout and resizing problems that you are most likely to encounter.

Form Widget General Concepts

You can use the Form widget just like a BulletinBoard widget (it is actually a subclass of BulletinBoard) by fixing the x and y resources of each child. However, this is rarely how programmers use the Form widget, because it provides much more powerful ways of placing its children.

Children are usually placed in the Form widget using a set of constraint resources provided by the Form. Each edge of a Form's child (left, right, top, and bottom) can be individually constrained in the following ways:

- The edge can be attached to an edge of the Form widget itself, perhaps offset by a certain distance.
- The edge can be attached to another child in the Form, again with an optional offset from the other child.
- The edge can be attached to a *position* that is a certain percentage from the left or top of the Form. If the Form is resized, a child using percentage offsets changes its size proportionally.

See Figures 9-9 and 9-10 for an illustration of these concepts. Each of these types of constraints can be mixed and matched within the same Form (indeed, different edges of a *single* child could use different methods of attachment). By using the right kinds of attachment, you can implement some very sophisticated layout and resize behavior.

Form Constraint Resources Used to Implement Placement

Each child of a Form gets the following constraint resources that can be used to specify the various kinds of edge attachment described:

> In the following discussion, there are times when I must refer to a set of resources with similar names such as `topWidget`, `bottomWidget`, `leftWidget`, and `rightWidget` resources. To simplify this discussion, I refer to such a group as "The *edge*Widget resources," where *edge* stands for any of top, bottom, left, or right.

Figure 9-9. Relative Constraints. Each child of a form has left, right, top, and bottom edges that can be attached to the Form itself or to other children. In this illustration, the dashed lines represent these constraints. So, for example, the left edge of CHILD A is attached 10 pixels from the left Form edge, the tops of both CHILD A and CHILD B are attached 5 pixels from the top Form edge. The left edge of CHILD B is attached to the right edge of CHILD A (offset by 5 pixels), and the right edge of CHILD B is attached to the right edge of the Form, offset by 10 pixels. Both children's bottom edges are attached 8 pixels from the bottom of the Form.

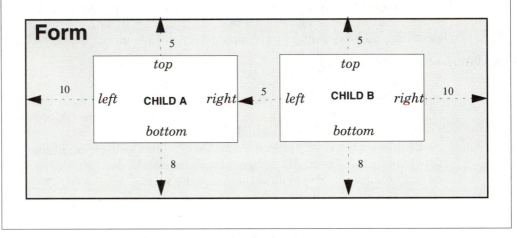

bottomAttachment, topAttachment, leftAttachment, rightAttachment

These resources allow you to set the general type of attachment you desire for each corresponding edge of the child. They can be set to one of the following:

- ATTACH_NONE. Do not attach this edge.
- ATTACH_FORM. Attach this edge to the corresponding edge of the Form itself. For example, bottomAttachment specifies an attachment to the bottom of the form, etc.
- ATTACH_WIDGET. Attach this edge to the corresponding edge of another child of the Form. The handle of that child must be stored in the *edge*Widget constraint resource. For example, if bottomAttachment is set to ATTACH_WIDGET, then the widget's handle is placed in the bottomWidget constraint resource.

> There are actually several other settings besides the ones I mention here, but I don't want to complicate matters at this point by going into fine details.

- ATTACH_POSITION. Attach this edge to a position a fixed percentage from the top or left of the form. The percentage is stored in the corresponding *edge*Position resource. For example, to specify that the bottom of a widget should be 50% of the way from the top of the Form, you would set bottomAttachment to ATTACH_POSITION and bottomPosition to 50.

bottomOffset, topOffset, leftOffset, rightOffset

If the corresponding *edge*Attachment resource is set to ATTACH_FORM or ATTACH_WIDGET, then these resources specify an offset from the form or widget edge. For example, if bottomAttachment is ATTACH_FORM and bottomOffset is 10, then the bottom edge of the child will be placed 10 pixels from the bottom edge of the form.

bottomWidget, topWidget, leftWidget, rightWidget

If the corresponding *edge*Attachment resource is set to ATTACH_WIDGET, then these resources hold the widget handle of the widget to use. Note that the widget used for relative placement must be an *immediate* child of the Form. For example, if bottomAttachment is ATTACH_WIDGET and bottomWidget is set to $CHILD,

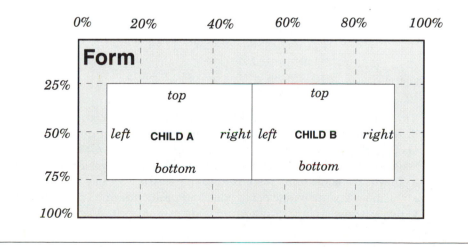

Figure 9-10. Positional Constraints. Here, edges of the children are attached to positions relative to the form. For example, the tops of both children are attached 25% of the way from the top of the form, the bottoms are attached 75% of the way from the top. The left edge of CHILD A is attached 10% of the way from the left of the Form, and the right edge of CHILD B is attached 90% of the way from the left of the Form. The right edge of CHILD A and the left edge of CHILD B are attached at the 50% point.

where $CHILD is the handle of some other child of the Form, then the widget's bottom edge will be placed adjacent to $CHILD's edge (assuming bottomOffset is 0).

bottomPosition, topPosition, leftPosition, rightPosition

If the corresponding *edge*Attachment resource is set to ATTACH_POSITION, then these resources specify a percentage from the left edge (for leftPosition and rightPosition) or top edge (for topPosition and bottomPosition) of the form. By default, you may set these resources to a number from 0 to 100. On resize, the relative position within the form will be maintained. For example, if you set bottomAttachment to ATTACH_POSITION and bottomPosition to 50, then the bottom edge of the widget will always be placed 50% of the way down from the top of the Form, even after resizing. The widget will be stretched or compacted if necessary to maintain this relationship.

It is possible to change the range of values these resources can be set to by setting the Form resource fractionBase. In that case, instead of percentage values, these resources specify form positions proportional to the value of fractionBase. For example, if you set fractionBase to 5 and set bottomPosition to 2, then the bottom of the widget would always be two-fifths (40%) of the way down from the top of the Form. The fractionBase resource always changes both horizontal and vertical positioning values; it is not possible to have different ranges of position for horizontal and vertical.

Setting Form Constraints the Easy Way

Let's say we have a Form whose handle is stored in the variable FORM. We could create a Label child of this Form whose top is fixed 5 pixels from the top of the form, and whose left edge is fixed 10 pixels from the left of the form, and whose right edge is attached 10 pixels from the right edge of the Form using:

```
XUlabel label1 $FORM \
    topAttachment:ATTACH_FORM \
    topOffset:5 \
    leftAttachment:ATTACH_FORM \
    leftOffset:10 \
    rightAttachment:ATTACH_FORM \
    rightOffset:10
```

That seems like a lot of work: to place one child in the form we had to type in six different resource settings. The XU convenience library provides a simpler way to specify Form constraints, the XUattach function. This function takes an easy-to-read specification of how you want a widget's edges attached and then prints the appropriate constraint resource settings. So, you use this inside of command substitution on your widget creation command line (or on an XUset command line if you want to set constraints after widget creation). For example, the following code does the same thing as the previous example, but is more readable and easier to type:

```
XUlabel label1 $FORM \
        $(XUattach top 5 left 10 right 10)
```

Note that `XUattach` is called inside of command substitution notation: `$( ... )`.

> In the old days, people used backquotes for command substitution. Backquotes are still supported by dtksh, but their use is discouraged and is considered obsolescent. The notation used above is superior from several perspectives: it is easier to read than backquotes, it nests easily, and you are less likely to use the wrong notation by mistake.

Also note that there are no quotes around the command substitution. This is because we want `XUattach` to print all the appropriate constraint resource settings in such a way that they become arguments to the `XUlabel` command. If you were to call `XUattach` on a line by itself like this:

```
XUattach top 5 left 10 right 10
```

then it would literally print this:

```
topAttachment:ATTACH_FORM
topOffset:5
leftAttachment:ATTACH_FORM
leftOffset:10
rightAttachment:ATTACH_FORM
rightOffset:10
```

You can specify any combination of edge attachments using `XUattach`. Its arguments can be one or more of the following:

XUattach Argument:	*Equivalent Constraint Resource Settings:*
`top` [*offset*]	`topAttachment:ATTACH_FORM` `topOffset:`*offset* (only if *offset* argument is present)
`bottom` [*offset*]	`bottomAttachment:ATTACH_FORM` `bottomOffset:`*offset* (only if *offset* argument is present)
`left` [*offset*]	`leftAttachment:ATTACH_FORM` `leftOffset:`*offset* (only if *offset* argument is present)

XUattach Argument:	*Equivalent Constraint Resource Settings:*
right [*offset*]	rightAttachment:ATTACH_FORM rightOffset:*offset* (only if *offset* argument is present)
under $*widget* [*offset*]	topAttachment:ATTACH_WIDGET topWidget:$*widget* topOffset:*offset* (only if *offset* argument is present)
over $*widget* [*offset*]	bottomAttachment:ATTACH_WIDGET bottomWidget:$*widget* bottomOffset:*offset* (only if *offset* argument is present)
leftof $*widget* [*offset*]	rightAttachment:ATTACH_WIDGET rightWidget:$*widget* rightOffset:*offset* (only if *offset* argument is present)
rightof $*widget* [*offset*]	leftAttachment:ATTACH_WIDGET leftWidget:$*widget* leftOffset:*offset* (only if *offset* argument is present)
toppos *offset*	topAttachment:ATTACH_POSITION topOffset:*offset*
bottompos *offset*	bottomAttachment:ATTACH_POSITION bottomOffset:*offset*
leftpos *offset*	leftAttachment:ATTACH_POSITION leftOffset:*offset*
rightpos *offset*	rightAttachment:ATTACH_POSITION rightOffset:*offset*

Note the slightly counterintuitive resource settings for the leftof and rightof arguments. If you think about it for a moment, the specifications outlined here are correct: if you want to put one widget to the left of another, then you would set its right edge attachment to that widget.

Using `XUattach` will save you from thumbing through Motif Form constraint reference manuals every five minutes, and also save you hours typing in half a dozen or more resource settings per Form child. It will be used in the remainder of this chapter whenever Form constraints need to be specified.

Relative Placement Strategies

Relative child placement is probably the most common Form layout technique. Using relative placement, you can create layouts that resize properly, but only if you do things the right way. The general technique can be summarized as follows:

1. Place the uppermost/leftmost child first. Attach its top and left edges to the form.

2. Work from left to right and top to bottom placing children. Use `under` and `rightof` to place children relative to each other—but children should be attached to each other *in one direction only*. In other words, if child A is `rightof` child B, don't also set child B to be `leftof` child A. The same goes for `over` and `under`. Doing so will confuse Motif (a example is shown shortly).

3. The bottommost/rightmost widgets should have their bottom and right edges attached to the form.

This technique specifies a left-to-right and top-to-bottom strategy. That's not the only one you can use, but I strongly recommend it. It is also possible to specify attachments in a right-to-left and top-to-bottom fashion, and even right-to-left and bottom-to-top, etc., but the point is this: choose a direction and stick to it.

A simple example of following the procedure I've outlined is shown in Listing 9-6. Here, three Label widgets are created using relative attachments. The Label called `FIRST` is attached to the left and top of the form, the Label called `SECOND` is attached to the right of `FIRST`, and to the top and right edges of the Form (remember, we're going left-to-right and top-to-bottom). Finally, `THIRD` is attached under and to the right of `FIRST`, and is attached to the Form's bottom edge.

Listing 9-6. Relative Placement in Forms (formrel1.sh).

```
. $XUTILDIR/xutil.sh

XUinitialize TOPLEVEL "Form" -title "Left to Right" "$@"
XUform FORM $TOPLEVEL

XUlabel FIRST $FORM \
    labelString:first \
    borderWidth:1 \
    $(XUattach left 20 top 10 )

XUlabel SECOND $FORM \
    labelString:second \
```

```
        borderWidth:1 \
        $(XUattach rightof $FIRST 10 top 10 right 5)

XUlabel THIRD $FORM \
        labelString:third \
        borderWidth:1 \
        $(XUattach under $FIRST 5 rightof $FIRST 5 bottom 10)

XUrealize $TOPLEVEL
XUmainloop
```

The resulting output is shown in Figure 9-11. An important thing to notice about this example is the placement of THIRD. It is both rightof and under FIRST. As you can see, a specification of rightof only affects the vertical placement of the widget, *it does not affect the horizontal placement* (that's done by under). Many novice Motif programmers mistakenly think that by specifying rightof a widget will move to the immediate right of the referenced widget in both the horizontal and vertical dimensions. In reality, you must specify both dimensions to get the desired results.

Figure 9-11. Relative Placement in Forms (formrel1.sh). On the left, the output of formrel1.sh as it initially appears. On the right, the appearance after resizing larger. Note the rightmost and bottom-most widgets are stretched to receive the extra space because the constraints used add widgets from left to right and top to bottom.

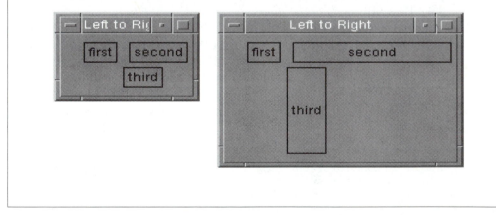

Resize Behavior of Relatively Placed Form Children

One interesting thing to notice about the output of this simple example is the resize behavior. When the Form was stretched wider, the widget FIRST did not change size, but SECOND and THIRD did. In the horizontal dimension, FIRST did not grow because SECOND was the last child in the "chain" of children going from left to right. In the vertical dimension, FIRST did not grow because THIRD was the last child in the "chain" of children going from top to bottom. Also, SECOND did not grow vertically because it does not have a bottom attachment.

So, the general rule is that when you use rightof to create a chain of children from left to right (with the first and last child in the chain attached to the Form left and right edges), then the last child in the chain (the rightmost child) is the only one resized horizontally when the Form changes size. The same rule applies when using under to arrange a top-to-bottom chain of children: the last (bottom-most) child is the one resized vertically.

Figure 9-12. Right to Left Placement (formrel2.sh). In this example, children are placed right to left (but still top to bottom). On the left, the program as it initially appears. On the right: after resizing, the rightmost widget (second) gets the extra horizontal space.

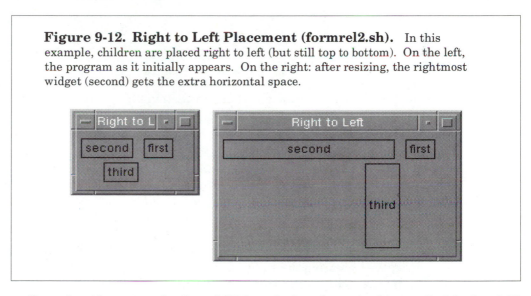

But what if we want the first child in a chain to be resized instead of the last? To do that, you can simply change the direction in which you build the chain. For example, in Listing 9-7 we build the horizontal chain from right to left instead of left to right as in the previous example.

The resulting output shown in Figure 9-12 confirms that reversing the order causes the leftmost child to be resized horizontally. In this example, only the horizontal chain was reversed, the top to bottom chain was left intact. It is also possible to build child attachments from bottom-to-top using over instead of under.

Listing 9-7. Right to Left Placement (formrel2.sh).

```
. $XUTILDIR/xutil.sh

XUinitialize TOPLEVEL Form -title "Right to Left" "$@"
XUform FORM $TOPLEVEL
```

```
XUlabel SECOND $FORM \
    labelString:first \
    borderWidth:1 \
    $(XUattach right 20 top 10 )
XUlabel FIRST $FORM \
    labelString:second \
    borderWidth:1 \
    $(XUattach leftof $SECOND 10 top 10 left 5)
XUlabel THIRD $FORM \
    labelString:third \
    borderWidth:1 \
    $(XUattach under $SECOND 5 leftof $SECOND 5 bottom 10)

XUrealize $TOPLEVEL
XUmainloop
```

Giving Space to an Intermediate Widget

OK, so we can make the first or last child in a horizontal or vertical chain of widgets the one to be resized. How about one in the middle? This is a more common case, and it takes a little more work. The strategy follows:

1. Build a chain of widgets as before, from top to bottom and right to left.
2. After the chain is complete, attach the bottom of the child that should receive vertical resize space to the bottom of the Form *offset by the height of all children below it in the chain*. You can calculate this height by using XUget on the `height` resources of the children below in the chain, adding in extra space for any offsets used in placing them. Do not set the bottom attachment for the last child in the chain.
3. The same technique can be used to specify a child to receive horizontal resize space by setting the right edge of that child to be attached to the Form offset by the width of all children to the right of it. You can use XUget to get the `width` resources of the children, adding any offsets as before. Analogously with the previous case, do not set the right attachment for the last child in the chain.

Listing 9-8 shows a simple example that creates three vertically stacked children in a Form and gives all extra resize space to the middle child. In this simple case, only one sibling needed to be queried for its height, but you can imagine more complex cases in which several children's heights would have to be accessed with the maximum of all height values used.

Listing 9-8. Mixing Attachments (formmix.sh). This program gives all vertical space to the center Label widget by fixing its bottom offset to the Form edge, leaving enough room for the bottom Label widget.

```
. $XUTILDIR/xutil.sh
XUinitialize TOPLEVEL "Form" -title "Mixing Attachments" "$@"
```

```
XUform FORM $TOPLEVEL

XUlabel TOP $FORM \
    labelString:"I am attached to the top, left,
and right edges of the form" \
    borderWidth:1 \
    $(XUattach top 10 left 10 right 10)

XUlabel MAIN $FORM \
    labelString:"I am attached under the widget
above me.  My left and right edges are
attached to the form.  My bottom edge
is attached to the form, but offset
an amount equal to the height of
the widget under me." \
    borderWidth:1 \
    $(XUattach under $TOP 0 left 10 right 10)

XUlabel BOTTOM $FORM \
    labelString:"I am attached under the widget
above me, and also to the left and
right edges of the form" \
    borderWidth:1 \
    $(XUattach under $MAIN 0 left 10 right 10)

XUget $BOTTOM height:hbottom
XUset $MAIN $(XUattach bottom $((hbottom+10)) )

XUrealize $TOPLEVEL
XUmainloop
```

The output resulting from this program (with an illustration of the resize behavior) is shown in Figure 9-13.

Positional Placement

The positional placement options of XUattach (leftpos, rightpos, toppos, bottompos) allow you to specify that an edge is attached a fixed percentage of the distance from the top or left edges of the Form. When a resize occurs, a positionally attached edge will move proportionately, maintaining the same relationship. So, for example, if a child's top edge is attached at position 50, then that edge will always be 50% of the way from the top of the Form regardless of resizing.

By default, Form positions go from 0 to 100, but the number of positions can be changed by setting the fractionBase resource of the Form to a positive integer, as mentioned previously. For example, if you set fractionBase to 10, then Form positions will go from 0 to 10 (both horizontally and vertically—there is no way to specify a different number of horizontal and vertical positions). In this case, setting the right position of a child to 5 would place that edge halfway from the left edge of the

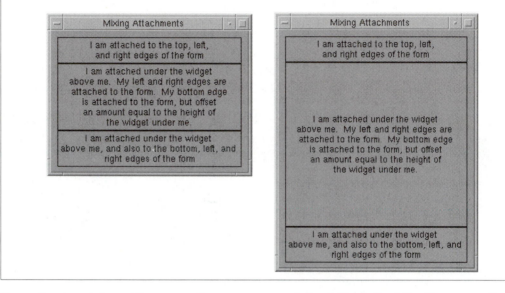

Figure 9-13. Output of formmix.sh.   On the left, the program as it first appears. On the right, the program after a resize. All new vertical space is given to the center Label.

Form (horizontal positions are always measured from the left of the Form, vertical from the Top).

It is useful to set `fractionBase` when there is a natural unit of measurement for positions. For example, if you were writing a checker game application and wanted to create an eight-by-eight array of widgets to represent the squares, a natural implementation would be to set `fractionBase` to 8 and attach all four edges of each child using positional attachments.

Positional attachments are appropriate when your application requires several different children to participate proportionately in resizing operations. If only one child of a Form needs to be resized (i.e., all the other children can remain a constant size) then it's usually better to use relative attachments as discussed earlier.

Listing 9-9 shows a simple example of specifying positional attachments. It sets `fractionBase` to 6, so the Form positions will go from 0 to 5 in each dimension. A combination of positional and relative specifications is used (the widget THIRD is specified to be under the widget FIRST).

Listing 9-9. Positional Placement in Forms (formpos.sh).

```
. $XUTILDIR/xutil.sh

XUinitialize TOPLEVEL Form -title "Positional Placement" "$@"
```

```
XUform FORM $TOPLEVEL \
    fractionBase:6

XUlabel FIRST $FORM \
    labelString:first \
    borderWidth:1 \
    $(XUattach leftpos 2 rightpos 4 bottompos 2 top 0 )

XUlabel SECOND $FORM \
    labelString:second \
    borderWidth:1 \
    $(XUattach leftpos 4 rightpos 6 toppos 2 bottompos 3)

XUlabel THIRD $FORM \
    labelString:third \
    borderWidth:1 \
    $(XUattach under $FIRST 5 leftpos 0 rightpos 4 bottompos 6)

XUrealize $TOPLEVEL
XUmainloop
```

The output of this example is shown in Figure 9-14. When the Form is resized, all three children of the Form are changed: they become proportionately smaller in the vertical dimension and proportionately larger in the horizontal dimension (because the Form has been resized to be wider and shorter)

Figure 9-14. Positional Placement in Forms (formpos.sh).

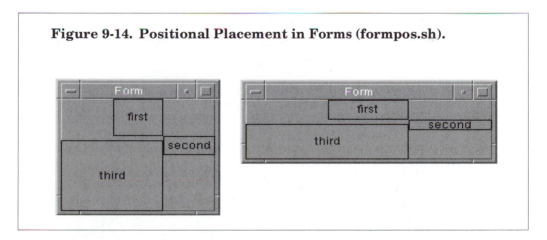

Contradictory Constraints

By far the most common problem programmers have with the Form widget is the dreaded *contradictory Form constraints* error. This error is caused by an illogical or circular set of Form constraints. Some kinds of contradictory constraints are easy to understand. Consider the following:

```
XUset $CHILD1 $(XUattach rightof $CHILD2)
XUset $CHILD2 $(XUattach rightof $CHILD1)
```

Clearly this is illogical: it is not possible for CHILD1 to be to the right of CHILD2 at the same time that CHILD2 is to the right of CHILD1. Most programmers will recognize this as an error. However, some kinds of contradictory constraints are more difficult to understand. Most programmers will not recognize this as an error:

```
XUset $CHILD1 $(XUattach rightof $CHILD2 10)
XUset $CHILD2 $(XUattach leftof $CHILD1 10)
```

Now, it may seem like this should not be a problem: CHILD1 is 10 pixels to the right of CHILD2, and CHILD2 is 10 pixels to the left of CHILD1. The specification is certainly redundant, but it seems like it should work. However, the Form widget won't accept this specification, it will complain of contradictory constraints. This is due to how the layout algorithms of the Form widget work. In general, any time you create redundant child relative specifications you will run into trouble. This is why I recommended earlier that when laying out children you pick a direction (left to right, top to bottom) and stick with it throughout the Form.

Listing 9-10 gives a slightly more subtle example of this problem. Here, two different widgets reference a third widget in opposite directions (one uses leftof and the other uses rightof). This should be an immediate tip-off that there will be problems: whenever you use both rightof and leftof (or both under and over) in the same Form to specify constraints, you are headed for trouble! The output that results from this program is shown in Figure 9-15. The terminal emulator from which the doomed program was run is shown underneath with a typical error message (it is generated by the Motif toolkit). On top, the "blown" screen is shown, clearly it is an erroneous result.

Listing 9-10. A Circular Specification (formbad.sh).

```
. $XUTILDIR/xutil.sh

XUinitialize TOPLEVEL "Form" -title "This Won't Work" "$@"
XUform FORM $TOPLEVEL

XUlabel FIRST $FORM \
    labelString:first \
    borderWidth:1 \
    $(XUattach left 20 top 10 )
XUlabel SECOND $FORM \
    labelString:second \
    borderWidth:1 \
    $(XUattach rightof $FIRST 10 top 10 right 5)

XUlabel THIRD $FORM \
```

```
        labelString:third \
        borderWidth:1 \
        $(XUattach under $FIRST 5 leftof $FIRST 5 bottom 10)

    XUrealize $TOPLEVEL
    XUmainloop
```

Figure 9-15. Contradictory Form Constraints (formbad.sh).

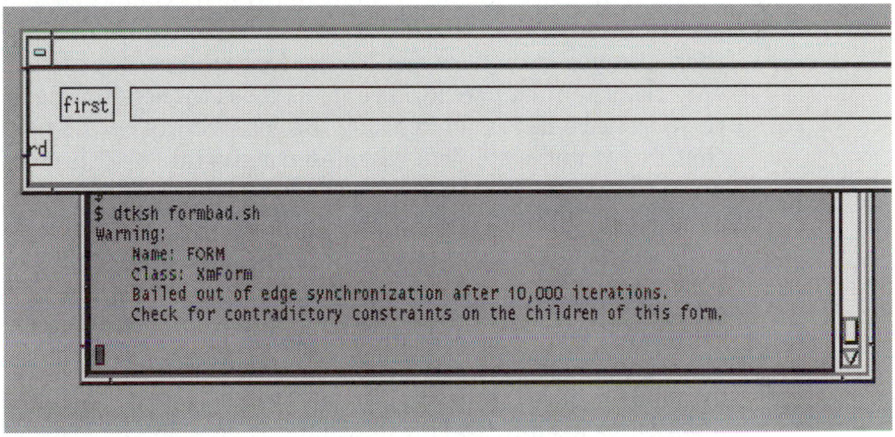

Other Form Resources

The horizontalSpacing and verticalSpacing resources of the Form widget can be used to specify defaults for offset constraints (top and bottom offsets for verticalSpacing and left and right offsets for horizontalSpacing). These defaults are only used if no value is specified for an individual child.

In addition, because Form is a subclass of BulletinBoard, all the BulletinBoard resources are available. Perhaps the most useful of these is the resizePolicy resource, which can be set to RESIZE_ANY, RESIZE_GROW, or RESIZE_NONE. See *Other General BulletinBoard Resources*, on page 185 for a full explanation.

Other Form Constraint Resources

Besides those already mentioned, the resizable resource can be set to either the value true or false for any Form child. The default is true, meaning the child is allowed to request a new size. If set to `false`, all child resize requests will be denied.

Note that this resource only affects requests initiated by the child itself—setting `resizable` to `false` does not prevent the Form from deciding to resize a child based on its constraints.

Form Widget Pitfalls—Summary

Here are the most common problems encountered when using the Form widget:

- **Using the wrong child**. A common error is to specify a constraint using a widget that is not an immediate child of the Form. Often a grandchild of the Form (a widget inside another manager widget in the form) is the culprit.

  A common cause of this is the use of ScrolledList or ScrolledText widgets in a Form. These are actually composite widgets composed of a List or Text widget inside a ScrolledWindow widget. The convenience functions that create these composites return the Text or List widget, not the ScrolledWindow parent. So, you must use XUparent on the returned handle to get the handle of the ScrolledWindow and specify the constraints on the parent instead. Note that this is not a problem when all constraints are specified at widget creation time—the Motif convenience functions properly pass the constraint resources on to the parent. This problem appears when you add or change constraints to a ScrolledText or ScrolledList following widget creation.

- **Contradictory constraints**. This is explained in detail in the previous section. It is caused by failing to stick with one direction when defining the constraints.

- **Too many immediate children**. Because of the complexity of the layout algorithms used by the Form widget, there can be performance problems if you add too many immediate children to a Form. A better strategy is to create other manager widgets for certain children in the Form that do not require fancy layout constraints, and specify constraints on that manager. For example, if several of the children in the layout only need to be stacked vertically, put them in a RowColumn that is in the Form. I have seen some screens display a factor of 10 or faster when using such a strategy (from 30 seconds to 3 seconds).

9.8 The ScrolledWindow Widget

The ScrolledWindow widget provides a viewport into a larger child. It provides horizontal and vertical ScrollBars to allow the user to change the part of the child being viewed. The ScrolledWindow is used when a large widget will not conveniently fit in a window. See Figure 9-16.

We've already seen some uses of the ScrolledWindow widget; the ScrolledList and ScrolledText widgets are really just List and Text widgets created as children of a ScrolledWindow widget.

The ScrolledWindow widget takes only one child; if you need to display more than one widget in a ScrolledWindow you can create another manager widget as the ScrolledWindow's child and attach as many widgets to that manager as you wish.

Ways to Use the ScrolledWindow Widget

There are two different ways to use the ScrolledWindow widget, controlled by the `scrollingPolicy` resource. That resource can take one of two values:

AUTOMATIC	The ScrolledWindow entirely takes care of scrolling the child.
APPLICATION_DEFINED	The application is entirely responsible for managing the ScrollBars and the view of the child. This involves registering callbacks on the ScrollBars to intercept and interpret motion, doing complicated geometry calculations, potentially intercepting exposure and resize events, and other tasks.

In this book, I will only cover automatic mode. The correct implementation and use of application-defined mode is quite complex—far too complex for a novice Motif programmer. I've done it a few times and I still have nightmares about it.

A good treatment of this advanced topic is given in [Heller and Ferguson 1994].

There is only one reason people subject themselves to using application-defined mode: performance. In some applications, the ScrolledWindow's child can be very large or complex, making scrolling slow. In other cases, an application might not be able to keep all the data to be displayed in memory at once, and application-defined mode can be used to display just the pieces that are required at the moment; data is brought into memory only if the user moves the ScrollBar to view it. In fact, this is how the ScrolledText widget works when it is used to view a large text file on disk. The ScrolledList and ScrolledText composite widgets use application-defined mode, but fortunately for us programmers they appear to work automatically. There is special code in the List and Text widgets that allows them to "know" that their parent is a ScrolledWindow.

A Basic ScrolledWindow Example

Listing 9-11 shows a simple example of using an automatic ScrolledWindow. It creates a ScrolledWindow with scrollingPolicy set to AUTOMATIC (unfortunately, the little used APPLICATION_DEFINED mode is the default). Then, a RowColumn widget is created that contains 64 Label widgets arranged in eight rows and eight columns. That's really all there is to it, all the work is performed by the ScrolledWindow automatically. Figure 9-16 shows the output produced by this program.

Listing 9-11. The ScrolledWindow Widget (scroll.sh).

```
. $XUTILDIR/xutil.sh

XUinitialize TOPLEVEL ScrolledWindow "$@"

XUscrolledwindow SCROLL $TOPLEVEL \
    scrollingPolicy:AUTOMATIC

XUrowcolumn RC $SCROLL \
    packing:PACK_COLUMN \
    orientation:HORIZONTAL \
    numColumns:8

for (( i = 0; i < 64; i++ ))
do
    XUlabel tmp $RC \
        labelString:"item number $i" \
        borderWidth:1
done

XUrealize $TOPLEVEL
XUmainloop
```

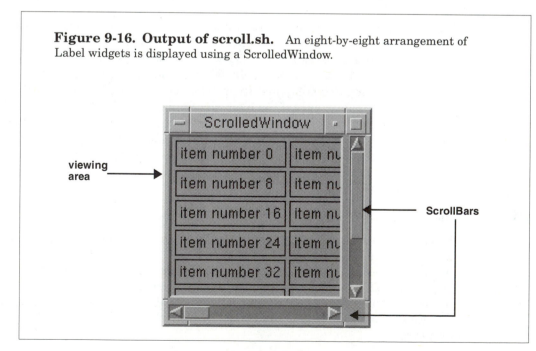

Figure 9-16. Output of scroll.sh.   An eight-by-eight arrangement of
Label widgets is displayed using a ScrolledWindow.

Handling Slow Scrolling

As I mentioned before, there are times when scrolling can be too slow using the ScrolledWindow widget in AUTOMATIC mode. I also mentioned that using the APPLICATION_DEFINED mode was highly complex and not for the faint of heart. So, what is the programmer to do? Fortunately, there is a way to make the Scrolled-Window perform acceptably with complex children even in AUTOMATIC mode.

The idea is to prevent the ScrolledWindow's ScrollBar from attempting to refresh the display every time the user drags the ScrollBar a single Pixel. What we'll do is cause the ScrollBar to update the display only when the user releases the mouse button. This will save many screen updates and make performance acceptable.

Note that this performance gain does not come without a cost—the user will not be able to see precisely where they'll end up until releasing the ScrollBar. But many fine applications use this strategy for coping with slow scrolling, so users have come to accept it; and it only takes a few lines of code to implement, and you can still use AUTOMATIC mode.

The strategy is to modify the underlying ScrollBar widgets that were created by the ScrolledWindow. Specifically, we will remove the callbacks that the ScrolledWindow set up on the ScrollBar that cause the display to be updated every time the Scrollbar is dragged. Modifying the scroll.sh example, we could disable pixel-by-pixel scrolling in the vertical direction by inserting these lines of code right before the XUrealize command:

```
XUget $SCROLL verticalScrollBar:vsb
XUremoveallcallbacks $vsb dragCallback
```

The call to XUget will retrieve the widget handle of the vertical ScrollBar component of the ScrolledWindow and store it in the variable vsb. The call to XUre-moveallcallbacks will remove the callbacks associated with the vertical ScrollBar's dragCallback resource. These are the callbacks that the ScrolledWindow added to take care of AUTOMATIC mode pixel-by-pixel scrolling. In the example program directory (available via anonymous ftp) there is a script called scroll2.sh that includes these lines. The best way to see how it works is to run the two different versions of the program.

After this code is inserted, the screen will refresh only when the user releases the vertical ScrollBar, not every movement during drag operations. Note that the horizontal ScrollBar will still work normally, updating on every pixel. You could perform the same strategy using the horizontalScrollBar resource of the ScrolledWindow to remove its dragCallback, in which case it would behave the same way as the vertical ScrollBar.

Changing the ScrollBar Increments

While we're on the subject of modifying resources of the underlying ScrollBar widgets, a few other resources of the ScrollBar bear mentioning.

As shown earlier, you can modify these resources by first retrieving the handle of the ScrollBar you want (either the `horizontalScrollBar` or the `verticalScrollBar` resource of the ScrolledWindow), then using `XUset` on the retrieved handle:

`increment`   When the user clicks the mouse on one of the ScrollBar arrow-heads, the ScrolledWindow will move the view by this amount (the default is 1 pixel). It is often convenient to increase this amount depending on what kind of data is being displayed in the ScrolledWindow.

`pageIncrement`   When the user clicks the mouse in the region between an arrow and the slider rectangle, the ScrolledWindow moves the view by this amount (the default is 10 pixels). This is supposed to be a "page" of information, where the notion of page is application defined.

Other ScrolledWindow Resources

Here are some other useful ScrolledWindow resources:

`scrollBarDisplayPolicy`   When this resource is set to STATIC, the ScrollBars always appear, even when they are not needed (i.e., when the child fits entirely on the screen). When set to AS_NEEDED, ScrollBars only appear when necessary. The default for automatic ScrolledWindow widgets is AS_NEEDED.

In some situations you can avoid "screen dance" syndrome by using STATIC, with the drawback that the ScrollBars themselves take up some room on the screen.

`scrollBarPlacement`   This resource determines where the Scroll-Bars are placed. Possible values are: TOP_LEFT, TOP_RIGHT, BOTTOM_LEFT, and BOTTOM_RIGHT. These values are self-explanatory.

You should not set these resources in your script; this is a user preference that is normally set in the user's `.Xdefaults` file globally for all applications.

`scrolledWindowMarginHeight,` `scrolledWindowMarginWidth`	These resources set the margin spacing between the ScrolledWindow edges and the child widget. The default for both is 0 pixels.
`spacing`	This resource sets the space between the ScrollBars and the child viewing area. The default is 4 pixels.
`visualPolicy`	If set to CONSTANT (the default for automatic ScrolledWindows), then the ScrolledWindow widget does not attempt to grow or shrink based on child resize requests. When set to VARIABLE, the ScrolledWindow itself may attempt to grow or shrink the viewing area in response to child resize requests.

ScrolledWindow Pitfalls

By far the most common ScrolledWindow widget programming mistake is to forget to set the `scrollingPolicy` resource to AUTOMATIC. The unmistakable symptoms of this error is that the ScrollBars appear even if they are not needed, and they do not do anything when you move them.

9.9 A Better Dialog for Checkbook Entry

Using the principles outlined in this chapter, we will now revisit the checkbook application's "Add Entry" screen. The idea is to modify it so the fields look like a real check.

So, for example, the check number will be placed in the upper left corner, the date will be in the upper right corner, the payee and amount fields will span the dialog across the middle, and the comment will appear in the lower left corner.

We have a couple of fields that don't normally appear on a real check, so for those we'll improvise. The category field is similar to a comment, so we'll put that above the comment field. The reconciled field will go in the lower right corner, simply because there happens to be space there for it. Metaphors are nice, but we must be practical as well!

We'll use the same XU library convenience functions to create captioned controls (`XUaddtextfield`, `XUadddatefields`, `XUaddmoney`, etc.). There is a problem though: those functions assume they will be adding their children to a RowColumn widget (or at least some widget that will stack the children horizontally). We solve this problem by creating RowColumn widgets within the Form widget to hold the captioned controls. So, all constraints will be placed on these RowColumn managers (because they are the immediate children of the Form). In some cases, like the payee and amount fields, it is sufficient for a single RowColumn to hold several controls because the controls naturally lie next to each other in the desired layout scheme. The revised `addCB` function that creates this layout is shown in Listing 9-12. This is the dialog that appears in the final version of the checkbook application, `chkbook.sh`.

Listing 9-12. Custom Checkbook Entry Dialog (chkbook.sh).

```
function addCB {    # [ record-to-edit ]  if no args, adds a new check
    if [[ ! "$ADDPOP" ]]
    then
        typeset labtmp numrc daterc payeerc categrc \
            commentrc amountrc recrc

        XUformdialog -u ADDPOP $TOPLEVEL \
            dialogTitle:"Add A New Entry"

        # Attach the Check number to the top left corner
        XUrow numrc $ADDPOP \
            $(XUattach left 5 top 5)
        XUaddtextfields $numrc \
            ADDPOP.CHECKNUM "Check Number:" : 8
        XUtextautoselect ${ADDPOP.CHECKNUM}

        # Attach the Date to the top right corner

        XUrow daterc $ADDPOP \
            $(XUattach right 5 top 5)
        XUadddatefields ${daterc} ADDPOP.DATE Date:

        # Add the payee and amount fields in a single row
        # 30 pixels under the check number row, and anchor
        # the left and right edges to the form

        XUrow payeerc $ADDPOP \
            $(XUattach under $numrc 30 left 5 right 5)
        XUaddtextfields ${payeerc} \
            ADDPOP.PAYEE Payee: : 30
        XUaddmoneyfields ${payeerc} \
            ADDPOP.AMOUNT   'Amount: $'   9 # Literal $

        # Add the category field under the payee
        # row, attached to the left of the form

        XUrow ADDPOP.CATEGRC $ADDPOP \
            $(XUattach under $payeerc 20 left 5)

        # sort the categories using set -s
        set "${!CATEGORIES[@]}"
        set -s
        XUaddoptionmenu ADDPOP.CATEG ${ADDPOP.CATEGRC} Category: \
```

```
        "${@}" "-" "New ..."
XUaddcallback ${ADDPOP.CATEG.CHILD[New ...]} \
    activateCallback "newcategCB"

# Add the comment field under the category,
# spanning the entire width of the form

XUrow comrc $ADDPOP \
    $(XUattach under ${ADDPOP.CATEGRC} 5 left 5 right 5)
XUaddtextfields ${comrc} \
    ADDPOP.COMMENT Comment: : 20

# Add the reconciled toggle button
# at the same vertical height as
# the comment, attached to the right of the form
XUrow recrc $ADDPOP \
    $(XUattach under $payeerc 20 right 5)
XUaddtogglefields ${recrc} \
    ADDPOP.RECON "Reconciled?" ""

XUtextallowchars \
    ${ADDPOP.PAYEE} "[!|]" \
    ${ADDPOP.COMMENT} "[!|]"

XUsettraversalorder ${ADDPOP} ${ADDPOP.CHECKNUM} \
    ${ADDPOP.ADD} \
    ${ADDPOP.DATE.MM} ${ADDPOP.DATE.DD} ${ADDPOP.DATE.YY} \
    ${ADDPOP.PAYEE} \
    ${ADDPOP.AMOUNT} ${ADDPOP.COMMENT}

# Create an action area under the reconcile row,
# and add buttons to it

XUaddactionarea ADDPOP.ACTION $ADDPOP $comrc
XUactionbuttons ${ADDPOP.ACTION} \
    -d ADDPOP.ADD      Save    "add_addCB $1" \
       ADDPOP.CLEAR    Clear   add_clearCB \
    -c ADDPOP.DISMISS  Dismiss add_dismissCB \
       ADDPOP.HELP     Help    \
                   'helpCB _context ${ADDPOP.WORK}'

addhelp \
    $ADDPOP                    add-entry \
    ${ADDPOP.DATE}            date-field \
    ${ADDPOP.DATE.LABEL}      date-field \
    ${ADDPOP.PAYEE}           payee-field \
    ${ADDPOP.PAYEE.LABEL}     payee-field \
    ${ADDPOP.AMOUNT}          amount-field \
    ${ADDPOP.AMOUNT.LABEL}    amount-field \
```

```
                    ${ADDPOP.CATEG}             category-field \
                    ${ADDPOP.CATEG.LABEL}       category-field

       fi
       add_clearCB  $1 # initialize fields
       XUmanage $ADDPOP
       XUsetfocus ${ADDPOP.CHECKNUM}
   }
```

One other aspect of this example should be explained. The command buttons are created in a two-step process: first an area is created for them using the function XUaddactionarea. That function takes as its arguments a variable that will receive the handle of the action area, the name of the Form parent to which the action area should be attached, and the handle of the bottom-most widget in the Form. The action area will be created below that widget. The action area is itself a Form, and it includes a Separator line. The XUaddactionarea function arranges for the action area to remain a fixed size even when its parent Form is resized. The output of this example is shown in Figure 9-17.

Figure 9-17. Checkbook Entry Dialog (chkbook.sh).

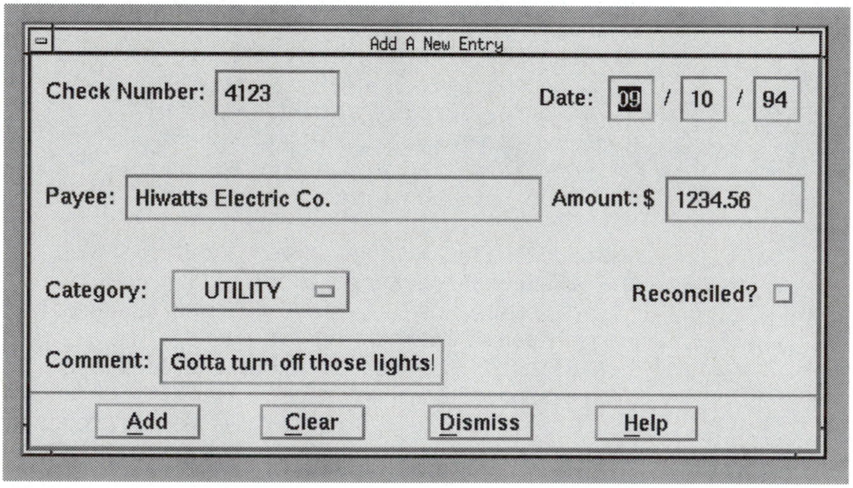

9.10 Multiple Screen Dialogs

There is often a need to create a dialog that has several different modes, each mode showing an entirely different set of fields. The user clicks on either an OptionMenu or one of a set of ToggleButtons to select which mode the dialog should be in, which changes the fields displayed. Figure 9-18 illustrates these ideas.

Figure 9-18. Elements of A Multiscreen Dialog. This diagram shows a typical layout used for a multiscreen dialog. When the user selects a mode ToggleButton at the top of the dialog, the fields displayed in the center area change.

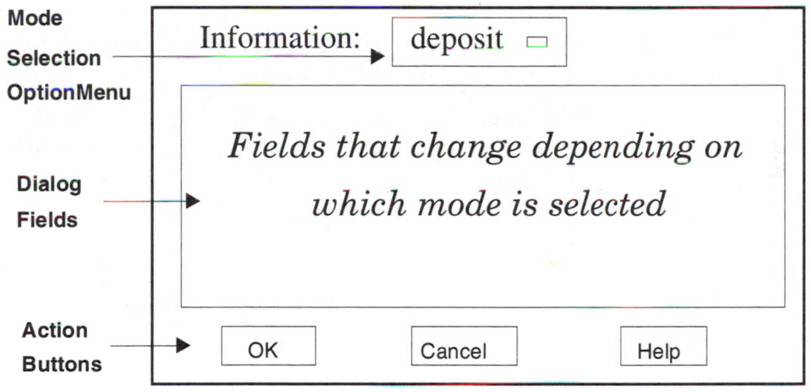

Mode

Selection

OptionMenu

Information: → deposit ▭

Fields that change depending on

which mode is selected

Dialog

Fields

Action

Buttons

OK   Cancel   Help

In the checkbook program, you could imagine different modes for the Add Entry screen: one for regular checks, another for deposits, perhaps a third for adjustments such as interest payments or bank service charges. The reason for this is convenience: some fields are irrelevant in the case of a deposit; for example, there is no check number field. There is also no particular reason for a deposit screen to look anything like the physical check metaphor we're using for regular check entries. Here is a summary of the multiscreen dialog strategy:

1. Create a Form widget that will server as the topmost manager in the dialog.

2. Create the OptionMenu that will be used to control which screen is displayed. It should be attached to the top of the form (XUattach top ...).

    > Some applications use a RadioBox with ToggleButtons inside instead of an OptionMenu to allow the user to choose which screen is displayed. This works as long as there are not too many screens and the ToggleButtons all fit nicely across the top of the window. The OptionMenu method works for any number of screens and so is presented here.

3. Create a ScrolledWindow widget as a child of the Form. Attach it under the ToggleButton, and also to the left and right edges of the form. If you don't need an action area, attach it to the bottom as well.

4. Create a RowColumn widget inside the ScrolledWindow. It will be used to hold each of the screens, but only one at a time will be managed.

5. Create each individual screen inside the RowColumn, as one individual child of the RowColumn.

6. Add callbacks on the OptionMenu buttons that will unmanage the currently displayed screen then manage the desired screen. It is helpful to keep track of the currently managed screen by storing its handle in a variable—that way you can simply unmanage the widget handle stored in the variable before managing the desired screen.

7. If needed, add an action area under the ScrolledWindow and attach it to the left, right, and bottom edges of the form.

Listing 9-13 presents a simple application with two screens that can be selected using a ToggleButton in this manner. It simulates an application that allows data input, and the ToggleButton chooses between personal information and employer-related information. The two different screens presented by the application are shown in Figure 9-19.

Listing 9-13. A Simple Multiscreen Application (multi.sh). This program uses the method outlined earlier for creating multiscreen dialogs.

```
. $XUTILDIR/xutil.sh

function selectCB {
    case "$1" in
    EMPLOYER)
        XUunmanage ${ALLSCREENS.PERSONAL}
        XUmanage ${ALLSCREENS.EMPLOYER}
        ;;
    PERSONAL)
        XUunmanage ${ALLSCREENS.EMPLOYER}
        XUmanage ${ALLSCREENS.PERSONAL}
        ;;
    esac
}


XUinitialize TOPLEVEL Multi-Select "$@"

XUform TOPFORM $TOPLEVEL

# Create the option menu that will select which screen
# of information is displayed.
XUrow tmp $TOPFORM \
    $(XUattach top 4 left 4 right 4)
XUaddoptionmenu MODE $tmp "Information Category:" \
    "Personal" "Employer"
```

```
# Add callbacks that change the screen when an option
# is selected
XUaddcallback ${MODE.CHILD[Personal]} \
    activateCallback "selectCB PERSONAL"
XUaddcallback ${MODE.CHILD[Employer]} \
    activateCallback "selectCB EMPLOYER"

# Create a ScrolledWindow widget that will hold all the screens
XUscrolledwindow SW $TOPFORM \
    scrollingPolicy:AUTOMATIC \
    $(XUattach under $tmp 4 left 4 right 4 bottom 4)

# Create a RowColumn widget that will hold each of the screens.
# Only one screen will be managed at a time.
XUcolumn ALLSCREENS $SW packing:PACK_COLUMN

INFO=    # initialize hierarchical variable to hold handles

# Create the PERSONAL information screen (unmanaged!)
XUrowcolumn -u ALLSCREENS.PERSONAL $ALLSCREENS
XUaddtextfields ${ALLSCREENS.PERSONAL} \
    INFO.NAME    Name:        ver_name    16 \
    INFO.ADDR    Address:     ver_addr    16 \
    INFO.PHONE   Telephone:   ver_phone   16
XUalign2col ${ALLSCREENS.PERSONAL}

# Create the EMPLOYER information screen (unmanaged!)
XUrowcolumn -u ALLSCREENS.EMPLOYER $ALLSCREENS
XUaddtextfields ${ALLSCREENS.EMPLOYER} \
    INFO.EMPLOYER   Employer:       ver_name    16 \
    INFO.YEARS      "Years There:"  ver_phone   16
XUalign2col ${ALLSCREENS.EMPLOYER}
selectCB PERSONAL    # set default to PERSONAL
XUrealize $TOPLEVEL
XUmainloop
```

The strategy used by this program is not the only one that will work, but it is a good one that I have used in many applications. It avoids "screen dance" by unmanaging and managing each screen as a unit. Because it uses a RowColumn widget with a ScrolledWindow parent, this program will also respond appropriately to resize requests by displaying ScrollBars when necessary.

9.11 Summary

Motif provides several widgets to arrange other (child) widgets in useful ways. When a child becomes managed, a complex negotiation takes place to determine its size and position in the manager.

Figure 9-19. Output of multi.sh. On the left, the application as it initially appears in Personal information mode. On the right, the application as it appears if the user selects "Employer" from the OptionMenu at the top of the screen.

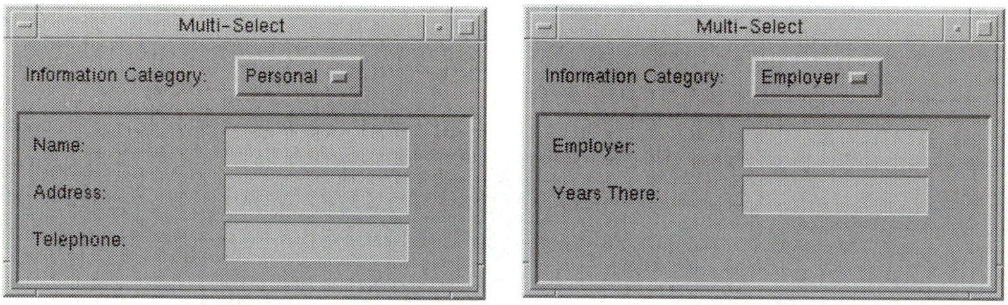

To avoid the overhead of negotiation as much as possible, you should create the manager widget in an unmanaged state (using the -u option of the XU library widget creation command), then create its children, then manage the manager using XU-manage.

Manager Widgets

Use RowColumn widgets whenever you can stack children in regular rows or columns.

Don't use the BulletinBoard widget unless you are writing a very sophisticated program that requires custom control over widget placement.

Use the Form widget when you need fine control over resize behavior or complex child relationships, but beware of adding too many children to a it. A Form widget should normally be used as the topmost level of manager in a Shell widget.

The PanedWindow widget can be used to provide separately sizable areas for two or more children. It's a good idea not to create more than two resizable panes.

The ScrolledWindow widget provides a view into a larger child. Unless you are an experienced Motif programmer you should use AUTOMATIC mode, in which the ScrolledWindow widget takes care of all scrolling chores.

Multiscreen Dialogs

When a dialog contains too many fields to fit conveniently on one screen, consider using a multiscreen approach in which the user selects from among several screens using an OptionMenu (or alternatively, a set of ToggleButtons). The general technique is to create all the screens as children of a RowColumn, but only manage the one the user selects.

10 *Providing Feedback During Long Callbacks*

10.1 Introduction

Time-consuming callback functions present a problem: while callback commands are executing, the X event loop cannot process events—it's waiting for the callback to return. That means that the graphical part of the application stops cold; buttons stop functioning, the mouse pointer cannot trigger further events, the keyboard doesn't respond, and if parts of the application become exposed they do not repaint.

Clearly, this is not an acceptable situation. At the very least, the user must get some indication that the application is temporarily "on hold" but even providing that level of feedback is not really acceptable for very long callbacks. This chapter will show you various strategies for dealing with time-consuming callbacks. In it, you will learn how to:

- Change the mouse pointer to a "busy" cursor
- Use a WorkingDialog to inform the user that they have to wait
- Provide a progress scale to indicate the percentage of the task that is complete
- Spawn a separate process to handle the time-consuming callback so the application can continue
- Display the "tail" of a logfile to show the user progress.

In the process of learning these techniques, you will also learn how to use timers and how to register input events that trigger when a file grows—techniques that are useful in many situations besides those discussed in this chapter.

10.2 General Concepts

Most callbacks take a very small amount of time. For example, a typical string validation callback for a TextField might take a few milliseconds.

219

The dtksh command interpreter can execute something on the order of 1000 built-in commands per second on an Intel 486 processor (even more on a RISC workstation), so even complex validation should only take a fraction of a second (assuming it can be done without spawning other processes).

Sometimes a callback must do a substantial amount of work; for example, formatting a complex print file or doing a lengthy set of calculations. In other instances, a callback could be delayed because it must wait for a slow device (for example, formatting a floppy disk might take up to a minute).

Long callbacks present a problem because of the way events are handled within an X application.

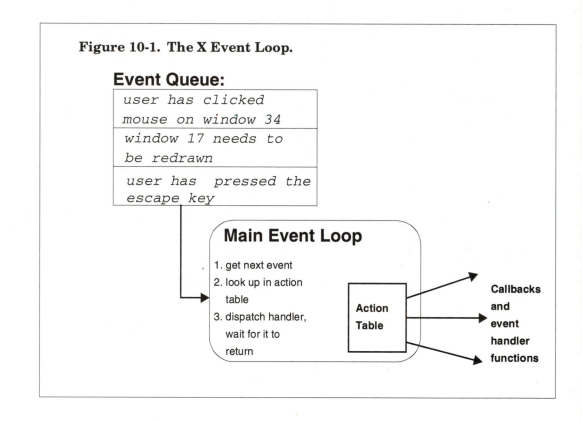

Figure 10-1. The X Event Loop.

The Event Loop

While a callback is executing, the entire graphical part of the application is frozen. That's because the driving force of the X application—the event loop—has stopped, it is waiting for the callback to return. This is illustrated in Figure 10-1. As the user interacts with the display server, events are sent to the client application.

These events queue up to be handled by the event loop (the function `XUmainloop` actually implements this loop in your script). These raw events are looked up in an action table.

The action table specifies the correct callback function or event handler function to execute in order to process the incoming event. While that callback or handler is executing, the event loop is not running (it's waiting for the function to return). Thus, no windows will redraw if they are exposed as a result of the user moving an obscuring window, no keyboard or mouse events will be processed, etc.

> I am simplifying the event, translation, and action table relationship in the foregoing explanation. For a more complete explanation, see Chapter 19, *Events, Translations, etc.*

The Importance of Feedback

If your application does not take special action to let the user know what's going on during a long callback, the user is likely to get confused. This confusion can lead to serious errors. The user might think the application is "hung" and will never start up again; they might terminate the program or even reboot the entire machine.

As a general rule, the longer a callback takes the more you as an application programmer need to do to let the user know things are still working as expected. With this in mind, I have developed the guidelines shown in Table 10-1.

Table 10-1. Guidelines for Providing Feedback

Maximum Expected Time for Callback Completion	Suggested Type of User Feedback
Less than 1 second	None required
1 to 10 seconds	Change the mouse pointer to a "busy" cursor.
10 to 30 seconds	Create a WorkingDialog to inform the user that the callback could take a significant amount of time.
30 seconds to 2 minutes	Consider spawning a background process to handle the callback. Create a feedback dialog that includes an indicator so the user knows approximately how much of the task is complete. Give the user a way to terminate the procedure.
More than 2 minutes	Strongly consider spawning a background process to handle the callback. Show the user both the elapsed time and the approximate percentage of the task completed. If possible, show the user intermediate steps that have completed successfully.

The following sections give examples of how to implement these various methods of providing feedback to the user. In most cases, I will simply use the dtksh `sleep` command to simulate a time-consuming callback; in this way the examples won't be cluttered with superfluous code.

10.3 Changing the Pointer to a Busy Cursor

The XU convenience library contains a function that changes the mouse pointer to a "busy" cursor. It also arranges for the cursor to change back to the standard arrow cursor when your callback returns:

```
XUbusy $widget
```

The pointer will change to the busy cursor only when it is within the specified *widget*. If the callback was spawned from a dialog, you would normally use the handle returned from the dialog creation routine. For callbacks executed from the main window of the application, you should give the handle of the MainWindow widget or whatever top level manager you are using.

Listing 10-1 shows how to use this function to provide feedback for a relatively short callback. It is helpful to run this program to see how it works. As suggested previously, changing the clock face to a busy cursor is sufficient for callbacks that will last up to a few seconds.

Listing 10-1. Using a Busy Cursor (feedbusy.sh).

```
. $XUTILDIR/xutil.sh

function callback { # A short callback
    XUbusy $TOPFORM

    long_work        # Simulated work
}

function long_work {
    sleep 5
}

XUinitialize TOPLEVEL Feedbusy "$@"
XUrowcolumn RC $TOPLEVEL \
    marginHeight:30 marginWidth:30
XUpushbutton PUSH $RC \
    labelString:"Execute Callback"
XUaddcallback $PUSH activateCallback callback

XUrealize $TOPLEVEL
XUmainloop
```

The output of this program (which is admittedly not very enlightening, you have to run it yourself) is shown in Figure 10-2.

10.4 Displaying a WorkingDialog

If a callback could last longer than a few seconds, up to about half a minute, you need to grab the user's attention and make sure they know they will have to be patient for a little while. The simplest way to do this is by using the Motif Working-Dialog. This dialog was discussed in Chapter 5, *The Standard Dialogs* (instructions for creating a WorkingDialog using the function XUworking are given on page 84).

In the simplest use of the WorkingDialog for this purpose, we don't really want to show any action buttons. That's because they won't work anyway—remember that our event loop is not running while the callback is in progress. Later in this chapter I'll show how to make buttons like this work by spawning the callback as a background process.

Giving the WorkingDialog a Chance to Display

The one really tricky part of using the WorkingDialog in this manner is that simply popping up the dialog before doing the real work of the callback is not sufficient. That's because the WorkingDialog you pop up will not receive any events (remember, we're still in the callback and the event loop is not running). One event is particularly important here: the one that tells the WorkingDialog to display itself! If

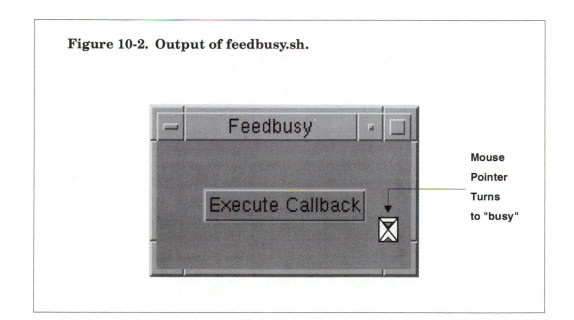

Figure 10-2. Output of feedbusy.sh.

we were to simply pop up the WorkingDialog, then do our work, then return from the callback, then the WorkingDialog would not actually display itself until after the work was finished and the event loop started up again—the user won't see the message until the work is done.

The XU library provides a simple way around this problem by providing this command:

```
XUdefer command
```

We'll discuss exactly how this works a little later in this chapter, for now suffice it to say that the *command* argument to XUdefer will be scheduled for execution after the event loop has processed any events already queued up. So, our callback handling strategy will be:

1. Display a WorkingDialog using XUworking.

2. Split off the real work of the callback into a separate function which is scheduled using XUdefer.

3. Return from the callback, allowing the event loop to process the redisplay events for the WorkingDialog. When it has nothing else to do, the event loop will execute the separate function previously scheduled with XUdefer.

This strategy is illustrated in Listing 10-2, with the resulting WorkingDialog displayed in Figure 10-3. Notice that no button definitions are given on the call to XUworking. The lack of button definitions causes XUworking to unmanage the buttons; they will not appear. Also notice that the WorkingDialog is dismissed by unmanaging its widget handle, which is stored in the variable _XU.Working-Dialog; this dismissal is also carried out using XUdefer.

If several commands are registered for deferred execution, they will execute in *last in/first out* order. This is why we scheduled the WorkingDialog unmanage call using XUdefer before we scheduled the work procedure—we want the work procedure to be executed first, then when it finishes, the WorkingDialog should be unmanaged.

Listing 10-2. Using a WorkingDialog (feedwd.sh).

```
. $XUTILDIR/xutil.sh

function callback {
    XUworking -m "Working" \
        "This may take a little while, so
        please be patient." \
        '' '' ''
    XUbusy $TOPLEVEL
    XUbusy ${_XU.WorkingDialog}
    XUdefer "XUunmanage ${_XU.WorkingDialog}"
```

```
    # Defer the actual work of the callback until
    # after the event loop has processed its queues,
    # this way the working dialog will appear since
    # its redisplay events will be handled

    XUdefer "long_work"      # Simulated work
}

function long_work {
    sleep 20     # simulated work
}

XUinitialize TOPLEVEL Feedwd "$@"
XUrowcolumn RC $TOPLEVEL \
    marginHeight:30 marginWidth:30
XUpushbutton PUSH $RC \
    labelString:"Execute Callback"
XUaddcallback $PUSH activateCallback callback

XUrealize $TOPLEVEL
XUmainloop
```

One thing you might notice is that this example also uses a busy cursor along with
the WorkingDialog. Two calls to the XUbusy command are necessary: the first
causes the main window to get a clock cursor, and the second causes the Working-
Dialog window to get a busy cursor. In general, you must call XUbusy on each shell
class widget separately (assuming you want to put the busy cursor on all windows
in the application).

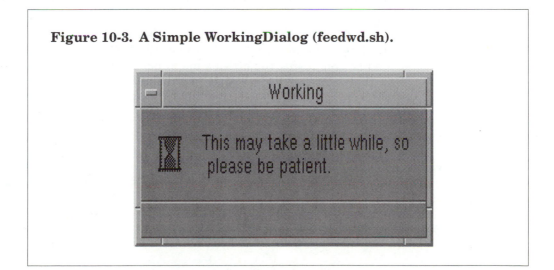

Figure 10-3. A Simple WorkingDialog (feedwd.sh).

10.5 Progress Indicators

For callbacks that will take even longer, perhaps a minute or two, it is necessary to provide an indication that progress is being made. A minute spent staring at a lifeless computer window can seem like an eternity to the user; the time passes more quickly if there is some motion. The motion and progress indication also assure the user that the application has not entered a hung state, and gives them a rough idea of how much longer they might have to wait.

A common technique in graphical programs is to use a Scale widget to display an estimate of the percentage of the task that is complete. The Scale is made to move as the callback executes. This may seem like a simple idea, but there are some complications:

- The Scale widget will not respond to events for the same reason that the rest of the application will not—the event loop is not running. For this reason, it is necessary to spawn the main work performed by the callback as a background process and communicate progress back to the parent so it can be displayed using the Scale.

- It is not always easy for the application to know how much of a task is complete. Often only a rough estimate is possible, and sometimes even a rough estimate is difficult to make.

The following sections offer some advice and solutions to these problems.

Spawning Work in the Background

The strategy here is to break the callback into two parts:

1. The first part will set up the progress feedback dialog and obtain any data values from the program that are necessary to perform the work of the callback.

2. The second part will be a separate script that takes the data values obtained by the first part and actually does the work. It will be spawned as a background process (using the dtksh & operator) so the first part can return and allow the event loop to start again. It will write a progress report to a temporary file that will be monitored by the progress feedback dialog set up by the first part.

One important note is that *the background script cannot directly perform any graphical operations*. This is a sad but true fact: when one piece of your dtksh script is spawned as a separate process, it cannot access any widgets back in the parent process, it cannot create new widgets controlled by the parent process, etc. If it wishes to do graphics at all, it must be written as a completely separate script that calls XUinitialize, etc., and become a separate graphical process in its own right.

The Progress Feedback Dialog Strategy

The progress feedback dialog will consist of an insensitive Scale widget and an action button that can cancel the task in progress (using the dtksh `kill` command to destroy the background process). You may also wish to create a `Help` button on this dialog. The dialog will also contain a Label area that can display the current subtask being performed by the background process (this gives the user an idea of what is happening at the moment).

Once per second, a timer will go off that will cause a file to be read. This file will be kept up to date by the background process that's doing the real work. The file will contain a single line which can be in one of these formats:

- A number from 0 to 100 followed by a a string. The number will be used to set the Scale widget's value, and the string will change the "current task" Label.

- Any string that does not start with a number is considered to be an error message. If this appears, the background process is assumed to have terminated—unable to complete the task. The progress dialog will pop up an ErrorDialog containing the error string.

In the rest of this chapter, I will refer to this file as the *communication file*.

Scheduling Timers

To poll the communication file, we need to learn about X timers. Timers are created and destroyed with these commands:

```
XUaddtimeout variable milliseconds command
XUremovetimeout $variable
```

The *variable* passed to `XUaddtimeout` will be set to a timer identifier that can be used to cancel the timer later using `XUremovetimeout`.

> Of course, you must cancel a timer event before it is actually executed.

The *milliseconds* argument is the length of time that should pass before *command* is executed. Note that once the *command* is executed, the timer is gone—if you want it to go off again in the future then the *command* should reschedule the timeout using `XUaddtimeout` again.

A Progress Dialog Example

The strategy just outlined is carried out by a program called `feedprog.sh`. The callback subroutine that creates the progress dialog is shown in Listing 10-3. The progress indicator is displayed in Figure 10-4.

This example is quite instructive, because the progress dialog presented is complete enough to use in a production application (I have used this general style of code in several production applications). Recall that the file used for communication can return either a percentage complete indicator (a number between 0 and 100), or an error message if something goes wrong in the background process. The error message is displayed using an ErrorDialog. Otherwise, a value of 100 indicates that the background procedure has completed normally. In any case, when the background process completes the communication file is removed.

Creating the Progress Dialog

The standard XU functions are used to create a simple two-column dialog (two-column dialogs are explained in detail in Chapter 6, *Prompting Using Custom Dialogs*). The communication filename is created in the /tmp directory. Its name ends with the process ID of the dtksh script's process (expanded using the special notation $$). In that way, we are sure the communication file will be unique to this application. The communication filename is passed to the background script (feed-bkgr.sh, which is explained later).

After the background process is started, its process ID is saved (the parameter $! in KornShell expands to the process ID of the last background process executed). Finally, a timer is registered that will poll the communication file. The timer is set to go off in 1000 milliseconds, which is 1 second.

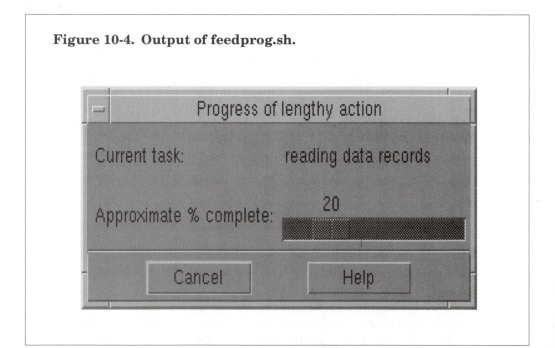

Figure 10-4. Output of feedprog.sh.

Listing 10-3. Creating the Progress Dialog (feedprog.sh).

```
. $XUTILDIR/xutil.sh

function callback {
    typeset tmp

    # create a progress dialog if it doesn't already exist
    if [[ ! "$PROGRESSPOP" ]]
    then
        XUsimpledialog PROGRESSPOP $TOPLEVEL \
            title:"Progress of lengthy action"
        XUset ${PROGRESSPOP.WORK} \
            entryAlignment:ALIGNMENT_BEGINNING
        XUlabel tmp ${PROGRESSPOP.WORK} \
            labelString:"Current task:"
        XUlabel PROGRESSPOP.TASK ${PROGRESSPOP.WORK} \
            labelString:""
        XUlabel tmp ${PROGRESSPOP.WORK} \
            labelString:"Approximate % complete:"
        XUscale PROGRESSPOP.SCALE ${PROGRESSPOP.WORK} \
            orientation:HORIZONTAL \
            showValue:true \
            minimum:0 \
            maximum:100
        XUalign2col ${PROGRESSPOP.WORK}

        XUactionbuttons ${PROGRESSPOP.ACTION} \
            -c PROGRESSPOP.CANCEL Cancel C  killbackgroundCB \
               PROGRESSPOP.HELP    Help   H  :

        XUinsensitive ${PROGRESSPOP.SCALE}
    fi
    XUset ${PROGRESSPOP.SCALE} value:0
    XUmanage $PROGRESSPOP

    # initialize a temporary file for the progress reports
    PROGRESSPOP.COMFILE=/tmp/PROGRESS$$
    print 0 > ${PROGRESSPOP.COMFILE}

    # spawn a background process that
    # actually does the work
    dtksh feedbkgr.sh ${PROGRESSPOP.COMFILE} &

    PROGRESS POP.PID=$!

    XUaddtimeout tmp 1000 "showprogress"
}
```

Showing Progress

Listing 10-4 gives the definition of the `showprogress` function, which is executed via a timer. This function starts by obtaining the contents of the communication file.

> The KornShell notation `$(<filename)` expands to the contents of a file; it is equivalent to `$(cat filename)`

If the file contains no data at all, then we have happened to read it exactly as the background process has begun writing data to the file, so we simply reschedule `showprogress` and return.

Otherwise, the contents are checked to see if they contain a new percentage and subtask string, or an error message. Appropriate actions are taken in either case.

Listing 10-4. Showing Progress (feedprog.sh).

```
function showprogress {
    typeset file contents tmp percent task

    file="${PROGRESSPOP.COMFILE}"
    contents=$(<$file)

    # if the file is empty, we've caught it at the
    # exact moment of a write by the background
    # process, so reschedule and return
    if [[ ! "$contents" ]]
    then
        XUaddtimeout tmp 1000 "$0 $*"
        return
    fi

    # if the progress popup is no longer
    # managed, don't display any more results
    if ! XUismanaged $PROGRESSPOP
    then return
    fi

    case "$contents" in
    100)
        # We are finished!
        XUinformation "Task is Complete" \
            "The task has completed successfully."
        XUunmanage ${PROGRESSPOP}
        rm $file
        ;;
    [0-9]*)
        # split up the contents using read
        print "$contents" | read percent task
```

```
          XUset ${PROGRESSPOP.SCALE} value:"$percent"
          XUset ${PROGRESSPOP.TASK} labelString:"$task"
          XUaddtimeout tmp 1000 "$0 $*"
          ;;
     *)
          XUunmanage $PROGRESSPOP
          XUerror Error "$contents"
          rm $file
          ;;
     esac
}
```

Terminating the Background Process on Demand

The progress dialog provides a button that gives the user the option of terminating the background process. Listing 10-5 shows the function that is called if that button is selected. It is rather simple: the previously saved process identifier is sent an interrupt signal using the KornShell `kill` command. After that, the progress dialog is unmanaged, the communication file is removed, and an informational message is displayed confirming that the process has been terminated.

Note that a real application might want to prompt the user for confirmation before actually terminating the background process. Techniques for asking the user for confirmation are discussed in *Using the QuestionDialog for Confirming Deletion* on page 89.

Listing 10-5. Terminating the Background Process (feedprog.sh).

```
function killbackgroundCB {
    kill -s INT ${PROGRESSPOP.PID}

    XUunmanage $PROGRESSPOP
    rm $file
    XUinformation "Action Terminated" \
        "The lengthy task was terminated at your request."
}
```

Designing the Background Process

There are some design decisions to make for the background process:

- How will it determine the percentage of work completed so it can keep the communication file up to date?
- How will it respond to being forcibly killed by the graphical program?

Estimating Task Percentage Complete

Determining the exact percentage of work completed is usually quite difficult. For-tunately, it is not necessary to give the user an exact figure, all the user needs is a general idea of how much of the task has been accomplished so far. However, even a rough estimate can be hard to figure out in some instances.

It's difficult for me to give you general advice on this subject, because the range of tasks you might be performing is unlimited. Here are some strategies that I have used in the past; they might give you some clues to the strategy that will best suit your application.

- **File vs. Byte Based Estimates.** If the work to be performed is related to a number of different files, it is often easier to use the percentage of files pro-cessed so far rather than the more accurate number of bytes processed. For example, if the work is to copy 100 files out to a floppy disk, you might want to increment the Scale by 1% for each file copied rather than trying to take into account the size of the files involved.

- **Estimates Based on Number of Steps in the Task.** If a task has several well-defined subtasks, say, 10, and the subtasks are not very data dependent in their relative execution times, then a simple approximation is to assign an estimated percentage to each task and increment the Scale after each sub-task is completed. If one or more of the subtasks is data dependent in its execution time, then you could make allowances for incrementing the Scale specially during that task (perhaps using one of the other strategies dis-cussed here).

- **Estimates Based on Previous Task Execution Time**. The idea of this strategy is that there is a task that is more or less identically executed by the user from time to time. So, your work procedure keeps track of how long the task took the last time the user executed it (perhaps it stores this time in a hidden file under the user's $HOME directory).

> The dtksh variable SECONDS is useful in this regard, that variable always holds the number of seconds since the dtksh process began executing. It can also be reset to any value by assignment.

In any case, your work procedure can simply divide the current amount of time spent doing work by the previous amount of time the total task took, then multiply by 100 to yield a percentage. It should never return more than 99 percent until the task is actually completed, however. So, if the task takes longer this time than last time, the user might be stuck looking at "99%" in the Scale widget for a long time; that's just a pitfall of doing a rough estimate like this. After the task is completed, the background process stores the new task time in the hidden file—presumably producing a better estimate for the next time.

Responding to Kill Requests

If the user decides to terminate the time-consuming task early, then the example feedback dialog will attempt to kill the background process. In many cases there will be some cleanup work to be performed by the background process before it dies.

The usual KornShell programming strategy works well here: use the `trap` command to intercept the signal and clean up. For example, the command:

```
trap cleanup INT
```

registers the shell function `cleanup` to be called when an `INT` (interrupt) signal is raised on the background process. The progress dialog displays an InformationDialog informing the user that the termination was carried out. See Figure 10-5.

Figure 10-5. Progress Feedback Background Termination.

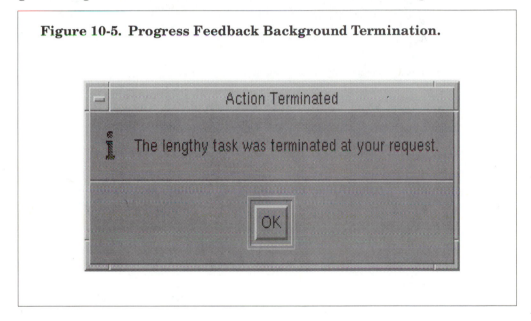

An Example Background Process

Listing 10-6 shows a complete example of a background process. As before, it doesn't actually do any real work, but simulates work in several places by using the `sleep` command.

In this example, the strategy of using subtasks to estimate work completed is used. For good measure, I also simulate an error condition that triggers randomly (using the `RANDOM` feature of dtksh) sometimes when the background process is run. In this way, it can be used to test the feedback dialog error display feature. An example of an error display triggered in this way is shown in Figure10-5. A `trap` command is also provided in this example; it does nothing but print a message to the standard output. For safety, a second `trap` command is used to intercept any error that occurs in the script (the ERR trap). This will trigger, for example, if there is a syntax error in the script. That `trap` sends an appropriate message to the communication file.

Listing 10-6. A Background Process (feedbkgr.sh).

```
trap 'print "I was interrupted" ; exit' INT

trap 'print "Fatal error occurred" > $file' ERR

file=$1

print "0 initializing" > $file

sleep 5

print "20 reading data records"  > $file

sleep 10

print "60 making updates" > $file

sleep 5

print "80 writing results" > $file

# Simulate an error condition about 50% of the time
# by choosing a random number.  This allows us to
# test the error handling portion of the feedback
# dialog
if [[ $RANDOM == *[0-4] ]]
then
    print "Error!  Unable to write results." > $file
else
    print 100 > $file
fi
```

10.6 Following a Logfile

Some tasks produce a detailed record of what they are doing by storing results in a logfile. In some applications, it is a good idea to allow the user to follow the progress of such a logfile by displaying it in a Text widget.

> This requires judgement on your part. If the messages written to the logfile are not likely to be intelligible to the average user of your application, you might not want to display it.

This is relatively simple to implement because X provides a capability that allows you to register a function to be called whenever there is input available from a file:

```
XUaddinput variable file-descriptor command
XUremoveinput $variable
```

The *variable* will receive an identifier that can be used to cancel the input handler by XUremoveinput. The *command* is executed whenever there is input available on the named *file-descriptor*. The file descriptor is an integer from 0 to 9 (where 0 is the standard input of the dtksh process, 1 is the standard output, and 2 is the standard error). To associate a file or device with a file descriptor, you can use the exec command. For example, to associate the file myfile with file descriptor 4, you could use:

```
exec 4<myfile
```

While the *command* is executing, the variable INPUT_LINE will contain the next line of data from the *file-descriptor*. The *command* is executed once for each line in the file.

> The XUaddinput command is actually more flexible than this. *It is possible to give it an option (-r) that causes it to be called whenever there is any input (whether a full line or not). But this process is much more difficult to use, since the programmer is then responsible for reading the data directly. See the reference material on XtAddInput on page 671 for more details.

An X Version of "tail -f"

The standard UNIX command tail has an option (-f) that allows it to *follow* a file—any lines appended to the file are displayed. It is typically used when a long task is writing intermediate results to a logfile (for example, when you use nohup on a long make command).

To illustrate how one might use XUaddinput to provide this same kind of feedback in a graphical program, we will now implement a similar command using dtksh. The command is called dttail.sh and it takes a filename as its argument and pops up a window to follow the output.

In order for this program to be used in conjunction with a cooperating task it has some other features. For example, if a line of the form __END__ appears in the file, the program will assume the task is complete. Also, dttail.sh will display the total elapsed time since it began following the file, and will stop counting time when it detects the __END__ directive. The time is tracked using the dtksh SECONDS variable, which always holds the number of seconds that have passed since the dtksh process started.

The dttail.sh program is shown in Listing 10-7. The input handler function is called getlineCB. It starts by testing to see if any input is really available. It is possible for the handler function to be called in some cases when there is no input,

so that has to be tested. This function calls another function, `showline`, to display
the next line of input in a ScrolledText widget. The functions involved here will be
explained more fully in Chapter 16, *Text and TextField Widgets*. Basically, they just
append the new line to the displayed text and then move the ScrollBars so the end
of the file is showing.

To test this program, write a short shell script that prints one line to a file every
few seconds, something like this:

```
while sleep 3
do
      print "another line of text"
done > file
```

Run this in the background, and then run:

```
dtksh dttail.sh file
```

At some point, you could stop your data generating loop and print the __END__ keyword onto the end of the file:

```
print "__END__" >> file
```

to test that feature. Some sample output is shown in Figure 10-6.

Figure 10-6. Output of dttail.sh.

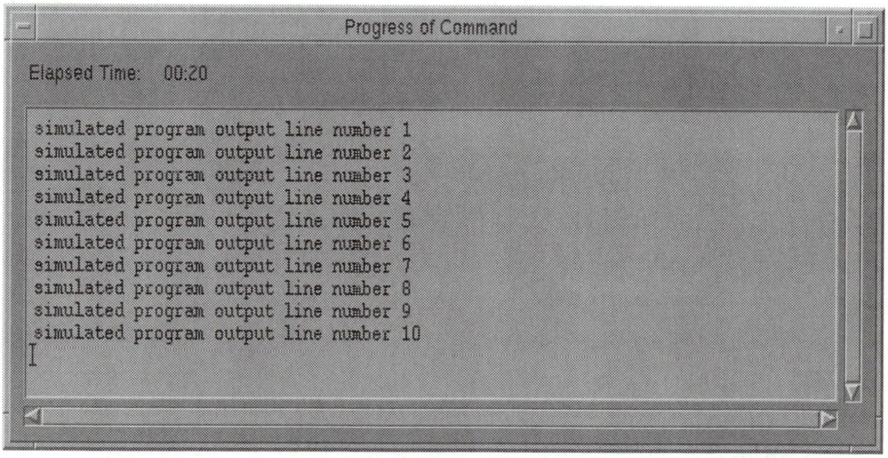

Listing 10-7. Following a Logfile (dttail.sh). This is a stand-alone program that will follow the end of a file provided as its first argument. It uses the XUaddinput command to register the file as an input source. It also displays the elapsed time it has been following the file, and if a line in the file contains the string __END__ it stops the elapsed time counter.

```
. $XUTILDIR/xutil.sh

getlineCB() {
    typeset line=$INPUT_LINE
    integer last

    # We could be called with nothing available
    if [[ ! "$line" ]]
    then return
    fi

    # When we see the end of the input (as signaled)
    # by the __END__ keyword) then write a message
    # to the text area and stop the timer clock
    if [[ $line == __END__ ]]
    then
        showline "----------End of Output----------"
        XUremovetimeout $TIMER
        XUset $TIMELABEL \
            labelString:"Final Elapsed Time:"
        return
    fi

    showline "$line"
}

function showline {
    typeset line=$1

    # stop displaying changes to the text window
    XUtextdisable $TEXT

    # append the line to the scrolled text window
    XUtextappend $TEXT "$line"$'\n'

    # Scroll to the last line
    XUtextgetlast last $TEXT
    XUtextshow $TEXT $last
    XUset $TEXT cursorPosition:$last

    # enable display again
    XUtextenable $TEXT
}
```

```
function showtimeCB {
    typeset -Z2 minute second # -Z2 pads with leading 0

    second=$((SECONDS%60))
    minute=$(( ((SECONDS-second)/60)%60 ))

    XUset $TIME labelString:"$minute:$second"
    XUaddtimeout TIMER 1000 showtimeCB
}

XUinitialize TOPLEVEL Feedfollow \
    -title "Progress of Command" "$@"

XUform FORM $TOPLEVEL

XUlabel TIMELABEL $FORM labelString:"Elapsed Time:" \
    $(XUattach left 10 top 10 )
XUlabel TIME $FORM labelString:"00:00" \
    $(XUattach rightof $TIMELABEL 10 top 10)
XUscrolledtext TEXT $FORM \
    editMode:MULTI_LINE_EDIT \
    columns:80 \
    rows:12 \
    $(XUattach left 10 right 10 bottom 10 under $TIMELABEL 10)

# Take input from first argument, if it's a readable file
if [[ ! -r "${ARGV[1]}" ]]
then
    print "Usage: $0 file" >&2
    exit 1
fi
exec 1<${ARGV[1]}
XUaddinput INPUT 1 getlineCB

SECONDS=0
XUaddtimeout TIMER 1000 showtimeCB

XUrealize $TOPLEVEL
XUmainloop
```

10.7 Using WorkProcs to Break Up a Task

There is an alternative to using background processes for time-consuming call-backs. This strategy is more difficult to implement, but it has the advantage that the procedure executing the task has full access to the application variables and the X objects defined in the application, so it can perform graphic operations as needed.

The strategy here is to break the task into small well- defined chunks; each chunk will do a little bit of the work, then will return back to the event loop so other application work can continue.

The X WorkProc mechanism allows the programmer to register a function that will be executed whenever there are no events available to be processed by the event loop. This is accomplished using the commands:

```
XUaddworkproc variable command
XUremoveworkproc $variable
```

After a call to `XUaddworkproc`, the variable will contain an identifier that can be used to cancel the WorkProc later using `XUremoveworkproc`. The *command* will be executed repeatedly by the event loop—whenever there are no other events to process. If the *command* ever returns a nonzero value it will be removed (just as if `XUremoveworkproc` had been called).

If more than one WorkProc is registered, only the last one registered will be executed until it is either removed using `XUremoveworkproc` or it returns a nonzero value; at that point the previous WorkProc is executed until it is removed or returns nonzero, etc. In effect, when a WorkProc is registered, it is pushed on top of a stack of WorkProcs, and only the top WorkProc on the stack is executed. When it is removed or returns nonzero it is popped off the stack, and the next WorkProc on the stack gets its turn.

The `XUdefer` command, described earlier in this chapter, is implemented using WorkProcs. The difference is that `XUdefer` arranges for its command to be executed exactly one time.

WorkProc Strategy

If you have a task that can be easily broken down into a series of quick subtasks (quick being a few milliseconds), then you might be able to avoid spawning a background process by using WorkProcs. The idea is to encapsulate enough state information in a variable or set of variables so that you can design a WorkProc that will execute a tiny fraction of the whole task, update the state variables, and return control to the event loop. When the task is complete, the WorkProc returns nonzero to cause itself to be unscheduled.

A WorkProc Example

In this example, we implement a WorkProc that calculates prime numbers using the sieve of Eratosthenes method. In this method of calculating prime numbers, a list of all numbers is created. Every second number starting at 4 is crossed off. Then every third number starting at 6 is crossed off; then every fourth number starting at 8, and so on. Eventually, only prime numbers remain.

This kind of repetitive calculation that requires minimal state information is ideal for implementation as a WorkProc. Our WorkProc will be designed so it "crosses out" exactly one number each time it is called.

Listing 10-8 shows the example program, called `dtsieve.sh`. The running program is shown in Figure 10-7.

The numbers are displayed in a 20-by-20 grid (all numbers between 1 and 400 will be displayed). Each number will be held in a Label widget. As numbers are "crossed out" the Labels that hold them will be unmanaged by the WorkProc. A button is provided that starts the calculation process. In addition, a TextField is displayed. Its purpose is to prove the application is still processing events smoothly. While the calculation is in progress, the user will still be able to interact with the application by typing in the TextField.

Figure 10-7. Output of dtsieve.sh. This snapshot was taken in the middle of the calculation. As shown, it is possible to type in the TextField to the right of the "Run Sieve" button, even while the calculation progresses. This proves that the event loop continues to run.

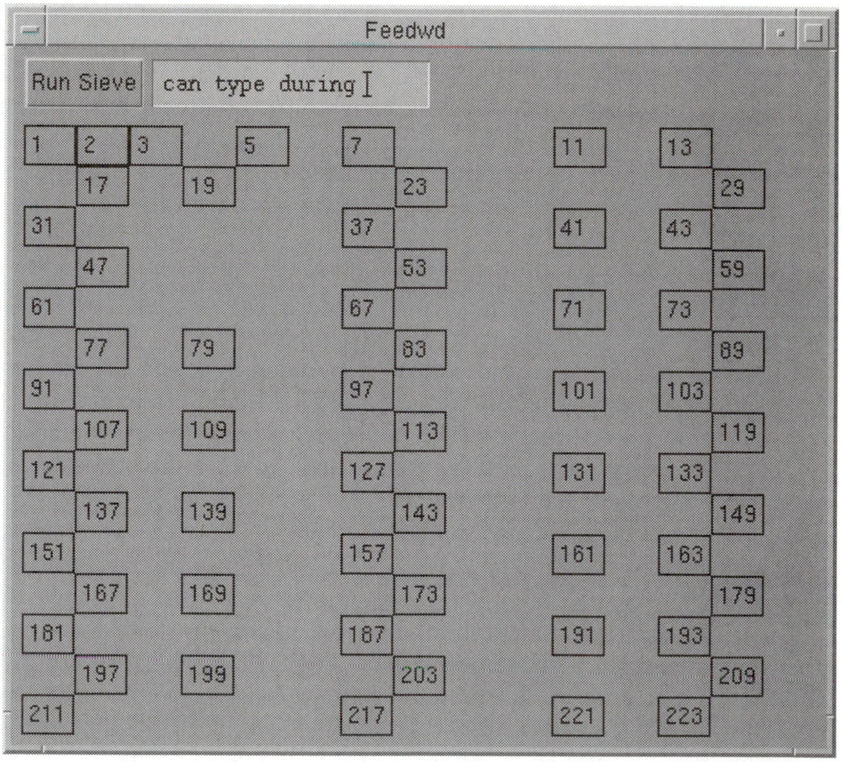

The WorkProc function is called `calc_sieve`. It keeps track of its state using a hierarchical variable called CONTEXT. That variable has two subfields: CONTEXT.CUR (which holds the current increment value) and CONTEXT.POS (which contains the current position in the array of numbers). It keeps these state variables up to date. The function is largely composed of tests on these state variables to determine which Label to unmanage. When all the work is done, this function returns 1 to remove itself from the WorkProc list.

Listing 10-8. A WorkProc Based Task (dtsieve.sh).

```
. $XUTILDIR/xutil.sh

function callback {
    # if there is a calculation in progress, remove
    # it and reset the labels
    if [[ $WORKID ]]
    then
        XUremoveworkproc $WORKID
        for (( i = 1; i <= MAXNUM; i++ ))
        do
            XUmap ${LABEL[i]}
        done
        XUset $STATUSLABEL labelString:""
    fi
    CONTEXT=          # Init parent variable
    CONTEXT.CUR=2     # Current number
    CONTEXT.POS=4     # Current position in array
    XUaddworkproc WORKID "calc_sieve CONTEXT"
}


# The function calc_sieve will be scheduled as
# a Work Proc.  It will perform 1 sieve calculation
# at a time, returning control to the event handler
# in between.  When it is finished, it returns 1
# to remove itself from the list of Work Procs.

function calc_sieve {
    nameref C=$1

    XUunmap ${LABEL[C.POS]}
    set +x
    (( C.POS += C.CUR ))
    if (( C.POS > MAXNUM ))
    then
        if (( ++C.CUR > MAXNUM/2 ))
        then
            XUset $STATUSLABEL labelString:FINISHED!
            return 1
```

```
            fi
            (( C.POS = C.CUR * 2 ))
        fi
        return 0
    }

    XUinitialize TOPLEVEL Feedwd "$@"
    XUcolumn COL $TOPLEVEL
    XUrow ROW $COL
    XUpushbutton PUSH $ROW \
        labelString:"Run Sieve"
    XUaddcallback $PUSH activateCallback callback
    XUtextfield TEXT $ROW
    XUlabel STATUSLABEL $ROW labelString:""

    XUrowcolumn RC $COL \
        orientation:horizontal \
        packing:PACK_COLUMN \
        spacing:0 \
        entryBorder:1 \
        numColumns:15

    integer MAXNUM=225

    for (( i = 1; i <= MAXNUM ; i++ ))
    do
        XUlabel LABEL[$i] $RC \
            labelString:$i
    done

    XUrealize $TOPLEVEL
    XUmainloop
```

10.8 Summary

Long callbacks pose a problem because they freeze an application. Depending on how long the callback takes, different levels of feedback should be given to the user (more elaborate feedback for longer periods of time). Feedback ranges from simply changing the cursor to a clock face for callbacks that will take a few seconds, all the way to providing highly detailed information about which step of a task is currently in progress.

For callbacks that will take more than a minute or two, it is advisable to spawn the work as a background process and provide the user with detailed feedback about the progress of the task. A Scale widget is often used to display an approximate percentage of the task that is complete.

Sometimes a task produces a detailed set of logfile entries showing its progress. A logfile can be "followed" by using the `XUaddinput` command.

When a task can be divided into many very small pieces that don't require very much state information, the X WorkProc mechanism can be used to execute the task without spawning a background process, while still allowing the application to continue processing events.

11   *Decoration Widgets*

11.1 Introduction

The Separator, Label, and Frame widgets are used mainly to decorate application windows. We've already used some of these widgets in previous chapters; in this chapter we'll explore more details of these relatively simple widgets, including:

- How to use the Separator widget or gadget to divide areas of a screen
- How to use the Label widget or gadget to display text or bitmap images
- How to use the Frame widget to place a border around a child.

None of these widgets interacts with the user in any way, yet they are still important to help organize and caption fields. This chapter will discuss how to use these widgets to achieve certain effects, and will discuss the most common mistakes programmers make when using them.

11.2 The Separator Widget

The Separator widget (or gadget) is quite simple; all it does is draw a horizontal or vertical line. You've seen this widget in previous chapters: it divides the work area and action button area in most dialogs, for example. You can create Separators using either of these commands:

```
XUseparator variable $parent [resource:value ...]
XUseparatorgadget variable $parent [resource:value ...]
```

Separator Widget Resources

The `orientation` resource can be set to either HORIZONTAL or VERTICAL and determines the direction of the line (the default is HORIZONTAL). The `margin`

resource determines how far the ends of the line are from the edges of the widget
(the default is 0, meaning the ends of the line touch their respective edges).

For horizontal Separators, the line is centered between the top and bottom of the
widget, and the ends of the line are offset from the left and right edges by the amount
held in the margin resource. For vertical Separators, the line is centered between
the left and right edges of the widget, and its ends are offset from the top and bottom
by the amount set in margin.

The shadowType resource determines how the line is drawn. It can take one of
the following values:

SINGLE_LINE	A line one pixel thick is drawn.
DOUBLE_LINE	A double line is drawn.
SINGLE_DASHED_LINE	A single dashed line.
DOUBLE_DASHED_LINE	A double dashed line.
NO_LINE	No line is drawn. This may seem bizarre, but it is occasionally useful for providing some extra whitespace between other widgets (perhaps in a RowColumn).
SHADOW_ETCHED_IN	This is the default shadowType. Lines are drawn such that the Separator appears to be etched into the window.
SHADOW_ETCHED_IN_DASH	Like above but a dashed line is drawn.
SHADOW_ETCHED_OUT	Lines are drawn such that the Separator appears to be coming out of the window.
SHADOW_ETCHED_OUT_DASH	Like above but a dashed line is drawn.

For the shadow-style separatorType settings, the resource shadowThickness
can be used to set the thickness of the line. See Figure 11-1 for an illustration of
these various resource settings.

Separator Pitfalls

When using one of the shadow-style separatorTypes, if you set the shadowThickness, be sure it is an even number. This is because the three-dimensional
effects are achieved by dividing the line in two pieces and shading them different
colors.

Another common mistake is the use of too many Separators in a dialog. For example, if the work area of a dialog consists of a widget that includes borders (like a

Figure 11-1. Separator Types (septypes.sh). This figure illustrates various styles of the Separator widget and gadget. For illustration purposes, I used a rather large setting for shadowThickness (8 pixels).

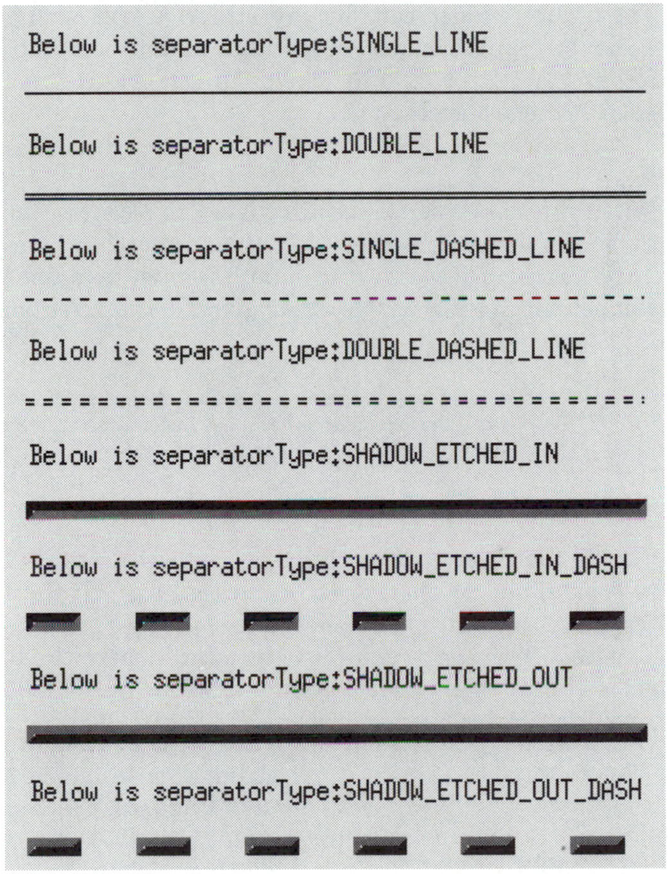

ScrolledWindow) then it is not necessary to include a Separator between that widget and the action button area (the ScrollBar already provides sufficient visual separation).

11.3 The Label Widget and Gadget

You've seen the Label widget used in many of the examples in previous chapters. Typically, it is used to caption control widgets or provide titles. Sometimes it is used to provide messages to the user (although an insensitive TextField is often used for this purpose as well). You create Label widgets or gadgets using:

```
XUlabel variable $parent [resource:value ...]
XUlabelgadget variable $parent [resource:value ...]
```

The Label widget can display either a text string or a pixmap. The resource labelType determines which kind of data the Label will display; it can be set to either STRING or PIXMAP (the default is STRING). The following sections describe each of these choices.

String Labels

When the labelType resource is set to STRING, the Label displays text. The text to be displayed is stored in the labelString resource. If you do not set the labelString resource, the default text is the name of the widget (which is the last component of the variable name given to the XUlabel call). The text may be multi-line.

> A good way to create a multiline Label is to use the dtksh ANSI string feature, using the \n notation for a newline character. To create an ANSI string, use single quotes prefixed by a dollar sign, like this:
>
> ```
> XUlabel LABEL $PARENT labelString:$'First line\nSecond line'
> ```

The font used to draw the text is stored in the fontList resource, and its color is determined by the foreground resource. If the Label widget is insensitive, its text takes on a stippled appearance.

The alignment resource determines where the text is drawn within the boundaries of the Label widget. It may take one of the following values:

ALIGNMENT_BEGINNING   The text is aligned at the beginning of the text string. For languages that read from left to right (like English), this means the text is left-aligned.

ALIGNMENT_CENTER   The text is centered.

ALIGNMENT_END   The text is aligned at the end of the text string. For languages that read left to right, this means the text is right-aligned.

Spacing in the Label is controlled by several other resources that determine margins of whitespace around the Label's text. The resource marginHeight specifies an equal amount of whitespace that should be placed at the top and bottom edges of the Label, and marginWidth similarly specifies an equal amount of space to be placed at the left and right edges. In addition to these margins, more space may be specified at any desired edge by setting any combination of `marginTop`, `margin-Bottom`, `marginLeft`, and `marginRight`. See Figure 11-2.

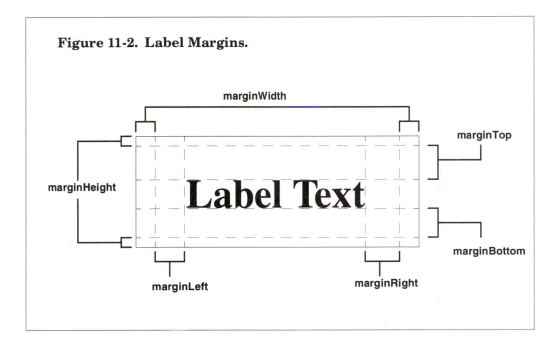

Figure 11-2. Label Margins.

If the Label's text is changed after the Label is created, then it will recalculate the amount of space it needs and request a geometry change from its parent. This behavior can be disabled by setting the resource `recomputeSize` to `false`. In that case, the Label will retain its original size regardless of changes to its `labelString` (or other resources that might affect size, such as `fontList`).

Pixmap Labels

When `labelType` is set to `PIXMAP`, the Label widget can display an image. In that case, the `labelPixmap` resource specifies a path to a Pixmap or Bitmap file that contains the image to be displayed when the Label is sensitive. Similarly, `labelInsensitivePixmap` specifies a path to a Pixmap or Bitmap to be displayed when the Label is insensitive.

> Pixmap and Bitmap format images can be created using the CDE `dticon` utility.

Listing 11-1 shows how to display an image using a Label. When the button is pressed, the Label is toggled from sensitive to insensitive (or vice versa). The two output states are shown in Figure 11-3.

Listing 11-1. A Pixmap Label (labelpix.sh).

```
. $XUTILDIR/xutil.sh

function togglesensitiveCB {
    if XUissensitive $LABEL
    then XUinsensitive $LABEL
    else XUsensitive $LABEL
    fi
}

XUinitialize TOPLEVEL Labelpix "$@"
XUcolumn COL $TOPLEVEL
XUaddbuttons $COL \
    PUSH "Change Sensitivity" C togglesensitiveCB

XUlabel LABEL $COL \
    labelType:PIXMAP \
    labelPixmap:./smiley.bmp \
    labelInsensitivePixmap:./frowny.bmp

XUrealize $TOPLEVEL
XUmainloop
```

Figure 11-3. Output of labelpix.sh. On the left, the program before pressing the button displays the default pixmap. On the right, the insensitive pixmap is displayed after pressing the button.

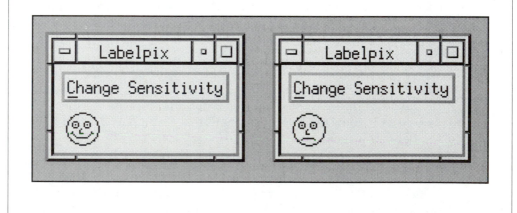

When displaying pixmaps, the resources `marginWidth`, `marginHeight`, `margin-Top`, `marginBottom`, `marginLeft`, `marginRight`, and `recomputeSize` also work as described in the previous section.

Label Widget Pitfalls

When used inside a RowColumn widget, the RowColumn's `entryAlignment` resource will override any Label child's `alignment` resource. To turn off this behavior, set the RowColumn's `isAligned` resource to false.

11.4 The Frame Widget

The Frame widget is a very simple manager. It draws a border around one child (called the work area child). It is often used with a RowColumn widget as its child, because the RowColumn widget is not able to draw a border. You can add additional children to the Frame widget to be used as titles for the work area child (these are called title children). You create a Frame widget using the command:

```
XUframe variable $parent [resource:value ...]
```

The Frame widget's `marginHeight` and `marginWidth` resources can be used to specify additional whitespace between the work area child and the edges of the border the Frame provides. By default, both are 0.

The appearance of the border can be selected by setting the `shadowType` resource to one of these values:

`SHADOW_IN`	Make the Frame border appear to be set into the screen.
`SHADOW_OUT`	Make the Frame border appear to be popping out of the screen.
`SHADOW_ETCHED_IN`	A double line is drawn for the border that appears to be etched into the screen.
`SHADOW_ETCHED_OUT`	A double line is drawn that appears to be coming out of the screen.

See Figure 11-4 for an illustration of these shadow types.

Creating a Title Child

In the simplest use of a Frame widget, a single work area child is created and the Frame provides it a border. However, an additional child can be added to provide a title (other children can be created that are not displayed).

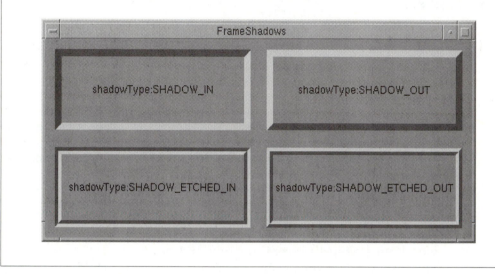

Figure 11-4. Frame Shadow Types (frmshdw.sh). Several different settings of the `shadowType` resource. For illustration purposes, I used an
unusually large setting for `shadowThickness` (8 pixels).

The title child is distinguished from the work area child using a constraint resource called `childType`. This resource can be set to one of the following values:

`FRAME_WORKAREA_CHILD`	The default setting, which specifies the child is the work area. There can be only one child of this type.
`FRAME_TITLE_CHILD`	The child is a title.
`FRAME_GENERIC_CHILD`	The child will not be displayed by the Frame widget. This is useful when you might display one of several different children in a Frame. You can select the child to display by changing which child is of type `FRAME_WORKAREA_CHILD`.

By default, the title child is placed on the top border line, centered vertically around
the shadow and aligned to the left edge of the Frame. This default placement of the
title child can be changed by setting several other constraint resources.

Placement of the Title

The constraint resource `childHorizontalAlignment` can be set to one of the values: `ALIGNMENT_BEGINNING`, `ALIGNMENT_CENTER`, or `ALIGNMENT_END`, with

meanings similar to those described above for the Label widget. The default is
`ALIGNMENT_BEGINNING`.

The resource `childHorizontalSpacing` controls how much whitespace should
be provided between the left and right edges of the title and the edges of the Frame's
border. The default is the same as the Frame's `marginWidth`.

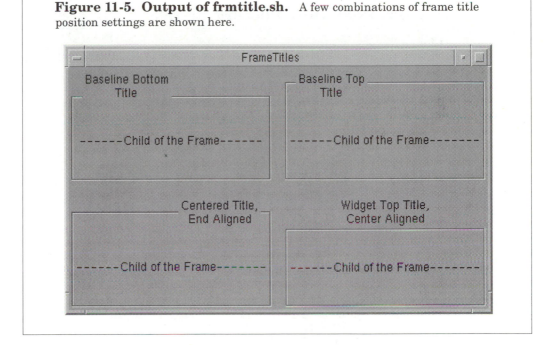

Figure 11-5. Output of frmtitle.sh. A few combinations of frame title
position settings are shown here.

The resource `childVerticalAlignment` changes the vertical position of the title child. It can be set to one of these values:

`ALIGNMENT_BASELINE_BOTTOM`	The baseline of the bottom line of text aligns vertically with the Frame's top shadow.
`ALIGNMENT_BASELINE_TOP`	The baseline of the first line of the title's text aligns with the Frame's top shadow.
`ALIGNMENT_WIDGET_TOP`	The top of the title area aligns with the top shadow of the Frame.
`ALIGNMENT_CENTER`	The title is vertically centered with the Frame's top shadow.

ALIGNMENT_WIDGET_BOTTOM The title's bottom edge is aligned vertically with the Frame's top shadow.

Note that the title child is assumed to be of a textual type (Label, TextField, or Text widget or gadgets) if one of the baseline vertical alignments is selected.

Listing 11-2 shows how to make Frame widgets with several different kinds of titles. Figure 11-5 shows the output of this program.

Listing 11-2. Frames with Titles (frmtitle.sh).

```
. $XUTILDIR/xutil.sh

XUinitialize TOPLEVEL FrameTitles "$@"

XUrow ROW $TOPLEVEL \
    packing:PACK_COLUMN numColumns:2 \
    spacing:16

XUframe BASEBOT $ROW
XUlabel BASEBOT.CHILD $BASEBOT \
    labelString:$'\n\n------Child of the Frame------\n\n'
XUlabel BASEBOT.TITLE $BASEBOT \
    labelString:$'Baseline Bottom\nTitle' \
    childType:FRAME_TITLE_CHILD \
    childVerticalAlignment:ALIGNMENT_BASELINE_BOTTOM

XUframe BASETOP $ROW
XUlabel BASETOP.CHILD $BASETOP \
    labelString:$'\n\n------Child of the Frame-------\n\n'
XUlabel BASEBOT.TITLE $BASETOP \
    labelString:$'Baseline Top\nTitle' \
    childType:FRAME_TITLE_CHILD \
    childVerticalAlignment:ALIGNMENT_BASELINE_TOP

XUframe CENTER $ROW
XUlabel CENTER.CHILD $CENTER \
    labelString:$'\n\n------Child of the Frame-------\n\n'
XUlabel CENTER.TITLE $CENTER \
    labelString:$'Centered Title,\nEnd Aligned' \
    childType:FRAME_TITLE_CHILD \
    childVerticalAlignment:ALIGNMENT_CENTER \
    childHorizontalAlignment:ALIGNMENT_END

XUframe WIDTOP $ROW
XUlabel WIDTOP.CHILD $WIDTOP \
    labelString:$'\n\n------Child of the Frame-------\n\n'
XUlabel WIDTOP.TITLE $WIDTOP \
    labelString:$'Widget Top Title,\nCenter Aligned' \
```

```
            childType:FRAME_TITLE_CHILD \
            childVerticalAlignment:ALIGNMENT_WIDGET_TOP \
            childHorizontalAlignment:ALIGNMENT_CENTER

   XUrealize $TOPLEVEL
   XUmainloop
```

Frame Widget Pitfalls

The Frame widget is reasonably foolproof; just make sure you create at most one work area child (no constraint resources need be set on the work area) and at most one title child.

11.5 Summary

The Separator widget and gadget can be used to provide a simple horizontal or vertical line in a dialog to separate items visually.

The Label widget is often used to provide captions and titles. It can display either a text string or a pixmap. Various resources are available to control the margins and alignment of the data displayed.

The Frame widget provides a border around one child, called the work area child. It may also have another child, called the title child, which provides a title at the top of the border. The `childType` constraint resource is used to set which child is the work area and which is the title. Other constraint resources can be set on the title child to select its margins, alignment, and vertical placement relative to the top shadow.

12 *Button, Button*

12.1 Introduction

Buttons are widely used in graphical programs. They are easy for the user to understand: you push a button and something happens, it's that simple. You've already seen several simple examples of buttons in previous chapters (PushButtons and ToggleButtons). In this chapter, you'll be introduced to some new kinds of buttons and you'll learn some new ways to use the buttons you've already seen. This chapter will teach you:

- How to display pixmap images on PushButtons and ToggleButtons to create a "button bar"
- How to use ArrowButtons to display a directional arrow
- How to create a set of ToggleButtons so that only one button is selected at a time
- How to create a set of ToggleButtons in which any combination of buttons can be selected.

Besides these uses, Buttons are employed in various kinds of menus. Those uses are discussed in Chapter 13, *Menu, Please*. This chapter concentrates on uses of buttons in a free-standing mode. Some buttons behave differently when they are in a menu, and I will point out cases like that in this chapter, deferring an in-depth description of the special behavior until the next chapter.

12.2 The PushButton Widget and Gadget

PushButton widgets and gadgets look and function identically, and in the descriptions that follow anything I describe for the "PushButton widget" should be assumed to apply equally to the gadget form unless specially noted.

The PushButton widget is a subclass of the Label widget. A PushButton displays either a text string or pixmap inside a shadowed border. When the user clicks the mouse button while the pointer is within a PushButton, its `activateCallback` is executed. This is the primary use of the PushButton. You can create PushButton widgets and gadgets using these commands:

```
XUpushbutton variable $parent [resource:value ...]
XUpushbuttongadget variable $parent [resource:value ...]
```

These work like all the other widget creation commands you have seen.

PushButton Appearance Resources

Because it is a subclass of Label, the PushButton supports all the resources of Label, including:

- `labelType`. This specifies whether the PushButton displays a text string or a pixmap image. It can be set to PIXMAP or STRING (which is the default).

- `labelString`. If `labelType` is set to STRING, this resource holds the text to be displayed. The text may be multiline.

  > A convenient way to specify a multiline string in dtksh is to use the notation for an ANSI string (single quotes prefixed by a dollar sign), and use the \n notation for a newline character: `labelString:$'first line\nSecond line'`

- `labelPixmap`. If `labelType` is set to PIXMAP, this resource should be set to a path to a pixmap definition file.

- `mnemonic`. This is a single character that can be used to select the button without using the mouse pointer *when it is in a menu*. On most keyboards, pressing ALT+*mnemonic* will activate the button. The mnemonic will appear underlined if `labelType` is STRING. Note: mnemonics only work inside MenuBar widgets.

Other less commonly used Label resources are also available: `recomputeSize`, `alignment`, `marginWidth`, `marginHeight`, `marginTop`, `marginBottom`, `marginLeft`, and `marginRight`. See *The Label Widget and Gadget* on page 247 for more details.

In addition to the resources inherited from Label, the PushButton defines some other resources that affect its appearance:

armPixmap   If `labelType` is PIXMAP, this resource specifies a pixmap file to display when the user presses and holds the mouse button while the pointer is on the PushButton.

fillOnArm   If set to true (the default) then the background of the Push-
                     Button is filled with the color specified by armColor (as dis-
                     cussed later) when the user presses and holds the mouse
                     button while the pointer is in the PushButton.

armColor   The color used to fill the PushButton if fillOnArm is set to
                     true. The default is a color halfway between the colors used
                     for the shadows around the PushButton.

showAsDefault   If set to a value greater than zero (default is 0), then the but-
                     ton will take on the appearance of a default button; its border
                     will become wider. If the resource defaultButtonShad-
                     owThickness is nonzero, then that resource specifies the
                     amount of extra space to leave around the button, otherwise
                     the value in showAsDefault is used.

In general, resources such as armColor and defaultButtonShadowThickness
should be set in resource files rather then being hard-coded in the application.

The showAsDefault resource is usually not set directly by programmers. It is
used by the BulletinBoard and Form widgets when a button handle is specified in
their defaultButton resource. Those manager widgets take care of activating the
default button when the ENTER key is pressed.

Creating Multiple Buttons

Often a program needs to create several buttons with a common parent. Also, when
you create buttons, you usually only need to specify a few resources such as the
labelString, mnemonic, and the action to occur when the button is pressed. The
XU library provides a command to fill this need:

```
XUaddbuttons $parent [variable label command ...]
```

This command's first argument is the *parent* for the buttons. Further arguments
are in sets of three. The first in each set is a *variable* name, which will receive the
widget handle of the new button, the second item is the *label* to display on the button. The final argument of each set of three is an arbitrary dtksh *command* that will
be executed when the button is selected.

In addition, the XU library provides a similar function for creating buttons that
will display a pixmap instead of a text label:

```
XUaddpixbuttons $parent [variable pixmap command ...]
```

This function takes the handle of the buttons' *parent* as its first argument, then
sets of three arguments that specify a *variable* name to receive the button's handle, a path to a *pixmap* file, and a dtksh *command* to execute when the button is
activated.

Listing 12-1 shows an example that creates several buttons in a column stacking RowColumn widget using `XUaddbuttons` and `XUaddpixbuttons`. The resulting output is shown in Figure 12-1.

Figure 12-1. PushButton Sampler (pushbut.sh).

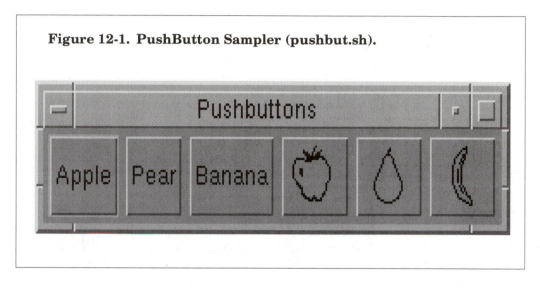

Listing 12-1. Creating PushButtons (pushbut.sh).

```
. $XUTILDIR/xutil.sh

XUinitialize TOPLEVEL Pushbuttons "$@"
XUrow ROW $TOPLEVEL

XUaddbuttons $ROW \
    BUTTON1 "Apple"  "print Apple" \
    BUTTON2 "Pear"   "print Pear" \
    BUTTON3 "Banana" "print Banana"
XUaddpixbuttons $ROW \
    BUTTON4 "$XUTILDIR/bitmaps/apple.bmp"  "print Apple" \
    BUTTON5 "$XUTILDIR/bitmaps/pear.bmp"   "print Pear" \
    BUTTON6 "$XUTILDIR/bitmaps/banana.bmp" "print Banana"

XUrealize $TOPLEVEL
XUmainloop
```

PushButton Callbacks

You're already familiar with `activateCallback`, which specifies functions to call when the user clicks the mouse on the PushButton. Two other callbacks are available for the PushButton that are occasionally useful:

armCallback   Specifies commands to call at the moment the user presses
                         the mouse button while the pointer is in the PushButton.

disarmCallback   Specifies commands to execute when the user releases the
                         mouse button following an arm. The release could be either
                         while the pointer is still inside the PushButton (in which
                         case an activate would have occurred), or it could occur
                         after the user has moved the pointer outside the PushBut-
                         ton while holding down the mouse button (in which case no
                         activate would occur).

If the user presses and releases (i.e., clicks) the mouse button in the PushButton, all
three callbacks—arm, activate, and disarm—will be executed (in that order). If the
user were to press the mouse button and hold it while within the PushButton, but
then move the mouse pointer outside the PushButton before releasing it, then the
arm and disarm callbacks would be executed, but not the activate callback.

Call Data During PushButton Callbacks

While any of the functions associated with the arm, activate, or disarm callback is
executing, the following useful variables are defined:

- CB_CALL_DATA.REASON

  This specifies which kind of callback is executing, and will be set to one of
  CR_ACTIVATE, CR_ARM, or CR_DISARM. This is useful because it allows you
  to write a single function and register it with any combination of these callbacks—your function can tell which kind of callback event triggered its execution by testing this variable.

- CB_CALL_DATA.EVENT.XBUTTON.STATE

  > Actually, many subfields of CB_CALL_DATA.EVENT are defined during execution of
  > these callbacks. I am showing you this one in particular because it is most often
  > useful. See Chapter 19, *Events, Translations, etc.* for complete details.

  This variable indicates which mouse button was used for the selection and
  whether any modifier keys such as SHIFT, CONTROL, or ALT were used in
  conjunction with the button press. This variable is composed of subfields
  separated by the pipe (|) symbol. So, for example, if the activateCall-
  back was invoked because the user clicked the PushButton using mouse
  button one while the Shift key was being held down, then this variable
  would be set to the value: Button1Mask|ShiftMask. Similarly, if the
  CONTROL key were pressed down then one of the subfields would be Con-
  trolMask. The ALT key is known as Mod1Mask. Multiple modifier keys can
  also be detected. If the user holds down both Shift and Control while click-

ing with mouse button one, this variable would be set to `Button1Mask|ShiftMask|ControlMask`.

> By default, only mouse button one can be used to select a PushButton. If a PushButton is contained in a RowColumn widget with certain settings, it is possible for other mouse buttons to trigger a PushButton.

During the execution of the `activateCallback` functions, the following variable is defined:

- `CB_CALL_DATA.CLICK_COUNT`

  If the PushButton resource `multiClick` is set to `MULTICLICK_KEEP` (the default when the button is not in a menu), then this variable will hold the number of clicks that have occurred within a specified time-out period.

  > The default time-out is 200 milliseconds, and you should not change it in your program since it is considered a user preference. For this reason dtksh does not provide a direct feature for changing this time interval.

  If the `multiClick` resource is set to `MULTICLICK_DISCARD` (the default when the PushButton is inside a menu) then `activateCallback` is never called on subsequent clicks inside the time-out period.

These call data values can be used to implement some different kinds of behavior for the PushButton widget, described in the following sections.

Multiple Click PushButtons

Sometimes it is desirable to require a double click to activate a PushButton. For example, if pressing the button will invoke some kind of time-consuming operation such as opening a large file, you may want to have a single click on the button display the size of the file, then only open the file on a double click.

This is easily accomplished by setting the `multiClick` resource to `MULTICLICK_KEEP` (which is the default as long as the button is not in a menu) then writing your activate callback function so it tests the value of `CB_CALL_DATA.CLICK_COUNT` to determine which action to perform. Listing 12-2 shows how this is done. A RowColumn widget is created and filled with buttons representing files in the current directory. If a button is clicked once, then the size of the file is displayed in a Label. If a button is multi-clicked within the multi-click time interval, then an `xterm` process is spawned to edit the file. The resulting output is shown in Figure 12-2.

Listing 12-2. Multiple Click Buttons (pbclick.sh).

```
. $XUTILDIR/xutil.sh

function showfileCB {
    typeset button=$1 file
```

```
        XUget $button labelString:file

        # If this is a single click, then show the size
        # of the file in the message area, else start
        # an xterm to edit the file

        if (( CB_CALL_DATA.CLICK_COUNT == 1 ))
        then
            XUset $MESSAGE labelString:"$(wc -c $file)"
        else
            xterm -e ${EDITOR:-vi} "$file" &
        fi
}

XUinitialize TOPLEVEL Pbclick "$@"
XUcolumn COL $TOPLEVEL

# Create a label to hold the file size message
XUlabel MESSAGE $COL labelString:" "

XUrow FILES $COL \
    packing:PACK_COLUMN numColumns:8

# For each readable file in the current directory,
# create a PushButton containing its name

for file in *
do
    if [[ -r $file ]] && [[ ! -d $file ]]
    then
        XUpushbutton tmp $FILES \
            labelString:"$file"
        XUaddcallback $tmp activateCallback "showfileCB $tmp"
    fi
done

XUrealize $TOPLEVEL
XUmainloop
```

Problems with Multiple Clicks

There is no convenient way to avoid executing the single-click action of a button that also has a multiple-click behavior. That's because the `activateCallback` will be called both on the first click and the subsequent click. In the example shown earlier, this did not matter since the single-click action simply updated a Label on the screen to show a file size.

Figure 12-2. Output of pbclick.sh. A single click on a button displays the size of the selected file, whereas a double click spawns an xterm process to edit the selected file (not shown).

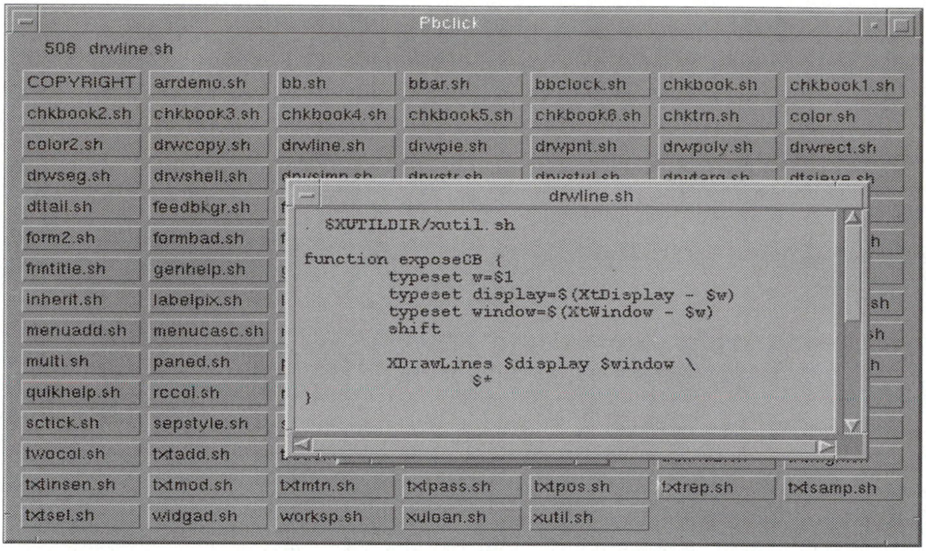

For this reason, it is a bad idea to use the number of clicks to choose between two radically different behaviors. My advice is to use the single-click selection for some fast, innocuous purpose (or don't use it at all), and use the multi-click selection for a more meaningful (possibly time-consuming) operation. Also note that your single-click callback must execute very quickly, otherwise it will delay the second button click outside the default detection range of 200 milliseconds, and the user will find it very difficult to execute the multi-click action.

Many users dislike using multiple clicks and find it nonintuitive. Your help screens and documentation must be sure to mention any special actions executed by multiple clicks.

Using Modifier Keys with PushButtons

In some cases you may want a PushButton to execute a slightly modified version of its usual action. For example, let's say you've got a button that when pressed copies a file from one directory to another. It might be convenient if that same button could be used for a "move" operation, which is very similar to a copy (it would save space on the screen to do this instead of have a separate button for "move"). One solution would be to specify that depressing the SHIFT key down while pressing the button causes a move instead of a copy.

I will caution that overuse of this technique leads to cryptic, nonintuitive programs. If there is enough screen real estate to display two buttons rather than overloading a single button using modifier keys, that is preferable. You may also want to use a menu instead of a set of buttons if there are too many actions.

If you do decide to use a modifier key with a PushButton, the technique is quite simple. Inside your `activateCallback`, just test the value of the `CB_CALL_DATA.EVENT.XBUTTON.STATE` variable (yes, it's a long name) to see if the appropriate mask is included. Possible masks are `ShiftMask`, `ControlMask`, and `Mod1Mask` (for ALT). You must handle the case where there are multiple masks separated by the pipe (|) symbol. This is easy enough by using dtksh pattern matching tests.

Listing 12-3 shows a simple program that detects which modifier keys were used when a PushButton is activated. The list of modifier keys is displayed in a Label widget. Note that you can specify actions for any combination of modifiers (CONTROL plus ALT at the same time, for example). You should test each pattern separately in this case rather than relying on the pipe-separated items coming out in the same order each time. The resulting output from this program is shown in Figure 12-3 (following a shifted selection).

Listing 12-3. PushButton Modifier Keys (pbmod.sh).

```
. $XUTILDIR/xutil.sh

function pushCB {
    typeset modifiers=""
    typeset mask=${CB_CALL_DATA.EVENT.XBUTTON.STATE} # Save typing

    if [[ $mask == *ShiftMask* ]]
    then modifiers="$modifiers Shift"
    fi
    if [[ $mask == *ControlMask* ]]
    then modifiers="$modifiers Control"
    fi
    if [[ $mask == *Mod1Mask* ]]
    then modifiers="$modifiers Alt"
    fi
    XUset $MESSAGE labelString:"${modifiers:-None}"
}

XUinitialize TOPLEVEL Pbclick "$@"
XUcolumn COL $TOPLEVEL

# Create a label to hold the message
XUlabel MESSAGE $COL labelString:" "

XUpushbutton tmp $COL \
    labelString:$'Push me with\nControl, Alt, or Shift\n(or a combination)'
```

```
XUaddcallback $tmp activateCallback pushCB

XUrealize $TOPLEVEL
XUmainloop
```

Figure 12-3. Output of pbmod.sh.   The program as it appears after the
button is selected while holding down only the SHIFT key.

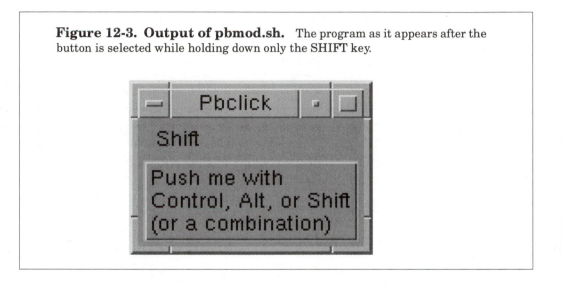

12.3 Creating a Button Bar

The MainWindow widget defines several standard areas such as a work area, menu
bar, and message area. It also defines something called the *command area* that sits
between the menu bar and work area. Traditionally, Motif programs used that area
for a Command widget (recall that a Command widget allows the user to type in
line-oriented commands to execute application functions and also provides a history
area with previous commands).

Very few modern programs provide a way to execute line-oriented commands, but
this area of the MainWindow is useful to provide a more popular feature: a *button
bar*. A button bar is simply a horizontal stack of pixmap style PushButtons. These
buttons can be used to execute actions that are also available in the menu bar
menus—they just provide a shortcut so users don't have to hunt for frequently used
commands in the menus.

It is quite simple to create such a feature by using XUaddpixbuttons. Actually,
the vast majority of the work is designing the pixmaps for the buttons. Quite a few
pixmaps are available in the public domain on the Internet and elsewhere, so you
may be able to use some existing designs rather than create your own from scratch.
Listing 12-4 shows an addition to the checkbook program that implements a simple
button bar. The resulting output is shown in Figure 12-4.

Figure 12-4. Checkbook with Button Bar (chkbook6.sh). Four
pixmap buttons are created that can execute functions found in the menus.
From left to right the pixmaps are Help, View Details, Delete, and New Check.

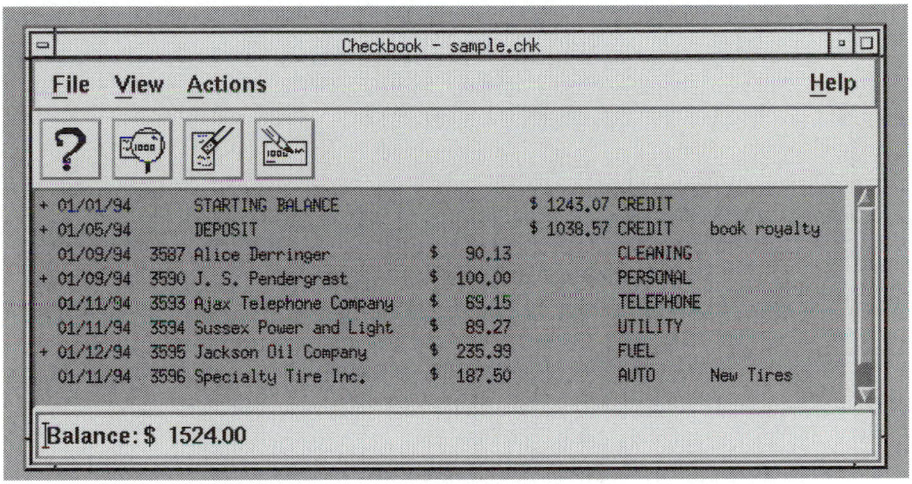

Listing 12-4. Checkbook ButtonBar (chkbook6.sh). This code was inserted in the
checkbook program in order to add a button bar. A row stacking parent (BB) is created as a
child of MAINWIN; pixmap buttons are added to it. Later, BB is registered as the commandWindow of MAINWIN using XUset.

```
XUrow BB $MAINWIN   # A button bar
XUaddpixbuttons $BB \
    BB.HELP    $XUTILDIR/bitmaps/help.bmp      "helpCB _hometopic" \
    BB.DETAILS $XUTILDIR/bitmaps/details.bmp   showdetailsCB \
    BB.DELETE  $XUTILDIR/bitmaps/delete.bmp    deleteCB \
    BB.ADD     $XUTILDIR/bitmaps/addcheck.bmp  addCB

XUset $MAINWIN \
    menuBar:$MB \
    workWindow:$WORK \
    messageWindow:$MESSAGE \
    commandWindow:$BB
```

12.4 The ArrowButton Widget and Gadget

The ArrowButton is quite similar to the PushButton. It displays a directional
arrow instead of a text label or pixmap. You would use it when an action has some

kind of directional meaning that would be conveyed by the ArrowButton's distinctive image. See Figure 12-5.

You can create ArrowButton widgets and gadgets using:

```
XUarrowbutton variable $parent [resource:value ...]
XUarrowbuttongadget variable $parent [resource:value ...]
```

There is no programming difference between the widget and gadget forms, and unless otherwise noted everything I describe next applies to both even though I will usually say "ArrowButton widget"

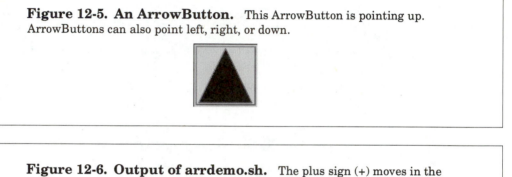

Figure 12-5. An ArrowButton.   This ArrowButton is pointing up. ArrowButtons can also point left, right, or down.

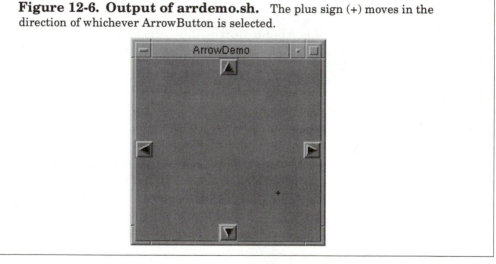

Figure 12-6. Output of arrdemo.sh.   The plus sign (+) moves in the direction of whichever ArrowButton is selected.

ArrowButton Resources

The ArrowButton is not a subclass of either the Label or the PushButton, but several of its resources and callbacks are similar. For example, it has an activate-Callback, armCallback, and disarmCallback that work identically to those of the PushButton (including the CB_CALL_DATA fields that are available). It also has a multiClick resource that works like the PushButton's.

Because it cannot display text (or a pixmap), it does not have resources such as `alignment`, `labelString`, `labelPixmap`, the various margins, etc.

The direction of the arrowhead is specified using the `arrowDirection` resource, which can be set to one of the following values: `ARROW_UP`, `ARROW_DOWN`, `ARROW_LEFT`, or `ARROW_RIGHT`.

A simple program that uses ArrowButton widgets is shown in Listing 12-5. Four ArrowButtons are created, one on each edge of a BulletinBoard. The `activateCall-back` of each is set up to move a Label widget within the confines of the BulletinBoard in each of the four directions indicated by their arrows. The resulting output is shown in Figure 12-5.

Listing 12-5. Using ArrowButtons (arrdemo.sh).

```
. $XUTILDIR/xutil.sh

function moveCB {
    integer curx cury
    XUget $TARGET x:curx y:cury
    case "$1" in
    up)      (( cury -= 10 )) ;;
    down)    (( cury += 10 )) ;;
    left)    (( curx -= 10 )) ;;
    right)   (( curx += 10 )) ;;
    esac
    XUset $TARGET x:$curx y:$cury
}

XUinitialize TOPLEVEL ArrowDemo "$@"

XUform FORM $TOPLEVEL borderWidth:0

XUarrowbutton LEFT $FORM \
    arrowDirection:ARROW_LEFT \
    $(XUattach toppos 45 bottompos 55 leftpos 0 rightpos 10)
XUaddcallback $LEFT activateCallback "moveCB left"

XUarrowbutton RIGHT $FORM \
    arrowDirection:ARROW_RIGHT \
    $(XUattach toppos 45 bottompos 55 leftpos 90 rightpos 100)
XUaddcallback $RIGHT activateCallback "moveCB right"

XUarrowbutton UP $FORM \
    arrowDirection:ARROW_UP \
    $(XUattach toppos 0 bottompos 10 leftpos 45 rightpos 55)
XUaddcallback $UP activateCallback "moveCB up"

XUarrowbutton DOWN $FORM \
    arrowDirection:ARROW_DOWN \
```

```
    $(XUattach toppos 90 bottompos 100 leftpos 45 rightpos 55)
XUaddcallback $DOWN activateCallback "moveCB down"

XUbulletinboard CANVAS $FORM \
    width:100 height:100 \
    $(XUattach toppos 12 bottompos 88 leftpos 12 rightpos 88)

XUlabel TARGET $CANVAS labelString:+ x:100 y:100

XUrealize $TOPLEVEL
XUmainloop
```

12.5 The ToggleButton Widget and Gadget

ToggleButtons are used to display an "on" or "off" state. Like PushButtons, they display a text string or pixmap label. However, they also contain a state indicator, a
small square or circular-shaped area to the left of the label. This state indicator can
be filled or check-marked to indicate that the ToggleButton is "on" or unfilled to
indicate "off." See Figure 12-5.

Figure 12-7. A Toggle Button.

State Indicator ————   Label

You can create ToggleButton widgets or gadgets using:

```
XUtogglebutton variable $parent [resource:value ...]
XUtogglebuttongadget variable $parent [resource:value ...]
```

These commands are just like any other widget creation commands provided by the
XU library.

ToggleButton Resources

Because it is a subclass of Label, the ToggleButton supports all the usual resources
for displaying text or pixmaps as described under *PushButton Appearance*

Resources on page 258. So, for example, you may set `labelString` to specify the text of a string label, or you could set `labelType` to `PIXMAP` and set `labelPixmap` to the path of a pixmap file. The ToggleButton also supports Label resources such as `alignment`, `marginWidth`, `marginHeight`, etc.

In addition, the ToggleButton has several resources that affect how its state indicator is displayed:

- `visibleWhenOff` specifies whether the state indicator should appear when the ToggleButton is in the off state. When the ToggleButton is in a menu, the default is `false`, otherwise it is `true`.

- `indicatorOn` specifies whether an indicator should appear at all. The default is `true`. If this is set to `false`, then the selected state is indicated by switching the shadow colors. On most displays, it is difficult to tell the difference, so I recommend you never set this to `false`.

- `fillOnSelect` is used to determine whether the indicator should be filled in with the color specified in the `selectColor` resource when the state is on (*selected* is another term used to indicate "on"). The default is the same as the setting of `indicatorOn` at widget creation time.

  > If you set `indicatorOn` to `false` and explicitly set `fillOnSelect` to `true`, then the `selectColor` will fill the entire background of the ToggleButton when it is selected.

- `selectColor`. See `fillOnSelect` entry. The `selectColor` defaults to a color half way between the two shadow colors. On many display devices this is not enough of a color change to really see the difference, so I suggest you use black instead (in your application's resource file, set:

  ```
  *selectColor: black
  ```

- `indicatorSize` specifies the size of the state indicator. By default a pleasing size is calculated based on the size of the label string or pixmap.

- `spacing` indicates the amount of space between the indicator and the label string or pixmap. The default is 4 pixels.

- `selectPixmap` and `selectInsensitivePixmap` can be used if `labelType` is `PIXMAP` to set a different pixmap to be displayed when the Toggle-Button is selected and either sensitive or insensitive, respectively.

- `set` is a boolean resource that indicates the ToggleButton's state. A value of `true` indicates that the ToggleButton state is on (selected).

Using these resources is straightforward. A simple program that displays some different combinations of settings is presented in Listing 12-6, with the resulting output shown in Figure 12-8.

Listing 12-6. Toggle Button Appearance (toggles.sh).

```
. $XUTILDIR/xutil.sh

XUinitialize TOPLEVEL Toggles "$@"
```

```
XUcolumn COL $TOPLEVEL

# ToggleButton using all defaults
XUtogglebutton NORMAL $COL \
    labelString:"All Defaults" set:true

# ToggleButton using visibleWhenOff:false
XUtogglebutton tmp $COL \
    labelString:"visibleWhenOff:false" \
    visibleWhenOff:false

# Pixmap ToggleButton using different pixmaps
# for selected vs. unselected
XUtogglebutton tmp $COL \
    labelType:PIXMAP \
    labelPixmap:"$XUTILDIR/bitmaps/frowny.bmp" \
    selectPixmap:"$XUTILDIR/bitmaps/smiley.bmp"

# Use background fill instead of indicator
XUtogglebutton tmp $COL \
    labelString:"Background Fill" \
    indicatorOn:false \
    fillOnSelect:true
XUrealize $TOPLEVEL
XUmainloop
```

Toggle Button Callbacks

Like the PushButton widget, the ToggleButton has an `armCallback` and `disarm-Callback`. However, instead of an `activateCallback`, the ToggleButton executes a callback named `valueChangedCallback` when it is selected.

The following call data variables are set during the scope of functions registered for any of these callbacks:

- `CB_CALL_DATA.REASON`

  This is set to `CR_ARM`, `CR_DISARM` or `CR_VALUE_CHANGED`, and indicates which type of callback invoked the function.

- `CB_CALL_DATA.SET`

  This holds the current state of the ToggleButton, and can either be the string `true` or `false`.

- `CB_CALL_DATA.EVENT`

  This variable has subfields that describe the X event that triggered the call-back. Events are discussed in Chapter 19, *Events, Translations, etc.* These values are rarely of use with the ToggleButton.

The previous example shows how the `valueChangedCallback` is used.

Figure 12-8. Output of toggles.sh. On the left, the program as it appears when all the buttons are "on." On the right, the appearance when all buttons are "off." From top to bottom: a ToggleButton created using only resource defaults, a ToggleButton with `visibleWhenOff` set to false (note the indicator does not appear on the right), a ToggleButton using a different `selectPixmap`, and a Togglebutton that uses a background color change instead of an indicator.

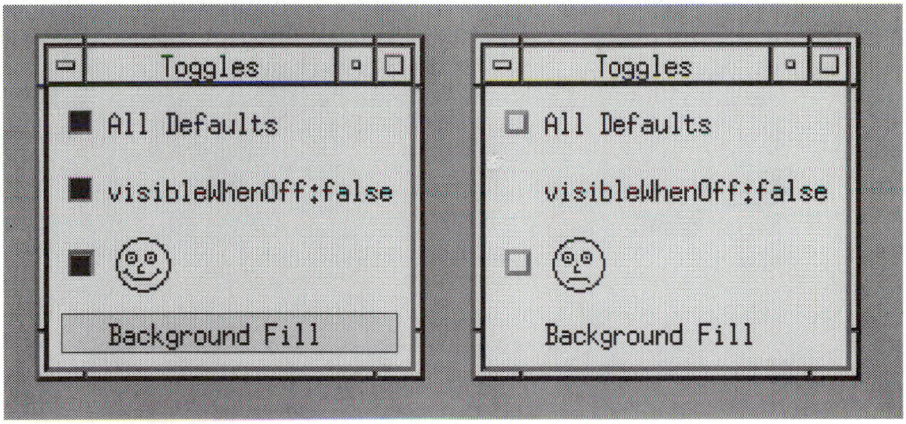

One thing to keep in mind is that in many cases the ToggleButton is used without even setting the `valueChangedCallback`. For example, when the ToggleButton is being used in a dialog to prompt for a yes/no value, there is no particular need to set any callbacks. When the dialog's OK button is selected, the ToggleButton can be queried for its state by using `XUget` on the `set` resource. You only need to set callbacks on a ToggleButton when you need some kind of side effect to occur when its state changes.

12.6 RadioButtons

As briefly mentioned before, the ToggleButton can be used as a way to select one of several choices. In this mode, the state indicator is changed to a circle. When the user selects one ToggleButton, the previously selected button automatically turns to the "off" state. The logic necessary to ensure that only one ToggleButton indicator is selected at a time is provided by a RadioBox manager widget (this is actually just a RowColumn widget with certain resource settings). When ToggleButton widgets are placed inside a RadioBox, they are termed RadioButtons.

You can create a RadioBox widget using the command:

```
XUradiobox variable $parent [resource:value ...]
```

Because it is just a specialized RowColumn, the RadioBox stacks its ToggleButton children in rows and columns. The `orientation` resource can be used to select either a `HORIZONTAL` or `VERTICAL` stacking. See *The RowColumn Widget* on page 171 for other ways of stacking children using a RowColumn widget.

The XU library provides a convenient function for adding multiple ToggleButton widgets to a single parent (such as a RadioBox):

```
XUaddtogglebuttons $parent [variable label command ...]
```

Like `XUaddbuttons`, this command's first argument is the handle of the parent to which the buttons are being added, and the rest of the arguments are in sets of three, one set per button. The first of each set is the name of a *variable* that will receive the handle of the newly created button, the second is the *label* that should appear on the button, and the last is a *command* that will be registered with the `valueChangedCallback`. You can use the dtksh colon command (`:`) which does nothing if you don't need a `valueChangedCallback`.

So, to create a set of RadioButtons that would allow the user to select one fruit from a list of choices, you could use this code:

```
XUradiobox RADIO $TOPLEVEL
XUaddtogglebuttons $RADIO \
    APPLETOG "Apple" : \
    PEACHTOG "Peach" : \
    PEARTOG  "Pear"  : \
    KIWITOG  "Kiwi"  :
```

The output produced by this piece of code (which is a part of a larger program called `togradio.sh` in the examples directory) is shown in Figure 12-9.

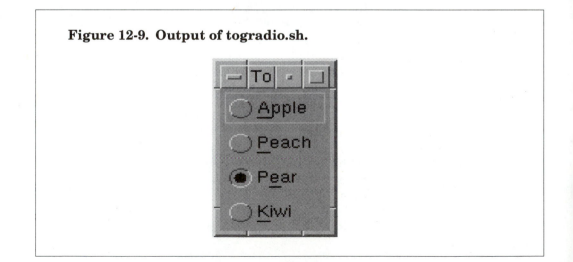

Figure 12-9. Output of togradio.sh.

The valueChangedCallback in RadioBoxes

When ToggleButtons are in a RadioBox, the manager automatically ensures that only one button is selected at a time. If the user selects a button, any previously selected button is set to off automatically. One mistake that many novice Motif programmers make is forgetting that any `valueChangedCallback` is triggered for *both* the old button and the newly selected button (it makes sense when you think about it, both buttons' values are changing after all).

You may need to check the `CB_CALL_DATA.SET` variable in your `valueChangedCallback` to see if the callback was triggered because the value is changing to off (it will be set to `false` in that case).

Setting the RadioButton State Programmatically

There are times when you need to set which ToggleButton is selected in a RadioBox. If you were simply to use `XUset` to change the `set` resource of one of the buttons to `true`, you will be disappointed to find that the state of the previously selected ToggleButton does not automatically change to `false`. You will end up with two buttons selected at the same time, clearly not what you desire.

The XU library provides a function that will set the state of a ToggleButton such that the one-of-many property is kept up to date:

```
XUtogglebuttonsetstate $widget [true|false]
```

In this command, `$widget` specifies the handle of the ToggleButton widget to change. The next argument is either `true` or `false`, and specifies the desired state of the ToggleButton. If the call results in a state change, then the `valueChangedCallback` of the named button is also triggered. It is as if the user actually pressed the named button to select the desired state.

In the previous example of selecting one of several fruits, we could insert this line of code following the `XUaddtogglebuttons` command to make "Pear" the selected item:

```
XUtogglebuttonsetstate $PEARTOG true
```

Forcing One Selected Button

The RadioBox resource `radioAlwaysOne` can be set to `true` to force one button to always be selected in the RadioBox. The default `value` is true. If you set this resource to false, then the user may click the current selection to toggle it off, leaving the RadioBox with no selected items. Note that this is a resource of the RadioBox, not the ToggleButtons, for example:

```
XUradiobox RADIO $TOPLEVEL radioAlwaysOne:false
```

Note that even if `radioAlwaysOne` is set to `true`, it is possible for the programmer to cause a situation in which there is no selected button. For example, you could unmanage the current selection, or destroy it, or use XUset to turn the current selection off explicitly.

12.7 CheckBoxes

Sometimes a plain RowColumn widget that contains several-of-many style Toggle-Buttons is called a CheckBox. The XU library provides two functions that allow you to create RowColumn widgets that stack children either horizontally or vertically that are suitable for this purpose:

```
XUrow variable $parent [resource:value ...]
XUcolumn variable $parent [resource:value ...]
```

These commands were explained in detail previously, see *Single Rows and Columns* on page 171.

After creating the desired orientation of RowColumn, you can simply attach the ToggleButtons to it using the previously discussed XUaddtogglebuttons command. Because these commands do not configure the RowColumn widget as a Ra-dioBox, any number of the ToggleButtons contained in it can be selected at once. This kind of arrangement is used when the user may select several choices simulta-neously.

As before, you can use the valueChangedCallback of each ToggleButton to per-form side effects.

12.8 The DrawnButton Widget

There is yet another button variation called the DrawnButton widget. This widget acts a lot like a PushButton, but it does not define any kind of label to display. It leaves a blank "canvas" for the programmer to draw whatever is desired on the but-ton. Arbitrary drawing on such a widget is an advanced topic and is discussed in Chapter 18, *Xlib: Low-Level Graphics*.

12.9 Summary

Buttons are simple for users to understand and use, and so are a popular method of allowing users to trigger actions.

PushButtons are used to execute an action on demand. They may display either text string labels or pixmap graphics. It is possible to define a different behavior for buttons selected with multiple clicks, and it is possible to detect when a modifier key such as SHIFT or CONTROL has been pressed while the button is selected to pro-vide alternate button actions.

The ArrowButton is similar to a PushButton, but it displays a directional arrow-head instead of text or a pixmap. The arrow can be made to point up, down, left, or right. It is used when there is a directional meaning to the action to be performed.

ToggleButtons are used to display an "on" or "off" state. They have a state indicator area, which is a small diamond or square next to their label (or pixmap). If this area is filled in, then the ToggleButton is said to be "on" or "selected."

When ToggleButtons are created inside a RadioBox widget (actually a RowColumn with certain resource settings), then only one button can be selected at a time. If the user selects a button, any previously selected button is automatically unselected.

13   *Menu, Please*

13.1 Introduction

Motif provides several different types of menus that are useful in diverse situations. You've already seen how to create simple systems of PullDownMenus in Chapter 4, *The Standard Main Window*, and you've learned how to create OptionMenus in Chapter 6, *Prompting Using Custom Dialogs*. In this chapter, I'll go into more depth on those kinds of menus, and I'll show you how to use another kind of menu: the PopupMenu (it is displayed by an application-defined event instead of a button widget). The topics discussed include:

- How to create PullDownMenus containing ToggleButtons
- How to create multilevel cascading menus
- Registering accelerators and mnemonics on menu items
- Creating tear-off menus
- How to create and use OptionMenus
- How to create, trigger, and position Popup menus.

13.2 PullDown Menus

In Chapter 4, *The Standard Main Window*, you learned how to use the `XUmenusys-tem` command to create a PullDownMenu system. Recall from Chapter 4, *The Standard Main Window* that this command has the following syntax:

```
XUmenusystem $menubar [variable label mnemonic action ...]
```

where the first argument is the handle of a MenuBar widget, and further arguments are sets of four that define menu items:

279

1. A *variable* that will receive the widget handle of the new menu item
2. A *label* that will appear on the menu
3. A single-character *mnemonic* that can be used to select the item without using the mouse
4. An *action* that is either a dtksh command to execute when the item is selected or a curly brace delimited group of further sets of four arguments of the same format that creates a cascading menu

In addition, if the set of four arguments is composed of four dashes (-), then a Separator is inserted at that point in the PullDown menu. If you don't recall these concepts, you should refresh your memory by looking over the examples presented in *The XUmenusystem Command* on page 56.

Multilevel Cascades

The XUmenusystem command allows multilevel cascading menus. This is accomplished by specifying a curly brace enclosed set of arguments instead of an action command. Such items will appear with an arrow next to them; when the user selects such an item, another level of menu will appear to the right of the item (this is sometimes called a *pull right* menu). Cascading menus can continue in this fashion for any number of levels, although it is considered poor style to nest more than two or three levels of menu.

The code presented in Listing 13-1 produces several regular menu items and one multilevel cascading button. The Print menu item has an opening curly brace instead of an action command; more sets of arguments are contained between that curly brace and the matching close curly brace. I indented this set of braces in the code to make the level of menu clear. An example of how this menu looks with the Print menu item expanded is shown in Figure 13-1.

Listing 13-1. A Multiple Level Cascade (menucasc.sh).

```
. $XUTILDIR/xutil.sh

XUinitialize TOPLEVEL MenuCasc "$@"

XUcolumn COL $TOPLEVEL
XUmenubar MB $COL
XUlabel LAB $COL labelString:$'\n\nA Menu With Cascades\n\n'

XUmenusystem $MB \
    FILE "File" F { \
            MB.OPEN    "Open"    O    openCB \
            MB.CLOSE   "Close"   C    closeCB \
            MB.PRINT   "Print"   P  { \
                MB.PRDEF "to default printer" t printdefCB \
                MB.PRCH  "choose printer..."  c printchooseCB \
```

```
                    } \
                    - - - - \
                    MB.EXIT    "Exit"    E    exitCB \
              }

        XUrealize $TOPLEVEL
        XUmainloop
```

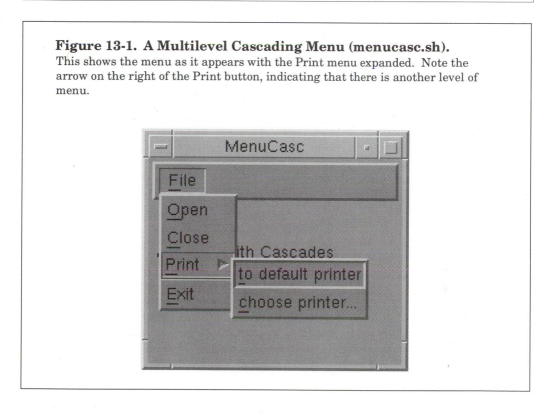

Figure 13-1. A Multilevel Cascading Menu (menucasc.sh).
This shows the menu as it appears with the Print menu expanded. Note the
arrow on the right of the Print button, indicating that there is another level of
menu.

13.3 Advanced Uses of XUmenusystem

Sometimes it is desirable to put ToggleButtons in a PullDownMenu. For example, if
a particular menu item is used to toggle between two different viewing options (like
the "View Details" mode of the checkbook program), then the status indicator contained in a ToggleButton is a good way to let the user know whether the option is
currently in effect or not.

The XUmenusystem command has an option, -t, that you can place before a set
of four arguments. This option causes the following set of four arguments to define
a ToggleButton instead of the usual PushButton. The *action* argument must be a
dtksh command (it will be registered with the ToggleButton's valueChangedCall-

back). For example, the code shown in Listing 13-2 would create two normal buttons, a Separator, and a ToggleButton. The menu resulting from this command is
shown in Figure 13-2.

Listing 13-2. A Menu with a ToggleButton (menutog.sh).

```
. $XUTILDIR/xutil.sh

XUinitialize TOPLEVEL MenuTog "$@"

XUcolumn COL $TOPLEVEL

XUmenubar MB $COL
XUlabel LAB $COL labelString:$'\n\nA Menu With a ToggleButton Item\n\n'

XUmenusystem $MB \
    VIEW "View" V { \
            MB.ALPHA    "Sort Alphabetically"    A    alphasortCB \
            MB.SIZE     "Sort by Size"           S    sizesortCB \
            - - - - \
        -t MB.DETAILS "Show Details"             D    detailsCB \
    }

XUrealize $TOPLEVEL
XUmainloop.
```

Figure 13-2. A Menu with a ToggleButton (menutog.sh).   On
the left, the menu as it initially appears. On the right, after selecting the "Show
Details" item, the menu is displayed a second time. Note the indicator that now
appears.

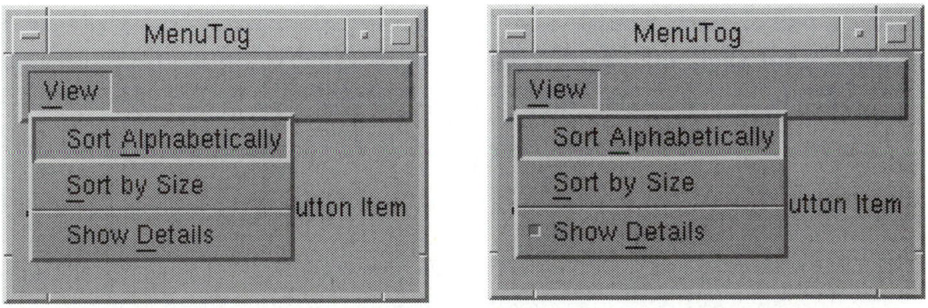

Using RadioButtons in a Menu

The previous example shows how to use a CheckBox style ToggleButton in a menu. There are also cases when it is desirable to use several ToggleButtons in a menu in RadioButton mode (only one button can be selected at a time).

The problem with this is that Motif does not provide a simple way to coordinate a set of exclusive ToggleButtons in a menu. The XUmenusystem command overcomes this by providing another option that can be used before a set of four arguments: -e *variable*. In this construct, the programmer must provide a unique dtksh variable name. All menu definitions preceded by the -e option with the same *variable* will be exclusive among themselves. By using different variables for different sets of items, it is possible to define several different sets of mutually exclusive ToggleButtons. When defining different sets of exclusive items, it is usually a good idea to divide each set visually using Separators. For example, the code in Listing 13-3 will create two sets of ToggleButtons, each set of which can have at most one active item.

Listing 13-3. Radio Buttons in a Menu (menurad.sh).

```
. $XUTILDIR/xutil.sh

XUinitialize TOPLEVEL MenuRadio "$@"

XUcolumn COL $TOPLEVEL
XUmenubar MB $COL
XUlabel LAB $COL labelString:$'\n\nA Menu With Some RadioButton Items\n\n'

XUmenusystem $MB \
    VIEW "View" V { \
            -e SORT MB.ALPHA "Sort Alphabetically" A     alphasortCB \
            -e SORT MB.SIZE  "Sort by Size"         S   sizesortCB \
            -e SORT MB.SIZE  "Sort by Date"         D   datesortCB \
            - - - - \
            -e TYPE MB.ALL   "All Items"            l   showallCB \
            -e TYPE MB.DEP   "Deposits Only"        e   showdepCB \
            -e TYPE MB.CHK   "Checks Only"          C   showcheckCB \
    }

# initialize defaults
XUtogglebuttonsetstate ${MB.ALPHA} true
XUtogglebuttonsetstate ${MB.ALL} true
XUrealize $TOPLEVEL
XUmainloop
```

The first set of three menu items (the "Sort" items) are coordinated using the variable SORT, whereas the second set of items, which are used to choose the kind of data displayed, is coordinated by the variable TYPE. The XU library uses these variables to keep track of the current item, so when a new item is selected it can shut off the previously selected item. Note the use of XUtogglebuttonsetstate to turn on the default items from each group. Figure 13-3 shows how this menu looks.

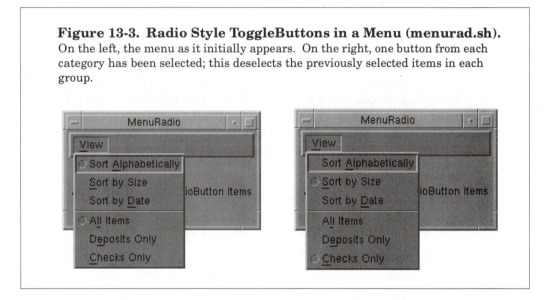

Figure 13-3. Radio Style ToggleButtons in a Menu (menurad.sh).
On the left, the menu as it initially appears. On the right, one button from each category has been selected; this deselects the previously selected items in each group.

13.4 Adding and Removing Menu Items

In some applications, it is necessary to add new menu items following the initial menu creation process.

Adding items is quite easy to do, again using the XUmenusystem command. All you need to do is use the handle of the PullDownMenu you want to add items to instead of using the MenuBar handle as the first argument. The PullDown menu's handle is the same as the handle of a button item with .PULLDOWN appended. Listing 13-4 shows how you might add items to the end of a File menu that allow the user to change quickly which file they are processing (this is a common feature of applications that allow the user to open multiple files). Each time the button labeled "Add an Item" is selected, another item is appended to the end of the File menu (this is just a simulation, a real application would perform this action whenever the user opens a new file). The function additemCB does this by calling XUmenusystem on ${FILE.PULLDOWN}, which is the PullDown menu handle associated with the File MenuBar button. The handles of the newly created menu items are stored in an array called NEWITEMS. The ${#NEWITEMS[@]} notation in that function returns the number of items in that array. In effect, this function increments that number when it adds a new item to the array by calling XUmenusystem. The output of this program is shown in Figure 13-4.

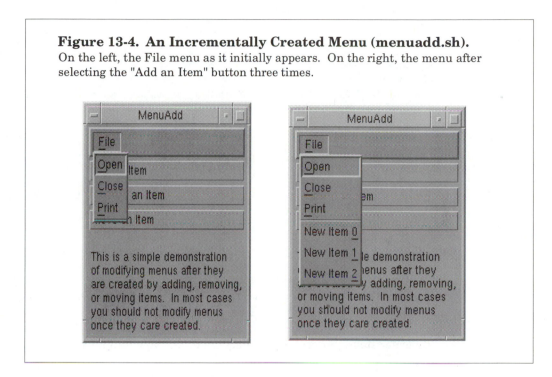

Figure 13-4. An Incrementally Created Menu (menuadd.sh).
On the left, the File menu as it initially appears. On the right, the menu after
selecting the "Add an Item" button three times.

Listing 13-4. Adding and Removing Menu Items (menuadd.sh).

```
. $XUTILDIR/xutil.sh

function additemCB {
    integer next=${#NEWITEMS[@]}

    XUmenusystem ${FILE.PULLDOWN} \
        NEWITEMS[$next] "New Item $next"  $next  "showitem $next"
}

function removeitemCB {
    integer last=$(( ${#NEWITEMS[@]} - 1 ))

    if (( last >= 0 ))
    then
        XUdestroy ${NEWITEMS[last]}
        unset NEWITEMS[last]
    fi
}
```

```
XUinitialize TOPLEVEL MenuAdd "$@"

XUcolumn COL $TOPLEVEL

XUmenubar MB $COL
XUaddbuttons $COL \
    ADD    "Add An Item"     additemCB \
    REMOVE "Remove An Item"  removeitemCB
XUmenusystem $MB \
    FILE "File" F { \
            MB.OPEN   "Open"    O    openCB \
            MB.CLOSE  "Close"   C    closeCB \
            MB.PRINT  "Print"   P    printCB \
            - - - - \
    }


XUrealize $TOPLEVEL
XUmainloop
```

The preceding example adds items to the end of the menu. It is also possible to add items in other positions by setting the positionIndex resource on the handle of the item following its creation. That resource specifies the position (starting at 0) that the item occupies in the menu. When counting positions, Separators count just like any other item. So, in the previous example, we could move NEWITEM[0] to the beginning of the menu using XUset:

```
XUset $NEWITEM[0] positionIndex:0
```

We could set it to be the fourth item from the top (position 3 since positions start at 0) using:

```
XUset $NEWITEM[0] positionIndex:3
```

Even though you *can* do this, it is usually not a good idea to move menu items around. Users get used to seeing items come up in the same order, and might be confused if items move. I am showing you this technique in case your application has some exceptional condition that makes moving items necessary. (For example, if you wanted to keep the list of opened files in alphabetical order rather than the order in which the user opened them, you could find the correct position in the list and insert the item there by resetting positionIndex.)

Removing Items from a Menu

It is generally considered bad style to remove items from menus dynamically. This is because users get used to seeing the same menu items in the same positions, and they might select the wrong item out of habit if there are dynamic changes taking place. There are exceptions (as always) to this general rule. For example, if you are adding newly opened files to a menu as shown in the preceding example, you also need to remove those items when the user closes the associated file.

If you need to remove an item from a menu, simply use XUdestroy on the handle of the item you wish deleted. In the preceding example, we could remove NE-WITEM[2] by simply calling:

```
XUdestroy $NEWITEM[2]
```

If you want to remove an item temporarily that you might want to add back later, you could use XUunmanage instead of XUdestroy. To bring such an item back later, use XUmanage on the handle.

The example program shown in Listing 13-4 includes a function, removeitemCB, which removes the last item added to the menu. This function is straightforward, it simply figures out the index of the last item and destroys the widget whose handle is stored in the last position of the NEWITEM array.

13.5 Creating PulldownMenus Without XUmenusystem

It is actually quite tedious to construct PullDownMenu systems like those shown in this chapter without using the XUmenusystem utility. Numerous Motif widgets are involved, including the PullDownMenu (actually just a special configuration of a RowColumn widget), the CascadeButton, the PushButton, and possibly ToggleButtons and Separators as shown earlier.

In practice, the XUmenusystem command gives you all the features you are likely to need in day-to-day PulldownMenu programming, so there's no need in particular to suffer through the traditional Motif method. However, for completeness I will outline the general method:

1. Create a MenuBar using XUmenubar. For each menu to be associated with this MenuBar, do all of the following steps.

2. Create a CascadeButton widget as a child of the MenuBar using XUcascadebutton, which takes the usual arguments for a widget creation command.

3. Create a PullDownMenu widget, using the command XUpulldownmenu (another widget creation command). A PullDownMenu is simply a RowColumn widget with certain resource settings to configure it appropriately for this purpose. The parent of this PullDownMenu should be the MenuBar.

4. Set the subMenuId resource of the CascadeButton to the widget handle of the PullDownMenu widget.

5. Add PushButtons or ToggleButtons to the PullDownMenu widget to implement the commands of the menu. It is also possible to add CascadeButtons to the PullDownMenu in order to create further cascading menus (they

would pull to the right). Such CascadeButtons would also need PullDown-Menu widgets associated with them using the subMenuId resource.

6. Repeat steps 2 through 5 for each menu to be added to the MenuBar.

13.6 Tear-Off Menus

Sometimes a menu contains items that are used so frequently that it would be convenient if the menu simply stayed visible all the time. Motif provides the concept of a *tear-off menu* for such cases. This is a PulldownMenu, but it contains a special button that looks like the perforations on a coupon. If the user clicks on the perforation, the menu actually detaches itself from the MenuBar and floats as a separate window. The user can select items as often as desired, and can dismiss the tear-off menu using the window manager menu in the upper left corner of the floating menu.

To make a certain PulldownMenu a tear-off menu, simply set the tearOffModel resource of the PulldownMenu to the value TEAR_OFF_ENABLED (the default is TEAR_OFF_DISABLED). It is possible to make all menus in the application tear-offs by setting *tearOffModel: TEAR_OFF_ENABLED in the application's resource file.

If you created the menu using XUmenusystem, the handle of the PulldownMenu is stored in the variable *cascadevariable*.PULLDOWN, where *cascadevariable* is the variable name you gave when specifying the start of the menu. For an example of this, see Listing 13-5. This will make the "View" menu a tear-off menu. The output of this program is shown in Figure 13-5.

Listing 13-5. A Tear-Off Menu (menutear.sh).

```
. $XUTILDIR/xutil.sh

XUinitialize TOPLEVEL MenuTear "$@"

XUcolumn COL $TOPLEVEL
XUmenubar MB $COL
XUlabel LAB $COL labelString:$'\n\nA Menu With a ToggleButton Item\n\n'

XUmenusystem $MB \
    VIEW "View" V { \
            MB.ALPHA   "Sort Alphabetically"   A   alphasortCB \
            MB.SIZE    "Sort by Size"           S   sizesortCB \
            - - - - \
        -t MB.DETAILS "Show Details"            D   detailsCB \
    }
XUset ${VIEW.PULLDOWN} tearOffModel:TEAR_OFF_ENABLED
XUrealize $TOPLEVEL
XUmainloop
```

Figure 13-5. Output of menutear.sh.   Above, the tear-off menu as it
appears in the MenuBar. Below, after the user has clicked the perforated item,
the menu floats as a free-standing window.

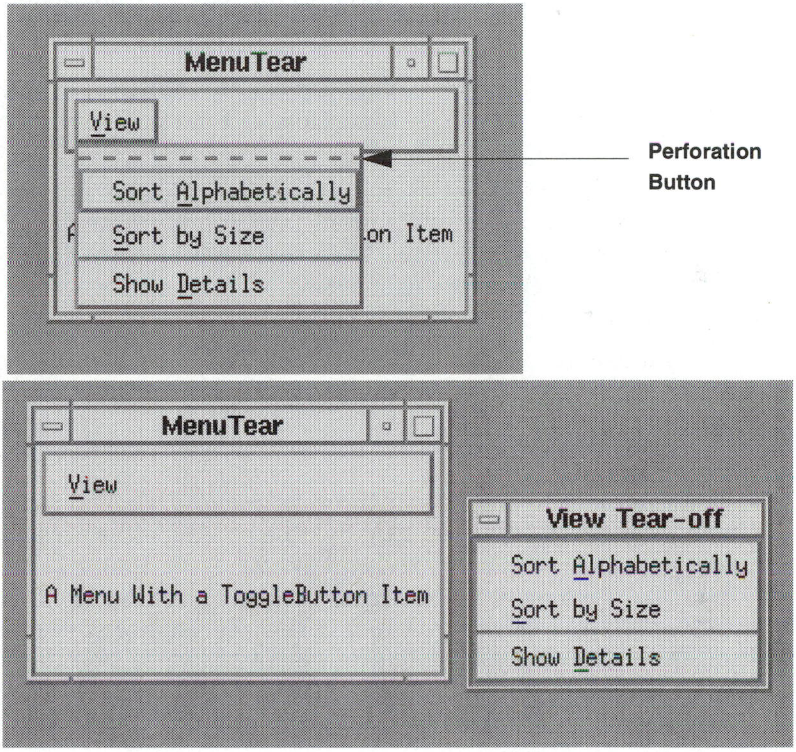

13.7 Accelerators

An *accelerator* is a keyboard sequence that can be used to select a menu item even
when it is not visible. These are shortcuts that are intended for frequently executed
operations. For example, you might specify that pressing the CONTROL key at the
same time as the letter O is equivalent to the File menu's Open item.

Accelerators are defined by setting two resources on the menu item:

- accelerator

  This resource can be set to a *translation specification* that defines the key
  sequence that will invoke the action. Translations are discussed in more

detail in Chapter 19, *Events, Translations, etc.*. However, some quick examples will suffice for the time being:

Ctrl<Key>O   Specifies the CONTROL key pressed at the
                 same time as the letter O.

Alt<Key>X   Specifies the ALT key pressed at the same
                 time as the letter X.

Ctrl<Key>F1   Specifies the CONTROL key pressed at the
                 same time as Function key 1.

- acceleratorText

  This is text that will appear to the right of the menu item label when the user views the menu. The usual notation is to specify the modifier key (CONTROL is the usual choice) followed by a +, followed by the letter. For example: Ctrl+C.

You can use XUset to set these resources on any menu item handles on which you desire accelerators. Alternatively, the XU library provides a convenience function:

    XUsetaccelerators [$*widget accelerator text* ...]

This command takes sets of three arguments, the first is the *widget* handle of a menu item (a PushButton usually), the second is the accelerator's translation specification, and the third is the accelerator *text* that will be displayed next to each item. For example, the program presented in Listing 13-6 creates a simple menu and installs accelerators on each of the items using XUsetaccelerators. The output from this program is shown in Figure 13-6.

Listing 13-6. Accelerators (menuacc.sh).

```
. $XUTILDIR/xutil.sh

XUinitialize TOPLEVEL MenuAcc "$@"

XUcolumn COL $TOPLEVEL
XUmenubar MB $COL
XUlabel LAB $COL labelString:$'\n\nA Menu With Accelerators\n\n'

XUmenusystem $MB \
    FILE "File" F { \
            MB.OPEN    "Open"    O    openCB \
            MB.CLOSE   "Close"   C    closeCB \
            - - - - \
            MB.EXIT    "Exit"    E    exitCB \
    }
```

```
XUsetaccelerators \
    ${MB.OPEN}  'Ctrl<Key>O' 'Ctrl+O' \
    ${MB.CLOSE} 'Ctrl<Key>C' 'Ctrl+C' \
    ${MB.EXIT}  'Ctrl<Key>E' 'Ctrl+E'

XUrealize $TOPLEVEL
XUmainloop
```

Figure 13-6. Output of menuacc.sh.

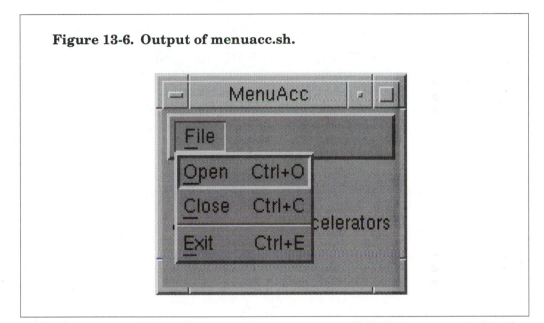

There is no need to provide accelerators for every menu item in an application. Usually only the most frequently used items should get accelerators. Accelerators can be installed on either PushButton style menu items or ToggleButton style items, but not cascading (pull-right) items.

13.8 Option Menus

Option menus allow the user to select one of several items, displaying the current item on a button-like control. If the user presses the button, a menu appears around it containing the possible choices. If the user selects one of the options with the mouse, it becomes the current selection and is displayed on the control.

In Chapter 6, *Prompting Using Custom Dialogs*, you learned how to use the XU library function XUaddoptionmenu to create a simple OptionMenu. The usage of this command is:

```
XUaddoptionmenu [-m] variable $parent label [item [mnemonic]...]
```

The *variable* is set to the handle of the newly created OptionMenu. The menu is created as a child of the *parent* widget handle. The *label* argument is a string that should appear on a Label widget that is also created as a child of the *parent* widget. One or more *item* arguments specify the text of various choices the user could made. If the -m option is provided, then a *mnemonic* character should appear after each item. For example:

```
XUaddoptionmenu -m OPTIONS $PARENT "Size:" \
    "Small"  S \
    "Medium" M \
    "Large"  L
```

By default, the first item specified is displayed as the current choice. The XU library arranges for the currently selected item's text label to be stored in ${*variable*.VALUE}. In the preceding example, if the user selected Medium, then ${OPTIONS.VALUE} would be set to the string "Medium."

However, this function can be used to change the current item:

```
XUsetoption $optionmenu item-index
```

In this command, the *optionmenu* is the handle of an OptionMenu widget, and *item-index* is the index (starting at zero) of the item you wish to make the current selection. Continuing with the preceding example, if you wanted to make Large the default item programatically, then after creating the menu you would call:

```
XUsetoption $OPTION 2
```

For an example of how to use these functions, see *Prompting for Multiple Choices* on page 114.

Manually Creating an OptionMenu

The XUaddoptionmenu command provided by the XU library creates a Label as a child of the parent widget first, then creates the OptionMenu. This is so it can be used conveniently in two-column dialogs (see Chapter 6, *Prompting Using Custom Dialogs*, for a discussion of two-column dialogs).

However, the Motif OptionMenu actually allows an internally defined Label (it is set to the empty string by XUaddoptionmenu). Using the internal Label is not desirable in a two-column dialog because there is no easy way to get it to align with other Labels in the dialog, but if you are creating a more customized layout it may be more convenient to use the internal Label.

You can do this by creating an OptionMenu manually, without using the XUaddoptionmenu command. The steps involved are as follows:

1. Create a PullDownMenu widget using XUpulldownmenu. It must be created unmanaged, so use the -u option.

2. Create an OptionMenu widget using `XUoptionmenu`. It too must be unmanaged when created, so again you should use the `-u` option. Set its `subMenuId` resource to the handle of the previously created PullDownMenu. Set its `labelString` resource to the desired label text that will appear to the left of the current selection.

3. Create PushButtons as children of the previously created PullDownMenu. You could add buttons one by one using `XUpushbutton`, or you could use `XUaddbuttons` to create multiple buttons. You can use the `activateCallback` to track the currently selected item; one convenient way to do this is to simply assign a variable to the current selection in the `activateCallback`.

4. Use `XUmanage` to manage the OptionMenu. You should not manage the PullDownMenu.

An example illustrating these steps is presented in Listing 13-7, with the resulting output shown in Figure 13-7.

Listing 13-7. A Manually Created OptionMenu (menuopt.sh). This program creates an OptionMenu following the manual steps outlined in this section. A button is created that prints the current item. This example uses the simple strategy of assigning a variable to the current selection when its `activateCallback` is invoked.

```
. $XUTILDIR/xutil.sh

XUinitialize TOPLEVEL MenuOpt "$@"

XUcolumn COL $TOPLEVEL

# create a PullDownMenu
XUpulldownmenu -u pull1 $COL
# create an OptionMenu, associate it with the
# PullDownMenu using the subMenuId.
XUoptionmenu -u SORT "$COL" \
        labelString:"Sort Order:" \
        subMenuId:"$pull1"
# add buttons to the PullDownMenu
XUaddbuttons $pull1 \
    SORT.ALPHA "Alphabetic" "SORT.CHOICE=ALPHA" \
    SORT.SIZE  "Size"       "SORT.CHOICE=SIZE"
XUmanage $SORT

XUaddbuttons $COL \
    tmp "Print Choice" 'print ${SORT.CHOICE}'

XUrealize $TOPLEVEL
XUmainloop
```

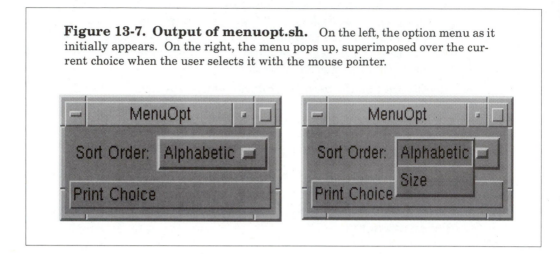

Figure 13-7. Output of menuopt.sh.   On the left, the option menu as it initially appears. On the right, the menu pops up, superimposed over the current choice when the user selects it with the mouse pointer.

13.9 Popup Menus

Popup menus are unlike any of the others we have seen so far; they are not invoked by selecting a visible control on the screen like a MenuBar item or an OptionMenu button. Instead, they are associated with individual widgets (note: widgets only, not gadgets), and are displayed when the user presses the osfMenu mouse button.

> The osfMenu mouse button is normally the rightmost button, unless the mouse has been customized as a left-handed mouse using the CDE Preferences screen.

Popups are used for a convenient list of actions that somehow uniquely apply to the widget with which they are associated.

According to the Motif style guide, it is not a good idea to make functions in your application available exclusively on a popup. Any function on a popup should also be available in some other way, perhaps as an action available in a MenuBar menu or some other control. The reason for this is that some users may not realize they can invoke the PopupMenu by pressing mouse button three.

Creating Popup Menus

To create a PopupMenu, first use XUpopupmenu (a typical widget creation command) to create an unmanaged popup, then associate menu items with it using XUmenusystem. For example:

```
XUpopupmenu -u POPUP $TOPLEVEL
XUmenusystem $POPUP \
    SHOWSIZE "Show Size" S showsizeCB \
    SHOWTYPE "Show Type" T showtypeCB
```

To associate a PopupMenu with any particular widget, you can use:

```
XUregisterpopup $widget $popup
```

After this command, if the user presses mouse button three while the pointer is over the named *widget*, then *popup* will be managed and positioned at the mouse pointer. The *widget* must actually be a widget, not a gadget

The handle of the widget that caused the PopupMenu to be invoked is stored in the variable ${_XU.EH_WIDGET} (the EH stands for Event Handler). This can be used within the PopupMenu's button activateCallbacks to identify which widget was selected by the user to bring up the PopupMenu.

A Popup Example

An example of how PopupMenus might be used is provided in Listing 13-8. This example program displays all the files in the current directory in Label widgets that are stacked in columns. If the user presses mouse button three while the pointer is over one of the Labels, then a PopupMenu is displayed next to the mouse pointer. Two actions are available in this menu: one will show the size of the file (using the UNIX wc command), the other will show the type of file (using the UNIX file command). The results of these actions are displayed in another Label widget (called RESULT). The output resulting from this program is shown in Figure 13-8.

Listing 13-8. Popup Menus (menupop.sh).

```
. $XUTILDIR/xutil.sh

function showsizeCB {
    typeset file

    XUget "${_XU.EH_WIDGET}" labelString:file
    XUset $RESULT value:"$(wc -c $file)"
}

function showtypeCB {
    typeset file

    XUget ${_XU.EH_WIDGET} labelString:file
    XUset $RESULT value:"$(file $file)"
}

XUinitialize TOPLEVEL MenuPop "$@"

XUcolumn COL $TOPLEVEL
XUtext RESULT $COL value:" " editable:false
XUrow FILES $COL packing:PACK_COLUMN numColumns:10
```

```
# create a PopupMenu
XUpopupmenu -u POPUP $TOPLEVEL whichButton:2
XUmenusystem $POPUP \
    SHOWSIZE "Show Size" S showsizeCB \
    SHOWTYPE "Show Type" T showtypeCB

for file in *
do
    XUlabel LABEL $FILES \
        labelString:"$file"
    XUregisterpopup $LABEL $POPUP
done

XUrealize $TOPLEVEL
XUmainloop
```

Figure 13-8. Output of menupop.sh. The rightmost mouse button has
been clicked on the first file name (the one in the upper left corner).

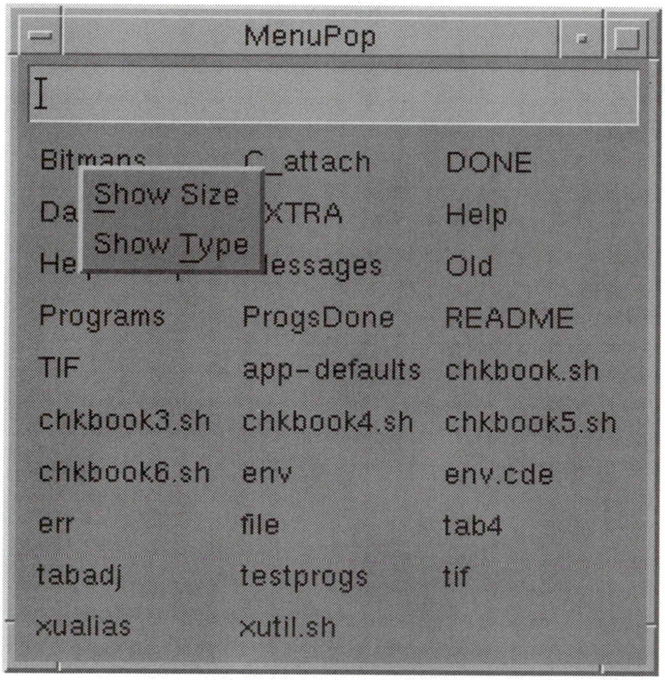

13.10 Summary

Motif provides several different kinds of menus that are used in different situations:

- PullDownMenus are used to create systems of menus used in MenuBars. They may contain PushButtons, ToggleButtons, and multilevel CascadeButtons. It is possible to enable a tear-off feature whereby the user may keep the menu displayed after a selection.

- OptionMenus allow the user to select one of several items. The current selection is displayed, but if the user holds down the mouse button on the OptionMenu, a menu appears that allows another selection to be made.

- PopupMenus are invoked by pressing mouse button three while it is on a widget that has registered such a menu. They are used to allow the user quick access to common commands that apply to the widget under the mouse pointer.

Menus can have single-letter mnemonics that allow items to be selected without using the mouse. In addition, accelerators can be installed on certain menu items to allow the user to execute the function provided by the item without even displaying it.

14 *The Scale Widget*

14.1 Introduction

The Scale widget can be used to prompt for numeric values between fixed upper and lower limits. It allows the user to grab a slider with the mouse and drag it to choose a new value. The user may increment or decrement the Scale value by clicking the mouse on either side of the slider (called the *trough*), or by using keyboard commands such as PAGE UP or PAGE DOWN keys. In this chapter, you will learn:

- Appropriate uses of the Scale widget
- Resources that control a Scale widget's appearance
- How to add tick marks and other decorations to a Scale widget
- How to use Scale widget callbacks.

Scale widgets can also be used as output-only widgets by making them insensitive. For example, in Chapter 10, *Providing Feedback During Long Callbacks*, you saw an example that used an insensitive Scale to show the user what percentage of a task was completed (see Listing 10-4 on page 230).

14.2 Creating the Scale Widget

You can create a Scale using this command:

```
XUscale variable $parent [resource:value ...]
```

This command works like all the other widget creation commands you have seen; it stores the handle of the newly created scale in the named `variable`.

Scale Value Resources

The current number displayed by the Scale is stored in a resource called `value`. This number is always between the numbers stored in the `minimum` and `maximum` resources. By default, the minimum is 0, the maximum is 100; value starts at 0. If the resource showValue is set to true, then the value is always displayed floating above the Scale's bar.

Internally, the Scale's value is an integer, but the decimalPoints resource allows the programmer to make it appear to display a fixed-point real number. That resource is an integer that defines the number of decimal digits that should display after a decimal point when showValue is true. For example, if value is set to 4250 and decimalPoints is set to 2, then the string 42.50 would be displayed floating over the slide bar. The value is still an integer; it is merely displayed differently. See the right slider in Figure 14-1.

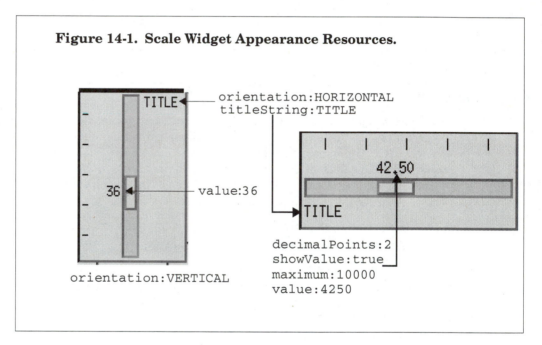

Figure 14-1. Scale Widget Appearance Resources.

The resource titleString can be used to display a string next to the Scale. For vertical Scales, the title appears in the upper right corner of the rectangle enclosing the scale. For horizontal Scales, the title appears in the lower left corner. See Figure 14-1.

14.3 Scale Widget Children

The Scale widget is a simple manager widget. Its children are spaced evenly along the Scale's bar. The primary use of children is to provide "tick" marks. For example, to place five evenly spaced ticks on a horizontal Scale, one could add Label widgets (or gadgets) to it that contain the pipe (|) character:

```
XUscale SCALE $TOPLEVEL orientation:horizontal
for i in 1 2 3 4 5
do
        XUlabelgadget tmp $SCALE labelString:'|'
done
```

For vertically oriented Scale widgets, dash characters (–) work nicely. Of course, you may also put numeric Labels in the Scale. A common practice is to put the `minimum` and `maximum` values as the first and last Labels, with a few tick marks spaced along the axis. It is also common to show the `minimum`, `maximum`, and middle values. These strategies are illustrated in Listing 14-1, with the resulting output shown in Figure 14-2.

Listing 14-1. Scale Tick Marks (sctick.sh).

```
. $XUTILDIR/xutil.sh

XUinitialize TOPLEVEL ScaleTicks "$@"

XUcolumn COL $TOPLEVEL spacing:25

# Create a scale with several tick marks
XUscale SCALE1 $COL \
    orientation:horizontal
XUlabel tmp $SCALE1 labelString:"|"
XUlabel tmp $SCALE1 labelString:"|"
XUlabel tmp $SCALE1 labelString:"|"
XUlabel tmp $SCALE1 labelString:"|"
XUlabel tmp $SCALE1 labelString:"|"

# Create a scale with minimum and maximum
# tick marks, with a few marks in between
XUscale SCALE2 $COL \
    orientation:horizontal
XUlabel tmp $SCALE2 labelString:0
XUlabel tmp $SCALE2 labelString:"|"
XUlabel tmp $SCALE2 labelString:"|"
XUlabel tmp $SCALE2 labelString:"|"
XUlabel tmp $SCALE2 labelString:100

# Create a scale with minimum, maximum and
# center numbers, with marks in between
XUscale SCALE3 $COL \
    orientation:horizontal
XUlabel tmp $SCALE3 labelString:0
XUlabel tmp $SCALE3 labelString:"|"
XUlabel tmp $SCALE3 labelString:50
XUlabel tmp $SCALE3 labelString:"|"
```

```
XUlabel tmp $SCALE3 labelString:100

XUrealize $TOPLEVEL
XUmainloop.
```

Figure 14-2. Scale Tick Mark Strategies.

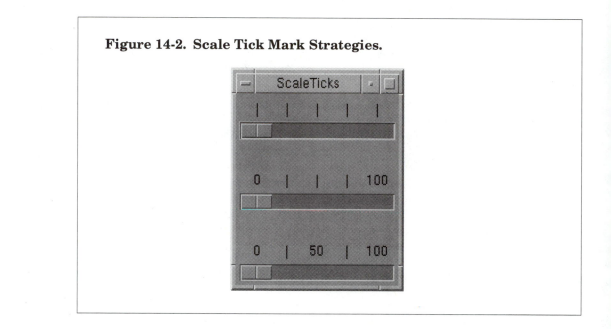

14.4 Scale Callbacks

There are two callbacks specific to the Scale widget:

dragCallback   This callback is triggered whenever the user drags
                                the Scale's slider. It may be executed many times
                                per second if the user rapidly moves the slider.

valueChangedCallback   This callback is triggered when the user releases
                                the slider after a drag, or otherwise causes the
                                Scale's value to change (for example, by using the
                                keyboard arrow keys or clicking in a trough area).

The following call data variables are set while any commands triggered by these
callbacks are executing:

- CB_CALL_DATA.REASON

  This indicates which of the callback types triggered the function, and is
  either CR_VALUE_CHANGED or CR_DRAG.

- `CB_CALL_DATA.EVENT`

  This variable contains subfields that indicate the X event that triggered the callback. For example, it would be possible to tell the difference between a value changed by a mouse click as opposed to a keyboard action such as using the arrow keys. Events are explained in Chapter 19, *Events, Translations, etc.*

- `CB_CALL_DATA.VALUE`

  This variable holds the new slider value.

An example of how to use these callbacks was presented way back in Chapter 2, *X Window Basics*. See Listing 2-4, *Variables In Callbacks (scales.sh)*, on page 31.

14.5 Other Scale Widget Resources

Here are some other Scale resources that are useful in some situations:

`processingDirection`	Specifies which side of the Scale the maximum value is on. For horizontally oriented Scales this can be either `MAX_ON_LEFT` (the default for languages that read left to right like English) or `MAX_ON_RIGHT`. For vertical Scales, this can be `MAX_ON_TOP` (the default) or `MAX_ON_BOTTOM`.
`scaleMultiple`	When the user clicks the mouse in the area between the slider and an end of the bar, the value increments or decrements by this amount. By default, this is 10% of the difference between the `minimum` and `maximum` values (but it is always at least `1`). For example, if the `minimum` is 100 and the `maximum` is 300 then the increment amount is (300 − 100)/10, which is 20.
`scaleHeight`, `scaleWidth`	These resources can be used to set the width and height of the slider bar. Note that the `width` and `height` resources set the width and height of the entire rectangular area that encloses the slider bar, the `titleString`, and any children of the Scale. These should normally be set only in a resource file.

14.6 Scale Widget Pitfalls

The Scale widget is relatively simple to use, but programmers do encounter some common problem:

- When using an insensitive Scale for displaying a number, it is not a good idea to add Label children as decorations or a `titleString`. This is because those elements will take on a stippled appearance that is hard to read.

- Any `dragCallbacks` that you add must execute quickly, because they could be called many times per second as the user rapidly moves the Scale. This means they must not spawn any UNIX commands; they must only execute dtksh built-ins. Your `dragCallback` should not exceed a few milliseconds of real time. You can use the dtksh `time` command to see how long your `drag-Callback` takes to execute when called in isolation.

- Scale widgets are not good to use for very wide ranges of numeric input. That's because the resolution of the slide bar depends on how many pixels wide the Scale is. For example, if you were to try to prompt for a number between 1 and 20,000 using a Scale that is 200 pixels wide, then each time the user moves the slider by one pixel its `value` will increment by 100! There is no easy way for the user to choose an arbitrary number in this case—you would be well advised to use a TextField widget setup for numeric input (for example, created using the `XUinteger` command).

14.7 Summary

The Scale widget can be used to prompt for numeric values between fixed ranges. It can be made to display fixed-point decimal numbers. It can include a title, and any number of children to decorate its slide bar. Callbacks are available that trigger when the Scale is dragged and when the user releases the slider.

15 *The List Widget*

15.1 Introduction

The List widget provides a simple way to allow the user to view and select items from a textual list. It can be created with a ScrollBar if there are too many items to fit it conveniently on the screen. Various options allow the programmer to control how the user selects items; for example, the programmer can specify that only one item can be selected at a time, or can specify that multiple items can be simultaneously selected. List widgets have been used in previous chapters, but here we will go into much more depth, and will cover topics such as:

- How to insert new items in a List
- How to delete or replace items in a List
- How to determine which item(s) are selected
- How to change which items are showing in a List with ScrollBars
- Examples of common applications of the List widget, such as using double lists for selecting items to be operated on
- Common mistakes programmers make when using Lists

15.2 Creating List Widgets

Normally, you should create a List widget with ScrollBars using

```
XUscrolledlist [-u] variable $parent [resource:value ...]
```

This is a typical XU library widget creation command. It stores the handle of the newly created widget in the given *variable* name. To create a List with no Scroll-Bars, use `XUlist` instead. By default, the ScrolledList will only display the Scroll-

Bars if they are needed, so there is no particular reason to use XUlist instead of XUscrolledlist.

Adding Form Constraints

One thing you must be aware of when using XUscrolledlist is that this command returns the handle of a List widget whose parent is a ScrolledWindow widget. Thus, if you needed to attach Form constraints to the ScrolledList after creating it, you'd have to get the parent of the returned *variable* (which is the ScrolledWindow) and attach the constraints to that widget instead. You can get the parent of a widget by using:

```
XUparent variable $widget
```

which stores the handle of the parent of $*widget* in *variable*. If *variable* is a dash (-) character, then the parent widget handle is printed to the standard output and could be used directly within another command. Here is a typical code fragment that creates a ScrolledList and adds some Form constraints to it using XUattach:

```
XUscrolledlist LIST $FORM
XUset $(XUparent - $LIST) \
      $(XUattach top left)
```

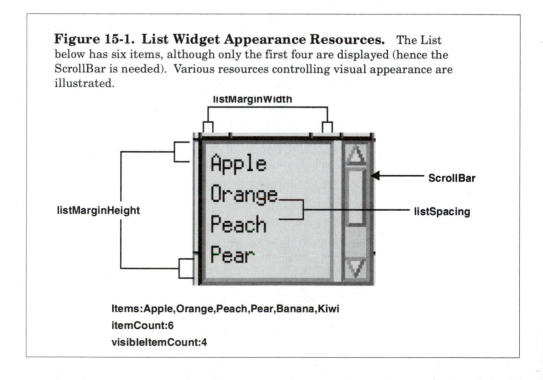

Figure 15-1. List Widget Appearance Resources.   The List below has six items, although only the first four are displayed (hence the ScrollBar is needed). Various resources controlling visual appearance are illustrated.

List Widget Appearance Resources

The following resources are straightforward in their use and affect the appearance of the List widget. See Figure 15-1 for some examples of how these resources affect the appearance of the List widget.

`fontList`	Specifies the font to use for the List items. If it is important in your application to align fields of items by text column position, then you should use a fixed-width font.

`itemCount,`
 	
`items`
	The `itemCount` resource specifies the number of items in the List. The `items` resource can be set to a comma-separated list of text items.
	
	These resources should be set at the same time. Function calls (explained later) are normally used to add items to a List rather than setting these items directly. For example:

```
XUset $LIST \
        itemCount:3 \
        items:"alpha,beta,gamma"
```

`selectedItemCount,`
 	
`selectedItems`
	Like the above resources, these specify the number of selected items in the list and the items themselves. Again, the items are specified as a comma-separated set of strings. These resources are usually not set directly by the programmer, but rather are set using convenience functions (explained later). Selected items appear in reverse video.

`listMarginHeight,`
 	
`listMarginWidth`
	These resources can be used to set the spacing between the top and bottom (`listMargin-Height`) or left and right (`listMarginWidth`) edges of the List. The default for both is 0 pixels.

`listSpacing`	Specifies the amount of space between items in the List. The default is 0 pixels.
`scrollBarDisplayPolicy`	When set to `AS_NEEDED` (the default) a ScrollBar appears when there are too many items to fit (assuming the List was created using

XUscrolledlist). When set to STATIC, the
ScrollBar is always displayed.

topItemPosition   The index of the item that is currently showing
                                                  at the top of the list. Indexes start at 1, and an
                                                  index of 0 is a special value that specifies the
                                                  last item in the List.

visibleItemCount   This is used to set the desired number of items
                                                  to display; it changes the default size of the
                                                  List.

As usual, several of these resources are best set in resource files rather than being
hard-coded in the application. Most notably, resources like fontList, listMargin-
Width, listMarginHeight, and listSpacing are almost always more appropriately
set in resource files.

15.3 List Widget Selection Models

The selectionPolicy resource controls how the user is allowed to make selections
from the List. It may take one of these values:

- SINGLE_SELECT

  At most one item can be selected at a time. If the user selects an item, any
  previously selected item becomes unselected. If the user selects an already
  selected item, it becomes unselected (i.e., it toggles from selected to unselected, leaving no item selected).

- BROWSE_SELECT

  Only a single item can be selected at a time, and there must always be a
  selected item. Also, the user may press and hold mouse button one while in
  the list, and the selection follows the movements of the pointer (by highlighting). If the user releases the mouse pointer while on an item, that item
  becomes selected, and any other selected item becomes unselected.

- MULTIPLE_SELECT

  Any number of items can be selected. Clicking on an item toggles its selection state.

- EXTENDED_SELECT

  This mode also allows multiple selections, but with the addition that the
  user may choose to drag the mouse pointer through several items while holding down button one, and all items dragged over become selected. In addition, individual items may be toggled without deselecting other items by
  holding down the CONTROL key while clicking. Clicking without holding
  down the CONTROL key will deselect any other selected items.

The choice of which mode to use is entirely dependent on how you intend the List to be used. When it is logical to only allow a single item to be selected, I prefer to use BROWSE_SELECT rather than SINGLE_SELECT, since it allows a convenient dragging select motion, and in many situations its feature of always requiring one item to be selected is desirable.

The choice of MULTIPLE_SELECT versus BROWSE_SELECT is not as clear-cut. When the user would normally choose several discontiguous items, MULTIPLE_SELECT is more convenient because it does not require any special modifier keys to avoid deselecting previous items. If it is more common for the user to select contiguous items, then EXTENDED_SELECT is more convenient because it allows the dragging operation to select multiple items.

Listing 15-1 shows a program that can be used to experiment with these selection models. It contains a RadioBox and a List. The ToggleButtons in the RadioBox can be used to choose any of the selectionPolicy settings described earlier. The output of this program is shown in Figure 15-2, although this program is best experienced by actually running it and playing with the various selection methods so you get a feel for what might be the most convenient for different situations.

Listing 15-1. List Selection Models (listsel.sh).

```
. $XUTILDIR/xutil.sh

function changemodeCB {
    XUset $LIST selectionPolicy:$1
}

XUinitialize TOPLEVEL ListSel "$@"

XUcolumn COL $TOPLEVEL

XUradiobox RADIO $COL orientation:horizontal

XUaddtogglebuttons $RADIO \
    TOG_SINGLE   "SINGLE"   S "changemodeCB SINGLE_SELECT" \
    TOG_BROWSE   "BROWSE"   B "changemodeCB BROWSE_SELECT" \
    TOG_MULTIPLE "MULTIPLE" M "changemodeCB MULTIPLE_SELECT" \
    TOG_EXTENDED "EXTENDED" E "changemodeCB EXTENDED_SELECT"

XUscrolledlist LIST $COL \
    visibleItemCount:6

XUlistappend $LIST \
    "Apple" "Orange" "Peach" "Pear" "Banana" "Kiwi" \
    "Mango" "Necterine" "Pineapple" "Grape"

XUtoggleselect $TOG_SINGLE  # Simulate a user selection of SINGLE
```

```
XUrealize $TOPLEVEL
XUmainloop
```

Figure 15-2. Output of listsel.sh. On top, the program shows single selection mode, in which at most one item can be selected. Below, in multiple selection mode the user can individually toggle items by selecting them. Browse select is similar to single select, but at least one item must always be selected, and it allows a dragging style select. Extended select allows ranges of items to be selected by dragging, and discontiguous items can be selected using the CONTROL key while selecting.

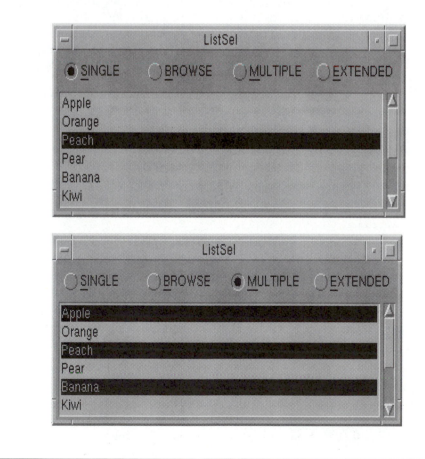

15.4 Modifying the List Items

It is perfectly all right for you to add or delete items in a List by setting the `items` and `itemCount` resources, but that's usually not the most convenient way. For one thing, setting `items` requires you to build a list of items separated by commas, and for another it is often not convenient to count the items in order to set `itemCount`. Finally, if you are incrementally adding items to an existing set, your only solution using these resources is to build the whole list from scratch with the new items added, then reset the whole set of items.

For these reasons, most programmers use convenience functions to modify the contents of the List widget. This section explains how to use all the convenience functions provided by the XU library.

Adding Items

The XU library provides two functions that simplify the task of adding items to a list:

```
XUlistappend $list [item ...]
XUlistadd $list index [item ...]
```

The `XUlistappend` function adds one or more items to the end of a List widget. For example, the following command will append three items to a List whose handle is stored in the variable `fruitlist`:

```
XUlistappend $fruitlist "Apple" "Orange" "Mango"
```

The `XUlistadd` function is similar, but it allows you to add items at an arbitrary position in the list, rather than at the end. The position is specified by the *index* argument. In List widgets, indexes start at 1, and the special index value of 0 specifies the last item in the List. The item to be added replaces the item at the specified position, pushing it and all items past it down in the List. So, this command is equivalent to the one above:

```
XUlistadd $fruitlist 0 "Apple" "Orange" "Mango"
```

This command would add an item at the beginning of the a List:

```
XUlistadd $fruitlist 1 "Banana"
```

Deleting Items

The XU library contains two functions for deleting items from a List:

```
XUlistdeleteall $list
XUlistdelete $list index [count]
XUlistdelete -s $list item ...
```

The XUlistdeleteall function does exactly what its name implies: all items are removed from the List widget provided as its argument. The XUlistdelete function removes an item by its *index*. The optional *count* argument can be used to remove several items starting at the *index* position. If count is not specified, it defaults to 1. With the -s option, the deletion is carried out by matching string items as opposed to numerical indexes. Any number of string items can be given, and all List items that exactly match any of the strings will be deleted. Note that case matters, and patterns are not allowed, only exact string matches.

For example, assume a List contains the following items (in this order): Apple, Pear, Kiwi, Mango, Banana. In that case, the following two lines of code will have the same effect:

```
XUlistdelete $list 2 3   # delete 3 items starting at position 2
```

and

```
XUlistdelete -s $list Pear Mango Kiwi  # order doesn't matter
```

Any string match must be exact, including case.

Replacing Items

You can replace the string on one or more items using:

```
XUlistreplace $list  position [item ...]
```

Starting at the index named by *position*, strings are replaced by the *items*. For example, if we have a List containing these items: Red, Green, Yellow, Blue, Black, then the following command would replace Green with Brown and Yellow with Magenta:

```
XUlistreplace $colorlist 2 Brown Magenta
```

It is important to note from these examples that the position is the starting point for the replace, and contiguous items are replaced from that point on. If there are not enough items in the starting list to accommodate all the new items, then any overflow items are appended to the list.

Changing the Selected Items

It is possible to change which items are selected programmatically (simulating a user selection) using:

```
XUlistselectall $list
XUlistselect [-s] [-n] $list item ...
XUlistdeselectall $list
XUlistdeselect [-s] $list item ...
```

The `XUlistselectall` and `XUlistdeselectall` commands force all items to be selected or deselected, respectively.

`XUlistselect` and `XUlistdeselect` can be used to change the selection state of individual items. The *item* arguments are position indexes by default, but with the `-s` option they may be an exact match of the List item's text. With the `-n` (notify) option, `XUlistselect` triggers any callbacks that would normally be called when a selection changes (thus exactly simulating a user-initiated selection or deselection).

Changing the View

For ScrolledLists, there are times when you need to change which items are currently visible. For example, if you have a List with a very large number of items, you might want to provide a search feature whereby the user types in an item string and the program finds it and scrolls to that area of the list. Two functions are available for changing the current item view:

```
XUlisttop [-s] $list item
XUlistbottom [-s] $list item
```

The first command changes the ScrollBars so the named item is the topmost one displayed. The second makes its item argument the bottom-most one displayed. The *item* argument is a List position index by default, but with the `-s` option it is an exact match of the item's text string.

A List Modification Example

Listing 15-2 presents a program that illustrates how to use all the XU library List modification commands. It creates buttons for each of the List modification functions that have been described here (`XUlistappend`, `XUlistdelete`, etc.). Fields are provided that allow the user to type in arguments for these commands: a string to be used for new items, a string to use to select an item from the list, and a numeric position index.

When a command button is selected, the corresponding XU library command is executed and displayed in a Label above the List—so this program can be used as a learning aid. For convenience, the program automatically changes the string argument after each command is executed (so you don't have to change it manual to get unique strings). Also, when the user selects an item from the list, the selected item's string and index are placed in the appropriate argument TextFields.

This program is best understood by running it. Typically, after first running the program you should add several items to the list by using the `Append` button, then experiment with the different command buttons.

The output of this program is shown in Figure 15-3.

Listing 15-2. List Modification Program (listmod.sh).

```
. $XUTILDIR/xutil.sh

# Execute the desired function, and put the command
# that performs the function in a label
function doit {
    XUget $W_STRING value:STRING
    XUget $W_INDEX value:INDEX
    XUget $W_SELSTRING value:SELSTRING
    XUset $SHOWCOMMAND labelString:"$(eval print $*)"
    eval "$(print $*)"

    # for convenience, change the default string

    XUset $W_STRING value:"New_Item_$((++NEXTITEM))"
}


# When the user selects an item, change the default index and
# string used for selection of items
function showitem {
    XUset $W_SELSTRING value:"${CB_CALL_DATA.ITEM}"
    XUset $W_INDEX value:"${CB_CALL_DATA.ITEM_POSITION}"
}


integer NEXITEM=0

XUinitialize TOPLEVEL ListMod "$@"

XUcolumn COL $TOPLEVEL

XUrow CONTROLS $COL packing:PACK_COLUMN numColumns:5

XUaddbuttons $CONTROLS \
  tmp "Append"            'doit XUlistappend \$LIST "\$STRING"' \
  tmp "Add at Index"      'doit XUlistadd \$LIST \$INDEX "\$STRING"' \
  tmp "Delete by Index"   'doit XUlistdelete \$LIST \$INDEX' \
  tmp "Delete by String"  'doit XUlistdelete -s \$LIST "\$SELSTRING"' \
  tmp "Delete All"        'doit XUlistdeleteall \$LIST' \
  tmp "Replace by Index"  'doit XUlistreplace \$LIST \$INDEX "\$STRING"' \
  tmp "Select by Index"   'doit XUlistselect \$LIST \$INDEX' \
  tmp "Select by String"  'doit XUlistselect -s \$LIST "\$SELSTRING"' \
  tmp "Select All"        'doit XUlistselectall \$LIST' \
  tmp "Deselect by Index" 'doit XUlistdeselect \$LIST \$INDEX' \
  tmp "Deselect by String"'doit XUlistdeselect -s \$LIST "\$SELSTRING"' \
  tmp "Deselect All"      'doit XUlistdeselectall \$LIST' \
  tmp "Top by Index"      'doit XUlisttop \$LIST \$INDEX' \
  tmp "Top by String"     'doit XUlisttop -s \$LIST "\$SELSTRING"' \
  tmp "Bottom by Index"   'doit XUlistbottom \$LIST \$INDEX' \
```

```
     tmp "Bottom by String"  'doit XUlistbottom -s \$LIST "\$SELSTRING"'

XUrow COMMANDS $COL

XUaddtextfields $COMMANDS \
    W_STRING "New string:" : 15
XUaddtextfields $COMMANDS \
    W_SELSTRING "Selection string:" : 15
XUaddintegerfields $COMMANDS \
    W_INDEX "Index:" 4

XUset $W_STRING value:"New_Item_0"
XUset $W_INDEX value:0

XUlabel SHOWCOMMAND $COL labelString:" "

XUscrolledlist LIST $COL \
    visibleItemCount:8 \
    selectionPolicy:EXTENDED_SELECT \
    extendedSelectionCallback:showitem

XUrealize $TOPLEVEL
XUmainloop
```

15.5 Querying the List

As with modifying items in a List widget, it is possible to search for a particular item string by first using XUget on the List's items resource, then parsing the comma separated list of items that comes back, then comparing each item with the desired string. There are complications, though. For example, if a List item actually contains a comma, it will come out preceded by a backslash (\) in the items resource, and you would have to take that into account when parsing.

Luckily, there's no need to bother doing all this, since Motif provides some commands that allow the List to be searched.

You can search for items in a List using the command:

```
    XUlistfind variable $list string
```

This command finds all occurrences of the *string* in the List widget whose handle is stored in *list*. The indexes of the items are stored in the provided *variable* name, separated by spaces if there is more than one match. The match must be exact. For example, if we have a List whose handle is stored in the variable colorlist with items Red, Green, Blue, Magenta, then the following command will store the number 2 in the variable var:

```
    XUlistfind var $colorlist "Green"
```

Figure 15-3. Output of listmod.sh. This program demonstrates the use of all the XU library List convenience functions. The user may type in a new item string, an item search string, or an item index then press one of the action buttons. The XU command that performs the action is displayed above the list. For convenience, new item strings are generated automatically, and if the user selects an item, its text and index are filled in the selection fields.

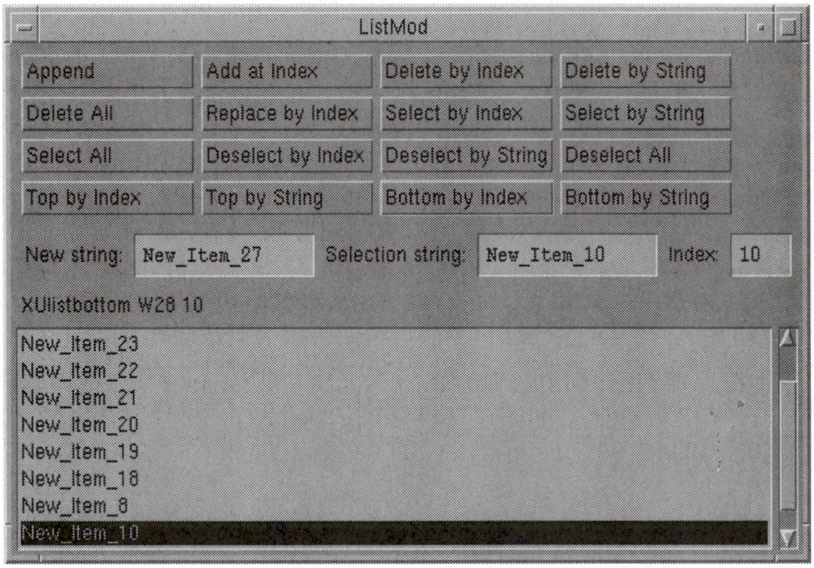

As with many dtksh commands, the variable may also be a dash (-), in which case the resulting indexes are printed to the command's standard output. This is often useful for use with a `for` loop:

```
for item in (XUlistfind - $list "$searchstring")
do
        etc.
```

The XUlistfind command also provides a return code of false (nonzero) if no items were found. In this context, it is useful in conditional commands:

```
if XUlistfind var $list "$searchstring"
then
        etc.
```

Getting the Text of an Item

As you can see, many of the commands described in this section return indexes of items. If you have an item index, and wish to get the text associated with the item at that position, you can use:

```
XUlistget variable $list index
```

The text of the item at position *index* in the named List is stored in the *variable*. If the *variable* argument is a dash (-), then the text of the item is printed to the standard output.

For example, the following code fragment will print all the items in a List to the standard output:

```
XUget $list itemCount:n
for (( i = 1; i < n; i++ ))
do
        XUlistget - $list $n
done
```

In addition, the XU library provides a command that will parse an item list separated by commas:

```
XUlistparse array itemstring
```

In this command, *array* is the name of a variable and *itemstring* is a comma-separated list of strings. This command correctly takes into account backslashed commas, and sets successive positions in the array to each item, starting at position 1 (it starts at position 1 instead of 0 for convenience in using other List commands).

For example, if a List whose handle is stored in the variable LIST contains items: Apple, Banana, and Cherry, then this code

```
XUget $LIST items:fruits
XUlistparse array "$fruits"
```

will set array[1] to Apple, array[2] to Banana, and array[3] to Cherry.

One limitation of this technique is that dtksh arrays are can have at most 4096 elements, so if you have a very large list of items you may not be able to parse them all into an array. There is still a solution: if you use a dash (-) instead of a variable name for the array, then the items are printed to the standard output, one per line. You could process items using a loop like this:

```
for item in $(XUlistparse - "$fruits")
do
        etc. ...
```

Finding Selected Items

The following command can be used to find the selected items in a List (assuming there are any):

```
XUlistgetselected variable $list
```

This command places the indexes of all the selected items contained in the given List widget in the *variable* name. If the variable is a dash (-), then the set of selected indexes is printed to the standard output. In either case, the indexes are separated by a space character.

If you need the strings associated with the items, you can use XUlistget on the returned indexes. For example, the following code will print the strings associated with each selected item:

```
for index in $(XUlistgetselected - $mylist)
do
       print $(XUlistget - $mylist $index)
done
```

15.6 List Widget Callbacks

Callbacks are available for the List widget that are triggered when the user selects or deselects items. The callback that you need to use depends on the selection-Policy you have set for the List widget:

Callback Name:	*Used When selectionPolicy Is:*
browseSelectionCallback	BROWSE_SELECT
extendedSelectionCallback	EXTENDED_SELECT
multipleSelectionCallback	MULTIPLE_SELECT
singleSelectionCallback	SINGLE_SELECT

Easy, right? Nonetheless, a very common mistake is to use the wrong callback. This often happens when you write a complete program using one kind of selection policy, then you decide to change the selection policy but forget to change the callbacks correspondingly.

Besides these callbacks, there is another one named defaultActionCallback that is executed if the user double-clicks on an item. This is useful for situations in which there are several different operations the user can perform on a selected item in a List, and one of the operations makes sense as a default. For example, in the checkbook program the user typically selects an item in the List of check entries, then clicks an action button or makes a menu selection that operates on the selected item. It would be reasonable to set up a default action that displays the check entry edit screen on a double-clicked item.

Call Data Values

When the command registered for any of the List widget callbacks is executing, the following call data variables are set:

- CB_CALL_DATA.REASON

  This specifies which of the callbacks was triggered, and is set to one of CR_BROWSE_SELECT, CR_DEFAULT_ACTION, CR_EXTENDED_SELECT, CR_MULTIPLE_SELECT, or CR_SINGLE_SELECT.

- CB_CALL_DATA.EVENT

  This variable has subfields that describe the X event that triggered the callback. Events are discussed in Chapter 19, *Events, Translations, etc.*

- CB_CALL_DATA.ITEM

  This is the text of the last item selected by the event that caused the callback. Multiple items can be selected by a drag operation in some selectionPolicy modes (see CB_CALL_DATA.SELECTED_ITEMS).

- CB_CALL_DATA.ITEM_LENGTH

  The length of the string held by ${CB_CALL_DATA.ITEM}.

- CB_CALL_DATA.ITEM_POSITION

  The position index of ${CB_CALL_DATA.ITEM}.

- CB_CALL_DATA.SELECTED_ITEMS

  A comma-separated list of the text of all the selected items.

- CB_CALL_DATA.SELECTED_ITEM_COUNT

  The number of selected items.

- CB_CALL_DATA.SELECTED_ITEM_POSITIONS

  A comma-separated list of the indexes of all selected items.

- CB_CALL_DATA.SELECTION_TYPE

  This indicates how the most recent selection was made by the user. If the selection was the first selection of an extended selection, they keyword INITIAL will be stored in this variable. If the user modified an existing set of selections, this will be set to MODIFICATION, and if the user clicked a noncontiguous item to add it to the selected items, this will be set to ADDITION. This call data variable is useful only for some sophisticated programs.

By far, the most useful of these call data parameters is the SELECTED_ITEMS and SELECTED_ITEM_POSITIONS fields. One problem with using these values is the comma separators.

In the case of the SELECTED_ITEM_POSITIONS field, you can use the dtksh string substitution feature to replace the commas with spaces, then process items using a simple `for` loop. This is possible because you know the numbers themselves contain no whitespace or commas (which is not necessarily true of the `SELECTED_ITEMS` field). For example:

```
items=${CB_CALL_DATA.SELECTED_ITEM_POSITIONS/,// }
```

This will set the variable `items` to a space-separated list of selected item indexes. The dtksh notation `${`*variable*`/`*pattern*`//`*replacement*`}` expands to the string contained in *variable* with *pattern* replaced by *replacement* everywhere. Thus, the preceding code simply substitutes a space for every comma in the selected item position's call data. You could then call `XUlistdelete` on the result. `XUlistdelete` expects each index to be a separate argument, the spaces accomplish that.

To parse the `SELECTED_ITEMS` field when the items might contain whitespace or backslashed commas, you can use the `XUlistparse` command, explained earlier, like this:

```
XUlistparse array "${CB_CALL_DATA.SELECTED_ITEM_POSITIONS}"
```

This will place each selected item's text in successive elements of the *array* variable, starting at position 1.

15.7 Example: The Double List

To illustrate some of the ideas explained in this chapter, I'll create a special dialog that is commonly used to allow the user to partition a set of items into two different categories: those that will be operated on, and those that will not. Two Lists will be used for this purpose:

- The *action list* will contain items to be operated on.

- The *no action list* will contain items that will not be operated on.

While this kind of division of items can be accomplished by a single list (where the items to be operated on are the selected ones), it is often more clear to the user what precisely will happen if two lists are used. ArrowButtons are provided that allow the user to move items between the two lists in either direction. In addition, we will allow a double-click on any item to move the item to the opposite List. We will also allow multiple selections and drag selections in the Lists.

This kind of dialog is quite commonly used in graphical programs. Listing 15-3 presents a complete program that uses such a dialog to select files to print using the `lp` command. It finds all text files (as determined by the `file` command) in the current directory, and initializes the action list to contain them. The resulting output is shown in Figure 15-4.

Figure 15-4. A Double List Selection Box (listdbl.sh).

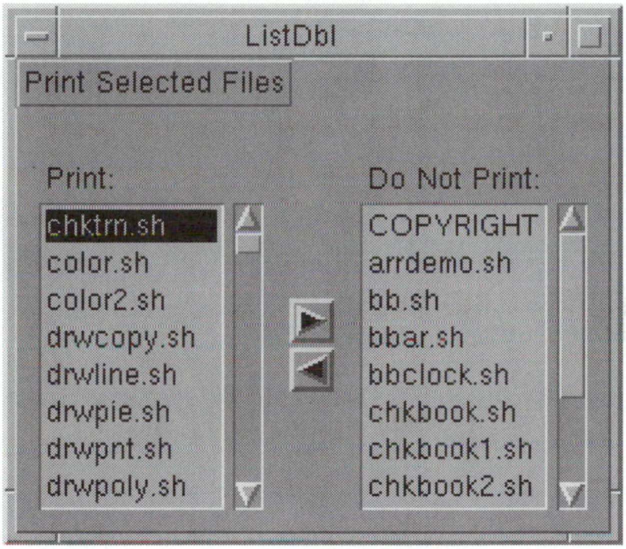

Listing 15-3. A Double List Selection Box.

```
. $XUTILDIR/xutil.sh

function printCB {
    typeset files array

    # print the action list items using "lp"
    XUget $ACTLIST items:files
    XUlistparse array "$files"

    lp "${array[@]}"
}

function moveCB {
    typeset fromlist=$1 tolist=$2
    typeset files array

    # get the selected items
    XUget $fromlist selectedItems:files
```

```
        XUlistparse array "$files"

        # append to the other list
        XUlistappend $tolist "${array[@]}"

        # remove selected items strings from the action list
        XUlistdelete -s $fromlist "${array[@]}"
}

XUinitialize TOPLEVEL ListDbl "$@"

XUform FORM $TOPLEVEL

XUpushbutton BUTTON $FORM \
    labelString:"Print Selected Files" \
    activateCallback:printCB \
    $(XUattach top left)

XUlabel ACTLAB $FORM \
    labelString:"Print:" \
    $(XUattach left 10 under $BUTTON 20)

XUscrolledlist ACTLIST $FORM \
    visibleItemCount:8 \
    selectionPolicy:EXTENDED_SELECT \
    defaultActionCallback:'moveCB $ACTLIST $NOACTLIST' \
    $(XUattach left 10 under $ACTLAB bottom 10)

XUarrowbutton MOVERIGHT $FORM \
    arrowDirection:ARROW_RIGHT \
    $(XUattach rightof $ACTLIST 10 toppos 50) \
    activateCallback:'moveCB $ACTLIST $NOACTLIST'

XUarrowbutton MOVELEFT $FORM \
    arrowDirection:ARROW_LEFT \
    $(XUattach rightof $ACTLIST 10 under $MOVERIGHT) \
    activateCallback:'moveCB $NOACTLIST $ACTLIST'

XUlabel NOACTLAB $FORM \
    labelString:"Do Not Print:" \
    $(XUattach rightof $MOVERIGHT 10 under $BUTTON 20)

XUscrolledlist NOACTLIST $FORM \
    visibleItemCount:8 \
    selectionPolicy:EXTENDED_SELECT \
    defaultActionCallback:'moveCB $NOACTLIST $ACTLIST' \
    $(XUattach rightof $MOVERIGHT 10 under $NOACTLAB right 10 bottom 10)

# Initialize the action list to contain all files in
```

```
# the current directory that are text files.  We use the
# "file" command in conjunction with grep to find these,
# then use "cut" to strip off the file name, which precedes
# a colon character in the output of the file command

XUlistappend $ACTLIST $(file * | grep text | cut -f1 -d:)

XUrealize $TOPLEVEL
XUmainloop
```

15.8 Limitations of the List Widget

The List widget is quite useful, but of course there are some things it cannot do. The following list includes some features that the List widget lacks which programmers often want to do. Often requested (but unprovided) features include

- There is no way to make different items different colors. All items share the same `foreground` and `background` colors.

- There is no way using dtksh to make different items different fonts, or to mix fonts within a single item. It is possible to do this in the C language interface for Motif, and this feature is likely to be supported in future releases of dtksh.

- There is no way to display bitmap graphics in a List item.

- There is no simple way to provide a title over the List items that aligns with fixed-width fields in the list data (in order to caption columns of data in the items). This can be simulated by putting a Label over the List widget and playing with offsets until things line up, but it is not easy to automate in such a way that font changes will result in proper alignment.

If you really must have one of these features, some of them can be simulated by creating Label widgets inside a RowColumn that is in a ScrolledWindow. Performance of such a conglomeration will not be as good as using a List widget, especially for large numbers of items, and the programming is likely to be much more difficult, especially if you wish to implement drag selections or other features of the List widget.

15.9 Summary

List widgets are useful for displaying groups of text items. Although the text items can be changed by modifying resources, it is simpler to use conveniences provided by Motif through the XU library to manipulate List items. Functions are available to add, delete, change, select, and deselect items in the List. In addition, the programmer can search for a particular text string and modify which items are displayed in the ScrolledWindow view of the List.

Several different selection mechanisms can be employed. It is possible to set up the List so only a single item can be selected at a time. It is also possible to allow drag selections or multiple selections to be made by toggling the selection state of clicked items. Callbacks are available that are triggered when items are selected or deselected in any of these ways.

16 *Text and TextField Widgets*

16.1 Introduction

This chapter describes the three Motif widgets that allow viewing and editing of text: the Text, ScrolledText, and TextField widgets. The Text widget provides a multiline area to view and edit text. The ScrolledText widget is really just a Text widget inside a ScrolledWindow widget; it gives the user a simple way to scroll through the data. The TextField widget is a single-line version of the Text widget that provides better performance because it doesn't have to handle multiple lines.

You saw a simple use of the ScrolledText widget in the section *Following a Logfile* on page 234; in that example lines from a logfile were appended to a Text widget to allow the user to "follow" the progress of a lengthy activity. You learned several uses of the TextField widget in Chapter 6, *Prompting Using Custom Dialogs*.

This chapter will explore some more sophisticated uses of the Text and TextField widgets, including:

- Inserting and deleting strings in a Text widget
- Searching for text strings
- Cutting and pasting text
- Intercepting keystrokes that modify Text or TextField widgets
- Prompting for passwords by hiding typed text
- Limitations of the Text and TextField widgets.

In the descriptions throughout this chapter, I will use the term Text widget to refer to any of the Text, ScrolledText, or TextField widgets, except where specifically noted. These widgets have almost identical features, except for the fact that the TextField widget can only have a single line.

16.2 General Features of Text Widgets

Even though the Text widget is a primitive widget class, that does not mean it is simplistic or trivial. In fact, the Text widget is one of the most sophisticated and feature-rich widgets in all of Motif.

Visually, the Text widget provides a panel on which text is displayed. The Text widget may have a border. It also has the concept of a *current position* marked by an *I-beam cursor*. The Text widget may be placed inside a ScrolledWindow to create what is known as a ScrolledText widget. In this case, the user may manipulate ScrollBars that automatically appear when needed.

The user may also sweep areas of text by holding down mouse button one while moving the pointer; such swept areas turn reverse video and define a piece of text that the user can operate on using other keyboard controls. This area is called the *selected text* (or simply the *selection*). See Figure16-1.

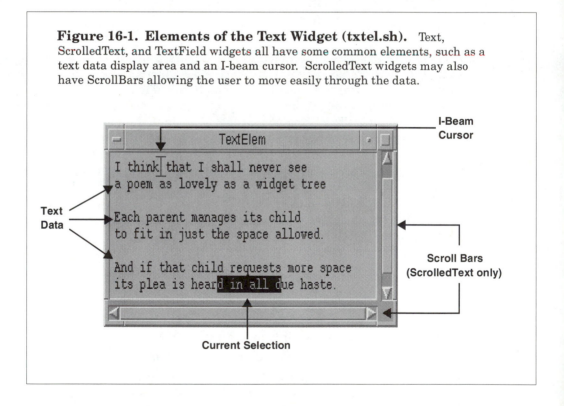

Figure 16-1. Elements of the Text Widget (txtel.sh). Text, ScrolledText, and TextField widgets all have some common elements, such as a text data display area and an I-beam cursor. ScrolledText widgets may also have ScrollBars allowing the user to move easily through the data.

User Initiated Navigation and Editing

The Text widget provides the user with numerous keyboard and mouse actions to navigate and modify text—all automatically with no need for programmer intervention. For example, the default keyboard bindings allow the user to perform these actions:

arrow key	Move the cursor in the direction of the arrow key (i.e., up one line for the UP ARROW, forward one character for RIGHT ARROW, etc.).
CONTROL+*arrow key*	For the UP ARROW and DOWN ARROW keys, move by paragraph; for the RIGHT ARROW and LEFT ARROW keys, move by word.
PAGE UP, PAGE DOWN	Move up or down one screen.
DELETE	If there is a selection, delete all the text contained in it, otherwise delete the character following the cursor.
BACKSPACE	Delete the character before the cursor.
mouse click	Move the cursor to the position of the mouse pointer.
mouse double-click	Select the current word.
mouse triple-click	Select the current line.
mouse quadruple-click	Select all the text in the Text widget.
press and drag mouse	Select text between the starting and ending point of the mouse pointer. The selection is completed by releasing the mouse button.
SHIFT+*arrow key*	Move the cursor in the indicated direction, and also extend the selection in that direction. For example, pressing SHIFT+RIGHT ARROW moves the cursor right and also selects the character that is moved over.
CONTROL+SHIFT+*arrow key*	Move by word (for LEFT ARROW or RIGHT ARROW) or paragraph (for UP ARROW and DOWN ARROW) and simultaneously extend the current selection.

There are other default bindings as well, see [Heller and Ferguson 1994] for complete details.

Text Widget Convenience Functions

Like the List widget discussed in the previous chapter, the Text, ScrolledText, and TextField widgets have many convenience functions that allow various useful operations to be performed easily. The bulk of this chapter explains and gives examples of the XU library interfaces to these Motif convenience functions.

One comment that I'll make up front is that in the traditional Motif commands there are entirely separate commands for the Text and TextField widgets (the ScrolledText is just a Text widget inside a ScrolledWindow widget, so you would use the Text versions with it). For example, in the traditional Motif functions, you must use the command XmTextGetSelection to get the selected data in a Text widget, but you must use XmTextFieldGetSelection to do the same thing for a TextField widget.

The XU library Text widget convenience functions are, well, more convenient than the Motif convenience functions. They all figure out which kind of Text widget you are using, and map to the appropriate underlying Motif convenience function.

For this reason, when you see functions described in this chapter, you can assume they apply to any of the Motif Text widgets (Text, ScrolledText, or TextField), unless the explanations specifically say they do not.

16.3 Creating Text Widgets

You can create Text widgets using these XU library commands:

```
XUscrolledtext [-u] variable $parent [resource:value ...]
XUtext [-u] variable $parent [resource:value ...]
XUtextfield [-u] variable $parent [resource:value ...]
```

These are typical XU library widget creation commands; they store the handle of the newly created widget in the variable. The -u option can be used to create the widget initially unmanaged.

The XUscrolledtext command creates a ScrolledText widget, which is actually just a ScrolledWindow widget with a Text widget child. You should use this function when the enclosed text could be too lengthy to fit on the screen. The XUtext command creates a Text widget that can be multiple lines long. The XUtextfield command creates a TextField widget; that variation must have exactly one line of text.

16.4 Text Widget Appearance Resources

The Text widget has numerous resources that affect how it looks. Besides the usual appearance resources like borderWidth, foreground, background, width, and height, these are available:

`autoShowCursorPosition`	If set to `true` (the default) then the cursor is always kept in view when it is moved (i.e., the ScrollBars of a ScrolledText widget are adjusted automatically).
`blinkRate`	The number of milliseconds between "blinks" of the cursor. You should not set this under most circumstances; it is a preference that you should allow the user to set in a resource file.
`columns, rows`	(The `rows` resource is not available for TextField widgets). The number of character columns wide and character rows tall the Text widget should be. Assuming no `width` resource has been specified, `columns` defaults to 20. Assuming no `height` resource has been specified, `rows` defaults to 1.
	Note: in order to create a multiline Text widget, you must set `rows` to a number greater than one *and* you must set `editMode` to `MULTI_LINE_EDIT` (see discussion later). Even experienced Motif programmers often forget to set `editMode`.
`cursorPositionVisible`	If set to `true` (the default), the cursor position is marked by a blinking I-beam.
`editMode`	(Not available for TextField widget). If set to `SINGLE_LINE_EDIT` (the default), the Text widget will only receive key bindings for actions that make sense on a single line. If set to `MULTI_LINE_EDIT`, key bindings are included that make sense for multiline Text widgets.
	One very irritating thing about the Text widget is that you must remember to set `editMode` to `MULTI_LINE_EDIT` in addition to setting `rows` to a value greater than one in order to make a multiline Text widget. If you forget to set `editMode`, you'll only get one line even if `rows` is set to a larger number.

`fontList`	The font used to display the text data.
`marginHeight,` `marginWidth`	Specifies the space between the left and right (`marginWidth`) and top and bottom (`margin-Height`) edges of the widget and the text it contains. The default for both is 5 pixels.
`topCharacter`	This resource is an integer that determines which character position is at the top of the Text window. Character positions start at zero, and count all characters, punctuation, NEWLINE, TAB, etc. in the Text widget's `value` buffer. For example, if `topCharacter` were set to 100 in a ScrolledText widget that contained 200 characters of data, the line containing character position 100 would be positioned at the top of the window (the ScrollBars would move accordingly).
`value`	This resource holds the string that is displayed in the Text widget. In the case of Text or ScrolledText widgets, it may contain newlines that are used to denote line breaks.

16.5 Text Widget Behavior Resources

The resources explained in the previous section all affect how the Text widget looks. There are some others that affect certain behavioral aspects of the widget:

`editable`	If set to `true` (the default), the user may edit the text data. Note that setting this to `false` is slightly different from setting the Text widget to the insensitive state, because the user will still be able to use the mouse and arrow keys to navigate a noneditable Text widget, while they can't do a thing to an insensitive one. Also, an insensitive Text widget will take on a hard-to-read stippled appearance.
`maxLength`	This is the maximum number of characters the user can enter in the Text widget from the keyboard. Note that it is not the maximum width of the displayed text data, but rather the actual maximum number of characters of data allowed. There could be fewer characters displayed, for

example, with ScrollBars appearing to allow more input. This resource also does not restrict the size of the `value` resource set programmatically using `XUset` or other convenience functions.

verifyBell

If `true` (the default), the terminal bell will ring if a validation fails on the Text widget. Validation is explained under the section *Text Widget Callbacks* on page 346.

resizeHeight,
resizeWidth

(Not available for ScrolledText) If `true` (default is `false`), the Text widget will automatically attempt to gain size horizontally (`resizeWidth`) or vertically (`resizeHeight`) to accommodate changes in entered data.

scrollLeftSide,
scrollTopSide

(Not available for TextField). These specify on which side of the screen the ScrollBars should appear. They are both boolean values that default to `false` (exception: in languages that read right to left `scrollLeftSide` defaults to `true`).

These should *never* be hard-coded into the application, they are user preferences that should be specified in the user's `.Xdefaults` file.

wordWrap

(Not available for TextField) If `true` (default is `false`), lines will automatically be broken at a SPACE or TAB to avoid overrunning the window's edge. Of course, you must have created a multiline Text widget for this to work.

16.6 Modifying Text

The string displayed by the Text widget is stored in the `value` resource. You can set `value` either at widget creation time on the `XUtext`, `XUscrolledtext`, or `XUtextfield` command line, or later using `XUset`. In the case of multiline Text widgets, embedded newlines in the `value` string delimit lines. The KornShell ANSI string notation is useful for specifying values with embedded newlines. To create an ANSI string, you use single quotes where the opening quote is prefixed by a dollar sign (`$`). Such a string may include embedded ANSI character symbols such as `\n` for NEWLINE or `\t` for TAB. For example, the following command creates a three-line text data value:

```
XUset $TEXT value:$'one\ntwo\nthree'
```

To display the contents of a file, the simplest thing to do is set the `value` resource using the KornShell notation for file expansion. The notation `$(<`*filename*`)` is a

KornShell idiom for "expand the entire contents of the file *filename* here." For example, this code will set a Text widget to display the contents of the password file:

```
XUset $TEXT value:"$(</etc/passwd)"
```

If you wish to modify the displayed text, it is possible to retrieve the value resource using XUget, modify the string using KornShell string handling functions, then set the value resource to the modified value.

> See *Other Kinds of Variable Expansion* on page 558 for a summary of KornShell string handling features. KornShell-93, on which dtksh is based, contains much more powerful string handling capabilities than previous versions of KornShell, so even if you are familiar with KornShell you might want to review these new features.

However, there is no need to go through all that work, because Motif contains a number of convenience functions to perform various modifications on the Text widget's value in a simpler and more expedient manner. These are explained in the next few sections.

Text Positions

All of the Motif Text modification commands use the notion of *text positions* to determine what piece of text data is being modified. The idea is that the text held in the value resource is one big string with character positions starting at zero, and including all NEWLINE, TAB, or other special characters. Text positions are conceptually places *between* characters (places where the I-beam cursor can sit). The spot right before the first character in the text data is position 0, the spot right after the first character is position 1, etc. For example, consider the following command:

```
XUset $TEXT value:$'first line\nsecond line\nthird line'
```

After this, the "f" in the word "first" is after position 0, and the "s" in "second" is after position 11 (the \n is a single NEWLINE character and counts for one position). The output of a program that uses this command is shown in Figure 16-2; some lines have been added that show a few position numbers.

To define a substring within the text data, two positions are required: the starting position and the ending position. All characters between those two positions define a unique substring within the Text widget's data. Because positions are between characters, there's no ambiguity about whether such ranges are inclusive or not. In the example shown in Figure 16-2, the word "line" on the first line of data is between starting position 6 and ending position 10.

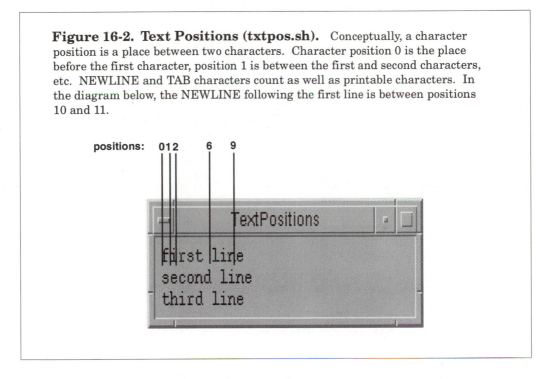

Figure 16-2. Text Positions (txtpos.sh).   Conceptually, a character position is a place between two characters. Character position 0 is the place before the first character, position 1 is between the first and second characters, etc. NEWLINE and TAB characters count as well as printable characters. In the diagram below, the NEWLINE following the first line is between positions 10 and 11.

Adding Text

These XU functions can be used to add new text to a Text widget:

```
XUtextappend $text string
XUtextinsert $text position string
```

The XUtextappend command adds the *string* to the end of any existing text in the widget $text. XUtextinsert allows you to specify a *position* at which the insertion will take place; any text following *position* will be pushed forward to accommodate the new *string*. For example, after this code executes the widget $TEXT will hold the string "the three little pigs":

```
XUset $TEXT value:"the little"
XUtextappend $TEXT " pigs"
XUtextinsert $TEXT 4 "three "
```

Deleting Text

You can delete text using:

```
XUtextdelete $text from-position to-position
```

This deletes all text between the text positions specified by *from-position* and *to-position*. For example, after the following code the widget $TEXT will contain the string "Little Hood":

```
XUset $TEXT value:"Little Red Riding Hood"
XUtextdelete $TEXT 7 18
```

Replacing Text

Replacing one piece of text with another is equivalent to doing a delete followed by an insert. You can do a replace in a single operation using:

```
XUtextreplace $text from-position to-position string
```

This first deletes the text between *from-position* and *to-position*, then inserts the new *string* at *from-position*. For example, after the following code the widget $TEXT will hold the string "Who's Afraid of the Big Bad Wolf?":

```
XUset $TEXT value:"Who's Afraid of Virginia Wolf?"
XUtextreplace $TEXT 16 24 "the Big Bad"
```

Optimizing Text Modifications

If you need to do several modifications to a Text widget at once, you might cause some "screen dancing" problems. That's because the Text widget will update its display after each of your modifications. For example, if you delete some text, and then add some text somewhere else, the user may see two repaints of the Text window—one for each operation.

Motif has commands that allow you to "turn off" the redisplay of text modifications temporarily, then turn them back on again after you have completed all of your operations. In that way, only one screen repaint occurs. The XU library provides these functions:

```
XUtextdisableredisplay $text
XUtextenableredisplay $text
```

The normal use is to call XUtextdisableredisplay on a Text widget handle, then do all your updates, then call XUtextenableredisplay. For example:

```
XUtextdisableredisplay $TEXT
XUtextappend $TEXT "$newstring"
XUtextreplace $TEXT 20 60 "$anotherstring"
XUtextenableredisplay $TEXT
```

If you are only doing a single modification, there is no advantage to using these functions.

16.7 The Text Selection and Insertion Point

The user may select (highlight) pieces of text using the mouse. Text selected by the user in this way can be replaced by typing new text or deleted by pressing the DELETE key. The user may change the position of the insertion cursor by simply clicking the mouse at the desired location.

It is also possible for you to manipulate programmatically the selected area in the Text widget and the insertion point. The resource `cursorPosition` specifies where the I-beam cursor should appear. This resource is an integer; the cursor will appear immediately *before* the position specified by this resource.

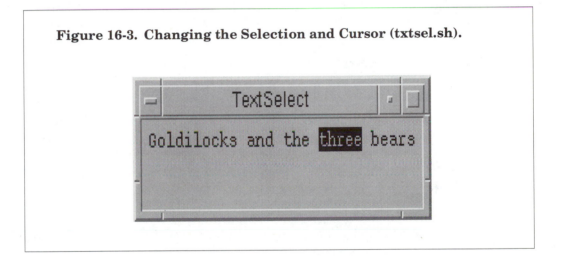

Figure 16-3. Changing the Selection and Cursor (txtsel.sh).

There are no resources that control the placement of the selection, you must use convenience functions. Several functions are provided by the XU library for manipulating the selection:

```
XUtextselect $text from-position to-position
XUtextdeselect $text
```

The first of these makes the text between positions *from-position* and *to-position* the primary selection. The third, `XUtextdeselect`, eliminates the selection (there will be no selected text following this command). For example, the following code will cause the word "three" to be selected, and will place the cursor immediately after the word "and":

```
XUset $TEXT value:"Goldilocks and the three bears"
XUtextselect $TEXT 19 24
XUset $TEXT cursorPosition:14
```

The output resulting from this code is shown in Figure 16-3.

There is also a convenience function that can be used to delete the text contained in the current selection (if there is a selection):

```
XUtextremove $text
```

There are two functions that allow you to retrieve the value of the current selection:

```
XUtextgetselection variable $text
XUtextgetselectionposition $text from-variable to-variable
```

The `XUtextgetselection` function stores the text string contained in the selection in the named *variable*. It returns success (zero) if there was an active selection. Thus, it can be used with conditional statements to test if there is any selection:

```
if XUtextgetselection selstring $TEXT
then
        etc.
```

The `XUtextgetselectionposition` function allows you to retrieve the starting and ending positions of the current selection (if any). Those values are stored in the variables named on the command line, *from-variable* and *to-variable*. This command also returns success if there was an active selection, and thus can be used with conditional commands.

Cut, Copy, and Paste

X contains a mechanism to allow data to be transferred between applications at the user's request. This is called the *clipboard* (sometimes referred to as the *cut buffer*). The way it works is that client application sends the display server a piece of data (the *selection*), which it stores until a request comes in to retrieve the data. The request to retrieve the data could come from the same application, or a different application. In fact, it could come from an application running on an entirely different machine!

The user could, for example, sweep out a selection, then press a button (or menu item) to *cut* the text. That text is automatically deleted from the Text widget and is stored on the X display server. Later, the user could go to an entirely different application's Text widget (or any other widget that supports text selection) and issue a *paste* command. That would insert the previously cut text at the cursor position in the new widget. It is not necessary to delete the text data from the original widget, it is also possible to do a *copy* operation to put data into the clipboard.

From the programmer's point of view, things are pretty simple. You can issue one of these commands from a menu item or button to access the clipboard:

```
XUtextcut $text
XUtextcopy $text
XUtextpaste $text
```

These commands all take only one argument, the handle of a Text widget. The `XUtextcut` and `XUtextcopy` commands operate on whatever text (if any) is currently selected in the Text widget. The `XUtextpaste` command inserts whatever text data is in the clipboard at the cursor position in the Text widget.

16.8 Text Widget Command Example

Listing 16-1 presents an example that illustrates the use of all these Text modification and selection manipulation commands. It creates a number of action buttons at the top of the window, and a ScrolledText widget at the bottom. Some fields are provided that allow the user to enter parameters to be used with the actions, such as a new text string or a position number.

When an action button is pressed, the associated Text modification function is printed to a Label and executed on the Text widget. In this way, you can see exactly what command line is used to implement the Text modification, along with the resulting action. For convenience, if the user clicks in the Text window the position field is changed to that spot in the Text widget. The resulting output is shown in Figure 16-4.

Listing 16-1. Modifying Text (txtmod.sh).

```
. $XUTILDIR/xutil.sh

# Execute the desired function, and put the command
# that performs the function in a label
function doit {
    XUget $W_STRING value:STRING
    XUget $W_POS value:POS
    XUget $W_POS2 value:POS2
    XUset $SHOWCOMMAND labelString:"$(eval print $*)"
    eval "$(print $*)"
}

# When the user moves the cursor, change the default position
function changepos {
    XUset $W_POS value:"${CB_CALL_DATA.NEWINSERT}"
    XUset $W_POS2 value:"$((CB_CALL_DATA.NEWINSERT + 5))"
}

XUinitialize TOPLEVEL TextMod "$@"

XUcolumn COL $TOPLEVEL
```

```
XUrow CONTROLS $COL packing:PACK_COLUMN numColumns:2

XUaddbuttons $CONTROLS \
    tmp "Append"          'doit XUtextappend \$TEXT "\$STRING"' \
    tmp "Insert"          'doit XUtextinsert \$TEXT \$POS "\$STRING"' \
    tmp "Delete"          'doit XUtextdelete \$TEXT \$POS \$POS2' \
    tmp "Delete Selection"  'doit XUtextremove \$TEXT' \
    tmp "Replace"         'doit XUtextreplace \$TEXT \$POS \$POS2 "\$STRING"' \
    tmp "Select"          'doit XUtextselect \$TEXT \$POS \$POS2' \
    tmp "Deselect"        'doit XUtextdeselect \$TEXT' \
    tmp "Cut"             'doit XUtextcut \$TEXT' \
    tmp "Paste"           'doit XUtextpaste \$TEXT' \
    tmp "Copy"            'doit XUtextcopy \$TEXT'


XUrow COMMANDS $COL

XUaddtextfields $COMMANDS \
    W_STRING "New string:" : 15
XUaddintegerfields $COMMANDS \
    W_POS "Start Position:" 4 \
    W_POS2 "End Position:" 4

XUset $W_STRING value:"=========="
XUset $W_POS value:0
XUset $W_POS2 value:10

XUlabel SHOWCOMMAND $COL labelString:" "

XUscrolledtext TEXT $COL \
    rows:5 \
    editMode:MULTI_LINE_EDIT \
    value:"AAAAAAAAAAAAAAAAAAAAAAAAAAA
BBBBBBBBBBBBBBBBBBBBBBBBBBB
CCCCCCCCCCCCCCCCCCCCCCCCCCC
DDDDDDDDDDDDDDDDDDDDDDDDDDD"

XUaddcallback $TEXT motionVerifyCallback changepos
XUrealize $TOPLEVEL
XUmainloop
```

16.9 Searching for Text

If a multiline Text widget could hold a large amount of text data, it is a good idea to give the user a way to search for strings within the Text. Motif has a Text widget search capability, which is provided through this XU library command:

```
XUtextfind [-b] variable $text start-position search-string
```

> **Figure 16-4. Output of txtmod.sh.** The result of inserting text using the Insert button is shown in this snapshot of `txtmod.sh`.
>

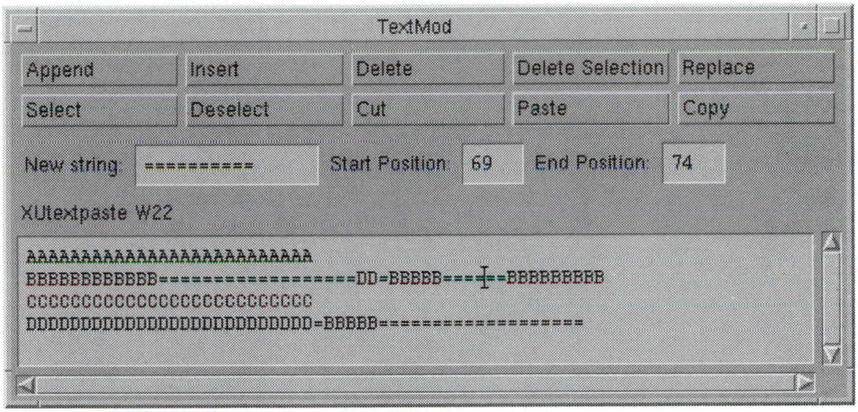

This searches for the given *search-string* within the widget $text. The search begins at *start-position* and goes forward through the text data. With the -b option, the search goes backward instead. If the search is successful, the position of the found string is stored in the *variable* and the command returns success (zero). Thus, it can be used with conditional statements to test whether there was a match. For example, this code will search for the string "Hansel" in a text widget starting at position 100 and going forward. If the search is successful, the position where the string was found is printed:

```
if XUtextfind found $TEXT 100 "Hansel"
then print "String found at position $found"
else print "Not found"
fi
```

Listing 16-2 gives a larger example of this command. Here, a ScrolledText widget is created and filled with an insightful piece of poetry. A TextField widget is used to prompt the user for a piece of text to search for. Two ArrowButtons are provided that allow the user to select the direction of the search: the upward-pointing arrow searches backward and the downward-pointing arrow searches forward; these correspond visually to the layout of the text displayed in the window. If the string is found in the desired direction, it is highlighted by setting the selection to the found text. The output from this program is shown in Figure 16-4.

Figure 16-5. Output of txtfind.sh.

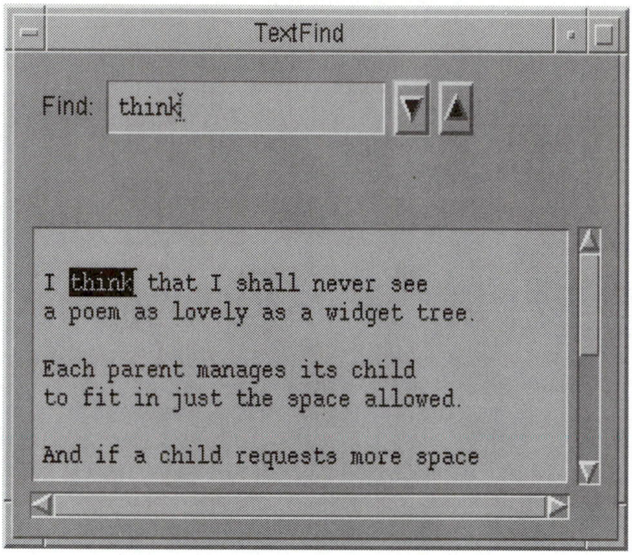

Listing 16-2. Search Program (txtfind.sh).

```
. $XUTILDIR/xutil.sh

POEM="
I think that I shall never see
a poem as lovely as a widget tree.

Each parent manages its child
to fit in just the space allowed.

And if a child requests more space
its plea is heard in all due haste.

But if this plea need be denied
no lack of love for the child is implied,

Managers would allow changes if they could
but sometimes deny for the child's own good.
"
```

```
function findCB {
    typeset direction=$1
    integer position start end result

    XUset $MESSAGE labelString:" "
    XUget $FIND value:pattern
    XUget $TEXT cursorPosition:position

    # If going backward and there is a current selection,
    # start the search from the beginning of the selection
    # so hitting the upward arrow button won't keep finding the same
    # thing over and over again.
    if [[ $direction == -b ]] && XUtextgetselectionposition $TEXT start end
    then position=$((start-1))
    fi

    if [[ ! $pattern ]]
    then
        XUset $MESSAGE \
            labelString:"Specify a string to find and try again"
        return
    fi

    if XUtextfind $direction result $TEXT $position "$pattern"
    then
        print result=$result end=$(( result + ${#pattern} ))
        XUtextselect $TEXT $result $(( result + ${#pattern} ))
    else
        XUset $MESSAGE \
            labelString:"There was no match for '$pattern'"
    fi
}

XUinitialize TOPLEVEL TextFind "$@"

XUform FORM $TOPLEVEL

XUrow CONTROLS $FORM \
    $(XUattach top 10 left 10)

XUlabel FINDLAB $CONTROLS \
    labelString:"Find:"
XUtextfield FIND $CONTROLS
XUaddcallback $FIND activateCallback "findCB"

XUarrowbutton NEXT $CONTROLS \
    arrowDirection:ARROW_DOWN \
    activateCallback:"findCB"
```

```
XUarrowbutton PREVIOUS $CONTROLS \
    arrowDirection:ARROW_UP \
    activateCallback:"findCB -b"

XUlabel MESSAGE $FORM \
    labelString:" " \
    alignment:ALIGNMENT_BEGINNING \
    $(XUattach left 10 under $CONTROLS 10)

XUscrolledtext TEXT $FORM \
    rows:8 \
    columns:40 \
    editMode:MULTI_LINE_EDIT \
    value:"$POEM" \
    $(XUattach under $MESSAGE 10 right 10 left 10 bottom 10)

XUrealize $TOPLEVEL
XUmainloop
```

This program largely consists of setting up the various widgets. The function findCB does the work of searching for text; it optionally takes an argument (-b) to specify a backward search. This argument is simply passed to the XUtextfind command.

The search begins at the current cursor position. In this way, the user can change the search point simply by clicking the mouse on a new position. One slightly tricky point is that if the user is searching backward and a current selection exists we must start the search at the character before the start of the selection. Without this refinement, multiple clicks on the backward search ArrowButton would keep finding the same string over and over instead of continuing back in the text.

If the search is not successful, a message is printed to a Label widget indicating that the string could not be found.

Limitations of XUtextfind

Unfortunately, this search capability provided by Motif does not provide some desirable features:

- There is no way to do a case-ignoring search.
- There is no capability to search for regular expressions, only fixed string searches are performed.
- There is no way to "anchor" the search to the beginning of a line.

The only solution to these problems is to implement the search "by hand" instead of using the XUtextfind command. In other words, you would need to use XUget to retrieve the value resource of the text string, then search through it using Korn-Shell pattern matching and string handling functions. The drawback of this approach is that for very large amounts of text data the KornShell functions could be too slow. In that case, you would have to attach custom C code to do the search. See Chapter 23, *Attaching C Code*, for more details.

Example: Implementing a Case Ignoring Search

Listing 16-3 shows how to perform a case-ignoring search using KornShell string functions. The function is called `caseignorefind`, and it takes the same order of arguments as `XUtextfind` (except it doesn't support a `-b` option). This function only searches forward, but it could be modified to search backwards without much trouble. It uses the `typeset` command with the `-u` option to make both the text data and the search string uppercase before doing comparisons. The example programs directory has a program called `txtfind2.sh` that uses this instead of `XUtextfind`.

The basic strategy is to step through the text data using the KornShell substring capability, which uses the notation:

```
${variable:start:number}
```

This expands to the contents of *variable* starting at character number *start* and going for *number* characters. If the `:number` part is left off, the substring goes to the end of the string. Character numbers start at zero in KornShell, as in C. For example, this sequence of code would print "Piper":

```
X="The Pied Piper of Hamlin"
print ${X:9:5}
```

And this code would print "Piper of Hamlin":

```
X="The Pied Piper of Hamlin"
print ${X:9}
```

The Search Algorithm

If we were to write this search simplistically, by stepping through each and every character of the text data then comparing the first part of the string to the search pattern, it would perform badly on long text data strings. For example, such a strategy would take 5 to 10 seconds to find a string at the end of a 500-line piece of text data with 50 characters on each line (on an Intel 486 computer running at 50 megahertz). Fortunately, there is a simple optimization that makes this search perform quite well on typical data. The idea is to use the KornShell pattern matching notations to strip off any leading substring of the text data that does not contain the first character of the search string. This notation will do the trick:

```
${variable#pattern}
```

It strips off a leading set of characters that match the *pattern* from *variable* and expands to the result. We will construct the pattern by placing an asterisk (*) that matches any characters in front of the first character of the search string.

Using this strategy, we skip over long sequences of characters that have no chance of matching the search string. In the previous example of a 500-line set of text data, a search starting at the beginning for a string at the end might only take 5 to 10 milliseconds as opposed to 5 to 10 seconds!

This is an important lesson: KornShell functions can usually be made to work with excellent performance—if you use the right strategy. In most cases "right" means avoiding process spawning and minimizing the number of commands that are executed in tight loops. This example program spawns no processes, and by using KornShell pattern matching functions to clip off characters that have no chance of matching the pattern, it greatly cuts down the number of built-ins that need to be executed.

Listing 16-3. Case-Ignoring Search (txtfind2.sh).

```
function caseignorefind {
    nameref retval=$1    # variable name to return result
    typeset widget=$2    # the text widget to search
    integer startpos=$3 # the starting position for search
    typeset -u pattern=$4    # the pattern to search for, in uppercase
    typeset -u alltext  # all the text of the widget, in uppercase
    integer origlen      # initial length of the string
    integer patlen=${#pattern}  # for convenience, the string length
    typeset firstchar=${pattern:0:1}    # for optimization

    XUget $widget value:alltext
    origlen=${#alltext}
    alltext=${alltext:startpos}      # start at startpos by taking substring

    while [[ $alltext ]]
    do
        # Optimization: clip off all leading characters of
        # the text that are not the same as the first character
        # in the pattern.  This is very fast.
        prevsize=${#alltext}
        alltext="${alltext#*$firstchar}"

        # If we clipped, the size of alltext will be different.
        # In that case, put back the first character (which would be
        # clipped off along with the rest)
        if (( prevsize != ${#alltext} ))
        then alltext="$firstchar$alltext"
        fi

        # See if we have a match
        if [[ "${alltext:curpos:patlen}" == "$pattern" ]]
        then
            # Found it!  Return the original length minus the
            # current length, that's the position in the text data
```

```
              # where it was found.
              (( retval=origlen-${#alltext} ))
              return 0
          else
              alltext=${alltext:1}       # skip first char and continue
          fi
      done
      retval=-1
      return 1      # not found
  }
```

16.10 Changing the View

By default, Text widgets will make sure the cursor is always in view. ScrolledText widgets will automatically change the ScrollBar settings to ensure this, and Text and TextField widgets will similarly change which part of the text data is being displayed. This is controlled by the autoShowCursorPosition resource, which defaults to true. Note that even programmatic changes of the cursor position will cause this automatic scrolling behavior if this resource is set to true. If you set this resource to false, then the cursor is allowed to go off-screen (this is rarely what you want).

For ScrolledText widgets and Text widgets whose text will not all fit in the window at once, there are times when you need to change which part of the text is being displayed without changing the cursor position. This is easily accomplished using the command:

        XUtextshowposition $*text position*

This will automatically scroll the Text widget so the indicated *position* is visible. It is also possible to ensure that a given position is at the top of the display by using:

        XUtextsettopposition $*text position*

The difference is that XUsettopposition ensures the named position is the top line of the display area, whereas XUtextshowposition just causes the named position to come into the view, but makes no guarantees about where precisely.

Finally, it is possible to scroll a Text widget by a certain number of lines using the command:

        XUtextscroll $*text numlines*

If *numlines* is positive, then the Text widget is scrolled forward (i.e., as if the user hit the DOWN ARROW key when on the last visible line). A negative value will scroll the Text widget display backward.

16.11 Text Widget Callbacks

The Text widget has several callbacks that are useful in a variety of situations:

- `activateCallback`

  Triggered when the user presses the ENTER key.

- `valueChangedCallback`

  Triggered after the text data are modified.

- `modifyVerifyCallback`

  Triggered before the text data are about to be modified, and gives the programmer a chance to stop the modification or alter it in some way.

- `motionVerifyCallback`

  Triggered before the cursor moves, and gives the programmer a chance to stop the motion.

- `focusCallback`, `losingFocusCallback`

  These are triggered when the Text widget has gained or lost focus.

- `gainPrimaryCallback`, `losePrimaryCallback`

  These are called when the Text widget has gained or is about to lose the selection. Only one widget at a time may have the selection.

Call Data Available During Text Callbacks

All Text widget callbacks support these variables while their functions are executing:

- `CB_CALL_DATA.REASON`

  The reason for the callback, which is one of `CR_ACTIVATE`, `CR_FOCUS` , `CR_GAIN_PRIMARY` , `CR_LOSE_PRIMARY`, `CR_LOSING_FOCUS`, `CR_MODIFYING_TEXT_VALUE` (for `modifyVerifyCallback`), `CR_MOVING_INSERT_CURSOR` (for `motionVerifyCallback`), or `CR_VALUE_CHANGED`. This can be used when you create a general subroutine to handle a variety of different callbacks; by testing this variable you can determine which callback event was triggered.

- `CB_CALL_DATA.EVENT`

  This variable, and its subfields, define the X event that caused the callback to be triggered. X events are discussed in Chapter 19, *Events, Translations, etc.*

The `losingFocusCallback` and `motionVerifyCallback` callbacks support these additional variables:

- `CB_CALL_DATA.DOIT`

  A boolean value that can be set to `true` or `false` by the callback function (it starts out set to `true`). If set to `false`, then the action will not occur (i.e., if the callback was `losingFocusCallback`, then the focus will not be lost, if it was `motionVerifyCallback`, then the motion will not occur). This is one of the few cases in Motif where a call data parameter can be modified within the callback function.

- `CB_CALL_DATA.CURRINSERT`

  The position of the cursor before the action that triggered the callback occurred.

- `CB_CALL_DATA.NEWINSERT`

  The proposed new value of the cursor that will be set if the `CALL_DATA.DOIT` variable holds the value true when the callback function returns.

The `modifyVerifyCallback` contains all of the preceding call data variables plus a few more:

- `CB_CALL_DATA.STARTPOS`, `CB_CALL_DATA.ENDPOS`

  These variables define the starting and ending position of the modified text. Text between these two values will be deleted as a result of the modification.

- `CB_CALL_DATA.TEXT.PTR`, `CB_CALL_DATA.TEXT.LENGTH`

  These variables contain the text value to be inserted at `CB_CALL_DATA.STARTPOS` and the length of the new text.

  > Of course, you could also get the length by simply using the KornShell string length notation: `${#CB_CALL_DATA.TEXT.PTR}`.

  If the modification is purely a deletion, then `CB_CALL_DATA.TEXT.PTR` will be set to the empty string and `CB_CALL_DATA.TEXT.LENGTH` will be 0.

Some examples of how to use most of these call data parameters and callbacks are shown in the next few sections.

The activateCallback

The `activateCallback` is triggered when the user presses the ENTER key while in the Text widget. It can be used for certain kinds of validation, as long as you realize that this callback may not be invoked at all (it is not invoked, for example, if the user moves out of the Text widget using a mouse click to give focus to another control).

This implies that you must run any validation commands when the data are actually used (such as when the user presses an OK button in a dialog). Other than this caveat, the use of this callback is straightforward.

The Focus Callbacks

The `focusCallback` and `losingFocusCallback` are triggered when the Text widget gains or losses focus by any means. This includes the user pressing the TAB key to traverse to a new field, or using the mouse to traverse to a new control.

There are a variety of uses for these callbacks. For example, by default, the cursor continues to be displayed even when the Text widget does not have focus. In an application that has many Text widgets in a dialog this tends to clutter the screen. It looks better if the cursor only appears when the Text widget has focus. The XU library function `XUtextautocursor` can be used to turn off the cursor when the Text widget does not have focus; it works by registering a `focusCallback` that does this:

```
XUset $CB_WIDGET cursorPositionVisible:true
```

and registering a `losingFocusCallback` that does this:

```
XUset $CB_WIDGET cursorPositionVisible:false
```

There are other similar uses for these callbacks. For example, I once wrote a system that used many Text widgets to prompt for information. The user of this system was somewhat farsighted, and was having a lot of trouble picking out which Text widget had focus (the blinking cursor was not very noticeable among the large set of fields).

> Some programmers might argue that it is not their program's responsibility to make up for poor eyesight and the user in this case should wear glasses. This is the wrong attitude—the user's problem is your problem and reasonable accommodations should be made for the user.

I changed the program so the `background` color of the Text widget with focus would turn yellow, while the others without focus would have a light gray background. This solved the problem nicely, and was done using the focus callbacks.

Another use of these callbacks might be to select automatically the text of a Text-Field when it gains focus. This would be useful when you would expect the user to almost always want to change the entire contents of a particular field after selecting it (i.e., they could just type any characters after using the mouse to focus on the field and the selected text would be deleted and replaced). The XU library command `XU-autoselect` sets up this behavior, again using the focus callbacks.

The motionVerifyCallback

It is possible to intercept user requests to change the cursor location and decide whether or not to honor those requests by using the `motionVerifyCallback`. This callback has a call data parameter, `CB_CALL_DATA.DOIT`, which can be set to either `true` or `false` by your callback function (it is initially set to `true`). If it is set to `false` by the time your callback function returns, then the motion request is denied. If the `verifyBell` resource is set to `true` (the default), then the terminal bell will ring when such a denial occurs. The call data parameter `CB_CALL_DATA.CURRINSERT` will be set to the current cursor position in the Text widget, and the variable `CB_CALL_DATA.NEWINSERT` will be set to the user's desired cursor position.

For example, if the cursor is at position 20 and the user presses the LEFT AR-
ROW key, then any functions registered for the `motionVerifyCallback` will be called
with `CB_CALL_DATA.CURRINSERT` set to 20 and `CB_CALL_DATA.NEWINSERT` set to 19. If
such a callback function were to set `CB_CALL_DATA.DOIT` to `false` before returning,
then the LEFT ARROW key would not function and by default the terminal bell
would ring.

Typical Uses of the motionVerifyCallback

This callback is usually used to check whether a cursor motion attempt by the user
should be denied. For example, consider a Text widget in which the user is supposed to enter some data, but where other areas of the text data should not be
changed or even entered. This could be accomplished by registering a `motionVeri-`
`fyCallback` that checks any attempted cursor position change and denies those
requests that would put the cursor in the forbidden area.

Listing 16-4 illustrates this concept. It creates a Text widget in which some fixed
heading information appears. A `motionVerifyCallback` is registered that will prevent the user from ever moving the cursor into that area. The callback function,
named `motionCB`, simply checks to see if the proposed new cursor position number
falls within the heading; if so then the motion request is denied by setting
`CB_CALL_DATA.DOIT` to `false`. The resulting output is shown in Figure 16-6.

Listing 16-4. Using a motionVerifyCallback (txtmtn.sh).

```
. $XUTILDIR/xutil.sh

function motionCB {
    integer noenterpos=$1    # disallow motion before this position

    if (( CB_CALL_DATA.NEWINSERT < noenterpos ))
    then CB_CALL_DATA.DOIT=false
    fi
}


HEADER="
Name               Address
----------------- -----------------------------
"
XUinitialize TOPLEVEL TextMotion "$@"

XUtext TEXT $TOPLEVEL \
    editMode:MULTI_LINE_EDIT \
    rows:10 \
    columns:50 \
    value:"$HEADER" \
    cursorPosition:"${#HEADER}"
XUaddcallback $TEXT \
```

```
        motionVerifyCallback "motionCB ${#HEADER}"

XUrealize $TOPLEVEL
XUmainloop
```

Figure 16-6. Motion Verification (txtmtn.sh). Because of the
`motionVerifyCallback`, it is impossible for the user to move into the header
lines (either by using the mouse or keyboard).

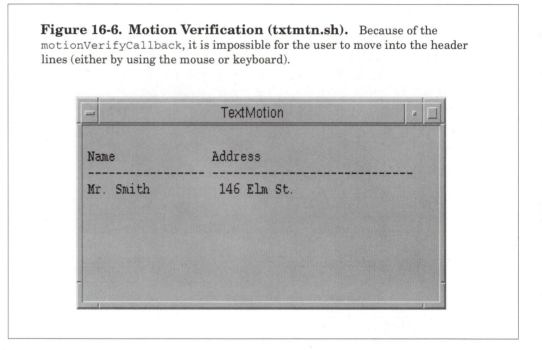

Besides denying potential motion requests, there are other uses for the `motionVer-`
`ifyCallback`. For example, the `XUautotraverse` convenience function uses this
callback to cause an automatic traversal from one Text widget to another when the
user types in the last position. This is very convenient for certain kinds of fixed
width data fields such as Social Security numbers.

The modifyVerifyCallback

Like the `motionVerifyCallback`, the `modifyVerifyCallback` allows the programmer to deny a user-requested change to the Text widget. In this case, an actual
modification to the Text widget may be denied rather than just a motion request.
Besides outright denial of the request, it is also possible to modify the request in
other ways that will be illustrated shortly.

Besides the call data variables provided by the `motionVerifyCallback`, the `mod-`
`ifyVerifyCallback` reports the location of the modified text in
`CB_CALL_DATA.STARTPOS` and `CB_CALL_DATA.ENDPOS`. Text between those positions
will be deleted by the pending request. Text to be inserted at `CB_CALL_DATA.START-`

POS is provided in the variable CB_CALL_DATA.TEXT.PTR, and the length of that text is supplied in CB_CALL_DATA.TEXT.LENGTH. These text insertion variables can be modified by your callback function, and if modified then the new text becomes the text to be inserted.

Figure 16-7. Output of txtpass.sh. Whatever the user types appears only as the letter X. The real password is maintained in a variable. For illustration purposes, the variable that holds the real password is displayed in a label below the Text widget. Obviously, a real application would not display the password in this way.

One practical illustration of modifying the text before allowing its insertion is shown in Listing 16-5. This program prompts for a password; for security reasons you don't want the text of the password to be displayed. The strategy will be to use the modifyVerifyCallback to intercept the characters being inserted by the user. Those characters will instead be inserted in a separate variable area. The CB_CALL_DATA.TEXT.PTR variable will be set to a string of x characters before returning from the callback, thus preventing the Text widget from showing the actual password. The output is shown in Figure 16-7.

> Security experts will point out that even displaying these X's gives away some information that would be useful to a hacker—the length of the password. Thus, this example would not pass the highest levels of security. Many users will be confused if there is absolutely no feedback, so I suggest using this technique whenever only modest security is needed. To implement a system in which there is no feedback, simply set the CB_CALL_DATA.TEXT.PTR to an empty string and set CB_CALL_DATA.TEXT.LENGTH to 0 before returning.
>
> Do not make the mistake of thinking you can turn off password feedback by changing the foreground color to be the same as the background color in the Text widget, because this would allow a sneaky hacker to use the cut buffer to steal the password! They could simply do a cut operation from the invisible password Text widget into some other application window where it will be displayed.

Listing 16-5. Intercepting Text Modifications (txtpass.sh).

```
. $XUTILDIR/xutil.sh

XVAR="XXXXXXXXXXXXXXXXXXXX"

function passwordCB {
    typeset newpw

    # start with the stuff before the changed text area
    newpw="${TEXT.PASSWORD:0:CB_CALL_DATA.STARTPOS}"

    # append the changed text
    newpw="${newpw}${CB_CALL_DATA.TEXT.PTR}"

    # append the stuff after the changed area
    newpw="${newpw}${TEXT.PASSWORD:CB_CALL_DATA.ENDPOS}"

    TEXT.PASSWORD=$newpw          # store back into password

    # Put X's in text before returning.  Substring enough X's from the
    # variable XVAR to fill the text length
    CB_CALL_DATA.TEXT.PTR=${XVAR:0:${#newpw}}

    # Display the hidden password for illustration purposes.
    # Obviously, you would not do this in a real program!!!
    XUset $MESSAGE labelString:"Hidden password: '${TEXT.PASSWORD}'"
}

XUinitialize TOPLEVEL TextPassword "$@"

XUcolumn COL $TOPLEVEL
XUrow ROW $COL
XUlabel LABEL $ROW labelString:"Enter Password:"
XUtextfield TEXT $ROW maxLength:20
XUaddcallback $TEXT modifyVerifyCallback passwordCB
TEXT.PASSWORD=  # Initialize actual password to nothing

XUlabel MESSAGE $COL labelString:" "

XUrealize $TOPLEVEL
XUmainloop
```

Other common uses of the `modifyVerifyCallback` include restricting the character set allowed in the Text widget or forcing the text data to be all uppercase or all lowercase. The XU library provides convenience functions for setting up these types of features on Text widgets. The `XUtextforcecase` function causes its Text widget arguments to automatically convert case while characters are typed (it has options to specify all uppercase or all lowercase). The `XUtextallowchars` function takes pairs of Text widget handles and KornShell character pattern matching specifications and arranges that only characters that match the given pattern are allowed in the Text widget. For example, to make a Text widget only accept integers, you could use:

```
XUtextallowchars $TEXT "[0-9]"
```

All of these XU library functions are explained in Chapter 6, *Prompting Using Custom Dialogs*.

Figure 16-8. Text Highlighting (txthigh.sh).

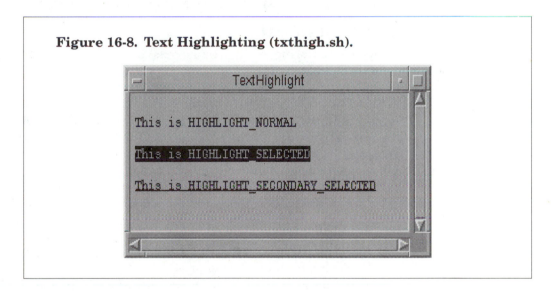

16.12 Highlighting Areas of Text

The Text widget allows pieces of text to be highlighted in several different ways. This highlighting can look similar to a selection, but it is not a selection. This feature can be used to decorate or emphasize certain portions of the text data. To highlight parts of the text, you can use:

```
XUtextsethighlight $widget start end [highlight-type]
```

This sets highlighting on text data between the *start* and *end* positions. The *highlight-type* argument, if provided, may be one of these values:

- HIGHLIGHT_NORMAL

  Turn off all special highlighting.

- HIGHLIGHT_SELECT
  Highlight in the same manner as selecting text, i.e., by reverse video.
- HIGHLIGHT_SECONDARY_SELECT
  Highlight by underlining. This is the default if no *highlight-type* is specified.

It is important to note that this command does not change the selection, it only changes the appearance of the text. The different types of highlighting are shown in Figure 16-8.

For example, to underline text between positions 10 and 20, you could use:

```
XUtextsethighlight $TEXT 10 20 HIGHLIGHT_SECONDARY_SELECT
```

16.13 Limitations of the Text Widget

While very useful for entering, editing, and displaying textual data, there are some limitations on the Text widgets that many novice Motif programmers stumble on, including:

- There is no way to mix colors in the Text widgets, you can have a background color, a foreground color (the color of the text itself), and you can cause certain pieces of text to be highlighted, but that's the extent of varying the look of the text.
- There is no way to mix fonts in the Text widget.
- Similarly, there is no way to make parts of the text superscripted or subscripted, or fully justified by varying the inter-character spacing, etc. Thus, the Text widget is not sufficient to create a fully functional word processing system that allows what-you-see-is-what-you-get display. Implementing a full word processor is a monumental task that requires custom widgets and sophisticated programming techniques.
- Many programmers try to use the Text widget as an output device for another program (i.e., they try to make it a kind of terminal emulator). Forget it, it won't work. The CDE widget libraries do provide a terminal emulator widget (an extension beyond the basic Motif widget set), but it is not provided by default from dtksh. See Chapter 23, *Attaching C Code*, for examples of how to accomplish this using dtksh.
- The lack of pattern matching and case-ignoring capabilities in the Text widget's search function means some search tasks must be written using relatively time-consuming KornShell string handling functions. If carefully written, it is possible to get acceptable performance in this way, but it would be a lot nicer if the Motif search function contained more realistic features.

16.14 Summary

The Text, ScrolledText, and TextField widgets automatically provide sophisticated editing and navigation for the end user. The programmer can register callbacks that allow text modification and navigation commands to be intercepted (and possibly modified or rejected); this very flexible interface allows you to customize the Text widget in a number of interesting ways.

Convenience functions are provided by Motif that allow the programmer to insert, delete, replace, and search for text, and to highlight portions of the text. Text is always referenced by character position, with positions starting at zero and including all characters, newlines, and special characters such as TAB that could appear to be more than one character on the display.

PART II   *Advanced Programming*

This section goes into detail on more advanced X concepts, and in most cases uses only the raw X commands provided by dtksh to get the work done. If you are a novice X programmer, you'd be well advised to master Part I before proceeding to this material.

Some of the material presented in this section describes how to add new built-in commands to the dtksh process. This is a powerful feature that allows you to optimize your programs or access features of X that are not directly provided by this release of dtksh. This material assumes you are a competent C language (or C++) programmer—and in some cases chapters in Part II even assume you know how to use the C language Motif interfaces—so these are the most advanced subjects.

17 *Traditional X Commands*

17.1 Introduction

This chapter is meant for programmers who have previously used the C language to write X programs. If you are not familiar with the C language X interfaces, this material will not be particularly enlightening and you should consider skipping it.

Specifically, I will discuss how the C language application programming interfaces for Motif, the Xt Intrinsics, and Xlib were mapped to the dtksh language. This chapter is included so that X programmers can use their existing skills to do dtksh programming. Topics covered in this chapter include:

- How the C language X functions were mapped to the dtksh language, and the rationale behind these mappings
- How call data, translations, and X events are accessible using dtksh hierarchical variables
- How resources are mapped from C to dtksh language.

Examples in this chapter will be geared toward showing you how C was mapped to dtksh, and are not meant to teach you C language X programming interfaces.

Reference Chapters

This chapter will not discuss every single X command provided by dtksh; it will provide general rules for how the commands are mapped from C to Shell to give you an intuitive feel for writing dtksh programs. Exhaustive information on individual commands is provided in these reference chapters:

- Chapter 32, *Desktop KornShell Built-in Commands*, provides an alphabetical list of every dtksh built-in extension above and beyond the base KornShell-93 language, with complete usage information and a short summary of the purpose of each argument.

- Chapter 34, *Motif Widget Reference*, provides an alphabetical list of all Motif and Xt widgets supported by dtksh, along with information on resources available from dtksh, their types, and summary information on their use, with cross references to discussions of those widgets in Part I of this book.

Those chapters are not meant to be read page-by-page; they are reference works meant to be used in daily programming.

17.2 Command Mapping General Concepts

Dtksh provides, as much as possible, a direct mapping to the underlying X functions. For this reason, programmers who already know the C language interfaces to X will find it quite easy to start using dtksh—once they know the few simple rules summarized in this chapter. This mapping from C functions to dtksh commands attempts to be as direct as possible, including the following:

- The *name* of the C function is identical to the dtksh command name.

- The *type* and *order* of arguments to the C function is the same as the type and order of arguments of the dtksh command, with a few logical and well-defined exceptions.

- The names of *resources* and *defined values* are the same as those that would be used in resource files (which are the names used in the C function with prefixes such as XmN or XtN dropped).

Where exceptions to these general rules exist, they are not arbitrary. All exceptions were designed to make sense in the context of using the commands from KornShell, and the exceptions themselves follow a few simple rules that are easily learned and remembered.

General Types of Command Mapping

There are four different ways in which an X function can be mapped to a dtksh command. The type of return value from the underlying C function completely determines which of the four kinds of mapping is used to determine how the equivalent dtksh command works. The next four subsections discuss these types of mapping and give examples of each, along with the rationale for why dtksh was designed in this way.

Void Function, Returns No Values

This includes only X functions that return void and do not return any values by reference (i.e., do not modify any passed-in pointer variables to contain a result). These map directly to dtksh commands in all respects; the number and order of arguments is identical. Here are some examples of such commands:

C Language Function Call	*Equivalent Dtksh Command*
`XRaiseWindow(dpy, window);`	`XRaiseWindow $dpy $window`
`XtMainLoop();`	`XtMainLoop`
`XtMapWidget(mywidget);`	`XtMapWidget $mywidget`
`XmUpdateDisplay(dpy);`	`XmUpdateDisplay $dpy`
`XmTextFieldSetString(text, "hello");`	`XmTextFieldSetString $text "hello"`

As you can see, this kind of mapping is quite straightforward. The differences are merely the result of syntactic variations between C and Shell, such as the need for parentheses and semicolons in C and the need for dollar sign variable expansions in dtksh.

Void Function, Returns Values by Reference

In this kind of command, the C function has a `void` return code, but does return results by reference (i.e., pointers to variables are passed in to the function and are filled in with results). These types of functions also map directly to dtksh commands. In any argument position that would take a pointer to a variable to be filled in with a result, the dtksh command should be given a dtksh variable name. Like its C counterpart, this dtksh variable will be filled in with the result of the command. Note that dtksh does not use the ampersand notation of C to pass a reference variable in this way. For example:

C Language Function Call	*Equivalent Dtksh Command*

`XmGetColors(widget, bgpixel, &fg,`
`        &topshadow, &bottomshadow,`
`        &select);`
	`XmGetColors $widget $bgpixel fg \`
	`        topshadow bottomshadow \`
	`        select`

`XmScaleGetValue(scalewid, &value);`	`XmScaleGetValue $scalewid value`

Function Returns a Boolean Value

C language functions that return a boolean value (`True` or `False`) are usually designed that way so they can be used conveniently with conditional statements such as `if` or `while`. This property is preserved in the mapping to dtksh built-in commands by using KornShell return codes as the result of the command. For example, a C function call that would return the boolean value `True` maps to a dtksh command that returns the KornShell success code.

> The KornShell success code is zero, which is the opposite of the C language, but that is not really important here. What is important is that the dtksh command return code can be used in a dtksh `if` statement in the same way that the C function return code can be used with the C `if` statement.

Once again, commands mapped in this way take arguments that correspond exactly to their C language brethren, for example:

C Language Statement	*Equivalent Dtksh Statement*
`if (XtIsManaged(widget))`	`if XtIsManaged $widget`
`{ etc. ...`	`then etc. ...`
`if (XmListItemExists(list, 3))`	`if XmListItemExists $list 3`
`{ etc. ...`	`then etc. ...`

Function Returns a Non-Boolean Value

These C functions return some non-boolean value as their result. Because the Korn-Shell return code mechanism is severely limited (it can only return a value from 0 to 255), it is not feasible to use it to return such a result. For this reason, in these cases dtksh adds a new argument, *which is always the first argument*, that is the name of a variable that will receive the result of the command. This is the only instance in which the dtksh built-in takes a different argument structure than the equivalent C function. However, there are a great many X functions that fall into this category (for instance, all the widget creation commands), so there are correspondingly many dtksh commands that use this mechanism to return results. We'll look at how widget creation commands are mapped in a moment, since they have some other differences from C. Some other examples include:

C Language Statement	*Equivalent Dtksh Statement*
`width = XWidthOfScreen(screen)`	`XWidthOfScreen width $screen`

C Language Statement	*Equivalent Dtksh Statement*
`class = XtClass(widget);`	`XtClass class $widget`
`parent = XtParent(widget);`	`XtParent parent $widget`
`s = XmTextGetString(textwid);`	`XmTextGetString s $textwid`

One interesting thing about this class of commands is that many of them allow the first argument to be a dash character (-) instead of a variable name (the exception is widget creation commands, discussed later). Such a construct causes the result of the command to be printed to the command's standard output instead of being stored in a variable name. This can be used in a variety of situations in which the result of the command is to be used immediately. For example, this code will destroy the parent of a widget whose handle is `$widget`:

```
XtDestroyWidget $(XtParent - $widget)
```

This construct allows you to avoid creating a temporary variable to hold the result that will be used immediately. Without this feature, you'd have to implement the preceding example with code like this:

```
XtParent tmp $widget
XtDestroy $tmp
```

Mix and Match

The types of mapping just discussed cover several general kinds of dtksh command argument structures, but there are combinations and variations of those. For example, some commands both return a boolean value and store some other result in a call-by-reference variable (like `XmTextFindString`). Other commands both return a non-boolean value and store results in other variables passed by reference. In such cases, dtksh does what you would expect; it remains consistent with the explanations given above for *both* kinds of function.

For example, the `XmListGetMatchPos` command both returns a value by reference and a boolean that can be used in a conditional. In the C language, you might use it like this:

```
if (XmListGetMatchPos(&position, listwidget, "A Label")) {
        etc. ...
```

whereas in dtksh, you would use it like this:

```
if XmListGetMatchPos position $listwidget "A Label"
then
        etc. ...
```

17.3 Exceptions for Convenience

Some of the C language function calls are not particularly convenient to use exactly as is when mapped to Shell. For example, X functions that take `Arg` parameters are more conveniently called using variable argument lists. Rather than blindly map such constructs, they were translated to a format that is more natural for shell programming. The next few subsections outline these conveniences.

Widget Creation Commands

In C, widgets may be created by a variety of functions, such as `XtCreateManaged-Widget()`, `XtCreatePopupShell()`, or the Motif convenience functions: `XmCreateWidgetClass()`. In addition, there are the variable argument versions of some of these commands, such as `XtVaCreateManagedWidget()`. In all cases, the C language widget creation command returns the newly created widget handle as its return value.

When mapped to dtksh, these commands fall into the category discussed in the section *Function Returns a Non-Boolean Value* on page 362. So, the equivalent dtksh command includes an extra argument, which is always the first argument: the name of a variable that will receive the newly created widget identifier (termed a *widget handle*).

The C language widget creation functions also take sets of resources and values to use as initial widget resource settings. The nonvariable argument versions of these commands typically use code like this to set up argument lists containing these values and then create the widget:

```
int n;
Arg args[5];;
Widget label;

n = 0;
XtSetArg(args[n], XmNlabelString, (XtArgVal) "Hello, World");
n++;
XtSetArg(args[n], XmNalignment, (XtArgVal) XmALIGNMENT_END);
n++;
label = XtCreateManagedWidget("mylabel",
                xmLabelWidgetClass,  parent,
                args, i);
```

Because of the verbosity of this type of code, most programmers prefer to use the variable argument versions when they are available. The same example using this style of programming would look like this:

```
Widget label;

label = XtVaCreateManagedWidget("mylabel",
                xmLabelWidgetClass, parent,
```

```
            XmNlabelString,  "Hello, World",
            XmNalignment,    XmALIGNMENT_END,
            NULL);
```

In this style, no separate `args[]` array needs to be declared, the programmer simply specifies the resource names and values directly in the function call, ending with the value `NULL` to mark the end of the resource list.

In dtksh, a notation similar to that used in resource files is used, and all resources are specified directly on the command line (like the variable argument style). As in a resource file, the name of the resource comes first, followed by a colon, followed by the value of the resource. Prefixes such as `XtN`, `XmN`, or `Xm` are left off of resource names or defined values, just as they would be in a resource file. The widget class name is also specified as it would be in a resource file; it takes the prefix `Xm` instead of `xm` and you leave off the `WidgetClass` suffix. The example just shown would be rendered like this in dtksh:

```
XtCreateManagedWidget label mylabel XmLabel $parent \
        labelString:"Hello, World" \
        alignment:ALIGNMENT_END
```

Notice the following:

- Instead of returning the widget identifier, this command takes an extra argument, the first argument, which is the name of a variable (`label`) to be set to the newly created widget identifier.

- Instead of `xmLabelWidgetClass`, the dtksh command uses `XmLabel` (the same as a resource file would use). For the gadget form, you would use `XmLabelGadget`.

- Instead of `XmNlabelString` and `XmNalignment`, the dtksh command uses `labelString` and `alignment` (the same as you would use in a resource file).

- Instead of `XmALIGNMENT_END`, the dtksh uses `ALIGNMENT_END` (again, the same as would be used in a resource file). Actually, for defined values like this, case does not matter, you could equally use `alignment_end` in the dtksh script (as you could in a resource file).

So, the rule is straightforward: Use the same kind of notation you would use in a resource file. One caveat on this rule is that each *resource*:*value* pair must be a single dtksh command argument. Thus, you must use KornShell quoting mechanisms if the *value* contains whitespace, and you should not put whitespace around the colon as you might in a resource file.

All resource conversions are automatic in dtksh. There is never a need to call the X converters yourself, as is sometimes necessary in C language X programming. Dtksh registers a number of new converters that are not usually available in the C language Motif libraries.

XtSetValues and XtGetValues

The `XtSetValues` and `XtGetValues` commands in dtksh use a notation similar to the widget creation commands for specifying resources to set or retrieve. In the case of `XtSetValues`, the notation is identical to that used on widget creation commands. For example:

```
XtSetValues $label marginWidth:3 labelString:"Goodbye, World"
```

Again, the *resource:value* notation is used, and resource names and values are specified in the same manner as in a resource file.

The `XtGetValues` command is slightly different, because it must *return* values of resources. It mimics the same type of notation, but instead of specifying values, you specify names of variables that will receive the values. For example:

```
XtGetValues $label marginWidth:w labelString:lab
print "marginWidth is $w and labelString is $lab"
```

The variable names you give can be simple names, as shown here, or they can be hierarchical names or arrays (indexed or associative).

List Function Exceptions

There are several List widget functions that take a different order of arguments than their C language counterparts:

- `XmListAddItems`
- `XmListAddItemsUnselected`
- `XmListReplaceItemsPos`
- `XmListReplaceItemsPosUnselected`

In each of these commands, the C language subroutine takes the following arguments, in this order:

1. A widget identifier
2. An array of string values
3. An integer specifying the number of items in the array of strings
4. An integer specifying the position in the List to start adding or replacing items.

In contrast, the dtksh equivalents to those commands take arguments in this order:

1. A widget identifier
2. An integer specifying the position in the List to start adding or replacing items.
3. Any number of string arguments.

For example, here is a typical C language call to `XmListAddItems`, where `items` is an array of `XmString` values that are to be added at position 10 in a List widget:

```
items[0] = XmStringCreateLocalized("first");
items[1] = XmStringCreateLocalized("second");
items[2] = XmStringCreateLocalized("third");
XmListAddItems(widget, items, 3, 10);
```

The dtksh equivalent would be:

```
XmListAddItems $widget 10 "first" "second" "third"
```

As you can see, there is good reason for the inconsistency between dtksh and C language argument ordering for these commands; the dtksh argument ordering is more convenient and natural for a shell command, and there's no need to count the number of string arguments. For this reason, the designers of dtksh decided to bend the usual rule of "map argument order exactly" for these List widget commands.

In addition, the following List widget commands, which are singular versions of some of the previous commands, take a different argument order:

- `XmListAddItem`
- `XmListAddItemUnselected`

In the dtksh version, the arguments are identical to the plural versions, except that only one string argument is allowed, whereas in the C language versions the position and string arguments are reversed:

```
XmListAddItem(widget, string, position);
```

versus

```
XmListAddItem $widget $position "$string"
```

The reason for the change is so the singular and plural versions of these commands would not be inconsistent with each other within dtksh; both take identical ordering of arguments. I always use the plural versions, since they can take one or more string arguments.

Xlib Drawing Commands

There is a whole chapter on the subject of Xlib commands that you should read if you aren't familiar with Xlib programming. In this section, I will only briefly discuss how certain aspects of the Xlib drawing commands, such as the graphics context, were mapped into shell language. For extensive tutorial information and complete examples, see Chapter 18, *Xlib: Low-Level Graphics*.

Xlib drawing functions such as `XDrawRectangles()` or `XFillPolygon()` take a graphics context (GC) argument. A graphics context is a set of parameters that specifies defaults for the graphics command such as colors, line thickness, etc. Typically, the C language programmer would use Xlib commands to allocate (or copy) a graphics context and modify parameters in it to suit the needs of the application.

The dtksh versions of these drawing commands use command line options to modify the GC. The GC modifications are normally used only for the duration of the command, and are then freed. For efficiency, however, it is possible for the dtksh programmer to specify that a GC should be kept (and not freed) for use with further drawing commands. For example, to draw a line with a two-pixel-wide line from coordinates 0,0 to 100,100 in a DrawingArea widget whose handle is stored in the variable CANVAS, you could use:

```
XtDisplay display $CANVAS
XtWindow window $CANVAS
XDrawLine $display $window -line_width 2  0 0  100 100
```

Notice that the -line_width 2 argument occurs in the same position in the argument list as the GC parameter would occur in the C language version of this command. Several of these context modification options can be specified in this position of the argument list. Not all GC elements are supported in the CDE 1.0 version of dtksh. Here are the GC options that are available:

-gc *variable*	Specify that the graphics context changes are to be saved in the named *variable*. If *variable* was previously set by another graphics drawing command, it is used as the base context for further modifications made by other options. This option must be first if it is specified.
-foreground *color*	Change the foreground to *color*.
-background *color*	Change the background to *color*.
-font *fontname*	Specify the font to use for text drawing commands.
-line_width *number*	Set the line width to *number*.
-line_style *style*	Set the line style. The *style* parameter can be one of: LineSolid, LineDoubleDash, or LineOnOffDash
-function *funcname*	Set the drawing function. The *funcname* parameter can be one of xor, or, clear, and, copy, noop, nor, nand, set, invert, equiv, andReverse, orReverse, or copyInverted.

17.4 Resource Mappings

As mentioned previously, dtksh does all resource conversions on your behalf. However, there are a few limitations as to which resources can be converted (typically in the `XtGetValues` direction). Some other things you need to know about resource conversions are also summarized.

Boolean Resources

In the C language interface to X, the programmer typically uses the defined values `True` and `False` to specify boolean values as arguments to X functions. In dtksh, any string that the X converter for String to Boolean understands can be used, which includes `True` and `False`, but also includes any other case combination you wish to use, like `TRUE` and `FALSE` or simply `true` and `false`. The converter will accept other strings as well, such as `Yes` and `No`, and even `1` and `0`!

However, when a boolean value is returned by `XtGetValues`, it is always returned as the all-lower case strings `true` and `false`. For this reason, I prefer to use the lowercase version for any command line arguments to dtksh commands that take boolean values as an argument; in that way confusion is avoided when testing booleans that are returned from functions.

Defined Values

For resources that take a fixed number of defined values, such as `alignment` (which can be one of: `ALIGNMENT_BEGINNING`, `ALIGNMENT_CENTER`, or `ALIGNMENT_END`), you can set the value using any case combination you wish.

Unlike boolean resources, however, these types of resources are always returned from `XtGetValues` as all-uppercase strings. For this reason, I suggest you always specify the values as all-uppercase strings to avoid confusing people who read your code. For example, if you were to set `alignment` using the string `alignment_beginning`, but later you did an `XtGetValues` and tested the result against the string `ALIGNMENT_BEGINNING`, someone reading your code might be confused. It is important to realize that when dtksh converts a value like this it becomes an integer internal to the widget, so there is no way for dtksh to maintain alternate case conventions on retrieval.

String Lists

Resources that are string tables, such as the items resource of the List widget, may be set directly, but are more commonly set using convenience functions such as `XmListAddItems`. If you set such a string table directly, you must use commas to separate items in the list of strings. If one of your items includes a comma, you can use backslash (`\`) to quote the comma. For example, this creates a List with two items, each of which includes a comma:

```
XtSetValues $list items:"alpha\,beta,gamma\,delta"
```

The list items would be `alpha,beta` and `gamma,delta`.

On retrieval using `XtGetValues`, the same kind of string is returned. KornShell string functions can be used to parse the comma-separated values. Examples of how to do this using the XU library convenience functions are shown under the heading *Getting the Text of an Item* on page 317.

CallbackLists

Resources of type `CallbackList` are supported by dtksh by allowing the programmer to set such resources to arbitrary dtksh command strings. You can directly set such resources using `XtSetValues`, or you can add callbacks using `XtAddCallbacks`. Dtksh also provides the `XtRemoveAllCallbacks` and `XtRemoveCallbacks` functions.

The client data argument to `XtAddCallbacks` is not necessary because you may pass any arbitrary dtksh command (in other words, you can define a dtksh function and pass it any arguments you wish). The call data argument is provided using hierarchical variables; that topic is discussed in more detail under the heading *Call Data Variables* on page 371.

For example, the following code registers an `activateCallback` on a button widget which executes a dtksh function called `pushCB`, passing it an argument:

```
XtAddCallback $button activateCallback "pushCB myargument"
```

Unsupported Resources

There are a few resources that are not fully supported by dtksh in the first version of the Common Desktop Environment. The lack of support for these resources is rarely a factor in practical programming tasks. Table 17-1 lists resources that are completely unsupported by dtksh; they can neither be set at creation time, nor set using `XtSetValues`, nor retrieved using `XtGetValues`.

Table 17-2 lists resources that can be set at widget creation time or using `XtSetValues`, but cannot be retrieved using `XtGetValues`. You can think of them as write-only resources. They cannot be retrieved because of certain technical problems that makes it very difficult to convert them to a sensible string value. Programs that might actually need to retrieve the values of these resources are rare.

In any case, it is possible to manipulate these resources by attaching custom C functions to dtksh. For more information, see Chapter 23, *Attaching C Code*.

Table 17-1. Unsupported Resources

Widget Class	Unsupported Resources
Core	accelerators, colormap
Composite	insertPosition, children
XmText	selectionArray, selectionArrayCount
ApplicationShell	argv
WMShell	iconWindow, windowGroup

Table 17-1. Unsupported Resources (continued)

Widget Class	Unsupported Resources
Shell	createPopupChildrenProc
XmSelectionBox	textAccelerators
Manager, Primitive, and Gadget	userData
XmFileSelectionBox	dirSearchProc, fileSearchProc, qualifySearchDataProc

Table 17-2. Set-Only Resources

Widget Class	Set-Only Resources
All widgets and gadgets	fontList (and other resources that set fonts), pixmap
Core	translations

17.5 Call Data Variables

Dtksh supports call data parameters to callback functions by creating local hierarchical variables that are defined only during the execution of the callback. All these hierarchical variables begin with the base CB_CALL_DATA. The CB_CALL_DATA variable itself is set to the address (in hexadecimal) of the C structure that holds the actual call data. This allows you to pass the call data structure to new built-in commands that you might write using the attachable C code features of dtksh (see Chapter 23, *Attaching C Code* for details on this feature).

For each C structure member of the call data, a hierarchical variable subfield is created below CB_CALL_DATA. The name of the hierarchical subfield is identical to the name of the C language structure member, except it is rendered in all-uppercase letters. Dtksh supports all fields of all call data parameters in Motif.

For example, consider the XmTextVerifyCallbackStruct of the Text widget. That call data structure is passed to several of the Text widget modification callbacks. It is defined as:

```
typedef struct {
        int             reason;
        XEvent          *event;
        Boolean         doit;
        XmTextPosition  currInsert, newInsert;
        XmTextPosition  startPos, endPos;
        XmTextBlock     text;
} XmTextVerifyCallbackStruct;
```

The `XmTextBlock` member is also a structure, defined as:

```
typedef struct {
        char        *ptr;
        int         length;
        XmTextFormat format;
} *XmTextBlock;
```

In the C language, you would declare an `XmTextVerifyCallbackStruct` locally in the callback handler function and assign the call data parameter passed into your function to it (casting as necessary). You can then reference fields as needed. For example, let's say you have declared an `XmTextVerifyCallbackStruct` variable named `cdata`. The following examples illustrate how you may reference fields in both C and dtksh:

C Language Reference	*Equivalent Dtksh Reference*
`cdata->reason`	`${CB_CALL_DATA.REASON}`
`cdata->startPos`	`${CB_CALL_DATA.STARTPOS}`
`cdata->text->ptr`	`${CB_CALL_DATA.TEXT.PTR}`

As you can see, any C language pointer dereferences (using the `->` notation) turn into periods separating hierarchical variable elements. One interesting point is that `${CB_CALL_DATA.TEXT}` will be set to the address of the `XmTextBlock` structure, in hexadecimal notation. This allows you to pass the address of this structure to an attached C function.

Call data structure members that can be set by a C language callback function can also be set by a dtksh callback function, and such an action will have the same effect as it would in C. For example, if you were to set:

```
CB_CALL_DATA.DOIT=false
```

in the `modifyVerifyCallback` of a Text widget, then the pending text modification would not occur.

Event Structures

The variable `CB_CALL_DATA.EVENT` is defined for all Motif widget call data structures, and it provides access to information about the X event that caused the callback to be triggered. Dtksh will set `CB_CALL_DATA.EVENT` to the address of the X event structure in hexadecimal (once again, so you could pass it to an attached C subroutine). In addition, some of the more useful subfields of `CB_CALL_DA-TA.EVENT` are available. Subfields are provided for the following X event union members:

- `XAny`
- `XButton`
- `XMotion`
- `XExpose`
- `XGraphicsExpose`
- `XKey`

Note that there are many other union members in the X event structure. Dtksh does not provide them all, only the ones listed above. For the union members listed above, though, dtksh provides complete coverage of all structure elements. For a complete list of event structure members supported by dtksh, see Appendix C.

The union members supported by dtksh were chosen because they are the most frequently needed ones in callbacks.

17.6 Event Handlers

Dtksh provides full access to event handling features of the Xt Intrinsics (`XtAddEventHandler` and `XtRemoveEventHandler`). In the context of an event handler function, the variable `EH_EVENT` will be defined, and it will hold the address of the X event structure that triggered the event. Subfields are also available that use `EH_EVENT` as a base, and those subfields include all of the X event union members described in the previous section.

See Chapter 19, *Events, Translations, etc.*, for more information on using events from dtksh.

17.7 Translations

Dtksh provides a generic translation function named `ksh_eval`, which takes one argument; the argument is a string that defines any arbitrary dtksh command. The dtksh command will be executed when the translation triggers. In the context of such a translation handling command, the variable `TRANSLATION_EVENT` is defined. It holds the address, in hexadecimal, of the X event that triggered the translation. The same X event union members described in the last section are available as subfields of the `TRANSLATION_EVENT` variable.

See Chapter 19, *Events, Translations, etc.*, for more information on using translations from dtksh.

17.8 Summary

Dtksh provides a great deal of X functionality, mapped directly from the C language X interfaces to KornShell built-in commands. Wherever possible, the order and types of arguments to the C function are the same as the order and types of arguments to the dtksh equivalent built-in command. In some cases an extra argument is added (always the first argument), which will be set to the result of the command. In a very small number of commands, the order of arguments differs between the C language and dtksh; this was done purely for the convenience of the shell programmer.

Dtksh automatically translates resource values as needed. A few resources are not supported, but they are rarely required for typical applications.

Dtksh provides callback commands with call data using hierarchical variables whose names mirror those used in C language call data structures (but all uppercase). This includes the most commonly needed subfields of the X event structure.

Dtksh supports definition of translations, and also event handlers, again passing information about X event structures using hierarchical variables.

18 *Xlib: Low-Level Graphics*

18.1 Introduction

This chapter explains how to use the lowest layer of the X application programming interface—Xlib. It teaches you all you need to know about Xlib, and only assumes you know shell programming techniques and X concepts to the depth discussed in Part I of this book.

In the Motif programming layer discussed in previous chapters, the programmer works by creating widgets. Widgets are high-level objects that are used for specific purposes such as displaying text or managing the layout of other widgets. Xlib provides a much lower level of detail. At this level, the programmer may draw arbitrary lines, circles, polygons, or text strings. The programmer must specify exactly where and how to draw these shapes—nothing is done on the programmer's behalf as at the widget level of programming. Topics discussed in this chapter include:

- How to use DrawnButton and DrawingArea widgets as a canvas for drawing
- How to draw various shapes such as lines, circles, arcs, and polygons
- How to change the parameters that affect how shapes are rendered, such as line styles, colors, and fonts
- How to create simple animation effects.

Xlib graphical programming is a huge subject, and this chapter cannot possibly cover it in full detail. Instead, a general overview of the commands is presented along with some simple examples. A more complete example is presented in Chapter 26, *Stock Chart Display*.

Why Use Xlib?

In general, Xlib-level programming is only used in relatively sophisticated dtksh programs. You can resort to Xlib if you need some kind of custom graphical display such as a pie chart or a bar chart or other specialized graphics.

There are commercially available and freeware widgets specifically made for charting purposes, and that's what I would suggest you use if you need very sophisticated graphing or charting for your application. It is possible to attach externally defined widgets to dtksh and use them as if they were built-in to dtksh (this is discussed in Chapter 23, *Attaching C Code*).

It would be necessary to use Xlib to create a video game, for example, or other kinds of animation effects.

But there's another important use for Xlib, one that's hard to master. Xlib can be used by an imaginative programmer to add a little spice to an application, to provide an element of fit and finish, to set the application apart so that it is no longer just a jumble of dialogs and buttons and menus, but a work of art. It's the little unexpected things that endear a program to its users. Xlib lets you do those unexpected things. Later in this chapter, the checkbook program that was developed in Part I will be extended to include some animation effects that fall into this category.

18.2 Xlib General Concepts

Before learning the Xlib commands, there are some general concepts you need to understand. Since you will be using Xlib to draw shapes, you need to understand the coordinate system. You need to know how X keeps track of different parameters that affect how shapes are drawn. This section will explain all these things. You may need to review some basic trigonometry in order to understand circular arc drawing (I never said this was going to be totally painless).

The Coordinate System

When you draw a shape using Xlib, you must specify x, y coordinates in order to position and size the shape. The coordinate system used by X is a little different from the one you learned in geometry class. The x axis runs horizontally across the screen, starting at zero on the left with increasing positive numbers going to the right. The y axis runs vertically, with the zero position starting at the *top* of the screen, with increasing positive numbers going *down*. The y axis numbering is the opposite of what you might be used to. See Figure 18-1. Distances and positions in Xlib are always measured in pixels.

The Aspect Ratio Problem

One problem with the X coordinate system is that there is no guarantee of a *unit aspect ratio*. That sounds very technical, but all it means is that one pixel in the horizontal dimension may not be exactly the same size as one pixel in the vertical dimension; it's hardware dependent. Most hardware has pixels that are nearly the same size horizontally and vertically, with perhaps a 1.2 to 1 ratio of horizontal to vertical pixel size. This problem will manifest itself most dramatically in the case of circles — they will seem flattened out on hardware that has a bad aspect ratio.

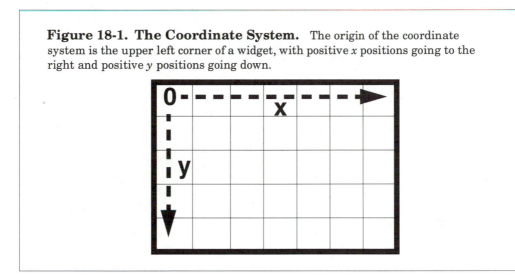

Figure 18-1. The Coordinate System. The origin of the coordinate
system is the upper left corner of a widget, with positive *x* positions going to the
right and positive *y* positions going down.

In practice, because most hardware is nearly correct you won't really need to take
any special action. For some highly precise rendering tasks, however, you should be
aware of this, and you may need to take corrective action.

Trigonometry Review

If you are not interested in drawing circles or circular arcs, or if you recall with complete clarity your high school trigonometry lessons, then you don't need to read this
section. Here, I review a few concepts that are useful for drawing and positioning
circles using Xlib:

- A circular arc is defined by an origin point, a radius, a starting angle, and an
  angular size. The arc sweeps a line from the first angle through the angular
  size a distance equal to the radius from the origin point.

- Angles start at zero at the three o'clock position, and are considered positive
  in the counterclockwise direction and negative in the clockwise direction.

- Angles are measured in either radians or degrees. A full circle has two times
  pi radians, or 360 degrees.

    > Pi is a constant with a value of about 3.1415926535. KornShell math functions like
    > `sin()` and `cos()` require radians as the unit of angular measure, while the Xlib
    > commands that render circular arcs require degrees.

- The coordinates of a point that is a distance `r` from the origin at an angle
  `theta` is given by the equations:

```
x = r*cos(theta)
y = r*sin(theta)
```

See Figure 18-2.

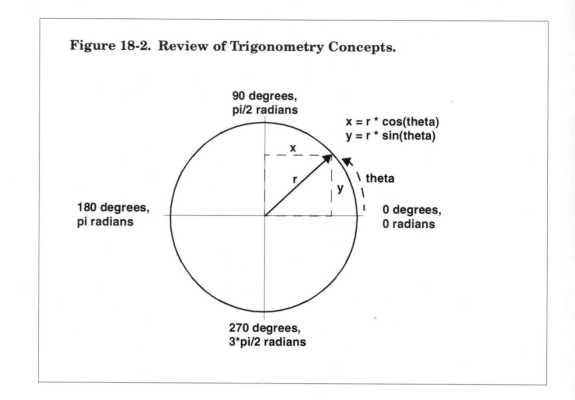

Figure 18-2. Review of Trigonometry Concepts.

The Graphics Context

Recall how X works: the client application (the dtksh script) sends messages to the X display server. These messages tell the server how to draw the various elements of the application's screen. Widgets use Xlib to draw themselves using these messages.

To draw even a simple shape, such as a line, a huge amount of detail is required. Obviously, the starting and ending coordinates of the line must be specified, but many other parameters are also necessary. What color will the line be? How thick should the line be drawn? Should the line be solid, or should it be dotted or dashed? Should the ends of the line be rounded off, or just drawn straight? Should the line's color be merged with other colors where it is drawn, or should it opaquely replace whatever happens to be there?

Now, if every single drawing request transmitted from the client to the display server had to describe every last detail of the shapes being drawn there would be a performance problem. The size of the message used to transmit the information from the client application to the display server would be enormous.

For this reason, X uses the concept of the *graphics context*, or GC for short. A graphics context is a data structure maintained by the display server that specifies all the parameters that might affect how a shape is drawn. There can be many different graphics contexts active for a given application. When a drawing request is sent to the display server, that request specifies only a small amount of information about the shape to be drawn, along with the identifier of the graphics context to use for all other parameters necessary to draw the shape. For example, to draw a line, a message is sent that contains the starting and ending coordinates of the line and an identifier of a graphics context; all other parameters such as line thickness or color are taken from the graphics context.

The application can create as many different graphics contexts as it needs to get its work done, but usually only a small number are necessary. The idea here is that many different shapes to be drawn will use the same few graphics contexts over and over again. This solves the performance problem—relatively little information needs to be transmitted to draw simple shapes.

How Dtksh Handles the Graphics Context

Traditional X programs use several Xlib commands to create, copy, or modify graphics contexts. Dtksh simplifies this process by providing a few command options on the Xlib shape drawing commands it supports. By default, dtksh maintains a single graphics context for all Xlib commands executed by the script, and will modify this context based on command line options. It resets the context back to its original (default) state after the shape drawing command is complete.

Programs that might draw very many shapes using several different contexts can do so by giving the dtksh Xlib commands an option that causes dtksh to maintain a graphics context after the command completes. The saved context can be used in subsequent drawing commands. There is no limit on the number of contexts a dtksh application can maintain in this way.

Here is a summary of the options supported by the dtksh shape drawing commands. Examples of how to use them will be presented when specific commands are discussed in the following sections.

`-foreground` *color*	Specifies the foreground *color* for the shape.
`-background` *color*	Specifies the background *color* for the shape.
`-line_width` *width*	Specifies the *width* of the line used to draw the shape. If *width* is zero, then the line will be drawn as thinly as possible on the display device.
`-line_style` *style*	This can be used to change how any lines in the shape are drawn. The *style* argument can be one of `LineSolid`, `LineDoubleDash`, or `LineOnOffDash`.

`-font` *fontname*	For text rendering Xlib commands, this changes the font used. The default is the application's default font.
`-function` *funcname*	This can be used to change how shapes are merged in with existing graphics on the screen. The *func-name* specifies a boolean operator that is used to combine bits in the screen with bits of the shape being drawn. On color displays, this boolean function applies to each of the red, green, and blue components. The *funcname* can be one of `xor`, `or`, `clear`, `and`, `copy`, `noop`, `nor`, `nand`, `set`, `invert`, `equiv`, `andReverse`, `orReverse`, or `copyInverted`.
`-gc` *variable*	If this option is present, it must be the first graphics context option. It specifies that the graphics context stored in *variable* should be used for this drawing command. If further options are given, they will modify the context specified by *variable*. If *variable* is unset, a GC will be created and stored in it. The GC is maintained for the life of the program. Without this option, any GC used by the drawing commands is freed immediately following the command's completion.

The Display, Screen, and Window Structures

X uses several data structures that pertain to graphical objects and the hardware on which they are rendered: the display, screen, and window data structures. It is beyond the scope of this discussion to go into exactly what each of these data structures is used for. All you need to know is that the Xlib functions need access to these structures to get their jobs done. All of these structures can be derived easily from the widget handle using these commands:

```
XtDisplay variable $widget
XtWindow variable $widget
XtScreen variable $widget
```

Each of these commands store the address of the relevant data structure associated with $*widget* in the *variable* name passed as the first argument (the address is stored as a hexadecimal number). The *variable* argument may also be a dash (-); in that case the result is printed to the function's standard output. This is sometimes useful for situations in which you will use the structure immediately.

The most common way to handle these variables is to retrieve them once at the beginning of a function you define to do drawing. It's also a good idea to use the same names always for such variables. I usually use these variables: `display`, `screen`, and `widget`. You can't get much clearer than that! For example:

```
function mydraw {     # first arg is widget to draw upon
    typeset w=$1
    # get X drawing data structures for later use
    # in this function.
    typeset display=$(XtDisplay - $w)
    typeset screen=$(XtScreen - $w)
    typeset window=$(XtWindow - $w)

    etc.
```

Using this strategy, you only need to get the structures once. Of course, it is possible to write a function that would draw on two different widgets at the same time. In that case, the window structure will be different and you'd need one variable for each widget you intend to draw on, but the display and screen will typically be the same.

Expose Events

It is important for you to have a mental model of how Xlib graphics work. The X display server does not maintain any information about how a certain window looks, it depends entirely on the client application for drawing. If a window overlaps your application, then is moved away again, then an expose event is generated by the X display server that informs the client program which pieces of the screen need to be redrawn.

> Certain modes can be used with the display server that cause it to save the screen image under a transient window such as a menu. However, the display server need not honor such a request and in general the application must be prepared to redraw any portion of itself at any time.

Each widget in the application knows how to redraw itself. When a widget is first managed and mapped onto the screen, there is an initial expose event generated to display the contents of the widget.

When you want to create custom graphics using Xlib commands, you must use one of the two widgets provided by Motif that allow arbitrary drawing: the Drawing-Area or the DrawnButton. Each of these widgets has a callback that allows you to use Xlib graphics to redraw them if an expose event occurs. These widgets are discussed next.

18.3 Widgets Used for Drawing

There are two Motif widgets, the DrawingArea and DrawnButton, whose sole purpose is to provide a canvas on which to draw using Xlib commands. The DrawingArea widget is a manager widget that provides callbacks for intercepting exposure events (exposeCallback) and keyboard or mouse input events (inputCallback). In addition, a callback is triggered whenever the size of the widget is changed (resizeCallback).

The DrawnButton widget provides PushButton-like capabilities, but does not draw anything in the label area. It also provides an exposeCallback and a resizeCallback, but it does not provide an inputCallback.

A Simple Example

The general strategy is to create one of the two drawing widgets and register an exposeCallback to draw whatever you wish upon it. Listing 18-1 shows a very simple example of Xlib drawing. I haven't explained precisely how to draw shapes yet, but this example is instructive at this point even if you don't yet know precisely how the drawing commands work. This program creates a DrawingArea widget, and displays a smiling face on it using Xlib commands for drawing circles and lines. The resulting output is shown in Figure 18-3.

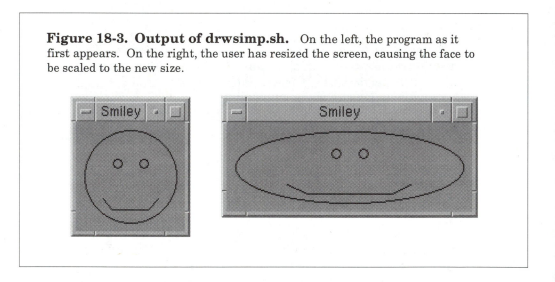

Figure 18-3. Output of drwsimp.sh.   On the left, the program as it first appears. On the right, the user has resized the screen, causing the face to be scaled to the new size.

After creating a DrawingArea widget, a function is registered as its expose-Callback, which draws the face. If you run this program, try covering part of the display by dragging another application window over it, then expose the face again by moving away the overlapping window. You will notice that the exposeCallback is triggered again (you know this because the face redraws). This function also takes into account the size of the DrawingArea, and scales the face to that size.

Listing 18-1. Using Exposure Callbacks (drwsimp.sh).

```
. $XUTILDIR/xutil.sh

typeset GC  # for efficiency, we'll use the same GC for all drawing

function exposeCB {
    # Draw a smiley face on the widget
    typeset w=$CB_WIDGET
    typeset display=$(XtDisplay - $w)
    typeset window=$(XtWindow - $w)
    integer margin=8
    integer height width

    # we need to scale to the size of the screen
    XUget $w height:h width:w

    XClearWindow $display $window -gc GC

    # Draw a circle, centered in the window

    integer circwidth=w-2*margin
    integer circheight=h-2*margin

    XDrawArc $display $window \
        -gc GC \
        $((margin)) $((margin)) \
        $((circwidth)) $((circheight)) \
        0 $((360*64))

    # Draw the eyes a little above the midline

    XDrawArc $display $window \
        -gc GC \
        $((w/2 - 2*margin)) $((h/2 - 2*margin)) \
        $((margin)) $((margin))  \
        0 $((360*64))

    XDrawArc $display $window \
        -gc GC \
        $((w/2 + margin)) $((h/2 - 2*margin)) \
        $((margin)) $((margin))  \
        0 $((360*64))

    # Draw the mouth
```

```
        XDrawLines $display $window \
            -CoordModeOrigin \
            -gc GC \
            $((w/4)) $((h*.7)) \
            $((w/3)) $((h*.8)) \
            $((2*w/3)) $((h*.8)) \
            $((3*w/4)) $((h*.7))
}

XUinitialize TOPLEVEL Smiley "$@"

XUdrawingarea CANVAS $TOPLEVEL \
    width:100 height:100 \
    exposeCallback:exposeCB

XUrealize $TOPLEVEL
XUmainloop
```

Using the DrawnButton Widget

The DrawnButton widget is virtually identical to the PushButton widget, but it does not have resources to display anything (labelString, labelPixmap, label-Type, alignment, etc.). Instead, it provides an exposeCallback, and it is up to your application to draw whatever is desired using that callback function. You would use this widget whenever one of the other button-type widgets (PushButton, ArrowButton, or ToggleButton) is not sufficient for your purposes.

You can use the activateCallback to perform an action when the user presses the DrawnButton, just as you do for the PushButton widget. One difference between using the DrawnButton and a PushButton is that you must size the DrawnButton by setting its width and height resources, whereas you normally allow the Push-Button to size itself. The reason for the difference is that the DrawnButton widget can't compute a reasonable starting size because it has no idea what you will be drawing on it. The PushButton has no such problem, because it can pick a reasonable starting size that depends on the label or graphic image to be displayed on it.

Using the DrawingArea Widget

The DrawingArea widget is more general than the DrawnButton widget. It is a Manager-class widget that provides an exposeCallback. It is possible to position children of the DrawingArea by setting their x and y resources (in other words, the DrawingArea acts a lot like a BulletinBoard widget).

Although you can add children to a DrawingArea widget, it is commonly used with no children at all — simply as a canvas on which to draw shapes. If you do add children to a DrawingArea, you must be careful not to draw over them; they will receive no indication that they may need to repaint themselves in such cases.

Besides the `exposeCallback`, the DrawingArea widget provides a callback that is triggered whenever there is keyboard or mouse input available, the `inputCall-back`. That callback is passed the X event that caused the input in the variable `CB_CALL_DATA.EVENT` and its subfields. See Chapter 19, *Events, Translations, etc.* for more information.

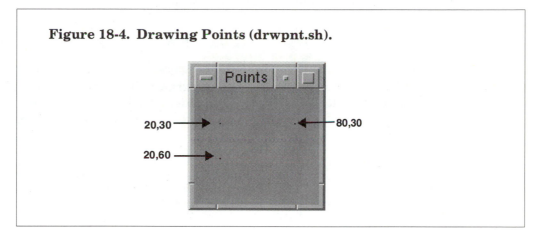

Figure 18-4. Drawing Points (drwpnt.sh).

18.4 Drawing Points

Points may be drawn using these commands:

```
XDrawPoint display window [GC args] x1 y1
XDrawPoints display window [mode] [GC args] x1 y1 [x2 y2 ...]
```

XDrawPoints draws multiple points. The *mode* argument must come before any *GC args* and may be one of these values:

- `-CoordModePrevious`

    The previous endpoint is used as the origin when determining the next point to draw. In other words, after the first point all further *x*, *y* coordinates are offsets from the previous point.

- `-CoordModeOrigin`

    This is the default, coordinates are always specified absolutely (relative to the origin).

For example, the following code will draw three points, one at the coordinate 20, 30, one at 80, 30, and one at 20, 60.

```
XDrawPoints $display $window \
    20 30 80 30 20 60
```

The output of a program that draws points using that command is shown in Figure 18-4.

18.5 Drawing Lines

The following functions can be used to draw lines:

```
XDrawLine display window [GC args] x1 y1 x2 y2
XDrawLines display window [mode] [GC args] x1 y1 x2 y2 [x3 y3 ...]
```

XDrawLine draws a single line from the point x1,y1 to the point x2,y2 on the given display and window. For example, to draw a line from the upper left corner to the lower right corner of a DrawingArea widget whose handle is stored in the variable DA and which is 100 pixels tall and 200 pixels wide, you could use:

```
XDrawLine $display $window \
    0 0 100 200
```

> All examples in this chapter will assume the display and window structures have already been retrieved for the drawing widget in question. In this example, you would use: XtDisplay display $DA and XtWindow window $DA to achieve this.

XDrawLines draws multiple, *connected* lines. Each set of two arguments defines a point, and all these points are connected in the order in which they are specified. The mode argument can be one of the two coordinate modes explained in the previous section: -CoordModePrevious or -CoordModeOrigin. For example, this command would draw the letter "L":

```
XDrawLines $display $window \
    20 20 20 100 50 100
```

That is, it draws a line from point 20, 20 to point 20, 100 (the downstroke of the "L") then it draws a line from point 20, 100 to point 50, 100 (the horizontal piece). The following command would do the same thing using relative coordinates:

```
XDrawLines $display $window -CoordModePrevious \
    20 20 0 80 30 0
```

Here, each set of coordinates is added to the previous point to get the new point. So, once again we start at point 20, 20 but the next point is derived by adding 0 to 20 to get the x coordinate (20) and then adding 80 to 20 to get the new y coordinate (100). This process is repeated for the following line.

Sometimes it is more convenient to use relative coordinates, sometimes absolute coordinates. Any number of connected lines may be drawn using XDrawLines.

The GC arguments may be any of the items described in the section: *The Graphics Context* on page 378. Of particular interest in the case of lines is the `-line_style` option. The following commands will draw one of each of the available line styles:

```
XDrawLine $display $window \
    -line_style LineSolid \
    0 0 100 0
XDrawLine $display $window \
    -line_style LineOnOffDash \
    0 50 100 50
XDrawLine $display $window \
    -line_style LineDoubleDash \
    0 100 100 100
```

The resulting output is shown in Figure 18-5. The `-line_width` option is also commonly used; its argument is the thickness, in pixels, of the line to be drawn. The default is zero, which is a special value meaning "draw the line as thinly as possible."

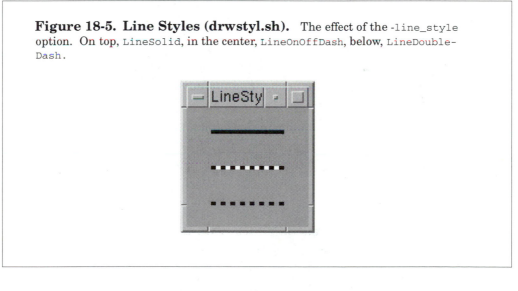

Figure 18-5. Line Styles (drwstyl.sh).   The effect of the `-line_style` option. On top, `LineSolid`, in the center, `LineOnOffDash`, below, `LineDouble-Dash`.

Disconnected Lines

It is possible to draw multiple disconnected lines by using:

```
XDrawSegments display window [GC args] x1 y1 x2 y2 [x3 y3 x4 y4 ...]
```

In this case, sets of four arguments define each line by its starting and ending coordinates. For example, this will draw two lines that will form the letter "X":

```
XDrawSegments $display $window \
    0 0 100 100 \
    100 0 0 100
```

This will draw a diagonal line from the upper left (point 0,0) to the lower right (point 100, 100), then another disjoint line from the upper right (point 100,0) to the lower left (point 0, 100). See Figure 18-6.

Figure 18-6. Line Segments (drwseg.sh).

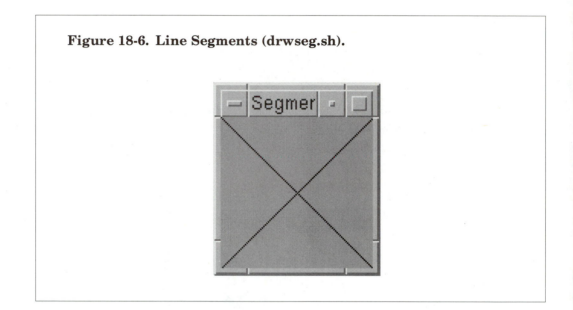

18.6 Drawing Rectangles

These commands can be used to draw a rectangle:

```
XDrawRectangle display window [GC args] x y width height
XFillRectangle display window [GC args] x y width height
```

Each of these commands defines a rectangle by the *x, y* coordinates of its upper left corner and its width and height. The XDrawRectangle command draws the outline of a rectangle. You can use the usual *GC args* to define the thickness and style of the line used to draw the outline (see *Drawing Lines* on page 386). The XFill-Rectangle command draws a solidly filled rectangle as opposed to just the outline of a rectangle.

For example, the following code will draw a small red, filled rectangular area surrounded by a larger blue rectangular outline:

```
XFillRectangle $display $window \
    -foreground red \
    40 50 100 50      # x=40 y=50 width=100 height=50
XDrawRectangle $display $window \
    -foreground blue \
    20 30 140 90      # x=20 y=30 width=140 height=90
```

The resulting output is shown in Figure 18-7 (the figure is in gray scale instead of color).

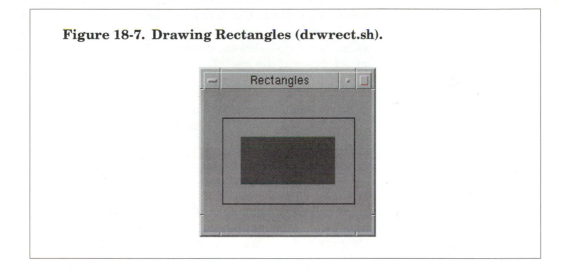

Figure 18-7. Drawing Rectangles (drwrect.sh).

18.7 Drawing Polygons

You can draw the outline of a polygon by using XDrawLines as explained above. You just need to make sure the ending point is the same as the starting point so the polygon forms a connected shape. To fill an area bounded by a polygon, you can use the command:

```
XFillPolygon display window [shape-hint] [mode] [GC args] x1 y1 ...
```

As with XDrawLines, the polygon is defined by a set of x, y coordinates which you can think of as being connected successively by lines. XFillPolygon will automatically connect the beginning and ending points if you fail to make them the same, thus ensuring that a closed area is filled. The *mode* argument is either -Coord-ModePrevious or -CoordModeOrigin as explained earlier for XDrawLines. The *GC args* can be used to specify the color of the filled area and other graphics context options.

One important argument is the `shape-hint`. This argument can be used to give `XFillPolygon` information about the shape being drawn so it can use the most efficient algorithm possible to fill the area. It can be one of these values:

-Complex   (The default). This option specifies that the shape is complex and may contain self-intersecting lines. This option causes `XFillPolygon` to use the most general, and slowest, algorithm to fill the area.

-Nonconvex   This option indicates that the shape does not have any self-intersecting lines, but may have concave areas. This allows `XFillPolygon` to use a faster algorithm than in the `-Complex` case. If you give this option when there really are crossing lines in the polygon the results are not defined.

-Convex   This option allows `XFillPolygon` to use the fastest algorithm of all. The shape must not have any self-intersecting lines or concave areas, otherwise it may not fill correctly.

If there is any question about the nature of the shape, it is safest to use `-Complex`.

The following example code will fill in a triangular area and a more complex shape:

```
XFillPolygon $display $window -Convex -CoordModeOrigin \
    20 20 100 20 100 100      # A triangle
XFillPolygon $display $window -Complex -CoordModeOrigin \
    120 20 220 20 200 100 140 10 130 100  # what is it?
```

Because a triangle is always a convex shape, this code may use the fast `-Convex` algorithm. The other shape (whatever it is) contains both self-intersecting lines and concave areas, and must use the slowest algorithm specified by `-Complex`. The resulting output is shown in Figure 18-8.

18.8 Drawing Circles and Arcs

Circles and circular arcs are drawn using these commands:

```
XDrawArc display window [GC args] x y width height angle anglesize
XFillArc display window [GC args] x y width height angle anglesize
```

Both of these commands define the arc to be drawn by the *x, y* coordinate of the upper left corner of the circular arc to be drawn, the *width* and *height* of the bounding box on which the arc resides, the *startangle,* which defines the beginning angle for the arc, and the *anglesize,* which determines the number of degrees through which the arc will sweep. The arc sweeps counterclockwise starting at *angle* and continuing to *angle+anglesize*. If *width* and *height* are the

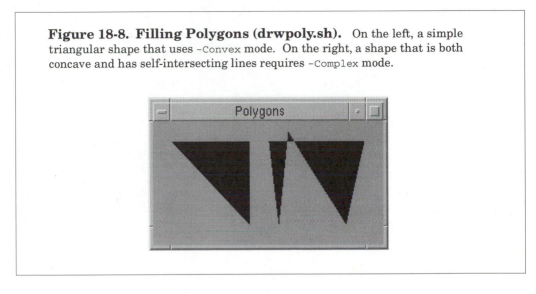

Figure 18-8. Filling Polygons (drwpoly.sh). On the left, a simple triangular shape that uses -Convex mode. On the right, a shape that is both concave and has self-intersecting lines requires -Complex mode.

same, then a circular arc is drawn, otherwise it will be elliptical. XDrawArc draws the outline of an arc, whereas XFillArc draws a pie-shaped filled area.

One tricky point is that the angles are defined by Xlib to be in units of 1/64th degrees. So, when calculating the angles, you need to multiply the number of degrees by 64 before calling XDrawArc or XFillArc.

For example, to draw the outline of a full circle centered in a box of size 100 by 100 whose upper left corner is at the point 10, 10, this code could be used:

```
XDrawArc $display $window \
    10 10 100 100 \
    0 $((360*64))
```

Note that I specified 0 as the starting angle and 360*64 as the size of the arc. There are 360 degrees in a full circle, and I had to multiply by 64 because Xlib wants angles specified in sixty-fourths of a degree. To draw a 60-degree-long pie-shaped filled area that extends counterclockwise starting from the 12 o'clock position, the following code could be used:

```
XFillArc $display $window \
    -foreground red \
    10 10 100 100 \
    $((90*64)) $((60*64))
```

The shapes drawn by these commands are shown in Figure 18-9. An example of drawing multiple arcs is shown in Listing 18-2. That program draws several arcs of different colors in a loop. In each loop iteration the size of the arc's radius is

Figure 18-9. Drawing Arcs (drwcirc.sh and drwpie.sh).   On the
left, a full circle is drawn. On the right, a pie shaped filled slice is shown.

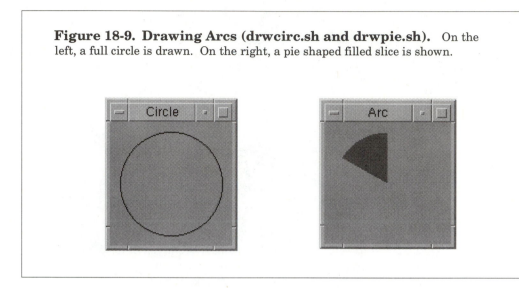

decreased by making the bounding box smaller. The starting angle is also changed
so each arc starts where the last one left off. Finally, the color is changed on each
iteration by using successive elements of an array of colors. The result looks something like a seashell, as you can see in Figure 18-10 (the figure shows the output in
gray scale instead of color).

Listing 18-2. Drawing Arcs (drwshell.sh).

```
. $XUTILDIR/xutil.sh

function exposeCB {
    typeset w=$CB_WIDGET
    typeset display=$(XtDisplay - $w)
    typeset window=$(XtWindow - $w)
    integer angle
    integer radius=100
    integer i=0 x=10 y=10 width=100 height=100
    typeset colors

    set -A color red green plum black brown blue grey yellow

    for (( angle = 0; angle < 360; angle += 45 ))
    do
        XFillArc $display $window \
            -foreground "${color[i++]}" \
            $x $y $width $height \
            $((angle*64)) $((45*64))
```

```
        (( x += 5 ))
        (( y += 5 ))
        (( width -= 10 ))
        (( height -= 10 ))
    done
}

XUinitialize TOPLEVEL SeaShell "$@"

XUdrawingarea CANVAS $TOPLEVEL \
    width:120 height:120 \
    exposeCallback:exposeCB

XUrealize $TOPLEVEL
XUmainloop
```

Figure 18-10. Output of drwshell.sh.

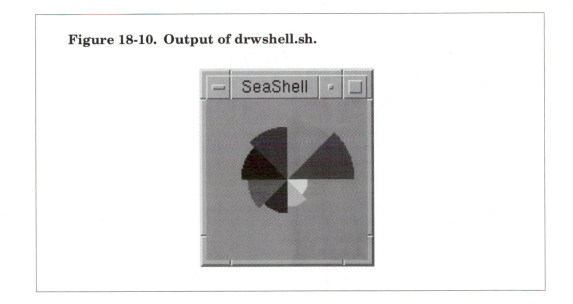

18.9 Drawing Strings

It is often necessary to render string data in an Xlib display. For example, labels may need to be placed along a graph axis. The following commands are useful for this purpose:

```
XDrawString display window [GC args] x y string
XDrawImageString display window [GC args] x y string
```

These commands draw their string argument starting at coordinate x, y. This coordinate names the position of the lower left corner of the string.

> Actually, this coordinate specifies the placement of the baseline of the string. Some characters, such as a lowercase letter j may extend slightly below this baseline.

The GC args can be used to change the font used to render the string, using the option -font *fontname*. For example, this set of code will print the string "Hello, World" at position 50, 100 using a constant width font:

```
XDrawString $display $window -font fixed \
      50 100 "Hello, World"
```

When positioning text, it is often necessary to know how many pixels wide a string will be when rendered in a particular font. This can be determined by using the command:

```
XTextWidth variable font string
```

This command stores the width of the given *string* as rendered using *font* in the named *variable*. For example, this code will horizontally center the string "Hello, World" at the point 50, 100 using a fixed-width font:

```
string="Hello, World"
XTextWidth w fixed "$string"
XDrawString $display $window -font fixed \
      $((50 - w/2)) 100 "$string"
```

As you see, I simply subtract half the width of the string from the desired *x* coordinate.

> Unfortunately, the first release of dtksh does not include any equivalent command to get the height of a text string, so it is not very easy to center a string vertically. Hopefully this will be corrected in a future release.

18.10 Copying and Clearing Areas

When redrawing parts of a display, it is often necessary to clear all graphics in a certain area. These commands are provided by dtksh to accomplish this:

```
XClearWindow display window
XClearArea display window [GC args] x y width height [true|false]
```

The XClearWindow command simply clears everything in the widget's window. The XClearArea command is more surgical, and allows a rectangle to be cleared. The rectangle is defined in the same way as in the XDrawRectangle command. The final argument to this command is either the string true or false. If true, then an exposure event is generated for the cleared area.

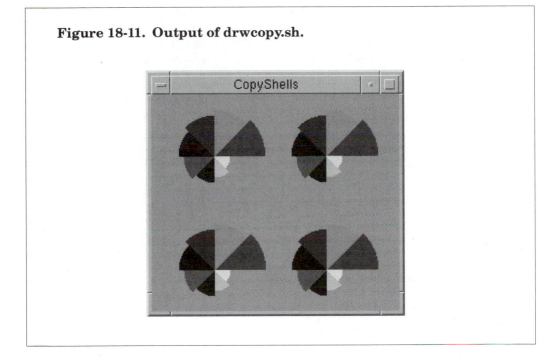

Figure 18-11. Output of drwcopy.sh.

Copying Areas

Besides clearing areas, it is sometimes convenient to copy graphics from one place in a window to another. Occasionally it is also desirable to copy graphics from one widget to another. Either of these operations can be performed using

```
XCopyArea display source-window dest-window \
    source-x source-y width height dest-x dest-y [GC args]
```

This copies graphics from a source widget's window to a destination widget's window. The rectangle defined by the points *source-x*, *source-y*, *width*, and *height* is copied to the destination widget position *dest-x*, *dest-y*.

For example, this code can be inserted in the `drwshell.sh` program to create four seashells stacked two by two as shown in Figure 18-11.

```
# First, copy to the right
XCopyArea $display $window $window \
    0 0 110 110 110 0
# Now, copy whole top row down to bottom
XCopyArea $display $window $window \
    0 0 220 110 0 110
```

This code would be inserted immediately after the initial seashell is drawn. First, a copy is made to the right of the original seashell, then both of those seashells are copied down to form the second row. Because circular arc fills are relatively expensive operations, this method (rendering one shell and then copying it to the other places) is far faster than rendering four separate seashells.

Animation

In this section, I present an extension to the checkbook program that adds a little pizzazz using animation techniques. In this extension, whenever a new check is added that causes the checkbook balance to go negative a warning will appear that tells the user the check could bounce. To drive the point home, the warning dialog will contain an animated area in which a ball will bounce!

Using the techniques outlined in this chapter, this is quite simple to implement. We will create a WarningDialog, and will add a work area child to it that will contain a DrawingArea widget. Using a timer, a small rectangle will be drawn in successive positions to simulate the motion of a ball (I use a rectangle instead of a circle for performance reasons). The formulas for gravity will be used to ensure that the simulation looks realistic (the ball will accelerate on the way down and decelerate on the way back up).

Listing 18-3 shows the code necessary to do this. It defines two functions:

- moveballCB calculates the next position of the ball, erases the old ball, then draws the new ball. It detects when the ball meets the edge of the Drawing-Area and "bounces" the ball in the opposite direction. It uses several state variables to keep track of the current x, y position of the ball, the current velocity in the x direction (which may be negative), and the current velocity in the y direction. At the end of this function, another call to XUaddtimeout is made to reschedule moveballCB.

- displayBounceWarning creates the WarningDialog that will display a message and a DrawingArea to display the bouncing ball. It sets up the initial state of the BALL.X, BALL.Y, BALL.XVEL, and BALL.YVEL variables. Those variables hold the ball's current position and its velocity in each dimension, respectively. This function then sets a timer to call moveballCB.

The checkbook program calls displayBounceWarning when it detects a negative balance. It will only display this warning one time (it could get irritating otherwise). The output of this dialog is shown in Figure 18-12, although it's meant to be viewed live.

It's important to note that I do not use the exposeCallback in this program. Instead, the program depends on the fact that the ball will be redrawn within a fraction of a second anyway. Some animation programs may require an exposeCallback to redraw background objects, etc.

Listing 18-3. Bounced Check Warning (chkbook.sh).

```
function moveballCB {
    typeset w=${BOUNCE.CANVAS}
    typeset display=$(XtDisplay - $w)
    typeset window=$(XtWindow - $w)
    integer width height

    if [[ ! "$w" ]]
    then return
    fi
    XUget $w width:width height:height

    # erase the old position
    XClearArea $display $window \
        ${BOUNCE.X} ${BOUNCE.Y} \
        ${BOUNCE.WIDTH} ${BOUNCE.HEIGHT}

    # update the position
    (( BOUNCE.X += BOUNCE.XVEL ))
    (( BOUNCE.Y += BOUNCE.YVEL ))

    # Draw the ball at the new position
    XFillRectangle $display $window \
        -foreground black \
        ${BOUNCE.X} ${BOUNCE.Y} \
        ${BOUNCE.WIDTH} ${BOUNCE.HEIGHT}

    # if the y coordinate is at the bottom, reverse
    # the y velocity to cause a bounce

    if (( BOUNCE.Y > height - BOUNCE.HEIGHT ))
    then
        (( BOUNCE.Y = height - BOUNCE.HEIGHT ))
        (( BOUNCE.YVEL = 0 - BOUNCE.YVEL ))
    fi

    # if the x coordinate is at either border
    # of the screen, reverse the x direction
    if (( BOUNCE.X < BOUNCE.WIDTH ||
        BOUNCE.X > width - BOUNCE.WIDTH ))
    then
        (( BOUNCE.XVEL = 0 - BOUNCE.XVEL ))
    fi

    # accelerate in the y dimension to simulate gravity
    (( BOUNCE.YVEL += 3 ))
    XUaddtimeout BOUNCE.TIMER 150 moveballCB
}
```

```
function displayBounceWarning {
    typeset button

    XUwarningdialog BOUNCE $TOPLEVEL \
        dialogTitle:"Negative Balance!" \
        messageString:$'Your Balance is negative.\nChecks may bounce!' \
        destroyCallback:'XUremovetimeout ${BOUNCE.TIMER}' \
        okCallback:'XUdestroy $BOUNCE'

    XUget $BOUNCE cancelButton:button
    XUunmanage $button

    XUdrawingarea BOUNCE.CANVAS $BOUNCE \
        width:100 height:100

    XUmanage $BOUNCE
    BOUNCE.X=10
    BOUNCE.Y=10
    BOUNCE.XVEL=5
    BOUNCE.YVEL=0
    BOUNCE.WIDTH=6
    BOUNCE.HEIGHT=6

    STATE.ALREADYBOUNCED=true
    XUaddtimeout BOUNCE.TIMER 150 moveballCB
}
```

Figure 18-12. Output of bouncing check animation (chkbook.sh).

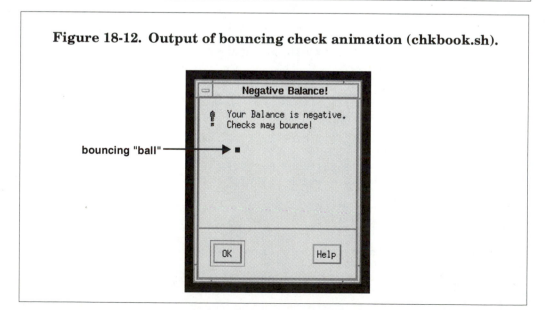

18.11 Details, Details

This chapter has only presented a brief overview of how to use Xlib. There are many other practical considerations. For example, how will your Xlib display respond to resizing? Should it scale to the size of the DrawingArea, or remain a fixed size and use a ScrolledWindow for scrolling? How should it determine which colors to use? Which fonts should you use?

These types of details make Xlib programming hard. I'll touch on some general principles in this section, but this is by no means a complete treatise. See the Bibliography for further references. Also, many of these issues are handled in the example presented in Chapter 26, *Stock Chart Display*.

Scaling

In cases where you want a graphic display to scale to the size of the window (i.e., when the user resizes the display and a DrawingArea widget grows or shrinks), you need to draw your graphics using a virtual set of coordinates that is scaled to the size of the window. The general strategy follows:

- Retrieve the `height` and `width` resources of the DrawingArea.
- Choose a virtual resolution, such as 1000 by 1000. Compute two scaling factors, `xscale` and `yscale`, which are the virtual sizes divided by the actual sizes in each dimension, i.e., `xscale=1000/width` and `yscale=1000/height`.
- Draw all graphics by using coordinates in the virtual scale divided by the scaling factors. In our example, which uses virtual coordinates of 1000 by 1000 to draw a point in the center of the screen, you would use virtual coordinates `500/xscale`, `500/yscale`.

This type of strategy can break down when drawing shapes that must maintain a unit aspect ratio, such as circles and squares. In that case, you could choose the smaller of the two dimensions to compute the scale in both dimensions, then use an offset in the larger dimension to recenter the display. For example, if the DrawingArea is 400 by 600, you can compute the scaling values both based on 400 (the smaller of the two dimensions), then offset all *y* coordinates by 100 (this is half of 600 minus 400) in order to center the drawings vertically.

It's a good idea in either case to define functions that do the virtual to physical coordinate scaling, such as:

```
function xphys {
    print $(($1/xscale + xoffset))
}

function yphys {
    print $(($1/yscale + yoffset))
}
```

Then use command substitution where you need to make virtual to physical translations:

```
XDrawLine $display $window \
         $(xphys 100) $(yphys 100) $(xphys 200) $(yphys 200)
```

That command would draw a line from virtual coordinate 100, 100 to virtual coordinate 200, 200. This code assumes the values xscale, yscale, xoffset, and yoffset have previously been calculated based on the width and height of the DrawingArea and the desired virtual resolution.

Fonts and Colors

You should avoid hard-coding fonts and colors into any program. This is relatively easy in the case of Motif widget programs because you can use resource files to define these for the application. For Xlib based parts of your program, this is not as simple, because dtksh does not have commands to make queries on resources in a resource file.

One solution is to define all colors and fonts using variables in a separate file that is read into your script using the Shell's dot command:

```
. $APPDIR/app-params.sh
```

You could allow a user to override this by first testing to see if the user has such a file in his or her $HOME directory, for example.

Performance Considerations

The dtksh interpreter is fast enough to draw moderately complex sets of shapes in a short period of time. For an example of this, you should try running the example program stock.sh, which can chart stock prices. A sample data file is provided called JNJ.stk that contains a few months of data for Johnson & Johnson Incorporated.

> While it is believed that the data in JNJ.stk is accurate, it is provided merely as example data for the stock.sh demonstration program, and you should not use it to make investment decisions.

This program draws hundreds of lines and rectangles, and it performs quite well even on low-end hardware.

There are some things to watch out for so your Xlib-based programs perform acceptably:

- Circular arcs can cause performance problems, especially on hardware that does not have built-in floating-point math support. Such hardware will not render circular arcs quickly even in C language Xlib programs.

- Instead of drawing many individual lines, such as by calling `XDrawLine` once for each line to be drawn, it is far faster to build an argument list and then make one call to `XDrawLines`.

- Lines that are more than one pixel wide draw far slower than single pixel width lines.

- Try to use the most efficient shape-hint possible when filling polygons.

- If you have a complex display inside a ScrolledWindow, severe performance problems can result if you use a simple "redraw everything" strategy in the `exposeCallback`. This is because every single pixel the user scrolls will cause an expose event. In a case like this, it is often best to disable drag scrolling using the techniques discussed in *Handling Slow Scrolling* on page 209.

- If you are drawing many graphical objects, it is far more efficient to save the graphics contexts you are using in variables using the `-gc variable` graphics context option. That causes dtksh to retain graphics contexts from one command to another. You may need several graphics contexts if you are drawing shapes with multiple colors (or other GC options that differ from shape to shape).

18.12 Summary

Xlib commands can be used to draw arbitrary shapes. Motif provides two widgets whose purpose is to serve as a canvas for drawing using Xlib: the DrawnButton and the DrawingArea. Drawing individual shapes is a much lower level of programming than using widgets directly, and is typically used only for special purposes such as graphical data display or adding special effects to programs to spice them up.

When a shape is drawn, much of the information that specifies how it will look is contained in a data structure called a graphics context, or GC. Dtksh provides access to the graphics context via command line options.

All Xlib drawing commands require addresses of data structures called the screen and window. These addresses can be derived from the widget being used as a canvas using the `XtScreen` and `XtWindow` commands.

Commands are available to draw text strings, points, lines, rectangles, filled polygons, and circular arcs. In addition, commands are available to clear and copy areas.

19 *Events, Translations, etc.*

19.1 Introduction

This chapter explores the different mechanisms provided by X for handling events, and shows you how to access these mechanisms using dtksh. This chapter does not assume you are an X expert, but you should have at least read Part I so you understand basic X programming techniques.

Events are the life-blood of a running X program. In previous chapters, you learned how to register callback functions that were triggered when events occurred. In this chapter, you will learn how to handle events at a lower level, including:

- How to register functions for handling keyboard and mouse translations
- How to register low-level handlers for arbitrary X events
- How to detect and respond to window manager-initiated events, such as the event that causes the application to terminate
- How to set up and use file input handlers
- How to use timers.

These subjects are typically useful in more sophisticated programs that need fine control over event handling. Most applications can get by very well using nothing other than callback functions for event handling.

19.2 General Concepts

Events drive all X programs. Events include user-initiated actions such as pressing a keyboard key or a mouse button, or moving the mouse pointer; events can also be triggered by timers, input arriving on a file descriptor, or operating system actions.

X handles events at several different levels. At the Xlib level, an event is described by an X event structure, which contains information about what kind of event occurred (button press, keyboard input, mouse motion, etc.) and other information specific to the kind of event (which mouse button was pressed, which keyboard key was entered, what the x, y coordinates of the mouse pointer were as it moved).

The Relationship Between Events, Translations, and Callbacks

When an event occurs, it is always relative to a particular widget. Each widget has a *translation table,* which specifies its events will be handled. For each event specified in the translation table, an *action* is defined that will be executed when the event occurs. Usually, the widget that has focus will handle an event, but if a widget has no translation table entry matching the event in question, its parent is given a chance to handle the event (this continues up the widget hierarchy until some widget handles the event; if none do then the event is discarded).

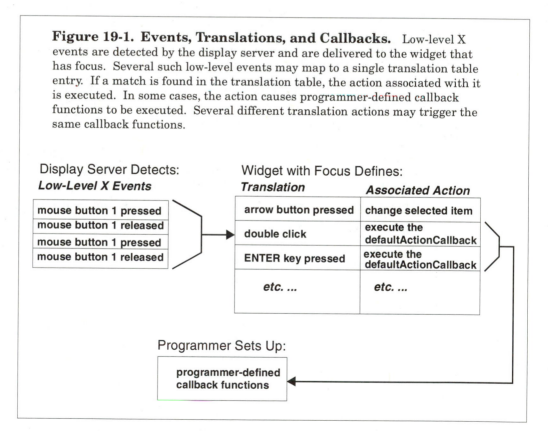

Figure 19-1. Events, Translations, and Callbacks.   Low-level X events are detected by the display server and are delivered to the widget that has focus. Several such low-level events may map to a single translation table entry. If a match is found in the translation table, the action associated with it is executed. In some cases, the action causes programmer-defined callback functions to be executed. Several different translation actions may trigger the same callback functions.

The translation table entries specify events at a higher level than that described by an X event structure. For example, it is possible to specify an action for a double-click in a translation table, whereas at the X event structure level several low-level events make up a double-click (user depresses mouse button one, releases it without moving very much, depresses it again within a short period of time, and releases it again without moving much).

Widgets typically map several translation table events so that they execute application-defined callbacks as their action. The programmer thinks of the callback function he or she registers as a handler for a widget-defined event. A widget's notion of an event is at an even higher level than the translation table's notion. For example, a Text widget's `motionVerifyCallback` is called when the user performs any action that would move the insertion point cursor in the Text widget. That could be caused by many different translation table entries (clicking the mouse, pressing an arrow key, etc.), and some of those translation table entries could be made up of multiple X events. This relationship between X events, translations, and callbacks is depicted in Figure 19-1.

19.3 Using Translations

As discussed earlier, each widget has a translation table that defines what action should occur when a particular event or set of events is detected. Most Motif widgets have a number of predefined translations. For example, the Text widget has translations that allow navigation by using arrow keys or the mouse pointer; it has other translations that allow modification of the text (such as by pressing the DELETE key).

Each widget has a resource called `translations` that holds the translation table. This resource can be set using `XtSetValues` (`XUset` for those of you using the XU library). However, it cannot be retrieved using `XtGetValues` (or `XUget`).

Translation Table Syntax

There is a fairly complicated syntax you can use to set a widget's `translations` resource. This syntax is quite powerful; it allows you to define an event or set of events that will trigger an action. There can be more than one translation table entry separated by newlines.

I'm not going to try to explain this syntax in complete detail here; rather, I will give you some general information and present some common examples of translation table syntax. If you want to learn all the gory details, an excellent treatment of the subject can be found in [Nye and O'Reilly 1993].

In its simplest form, each translation table entry line takes the following format:

```
[modifier]<event>[details]:action([args ...])
```

In this specification,

* *modifier* is a set of key modifiers such as `Ctrl` (the CONTROL key), `Shift`, `Alt`, or `Button1` (mouse button 1 is depressed). If such a modifier is present, then the specified modifier key or button must be depressed for the event to be detected.

- *event* is a string that specifies the type of event being selected, such as `BtnDown` (any mouse button is selected), `Btn1Down` (mouse button 1 is selected), `Key` (any key has been pressed), `Enter` (the mouse pointer has entered the widget's window), `FocusIn` (the widget has received the keyboard focus), etc.

- *details* is a string that further narrows down the event to be selected. For example, if the event was `Key`, then details could be the letter "k" meaning that specifically one of the letters k or K is desired (if you wanted capital K only, then you need to specify a *modifier* of `Shift`).

- *action* is an action command string. This can be any action that is available for the widget class in question, or the special action `ksh_eval`. The `ksh_eval` action is provided automatically by dtksh, it takes one argument which is a string that is any valid dtksh command.

> Besides `ksh_eval`, you can use any of the predefined translation actions defined for the widget you are using. For complete details on all translation actions available for the Motif widgets, see [Ferguson and Brennen 1993].

Simple Examples

Tthe following translation table specification would cause the string "entered" to be printed to the standard output when the mouse pointer moves inside a widget:

```
<Enter>:ksh_eval("print entered")
```

The next specification will print the string "ENTERED" if the mouse pointer moves inside a widget while the SHIFT key is depressed:

```
Shift<Enter>:ksh_eval("print ENTERED")
```

Finally, this specification will print the string "Alt-q pressed" if the letter q or Q is typed while the ALT key is depressed while in a widget:

```
Alt<Key>q:ksh_eval("print Alt-q pressed")
```

It is important to note that `ksh_eval` takes exactly one argument, which must be a string quoted using double quotes. I strongly suggest you make this argument a single function call to a dtksh function you define elsewhere; in this way you avoid quoting problems. If you must include a double quote within the command string, it should be backslashed, like this:

```
Shift<Leave>:ksh_eval("print \"LEAVING\"")
```

More Complex Translation Specifications

Besides the relatively simple specifications already discussed, the general translation table syntax allows higher level events to be detected. The following list of examples is meant to give you an idea of the powerful combinations of specifications available. For a thorough review of the full range of translation table syntax allowed by X, see [Nye and O'Reilly, 1993].

Specification	*Result*
`<Btn1Down>,<Btn1Up>:`*action*	Execute *action* on a single click.
`<Btn1Down>,<Btn1Down>:`*action*	Execute *action* on a double click.
`<Btn1Down>(2):`*action*	Execute *action* on a double click. Note the use of a repeat count in parentheses.
`Shift<Btn1Down>(2):`*action*	Execute *action* on a double click while the SHIFT key is depressed.
`<Key>q:`*action*	Execute *action* if either the letter q or Q is pressed.
`Shift<Key>q:`*action*	Execute *action* if the letter Q is pressed.
`~Shift<Key>q:`*action*	Execute *action* if the letter q is pressed. Note that the `~Shift` notation means the SHIFT key *must not* be held down.
`None<Key>q:`*action*	Execute *action* if the letter q is pressed and no other modifier keys are selected (i.e., none of the keys ALT, SHIFT, CONTROL, mouse buttons, etc.)
`Button2<Motion>:`*action*	Execute *action* when the mouse pointer is moved while mouse button 2 is held down.
`"dtksh":`*action*	Execute *action* if the letters d, t, k, s, and h are pressed, in that order. This is equivalent to specifying: `<Key>d,<Key>t,<Key>k,<Key>s,<Key>h`

Variables Available During Action Execution

While your action command is executing, the following variables are defined:

- `TRANSLATION_WIDGET` is set to the handle of the widget on whose behalf the translation action was triggered.
- `TRANSLATION_EVENT` is set to the address of the X event that triggered the translation. Subfields of this variable are also available that describe the

event. For example, `TRANSLATION_EVENT.TYPE` contains the type of event. The complete list of available subfields is detailed in Appendix C.

Modifying Translations

It is possible for you to replace a widget's translation table by setting the widget's translation resource, but that's not the preferred method because you usually don't want to wipe out all the existing translations defined for a widget, instead you might just want to add a few new entries or modify a few old ones. This can be accomplished using these dtksh commands:

```
XtAugmentTranslations $widget translation-spec
XtOverrideTranslations $widget translation-spec
```

`XtAugmentTranslations` will add new translations specified in the `transla-tion-spec` to the widget. However, if a translation is included in the `transla-tion-spec` that already exists in the widget's translation table, then the existing translation takes precedence. `XtOverrideTranslations` works the same way, except that the new translations specified in `translation-spec` take precedence over existing translations.

For example, the following code will set translations on a Label widget that will print messages when the mouse pointer moves into or out of the widget's window:

```
XtOverrideTranslations $LABEL \
    '<Enter>:ksh_eval("print entering")
    <Leave>:ksh_eval("print leaving")'
```

This code is contained in the file `trnlab.sh` in the examples directory. Notice that I put a backslash at the end of the first line, then added two translation table entries between single quotes, with no additional blank lines in between. That's important—the translation table entry parser is picky about things like extra blank lines. Also, there must be no whitespace between the colon and the action.

A Larger Example

The checkbook program displays a button bar that shows icons for commonly executed actions. Sometimes users don't like button bars because they can't figure out what the icons mean. Usually the user only has this problem the first few times they use the application (if the icons are well designed, that is). A common solution to this problem is to provide one line of help whenever the mouse pointer enters the icon—this serves as a quick reminder of the button's function.

Listing 19-1 shows code to accomplish this. A function, `iconhelp`, is defined that will display a short help string. It tests the value of `TRANSLATION_WIDGET` to determine which help string to display. It also takes a special argument, `CLEAR`, which causes it to clear the help string. After the button bar buttons are defined, translations are added so that the `iconhelp` function is called when the mouse pointer enters any of the buttons. Also, when the mouse pointer exits a button, the iconhelp function is called with the CLEAR argument. A sample of the output is shown in Figure 19-2.

Figure 19-2. Checkbook Icon Help (chkbook.sh). A help string appears to the right of the button bar buttons that describes the button on which the mouse pointer is sitting. Here, the mouse pointer (the black arrow) is on the third button from the left, which is the delete check icon.

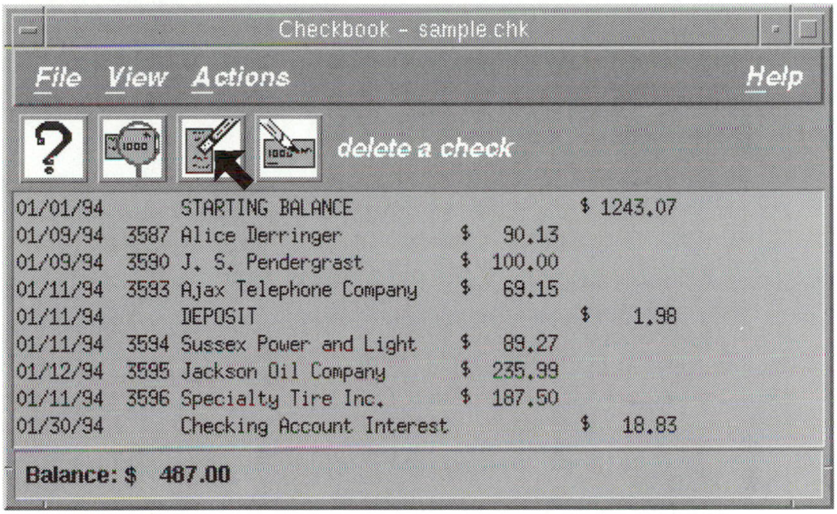

Listing 19-1. Checkbook Icon Help (chkbook.sh).

```
function iconhelp {
    if [[ $1 == CLEAR ]]
    then
        XUset $BBHELP labelString:""
        return
    fi

    # Depending on which button widget the cursor
    # is on, display different single-line help
    # messages in the quick help area

    case "$TRANSLATION_WIDGET" in
    ${BB.HELP})
```

```
            XUset $BBHELP labelString:"display help"
            ;;
        ${BB.DETAILS})
            XUset $BBHELP labelString:"display check details"
            ;;
        ${BB.DELETE})
            XUset $BBHELP labelString:"delete a check"
            ;;
        ${BB.ADD})
            XUset $BBHELP labelString:"add new checks"
            ;;
        esac
}


# Add translations to each button bar widget
# to provide help when the mouse pointer
# enters the widget.

for button in ${BB.HELP} ${BB.DETAILS} \
                ${BB.DELETE} ${BB.ADD}
do
    XtOverrideTranslations $button \
        '<Enter>:ksh_eval("iconhelp")
         <Leave>:ksh_eval("iconhelp CLEAR")'
done
```

19.4 Event Handlers

The previous section explained how you can create and modify translation tables in
order to customize event handling on certain widgets. Besides adding new translations, it is also possible for your application to receive notification directly of low-
level X events. This is rarely necessary, since the translation mechanism can detect
any event you need, and offers greater flexibility for defining sequences of events.
One plausible use might be to handle a very high volume event such as mouse
pointer motion, in which case a directly registered event handler might perform
slightly better than the translation mechanism.

Because there are very few situations when you might want to use an event handler, I'm not going to go into great detail here. For more information, see [Nye and
O'Reilly, 1993].

Adding an Event Handler

The following command is provided by dtksh to register an event handler:

```
XtAddEventHandler $widget event-mask nonmaskable-flag command
```

This causes the events specified by the *event-mask* to trigger the given dtksh *command*. The *event-mask* argument is a set of pipe separated event mask names. Any of the event mask names specified will trigger the *command*. Some examples of event mask names are KeyPressMask, KeyReleaseMask, ButtonPress-Mask, ButtonMotionMask, Button1MotionMask, FocusChangeMask, EnterWindowMask, and LeaveWindowMask. Most of these are self-explanatory, but for more detail see [Nye and O'Reilly 1993]. The *nonmaskable-flag* can take the values true or false, and specify whether the handler should be called for certain kinds of events that are always sent to a client. This is an advanced topic; if you don't understand what I mean by a nonmaskable event, just set this to false.

For example, the following code will register an event handler command that will trigger when the mouse pointer is moved while mouse button 1 or mouse button 2 is held down:

```
XtAddEventHandler $CANVAS 'Button1Motion|Button2Motion' \
    false 'print moving!'
```

Notice the use of the pipe symbol to specify that either of the two masks should trigger the command. Because the pipe symbol has special meaning to the shell, this must be quoted. I set the *nonmaskable-flag* to false because I do not wish to receive nonmaskable events.

Variables Available During Event Handler Execution

As with translation handlers, variables are defined during the execution of your event handler function that provide you with useful information:

- EH_WIDGET is set to the handle of the widget on whose behalf the event handler was triggered.

- EH_EVENT is set to the address of the X event that triggered the event handler. Subfields of this variable are also available that describe the event. The complete list of available subfields is detailed in Appendix C.

For example, if you register a handler for a ButtonPress event, you could access the *x, y* coordinates of the mouse pointer at the time of the button press as follows:

```
print "x=${EH.EVENT.XBUTTON.X} y=${EH.EVENT.XBUTTON.Y}"
```

19.5 Window Manager Protocols

X provides a mechanism for the window manager to communicate with the client application. By default, window manager actions such as closing or resizing the window associated with the client application all occur automatically. There are times when your application needs to know that some window manager action has occurred. For example, many applications need to catch the "close" action in order to do application-specific cleanup before exiting.

To intercept window manager protocols, the application must register a protocol callback with the window manager. A protocol callback is a function that is executed when a specific window manager action is performed. You can register such a callback using the following command:

    XmAddWMProtocolCallback $*shell-widget protocol-atom command*

The first argument to this command is the handle of a Shell-class widget. The next argument is an X atom that describes which window manager function should trigger the dtksh *command*. An X atom is simply the internal representation of a string value used for communication. You must retrieve X atoms using:

    XmInternAtom *variable display string flag*

The *display* argument should be obtained using the XtDisplay function. The atom associated with *string* is stored in *variable*. The *flag* should be either true or false, and indicates whether a new atom for string should be created if none already exists.

The following strings can be translated into atoms that are useful with the XmAddWMProtocolCallback:

- WM_DELETE_WINDOW indicates that the user is attempting to delete one of your application's windows using a window manager menu item.

- WM_SAVE_YOURSELF indicates that the user is attempting to close your application. This protocol can be used to save data before the window manager kills your application; after your callback is executed the application will be killed unless you set the deleteResponse resource of your root widget to DO_NOTHING. In that case, you could choose whether or not to exit from the application.

- WM_TAKE_FOCUS indicates that the window manager is giving focus to your application. You could use this to perform some special processing such as setting the initial focus to a particular widget.

Listing 19-2 shows an example of how to intercept the window manager close message. The user is told that data have changed and is given a chance to cancel the close or save the data before exiting.

A related subject bears mentioning here. CDE has a feature called the session manager that allows applications to save their state so that the next time the user logs in the application comes back up the same way that the user left it. To make your application participate in session management, you need to take some special actions. This subject is described in detail in Chapter 21, *The Session Manager*.

Listing 19-2. Intercepting the Close Protocol (evproto.sh).

```
function closeCB {
    XUconfirm "Data not saved" \
```

```
            "Do you wish to save data before closing?" \
            do_save exit helpCB
   }

   # Register a window manager callback for the "close" action
   XtDisplay display $TOPLEVEL
   XmInternAtom DEL_ATOM $display WM_DELETE_WINDOW false
   XmAddWMProtocolCallback $TOPLEVEL $DEL_ATOM closeCB

   # Set things up so application is not automatically killed on a close
   XUset $TOPLEVEL deleteResponse:DO_NOTHING
```

19.6 Input Handlers

It is possible to register a callback when input is available on a device or file. This is useful in a number of situations, such as following the output going into a log file, or communicating with a device or named pipe. You can register an input event using the command:

```
    XtAddInput variable [-r] descriptor command
```

In this command, a file *descriptor* number is registered as an input source. Whenever input is available on that descriptor, the *command* is executed. An input source identifier is stored in the *variable* that can be passed later to the command:

```
    XtRemoveInput $variable
```

to terminate the input source. With the -r option, the input handler command is placed in raw mode. In raw mode, your handler command must do all processing to parse the incoming data. Raw mode is explained later.

By far, the most common way dtksh programmers use XtAddInput is to let dtksh parse the input stream into lines—this happens by default if you do not use the -r option, and is also explained later.

The file descriptor you pass to XtAddInput is typically derived by using the KornShell exec command to connect a file or device to a file descriptor number. For example, this command connects descriptor 4 with the file /tmp/logfile:

```
    exec 4</tmp/logfile
```

The file descriptor number you choose must be between 0 and 9, and it's often not a good idea to use 0, 1, or 2, which are normally connected to the standard input, standard output, and standard error descriptors, respectively. This means there is a pretty small limit on the number of input sources your dtksh script can have open simultaneously. In practice, however, this is a sufficient number.

Variables Available During Input Handler Execution

The following variables are defined in the context of your input handler function:

- INPUT_ID contains the input handler descriptor that was originally returned in the variable passed to XtAddInput. It can be used to unregister the input source from within your handler.

- INPUT_SOURCE contains the file descriptor number from which input is being taken; it is the same as the descriptor originally passed to the XtAdd-Input call. If you are using the raw mode (-r option) then your handler is responsible for reading this descriptor to obtain data.

If you are not using raw (-r) mode, then dtksh automatically sets these additional variables in the context of your handler command:

- INPUT_LINE contains the full text of the next input line received from the file descriptor. This variable could be empty if the end of the file has been reached (see INPUT_EOF).

- INPUT_EOF is set to the string true if the end of the file has been reached. This gives you a chance to clean up your handler using XtRemoveInput, close the file descriptor, or take other actions.

Allowing Dtksh to Break Lines

In the default mode of operation, when you do not use the -r option to XtAddInput, dtksh will break lines for you and place them in the INPUT_LINE variable. Any unescaped newline character is used to delimit the line. The input handler command you registered will not be called unless a full line of text is available or the end of the file has been reached.

This is by far the easiest way to use input sources, and is convenient whenever you wish to handle the data one line at a time. An example of using this type of input handler appears under *An X Version of "tail -f"* on page 235. In that example, the XU library function XUaddinput is used; that is simply an alias for XtAddInput.

Using Raw Mode

If you supply the -r option to XtAddInput, then raw mode is enabled. In this mode, you're on your own. Dtksh will assume you do not wish to use line-oriented input. You could use this mode, for example, if binary data are being read from the file, or if some character other than newline is used to delimit records. Your handler function could be called when there is less than one line of input, and it must read data from the file descriptor.

The KornShell read command has some options that can be useful in this situation:

- -u *descriptor*

   This option reads input from the named file *descriptor*.

- -d *delimiter*

  This option changes the delimiter used to break records from the default, newline, to the specified *delimiter*.

For example, to parse records delimited by a pipe symbol, you could use this code in a raw input handler command to place the next record in the variable LINE:

```
read -u $INPUT_SOURCE -d '|' LINE
```

In cases where there is no delimiter for the data (perhaps the data are binary with fixed-length records) it will usually be necessary for you to use attached C code to parse the input data. See Chapter 23, *Attaching C Code*, for more information on using attached functions.

19.7 Timers

You may register a command to be executed after a specific amount of time has passed using:

```
XtAddTimeOut variable milliseconds command
```

This registers the specified *command* to be executed approximately *milliseconds* in the future. An identifier is stored in *variable* that can be used to remove the timer later using:

```
XtRemoveTimeOut $variable
```

The operating system may limit the resolution of timers available. For example, some operating systems may limit resolution to 100-millisecond increments. In that case, X will round the timer to the nearest available number of milliseconds.

Once the command registered for the timer is executed, the timer event is gone—if you want the command to be executed repeatedly then you must register another timer event before returning from the command.

An example of using timers for a simple animation task is given in the section *Animation* on page 396. In that example, the XU library function XUaddtimeout is used; that is simply an alias for XtAddTimeOut.

19.8 Summary

Several different mechanisms are available for handling different kinds of events, including:

- Widget-level translation tables
- Low-level X event handlers
- Window manager protocol handlers
- Input source handlers

- Timers.

These various types of events are triggered in different ways, but all have similarities: in each case you specify a dtksh command that is called when something special happens, and that command is passed data describing the event.

Many dtksh scripts use few, or none, of these mechanisms. They are mainly used in more sophisticated programs.

20 *The Workspace Manager*

20.1 Introduction

The CDE desktop contains a control panel that allows the user to manage multiple workspaces. Each workspace acts as a separate "room" so to speak; different applications can reside in different workspaces. The user can change the current workspace with a single click of the mouse. It is also possible for the user to put the same application in more than one workspace. This is useful for applications like a clock that the user wishes to be in view regardless of which workspace is currently selected. CDE contains a subsystem called the workspace manager that coordinates these workspaces.

Most applications don't need to know anything about workspaces, or which workspace they reside in, or how many workspaces there are, etc. Sometimes, there is a need for certain kinds of applications to interact with the workspace manager. For example, let's say you've written an application that monitors the UNIX system, attempting to detect error conditions such as a file system running low on space. If an error condition occurs, this application might pop up a warning message of some kind. In a case like this, the application would like to know that such a warning message will be seen by the user; so it would be necessary to find out which workspace the user is currently viewing and pop the message up there.

Dtksh contains a complete set of commands to interact with the workspace manager. This chapter shows you how to use these commands to perform functions like:

- Querying the workspace manager to get a list of available workspaces
- Retrieving the name of the current workspace
- Registering a callback that is triggered when the user changes workspaces
- Changing the user's current workspace

- Finding out which workspaces the application currently occupies, or changing which workspaces the application occupies, or causing it to occupy all available workspaces.

20.2 Workspace General Concepts

Users refer to workspaces by names. These names are ASCII strings that the user defines. For example, a user may wish to create different workspaces for different projects in which they are currently involved, and they may wish to name the workspaces in a way that indicates their use.

When communicating with the workspace manager, an application cannot use these names directly, but must instead use X atoms. X atoms are integers that map to strings; they allow the X communication protocols to ship around less data. The atom (number) that maps to a given string remains constant over the life of a CDE session, but may change in subsequent sessions. Dtksh provides functions that allow the programmer to convert strings to X atoms and vice versa:

```
XmGetAtomName variable display atom
XmInternAtom variable display string [true|false]
```

The `XmGetAtomName` function sets the *variable* argument to the string represented by the given *atom* on the named *display.* The `XmInternAtom` command does exactly the opposite—given a *string* and a *display* it sets the *variable* to the equivalent atom number. The final argument, either the string `true` or `false`, indicates whether a new atom should be created if no atom already exists for the *string*.

The *display* argument to either of these commands can be derived as follows:

```
XtDisplay display $TOPLEVEL
```

That command places the display structure address associated with the root widget of your application in the variable `display` (the code here assumes you have used the conventional variable `TOPLEVEL` to store the root widget of your application).

In addition, some workspace commands require the window of your root widget as an argument. This can be obtained using:

```
XtWindow window $TOPLEVEL
```

Again, this stores the window data structure pointer associated with the root widget of your application in a variable named `window`.

The examples in the rest of this chapter will assume that the variables `display` and `window` have already been set up using these commands.

The Root Window

Some workspace commands require the *root window* as a parameter. This is the window of the backdrop for the entire display, and should not be confused with the window of the root widget of your application. To get the root window, you can use code like this:

```
XRootWindowOfScreen rootwin $(XtDisplay - $TOPLEVEL)
```

After this executes, the window identifier of the root window will be stored in the variable `rootwin`. If your program will use workspace commands, it is convenient to get the values of these window and display variables right after the `XtRealize-Widget` command is executed (`XUrealize` for those of you using the XU library functions).

20.3 Querying the Workspace Manager

Several commands are available that allow your dtksh script to find out useful information about workspaces. It is possible to get a list of all the current workspaces using the command:

```
DtWsmGetWorkspaceList display root-window variable
```

The workspace that the user is currently viewing can be obtained using:

```
DtWsmGetCurrentWorkspace display root-window variable
```

The following command can be used to retrieve a list of all workspaces currently occupied by any Shell-class widget in the application:

```
DtWsmGetWorkspacesOccupied display shell-window variable
```

It is possible to set up a callback command that is executed whenever the user changes the current workspace by using the command:

```
DtWsmAddCurrentWorkspaceCallback variable shell-widget command
```

The `variable` will receive an identifier that can be used to remove the callback using:

```
DtWsmRemoveCurrentWorkspaceCallback shell-widget command $variable
```

20.4 Modifying Occupied Workspaces

Two commands are available to change the workspaces occupied by the application:

```
DtWsmSetWorkspacesOccupied display shell-window atom-list
DtWsmOccupyAllWorkspaces display shell-window
```

The `DtWsmSetWorkspacesOccupied` command causes the Shell-class widget identified by *display* and *shell-window* to occupy the workspaces associated with the comma-separated *atom-list*.

The `DtWsmOccupyAllWorkspaces` command causes the Shell-class widget identified by `display` and `shell-window` to occupy all workspaces. This includes any workspaces the user creates later; thus this command is not equivalent to calling `DtWsmSetWorkspacesOccupied` with a list of all workspace atoms.

20.5 Other Workspace Commands

It is possible to change forcibly the current workspace being viewed by the user with the command:

```
DtWsmSetCurrentWorkspace widget atom
```

This command's return code can be tested to determine whether or not it succeeded. Note that applications should not normally change the current workspace, because that might irritate the user.

Workspace Menu Functions

The window manager menu for most applications does not contain items to allow the user to change the workspaces in which the application appears. It is possible to add such items to the window manager menu by calling the command:

```
DtWsmAddWorkspaceFunctions display shell-window
```

The workspace window manager menu functions can be removed using:

```
DtWsmRemoveWorkspaceFunctions display shell-window
```

In both cases, these functions only work for Shell-class widgets, and must be called when the widget is popped down.

20.6 Common Mistakes

Certain mistakes are made by virtually every programmer who uses the workspace commands for the first time:

- It is tempting to set up the variable `DISPLAY` to hold the display structure of the `TOPLEVEL` shell widget. Don't do it: `DISPLAY` is used by X to hold the name of the display device. A common variable name used by X programmers to hold this value is `DPY`, or the lowercase versions: `display` or `dpy`.
- It is common to make the "s" in "Workspace" upper case by accident. For example, this is wrong: `DtWsmSetCurrentWorkSpace`. Workspace is considered a single word, and the "s" is always lowercase.
- Often, programmers will use the window of their application's root widget instead of the root window of the display for the commands `DtWsmGetWorkspaceList` and `DtWsmGetCurrentWorkspace`.

- The `DtWsmSetCurrentWorkspace` command is inconsistent with the other workspace commands in that it takes a widget handle as its argument instead of a window; this often leads to errors.

- Unlike most other dtksh X commands, the name of a variable that receives the result is the *last* argument to workspace functions.

Figure 20-1. Output of worksp.sh.   This is the display after pressing the "Show Workspaces Occupied" button. The results are presented in both atom and string form.

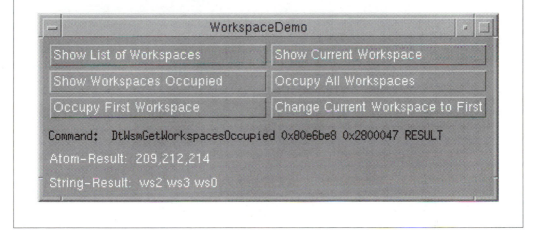

20.7 Workspace Example

Listing 20-1 presents a program that exercises most of the workspace commands. It provides a set of command buttons that can be used to execute various workspace functions, and a viewing area that displays results of some commands. The best way to experience this program is to actually run it on a CDE system; in that way you can see how the windows are moved from one workspace to another. The main screen created by this program is shown in Figure 20-1.

The program stores the root window in a variable called ROOTWDW, and stores the window and display associated with the TOPLEVEL widget in the variables WDW and DISPLAY. After that, it's just a matter of calling the functions with the correct sequences of arguments. The results are shown both in atom number format and string format. String conversions are performed by using XmInternAtom. Notice that the formatting takes place in a `for` loop in which the atom list (which is comma separated) is changed to a space-separated list using the string substitution feature of dtksh.

Listing 20-1. Workspace Demonstration (worksp.sh).

```
. $XUTILDIR/xutil.sh

# Execute the desired function, and put the command
# that performs the function in a label
function doit {
    RESULT=
    XUset $SHOWCOMMAND labelString:"Command:  $*"
    eval "$(print $*)"
    print result="'$RESULT'"
    if [[ "$RESULT" ]]
    then
        XUset $OUTPUT labelString:"Atom-Result:  $RESULT"
        typeset s strings=
        for atom in ${RESULT//,/ }
        do
            XmGetAtomName s $DPY $atom
            strings="$strings $s"
        done
        XUset $STROUTPUT labelString:"String-Result: $strings"
    else
        XUset $OUTPUT labelString:" "
        XUset $STROUTPUT labelString:" "
    fi
}

XUinitialize TOPLEVEL WorkspaceDemo "$@"

XUcolumn COL $TOPLEVEL

XUrow CONTROLS $COL packing:PACK_COLUMN numColumns:5

XUaddbuttons $CONTROLS \
    tmp "Show List of Workspaces"   \
        'doit DtWsmGetWorkspaceList $DPY $ROOTWDW RESULT' \
    tmp "Show Current Workspace" \
        'doit DtWsmGetCurrentWorkspace $DPY $ROOTWDW RESULT' \
    tmp "Show Workspaces Occupied" \
        'doit DtWsmGetWorkspacesOccupied $DPY $WDW RESULT' \
    tmp "Occupy All Workspaces" \
        'doit DtWsmOccupyAllWorkspaces $DPY $WDW' \
    tmp "Occupy First Workspace" \
        'DtWsmGetWorkspaceList $DPY $ROOTWDW RESULT;
         doit DtWsmSetWorkspacesOccupied $DPY $WDW ${RESULT%%,*}' \
    tmp "Change Current Workspace to First" \
        'DtWsmGetWorkspaceList $DPY $ROOTWDW RESULT;
         doit DtWsmSetCurrentWorkspace $TOPLEVEL ${RESULT%%,*}'
```

```
XUlabel SHOWCOMMAND $COL labelString:" " foreground:black fontList:fixed

XUlabel OUTPUT $COL labelString:" "
XUlabel STROUTPUT $COL labelString:" "

XUrealize $TOPLEVEL
XtDisplay DPY $TOPLEVEL
XtWindow WDW $TOPLEVEL
XtScreen SCR $TOPLEVEL
XRootWindowOfScreen ROOTWDW $SCR

XUmainloop
```

20.8 Summary

Dtksh provides commands that can query the workspace manager, change which workspaces windows of the application occupy, register callbacks that are triggered when the user changes workspaces, and perform other related functions. These commands identify workspaces based on atom representations of the workspace name, so the programmer must sometimes do conversions between atoms and strings or vice versa to get the job done. These commands also often require the programmer to provide pointers to the window and display data structures associated with Shell-class widgets. Other than these caveats, the workspace commands are generally straightforward to use.

21 *The Session Manager*

21.1 Introduction

The CDE session manager allows the user to log out of the desktop, then log back in again with applications restored to their previous state. This is a great feature because it allows the user to become productive again immediately on logging into the CDE; they don't have to go through the effort of launching applications over again, reopening files, and setting application options the way they prefer.

There is only one problem with this rosy scenario: the application must be written to cooperate with the session manager; applications that do not cooperate will not be relaunched, and their state will not be restored.

This chapter teaches you:

- How to register interest with the session manager so the application is notified when it needs to save state
- How to communicate with the session manager to save the state
- Which elements of the application are necessary to save, with advice on how to save them
- Strategies for restoring the application's state.

It is well worth investing the time to make your application cooperate with the session manager. The amount of code involved could be as little as a dozen lines, or could be much more depending on how much state you need to save.

21.2 Session Manager General Concepts

The session manager feature of CDE allows your application to be launched automatically when the user logs in, and further allows your application to return to the same state it was in when the user was last logged in. Several steps are necessary for an application to become session management aware:

1. The application must register with the session manager so it can be notified when the user logs out, allowing the application to save its state.

2. A function must be created that can write the current state of the application to a file.

3. When the application is notified that it must save its state, it uses the state-saving function discussed earlier to write the state information to a file; the filename that should be used is provided by the session manager. The application must then communicate with the session manager, passing it a command line that can be used by the session manager later to launch the application and restore its previous state.

4. When the application is launched, it must be able to detect whether it is being spawned by the session manager so it knows whether or not to restore its state from a file. Typically this is accomplished by creating a command line option specifically for this purpose. Such a command line option should take an argument; this argument is a path to a file containing the previously saved state information.

5. A function must be created that can restore the application's state from a previously created state-saving file. This function is called when the application detects that it has been launched by the session manager.

Examples of each of these steps are presented in this chapter.

What Constitutes Application State?

It is important to understand that the session manager feature only provides a mechanism for the application to retain its state — it is entirely up to the application to determine what "state" is important to save. For example, consider the checkbook program that is used as a running example in this book. The state of the checkbook application includes:

- The path of the checkbook file currently being displayed, and whether there are any unwritten modifications
- The placement of the ScrollBars in the check display list (i.e., which check is currently at the top of the display List)
- The state of viewing options such as whether detailed viewing mode is selected, and how the user is currently sorting the checks
- Whether or not the checkbook program is iconified
- Which work spaces are currently occupied by the checkbook program.

Some of these state items are stored in the application's internal variables and data structures, some can be derived by using X commands. The various methods for deriving different kinds of state information are discussed later.

How Much State Should Be Saved?

The level of state detail you choose to save depends on how ambitious you are as a programmer, and what the needs of your users are. For some complex applications, it might be prohibitive to save every last detail of the application's state. You must balance how practical it is to save different pieces of state versus how irate your users will be if they find certain aspects of the application incompletely restored.

For example, most users probably won't mind much if the ScrollBars are not reset to their previous positions, but they will probably not be happy if the file they last opened is not restored, or if their preferred viewing options mysteriously change back to application defaults. You should use your judgment here, and in cases that are unclear it's a good idea to ask the users what they need.

21.3 Registering Interest with the Session Manager

After the application's root widget is realized, but before XtMainLoop is invoked, the application needs to register a window manager protocol handler so it is informed when a state-saving action is needed. This requires you to retrieve the WM_SAVE_YOURSELF atom, and register a state-saving function. The code to do this for the checkbook.sh program is shown in Listing 21-1. This activates the window manager protocols for a WM_SAVE_YOURSELF event and registers a function, sessionsaveCB, to handle such an event. This is very similar to catching a close notification as discussed in *Window Manager Protocols* on page 411 — for more details see that section.

Listing 21-1. Session Management Interest (chkbook.sh).

```
# Get the atom for WM_SAVE_YOURSELF
XmInternAtom SAVE_ATOM $(XtDisplay - $TOPLEVEL) \
    WM_SAVE_YOURSELF false
# Ask to be informed when a WM_SAVE_YOURSELF event occurs
XmAddWMProtocols $TOPLEVEL $SAVE_ATOM
# Register a state saving function for WM_SAVE_YOURSELF
XmAddWMProtocolCallback $TOPLEVEL $SAVE_ATOM sessionsaveCB
```

21.4 Saving State

When the state-saving function is called, your application must perform the following actions:

1. Ask the session manager for a filename to which you can write the application's state.
2. Write the application's state to the file thus obtained.
3. Inform the session manager how the application should be launched.

These steps are detailed in the following sections.

Obtaining a State-Saving File

The session manager is responsible for allocating and managing files used to track application state. You can ask the session manager to provide you with such a file using the dtksh command:

```
DtSessionSavePath $root-widget path-variable file-variable
```

The first argument to this command is the widget handle of the root widget returned by `XtInitialize` (`$TOPLEVEL` by convention). The `path-variable` argument is the name of a variable that will be set to the full path of the allocated file. The `file-variable` is another variable name that will be set to the filename portion of the full path (i.e., just the last element of the path). The `file-variable` argument is rarely useful, but you must provide it anyway. This command's return code can be tested to find out if it succeeded.

> The command might fail for several reasons, such as inability to communicate with the session manager, or a file system being out of space, etc. The return code should always be tested, and if this command fails your application will not be able to save state and should simply print an error message and exit.

For example, the following command will attempt to set the variable SAVEPATH to the full path of a newly allocated session manager state-saving file. It will print a message to the standard error and exit if unsuccessful:

```
if ! DtSessionSavePath $TOPLEVEL savepath savefile
then
        print "Unable to save state of $DTKSH_APPNAME" >&2
        exit 1
fi
```

If this command is successful, the variable `savefile` will be the same as the last file component stored in the variable `savepath`. For example, if `savepath` were set to `/usr/tmp/session102` then `savefile` would be simply `session102`.

Writing Application State to the File

Once a suitable path has been obtained, how should the application write out its state? There are several different strategies you could use, but it's a good idea to keep in mind that whatever format you use to save state should be easy to write and easy to parse back later when the state is to be restored.

One very simple and obvious method is simply to write single-line records to the state-saving file that contain different elements of the state, in a fixed order. Such a file can be read back one line at a time in the same order later to restore the state.

Another method, one I believe is more powerful, is to write out the file in a format that can be brought back into your script later with the KornShell dot command. For example, you could write out lines of the form:

```
variable=value
```

Later, no parsing is necessary, you simply dot the state-saving file into your script and perform any auxiliary actions necessary to redisplay the application based on the values of the newly set variables. It may even be convenient to write other dtksh commands besides simple variable assignments to the state-saving file.

For example, the checkbook example program keeps the name of the checkbook data file currently being viewed in a variable called STATE.CURFILE. The following code could be used to append that crucial piece of information to the state-saving file:

```
{
    print "STATE=''"      # initialize hierarchical root
    print "STATE.CURFILE='${STATE.CURPATH}'"
    print "STATTE.PWD='$PWD'"
} >> $savepath
```

Note the cautionary use of single quotes embedded in the command written out to the state-saving file (whose name is stored in the variable savepath). Also note that for convenience, all the print commands are executed inside of curly braces (command grouping) and the output of the whole group is appended to the state-saving file. After these commands execute, the state-saving file would contain something like this:

```
STATE=''
STATE.CURPATH='sample.chk'
STATE.PWD=/home/pend/dtksh.examples
```

This method is quite straightforward, and is easy to use for any kind of state stored in application variables. The next few subsections give details about how to save state for some special attributes.

Saving the Iconic State

You can find out if your application is iconified using the command:

```
DtShellIsIconified $root-widget
```

This command returns success (zero) if the application is currently iconified; thus this command can be conveniently used in conjunction with the KornShell if statement. For example, this code can be used to append a state variable to the state-saving file that indicates whether the application is iconified:

```
if DtShellIsIconified $TOPLEVEL
then print "STATE.ICONIC=true"
else print "STATE.ICONIC=false"
fi >> $SAVEFILE
```

Saving the List of Occupied Workspaces

The list of atoms associated with the currently occupied workspaces can be retrieved using the DtWsmGetWorkspacesOccupied command. This command is discussed in detail in Chapter 20, *The Workspace Manager*. One problem with this command is that it returns a comma-separated list of atoms. Atoms are numbers that map to strings: the user defines workspace names as strings, the atoms are used internally by CDE to communicate information about workspaces. However, the numeric atom representation of a string may not stay the same from session to session. Thus, you must convert these atoms into strings again before saving them to the state-saving file. This conversion can be carried out using the command XmGetAtomName.

The following code retrieves the comma-separated list of atoms that represents occupied workspaces, then changes the commas to spaces using KornShell string substitution so they can be easily used with a for loop. In the for loop, the atoms are converted to strings, and are output to the state-saving file as array variable elements:

```
XtDisplay display $TOPLEVEL
if DtWsmGetWorkspacesOccupied $display WORK_ATOMS
then
        integer i=0
        for atom in ${WORK_ATOMS//,/ }   # change "," to space
        do
            XmGetAtomName string $display $atom
            print "STATE.WORKSPACE[$((i++))]='$string'"
        done >> $SAVEPATH
fi
```

Registering a Launch Command

After all the state attributes have been written to the file, the only thing left to do is inform the session manager how the application is to be launched when the user logs back in. The simplest way to handle this is to make your application recognize an option specifically designed for session manager use; this option should take an argument that is the path to the state-saving file. For example, the checkbook application uses the option -restore *path* for this purpose. To inform the session manager of the complete launch command, you should use:

```
DtSetStartupCommand $root-widget command
```

The checkbook application uses this code to register a launch command:

```
DtSetStartupCommand $TOPLEVEL \
    "$XUTILDIR/Programs/chkbook.sh -restore $savepath"
```

Note the use of a full path to execute the checkbook program. It is safest to use a full path unless you are certain the application will be stored in a directory that is contained in the user's PATH variable.

21.5 Restoring State

By using the strategy outlined in the previous section to save state, restoring state is quite simple, involving these steps:

1. Decode the arguments to your application to get the path of the state-saving file.

2. Dot in the state-saving file.

3. Take any actions necessary to refresh the application display from the state variables that are set as a result of dotting in the file.

Decoding the arguments is straightforward, you simply test for the option that indicates a session restore should occur. Restoring the iconic state and work space occupation state requires some special action, as discussed in the following sections.

Restoring Iconic State

To restore the iconic state of your application, you must use the command:

```
DtSetIconifyHint $root-widget [true|false]
```

This command tells the window manager whether or not the application wishes to be iconified. There are some restrictions on the use of this command; it cannot be called at any arbitrary time during your application. Specifically, `DtSetIconify-Hint` must be called after realizing the widget hierarchy but before the windows of your application are mapped. This means you must take action to avoid mapping the root widget before you realize it, then call `DtSetIconifyHint`, then map the root widget. For example:

```
XtInitialize TOPLEVEL MyApp myapp "$@"
# arrange for windows not to be automatically mapped
XtSetValues $TOPLEVEL mappedWhenManaged:false
XtRealizeWidget $TOPLEVEL
DtSetIconifyHint $TOPLEVEL true  # iconify
XtPopup $TOPLEVEL   # now map the windows
```

An example of how to use this in the context of a session restore operation is given later in this chapter.

Restoring Occupied Workspaces

To restore the set of workspaces the application occupies, you must use the `DtWsm-SetWorkspacesOccupied` function, as explained in Chapter 20, *The Workspace Manager*. The general procedure is to convert each workspace name into an atom, then string all the atoms together separated by commas, then call `DtWsmSetWork-spacesOccupied`. For example:

```
comma=""
atomlist=""
for name in "${STATE.WORKSPACES[@]}"
do
    XmInternAtom atom $display "$name" false
    atomlist="$atomlist$comma$atom"
    comma=,
done
DtWsmSetWorkspacesOccupied $display $window "$atomlist"
```

One trick used here is to initialize a variable called comma to the empty string; in the first iteration of the loop both $atomlist and $comma will thus be empty. The variable comma is then set to an actual comma character. In this way, you can avoid putting a superfluous comma at the beginning of the atom list.

21.6 A Complete Example

In this section, I present excerpts of code from the checkbook application that implement all aspects of session management that we have discussed.

Listing 21-2 presents a complete state-saving function. Listing 21-3 shows the corresponding state-restoring function. Listing 21-4 shows the code that registers interest in session management notification, followed by the code that detects the session restoration argument and calls the state-restoring function. All the actions taken by these functions have been explained throughout this chapter, but it's good to see the complete picture to understand the flow of the code.

Listing 21-2. A State-Saving Function. This function is called when a window manager WM_SAVE_YOURSELF event is generated. If it is called with a file argument, then it saves state to that file, otherwise it obtains a file from the session manager. It then prints *variable=value* pairs to the file, saving various aspects of its state.

```
function sessionsaveCB {
    typeset savepath savefile workatoms

    if [[ $1 ]]
    then
        savepath=$1 # for testing purposes
        > $savepath
    else
        if ! DtSessionSavePath $TOPLEVEL savepath savefile
        then
            print "Unable to save state for ${APPNAME}" 2>&1
            exit 1
        fi
    fi

    {
        # print out state values
        print "STATE.DETAILS='${STATE.DETAILS}'"
```

```
        print "STATE.SORTORDER='${STATE.SORTORDER}'"
        print "STATE.CURPATH='${STATE.CURPATH}'"

        # print out iconic state
        if DtShellIsIconified $TOPLEVEL
        then print "STATE.ICONIC=true"
        else print "STATE.ICONIC=false"
        fi

        # print out occupied workspaces
        if DtWsmGetWorkspacesOccupied \
            "${TOPLEVEL.DISPLAY}" \
            "${TOPLEVEL.WINDOW}" \
            workatoms
        then
            integer i=0
            typeset atom

            # Substitute commas with spaces in the
            # workatoms variable for ease of use with
            # the "for" statement
            for atom in ${workatoms//,/ }
            do
                XmGetAtomName \
                    name \
                    ${TOPLEVEL.DISPLAY} \
                    $atom
                print "STATE.WORKSPACES[$((i++))]='$name'"
            done
        fi
    } > $savepath

    # Register the start-up command.  Assumes XUTILDIR is
    # set in the user's .dtprofile
    if ! DtSetStartupCommand $TOPLEVEL \
        "$XUTILDIR/Programs/chkbook.sh -restore $savepath"
    then
        print startup set failed!
    fi
}
```

Listing 21-3. A State-Restoring Function. This function's argument is the path to a previously saved state-file. That file is dotted into the script to set variables that are then used to restore the iconic state, the occupied workspaces, and the file being edited.

```
function sessionrestoreCB {
    if [[ ! -r "$1" ]]
    then
```

```
        print "Could not restore state for $DTKSH_APPNAME"
        return
fi

# dot in the save path to reset variables
. $1

# restore the iconic state

DtSetIconifyHint $TOPLEVEL ${STATE.ICONIC}

# restore the work spaces occupied. First, build a list
# of atom names

typeset workspace atoms="" a
typeset comma=""  # no comma on first item

for workspace in "${STATE.WORKSPACES[@]}"
do
    XmInternAtom \
        a \
        ${TOPLEVEL.DISPLAY} \
        "$workspace" \
        false
    atoms="$atoms$comma$a"
    comma=","    # after first item, add a comma
done

DtWsmSetWorkspacesOccupied \
    ${TOPLEVEL.DISPLAY} \
    ${TOPLEVEL.WINDOW} \
    $atoms

# open checkbook file and redisplay using new settings

open_checkbook "${STATE.CURPATH}"
}
```

Listing 21-4. Setting Up Session Management (chkbook.sh). This code is placed shortly after the XUinitialize call. It registers interest in being notified of window manager WM_SAVE_YOURSELF events. Then, after arranging for the application's top-level shell to remain unmapped, it realizes the widget hierarchy, then tests to see if the -restore argument is present. If so, then the state-restoring function, sessionrestoreCB, is called.

```
# Get the atom for WM_SAVE_YOURSELF

XmInternAtom SAVE_ATOM \
    ${TOPLEVEL.DISPLAY} \
```

```
        WM_SAVE_YOURSELF \
        false

# Ask to be informed when a WM_SAVE_YOURSELF event occurs

XmAddWMProtocols $TOPLEVEL $SAVE_ATOM

# Register a state-saving function

XmAddWMProtocolCallback \
    $TOPLEVEL \
    $SAVE_ATOM \
    sessionsaveCB

# Because we may need to restore the iconic state, arrange
# for the TOPLEVEL widget not to automatically map itself

XUset $TOPLEVEL mappedWhenManaged:false
XUrealize $TOPLEVEL
XtWindow TOPLEVEL.WINDOW $TOPLEVEL

# If we get the -restore option, attempt to restore
# state from the argument, a save-file path

if [[ ${DTKSH_ARGV[1]} == -restore ]]
then
    sessionrestoreCB "${DTKSH_ARGV[2]}"
    shift 2
else
    open_checkbook "${DTKSH_ARGV[1]}"
fi

# now it is safe to map $TOPLEVEL
XUpopup $TOPLEVEL

XUmainloop
```

21.7 Debugging Considerations

Testing whether your application properly responds to session management requests can be tedious—you must run your application, change some aspects of its state, exit the CDE desktop, then log back in again. This can be time consuming and frustrating; simple syntax errors in your save and restore functions can take several iterations to iron out. Further, you will not get any error messages unless you take special action.

A better way to debug session management is to first test your state-saving and state-restoring functions by directly calling them from within your script. You could, for example, temporarily add menu items to your script that exercise these functions. It's a good idea to turn on KornShell tracing in both of these functions until they are debugged. Tracing can be turned on by making the first line of each function read:

```
set -x
```

Once you are satisfied that the state-saving and state-restoring functions operate properly in this stand-alone mode, you can then do a final test by actually exiting CDE and logging back in again.

A suitable menu item is shown in Listing 21-5. This code is only executed if the variable DTKSH_DEBUG is set in the environment before executing the checkbook program.

Listing 21-5. Debugging Menu Item (chkbook.sh). This code adds a menu item to the checkbook program to test the state-saving function. This code is only executed if the variable DTKSH_DEBUG is set, hence the menu item normally does not appear in the program. By setting and exporting this variable before running the checkbook program, you can debug the state-saving function without actually exiting the desktop. You could then check the restore function by invoking the checkbook program with the -restore option, passing the argument $HOME/SESSION.TEST.

```
if [[ "$DTKSH_DEBUG" ]]
then
    XUmenusystem $MB \
        MB.TEST "Test Session" T { \
            MB.TEST.SAVE "Save State" S \
                "sessionsaveCB $HOME/SESSION.TEST" \
            }
fi
```

21.8 Summary

The CDE session manager provides a mechanism for an application to save its state when the user logs out of CDE. When the user logs back in, the session manager will launch the application, including an option informing it how to restore its state. It is entirely up the application to determine how to save its own state, and what details of its state are important to the user. Some state items that are commonly saved include whether or not the application is iconified, which workspaces it occupies, what application data files are open, and application options.

22 *Message Catalogs*

22.1 Introduction

We live in the age of a global economy. Most large software companies derive a large portion of their revenue from sales in other countries, often more than half. For this reason, it's a good idea to think about writing an application with internationalization in mind from the start if there is a chance the application might someday be used by people who speak other languages. This means that any message string or label that will be displayed to the end user must not be hard-coded into the application.

The *message catalog* mechanism allows your program to display different strings depending on what language the user speaks. It is possible for the same program to be run with different sets of message strings. These strings may use a completely different character set than your program originally used—for example, they could be composed of Japanese Kanji characters. In this chapter, you learn how to:

- Create a message catalog using the `gencat` utility
- Retrieve message catalog entries in your dtksh script using the `catopen` and `catgets` utilities
- Use the KornShell internationalized string notation to make a list of message strings.

Internationalization is a huge topic that includes more than just changing the message strings the user sees; alas, this book just doesn't have room to cover the more esoteric topics. For a more complete description, see [CDE Internationalization 1994].

22.2 Message Catalog General Concepts

A *message catalog* is a file that contains message strings that can be referenced using identifier numbers. The UNIX utility `gencat` can be used to create a message catalog out of a message source file (gencat is discussed later). Two different numbers are required to identify a message uniquely:

- A *message set* number
- A *message identifier* number.

These numbers can be between 0 and 32767. The idea behind having two different numbers is that the application could divide its messages into several different broad categories using the message set number, and then within each set messages are identified using message identifier numbers. This would be useful, for example, if several different programmers were working on different subsystems in a large application. Each subsystem could be assigned a message set number for all of its messages, avoiding potential collisions with other subsystems.

The messages themselves are entered using whatever keyboard techniques apply to the language. Special keyboards are necessary in many cases to produce message files for oriental languages, or other languages that use alternate character sets. In many cases, the characters are multibyte values. Dtksh is capable of handling up to four-byte multibyte characters in strings, which as of this writing is sufficient for any language.

Message Catalog Commands

The C language has several standard functions that are used to access message catalogs, and these commands have been mapped to the dtksh language and are thus available for use in Shell scripts. The catopen function opens a message catalog file, the catgets command retrieves a string from the catalog based on the message identifier, and the catclose function closes a previously opened catalog.

The precise syntax of these commands is discussed in detail later. The general strategy is to open the message catalog file using catopen once at the beginning of your application, then use catgets throughout your application to retrieve strings as they are needed. Most applications don't need to close message catalogs until they exit. It is possible to open and use more than one message catalog file in the same application.

Selecting a Language

An environment variable called LANG defines what language the user desires to use. For U. S. English, this variable is usually set to the value C. By using this variable's value as a component of a directory path, it is possible to select different message catalog files.

For example, let's say your application-specific files are stored in a directory pointed to by the variable MYAPP. You could create a directory under that one called Messages, then under that directory could be subdirectories for various languages, such as C. Then, when opening the message catalog you could use the path $MYAPP/Messages/$LANG as the directory to search for the catalog file. Users who speak different languages will have different values for $LANG, and thus will pick up the correct message catalog.

22.3 Creating Message Catalogs

Message catalogs are created by the UNIX gencat utility, which takes these arguments:

```
gencat catalog message-source ...
```

This command takes as input one or more *message-source* files and stores the resulting message catalog in an output file named *catalog*. The *message-source* file contains lines made up of ASCII fields separated by a single space or tab character. Some lines are directives that start with a dollar sign ($). Each line should be in one of the following formats:

$set *number comment*
: This directive defines the message set *number* for all subsequent message strings, until the next $set directive. After the *number*, any further characters are considered a *comment*.

number message-string
: Any line beginning with an integer defines a message. The *number* is the message identifier, which in combination with the current message set uniquely identifies the *message-string* to be displayed to the user.

$ *comment*
: Any line beginning with a dollar sign followed by whitespace and any other characters is a *comment*.

$quote [*character*]
: By default, there is no notion of quoting, making it impossible to define null messages or messages with trailing whitespace characters. This command defines *character* as a quotation mark. If *character* is left out, then the current quotation character is removed.

$delset *number comment*
: If gencat is being run on an existing message file, this directive can be used to delete the whole existing message set *number*.

Empty lines are ignored. For more information on the fine points of message input files, see the UNIX manual page gencat(1).

Example

As a running example in this chapter, we will convert the "hello, world" program to use message catalogs. This program is called ihello.sh (the "i" is for international) in the example programs directory. A directory called `$XUTILDIR/Messages` is the root directory for our message files. Under that directory, there are two subdirectories:

- `C`, which holds message catalogs for U. S. English, and
- `PIGLATIN`, which holds message catalogs for the venerable play language most of us learned in grade school.

> In this pseudo-language, you speak by moving any leading consonant sound to the end of the word, then append the sound "ay." For example, " *Iay inkthay Iay allshay evernay eesay*," which translates to "I think that I shall never see ... ." Using this language in the examples has the advantage that you can understand the words without having to know another language.

Under each of these directories, there are message source files called `hello.C` and `hello.PIGLATIN`, respectively. These message source files are translated, using `gencat`, into message catalogs named `hello`, using commands like this:

```
cd $XUTILDIR/Messages/C
gencat hello hello.C
cd ../PIGLATIN
gencat hello hello.PIGLATIN
```

Listing 22-1 shows the `hello.C` input file, whereas Listing 22-2 shows the `hello.PIGLATIN` equivalent. Each of these files uses a message set number of 10, and each contains a single message using message identifier number 1.

Listing 22-1. U.S. English Message Catalog (hello.C).

```
$   Message Catalog for international hello world program
$   U.S. English Version

$set 10
1 hello, world
```

Listing 22-2. Pig Latin Message Catalog (hello.PIGLATIN).

```
$   Message Catalog for international hello world program
$   Pig Latin Version

$set 10
1 ellohey, orldway
```

22.4 Using Catalogs in a Program

Three commands are used to access message catalog entries:

```
catopen variable path
catclose catalog-id
catgets variable catalog-id set-number message-number default-string
```

The `catopen` command opens the message catalog file named by *path*, and stores a catalog identifier in *variable*. The `catclose` command can be used to close a catalog; its argument is a catalog identifier previously returned in the *variable* argument to `catopen`.

The `catgets` command retrieves a message given a *catalog-id,* which was previously obtained using `catopen`, a *set-number*, and a *message-number*. In addition, its final argument, *default-string,* is a message that should be returned if for some reason the catalog entry cannot be retrieved. In this way, your program might still work even if the message catalogs are not installed properly. The retrieved catalog message is stored in *variable*. If *variable* is a dash character (-), then the retrieved message is printed to the standard output.

An Example

Listing 22-3 shows how this works. It implements a version of the "hello, world" program that uses message catalogs. The resulting outputs, with the LANG variable set alternatively to C and PIGLATIN, is shown in Figure 22-1.

The message catalog is opened using a path that varies depending on LANG, as explained earlier. The catalog identifier is stored in a variable called CATID. A function is defined to make a catalog look-up. Because this function will often be called within a list of command arguments, it has a very short name, M (for Message). It takes as its arguments a message number and a default string. It assumes the message set number is always the same (this is true in many short programs). Any arguments after the first one are concatenated to make the default string, thus quoting is not necessary when the function is called.

When the Label widget that displays the message string is created, it sets the labelString resource using command substitution—the output of the function call to M.

Listing 22-3. International Hello World (ihello.sh).

```
# Internationalized version of hello.sh

. $XUTILDIR/xutil.sh

DEFAULT_SET=10

# Attempt to open the catalog

catopen CATID $XUTILDIR/Messages/$LANG/hello || {
    print "WARNING: Cannot open message catalog" 2>&1
}
```

```
# Define a function that uses a default message set and the
# previously opened catalog id

function M {
    typeset r
    catgets r "$CATID" "$DEFAULT_SET" "$1" "${*:2}"
    print $r
}

XUinitialize TOPLEVEL Ihello "$@"

XUlabel LABEL $TOPLEVEL labelString:"$(M 1 "hello, world")"
XUrealize $TOPLEVEL
XUmainloop
```

Figure 22-1. Outputs of ihello.sh.   On the left, the program as it appears when LANG=C, on the right, the appearance with LANG=PIGLATIN.

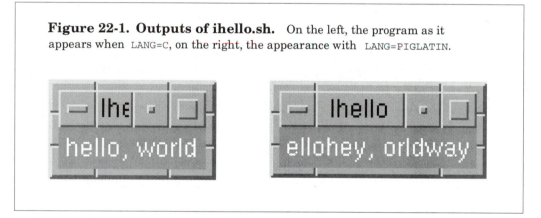

22.5 Using Internationalized String Notation

KornShell-93 has a new kind of string quoting mechanism that allows you to create easily the initial catalog for an application. This notation uses double quotes prefixed by a dollar sign. For example:

```
msg=$"International Message"
```

This type of string quoting is just like regular double quoting, except that dtksh marks the string as an international message. Any string thus marked can be dumped out to standard output by running dtksh with the -d option.

So, if we had used this line in the ihello.sh program:

```
XUlabel LABEL $TOPLEVEL labelString:"$(M 1 $"hello, world")"
```

then we could run dtksh like this:

```
dtksh -d ihello.sh > message_list
```

after which the file `message_list` would contain the string:

```
"hello, world"
```

This clearly makes creating the initial catalog easier. You would still need to add the message set directive and message numbers to each line of a file thus produced, but at least you would not need to painstakingly scan your entire program looking for message strings.

> It is also convenient to use this technique to dump all your message strings for proofreading purposes.

One tricky point is that if you create a new release of your program sometime later, you need to be sure any new strings created are added at the end of each message set. This is because you should try not to disturb the catalog numbers of existing messages (otherwise you'll drive the people who do the translations crazy). It is quite easy to create a simple utility that takes the old version of the catalog and a list of international strings from a new version of an application and prints a list of just the new strings. This is left as a KornShell programming exercise for the reader.

> Hint: the associative array feature of KornShell-93 is quite useful for creating a utility like this.

22.6 Other Considerations

Besides message strings, several other aspects of your program are affected by internationalization concerns:

- The character used as a decimal point in floating-point numbers is a comma in some languages instead of a period. If you use the dtksh built-in command `printf` to format numbers, or if you simply use dtksh's floating point output, this will be taken care of for you.

- The order of fields in dates differs in many countries. In the United States, the order is usually month, day, year. In Europe, it is often: day, month, year. It's a good idea to format dates in a subroutine that can take an option for the preferred format.

- Icons used in your program should also be stored in a directory structure that uses the LANG variable as one of its components. Some icons are culturally biased. For example, in the United States you will often see a mailbox icon used to denote electronic mail. That icon is meaningless in some countries that do not use mailboxes that look anything like the ones used in the United States.

Going Further

Even these considerations are just the tip of the iceberg, unfortunately. To write an application that is truly general and can be localized to any language on earth is no small task. All the necessary tools are provided by dtksh, Motif, and CDE to support most languages, including languages that read right-to-left (such as Hebrew) or top-to-bottom (several Oriental languages).

Using message catalogs in your application is a necessary first step no matter what language you are trying to support, but I've given you enough information in this chapter only for European languages. If you want to write an application with a truly global viewpoint, you should read the Internationalization chapter in [Heller and Ferguson 1994] for details of how Motif handles these issues, and also [CDE Internationalization 1994], which discusses all the issues you are likely to run across.

22.7 Summary

Dtksh supports wide character sets, message catalogs, and other aspects of internationalization such as decimal point conversion. Message catalogs can be used to define sets of messages used in an application. Messages are uniquely identified by two numbers: the message set and the message identifier. The UNIX `gencat` utility can be used to create a message catalog from a simple ASCII input file. The user's `LANG` variable can be used to select an appropriate catalog. Messages are retrieved using the `catgets` command.

Internationalization is a broad topic that really includes many other techniques and issues besides just defining message catalogs.

23   *Attaching C Code*

23.1 Introduction

One of the most powerful features of dtksh is its ability to be extended using shared libraries. This feature allows the C-knowledgable programmer to create new built-in commands and add them to the dtksh process on-the-fly. It also allows such a programmer to register new widget definitions with dtksh, and those widgets become usable just as if they were built in to dtksh from the start.

This chapter assumes you know how to program in the C language, and parts of it assume you understand how to program using the C interfaces of Motif and X. In it, you learn:

- Shared library concepts
- How to create new built-in commands for dtksh
- How to access the dtksh environment from within your attached C code in order to get and set variables and call the dtksh interpreter
- How to use X functions from within your attached C code
- How to register a new widget definition with dtksh
- Limitations and common problems encountered when using the shared library features of dtksh.

This is the most advanced material in this book. It is only for readers who know how to program using the C language. The sections on attaching new widget definitions assume you are familiar with C language X programming.

Reasons to Attach C Code to Dtksh

There are several major reasons why you might want to attach C code to dtksh:

- If you have developed a dtksh application, but some aspect of the application performs too slowly, you can often create a few new built-in commands that

445

optimize away the bottlenecks. Often just rewriting a small percentage of your shell code using attached C does the trick.

- If you have a C language library that provides some specialized functionality such as database access or communications, it is usually possible to make that functionality available via shell built-in commands. In this case, you can make small wrapper functions that meet the requirements of a shell built-in function—these functions simply decode arguments then call routines in the underlying library in which you are interested.

- When writing very advanced X programs, you may need access to some X function that is not directly provided by dtksh; you can overcome this limitation by attaching a C function that calls the desired function.

- You may need to use a widget that is not distributed with Motif; in this case you can attach the widget's definition to dtksh (some limitations are discussed next).

Drawbacks of Using Attached Code

Before you decide to attach C functions to the dtksh process, you should consider the trade-offs involved:

- Once you attach C functions to dtksh, the script loses a good measure of its portability. If you move your application to a different type of hardware, you will have to port your C code, whereas if the script were entirely written in shell it should run unchanged on any CDE-compliant system regardless of hardware type.

- Attached C code can be hard to debug—different versions of UNIX debugging tools have different levels of support for debugging shared libraries. Also, it will not be possible for you to single step through the dtksh internal routines when debugging your code. One solution is to debug any attached functions outside of dtksh by writing a simple `main()` that calls your attached functions.

- The more C code you write, the smaller the productivity gains from using dtksh.

My aim is not to discourage you from using the attachable code features of dtksh — it is one of the most powerful features of the entire language. I just want you to be aware of the trade-offs involved. Using an intelligent combination of C and dtksh code is still far more productive than writing an application entirely in C, and such a hybrid application is usually much easier to customize and extend than one written in C.

23.2 Shared Library General Concepts

Dynamic shared libraries are similar to standard archive libraries, but with one important feature—they can be loaded into a *running* process. The symbols in the shared library are available to the process to which the library is attached.

In this chapter, I will use the term *shared library* for brevity, but in all cases I am referring to dynamic shared libraries (also called shared objects by some people). There is another kind of shared library—the static shared library—which requires the executable to be statically linked with the library before being executed. Static shared libraries are generally not as powerful as dynamic shared libraries. Very few modern versions of UNIX lack dynamic shared libraries, so the features described in this chapter will usually be available. For example, Hewlett-Packard's HP/UX, IBM's AIX, Sun Microsystems SunOs and Solaris, Digital Equipment Corporation's OSF/1 and Novell's UnixWare operating systems all support dynamic shared libraries.

The KornShell language, on which dtksh is based, has the ability to attach a shared library and register the C functions in that library as new built-in commands (subject to some constraints that will be explained below).

You might think it would be difficult to create these types of libraries, but nothing could be further from the truth. As you will see in the next section, all you must do is use the proper compilation and loading options, and you will magically be in possession of a shared library!

How Shared Libraries Work

This material is presented as background information, you don't really need to know it in order to use shared libraries, but it might help to give you a mental model of how they work that will be helpful.

Although the exact mechanism varies somewhat from vendor to vendor, the basic idea behind how shared libraries work goes something like this:

- The object code to be used in a shared library is compiled so that it only uses relative addressing — no absolute branches.

- When a process loads a shared library, the object code contained in the library is mapped into the address space of the process, just as if it had been compiled in. This works because there are no absolute branches, so the code can be moved to any address with minimal work.

- The text of the shared library may be mapped by any number of processes, and only one copy of it is maintained in-core (hence the "shared"). Any data that the shared library uses are copied into the processes' address space if it is modified.

- The process that attached the shared library can do symbol table look-ups to find the addresses of functions that it desires to call. These functions can be executed just as if they had originally been compiled into the process.

23.3 Compilation on Different Operating Systems

Different operating systems require different compiler and loader options in order to create shared libraries. Also, different operating systems have different naming conventions for shared libraries. This section explains how you can compile shared libraries on several major vendor versions of UNIX. If your version of UNIX is not mentioned here, you must consult the documentation supplied with the compilation system to find out if shared libraries are supported and what options are required to create them.

In the next few subsections, I use an example to illustrate how to compile shared objects. In this example, we wish to create a shared object file from two C language files: funcs1.c and funcs2.c. When I present these examples, I will be using bare minimum compiler options, so it may be necessary for you to include other options depending on how you need to compile your particular code. For example, you may need to use the -I option to specify an include file directory.

SunOs 4

Sun Microsystem's SunOs 4 series uses the following conventions:

- Shared libraries use the suffix .so (**shared o**bject). For example: lib-funcs.so.

- To compile a shared library, you first compile all the object files so they are position independent. This is accomplished by using the -PIC option. Then, you simply load all the object files into a name that ends in .so, like this:

```
cc -c -PIC funcs1.c
cc -c -PIC funcs2.c
ld -o libfuncs.so funcs1.o funcs2.o
```

Solaris (SunOs 5)

Sun Microsystem's Solaris series (also known as SunOs 5) uses the System V Release 4 style of creating shared objects, which is slightly different from that just described:

- As above, shared libraries use the suffix .so.

- As above, you compile all the object files so they are position independent. However, in this case the option is slightly different: -K PIC. To create the shared object, use the cc command with the option -G. For example:

```
cc -c -K PIC funcs1.c
cc -c -K PIC funcs2.c
cc -G -o libfuncs.so funcs1.o funcs2.o
```

UnixWare (Version 1 or 2)

Novell's UnixWare operating system is based on System V Release 4, and so uses the same procedure as outlined above for Solaris.

HP/UX

Hewlett-Packard's HP/UX operating system uses the following conventions to create a share library:

- Shared libraries use the suffix `.sl`. For example: `libfunc.sl`.
- Source files must be compiled using position-independent code using the `+z` option to cc. When creating the object file, you must use the `+s` and `-b` options to create a shared library. For example:

```
cc -c +z funcs1.c
cc -c +z funcs2.c
ld +s -b -o libfuncs.sl funcs1.o funcs2.o
```

AIX

Creating shared libraries using IBM's AIX operating system is more difficult than the others discussed here. You must specify exactly which symbols are imported and exported from each shared library using a separate file. Each line of this file is the name of a C function to be exported or imported. Here is a summary of the conventions:

- Shared libraries are usually named the same as regular archive libraries, using the suffix `.a`. You can actually use any naming convention you want, some people use `.sl` for AIX.
- When loading the object files, you must use the options: `-bM:SRE`. Most people also use the options `-T512` and `-H512` (see IBM documentation).
- You must create a symbol file, which contains a list of function names you wish to export to dtksh, one function per line. In our example, we assume this file is called `funcs.exp` (export).
- When creating the shared library, you must specify the export file using the option `-bE:filename`. You must create a load map file using the option:

```
-bloadmap:loadfilename
```

By convention, the load map file should end in the extension `.map`, and in our example I use `funcs.map`. For example:

```
cc -c funcs1.c
cc -c funcs2.c
ld -bM:SRE -T512 -H512-bE:funcs.exp \
        -bloadmap:funcs.map -o libfuncs.a
        funcs1.o funcs2.o
```

Referencing Other Libraries

It is important that any other shared libraries that the functions in your shared library might reference be included at the end of the `ld` or `cc` command you use to create your shared library. If you fail to do this, then symbols may not be found at run-time when the library is attached. Even libraries that you expect to be already loaded in dtksh, such as the standard `libc` library, should be included for safety.

23.4 Creating New Dtksh Built-in Commands

As previously mentioned, dtksh allows you to write new built-in commands in C, compile them into a shared library, and use them in your dtksh script just like any other built-in command. A C function must meet several requirements in order for it to function properly as a new built-in dtksh command:

1. The function must return `int`, and should return 0 for success and nonzero for failure (which is true of any dtksh built-in command).

2. The function must take two arguments, `int argc` and `char *argv[]`, just like a C `main` function. When the function is called, `argv[0]` will contain the name of the function, and any further elements of the `argv` array will contain the arguments passed to your function by the user's script.

3. The function's name must be prefixed by `b_`, which is the convention internally in dtksh for built-in command function names. The part of the name following the `b_` will be the name of the built-in command that the script writer would use to invoke your function.

Listing 23-1 is a trivial function that meets the requirements to become a built-in command. This function simply prints its arguments, followed by the number of characters of arguments passed to it.

> Being from the old school, I use traditional C for these examples. If you wish to use ANSI C instead, feel free to do the translation.

Listing 23-1. A Function Suitable for a Built-in (simp.c).

```
#include <stdio.h>

int
b_simpcmd(argc, argv)     /* name must start with "b_" */
int argc;                 /* takes "main" style argc, argv parameters */
char *argv[];
{
    register int i;
    register int total = 0;
    int strlen();

    /*
     * Print arguments using printf.
     */
    for (i = 0; i < argc; i++) {
        printf("argv[%d]='%s'\n", i, argv[i]);
        total += strlen(argv[i]);
    }
    printf("total characters in args=%d\n", total);
    return(0);   /* shell standard: 0 for "success" */
}
```

Registering the Command as a Built-in

Once you have written a function that is suitable as a built-in command, you must compile it into a shared library. See *Compilation on Different Operating Systems* on page 447 above for details of how to do this on several popular operating systems. In the remainder of this section, I will assume you have compiled the `simp.c` program just shown into a shared library called `libsimp.so`.

> On some operating systems, the convention for naming shared objects is different. For example, on HP/UX shared objects end in `.sl`, while on IBM's AIX many people use the convention that shared libraries end in `.a` just like normal archive libraries. For simplicity, I use only the `.so` suffix in the rest of this chapter, since that is the most common convention.

Within the dtksh script, you can register your new built-in command using this command:

```
builtin [-f library-name] command-name ...
```

The `-f` option can be used to specify a shared library name to attach to the dtksh process. After that, any number of command names can be specified. All attached shared libraries will be searched for a symbol that is the same as a *command-name* prefixed by b_. After the `builtin` command executes, you can begin using these new commands as if they were normal dtksh built-in commands.

For example, assuming you have compiled the `simp.c` example shown previously into a shared library called `libsimp.so`, this sequence could be used to register and invoke the new built-in command:

```
builtin -f ./libsimp.so  simpcmd
simpcmd try this out
```

The output from this code would be:

```
argv[0]=simpcmd
argv[1]=try
argv[2]=this
argv[3]=out
total characters in args=10
```

Note that you need not attach the shared library and register the new built-ins in the same command. For example, this will work:

```
builtin -f ./libsimp.so
builtin simpcmd
```

The shared libraries that have been attached using the `-f` option of `builtin` are searched in reverse order until the function symbol is found.

Standard I/O

Dtksh arranges for all the standard I/O C functions used in your shared library to be replaced by internal dtksh routines that act appropriately. For example, if you use `printf` in a subroutine registered as a built-in, the output will go wherever the script has redirected standard output. Similarly, if you were to use `getchar` in such a subroutine, your command will correctly take its input from an incoming pipeline used in the script.

23.5 Accessing the KornShell Environment

From within your built-in command, you will be able to call certain subroutines that are defined internally to dtksh to access the shell environment.

> Warning: the CDE companies do not officially support these subroutine interfaces. These subroutine interfaces are documented in the predecessor to dtksh (called wksh), and as of this writing these functions appear to work properly in dtksh as well. However, because these interfaces are not officially supported, there is no guarantee they will continue to exist in future versions of CDE, although it is likely that some equivalent functionality will eventually be agreed on and documented by the member companies. These interfaces are very powerful and make attached C code far more useful, so I decided to document them here.

Here is a list of function calls you can use from attached code:

`char *`
`env_get(varname)`
`char *varname;`
	This function retrieves the value of the dtksh variable named `varname` in the current dtksh scope, and returns the value as a string. The *varname* may be a subscripted or hierarchical variable.

`void`
`env_set(vareqval)`
`char *vareqval;`
	This function sets dtksh variables. The `vareqval` argument is of the form *variable=value*. In such a specification, the *variable* may be a subscripted or hierarchical variable name.

`int`
`ksh_eval(command)`
`char *command;`
	This function invokes the dtksh command interpreter on the string held in the *command* argument. The exit code of the *command* is returned as the value of this function call. In other words, you can attach a piece of C code to your dtksh script, then call it from the dtksh interpreter, then have that C code make calls back into the dtksh interpreter!

Here are some examples of these subroutines in action:

```
val = env_get("foo[3]");    /* get the value of ${foo[3]} */
env_set("foo[3]=hello there");
ksh_eval("unset foo");      /* execute a dtksh unset command */
```

These subroutines allow your built-in command to access the dtksh variable space or perform necessary side effects. For example, if you wanted to write a command that would perform some calculation then return the result in a variable name passed in as its first argument, you would simply use env_set().

23.6 Using X from Attached Code

Attached built-in commands can be used to access X functions that are not directly available in dtksh. A function is provided which allows you to translate a dtksh widget handle into an X widget identifier:

```
Widget handle_to_widget(char *comname, char *handle);
```

This function takes two arguments. The comname argument is the name of the command that is invoking handle_to_widget. It should be the value stored in argv[0] when your command was invoked. It is used to print an appropriate error message if the conversion fails.

Event Structures and Call Data

Sometimes you wish to pass a call data or event structure to an attached piece of code. In this case, we assume the attached command is being invoked from within a dtksh callback command, translation handler command, or event handler command. In a callback, the address of the call data structure is stored in the variable CB_CALL_DATA as a hexadecimal value. Similarly, in a translation handler the variable TRANSLATION_EVENT holds the address of the event that triggered the translation in hexadecimal, and in an event handler the variable EH_EVENT holds the address of the event that triggered the event handler command, also in hexadecimal.

If you pass the value of any of these variables to a built-in command function, you can translate the value back into an address by using the strtoul function, then casting the value appropriately. For example, let's say you expect the first argument to your command function to be the value of EH_EVENT. Then, you can gain access to the event structure using code like this:

```
XEvent *event;

event = (XEvent *)strtoul(argv[1], 0);
```

Similar code can be used for various kinds of call data.

23.7 Attached Code Caveats and Pitfalls

There are several pitfalls involved in writing your own built-in commands:
- You must never modify the argv[] strings passed into your function. Doing so will cause wild behavior from the dtksh interpreter. For example, this

means you must never use standard C functions such as `strtok` directly on a member of `argv[]`, because `strtok` modifies its arguments. In a case like this, you must first copy the argument using `strdup`.

- If your attached C code has a bug, you can core dump the dtksh process, or corrupt dtksh's memory causing undefined results. It can be difficult to debug problems in this situation. On most operating systems, you can compile your shared library with debugging enabled and run a debugger on the dtksh command. However, you will not be able to single step through the dtksh code itself, only your own code. On some operating systems debuggers don't work well with shared libraries, though.

23.8 Registering New Widgets

If you have written a new widget that is compatible with the Motif widget set, or if you have obtained a widget that someone else has written, it is possible to attach the new widget to the dtksh process and register it as a new widget type.

> Many public domain widgets are available on the Internet that can be attached in this manner, and several high-quality commercial widgets are available for specific purposes.

The process involved is straightforward:

1. The new widget's class record and method functions must be compiled into a shared library.

2. You must attach to the shared library using the command:

```
builtin -f library
```

3. You must register the class record of the new widget using the command:

```
DtLoadWidget class-record-name dtksh-name
```

In this command, the *class-record-name* is the name of the C symbol that holds the widget's class record, and the *dtksh-name* argument is a string that determines the name of the widget from a dtksh programmer's point of view.

For example, if you have a new widget whose class record symbol is `xyWonderful-WidgetClass`, and whose code is stored in a shared library named `libmywid.so`, then you can register this widget using this code in your dtksh script:

```
builtin -f ./libmywid.so
DtLoadWidget xyWonderfulWidgetClass XyWonderful
```

Dtksh uses the convention that the dtksh programmer references a widget-class name using the same notation as would be used in a resource file, thus the name used by the programmer normally has an initial uppercase letter, and the suffix `WidgetClass` is left off.

Limitations of Attached Widgets

There are several limitations to your ability to attach new widgets and use them effectively in dtksh:

- The attached widget must contain string-to-type and type-to-string converters for any resource types for which there are no standard converters. Dtksh uses these converters to prepare argument lists for widget creation, `XtSetValues`, and `XtGetValues` commands. Any resource that does not have the appropriate converters cannot be used from the dtksh script.

- The widget must report all of its resources when queried by `XtGetResources`. Dtksh uses `XtGetResources` to find out what resources are available. Some widgets do not report all their resources when they are queried.

- Dtksh currently has no mechanism to allow you to map call data parameters to variables for your attached widgets. The address of the call data structure will be passed to any dtksh callback commands in the `CB_CALL_DATA` variable. As a work-around, you could write a new built-in command that would take that address and set up call data variables appropriately.

  > A feature to allow the programmer to map call data parameters to variables is being considered for a future release of dtksh.

- Widgets that are incompatible with the Motif widget set cannot be attached. For example, if a widget is a subclass of another widget that redefines VendorShell, there will be problems. There could also be problems if function names in the new widget collide with functions in the Motif widget set, etc.

- Widgets that rely on many convenience functions for their operation will require you to do some work before they can be used effectively. You will have to define new built-in commands that map the functionality of the widget's convenience functions to the shell language.

There are many widgets for which these limitations do not seriously impede use from dtksh. In any case, you can overcome most of these limitations by writing additional code. For example, if a widget does not provide a suitable converter for one or more of its resources, you could write a converter and register it with X using an attached built-in command. You could also write a command to set up variables with call data values. The limitation regarding unreported resources is not easy to overcome in this release of dtksh, but many widgets do not exhibit that behavior.

I have attached some widgets, such as the `xmpTable` widget from the WCL library, and used them immediately from dtksh with no further work. Other widgets require extensive work to use from dtksh because of reliance on many convenience functions or the use of exotic resource types that have no predefined converters to and from String. Most widgets fall somewhere in between these two extremes.

23.9 Summary

Dtksh allows the sophisticated programmer to attach C code compiled into shared libraries to the dtksh process. Functions in this attached C code can be registered as new dtksh built-in commands if they conform to certain requirements. Widget class records contained in shared libraries can also be registered as new widget types recognized by dtksh, with a few limitations.

24 *Nongraphical Interfaces*

24.1 Introduction

Dtksh contains several CDE application programming interfaces that are not graphical in nature. For completeness, I will mention these interfaces briefly in this chapter, just to give you a feel for when you might use them. This chapter does not provide extensive tutorial information on these interfaces, and does not provide programming examples for these interfaces — that is beyond the scope of this book. After all, the title is *Desktop KornShell Graphical Programming*!

Some of the topics mentioned here require an entire book of their own to explain properly (such as ToolTalk); in such cases, references are provided to C language documentation provided with CDE.

All of the commands provided by dtksh for these various interfaces are listed, with terse explanations, in Chapter 32, *Desktop KornShell Built-in Commands*.

24.2 The Action/Invocation Mechanism

The CDE supports the notion of *actions*. An action is a named procedure that can be defined by a user or by an application. An action can be invoked with arguments, and those arguments can be filenames. The files need not reside on the same machine; actions support the notion of networked files.

Few dtksh scripts need to use actions; the CDE already allows the user to launch actions by double-clicking on an icon associated with the action.

The Action Database

Actions are stored in a database. You can load this database in your dtksh script using the command:

```
DtDbLoad
```

This command takes no arguments, and it must be called before any other action database commands are used. It is possible for new actions to be added to the database after your script has called `DtDbLoad`. In that case, your script might not realize that certain actions exist. It is possible to register a command that will be called when a change occurs in the action database, using:

```
DtDbReloadNotify command
```

The command will be invoked whenever the action database changes. Typically, the command is simply a call to `DtDbLoad`, which reloads the database.

Obtaining Information About Actions

Each action has a *name*, and also several other *attributes*. Attributes are pieces of data associated with actions that describe the action. Two attributes that your program may need include the `LABEL` that should appear to the user describing the action, and the `DESCRIPTION` of an action.

You can find out if an action exists using the command:

```
DtActionExists action-name
```

This command returns success (zero) if the given `action-name` exists in the database. Thus, it can be used with the KornShell `if` statement as a conditional.

You can retrieve the `DESCRIPTION` and `LABEL` attributes of an action using these commands:

```
DtActionDescription variable action-name
DtActionLabel variable action-name
```

These commands store the retrieved information in the `variable` argument.

Invoking Actions

The following command invokes an action, passing it arguments which are files that exist on some host (or hosts) on the network:

```
DtActionInvokeOnFiles widget action-name term-options \
    execution-host context-host context-directory \
    use-indicator [file type host ...]
```

This invokes `action-name` on the machine `execution-host` using context from `context-host` with current working directory `context-directory`. The `use-indicator` option can be `true` or `false`, and determines whether the indicator light should flash during the action's invocation. There can be any number of triplets following `use-indicator`. These triplets identify files that are to be used as arguments for the action. The first item in each triplet is the `file` name; the second is the `type` of file, and the third is the `host` machine on which the file resides.

The *type* and *host* arguments may be empty strings ("") if you don't wish to specify them.

24.3 The Data Type Database

CDE contains a mechnism to define *data types*. A data type is associated with a file or directory. A data type has *attributes* associated with it. The available attributes vary depending on the data type. Data types are stored in a database; the database also tracks the various attributes available with each data type.

Loading the Data Type Database

You must load the data type database before using any other data typing command, by using:

```
DtLoadDataTypes
```

This command takes no arguments.

Setting a File's Data Type

This command can be used to set a data type on a file:

```
DtsSetDataType variable file data-type override
```

The named *file* is set to *data-type* if it does not currently have a type. If it does currently have a type, then the type is changed to *data-type* only if the *override* argument is the value `true`. The data type name associated with the *file* following execution of this command is stored in *variable*.

Finding Data Types

The following commands can be used to find out about data types:

```
DtDtsFileToDataType variable file
DtDtsDataTypeNames variable
DtDtsFindAttribute variable attribute-name attribute-value
```

The `DtDtsFileToDataType` command stores the data type associated with the named file in the variable. The `DtDtsDataTypeNames` command stores a space-separated list of all known data types in *variable*. The `DtDtsFindAttribute` command stores a space separated list of data type names in variable; only data types that have an attribute called *attribute-name*, which is set to *attribute-value*, are returned.

Finding Attributes

These commands can be used to find out about attributes associated with data types:

```
DtDtsDataTypeToAttributeList variable data-type option-name
DtDtsFileToAttributeList variable file
```

The first of these gets a list of attributes associated with a `data-type` and stores it in the `variable`; the second does the same but finds the attributes associated with a `file` (the file presumably has a data type).

You can retrieve the value of an attribute using these commands:

```
DtDtsDataTypeToAttributeValue variable data-type \
                    attribute-name option-name
DtDtsFileToAttributeValue variable file attribute-name
```

The first of these commands gets the value associated with an `attribute-name` of a `data-type`; the second does the same, but gets the value of `attribute-name` associated with a `file`. Both store the result in the `variable` argument.

24.4 ToolTalk

ToolTalk is a rich set of application programming interfaces that allows interprocess communication, automatic application launch, routing of messages to specific applications or classes of applications, and many other features.

The entire ToolTalk programming interface contains hundreds of function calls. Dtksh provides a very small subset of ToolTalk functions, about 20 commands. Dtksh does not contain any ToolTalk commands that allow the application to create new ToolTalk messages, it only contains commands to allow a dtksh script to participate in a predefined ToolTalk message set.

ToolTalk is beyond the scope of this book. See [CDE ToolTalk 1995] for more information on ToolTalk, and see [CDE Dtksh Guide 1995] for some information on the mapping of ToolTalk functions to dtksh commands. All the ToolTalk commands supported by dtksh begin with the prefix tt, and are listed with terse explanations in Chapter 32, *Desktop KornShell Built-in Commands*.

24.5 Summary

Dtksh provides numerous commands to access nongraphical aspects of the CDE. The action/invocation mechanism can be used to query a database of actions that define stored procedures the user may want to execute. The file typing mechanism allows your program to determine the type of a file, and the ToolTalk mechanism allows you to communicate with other applications, which can be local or on other machines.

PART III *Utilities and Applications*

Programs presented in this part are longer than those presented in earlier sections. This section includes the complete code for the XU library, a final version of the checkbook application developed in Part I, and an Xlib layer program that displays stock charts.

Each chapter begins by explaining the requirements for the program, then discusses the general strategies used in the program to implement those requirements. Finally, the code for the program is presented.

25 *Checkbook Application*

25.1 Introduction

The checkbook application was constructed during Parts I and II of this book. At each stage, new dtksh programming techniques were introduced and illustrated by adding features and functions to this program. In this chapter, I present the entire program.

Some aspects of this program were not discussed in previous chapters, usually because they just reused a concept that had already been introduced. For example, when the user adds a new check and wants to create a new category, this program allows the user to choose a special OptionMenu choice labeled "New ...." Once selected, that choices pops up a dialog that allows a new category to be created. Because this feature just rehashes previously discussed concepts such as OptionMenu selection and dialog creation, it was not discussed in the main line text.

Not Ready for Prime Time

This application is meant for illustrative purposes only. I don't want to pretend it is complete by any means, and I don't particularly want people balancing their real check book using it. For that reason, I have purposely left out some vital functions, such as a command to print checks, or a command to print a list of missing checks. The help files are also incomplete; they don't cover every field and screen in the program, and some help screens only consist of a title with no text.

It might be a useful exercise for you to try to extend this program to include some of that missing functionality.

Still, this program packs quite a lot of functionality into about 1000 lines of code, and is a testament to the compactness of dtksh applications.

25.2 Techniques Illustrated

This example presents a complete application that attempts to be a good desktop citizen. It is meant to illustrate many different concepts, such as:

- Interacting with the session manager to save and restore state
- How to store data in a simple flat-file database
- Techniques for prompting the user for data entry
- Building a menu bar
- Using the List widget to display data
- How to pop up warnings and errors
- Using the CDE Help system to provide context-sensitive help
- How to create a button bar
- How to do simple animation using Xlib drawing commands and timers
- Intercepting a window manager close directive in order to prompt the user to save unwritten changes.

Most of these techniques are of great practical imporatance to almost any graphical program.

25.3 Source Code

```
#!/usr/dt/bin/dtksh

. $XUTILDIR/xutil.sh

# Database Field definitions

readonly MM=0 DD=1 YY=2 PAYEE=3 CHECKNUM=4 AMOUNT=5 \
    CATEG=6 RECON=7 COMMENT=8 NUMFIELDS=9

typeset STATE=""
integer STATE.DETAILS=0                # 1 = more details displayed
integer STATE.ALREADYBOUNCED=0         # only display bounce-check warning
once
typeset STATE.SORTORDER=DATE           # method of sorting

typeset -A CATEGORIES   # hash table of all categories

function show_error {    # error-string
    typeset errstr=$1

    XUinformation "Error Details" "$errstr" :
}

function update_display {
```

```
    integer running
    typeset f line errors=""

    STATE.MAXCHECK=-1

    CATEGORIES[MISC]=1
    CATEGORIES[CREDIT]=1
    CATEGORIES[VOID]=1

    case "${STATE.SORTORDER}" in
    DATE)
        XUdbsort DB -n \
            +$((YY)) -$((YY+1)) \
            +$((MM)) -$((MM+1)) \
            +$((DD)) -$((DD+1)) \
            +$((CHECKNUM)) -$((CHECKNUM+1)) \
        ;;
    CATEG)
        XUdbsort DB \
            +$((CATEG)) -$((CATEG+1)) \
            -n \
            +$((YY)) -$((YY+1)) \
            +$((MM)) -$((MM+1)) \
            +$((DD)) -$((DD+1)) \
            +$((CHECKNUM)) -$((CHECKNUM+1)) \
        ;;
    esac

    XUlistdeleteall $WORK
    for (( i = 0; i < ${#DB.record[@]}; i++ ))
    do
        XUdbsplit DB $i f
        if ! check_record errors $((i+1)) "${f[@]}"
        then continue
        fi
        if [[ ${f[CATEG]} == CREDIT ]]
        then
            (( running += f[AMOUNT] ))
        else
            (( running -= f[AMOUNT] ))
        fi
        if [[ "${f[CHECKNUM]}" != " " ]] && (( f[CHECKNUM] >
STATE.MAXCHECK))
        then STATE.MAXCHECK=${f[CHECKNUM]}
        fi

        CATEGORIES[${f[CATEG]}]=1
        XUlistappend $WORK "$(format_record "${f[@]}")"
    done
```

```
        if [[ "$errors" ]]
        then
            XUwarning "Warning" \
                "Some records appear to be bad.
                They have been skipped.
                For more information, press Help" \
                : "" "show_error '$errors'"
        fi
        XUset $MESSAGE \
            value:"$(printf "Balance: \$%9.2f" $running)"
        XUset $TOPLEVEL title:"Checkbook - ${DB.file}"
        STATE.CURPATH="$PWD/${DB.file}"

        if (( running < 0 && STATE.ALREADYBOUNCED == 0 ))
        then displayBounceWarning
        fi
}

function moveballCB {
        typeset w=${BOUNCE.CANVAS}
        typeset display=$(XtDisplay - $w)
        typeset window=$(XtWindow - $w)
        integer width height

        if [[ ! "$w" ]]
        then return
        fi
        XUget $w width:width height:height

        # erase the old position
        XClearArea $display $window \
            ${BOUNCE.X} ${BOUNCE.Y} \
            ${BOUNCE.WIDTH} ${BOUNCE.HEIGHT}

        # update the position
        (( BOUNCE.X += BOUNCE.XVEL ))
        (( BOUNCE.Y += BOUNCE.YVEL ))

        # Draw the ball at the new position
        XFillRectangle $display $window \
            -foreground black \
            ${BOUNCE.X} ${BOUNCE.Y} \
            ${BOUNCE.WIDTH} ${BOUNCE.HEIGHT}

        # if the y coordinate is at the bottom, reverse
        # the y velocity to cause a bounce

        if (( BOUNCE.Y > height - BOUNCE.HEIGHT ))
        then
```

```
            (( BOUNCE.Y = height - BOUNCE.HEIGHT ))
            (( BOUNCE.YVEL = 0 - BOUNCE.YVEL ))
        fi

        # if the x coordinate is at either border
        # of the screen, reverse the x direction
        if (( BOUNCE.X < BOUNCE.WIDTH ||
            BOUNCE.X > width - BOUNCE.WIDTH ))
        then
            (( BOUNCE.XVEL = 0 - BOUNCE.XVEL ))
        fi

        # accelerate in the y dimension to simulate gravity
        (( BOUNCE.YVEL += 3 ))

        XUaddtimeout BOUNCE.TIMER 200 moveballCB
    }

    function displayBounceWarning {
        typeset button

        XUwarningdialog -u BOUNCE $TOPLEVEL \
            dialogTitle:"Negative Balance!" \
            messageString:"Your Balance is negative.
                        Checks may bounce." \
            destroyCallback:'XUremovetimeout ${BOUNCE.TIMER}' \
            okCallback:'XUdestroy $BOUNCE'

        XUget $BOUNCE cancelButton:button
        XUunmanage $button

        XUdrawingarea BOUNCE.CANVAS $BOUNCE \
            width:100 height:100

        XUmanage $BOUNCE
        BOUNCE.X=10
        BOUNCE.Y=10
        BOUNCE.XVEL=5
        BOUNCE.YVEL=0
        BOUNCE.WIDTH=6
        BOUNCE.HEIGHT=6

        STATE.ALREADYBOUNCED=1
        XUaddtimeout BOUNCE.TIMER 150 moveballCB
    }

    function check_record {
        # usage: check_record var line-number field1 field2 ...
```

```
    nameref e=$1
    typeset line=$2
    typeset f
    set -A f "${@:3}"    # set array f to all args past third

    if (( ${#f[@]} < NUMRECORDS ))
    then
        e=$(print "$e\nLine $line: too few fields")
        return 1
    fi
    if ! XUisinteger "${f[RECON]}"
    then
        e=$(print "$e\nLine $line: bad reconciled field")
        return 1
    fi
    if ! XUisdate "${f[MM]}" "${f[DD]}" "${f[YY]}"
    then
        e=$(print "$e\nLine $line: bad date")
        return 1
    fi
    if ! XUisfloat "${f[AMOUNT]}"
    then
        e=$(print "$e\nLine $line: bad amount")
        return 1
    fi
    return 0
}

function format_record {  # args are fields
    typeset f
    set -A f "$@"

    if [[ ${f[CATEG]} == CREDIT ]]
    then fmt="           \$%8.2f"
    else fmt="\$%8.2f           "
    fi
    if (( STATE.DETAILS ))  # Show all details
    then
        if (( f[RECON] ))
        then recon="+"
        else recon=" "
        fi
        printf \
            "%s %2.2d/%2.2d/%2.2d %5.5s \
%-25.25s $fmt %-9.9s %-16.16s" \
            "$recon" \
            ${f[MM]} \
            ${f[DD]} \
            ${f[YY]} \
```

```
                    "${f[CHECKNUM]}" \
                    "${f[PAYEE]}" \
                    ${f[AMOUNT]} \
                    "${f[CATEG]}" \
                    "${f[COMMENT]}"
        else
            printf "%2.2d/%2.2d/%2.2d %5.5s %-25.25s $fmt" \
                    ${f[MM]} \
                    ${f[DD]} \
                    ${f[YY]} \
                    "${f[CHECKNUM]}" \
                    "${f[PAYEE]}" \
                    ${f[AMOUNT]}
        fi
}

function open_checkbook {    # path
    typeset path=$1

    if [[ "$path" ]]
    then cd ${path%/*}
    fi

    XUdbopen DB "${path##*/}" "|" && STATE.CURPATH="$path"

    update_display
}

function showdetailsCB {
    STATE.DETAILS=!STATE.DETAILS      # logical not
    # change the menu label appropriately
    if (( STATE.DETAILS ))
    then
        XUset ${MB.VIEW.DETAILS} \
            labelString:"Don't Show Details"
    else
        XUset ${MB.VIEW.DETAILS} \
            labelString:"Show Details"
    fi
    update_display
}

function open_okCB {
    typeset path=${CB_CALL_DATA.VALUE}

    open_checkbook "$path"
    XUdestroy $CB_WIDGET
}
```

```
function openCB {
    if [[ ! $OPENDIALOG ]]
    then
        XUfileselectiondialog OPENDIALOG $TOPLEVEL \
            dialogTitle:"Open File" \
            pattern:"*.chk" \
            directory:"$PWD" \
            okCallback:open_okCB \
            cancelCallback:'XUdestroy $OPENDIALOG' \
            helpCallback:"helpCB file-menu"
    else
        XUmanage $OPENDIALOG
    fi
}

function saveas_okCB {
    typeset path=${CB_CALL_DATA.VALUE}

    if [[ -f $path && $path != ${DB.file} ]]
    then
        XUquestion -m "File Exists" \
            "Overwrite existing file $path?" \
            "_saveas '$path'" \
            : \
            "helpCB overwrite-warning"
        return
    fi
    _saveas "$path"
}

function _saveas {   # path
    DB.file=$path
    STATE.CURPATH="$PWD/$path"
    XUdbsync DB
    XUset $TOPLEVEL title:"Checkbook - ${DB.file}"
}

function saveasCB {
    if [[ ! $SAVEDIALOG ]]
    then
        XUpromptdialog SAVEDIALOG $TOPLEVEL \
            dialogTitle:"Save File" \
            selectionLabelString:"Save Checkbook To:" \
            textString:"${DB.file}" \
            okCallback:saveas_okCB \
            cancelCallback:'XUdestroy $SAVEDIALOG' \
            helpCallback:"helpCB save-as"
    fi
    XUset $SAVEDIALOG textString:"${DB.file}"
```

```
        XUmanage $SAVEDIALOG
}

function saveCB {
    XUdbsync DB
}

function deleteCB {
    integer index f

    XUlistgetselectedpos index $WORK
    let index--

    XUdbsplit DB $index f

    XUquestion -m "Confirm Delete" \
        "Really delete check:
        $(format_record "${f[@]}")" \
        "_delete $index" : "helpCB delete-confirm"
}

function _delete {   # index
    integer index=$1

    XUdbdelete DB $index
    update_display
}

function showcategCB {
    integer i
    typeset f

    if [[ ! $SELCATEG ]]
    then
        XUselectiondialog SELCATEG $TOPLEVEL \
            dialogTitle:"Select a Category for Display" \
            okCallback:'showcateg_okCB' \
            applyCallback:'showcateg_applyCB' \
            cancelCallback:'XUdestroy $SELCATEG' \
            helpCallback:'helpCB category-selection'
        XUselectionchildren SELCATEG
    fi

    XUset ${SELCATEG.LIST_LABEL} \
        labelString:"Choose a Category:"

    XUlistdeleteall ${SELCATEG.LIST}
    # sort the categories by cleverly using set -s
    set "${!CATEGORIES[@]}"
```

```
        set -s
        XUlistappend ${SELCATEG.LIST} "${@}"
        XUmanage $SELCATEG
}

function showcateg_okCB {
    showcateg_applyCB
    XUdestroy $CB_WIDGET
}

function showcateg_applyCB {
    integer i
    float total

    if [[ ! $SHOWCATEG ]]
    then
        XUselectiondialog SHOWCATEG $TOPLEVEL \
            dialogTitle:"Records in Selected Category:" \
            cancelCallback:'XUdestroy $SHOWCATEG' \
            cancelLabelString:"Dismiss"

        XUselectionchildren SHOWCATEG
        XUunmanage \
            ${SHOWCATEG.TEXT} \
            ${SHOWCATEG.APPLY_BUTTON} \
            ${SHOWCATEG.OK_BUTTON}
    fi

    XUlistdeleteall ${SHOWCATEG.LIST}
    for (( i = 0; i < ${#DB.record[@]}; i++ ))
    do
        XUdbsplit DB $i f
        if [[ ${f[CATEG]} == ${CB_CALL_DATA.VALUE} ]]
        then
            XUlistappend ${SHOWCATEG.LIST} \
                "$(format_record "${f[@]}")"
            (( total += f[AMOUNT] ))
        fi
    done
    XUset ${SHOWCATEG.SELECTION_LABEL} \
        labelString:"$(printf \
                    'Category total: $%8.2f' $total)"
}

function addhelp {
    while (( $# ))
    do
        XUaddcallback $1 helpCallback "helpCB '$2'"
        shift 2
```

```
            done
    }

    function helpCB {
        if [[ ! "$HELPPOP" ]]
        then
                XUhelpdialog -u HELPPOP $TOPLEVEL \
                    dialogTitle:"Checkbook Help" \
                    rows:5 \
                    columns:40
        fi
        case "$1" in
        _context)
                XUwidgethelp $2
                return
                ;;
        _onhelp)
                XUset $HELPPOP \
                    helpType:HELP_TYPE_TOPIC \
                    helpVolume:Help4Help \
                    locationId:_hometopic
                ;;
        *)
                XUset $HELPPOP \
                    helpType:HELP_TYPE_TOPIC \
                    helpVolume:$XUTILDIR/Help/Chkbook.sdl \
                    locationId:"$1"
                ;;
        esac
        XUmanage $HELPPOP
    }

    function newcategCB {
        if [[ ! $NEWCATDIALOG ]]
        then
            XUpromptdialog NEWCATDIALOG $TOPLEVEL \
                dialogTitle:"Create a New Category" \
                selectionLabelString:"New Category Label:" \
                okCallback:newcat_okCB \
                cancelCallback:newcat_cancelCB \
                helpCallback:"helpCB new-category"
        fi
        XUmanage $NEWCATDIALOG
    }

    function newcat_okCB {  # no args
        typeset -u newcat

        XUget $NEWCATDIALOG textString:newcat
```

```
        CATEGORIES[$newcat]=1

        # Destroy the old option menu
        XUdestroy ${ADDPOP.CATEG}

        # Create a new one with the new category as a default
        set "${!CATEGORIES[@]}" # sort the categories
        set -s
        XUaddoptionmenu ADDPOP.CATEG ${ADDPOP.CATEGRC} "" \
            "${@}" "-" "New ..."
        XUaddcallback ${ADDPOP.CATEG.CHILD[New ...]} \
            activateCallback "newcategCB"
        XUset ${ADDPOP.CATEG} \
            menuHistory:${ADDPOP.CATEG.CHILD[$newcat]}

    XUdestroy $NEWCATDIALOG
}

function newcat_cancelCB {
        XUdestroy $NEWCATDIALOG
        XUset ${ADDPOP.CATEG} \
            menuHistory:${ADDPOP.CATEG.CHILD[MISC]}
}

function editCB {
    integer index

    XUlistgetselectedpos index $WORK
    let index--

    addCB $index
}

function addCB {    # [ record-to-edit ]  if no args, adds a new check
    if [[ ! "$ADDPOP" ]]
    then
        typeset labtmp numrc daterc payeerc categrc \
            commentrc amountrc recrc

        XUformdialog -u ADDPOP $TOPLEVEL \
            dialogTitle:"Add A New Entry"

        # Attach the check number to the top left corner
        XUrow numrc $ADDPOP \
            $(XUattach left 5 top 5)
        XUaddtextfields $numrc \
            ADDPOP.CHECKNUM "Check Number:" : 8
        XUtextautoselect ${ADDPOP.CHECKNUM}
```

```
# Attach the date to the top right corner

XUrow daterc $ADDPOP \
    $(XUattach right 5 top 5)
XUadddatefields ${daterc} ADDPOP.DATE Date:

# Add the payee and amount fields in a single row
# 30 pixels under the check number row, and anchor
# the left and right edges to the form

XUrow payeerc $ADDPOP \
    $(XUattach under $numrc 30 left 5 right 5)
XUaddtextfields ${payeerc} \
    ADDPOP.PAYEE Payee: : 30
XUaddmoneyfields ${payeerc} \
    ADDPOP.AMOUNT   'Amount: $'   9 # Literal $

# Add the category field under the payee
# row, attached to the left of the form

XUrow ADDPOP.CATEGRC $ADDPOP \
    $(XUattach under $payeerc 20 left 5)

# sort the categories using set -s
set "${!CATEGORIES[@]}"
set -s
XUaddoptionmenu ADDPOP.CATEG ${ADDPOP.CATEGRC} Category: \
    "${@}" "-" "New ..."
XUaddcallback ${ADDPOP.CATEG.CHILD[New ...]} \
    activateCallback "newcategCB"

# Add the comment field under the category,
# spanning the entire width of the form

XUrow comrc $ADDPOP \
    $(XUattach under ${ADDPOP.CATEGRC} 5 left 5 right 5)
XUaddtextfields ${comrc} \
    ADDPOP.COMMENT Comment: : 20

# Add the reconciled toggle button
# at the same vertical height as
# the comment, attached to the right of the form
XUrow recrc $ADDPOP \
    $(XUattach under $payeerc 20 right 5)
XUaddtogglefields ${recrc} \
    ADDPOP.RECON "Reconciled?" ""

XUtextallowchars \
    ${ADDPOP.PAYEE} "[!|]" \
```

```
                    ${ADDPOP.COMMENT}  "[!|]"

          XUsettraversalorder ${ADDPOP} ${ADDPOP.CHECKNUM} \
              ${ADDPOP.ADD} \
              ${ADDPOP.DATE.MM} ${ADDPOP.DATE.DD} ${ADDPOP.DATE.YY} \
              ${ADDPOP.PAYEE} \
              ${ADDPOP.AMOUNT} ${ADDPOP.COMMENT}

          # Create an action area under the reconcile row,
          # and add buttons to it

          XUaddactionarea ADDPOP.ACTION $ADDPOP $comrc
          XUactionbuttons ${ADDPOP.ACTION} \
              -d ADDPOP.ADD       Save      "add_addCB $1" \
                 ADDPOP.CLEAR     Clear     add_clearCB \
              -c ADDPOP.DISMISS   Dismiss   add_dismissCB \
                 ADDPOP.HELP      Help      \
                                  'helpCB _context ${ADDPOP.WORK}'

          addhelp \
              $ADDPOP                     add-entry \
              ${ADDPOP.DATE}              date-field \
              ${ADDPOP.DATE.LABEL}        date-field \
              ${ADDPOP.PAYEE}             payee-field \
              ${ADDPOP.PAYEE.LABEL}       payee-field \
              ${ADDPOP.AMOUNT}            amount-field \
              ${ADDPOP.AMOUNT.LABEL}      amount-field \
              ${ADDPOP.CATEG}             category-field \
              ${ADDPOP.CATEG.LABEL}       category-field

      fi
      add_clearCB  $1 # initialize fields
      XUmanage $ADDPOP
      XUsetfocus ${ADDPOP.CHECKNUM}
  }

  function add_addCB {
      typeset replace=$1
      typeset f record
      integer i

      XUget ${ADDPOP.DATE.MM} value:f[MM]
      XUget ${ADDPOP.DATE.DD} value:f[DD]
      XUget ${ADDPOP.DATE.YY} value:f[YY]
      XUget ${ADDPOP.PAYEE} value:f[PAYEE]
      XUget ${ADDPOP.AMOUNT} value:f[AMOUNT]
      XUget ${ADDPOP.COMMENT} value:f[COMMENT]
      f[CATEG]="${ADDPOP.CATEG.VALUE}"
      XUget ${ADDPOP.RECON} set:f[RECON]
```

```
# check to make sure all the data are ok
if ! XUisdate "${f[MM]}" "${f[DD]}" "${f[YY]}"
then
    XUerror "Bad Date" \
        "Cannot save record -- date fields are invalid"
    XUsetfocus ${ADDPOP.DATE.MM}
    return
elif XUisblank "${f[PAYEE]}"
then
    XUerror "No Payee" \
        "Cannot save record -- fill in PAYEE and try again"
    XUsetfocus ${ADDPOP.PAYEE}
    return
elif XUisblank "${f[AMOUNT]}"
then
    XUerror "No Payee" \
        "Cannot save record -- fill in AMOUNT and try again"
    XUsetfocus ${ADDPOP.AMOUNT}
    return
fi

# The reconciled field is either a 1 or 0 in
# the checkbook flat file, so translate it
# appropriately.

if [[ ${f[RECON]} == true ]]
then f[RECON]=1
else f[RECON]=0
fi

record=
for (( i = 0; i < NUMFIELDS; i++ ))
do
    record="$record|${f[i]}"
done
record=${record:1}

if [[ $replace ]]
then
    DB.record[$replace]="$record"
else
    XUdbappend DB "$record"
fi
update_display
add_clearCB KEEPDATE
XUunmanage $ADDPOP
}
```

```
function add_clearCB {
    typeset f

    if [[ $1 ]]
    then
        XUdbsplit DB $1 f
        XUset ${ADDPOP.DATE.MM} value:"${f[MM]}"
        XUset ${ADDPOP.DATE.DD} value:"${f[DD]}"
        XUset ${ADDPOP.DATE.YY} value:"${f[YY]}"
        XUset ${ADDPOP.PAYEE} value:"${f[PAYEE]}"
        XUset ${ADDPOP.AMOUNT} value:"${f[AMOUNT]}"
        XUset ${ADDPOP.COMMENT} value:"${f[COMMENT]}"
        XUset ${ADDPOP.CATEG} \
            menuHistory:${ADDPOP.CATEG.CHILD[${f[CATEG]}]}
        if (( f[RECON] ))
        then XUset ${ADDPOP.RECON} set:true
        else XUset ${ADDPOP.RECON} set:false
        fi
        return
    fi

    # Initialize date to current day.
    if [ "$1" != KEEPDATE ]
    then
        XUset ${ADDPOP.DATE.MM} value:"$(date +%m)"
        XUset ${ADDPOP.DATE.DD} value:"$(date +%d)"
        XUset ${ADDPOP.DATE.YY} value:"$(date +%y)"
    fi
    XUset ${ADDPOP.PAYEE} value:""
    XUset ${ADDPOP.AMOUNT} value:""
    XUset ${ADDPOP.COMMENT} value:""
    XUset ${ADDPOP.CATEG} \
        menuHistory:${ADDPOP.CATEG.CHILD[MISC]}
    XUset ${ADDPOP.RECON} set:false

    # Add one to the highest check number seen, that's the default

    XUset ${ADDPOP.CHECKNUM} value:"$((STATE.MAXCHECK+1))"

    XUsetfocus ${ADDPOP.CHECKNUM}
}

function add_dismissCB {
    XUdestroy $ADDPOP
}

function helpcontextCB {
    typeset widget result
```

```
        DtHelpReturnSelectedWidgetId result $TOPLEVEL widget
        XUwidgethelp $widget
}


function exitconfirmCB {
    typeset confirmmessage="\
You have made changes to ${DB.file} since
it was last saved.

Do you wish to save these changes before exiting?"

    if [[ ${DB.needsync} == TRUE ]]
    then
        XUquestiondialog -u EXITCONF $TOPLEVEL \
            dialogTitle:"Changes not saved!" \
            messageString:"$confirmmessage" \
            okCallback:saveCB \
            okLabelString:$'Save\nChanges' \
            helpCallback:"helpCB no-save"

        typeset tmp
        XUpushbutton tmp $EXITCONF \
            labelString:$'Discard\nChanges' \
            activateCallback:exit
        XUmanage $EXITCONF
    else
        exit 0   # no need to ask, there were no pending changes
    fi
}

function sessionsaveCB {
    typeset savepath savefile workatoms

    if [[ $1 ]]
    then
        savepath=$1 # for testing purposes
        > $savepath
    else
        if ! DtSessionSavePath $TOPLEVEL savepath savefile
        then
            print "Unable to save state for ${APPNAME}" 2>&1
            exit 1
        fi
    fi

    {
        # print out state values
```

```
            print "STATE.DETAILS='${STATE.DETAILS}'"
            print "STATE.SORTORDER='${STATE.SORTORDER}'"
            print "STATE.CURPATH='${STATE.CURPATH}'"

            # print out iconic state
            if DtShellIsIconified $TOPLEVEL
            then print "STATE.ICONIC=true"
            else print "STATE.ICONIC=false"
            fi

            # print out occupied workspaces

            if DtWsmGetWorkspacesOccupied \
                "${TOPLEVEL.DISPLAY}" \
                "${TOPLEVEL.WINDOW}" \
                workatoms
            then
                integer i=0
                typeset atom

                # Substitute commas with spaces in the
                # workatoms variable for ease of use with
                # the "for" statement
                for atom in ${workatoms//,/ }
                do
                    XmGetAtomName \
                        name \
                        ${TOPLEVEL.DISPLAY} \
                        $atom
                    print "STATE.WORKSPACES[$((i++))]='$name'"
                done
            fi
    } > $savepath

    # Register the start-up command.  Assumes XUTILDIR is
    # set in the user's .dtprofile
    if ! DtSetStartupCommand $TOPLEVEL \
        "$XUTILDIR/Programs/chkbook.sh -restore $savepath"
    then
        print startup set failed!
    fi
}

function sessionrestoreCB {
    if [[ ! -r "$1" ]]
    then
        print "Could not restore state for $DTK_APPNAME"
        return
    fi
```

```
        # dot in the save path to reset variables
        . $1

        # restore the iconic state

        DtSetIconifyHint $TOPLEVEL ${STATE.ICONIC}

        # restore the workspaces occupied. First, build a list
        # of atom names

        typeset workspace atoms="" a
        typeset comma=""  # no comma on first item

        for workspace in "${STATE.WORKSPACES[@]}"
        do
            XmInternAtom \
                a \
                ${TOPLEVEL.DISPLAY} \
                "$workspace" \
                false
            atoms="$atoms$comma$a"
            comma=","   # after first item, add a comma
        done

        DtWsmSetWorkspacesOccupied \
            ${TOPLEVEL.DISPLAY} \
            ${TOPLEVEL.WINDOW} \
            $atoms

        # open checkbook file and redisplay using new settings

        open_checkbook "${STATE.CURPATH}"
}

function sortcategCB {
    STATE.SORTORDER=CATEG
    update_display
}

function sortdateCB {
    STATE.SORTORDER=DATE
    update_display
}


XUinitialize TOPLEVEL Checkbook "$@"

# Request not to be killed when user closes window using
```

```
        # the window manager menu (we want to confirm whether pending
        # changes should be saved before exiting).

        XUset $TOPLEVEL deleteResponse:DO_NOTHING

        # Create the main window

        XUmainwindow MAINWIN $TOPLEVEL
        XUmenubar MB $MAINWIN
        XUmenusystem $MB \
            MB.FILE "File" F { \
                MB.FILE.OPEN    "Open" O openCB \
                MB.FILE.SAVE    "Save" S saveCB \
                MB.FILE.SAVEAS "Save As..." A saveasCB \
                - - - - \
                MB.FILE.PRINT   "Print ..." P printCB \
                - - - - \
                MB.FILE.EXIT    "Exit" E exitconfirmCB \
            }

        XUmenusystem $MB \
            MB.VIEW "View" V { \
                MB.VIEW.CHECK   "Sort by Category" C sortcategCB \
                MB.VIEW.CHECK   "Sort by Date and Check" D sortdateCB \
                - - - - \
                MB.VIEW.CATEG "Show A Category" S showcategCB \
                - - - - \
                MB.VIEW.DETAILS "Show Details" e showdetailsCB \
            }

        XUmenusystem $MB \
            MB.ACT "Actions" A { \
                MB.ACT.ADD  "Add Entry"              A addCB \
                MB.ACT.EDIT "Edit Selected Entry"    E editCB \
                - - - - \
                MB.ACT.DEL  "Delete Selected Entry" D deleteCB \
            }

        XUmenusystem $MB \
            MB.HELP "Help" H { \
                    MB.HELP.CS  "Context-Sensitive Help" C \
                                    "helpCB _context $TOPLEVEL" \
                    MB.HELP.OV  "Overview"      O \
                                    "helpCB _hometopic" \
                    MB.HELP.KB  "Keyboard"      K \
                                    "helpCB keyboard" \
                    MB.HELP.UH  "Using Help"    H \
                                    "helpCB _onhelp" \
                    MB.HELP.PI  "Product Information"    P \
```

```
                                    "helpCB _copyright" \
        }

    if [[ "$DTKSH_DEBUG" ]]
    then
        XUmenusystem $MB \
            MB.TEST "Test Session" T { \
                MB.TEST.SAVE "Save State" S \
                    "sessionsaveCB $HOME/SESSION.TEST" \
                }
    fi

    XUset $MB menuHelpWidget:"${MB.HELP}"

    XUlist WORK $MAINWIN \
        visibleItemCount:8 \
        listSizePolicy:RESIZE_IF_POSSIBLE

    XUtextfield MESSAGE $MAINWIN \
        editable:false \
        cursorPositionVisible:false

    function iconhelp {
        if [[ $1 == CLEAR ]]
        then
            XUset $BBHELP labelString:""
            return
        fi

        # Depending on which button widget the cursor
        # is on, display different single-line help
        # messages in the quick help area
        case "$TRANSLATION_WIDGET" in
        ${BB.HELP})
            XUset $BBHELP labelString:"display help"
            ;;
        ${BB.DETAILS})
            XUset $BBHELP labelString:"display check details"
            ;;
        ${BB.DELETE})
            XUset $BBHELP labelString:"delete a check"
            ;;
        ${BB.ADD})
            XUset $BBHELP labelString:"add new checks"
            ;;
        esac
    }

    XUrow BB $MAINWIN    # A button bar
```

```
BMDIR=$XUTILDIR/Bitmaps # Bitmap directory

XUget $TOPLEVEL depth:depth

# If the display has depth 1, then we must use
# monochrome buttons, otherwise we can use
# color buttons.
if ((depth == 1))
then ext=bmp     # bitmap (monochrome)
else ext=xpm     # pixmap (multi-color)
fi

# Set the icon pixmap

XUset $TOPLEVEL iconPixmap:$XUTILDIR/Bitmaps/addcheck.$ext

# Add the button bar buttons

XUaddpixbuttons $BB \
    BB.HELP     $BMDIR/help.$ext       "helpCB _hometopic" \
    BB.DETAILS  $BMDIR/details.$ext  showdetailsCB \
    BB.DELETE   $BMDIR/delete.$ext   deleteCB \
    BB.ADD      $BMDIR/addcheck.$ext addCB

XUlabel BBHELP $BB labelString:" "

# Add translations to each button bar widget
# to provide help when the mouse pointer
# enters the widget.

for button in ${BB.HELP} ${BB.DETAILS} \
              ${BB.DELETE} ${BB.ADD}
do
    XtOverrideTranslations $button \
        '<Enter>:ksh_eval("iconhelp")
         <Leave>:ksh_eval("iconhelp CLEAR")'
done

XUset $MAINWIN \
    menuBar:$MB \
    workWindow:$WORK \
    messageWindow:$MESSAGE \
    commandWindow:$BB

addhelp \
    $MAINWIN    _hometopic \
    $MB         menu-bar \
    $WORK       check-list \
```

```
    $MESSAGE      balance-area \
    ${MB.FILE}    file-menu \
    ${MB.VIEW}    view-menu \
    ${MB.ACT}     actions-menu \
    ${MB.HELP}    help-menu

# Prepare for Session Manager Notification

XtDisplay TOPLEVEL.DISPLAY $TOPLEVEL

# Get the atom for WM_SAVE_YOURSELF

XmInternAtom SAVE_ATOM \
    ${TOPLEVEL.DISPLAY} \
    WM_SAVE_YOURSELF \
    false

# Get the atom for WM_DELETE_WINDOW

XmInternAtom DELETE_ATOM \
    ${TOPLEVEL.DISPLAY} \
    WM_DELETE_WINDOW \
    false

# Ask to be informed when a WM_SAVE_YOURSELF event occurs

XmAddWMProtocols $TOPLEVEL $SAVE_ATOM

# Ask to be informed when being deleted by window manager

XmAddWMProtocols $TOPLEVEL $DELETE_ATOM

# Register a state-saving function

XmAddWMProtocolCallback \
    $TOPLEVEL \
    $SAVE_ATOM \
    sessionsaveCB

# Register a function to check for unwritten data before exiting

XmAddWMProtocolCallback \
    $TOPLEVEL \
    $DELETE_ATOM \
    exitconfirmCB

# Because we may need to restore the iconic state, arrange
# for the TOPLEVEL widget not to map itself automatically
```

```
XUset $TOPLEVEL mappedWhenManaged:false
XUrealize $TOPLEVEL
XtWindow TOPLEVEL.WINDOW $TOPLEVEL

# If we get the -restore option, attempt to restore
# state from the argument, a save-file path

if [[ ${DTKSH_ARGV[1]} == -restore ]]
then
    sessionrestoreCB "${DTKSH_ARGV[2]}"
    shift 2
else
    open_checkbook "${DTKSH_ARGV[1]}"
fi

# now it is safe to map $TOPLEVEL
XUpopup $TOPLEVEL
XUmainloop
```

26 *Stock Chart Display*

26.1 Introduction

This chapter presents an Xlib-oriented program that reads a data file containing stock price information and draws a graph. The graph is a traditional high-low-close style stock chart. The program also displays two different moving averages (10-day and 50-day averages).

The program is called `stock.sh` in the example programs directory. A sample data file is provided called `JNJ.stk`—it contains a few months of data for Johnson & Johnson Corp. The data file consists of lines containing tab-separated fields:

```
date    high    low    close
```

Where the date can be any string label not containing whitespace, the high, low, and close are floating-point numbers that represent stock price data for the day in question.

To run the program on the sample file, you would do this:

```
dtksh stock.sh JNJ.stk
```

The resulting output is shown in Figure 26-1.

26.2 Techniques Illustrated

This program is meant to concentrate on Xlib functionality, so it lacks niceties such as the ability to read a new data file later or change the moving average time intervals on the fly. The techniques that are illustrated include:

- Computing coordinates of lines in a display
- Condensing multiple lines into a single drawing command
- Saving Xlib commands so repaints do not need to reperform calculations
- Using different colors, line styles, and other GC components.

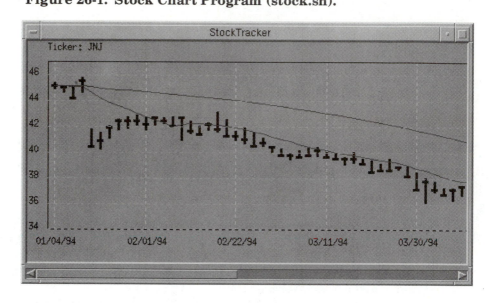

Figure 26-1. Stock Chart Program (stock.sh).

26.3 Source Code

```
. $XUTILDIR/xutil.sh

# Default drawing values for the stock chart

STOCKDEFS=
STOCKDEFS.FONT=fixed                    # font used to draw labels
STOCKDEFS.MA1INTERVAL=10                # number of days in the first moving
avg.
STOCKDEFS.MA2INTERVAL=50                # number of days in the second moving
avg.
STOCKDEFS.MA1COLOR=red                  # color of the first moving avg. line
STOCKDEFS.MA2COLOR=yellow               # color of the second moving avg. line
STOCKDEFS.LINEWIDTH=3                   # width of the vertical stock line
STOCKDEFS.STROKEWIDTH=4                 # width of the "close" cross stroke
STOCKDEFS.SPACING=8                     # pixels between each price bar
STOCKDEFS.BACKGROUND=lightgrey          # background of the chart


#
# Usage: WriteStockCommands $drawingarea [label high low close ...]
#
```

```
# Prints a list of commands that will draw the stock data to
# standard output.  That way, you can capture the commands in a file
# and repaint the screen quickly, without recomputing all the
# coordinates and scaling each time.  You must execute this command
# again if the size of the widget changed, or if the data changed.
#

function WriteStockCommands {
    typeset w=$1
    typeset dpy=$(XtDisplay - $w)
    typeset win=$(XtWindow - $w)
    typeset label
    float high low close ma1 ma2
    integer width height
    float scale               # scaling factor for drawing
    integer i h c l x y oldm1 oldm2 oldx
    float maxdata mindata
    integer totbars
    integer margin=$(XTextWidth - ${STOCKDEFS.FONT} "999 ")
    integer spacing=${STOCKDEFS.SPACING}
    integer barwidth=${STOCKDEFS.LINEWIDTH}
    integer strokewidth=${STOCKDEFS.STROKEWIDTH}

    XUget $w width:width height:height

    # The rest of the args are of the form: label high low close

    shift
    print "reading stock data" >&2
    i=0
    while (( $# > 4 ))
    do
        label[i]="$1"
        high[i]="$2"
        low[i]="$3"
        close[i]="$4"

        if (( i == 0 ))
        then
            (( ma1[i]=close[i]*STOCKDEFS.MA1INTERVAL ))
            (( ma2[i]=close[i]*STOCKDEFS.MA2INTERVAL ))
        else
            if (( i < STOCKDEFS.MA1INTERVAL ))
            then
                (( ma1[i]=ma1[i-1]+close[i]-close[0] ))
            else
                (( ma1[i]=ma1[i-1]+close[i]-close[i-STOCKDEFS.MA1INTERVAL]
))
            fi
```

```
                    if (( i < STOCKDEFS.MA2INTERVAL ))
                    then
                         (( ma2[i]=ma2[i-1]+close[i]-close[0] ))
                    else
                          (( ma2[i]=ma2[i-1]+close[i]-close[i-STOCKDEFS.MA2INTERVAL]
        ))
                    fi
            fi

            shift 4
            i=i+1
        done

        # run through the data, find the maximum and minimum

        print "computing min and max" >&2
        maxdata=0
        mindata=1000000
        for i in "${high[@]}" "${low[@]}"
        do
            if (( i > maxdata ))
            then maxdata=i
            elif (( i < mindata ))
            then mindata=i
            fi
        done

        # move min and max a couple of bucks to allow
        # some empty space near margins
        if (( mindata < 2 ))
        then (( mindata = 0 ))
        else (( mindata = mindata - 2 ))     # note! cannot use -- on float
        fi
        (( maxdata = maxdata + 2 ))              # note! cannot use ++ on float

        # There's no easy way to figure out the height of a font.
        # We just need a rough estimate so we know how many lines high
        # the screen is, and it's ok for the estimate to be too high.
        # So, we'll take double the width of the letter M to be an
        # approximate height.

        integer textheight=$(( $(XTextWidth - ${STOCKDEFS.FONT} M) * 2 ))
        totbars=${#high[@]}

        # calculate the scaling factor used for drawing the chart

        (( scale = (height - 2*margin)/(maxdata-mindata) ))

        if ((scale == 0))
```

```
then scale=1
fi

# Make the drawing area wide enough to accommodate all data

(( width = (2*margin + (spacing+barwidth)*(totbars+1)) ))
XUset $w width:$width

# Prepare for drawing by clearing the window

print "XClearWindow $dpy $win"

# Draw the bars

typeset barsegments ma1segments ma2segments

print "computing line segments" >&2
i=0
while (( i < totbars ))
do
    (( h = height-margin-(high[i]-mindata)*scale )) # x coord of high
    (( l = height-margin-(low[i]-mindata)*scale ))  # x coord of low
    (( c = height-margin-(close[i]-mindata)*scale )) # x coord of close
    (( oldm1 = m1 ))    # save old moving avgs.
    (( oldm2 = m2 ))
    (( m1 = height-margin-(ma1[i]/STOCKDEFS.MA1INTERVAL-mindata)*scale ))
    (( m2 = height-margin-(ma2[i]/STOCKDEFS.MA2INTERVAL-mindata)*scale ))

    # Calculate the new x position after saving old position
    (( oldx = x ))
    (( x = i * (barwidth+spacing) + margin + spacing ))

    # Draw the line from low to high

    barsegments="$barsegments $x $l $x $h"

    # Draw a tick through close

    barsegments="$barsegments $((x-strokewidth)) $c $((x+strokewidth)) $c"

    # Draw moving average lines

    if (( i > 0 ))
    then
        ma1segments="$ma1segments $oldx $oldm1 $x $m1"
        ma1segments="$ma1segments $oldx $oldm2 $x $m2"
    fi

    # Draw the label, centered in the middle of the bar
```

```
        if (( (i % 10 ) == 0 )) # avoid crowding: draw every tenth label
        then
            # Center the label by subtracting half its width from x
            XTextWidth labwidth ${STOCKDEFS.FONT} "${label[i]}"
            print XDrawString $dpy $win \
                -font ${STOCKDEFS.FONT} \
                $(( x + barwidth - labwidth/2 )) \
                $(( height - margin + textheight + 6 )) \
                '"'${label[i]}'"'

            print XDrawLine $dpy $win \
                -foreground lightgrey \
                -line_style LineOnOffDash \
                $x $margin $x $((height-margin))
        fi
        i=i+1
done

print "drawing segments" >&2
# Draw the lines and close strokes

print XDrawSegments $dpy $win \
    -line_width ${STOCKDEFS.LINEWIDTH} \
    ${barsegments}

# Draw the moving averages

print XDrawSegments $dpy $win \
    -line_width 0 \
    -foreground ${STOCKDEFS.MA1COLOR:-red} \
    $ma1segments

print XDrawSegments $dpy $win \
    -line_width 0 \
    -foreground ${STOCKDEFS.MA2COLOR:-yellow} \
    $ma2segments

# Draw the border

print XDrawRectangle $dpy $win \
    $((margin)) \
    $((margin)) \
    $((width-2*margin)) \
    $((height-2*margin))

print "drawing labels" >&2

# Draw the title
```

```
print XDrawString $dpy $win \
    -font ${STOCKDEFS.FONT} \
    $((margin)) 10 '"'${STOCKDEFS.TITLE}'"'

#
# Draw the y axis Labels
#

# figure the maximum number of lines displayable

integer maxlines='(height-2*margin)/(textheight)'

if (( maxlines < 2 ))
then
    # Can't do much with only 2 lines worth of space
    return
fi

# figure out how many dollars correspond to the maximum
# number of y axis labels we can draw.

integer ydelta='(maxdata-mindata)/maxlines'

# Round the final digit of the ydelta to a "nice" number

case "${ydelta:${#ydelta}-1}" in
0|2|5)
    # already nice
    ;;
1)
    ydelta=${ydelta/%[0-9]/2}    # substitute last digit with 2
    ;;
3|4)
    ydelta=${ydelta/%[0-9]/5}    # substitute last digit with 5
    ;;
6|7|8|9)
    ydelta=${ydelta/%[0-9]/0}    # substitute last digit with 0
    let ydelta+=10                   # and add 10
    ;;
esac

integer yscale='ydelta*scale'

# find the low end of the range
i=mindata
until (( (i % ydelta) == 0 ))
do
    let i--
```

```
        done
        y=$((height-margin))
        while (( y > margin ))
        do
            print XDrawString $dpy $win \
                -font "${STOCKDEFS.FONT}" \
                2 $((y)) $((i))
            print XDrawString $dpy $win \
                -font "${STOCKDEFS.FONT}" \
                $((width-margin+margin/2)) $((y)) "$((i))"
            print XDrawLine $dpy $win \
                -foreground lightgrey \
                -line_style LineOnOffDash \
                $margin $y $((width-margin)) $y
            (( y = y - yscale ))
            (( i = i + ydelta ))
        done
}

XUinitialize TOPLEVEL StockTracker "$@"
XUset $TOPLEVEL title:"StockTracker"
XUscrolledwindow SW $TOPLEVEL \
    scrollingPolicy:AUTOMATIC
XUget $SW horizontalScrollBar:hsb
XUget $SW verticalScrollBar:vsb
XUremoveallcallbacks $hsb dragCallback
XUremoveallcallbacks $vsb dragCallback

# For repaint speed, we will calculate the
# drawing commands once, storing them in a file
# whose name is stored in the variable STOCKCOMMANDS.
# When an expose event comes in, we simply dot in
# that file, which has all the coordinates precomputed.

STOCKCOMMANDFILE=/tmp/stock$$

XUdrawingarea CANVAS $SW \
    exposeCallback:'. $STOCKCOMMANDFILE' \
    width:500 height:300

XUrealize $TOPLEVEL

if [[ -f ${DTKSH_ARGV[1]} ]]
then
    STOCKFILE=${DTKSH_ARGV[1]}
    STOCKDEFS.TITLE="Ticker: ${STOCKFILE%%.*}"
    WriteStockCommands $CANVAS $(<$STOCKFILE) > $STOCKCOMMANDFILE
else
    print "Usage: $0 datafile.stk"
```

```
        exit 1
fi

XUmainloop
```

27 *The X Utilities*

27.1 Introduction

The X Utilities library (or XU library) was used in Part I to introduce novice X programmers to X application programming in a less painful way. The XU library is contained in the file `xutil.sh` in the example programs directory, and is a freely redistributable source file—you can use it in your own programs, ship it to other people, or use it in any way you see fit without having to worry about royalties or legal entanglements.

The `xutil.sh` file is meant to be brought into your dtksh script using the dot command of KornShell. The file contains a set of functions that simplifies the development of X applications by providing commonly needed procedures. It also harmonizes naming of functions so the novice programmer doesn't have to remember which functions begin with `Xt`, which with `Xm`, etc. Even professional X programmers will find many of the functions in the XU library useful for day-to-day programming tasks.

27.2 Techniques Illustrated

Besides offering useful utility functions, this file uses a grab bag of X and KornShell programming techniques that are highly instructive to study. For example, the `XUtextautoselect` function sets up a Text or TextField widget so the text is selected whenever the widget gains focus; this illustrates how to use the `focusCallback` and how to select text. There are too many different techniques used in this program to neatly summarize.

27.3 Source Code

```
# <NOTICE>
#
# Copyright (C) 1995 Addison-Wesley Publishing Company
# Permission is granted to distribute this program code without
# fee as long as this notice appears in its entirety.
#
# This code is distributed in "as is" condition, and no warranty
# is expressed or implied, including merchantability or use for any
# particular purpose.  Addison-Wesley Publishing Company will not
# held liable for any damages, whether actual or consequential,
# arising from the use of this code.
#
# This code is explained in the book:
#
#    "Desktop KornShell Graphical Programming
#      in the Common Desktop Environment"
#
#    By J. Stephen Pendergrast, Jr.
#    Published by Addison-Wesley Publishing Company
#    ISBN 0-201-63375-X
#
# <END-OF-NOTICE>

# This file contains general purpose utility functions for
# the CDE Desktop KornShell.  It is designed to be sourced into
# a shell script using the dot command, as:
#
#    . $XUTILDIR/xutil.sh
#
# where XUTILDIR is a variable set to the directory where this
# file resides.

# Global context:  The variable _XU is used as a global base for all
# XU library global variables

_XU=                    # initialize parent variable
_XU.VERSION=1.0         # for future compatibility

# Section #1 Aliases.
#
# Many of the XU convenience functions are simple aliases for other
# X commands.  These aliases are easier to remember because they all have
# the same XU prefix and are easier to type because their names
# don't involve multiple case changes.

alias \
    XUbell=XBell \
    XUcleararea=XClearArea \
```

```
XUclearwindow=XClearWindow \
XUcopyarea=XCopyArea \
XUdefinecursor=XDefineCursor \
XUdrawarc=XDrawArc \
XUdrawimagestring=XDrawImageString \
XUdrawline=XDrawLine \
XUdrawlines=XDrawLines \
XUdrawpoint=XDrawPoint \
XUdrawpoints=XDrawPoints \
XUdrawrectangle=XDrawRectangle \
XUdrawsegments=XDrawSegments \
XUdrawstring=XDrawString \
XUfillarc=XFillArc \
XUfillpolygon=XFillPolygon \
XUfillrectangle=XFillRectangle \
XUflush=XFlush \
XUheightofscreen=XHeightOfScreen \
XUraisewindow=XRaiseWindow \
XUrootwindowofscreen=XRootWindowOfScreen \
XUsync=XSync \
XUtextwidth=XTextWidth \
XUundefinecursor=XUndefineCursor \
XUwidthofscreen=XWidthOfScreen \
XUaddwmprotocolcallback=XmAddWMProtocolCallback \
XUaddwmprotocols=XmAddWMProtocols \
XUcommandappendvalue=XmCommandAppendValue \
XUcommanderror=XmCommandError \
XUcommandgetchild=XmCommandGetChild \
XUcommandsetvalue=XmCommandSetValue \
XUfileselectionboxgetchild=XmFileSelectionBoxGetChild \
XUfileselectiondosearch=XmFileSelectionDoSearch \
XUgetatomname=XmGetAtomName \
XUgetcolors=XmGetColors \
XUgetfocuswidget=XmGetFocusWidget \
XUgetpostedfromwidget=XmGetPostedFromWidget \
XUgettabgroup=XmGetTabGroup \
XUgettearoffcontrol=XmGetTearOffControl \
XUgetvisibility=XmGetVisibility \
XUinternatom=XmInternAtom \
XUistraversable=XmIsTraversable \
XUlistadditem=XmListAddItem \
XUlistadditemunselected=XmListAddItemUnselected \
XUlistadditems=XmListAddItems \
XUlistadd=XmListAddItems \
XUlistadditemsunselected=XmListAddItemsUnselected \
XUlistdeleteallitems=XmListDeleteAllItems \
XUlistdeleteall=XmListDeleteAllItems \
XUlistdeleteitem=XmListDeleteItem \
XUlistdeleteitems=XmListDeleteItems \
```

```
XUlistdeleteitemspos=XmListDeleteItemsPos \
XUlistdeletepos=XmListDeletePos \
XUlistdeletepositions=XmListDeletePositions \
XUlistdeselectallitems=XmListDeselectAllItems \
XUlistdeselectall=XmListDeselectAllItems \
XUlistdeselectitem=XmListDeselectItem \
XUlistdeselectpos=XmListDeselectPos \
XUlistgetkbditempos=XmListGetKbdItemPos \
XUlistgetmatchpos=XmListGetMatchPos \
XUlistgetselectedpos=XmListGetSelectedPos \
XUlistitemexists=XmListItemExists \
XUlistitempos=XmListItemPos \
XUlistposselected=XmListPosSelected \
XUlistpostobounds=XmListPosToBounds \
XUlistreplaceitemspos=XmListReplaceItemsPos \
XUlistreplace=XmListReplaceItemsPos \
XUlistreplaceitemsposunselected=XmListReplaceItemsPosUnselected \
XUlistselectitem=XmListSelectItem \
XUlistselectpos=XmListSelectPos \
XUlistsetaddmode=XmListSetAddMode \
XUlistsetbottomitem=XmListSetBottomItem \
XUlistsetbottompos=XmListSetBottomPos \
XUlistsethorizpos=XmListSetHorizPos \
XUlistsetitem=XmListSetItem \
XUlistsetkbditempos=XmListSetKbdItemPos \
XUlistsetpos=XmListSetPos \
XUlistupdateselectedlist=XmListUpdateSelectedList \
XUmainwindowsep1=XmMainWindowSep1 \
XUmainwindowsep2=XmMainWindowSep2 \
XUmainwindowsep3=XmMainWindowSep3 \
XUmainwindowsetareas=XmMainWindowSetAreas \
XUmenuposition=XmMenuPosition \
XUmessageboxgetchild=XmMessageBoxGetChild \
XUoptionbuttongadget=XmOptionButtonGadget \
XUoptionlabelgadget=XmOptionLabelGadget \
XUprocesstraversal=XmProcessTraversal \
XUremovewmprotocolcallback=XmRemoveWMProtocolCallback \
XUremovewmprotocols=XmRemoveWMProtocols \
XUscalegetvalue=XmScaleGetValue \
XUscalesetvalue=XmScaleSetValue \
XUscrollbargetvalues=XmScrollBarGetValues \
XUscrollbarsetvalues=XmScrollBarSetValues \
XUscrollvisible=XmScrollVisible \
XUselectionboxgetchild=XmSelectionBoxGetChild \
XUtextclearselection=XmTextClearSelection \
XUtextdisableredisplay=XmTextDisableRedisplay \
XUtextdisable=XmTextDisableRedisplay \
XUtextenableredisplay=XmTextEnableRedisplay \
XUtextenable=XmTextEnableRedisplay \
```

```
        XUtextfieldclearselection=XmTextFieldClearSelection \
        XUtextfieldcopy=XmTextFieldCopy \
        XUtextfieldcut=XmTextFieldCut \
        XUtextfieldgetbaseline=XmTextFieldGetBaseline \
        XUtextfieldgeteditable=XmTextFieldGetEditable \
        XUtextfieldgetinsertionposition=XmTextFieldGetInsertionPosition \
        XUtextfieldgetlastposition=XmTextFieldGetLastPosition \
        XUtextfieldgetmaxlength=XmTextFieldGetMaxLength \
        XUtextfieldgetselection=XmTextFieldGetSelection \
        XUtextfieldgetselectionposition=XmTextFieldGetSelectionPosition \
        XUtextfieldgetstring=XmTextFieldGetString \
        XUtextfieldinsert=XmTextFieldInsert \
        XUtextfieldpaste=XmTextFieldPaste \
        XUtextfieldpostoxy=XmTextFieldPosToXY \
        XUtextfieldremove=XmTextFieldRemove \
        XUtextfieldreplace=XmTextFieldReplace \
        XUtextfieldsetaddmode=XmTextFieldSetAddMode \
        XUtextfieldseteditable=XmTextFieldSetEditable \
        XUtextfieldsethighlight=XmTextFieldSetHighlight \
        XUtextfieldsetinsertionposition=XmTextFieldSetInsertionPosition \
        XUtextfieldsetmaxlength=XmTextFieldSetMaxLength \
        XUtextfieldsetselection=XmTextFieldSetSelection \
        XUtextfieldsetstring=XmTextFieldSetString \
        XUtextfieldshowposition=XmTextFieldShowPosition \
        XUtextfieldxytopos=XmTextFieldXYToPos \
        XUtextfindstring=XmTextFindString \
        XUtextgetbaseline=XmTextGetBaseline \
        XUtextgeteditable=XmTextGetEditable \
        XUtextgetinsertionposition=XmTextGetInsertionPosition \
        XUtextgetlastposition=XmTextGetLastPosition \
        XUtextgetlast=XmTextGetLastPosition \
        XUtextgetmaxlength=XmTextGetMaxLength \
        XUtextgetselection=XmTextGetSelection \
        XUtextgetselectionposition=XmTextGetSelectionPosition \
        XUtextgetstring=XmTextGetString \
        XUtextgettopcharacter=XmTextGetTopCharacter \
        XUtextinsert=XmTextInsert \
        XUtextpostoxy=XmTextPosToXY \
        XUtextremove=XmTextRemove \
        XUtextreplace=XmTextReplace \
        XUtextscroll=XmTextScroll \
        XUtextsetaddmode=XmTextSetAddMode \
        XUtextseteditable=XmTextSetEditable \
        XUtextsetinsertionposition=XmTextSetInsertionPosition \
        XUtextsetmaxlength=XmTextSetMaxLength \
        XUtextsetselection=XmTextSetSelection \
        XUtextsetstring=XmTextSetString \
        XUtextsettopcharacter=XmTextSetTopCharacter \
        XUtextshowposition=XmTextShowPosition \
```

```
XUtextshow=XmTextShowPosition \
XUtextxytopos=XmTextXYToPos \
XUtogglebuttongadgetgetstate=XmToggleButtonGadgetGetState \
XUtogglebuttongadgetsetstate=XmToggleButtonGadgetSetState \
XUtogglebuttongetstate=XmToggleButtonGetState \
XUupdatedisplay=XmUpdateDisplay \
XUaddcallback=XtAddCallback \
XUaddeventhandler=XtAddEventHandler \
XUaddinput=XtAddInput \
XUaddtimeout=XtAddTimeOut \
XUaddworkproc=XtAddWorkProc \
XUaugmenttranslations=XtAugmentTranslations \
XUcallcallbacks=XtCallCallbacks \
XUclass=XtClass \
XUcreateapplicationshell=XtCreateApplicationShell \
XUcreatemanagedwidget=XtCreateManagedWidget \
XUcreatepopupshell=XtCreatePopupShell \
XUcreatewidget=XtCreateWidget \
XUdestroywidget=XtDestroyWidget \
XUdisplay=XtDisplay \
XUdisplayofobject=XtDisplayOfObject \
XUgetvalues=XtGetValues \
XUhascallbacks=XtHasCallbacks \
XUismanaged=XtIsManaged \
XUisrealized=XtIsRealized \
XUissensitive=XtIsSensitive \
XUisshell=XtIsShell \
XUissubclass=XtIsSubclass \
XUlasttimestampprocessed=XtLastTimestampProcessed \
XUmainloop=XtMainLoop \
XUmanagechildren=XtManageChildren \
XUmapwidget=XtMapWidget \
XUnametowidget=XtNameToWidget \
XUoverridetranslations=XtOverrideTranslations \
XUparent=XtParent \
XUpopdown=XtPopdown \
XUrealizewidget=XtRealizeWidget \
XUremoveallcallbacks=XtRemoveAllCallbacks \
XUremovecallback=XtRemoveCallback \
XUremoveeventhandler=XtRemoveEventHandler \
XUremoveinput=XtRemoveInput \
XUremovetimeout=XtRemoveTimeOut \
XUremoveworkproc=XtRemoveWorkProc \
XUscreen=XtScreen \
XUsetsensitive=XtSetSensitive \
XUsetvalues=XtSetValues \
XUuninstalltranslations=XtUninstallTranslations \
XUunmanagechildren=XtUnmanageChildren \
XUunmapwidget=XtUnmapWidget \
```

```
    XUunrealizewidget=XtUnrealizeWidget \
    XUwindow=XtWindow

# Some of the aliases are shorter versions of the corresponding
# X command; if the last "word" of the X command is redundant or adds no
# clarification of the command's usage, it is left out.  For example:
#
#       XtManageWidget   becomes XUmanage
#
# because the only thing you *can* manage is a widget, the last word is
# not necessary.  Similarly, XtSetValues becomes XUset, XtGetValues becomes
# XUget, etc.

alias \
    XUset=XtSetValues \
    XUget=XtGetValues \
    XUmanage=XtManageChildren \
    XUunmanage=XtUnmanageChildren \
    XUmap=XtMapWidget \
    XUunmap=XtUnmapWidget \
    XUrealize=XtRealizeWidget \
    XUunrealize=XtUnrealizeWidget \
    XUdestroy=XtDestroyWidget \
    XUlistdeleteall=XmListDeleteAllItems

# Section 2:  Minor Conveniences
#
# These functions mimic some X commands, but add some minor value
# such as defaulting certain parameters that are not provided.

# XUpopup - exactly like XtPopup but defaults the mode to
# GrabNone if not given and if the widget is not a shell-
# class widget looks up the hierarchy to find a shell.
#
# Usage: XUpopup $widget [grab-type]
#
# If grab-type is not specified, it defaults to GrabNone

function XUpopup {
    typeset widget=$1
    typeset mode=$2

    while ! XtIsShell $widget && [[ $widget != "(null)" ]]
    do
        XtParent widget $widget
    done
    XtPopup $widget ${mode:-GrabNone}
}
```

```
# XUinitialize - like XtInitialize but assumes app-name is
# same as app-class lowercased.
#
# Usage: XUinitialize variable AppClass [other-args]

function XUinitialize {
    typeset -l lower="$2"
    XtInitialize "$1" "$lower" "$2" "${@:3}"
    eval "_XU.TOPLEVEL=\${$1}"
    if (( ${#ARGV[@]} ))
    then
        # If ARGV has stuff in it, then this user is running
        # the BETA version of CDE.  In the final product,
        # the name of ARGV was changed
        # to DTKSH_ARGV, and the name of TOPLEVEL was changed to
        # DTKSH_TOPLEVEL, and APPNAME was changed to DTKSH_APPNAME.
        # For convenience, we'll set things up
        # the way they are in the final CDE 1.0 product.

        set -A DTKSH_ARGV "${ARGV[@]}"
        DTKSH_TOPLEVEL="$TOPLEVEL"
        DTKSH_APPNAME="$APPNAME"
    fi
}

# XUsensitive - convenient way to make multiple widgets
# sensitive
#
# Usage: XUsensitive $widget ...

function XUsensitive {
    typeset w
    for w in "$@"
    do
        XtSetSensitive $w true
    done
}

# XUinsensitive - convenient way to make multiple widgets
# insensitive
#
# Usage: XUinsensitive $widget ...

function XUinsensitive {
    typeset w

    for w in "$@"
    do
        XtSetSensitive $w false
```

```
        done
}

# XUcolumn, XUrow:  make a RowColumn widget for stacking vertically
# or horizontally.
#
# Usage: XUcolumn variable $parent [resource:value ...]
# Usage: XUrow variable $parent [resource:value ...]

alias XUcolumn=XUrowcolumn

function XUrow {
    _XUcreateobject XmCreateRowColumn "$@" orientation:horizontal
}

# XUtogglebuttonsetstate:  like XmToggleButtonSetState but defaults state
to
# true.
#
# Usage: XUtogglebuttonsetstate $widget [true|false]

function XUtogglebuttonsetstate {
    typeset w=$1 state=$2 notify=$3
    XmToggleButtonSetState $w $state ${notify:-true}
}

# XUtoggleselect: programmatically simulate a toggle button press
#
# Usage: XUtoggleselect $widget

function XUtoggleselect {
    XmToggleButtonSetState $1 true true
}

# Section #3: Value Added Commands
#
# These commands have no equivalent in the standard X functions
# and add value by making commonly needed procedures available as
# simple functions.

# XUtextappend: append text to the end of a Text or TextField widget
#
# Usage: XUtextappend $widget text-string

function XUtextappend {
    typeset w=$1 text=$2
    integer pos
    typeset c=$(XtClass - $w)
```

```
      ${c}GetLastPosition pos $w
      ${c}Insert $w $pos "$text"
}

# XUtextfind:  search for a string in a Text or TextField widget
#
# Usage: XUtextfind [-b] variable $widget start-position pattern
#
#    -b option searches backward instead of the default of forward

function XUtextfind {
    if [[ $1 == -b ]]
    then
        _direction=TEXT_BACKWARD
        shift
    fi
    XmTextFindString "$2" "$3" "$4" "${_direction:-TEXT_FORWARD}" "$1"
}

# XUbusy - change the cursor to a busy cursor for $widget.
# Schedule a WorkProc to change it back automatically when the subroutine
# returns.
#
# Usage: XUbusy [$widget]
#
#    if the widget argument is not provided, the root widget is used

function XUbusy {
    typeset w=$1 tmp
    w=${w:-$DTKSH_TOPLEVEL}
    typeset dpy=$(XtDisplay - $w)
    typeset win=$(XtWindow - $w)

    if [[ ! "${_XU.HourGlassCursor}" ]]
    then DtGetHourGlassCursor _XU.HourGlassCursor $(XtDisplay - $w)
    fi
    XDefineCursor $dpy $win ${_XU.HourGlassCursor}
    XFlush $dpy
    XUdefer "XUundefinecursor $dpy $win"
}

# XUdefer:  defer a command until the next time through the event loop
#
# Usage: XUdefer dtksh-command

function XUdefer {
    typeset tmp

    XtAddWorkProc tmp "_XUdefer '$@'"
```

```
}

# _XUdefer: work routine used in XUdefer which evals args and unschedules
# the worproc by returning 1.

function _XUdefer { # dtksh-command
    eval "$@"
    return 1
}

# XUlistselectall: select all items in a List widget
#
# Usage: XUlistselectall $widget

function XUlistselectall {
    integer i n

    XtGetValues $1 itemCount:n
    for (( i = 1; i <= n; i++ ))
    do
        XmListPosSelected $1 $i || XmListSelectPos $1 $i false
    done
}

# XUlistappend: append items to a List
#
# Usage: XUlistappend $widget item ...

function XUlistappend {
    XmListAddItems "$1" 0 "${@:2}"
}

# XUlistdelete: delete items from a list
#
# Usage (to delete by position):  XUlistdelete $widget start-item count
# Usage (to delete by string match): XUlistdelete -s $widget string ...

function XUlistdelete {
    if [[ $1 == '-s' ]]
    then
        shift
        typeset list=$1
        XmListDeleteItems "$@"
    else
        typeset list=$1 item=$2 count=$3
        XmListDeleteItemsPos "$list" "${count:-1}" "$item"
    fi
}
```

```
# XUlistselect:  select items in a List
#
# Usage:  XUlistselect [-n] [-s] $widget item ...
#
#   -s option means items are strings to match,
#       otherwise they are indexes
#
#   -n option causes notification by calling selection callbacks

function XUlistselect {
    typeset stringflag=Pos notifyflag=false

    while [[ $1 == -* ]]
    do
        case "$1" in
        -s) stringflag=Item; shift ;;
        -n) notifyflag=true; shift ;;
        esac
    done
    typeset list=$1
    shift
    while (( $# ))
    do
        XmListSelect$stringflag $list $1 $notifyflag
        shift
    done
}


# XUlistdeselect:  deselect items in a List
#
# Usage:  XUlistdeselect [-n] [-s] $widget item ...
#
#   -s option means items are strings to match,
#       otherwise they are indexes
#
#   -n option causes notification by calling selection callbacks

function XUlistdeselect {
    typeset stringflag=Pos notifyflag=false

    while [[ $1 == -* ]]
    do
        case "$1" in
        -s) stringflag=Item; shift ;;
        -n) notifyflag=true; shift ;;
        esac
    done
    typeset list=$1
    shift
```

```
            while (( $# ))
            do
                XmListDeselect$stringflag $list $1
                shift
            done
    }

    # XUlisttop: set the topmost item in a (presumably scrolled) List
    #
    # Usage: XUlisttop [-s] $list item
    #
    #   -s option means items are strings to match,
    #       otherwise they are indexes

    function XUlisttop {
        if [[ $1 == '-s' ]]
        then
            shift
            XmListSetItem "$@"
        else
            XmListSetPos "$@"
        fi
    }

    # XUlistbottom: set the bottommost item in a (presumably scrolled) List
    #
    # Usage: XUlistbottom [-s] $list item
    #
    #   -s option means items are strings to match,
    #       otherwise they are indexes

    function XUlistbottom {
        if [[ $1 == '-s' ]]
        then
            shift
            XmListSetBottomItem "$@"
        else
            XmListSetBottomPos "$@"
        fi
    }

    # XUlistfind: find items in a list, returning indexes of matching items
    #
    # Usage: XUlistfind variable $widget search-string

    function XUlistfind {
        if [[ $1 != - ]]
        then nameref var=$1
        fi
```

```
        typeset list=$2 string=$3
        typeset matches

        XmListGetMatchPos matches "$list" "$string"
        matches=${matches//,/ }
        if [[ $1 == - ]]
        then print $matches
        else var="$matches"
        fi
}

# XUlistgetselected: find selected items in a list,
# printing indexes to standard out.
#
# Usage: XUlistgetselected variable $list-widget

function XUlistgetselected {
        typeset var=$1 list=$2
        typeset matches

        XmListGetSelectedPos matches "$list"
        matches=${matches//,/ }       # substitute spaces for commas
        if [[ $var == - ]]
        then print $matches
        else eval "$var='$matches'"
        fi
}

# XUlistget: get the text of a particular list item at an index, storing
# it in a variable.
#
# Usage: XUlistget variable $list-widget index

function XUlistget {
        typeset var=$1 list=$2 index=$3
        typeset items item array

        XtGetValues $list items:items
        n=0
        while (( ++n != index )) && [[ "$items" ]]
        do
            items=${items#*[!\\],}
        done
        item=${items%%[!\\],*}
        item="$item${items:${#item}:1}"
        item=${item//\\,/,}
        if [[ $var == - ]]
        then print "$item"
        else eval "$var='${item}'"
```

```
        fi
}

# XUlistparse: parse a comma-separated list of items into individual
# elements of an array.
#
# Usage: XUlistparse array item-list

function XUlistparse {
    nameref array=$1
    typeset items=$2 item
    integer n num

    n=0
    while :
    do
        item=${items%%[!\\],*}
        item="$item${items:${#item}:1}"
        item=${item//\\,/,}
        if [[ $array != - ]]
        then array[n++]=$item
        else print "$item"
        fi
        prev=$items
        items=${items#*[!\\],}
        if [[ $prev == $items ]]
        then
            break
        fi
    done
}

# XUtextdelete: delete a string from a Text widget
#
# Usage: XUtextdelete $text-widget string

function XUtextdelete {
    XmTextReplace "$@" ''
}

# XUtextselect: set the selected portion of a Text widget
#
# Usage: XUtextselect $text-widget start-pos end-pos

function XUtextselect {
    typeset t=$(XtLastTimestampProcessed - $(XtDisplay - $1))
    XmTextSetSelection "$@" $t
}
```

```
# XUtextdeselect: clear the selected portion of a Text widget
#
# Usage: XUtextdeselect $text-widget

function XUtextdeselect { # $text-widget
    typeset t=$(XtLastTimestampProcessed - $(XtDisplay - $1))
    XmTextClearSelection "$@" $t
}


# XUsettraversalorder: allow Enter key to traverse widgets instead of
# executing default action
#
# Usage: XUsettraversalorder $form-widget $default-widget $widget ...

function XUsettraversalorder {
    typeset form=$1 default=$2
    shift 2

    while (( $# > 1 ))
    do
        XtAddCallback $1 focusCallback \
         "XtSetValues $form defaultButton:NULL"
        XtAddCallback $1 losingFocusCallback \
         "XtSetValues $form defaultButton:$default"

        XtOverrideTranslations $1 \
            "Ctrl<Key>Return:ksh_eval(\"XmProcessTraversal $1
TRAVERSE_NEXT_TAB_GROUP; XtCallCallbacks $1 activateCallback\")
        <Key>Return:ksh_eval(\"XmProcessTraversal $1
TRAVERSE_NEXT_TAB_GROUP; XtCallCallbacks $1 activateCallback\")"
    shift
    done
}


# XUregisterpopup: add an event handler to a widget that
# allows button 2 to pop up a menu.
#
# Usage: XUregisterpopup $widget $popupmenu-widget

function XUregisterpopup {
    XtAddEventHandler $1 ButtonPressMask false "_registerpop $2"
}


# _registerpopup: position and popup a menu

function _registerpop { # $popupmenu-widget
    if [[ ${EH_EVENT.XBUTTON.BUTTON} == Button[23] ]]
    then
        XmMenuPosition $1 ${EH_EVENT}
```

```
            _XU.EH_WIDGET=${EH_WIDGET}
            XtManageChild $1
    fi
}

# XUregisterwindowclose: register a command to be called when the window
# manager tries to close the application, and prevent the window manager
# from forcibly killing the application.
#
# Usage: XUregisterwindowclose command

function XUregisterwindowclose {
    XmInternAtom DELETE_ATOM \
        $(XtDisplay - ${_XU.TOPLEVEL}) WM_DELETE_WINDOW false
    XmAddWMProtocolCallback ${_XU.TOPLEVEL} $DELETE_ATOM "$*"
    XtSetValues ${_XU.TOPLEVEL} deleteResponse:DO_NOTHING
}

# XUtextautocursor:  arrange for the cursor to be invisible when a
# Text or TextField widget does not have focus.
#
# Usage: XUtextautocursor $text-widget ...

function XUtextautocursor {
    while (( $# ))
    do
        XtAddCallback $1 focusCallback \
            "XtSetValues $1 cursorPositionVisible:true"
        XtAddCallback $1 losingFocusCallback \
            "XtSetValues $1 cursorPositionVisible:false"
        shift
    done
}

# _XUtextforcecase: used to force case from a callback

function _XUtextforcecase { # [-u|-l]
    typeset $1 v=${CB_CALL_DATA.TEXT.PTR}

    CB_CALL_DATA.TEXT.PTR=$v
}

# Force the case of a text or textfield widget
#
# Usage: XUtextforcecase [-u|-l] $text-widget ...

function XUtextforcecase {  # [-u|-l] text-widget ...
    typeset casearg=$1
    shift
```

```
    while (( $# ))
    do
        XtAddCallback $1 modifyVerifyCallback "_XUtextforcecase '$casearg'"
        shift
    done
}


# Used to disallow characters during a modifyVerifyCallback

function _XUtextallowchars {      # pattern
    typeset pattern=$1
    typeset v=${CB_CALL_DATA.TEXT.PTR}
    typeset orig_v=$v
    integer i

    for (( i = 0; i < ${#v}; i++ )) # check each character
    do
        if [[ "${v:i:1}" != $pattern ]]
        then
            v="${v:0:i}${v:i+1}"
        fi
    done
    if [[ "$orig_v" != "$v" ]]
    then
        CB_CALL_DATA.TEXT.PTR="$v"
        CB_CALL_DATA.TEXT.LENGTH="${#v}"
        XBell $(XtDisplay - ${_XU.TOPLEVEL}) 0
    fi
}


# XUtextallowchars:  set up Text or TextField widgets so only a specific
# set of characters are allowed.
#
# Usage: XUtextallowchars [$widget pattern] ...
#
#    any number of pairs of widgets and patterns may be specified.

function XUtextallowchars {
    while (( $# ))
    do
        XtAddCallback $1 modifyVerifyCallback "_XUtextallowchars '$2'"
        shift 2
    done
}


# XUwidgethelp: turn the cursor to a question mark, when user selects a
widget,
```

```
# call its associated helpCallback.  If it has no helpCallback, look back
up
# the widget hierarchy until one is found.
#
# Usage: XUwidgethelp $parent-widget
#
#    the argument is usually a top-level Dialog or Shell widget handle.

function XUwidgethelp { # $1 = widget id
    typeset _parent=$1 widget result

    DtHelpReturnSelectedWidgetId result $_parent widget || return

    while [[ $widget ]] && [[ $widget != "(null)" ]]
    do
        XtHasCallbacks result $widget helpCallback
        if [[ $result == CallbackHasSome ]]
        then
            print $result
            XtCallCallbacks $widget helpCallback
            return
        fi
        XtParent widget $widget || return
    done
}


# XUsethelp: conveniently set help callbacks for multiple widgets
#
# Usage: XUsethelp [$widget command] ...
#
#    arguments are pairs of widgets and help commands.
#

function XUsethelp {
    while (( $# ))
    do
        XtSetValues "$1" helpCallback:"$2"
        shift 2
    done
}


# XUsetaccelerators:  conveniently set accelerators and accelerator text
# for multiple widgets.
#
# Usage: XUsetaccelerators [$widget accelerator accelerator-text] ...
#
#    any number of triples of widget handles, accelerators, and
#    accelerator-text may be specified
```

```
function XUsetaccelerators {
    while (( $# ))
    do
        XtSetValues "$1" accelerator:"$2" acceleratorText:"$3"
        shift 3
    done
}

# XUsetfocus:  set the focus to a particular widget
#
# Usage: XUsetfocus $widget [direction]
#
#    if direction is not specified, the widget itself gets focus

function XUsetfocus {
    direction=$2

    XmProcessTraversal $1 ${direction:-TRAVERSE_CURRENT}
}


#
# XmCreateSimpleDialog: a fake routine used by XUcreatesimpledialog
#
# Creates a DialogShell with a Form child containing a RowColumn
# and action area.
#
# Same arguments as the XmCreate... commands

function XmCreateSimpleDialog {
    nameref _w=$1
    typeset _d

    XmCreateDialogShell _d "$2" dialogshell "${@:4}"
    XtCreateWidget $1 "$1" XmForm $_d
    XtCreateManagedWidget $1.WORK work_area XmRowColumn "${_w}" \
        orientation:horizontal \
        packing:PACK_COLUMN \
        entryAlignment:ALIGNMENT_END \
        $(XUattach top 0 left 0 right 0)
    XUaddactionarea $1.ACTION $_w ${_w.WORK}
}

# XUaddactionarea: create a manager suitable for action area buttons.
#
# Usage: XUaddactionarea variable $form-widget $under-widget
#
# creates a Separator below the $under-widget, then creates a Form
# widget underneath the separator.  Anchors the bottom, left, and
# right of the Form, and returns its handle in the variable
```

```
function XUaddactionarea {
    typeset name=$1 _parent=$2 under=$3
    eval $name=
    XtCreateManagedWidget ${name}.SEPARATOR \
        separator XmSeparator "${_parent}" \
        $(XUattach under $under 0 left 0 right 0)
    nameref sep=${name}.SEPARATOR
    XtCreateWidget $name action XmForm ${_parent} \
        $(XUattach bottom 4 left 4 right 4 under ${sep} 4)
}

# XUattach: simplified way to specify form constraints
#
# Usage: XUattach [left|right|top|bottom] [offset] ...
# Usage: XUattach [leftpos|rightpos|toppos|bottompos] [offset] ...
# Usage: XUattach [under|over|leftof|rightof] widget [offset] ...
#
#    multiple options may be mixed: XUattach left 5 under $w 3

function XUattach {
    typeset edge

    while (( $# ))
    do
        case "$1" in
        left|right|top|bottom)
            print "${1}Attachment:ATTACH_FORM"

            if [[ $2 == [0-9]* ]]
            then
                print "${1}Offset:${2}"
                shift 2
            else
                shift
            fi
            ;;
        leftpos|rightpos|toppos|bottompos)
            edge=${1%%pos}
            print "${edge}Attachment:ATTACH_POSITION"
            shift
            if [[ $1 == [0-9]* ]]
            then
                print "${edge}Position:${1}"
                shift
            fi
            ;;
        under)
            print "topWidget:$2 topAttachment:ATTACH_WIDGET"
```

```
                shift 2
                if [[ $1 == [0-9]* ]]
                then
                    print "topOffset:${1}"
                    shift
                fi
                ;;
        over)
                print "bottomWidget:$2 bottomAttachment:ATTACH_WIDGET"
                shift 2
                if [[ $1 == [0-9]* ]]
                then
                    print "bottomOffset:${1}"
                    shift
                fi
                ;;
        leftof)
                print "rightWidget:$2 rightAttachment:ATTACH_WIDGET"
                shift 2
                if [[ $1 == [0-9]* ]]
                then
                    print "rightOffset:${1}"
                    shift
                fi
                ;;
        rightof)
                print "leftWidget:$2 leftAttachment:ATTACH_WIDGET"
                shift 2
                if [[ $1 == [0-9]* ]]
                then
                    print "leftOffset:${1}"
                    shift
                fi
                ;;
        *)
                print "$0: unknown argument skipped: $1" 1>&2
                shift
                ;;
        esac
    done
}

# XUalign2col: align a RowColumn widget into two columns
#
# Usage: XUalign2col $widget

function XUalign2col {
    typeset n
```

```
    XtGetValues $1 numChildren:n
    XtSetValues $1 \
        packing:PACK_COLUMN \
        numColumns:$((n/2)) \
        orientation:HORIZONTAL
}

# XUalignlabels: make all label widget arguments the same width
#
# Usage: XUalignlabels $widget ...

function XUalignlabels {
    integer max=0 width
    typeset w
    for w in "$@"
    do
        XtGetValues $w width:width
        if (( width > max ))
        then max=width
        fi
    done
    for w in "$@"
    do
        XtSetValues $w width:$max
    done
}

# XUaddtogglefields: add multiple labeled ToggleButtons to a parent
#
# Usage: XUaddtogglefields $parent [variable caption label] ...

function XUaddtogglefields {
    typeset _parent=$1

    shift
    while (( $# ))
    do
        eval $1=
        XtCreateManagedWidget $1.LABEL label XmLabel $_parent \
            labelString:"$2"
        XtCreateManagedWidget $1 toggle XmToggleButton $_parent \
            labelString:"$3" fillOnSelect:true
        shift 3
    done
}

# XUaddtextfields: add multiple captioned TextField widgets to a parent
#
# Usage: XUaddtextfields $parent [variable caption verify-command columns]
```

```
function XUaddtextfields {
    typeset _parent=$1

    shift
    while (( $# ))
    do
        eval $1=
        XtCreateManagedWidget $1.LABEL label XmLabel $_parent \
            labelString:"$2"
        XtCreateManagedWidget $1 textfield XmTextField $_parent \
            activateCallback:"$3" columns:$4 \
            cursorPositionVisible:false \
            focusCallback:"XtSetValues \${$1} cursorPositionVisible:true" \
            losingFocusCallback:"XtSetValues \${$1}
cursorPositionVisible:false"
        shift 4
    done
}


# XUaddoptionmenu: create a simple captioned option menu
#
# Usage: XUaddoptionmenu variable $parent caption [ label ... ]
#
# Instead of a label defining a button, a dash "-" will put a separator
# in the menu.

function XUaddoptionmenu {
    typeset var=$1 _parent=$2 label=$3
    typeset tmp pull

    eval $var=
    XtCreateManagedWidget $var.LABEL label XmLabel $_parent \
        labelString:"$label"
    XmCreatePulldownMenu pull $_parent pull
    XmCreateOptionMenu "$var" "$_parent" $var \
        labelString:"" \
        subMenuId:"$pull"
    eval "typeset -A $var.CHILD"
    shift 3
    while (( $# ))
    do
        case "$1" in
        -)
            XtCreateManagedWidget tmp tmp XmSeparatorGadget $pull
            shift
            ;;
        *)
            XtCreateManagedWidget "${var}.CHILD[$1]" \
```

```
                    push XmPushButtonGadget \
                    "$pull" \
                    labelString:"$1" \
                    activateCallback:"$var.VALUE='$1'"
                shift
                ;;
        esac
    done
    eval tmp="\${$var}"
    XtManageChild $tmp
}

# XUactionbuttons: add buttons suitable for an action area
# to a parent widget.  A parent created by XUaddactionarea is
# a good choice.  Arranges for the labels to be nicely laid out.
#
# usage: XUactionbuttons $form [ variable label command ] ...

function XUactionbuttons {
    typeset _parent=$1
    integer i=1 numbuttons=0
    typeset defbut canbut

    shift

    while (( $# ))
    do
        case "$1" in
        -d) defbut=$2; shift ;;
        -c) canbut=$2; shift ;;
        esac
        XtCreateManagedWidget "$1" actionbutton XmPushButton $_parent \
            labelString:"$2" \
            activateCallback:"$3" \
            $(XUattach leftpos $i rightpos $((i+2)) )
        (( numbuttons++ ))
        shift 3
        i=i+3
    done
    XtSetValues $_parent fractionBase:$(( numbuttons*3+1 ))
    typeset grandparent
    XtParent grandparent $_parent
    if [[ "$defbut" ]]
    then
        nameref _def=$defbut
        XtSetValues $grandparent defaultButton:$_def
    fi
    if [[ "$canbut" ]]
    then
```

```
            nameref _can=$canbut
            XtSetValues $grandparent cancelButton:$_can
        fi
        XtManageChild $_parent
}


# XUaddintegerfields: add captioned fields suitable for integer display
#
# Usage: XUaddintegerfields $parent [variable label columns ...]

function XUaddintegerfields {
    typeset _parent=$1 _r
    shift
    while (( $# ))
    do
        XUaddtextfields $_parent "$1" "$2" XUverifyinteger "$3"
        eval _r=\${$1}
        XUtextallowchars ${_r} '[0-9]'
        shift 3
    done
}


# XUverifymoney: verify that the CB_WIDGET is of the form suitable
# for currency (2 decimal digit number). This function is suitable as
# a verification callback for a Text or TextField widget.
#
# Usage: XUverifymoney

function XUverifymoney {
    typeset v=

    XtGetValues $CB_WIDGET value:v
    case "$v" in
    +([0-9]))
        XtSetValues $CB_WIDGET value:"$v.00"
        ;;
    +([0-9]).[0-9])
        XtSetValues $CB_WIDGET value:"${v}0"
        ;;
    +([0-9]).[0-9][0-9])
        ;;
    *)
        XUverifyerror "Bad monetary value" "$v"
        XUdefer "XmProcessTraversal $CB_WIDGET TRAVERSE_CURRENT"
        ;;
    esac
}


# XUaddmoneyfields: add captioned fields suitable for money
```

```
#
# Usage: XUaddmoneyfields $parent [variable label columns ...]

function XUaddmoneyfields {
    typeset _parent=$1
    shift
    while (( $# ))
    do
        XUaddtextfields "$_parent" "$1" "$2" XUverifymoney "$3"
        eval _r=\${$1}
        XUtextallowchars ${_r} '[0-9.]'
        shift 3
    done
}

function XUverifyerror {
    XUerror "Error" "$1: $2" :
    XBell $(XtDisplay - ${_XU.TOPLEVEL}) 50
}

function XUverifyfloat {
    typeset v

    XtGetValues $CB_WIDGET value:v
    if [[ $v != *([0-9])?(.*([0-9])) ]]
    then
        XUverifyerror "Bad Floating Point Value" "$v"
    fi
}

# XUverifyinteger: verify that CB_WIDGET holds an integer
#
# Usage: XUverifyinteger

function XUverifyinteger {
    typeset v

    XtGetValues $CB_WIDGET value:v
    if [[ $v != *([0-9]) ]]
    then
        XUverifyerror "Bad Integer Value" "$v"
    fi
}

# XUaddfloatfields: add captioned TextFields suitable for floating-
# point values.
#
# Usage: XUaddfloatfields $parent [variable label columns ...]
```

```
function XUaddfloatfields {
    typeset _parent=$1
    shift
    while (( $# ))
    do
        XUaddtextfields "$_parent" "$1" "$2" XUverifyfloat "$3"
        eval _r=\${$1}
        XUtextallowchars ${_r} '[0-9.]'
        shift 3
    done
}


# subroutine used by XUtextautoselect to select all of a text
# widget when it gains focus

function _XUtextautoselect {        # no args
    typeset widget=$CB_WIDGET
    typeset v

    XtGetValues $widget value:v
    XmTextFieldSetSelection $widget \
        0 ${#v} \
        $(XtLastTimestampProcessed - $(XtDisplay - $widget))
}

# XUtextautoselect: set up TextFields so when they gain focus
# the text is selected (allowing type-over)
#
# Usage: XUtextautoselect $widget ...

function XUtextautoselect {
    while (( $# ))
    do
        XtAddCallback $1 focusCallback "_XUtextautoselect"
        XtSetValues $1 cursorPositionVisible:false
        shift
    done
}


# Subroutine used by XUtextautotraverse to traverse to the next
# widget when a maximum character position is exceeded.

function _XUtextautotraverse {   # max-width
    typeset width=$1 widget=$CB_WIDGET
    typeset p
    XtGetValues $widget cursorPosition:p
    if (( p >= width ))
    then XmProcessTraversal $widget TRAVERSE_NEXT_TAB_GROUP
    fi
```

```
    }

    # XUtextautotraverse: set up TextField widgets to traverse
    # automatically when a maximum character position is exceeded.
    #
    # Usage: XUtextautotraverse [$widget numchars ...]

    function XUtextautotraverse {
        while (( $# ))
        do
            XtAddCallback $1 valueChangedCallback "_XUtextautotraverse $2"
            shift 2
        done
    }


    # Subroutine used to validate a date.

    function _XUdatevalidate {   # [MM|DD|YY] month day year
        typeset widget=$CB_WIDGET
        typeset valtype=$1 mm=$2 dd=$3 yy=$4
        typeset p v m d y

        XtGetValues $widget cursorPosition:p value:v
        case "$1" in
        DD)
            if ((v > 31 || v < 1))
            then
                XUverifyerror "Bad day, must be between 1 and 31" "$v"
                XtSetValues $CB_WIDGET cursorPosition:0
                XmProcessTraversal $CB_WIDGET TRAVERSE_CURRENT
                return
            fi
            ;;
        MM)
            if ((v > 12 || v < 1))
            then
                XUverifyerror "Bad month, must be between 1 and 12" "$v"
                XtSetValues $CB_WIDGET cursorPosition:0
                XmProcessTraversal $CB_WIDGET TRAVERSE_CURRENT
                return
            fi
            ;;
        YY)
            XtGetValues $mm value:m
            XtGetValues $dd value:d
            XtGetValues $yy value:y
            if ! XUisdate $m $d $y
            then
                XUverifyerror "Bad date" "$m/$d/$y"
```

```
            XtSetValues $mm cursorPosition:0
            XmProcessTraversal $CB_WIDGET TRAVERSE_CURRENT
            return
        fi
        ;;
    esac
    if (( p >= 2 ))
    then XmProcessTraversal $widget TRAVERSE_NEXT_TAB_GROUP
    fi
}


# XUadddatefields: add TextField widgets capable of holding
# a date.  All validation is set up for you.
#
# Usage: XUadddatefields $parent [variable label ...]
#
#   subvariables hold individual components: variable.MM, variable.DD,
#   and variable.YY

function XUadddatefields {
    typeset _parent=$1

    shift
    while (( $# ))
    do
        eval $1=
        nameref tmp=$1 _m=$1.MM _d=$1.DD _y=$1.YY
        XtCreateManagedWidget $1.LABEL label XmLabel $_parent \
            labelString:"$2"

        XtCreateManagedWidget $1 rc XmRowColumn $_parent \
            orientation:horizontal
        XtCreateManagedWidget $1.MM textfield XmTextField $tmp \
            valueChangedCallback:"_XUdatevalidate MM \
                \${$1.MM} \${$1.DD} \${$1.YY}" \
            columns:2
        XtCreateManagedWidget lab lab XmLabelGadget $tmp labelString:"/"
        XtCreateManagedWidget $1.DD textfield XmTextField $tmp \
            valueChangedCallback:"_XUdatevalidate \
                DD \${$1.MM} \${$1.DD} \${$1.YY}" \
            columns:2
        XtCreateManagedWidget lab lab XmLabelGadget $tmp labelString:"/"
        XtCreateManagedWidget $1.YY textfield XmTextField $tmp \
            losingFocusCallback:"_XUdatevalidate \
                YY \${$1.MM} \${$1.DD} \${$1.YY}" \
            columns:2
        XUtextallowchars $_m '[0-9]' $_d '[0-9]' $_y '[0-9]'
        XUtextautoselect $_m $_d $_y
        XUtextautocursor $_m $_d $_y
```

```
            XUtextautotraverse $_y 2
            shift 2
      done
}

# XUtextcut: cut selected text from a Text or TextField widget
#
# Usage: XUtextcut $widget

function XUtextcut {
    typeset t=$(XtLastTimestampProcessed - $(XtDisplay - $1))
    typeset c=$(XtClass - $1)    # XmText or XmTextField

    ${c}Cut "$@" $t
}

# XUtextpaste: paste text to a Text or TextField widget
#
# Usage: XUtextpaste $widget

function XUtextpaste {
    typeset c=$(XtClass - $1)
    ${c}Paste "$@"
}

# XUtextcopy: copy selected text from a Text or TextField widget
#
# Usage: XUtextcopy $widget

function XUtextcopy {
    typeset t=$(XtLastTimestampProcessed - $(XtDisplay - $1))
    typeset c=$(XtClass - $1)

    ${c}Copy "$@" $t
}

# XUtextsethighlight: set the highlight mode for text in a
# Text or TextField widget
#
# Usage: XUtextsethighlight $widget start-pos end-pos [type]
#

function XUtextsethighlight {
    typeset widget=$1 left=$2 right=$3 type=$4
    typeset c=$(XtClass - $1)

    type=${type:-HIGHLIGHT_SECONDARY_SELECTED}
    ${c}SetHighlight $widget "$left" "$right" "$type"
}
```

```
# XUselectionchildren: get the children of a SelectionDialog
#
# Usage: XUselectionchildren variable
#
#    the variable should hold a SelectionDialog handle, and
#    subvariables are created for each child

function XUselectionchildren {
    nameref _w=$1
    typeset child

    for child in CANCEL_BUTTON DEFAULT_BUTTON HELP_BUTTON \
        APPLY_BUTTON LIST LIST_LABEL OK_BUTTON SELECTION_LABEL \
        SEPARATOR TEXT WORK_AREA
    do
        XmSelectionBoxGetChild ${!_w}.$child $_w DIALOG_$child
    done
}

# XUmenusystem: create a menu system
#
# Usage: XUmenusystem $parent [variable label mnemonic action ...]
#    ...
#
# action can be either a ksh command string or an open curly brace,
# in which case a submenu is created up to the matching close curly brace.
# Menus may be nested in this manner to any depth.

function XUmenusystem {
    typeset _parent="$1" tmp menu buttontype exclusivevar
    integer level

    shift

    while (( $# != 0 ))
    do
        if [[ $1 == "{" ]] || [[ $1 == "}" ]]
        then return
        fi
        buttontype=XmPushButtonGadget
        exclusivevar=""
        if [[ $1 == -t ]]
        then buttontype=XmToggleButtonGadget
            shift
        elif [[ $1 == -e ]]
        then buttontype=XmToggleButtonGadget
            exclusivevar=$2
            shift 2
```

```
fi
if [[ $1 == "-" ]]
then
    XtCreateManagedWidget tmp tmp XmSeparator $_parent
    shift 4
elif [[ $4 = "{" ]]
then
    XmCreatePulldownMenu menu "$_parent" menu
    XtCreateManagedWidget "$1" "$1" XmCascadeButton \
        "$_parent" \
        labelString:"$2" \
        subMenuId:"$menu" \
        mnemonic:"$3"
    eval "$1.PULLDOWN=$menu"
    shift 4
    XUmenusystem $menu "$@"
    level=1
    while (( level > 0 && $# > 0 ))
    do
        if [[ $1 == "{" ]]
        then let level++
        elif [[ $1 == "}" ]]
        then let level--
        fi
        shift
    done
else
    if [[ $buttontype == XmPushButtonGadget ]]
    then
        XtCreateManagedWidget "$1" "$1" $buttontype \
            "$_parent" \
            labelString:"$2" \
            mnemonic:"$3" \
            activateCallback:"$4"
    else
        XtCreateManagedWidget "$1" "$1" $buttontype \
            "$_parent" \
            labelString:"$2" \
            mnemonic:"$3" \
            valueChangedCallback:"$4"
        if [[ "$exclusivevar" ]]
        then
            eval tmp="\${$1}"
            eval "$exclusivevar=\"\${$exclusivevar} $tmp\""
            XtAddCallback $tmp valueChangedCallback \
                "_XUmenuexclusive $tmp \"\${$exclusivevar}\""
            XtSetValues $tmp indicatorType:ONE_OF_MANY
        fi
    fi
```

```
                shift 4
            fi
        done
}


# Subroutine used to implement exclusive togglebuttons in a
# menu

function _XUmenuexclusive { # $toggle-widget other-widgets
    typeset s widget

    XtGetValues $1 set:s
    if [[ $s == true ]]
    then
        for widget in $2
        do
            if [[ $widget != $1 ]]
            then XtSetValues $widget set:false
            fi
        done
    fi
}


#
# Widget creation commands.
#
# All use the  _XUcreateobject routine to create different widgets.
# The general usage is:
#
# Usage: XU<widgetname> [-u] variable $parent [resource:value ...]
#
# Where <widgetname> is the lower case of the widget name, and the -u
option
# can be used to create the widget unmanaged.  For example:
#
# XUlabel mylabel $rowcol labelString:"hello"
#


#
# Names for widgets created by _XUcreateobj are composed of the
# last element of the variable that holds them.  This function strips
# out any hierarchical parents of the variable, and strips off any
subscript
# so it forms a legal widget name.  For example, the variable:
#
# MB.FILE[1]  would become a widget name:  FILE.
#


# Subroutine: strip a variable down to its last component, with no
```

```
# index

function _XUstripvar {   # variable-name
    typeset wname=$1
    wname=${wname##*.}
    wname=${wname%%\[*]}
    print "$wname"
}


# Subroutine used to create an object.

function _XUcreateobject {   # command [-u] args...
    integer nomanage=0

    if [[ $2 == "-u" ]]
    then
        nomanage=1
        set "$1" "${@:3}"
    fi
    typeset _c=$1 _n=$2 _p=$3 _r
    shift 3
    typeset _wname=${_n##*.}
    _wname=${_wname%%\[*]}
    $_c "$_n" "$_p" "$_wname" "${@}"
    eval _r=\"\${$_n}\"
    XtAddCallback $_r destroyCallback "unset $_n"
    (( nomanage )) || XtManageChild $_r
}


# Aliases are used to map every widget creation command to a call to
# _XUcreateobject

alias XUhelpdialog='_XUcreateobject DtCreateHelpDialog'
alias XUquickhelpdialog='_XUcreateobject DtCreateQuickHelpDialog'
alias XUarrowbutton='_XUcreateobject XmCreateArrowButton'
alias XUarrowbuttongadget='_XUcreateobject XmCreateArrowButtonGadget'
alias XUbulletinboard='_XUcreateobject XmCreateBulletinBoard'
alias XUbulletinboarddialog='_XUcreateobject XmCreateBulletinBoardDialog'
alias XUcascadebutton='_XUcreateobject XmCreateCascadeButton'
alias XUcascadebuttongadget='_XUcreateobject XmCreateCascadeButtonGadget'
alias XUcommand='_XUcreateobject XmCreateCommand'
alias XUdialogshell='_XUcreateobject XmCreateDialogShell'
alias XUdrawingarea='_XUcreateobject XmCreateDrawingArea'
alias XUdrawnbutton='_XUcreateobject XmCreateDrawnButton'
alias XUerrordialog='_XUcreateobject XmCreateErrorDialog'
alias XUfileselectionbox='_XUcreateobject XmCreateFileSelectionBox'
alias XUfileselectiondialog='_XUcreateobject XmCreateFileSelectionDialog'
alias XUform='_XUcreateobject XmCreateForm'
alias XUformdialog='_XUcreateobject XmCreateFormDialog'
```

```
alias XUframe='_XUcreateobject XmCreateFrame'
alias XUinformationdialog='_XUcreateobject XmCreateInformationDialog'
alias XUlabel='_XUcreateobject XmCreateLabel'
alias XUlabelgadget='_XUcreateobject XmCreateLabelGadget'
alias XUlist='_XUcreateobject XmCreateList'
alias XUmainwindow='_XUcreateobject XmCreateMainWindow'
alias XUmenubar='_XUcreateobject XmCreateMenuBar'
alias XUmenushell='_XUcreateobject XmCreateMenuShell'
alias XUmessagebox='_XUcreateobject XmCreateMessageBox'
alias XUmessagedialog='_XUcreateobject XmCreateMessageDialog'
alias XUoptionmenu='_XUcreateobject XmCreateOptionMenu'
alias XUpanedwindow='_XUcreateobject XmCreatePanedWindow'
alias XUpopupmenu='_XUcreateobject XmCreatePopupMenu'
alias XUpromptdialog='_XUcreateobject XmCreatePromptDialog'
alias XUpulldownmenu='_XUcreateobject XmCreatePulldownMenu'
alias XUpushbutton='_XUcreateobject XmCreatePushButton'
alias XUpushbuttongadget='_XUcreateobject XmCreatePushButtonGadget'
alias XUquestiondialog='_XUcreateobject XmCreateQuestionDialog'
alias XUradiobox='_XUcreateobject XmCreateRadioBox'
alias XUrowcolumn='_XUcreateobject XmCreateRowColumn'
alias XUscale='_XUcreateobject XmCreateScale'
alias XUscrollbar='_XUcreateobject XmCreateScrollBar'
alias XUscrolledlist='_XUcreateobject XmCreateScrolledList'
alias XUscrolledtext='_XUcreateobject XmCreateScrolledText'
alias XUscrolledwindow='_XUcreateobject XmCreateScrolledWindow'
alias XUselectionbox='_XUcreateobject XmCreateSelectionBox'
alias XUselectiondialog='_XUcreateobject XmCreateSelectionDialog'
alias XUseparator='_XUcreateobject XmCreateSeparator'
alias XUseparatorgadget='_XUcreateobject XmCreateSeparatorGadget'
alias XUtext='_XUcreateobject XmCreateText'
alias XUtextfield='_XUcreateobject XmCreateTextField'
alias XUtogglebutton='_XUcreateobject XmCreateToggleButton'
alias XUtogglebuttongadget='_XUcreateobject XmCreateToggleButtonGadget'
alias XUwarningdialog='_XUcreateobject XmCreateWarningDialog'
alias XUworkarea='_XUcreateobject XmCreateWorkArea'
alias XUworkingdialog='_XUcreateobject XmCreateWorkingDialog'
alias XUsimpledialog='_XUcreateobject XmCreateSimpleDialog -u'

function XUtoplevelshell {
    XtCreatePopupShell $1 $1 TopLevelShell "${@:2}"
}

# XUaddtogglebuttons: add ToggleButtons to a parent, with mnemonics
#
# Usage XUaddtogglebuttons $parent [variable label mnemonic command ...]

XUaddtogglebuttons()
{
   typeset _parent=$1 callback
```

```
    shift

    while (( $# > 2 ))
    do
        typeset v=$(_XUstripvar $1)
        XtCreateManagedWidget "$1" "$v" XmToggleButton "$_parent" \
            labelString:"$2" mnemonic:"$3" valueChangedCallback:"$4" \
            fillOnSelect:true selectColor:black
            shift 4
    done
}

# XUaddbuttons: add PushButtons to a parent
#
# Usage: XUaddbuttons $parent [variable label command ...]

XUaddbuttons()
{
    typeset _parent=$1 callback
    shift

    while (( $# > 2 ))
    do
        XtCreateManagedWidget "$1" "$1" XmPushButton "$_parent" \
            labelString:"$2" activateCallback:"$3"
            shift 3
    done
}

# XUaddpixbuttons: add PushButtons that display pictures to a parent
#
# Usage: XUaddpixbuttons $parent [variable pixmap command ...]

XUaddpixbuttons()
{
    typeset _parent=$1 callback
    shift

    while (( $# > 2 ))
    do
        XtCreateManagedWidget "$1" "$1" XmPushButton "$_parent" \
            labelType:PIXMAP labelPixmap:"$2" activateCallback:"$3"
            shift 3
    done
}

. ${SCRIPT:-/usr/dt/scripts}/DtFuncs.dtsh

# Usage: XUwarning [-m] title message ok-cb quit-cb help-cb
```

```
function XUwarning {
    typeset mode=DIALOG_MODELESS
    if [[ "$1" == -m ]]
    then mode=DIALOG_PRIMARY_APPLICATION_MODAL; shift
    fi
    DtkshDisplayWarningDialog "$1" "${2//  /}" "$3" "$4" "$5" $mode
}


# Usage: XUquestion [-m] title message ok-cb quit-cb help-cb

function XUquestion {   # [-m] title message ok-cb quit-cb help-cb
    typeset mode=DIALOG_MODELESS
    if [[ "$1" == -m ]]
    then mode=DIALOG_PRIMARY_APPLICATION_MODAL; shift
    fi
    DtkshDisplayQuestionDialog "$1" "${2// /}" "$3" "$4" "$5" $mode
}


# Usage: XUinformation [-m] title message ok-cb quit-cb help-cb

function XUinformation {   # [-m] title message ok-cb quit-cb help-cb
    typeset mode=DIALOG_MODELESS
    if [[ "$1" == -m ]]
    then mode=DIALOG_PRIMARY_APPLICATION_MODAL; shift
    fi
    DtkshDisplayInformationDialog "$1" "${2//  /}" "$3" "$4" "$5" $mode
}


# Usage: XUerror [-m] title message ok-cb quit-cb help-cb

function XUerror {   # [-m] title message ok-cb quit-cb help-cb
    typeset mode=DIALOG_MODELESS
    if [[ "$1" == -m ]]
    then mode=DIALOG_PRIMARY_APPLICATION_MODAL; shift
    fi
    DtkshDisplayErrorDialog "$1" "${2//    /}" "$3" "$4" "$5" $mode
}


# Usage: XUworking [-m] title message ok-cb quit-cb help-cb

function XUworking {   # [-m] title message ok-cb quit-cb help-cb
    typeset mode=DIALOG_MODELESS
    if [[ "$1" == -m ]]
    then mode=DIALOG_PRIMARY_APPLICATION_MODAL; shift
    fi
    DtkshDisplayWorkingDialog "$1" "${2//  /}" "$3" "$4" "$5" $mode
    if [[ ! "$3" ]]
    then
```

```
        XtUnmanageChild $(XmMessageBoxGetChild - \
               $_DT_WORKING_DIALOG_HANDLE \
               DIALOG_OK_BUTTON)
    fi
    _XU.WorkingDialog=$_DT_WORKING_DIALOG_HANDLE
}


#
# Functions for simple flat-file database access and updates
#

# XUdbopen -   open a file, reading in records into an array.
# The user can specify the field delimiter, it defaults
# to a pipe "|" symbol.
#
# This must step through each line of the file, and thus the read time
# grows proportionately with the file size.  It was clocked at about 250
# lines per second on an Intel 486/66 (6 records per line, lines about 80
# characters long each).

# Usage: XUdbopen variable file [delimiter]

function XUdbopen {
    nameref handle=$1
    typeset file=$2 delimiter=$3

    delimiter=${delimiter:-|}
    unset handle
    handle=
    handle.file=${file:-NoName}
    typeset -L1 handle.delimiter=$delimiter
    handle.needsync=FALSE
    if [[ -r ${handle.file} ]]
    then XUdbread handle < ${handle.file}
    fi
}


# Usage: XUdbread db-variable

function XUdbread { # dbhandle
    nameref handle=$1
    typeset line
    integer recnum=0

    unset handle.record
    while read line
    do
        handle.record[recnum++]=$line
    done
```

```
}

# Do a lookup based on an arbitrary pattern anywhere in the record.
# This requires a linear search.  On a 486/66 this can scan about 500
# records per second.

# Usage: XUdbfindpattern db-variable pattern

function XUdbfindpattern {  # DBhandle pattern
    nameref handle=$1
    typeset pattern=$2

    for ((i = 0; i < ${#handle.record[@]}; i++))
    do
        if [[ ${handle.record[i]} == $pattern ]]
        then
            print ${handle.record[i]}
        fi
    done
}

# This function writes any pending DB changes back out to the file
#
# It was clocked at about 300 records per second on an Intel 486/66.

# Usage: XUdbsync db-variable

function XUdbsync { #  DBhandle
    nameref handle=$1
    integer i

    if [[ ${handle.needsync} == FALSE ]]
    then return
    fi

    XUdbwrite handle > "${handle.file}"
    handle.needsync=FALSE
}

#
# Write all records, in order, to the standard output
#
# Usage: XUdbwrite db-variable

function XUdbwrite {      # DBhandle
    nameref handle=$1
    typeset outfile=$2
    integer i
```

```
        for ((i = 0; i < ${#handle.record[@]}; i++))
        do
            print ${handle.record[i]}
        done
    }


    #
    # Delete a record.  Quite fast since it uses array functions.
    #
    # Usage XUdbdelete db-variable index

    function XUdbdelete {    # DBhandle index
        nameref handle=$1
        typeset index=$2

        set -A handle.record \
            "${handle.record[@]:0:index-1}" "${handle.record[@]:index+1}"
    }


    #
    # Append a new record.
    #
    # Usage: XUdbappend db-variable record

    function XUdbappend {    # DBhandle record
        nameref handle=$1
        typeset record=$2

        handle.record[${#handle.record[@]}]=$record
        handle.needsync=TRUE
    }


    #
    # Uses sort(1) to sort the database.  Since it requires several operations
    # to perform this, it is fairly slow.  It can process about 100 records
    # per second on a 486/66.
    #
    # Example:
    #
    #   XUdbsort $DB -f +3  # sort by field 3, case insensitive (-f)
    #
    # Usage: XUdbsort db-variable [sort-options]

    function XUdbsort { #  DBhandle sort-options
        nameref handle=$1

        XUdbwrite handle | \
            sort -t"${handle.delimiter}" "${@:2}" | \
            XUdbread handle
```

```
}

# Usage: XUdbsplit db-variable index array-variable

function XUdbsplit {     # DBhandle index variable
    nameref handle=$1
    typeset IFS=${handle.delimiter}

    set -A $3 ${handle.record[$2]}
}

#
# Validation Functions
#

# Usage: XUisinteger string ...

function XUisinteger {  # strings ...
    typeset s

    for s
    do
        if [[ $s != +([0-9]) ]]
        then return 1
        fi
    done
    return 0
}

# Usage: XUisblank string ...

function XUisblank {  # strings
    typeset s

    for s in "$@"
    do
        if [[ $s ]] || [[ $s != +([    ]) ]]
        then return 1
        fi
    done
    return 0
}

# Usage: XUisfloat string ...

function XUisfloat {  # strings ...
    typeset s

    for s
```

```
        do
            if XUisblank "$s" || [[ $s != ?(+([0-9]))?(.+([0-9])) ]]
            then return 1
            fi
        done
        return 0
    }

set -A _XU.MONTHDAYS 0 31 29 31 30 31 30 31 31 30 31 30 31

# Usage: XUisdate mm dd yy

function XUisdate { # mm dd yy
    typeset mm=$1 dd=$2 yy=$3

    if ! XUisinteger "$mm" "$dd" "$yy"
    then return 1
    fi
    if (( mm < 1 || mm > 12 || dd < 1 || dd > _XU.MONTHDAYS[mm] || yy < 0 ))
    then return 1
    fi
    # hard code the test for leap years
    if (( mm == 2 && dd == 29 && ((1900+yy)%4) != 0 ))
    then return 1
    fi
    return 0
}
```

PART IV *Reference*

In this section, reference material is presented on KornShell-93, all additional dtksh built-ins, all Motif widgets, and other miscellaneous subjects. Most of this material is not meant to be read cover to cover, but rather used on an as-needed basis.

The format is terse and compact by necessity, especially in the case of the Motif widget reference material. Unfortunately, the information presented here cannot completely substitute for the full Motif widget manual pages, but it is nonetheless quite useful for day-to-day programming chores.

28 *KornShell Language Review*

28.1 Introduction

This chapter presents a review of the KornShell programming language. If you know nothing about shell programming, this chapter probably won't go into enough depth and you should consider reading a more comprehensive tutorial such as [Bolsky and Korn 1995]. However, if you already know some kind of shell language such as Bourne shell, csh, or older versions of the KornShell, then this chapter should be sufficient.

The focus here will be on using the KornShell as a programming language, so I won't be discussing its numerous interactive features such as job control, command history, and command editing. There is a summary of that information in Chapters 30 and 31, but if you intend to use dtksh as an interactive shell, you might want to read tutorials that cover that aspect in greater depth.

 This chapter covers the version of KornShell used as a base for the dtksh language, KornShell-93. If you are familiar with an older version such as KornShell-88 or earlier, then you will want to review this chapter looking for the KSH93 margin marker shown here, which denotes features that are new in KornShell-93.

28.2 Cast of Characters

In many places in this chapter I'll have to refer to individual characters, because many characters have special meaning in the syntax of the shell. Different people use different names for some punctuation characters. The convention I'll use will be to give the name of the character (as a word), followed by the character in parentheses. For example:

The semicolon (;) can be used to break lines.

The exception is that nonprintable characters such as spaces, tabs, and newlines will not appear in quotes following the name, and neither will parentheses (that would look confusing).

28.3 Basic Definitions

This section defines some basic terms that will be used in the rest of this chapter. It isn't necessary for you to memorize these because numerous examples will be presented that should give you an intuitive feel for KornShell syntax. These definitions are included for completeness.

blank   A space character or a tab character.

metacharacter   A character that the shell treats specially when parsing commands. One of semicolon (;), ampersand (&), parentheses , the pipe symbol (|), angle brackets (<>), newline, space, or tab.

quote   There are times when you want to turn off the special meaning of one or more metacharacters. This is called *quoting*. The three ways to quote are by using double quotes around a string, using single quotes around a string, or preceding a single character by a backslash (\) character. Double quotes turn off the special meanings of blanks and some metacharacters but allow certain other kinds of special processing (see variable expansion and command expansion later). Single quotes turn off all special processing. The backslash character turns off the special meaning of the one character that follows it.

word   A word is a sequence of characters separated by metacharacters that have not been quoted. The simplest case is alphabetic characters separated by blanks, but any of the metacharacters can break a string into words.

command   A command is a set of words and metacharacters. The first word of a command is the name of the command, other words are arguments to the command.

                   Commands carry out specific tasks, such as the `print` command that prints out strings or the `typeset` command that declares variable types. Those are examples of built-in commands which are a part of the shell itself. Some commands are actually executables that the shell runs as separate processes, such as the `sed` command that edits a data stream or the `more` command that breaks data into easily viewed pages.

If you're a little unclear on some of those definitions, don't worry, because there will be plenty of examples below that should clarify them. The following sections cover specifics of the KornShell language.

28.4 Comments

Any word that begins with a pound sign (#) starts a comment. Comments continue until the end of the line on which they began. So, a line that begins with a pound sign is entirely a comment, and a comment may follow a command on the same line. Listing 28-1 shows a valid comment; it also shows an example of a pound sign embedded inside a word that does not form a coment.

Listing 28-1. Comments. The first line below shows a valid comment after the pound sign (#). The second line does not form a valid comment because the pound sign does not start a word, it will literally print: `example#no_comment`.

```
print example          # this is a valid comment

print example#no_comment
```

28.5 Command Execution

The most basic task performed by KornShell is command execution. Some commands are executed by starting other UNIX processes, and some commands are built in to the KornShell and do not cause other processes to spawn. You should try to use the built-in commands in KornShell instead of other UNIX commands that start processes because built-in commands are far faster. Some of the more commonly used built-in commands are explained later in this chapter. Complete reference information on all the built-in KornShell commands is contained in Chapter 31.

Commands return an integer value. The shell treats a return value of zero as "true" or "success" and nonzero as "false" or "failure." Note that this is the opposite of the C programming language.

In addition to the return code, some commands print data to the standard file descriptors `stdout` and `stderr`, and some commands take input from the `stdin` file descriptor.

There are several classes of command, each one is explained in the following sections.

Simple Command

A *simple command* is a sequence of blank-separated words, optionally preceded by a variable assignment list. Variables set in such an assignment list take on the given values only for the duration of the execution of the simple command. An example of this is shown in Listing 28-2.

Actually, there are a few exceptions to this for historical reasons. Some built-in commands are called special built-ins, and for those commands assignments preceding the command continue to be in effect after the command is executed. Chapter 31 lists all the special built-ins.

The first word in the sequence is the name of the command to be executed. Simple commands return values in the range 0 to 255 if they terminate normally, or if killed by a signal they return 256 plus the signal number.

Listing 28-2. Simple Commands. The first line assigns the string "Presley" to the variable `Singer`. The second line will print `Elvis Costello` because of the temporary assignment that precedes the call to a secondary `dtksh` process that executes a `print` command. The third line will print `Elvis Presely`. This shows that the variable assignment preceding the `dtksh` command was only temporary.

```
function show {
     print $1
}

Singer="Presely"
Singer="Costello" dtksh -c 'print "Elvis $Singer"'
print "Elvis $Singer"
```

Command Pipeline

A *command pipeline* is a sequence of one or more commands separated by the pipe symbol (|). The standard output of each command in the pipeline is connected to the standard input of the next command in the pipeline. The return value from the pipeline is the return code from the last command in the pipeline.

Listing 28-3. A Command Pipeline. The standard output of the first `grep` command will contain all lines from the file `composers` that contains the string `Bach`. Those lines will be fed into the standard input of the second `grep` command, which will strip out any lines containing the pattern `P.D.Q.`. The resulting lines will be fed into the `more` command, which will display one screen full of information at a time

```
grep "Bach" composers | grep -v "P.D.Q." | more
```

Arithmetic Command

Arithmetic commands can be used to evaluate mathematical expressions. They are formed by starting a word with double open parentheses: ((, followed by a valid arithmetic expression, closed by double close parentheses:)) . The syntax for valid arithmetic expressions is discussed below.

Arithmetic commands return zero if the expression evaluates to nonzero, nonzero otherwise. This may seem confusing, but it stems from the fact that zero is the success return code in Shell. This will be discussed in more detail when conditional statements are covered below.

Listing 28-4. Arithmetic Commands. These commands are used to evaluate mathematical expressions. They are often used in conjunction with the `if` or `while` statements. Note that it is unecessary to put the `$` character in front of variables in arithmetic commands.

```
(( A = B + C*D*2.7 + cos(THETA) ))

if (( A > MAX || A < MIN ))
then print "Range error"
fi
```

Command Lists

A *command list* is one or more pipelines (or simple commands) separated by one of the following separators. In the explanations below I'll use the word *command* interchangebly for the phrase "command or pipeline."

command `;` *command*

Commands separated by semicolons are executed sequentially. You can also use newlines instead of semicolons to execute commands sequentially. Example:

```
print hello; print world
```

command `&`

The preceding command is executed in the background, the KornShell does not wait for it to complete before going on to the next command. Example:

```
find . -print &
print "didn't wait for the find"
```

command `|&`

The preceding command is executed in the background, but a two-way pipeline is created so the KornShell can communicate with it. This is called a coprocess. Coprocesses are an advanced topic, see [Bolsky and Korn 1995].

command `&&` *command*

The command following the double ampersand is executed only if the preceding command returned a successful (zero) value.
Example:

```
grep income file && print "I found it!"
```

command `||` *command*

The command following the double pipe is executed only if the preceding command returned an unsuccessful (nonzero) value.

Example:

```
initialize || print "Failed!"
```

<code>(command-list)</code>   A command list inside of regular parentheses is executed in a separate environment. This means that variables set inside the list are local to that set of commands, files opened inside the list do not remain open when the list ends, if the current working directory is changed via the cd command inside the list it is not changed when the list ends, etc. This is usually accomplished by executing the list in a subshell, although the KornShell is smart enough to avoid the overhead of spawning another process if possible. Note that parentheses are metacharacters, meaning that they don't require blanks around them or to start a line to be recognized. Also note that if you want to nest these you need to put whitespace between two consecutive open parentheses in order to avoid confusion with arithmetic substitution. For an example, see Listing 28-5.

<code>{ command ; }</code>   Curly braces may be used to group items in a list. They can avoid precedence problems.   Example:

```
grep apple orchard && {
        initialize || print "Failed!"
}
```

Unlike parentheses, curly braces are not metacharacters, they must be separate words to be recognized (i.e., you need whitespace between them and other words). The closing curly brace must be at the beginning of a line (or after a semicolon) to be recognized.

The simplest way to avoid problems is to always use the convention that both curly braces and regular parentheses should be on lines by themselves.

Listing 28-5. Command Lists in Parentheses. Parentheses can be used to execute commands in another environment. Variable assignments, directory changes, etc., do not affect commands following the close parenthesis.

```
VAR=OLD
cd /tmp
(
        cd $newdir
```

```
            VAR=NEW
)

print "$VAR"            # will print: OLD
pwd                     # will print: /tmp
```

Listing 28-6. Command Grouping. Curly braces need to be surrounded by whitespace to be recognized, and must be the first word of a command. The first line below fails because there is no blank after the open curly brace. The second line fails because there is no semi-colon following "unum." The final set of lines is easy to read and works, thus it is a good format to use to avoid problems.

```
{print "E. Pluribus"; print "Unum"; }

{ print "E. Pluribus"; print "Unum" }

{
    print "E. Pluribus"
    print "Unum"
}
```

Precedence of Command List Separators

The && and || separators have equal precedence and are of higher precedence than ;, &, and |& (which are also of equal precedence among themselves). If there's any question about the precedence, you should probably use curly braces to group commands unambiguously. Doing so will avoid readability problems and subtle errors. Among separators of equal precedence, evaluation occurs left to right.

Listing 28-7 illustrates these concepts by using the true and false built-in commands in simple combinations with the && and || operators.

Listing 28-7. Precedence of Command Lists. The false command always returns a failure code, while the true command always returns success. Thus, the first line prints no and the second prints yes. The third line will print no first, but because the subcommand false || print no is successful it then prints yes as well. The fourth line prints yes, but since the subcommand true && print yes is successful it does not go on to print no. For similar reasons, the fifth line prints only no.

```
false || print no                       # prints: no
true && print yes                       # prints: yes
false || print no && print yes          # prints: no then yes
true && print yes || print no           # prints: yes
false && print yes || print no          # prints: no
```

Input and Output Redirection

Besides connecting the output of one command to the input of another command using pipelines, you can also redirect input and output from a command to files. In addition, you can open and close numeric file descriptors and connect them to files. To accomplish these feats, you need only put one or more of the following notations anywhere on the same line as any simple command. Note that even though you can put these anywhere on the line, by convention most programmers use these at the end of a command.

`<`*filename*	Take input from *filename*. Example:

```
wc -l <reportfile
```

`>`*filename*	Use *filename* as the standard output (file descriptor 1). If the *filename* does not exist it is created. If *filename* exists it is truncated unless KornShell was started with the `noclobber` option, in which case an error occurs. This will be explained more fully under the `set` built-in command later, but basically this is a safety option to prevent users from accidentally wiping out files.

Examples:

```
>byebye          # truncate the file byebye

wc -l reportfile >numlines
```

`>`|*filename*	This is the same as `>`*filename*, except it truncates existing files regardless of whether `noclobber` is set. This is a way to override the safety feature when you are sure of what you're doing.

Example:

```
>|byebye  # truncate even if noclobber set
```

`>>`*filename*	This is similar to `>`*filename*, except instead of truncating an existing file it seeks to the end of the file and appends the output to it. Example:

```
rm suspects
cat hadmotive >> suspects
cat hadweapon >> suspects
```

`<>`*filename*	Opens filename for both reading and writing as the standard input. This is rarely useful, so don't ponder it too long.
`<<[-]`*word*	This is called a *here document*. It allows you to specify some input to the command right there in the script without resort

ing to writing a temporary file. The *word* is used as a delimiter. Lines are read and stored until *word* is found on a line by itself. These lines then become the standard input to the command. If the optional – is appended to the <<, then leading tabs are stripped from the input lines and from *word*. The usual shell substitutions are carried out on the input lines unless some character of *word* is quoted. Most programmers use the convention of putting a backslash in front of the first character of *word* when they want to supress substitutions within the here document. See Listing 28-8 for examples.

<&digit   This duplicates standard input from the file descriptor specified by *digit*. The *digit* has a maximum value of 9. So, whatever is connected to the file descriptor *digit*, whether it be a file, device, here document, etc., will become the standard input to the command. The exec built-in command can be used to connect files or devices to a file descriptor. Example:

```
exec 5<suspects     # connect file to 5
grep Butler <&5     # search suspects file
```

>&digit   This duplicates the standard output to file descriptor digit. Digit can be no greater than 9. Example:

```
exec 6>evidence    # connect file to 6
print "gun" >&6    # append to evidence file
```

<&-   This closes the standard input.

>&-   This closes the standard output.

>&p   The standard input from the coprocess is moved to standard input. Coprocesses will be explained in a section all their own, they are an advanced feature.

<&p   The output to the coprocess is moved to standard output.

Listing 28-8. Here Documents. In the first cat command, the terminating string END is not quoted, thus the variable expansion $BRIBE will appear in the output as 1000. In the second cat command, the first character of END is quoted with a backslash character, thus the $1 string will literally print out as "$1". If END were not quoted the $1 would have expanded to the first argument of the script, which is not what was desired in this case.

```
BRIBE=1000
cat <<END
   A bribe of $BRIBE dollars was offered to the detective,
```

```
   strongly implicating the Butler.
END

cat <<\END
   The Maid, however, offered only $1, so we arrested her.
END
```

In addition, you can precede any of these by a digit from 0 to 9, in which case that file descriptor is used instead of the default standard input or standard output. For example, in the command:

```
ls file 2>&1
```

the standard error (file descriptor 2) is duplicated for writing as standard output (file descriptor 1). This means that the standard error's data will go wherever the standard output's go for that command.

If you include more than one redirection notation on a command, you must be aware of a tricky point: the order matters. These redirections are evaluated from left to right. Listing 28-9 illustrates this.

Listing 28-9. Order of Redirection Matters. In the first line below, the standard output is first sent to the file, then standard error is sent to where the standard output is going, which is also the same file. In the second example, first the standard error is sent to where the stnadard output is going (the terminal), then the standard output is sent to a file, so the two descriptors are now going to different places.

```
ls /tmp 1>file 2>&1

ls /tmp 2>&1 1>file
```

28.6 Variables

Variable names are formed in accordance with the following definitions:

simple name   A sequence of letters, digits, or underscores starting with a letter or underscore.

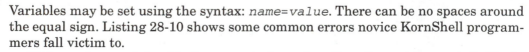

compound name   A sequence of one or more simple names separated by periods. A compound name may also start with a period.

Variables may be set using the syntax: *name=value*. There can be no spaces around the equal sign. Listing 28-10 shows some common errors novice KornShell programmers fall victim to.

If the *value* contains blanks or metacharacters then it must be quoted. Single quotes turn off all special meanings of metacharacters between them, double quotes allow variable and command expansion but turn off all other metacharacters, and a backslash character can be used to turn off the special meaning of the following character.

Listing 28-10. Variable Assignment. Unlike languages like C, the Shell is picky about blanks when it comes to assignment.

```
A = "A Sunny Day"           # fails, spaces not allowed around =
A=A Sunny Day               # fails, need quotes around blanks
A="A Sunny Day"             # Yes!  Single quotes would work too
```

Variables may be cleared using the unset built-in command which takes the syntax:

```
unset name ...
```

Unsetting a variable is not the same as simply setting it to the empty string; an unset variable doesn't exist in the system at all (for example, the env built-in will no longer even list an unset variable).

   The value of a variable can be substituted anywhere within a command by using the syntax ${name}. If a variable has a simple name (i.e., a name that does not contain periods) then the curly braces may be left out. However, there can be cases when you need the curly braces in order to avoid ambiguities inside of strings. For example, if there's an alphabetic character immediately following the variable name in the string, you must use the curly braces:

```
print "${A}BCDEFG"
```

KSH93 > Either simple or compound names can be used for variable names. The ability to use compound names for variables and functions is new in KornShell-93; in previous versions of KornShell there could be no periods in variable or function names. This is an important addition to the language, because it allows programmers to group related pieces of data into logical chunks, much like structures in the C language.

Listing 28-11. Using Compound Variables. All elements of the compound name must exist before setting a submember, which is why the first line is necessary. Compound variables are useful for grouping related data, just as structures are used in the C language.

```
BALL=                       # initialize base variable

BALL.X=0
BALL.Y=0
BALL.X.VELOCITY=10
BALL.Y.VELOCITY=-5
BALL.DIAMETER=5
```

One restriction on the use of compound names is that you can't set a compound variable to a value unless all the preceding elements of the compound name are also set. This is illustrated in Listing 28-12.

KSH93 ⟩ **Listing 28-12. Setting Compound Variables.** All elements of the compound name must exist before setting a submember, otherwise an error occurs.

```
unset CANNOT                    # Just making sure!

CANNOT.DO=7                     # Fails! Variable CANNOT is not set.

CAN=
CAN.DO=7                        # Works, CAN is set above
CAN.DO.ALSO=9                   # Works, both CAN and CAN.DO are set
CAN.NOT.DO=14                   # Fails! CAN.NOT was never set
```

Typed Variables

By default, KornShell variables hold string values. By using the typeset command, you can specify that a variable should hold one of several other types of values. Declaring the type of a variable is a good idea because KornShell will use a more efficient internal representation for the data the variable holds. In addition, if the wrong kind of value is assigned to a typed variable, then a run-time error will be generated, alerting you that there is a problem with the program. In addition, it is possible to define local variables inside of KornShell functions using the typeset command (see *Functions* on page 575).

There are many different options on the typeset command (see Chapter 31, *KornShell Command Reference*); some of the more common ones are illustrated in Listing 28-13.

Listing 28-13. Declaring Variable Types. The typeset command can be used to enforce data typing on variables. Several aliases are provided by KornShell for the typeset command to increase readability of declarations (float, integer, etc.)

```
typeset -i i=0      # Variable i is declared as an integer
integer i=0         # The same thing using the "integer" alias

typeset -E x y      # Variables x and y declared floating point
float x y           # The same thing using the "float" alias

typeset -L10 left   # Variable left will be left justified,
                    # 10 characters wide.  There is a -R option
                    # for right justification that works similarly
typeset -r SAFE     # Variable SAFE becomes read-only
readonly SAFE       # The same thing using the "readonly" alias
```

KSH93 ⟩

Name Reference Variables

KSH93 > There are times when it is convenient to have one variable "point" to another variable. Using the `typeset` command with the `-n` option (or the `nameref` alias), you can specify that one variable really refers to another variable. References or stores into the first variable actually affect the referenced variable. This feature is especially useful in conjunction with functions, and that aspect is discussed more fully under *Functions* on page 575.

Listing 28-14. Name Reference Variables. Using `typeset` with the `-n` option, or the equivalent alias `nameref` as shown below, one can create a variable that "points" to another variable. This is especially useful for passing values back from function calls, as is explained later.

```
A=9
nameref B=A            # Variable B now references variable A

print "$B"             # Prints 9, the value of $A

B=15
print "$A"             # Prints 15, the assignment to B above set A!
```

Math on Variables

If you declare a variable to be an integer or a floating-point type using the `typeset` command or one of its aliases (`integer` or `float`), then you can directly assign expressions to them. If you don't declare a variable using `typeset`, you can still compute mathematical expressions using either the arithmetic evaluation command, `(( expression ))`, or by using the `let` command.

Indexed Array Variables

KornShell supports single dimensional arrays. By default, arrays take integer subscripts (this is called an indexed array). Indexed array elements are set using the notation:

        arrayname[*expression*]=*value*

The *expression* may be any valid arithmetic expression, and *arrayname* may be either a simple name or a compound name. The value of an array element can be expanded using the notation `${`*arrayname*`[`*expression*`]}`. The curly braces are mandatory even if the *arrayname* is a simple name. One shorthand notation is that `$`*arrayname* is the same as `${`*arrayname*`[0]}`.

Listing 28-15. Indexed Array Notation. One common mistake novice KornShell programmers make with arrays is forgetting to use curly braces when substituting the value.

```
A[0]="Mozart"          # Works.
A[1]="Beethoven"       # Works.
```

```
A[1+1]="Liszt"            # Works, sets A[2].

print "$A[1]"             # Fails! Prints: Mozart[1] because $A is
                          # equivalent to ${A[0]}

print "${A[1]}"           # Works, prints: Beethoven

X=2
print "${A[X]}"           # Works, prints: Liszt
print "${A[$X]}"          # Also works, prints: Liszt
```

Array names can be compound names, but the index must be the last element of the name. You cannot put an index within a compound name.

KSH93 ▷   **Listing 28-16. Compound Names and Arrays.** It is illegal to put an array index within a compound name, and there can only be a single array index.

```
PLAYER=                      # Set the base variable
PLAYER.NAME[1]="Babe Ruth"   # This works as expected
PLAYER.NAME[1].HOMERS=714    # Fails!  Cannot embed an array index
```

Associative Array Variables

KSH93 ▷   In addition to indexed arrays, KornShell-93 supports associative arrays. Associative arrays use the same syntax as indexed arrays, except that they don't use mathematical expressions as their subscripts; instead any arbitrary string can be used. This is similar to the way arrays in the awk language work.

To make an array associative, you must declare it using the typeset command with the -A option. Whitespace matters inside the square braces for associative arrays. Variable expansion is carried out between the square braces unless quoting is used.

Associative arrays are very powerful—in effect they give you a ready-made hash table that can be used to do fast data look-ups.

There is a special notation that can be used with associative arrays to get the list of indexes that are available (i.e., all the strings that have ever been used as indexes):

> "${!*arrayname*[@]}"

This is often useful cycling through all the elements of the array using a for loop. Note that the order of the items produced by this construct is indeterminate.

KSH93 ▷   **Listing 28-17. Associative Arrays.**

```
typeset -A Taste         # Make Taste associative
Taste[lemon]="tart"      # Associate string lemon with tart
```

```
Taste[sugar ]="sweet"              # Watch out! The blank counts!
print "${Taste[lemon]}"           # As expected, prints: tart
print "${Taste[sugar]}"           # Prints nothing! The blank is missing.

food=lemon
print "${Taste[$food]}"           # Prints: tart

# loop through all the items, printing the indexes and values

for food in "${!Taste[@]}"
do
        print "$food ${Taste[food]}"
done
```

Positional Parameters

The arguments that were given to the shell script are available in special environment variables of the form $0, $1, $2, etc. The name of the command that invoked the KornShell is stored in $0, and each parameter passed to the shell is stored in order in $1, ... etc.   If there is more than one digit in the number following the dollar sign, then you must use curly braces: ${12}.   The variable $# holds the number of parameters.

In addition, the special variable $* expands to all the positional parameters, and the notation "$@" expands to all the parameters properly quoted. Note the double quotes around "$@", if you leave them out then $* and $@ are equivalent. A subset of the parameters can be expanded using the notation:

KSH93 ⟩

```
"${@:start:number}"
```

where *start* is the index of the first parameter desired, and *number* is the number of parameters to include. If the :*number* part is left off then all the items following *start* are included. So, the following two lines of code are equivalent:

```
print "${@:2:3}"
print "$2" "$3" "$4"
```

The built-in command shift may be used to move the parameters down by one or more positions. The built-in command set may be used to set a new parameter list.

Listing 28-18. Positional Parameter Examples.

```
set "a" "b" "c" "d" "e" "f" "g"            # Reset the parameters

print "$1"                        # Prints: a
print "$#"                        # Prints the number of parameters: 7
print "$*"                        # Prints: a b c d e f g
```

```
           shift
           print "$1"                   # Because of the shift, prints: b
           shift 2
           print "$1"                   # Likewise, prints: d
 KSH93     print "${@:1:2}"             # Prints: e f
           print "${@:2}"               # Prints: f g
           set "$*"                     # Turns all params into a single param!
           print "$1"                   # Prints: d e f g
           set $*                       # No quotes, the items are separate again
           print "$1"                   # Prints: d
```

Other Kinds of Variable Expansion

The notation `${name}` to expand the value of a variable is just one example of expansion. The KornShell allows a number of other notations, all beginning with the dollar sign (`$`), that perform other useful kinds of expansion:

`${#variable}`

Expands to the length of the string stored in the named variable. If `@` or `*` is used for the variable, prints the number of positional parameters, same as `$#`.

Example:

```
V="ABCDEFG"
print "${#V}"    # Prints: 7
```

 `${variable:offset}`

Expands to the part of the value of the *variable* starting at character position offset and going to the end of the value. In effect, allows you to clip off a leading part of the value of the *variable*. Note that *offset* can be any expression.

Example:

```
V="ABCDEFG"
print "${V:2}"    # Prints: CDEFG
```

KSH93 `${variable:offset:len}`

Similar to above, but only expands at most *len* characters. Both *offset* and *len* may be expressions.

```
V="ABCDEFG"
print "${V:3:2}"  # Prints: DE
```

`${array[*]}`

Expands to all the elements of the array. The subscript may also be an at sign (@), and in that case if this expression is enclosed in double quotes then quoting is preserved during the expansion. Example:

```
set -A A "A" B" "C"
print "${A[*]}"    # Prints: A B C
```

`${#array[*]}`

Expands to the number of elements set in the named array. Example:

```
set -A A "A" "B" "C"
print "${#A[*]}"    # Prints: 3
```

`${!array[@]}`

Expands to the list of subscripts that are set for the array. This is especially useful for associative arrays, since you can retrieve the list of indexes that have been used to set elements of the array.

> KSH93 `${array[@]:offset}`

Expands to the elements of the named array starting at index offset. You can also use an asterisk (*) instead of an at sign (@).

```
set -A A "A" "B" "C"
print "${A[@]:1}"  # Prints: B C
```

> KSH93 `${array[@]:offset:len}`

As above, but print at most *len* elements of the array.

```
set -A A "A" "B" "C" "D"
print "${A[@]:0:2}" # Prints: A B
```

> KSH93 `${!variable}`

If the named variable is a name reference type of variable, then the name of the indirect variable is expanded.

```
B=2
nameref A=B
print $A       # Prints: 2
print ${!A}    # Prints: B
```

`${variable:-string}`

If the named variable is set and not the empty string, expands to the value of the variable; oth erwise expands to the given string. Expansion is carried out in the string if it is used.

Example:

```
A=17
print ${A:-99}   # Prints: 17
unset A
print ${A:-99}   # Prints: 99
B=4
print ${A:-$B}   # Prints: 4
```

${*variable*:=*string*}

If the variable is not set or is set to the empty string, set it to the string and then expand to string. You can't set the positional parameters $0, $1, ... in this way.

```
unset A
print ${A:=YES}   # Prints: YES
print $A          # Prints: YES
```

${*variable*:?*string*}

If the variable is not set or is set to the empty string, print the given string and exit from the shell. If the string is empty, a standard message is printed.

${*variable*:+*string*}

If the variable is set and not the empty string, substitute string, otherwise nothing.

Example:

```
A=YES
print ${A:+NO}   # Prints: NO
unset A
print ${A:+NO}   # Nothing printed
```

 ${*variable*/*pattern*/*string*}

Substitute the first occurrence of the given *pattern* (see *Patterns* on page 569) with the substitution *string*. Example:

```
A=xyzxyz
print ${A/x/q}   # Prints: qyzxyz
```

 ${*variable*//*pattern*/*string*}

As above, but substitute all occurrences of the *pattern*.

Example:

```
A=xyzxyz
print ${A//x/q} # Prints: qyzqyz
```

${*variable*#*pattern*}   If the *variable*'s value starts with a match of
the given pattern, clip off that part of the value
and print the rest. A minimal match of the pattern is clipped off. Example:

```
F=s.file.c
print ${F#s.}    # Prints: file.c
```

${*variable*##*pattern*}   As above, but strips off a maximal match of the
pattern. Example:

```
A=xxxyyy
print ${A#*x}   # Prints: xxyyy
print ${A##*x} # Prints: yyy
```

${*variable*%*pattern*}   If the last portion of *variable*'s value matches
the pattern, expands to the value with the
matching portion stripped off. A minimal
match of the pattern is stripped.

Example:

```
F=s.file.c
print ${F%.c}   # Prints: s.file
```

${*variable*%%*pattern*}   Same as above, but a maximal match of the pattern is stripped.

Example:

```
A=xxxyyy
print ${A%y*}    # Prints: xxxyy
print ${A%%y*}  # Prints: xxx
```

For all of the preceding expansions which contain a colon (:) and check whether the
variable is unset or set to an empty string, you can leave out the colon. Doing so
has the same behavior, but the variable is only checked to see if it's set, being set to
the empty string still "counts." For example:

```
A=""                    # A is set to the empty string
print ${A:-not set}     # Prints: not set
print ${A-not set}      # Prints nothing
```

```
unset A
print ${A:-not set}        # Prints: not set
print ${A-not set}         # Prints: not set
```

Other Expansions

Besides the expansion notations illustrated in the previous section, two other kinds of expansion are allowed by the shell:

$(command)
This is called command substitution. The command between the parentheses is run in a subcontext and its standard output is substituted. Note that you can achieve the same effect by enclosing a command in backquotes: `command`. However, this is considered an obsolete construct. The method using dollar-open parenthesis is more readable (it is easy to mistake backquotes for normal quotes when reading code). In addition, the dollar-parenthesis method nests easily without worrying about quoting. There is one special idiom that can be used with this notation: $(<file) expands to the entire contents of the named file.

$((expression))
This is called arithmetic substitution. The expression is evaluated, and its value is substituted.

28.7 Conditional Statements

This section discusses the conditional statements in KornShell: if and case. This subject also requires some background on the [[condition]] command and the subject of pattern matching, so you'll learn those features here as well, even though they can also be used outside of conditional statements. In addition, arithmetic commands that evaluate mathematical expressions are often used inside of if statements, so that topic is covered here too.

The if Statement

The if statement is used to test conditions and execute code based on the result of the comparison. It has this syntax:

```
if conditional-command-list
then command-list
[ elif command-list
then command-list ]
[ else command-list ]
fi
```

Note that `fi` is `if` spelled backwards. If the *conditional-command-list* returns success (zero), then the *command-list* following the `then` keyword is executed. There may be zero or more `elif` clauses that are a shorthand for a nested combined `else-if`. There may be one `else` clause, which is executed if none of the other conditions succeeds.

Listing 28-19. Examples of the `if` Statement.

```
if grep love file              # A typical if/else statement
then print "found love"
else print "cannot find love"
fi


# An example of multiple elif clauses:

if mount $DEVICE1 /install
then print "Mounted $DEVICE1"
elif mount $DEVICE2 /install
then print "Mounted $DEVICE2"
elif mount $DEVICE3 /install
then print "Mounted $DEVICE3"
else print "Could not mount any devices"
fi


# Using semicolons instead of newlines:

if mycommand ; then print succeeded ; fi

# However, the following does the same thing and reads better:

mycommand && print succeeded
```

Arithmetic Commands as Conditionals

Although any command can be used as the condition in an `if` statement, it is common to use an arithmetic command as the condition. You might recall that an arithmetic command has the form:

```
(( expression ))
```

where there can be no spaces between the double parentheses. The *expression* uses the same syntax as the C language for expressions, and allows all the same operators as the C language. If variables are referenced in the expression, they need not be expanded using `$`. Appendix A contains a complete list of operators and precedence rules.

⟩   Expressions are evaluated using double-precision floating-point math. Floating-point constants follow ANSI-C notation conventions:

$$[+|-]\textit{digits}[.\textit{digits}][\texttt{E}[+|-]\textit{digits}]$$

For example, the following numbers are all the same:

```
3215.4
3.2154E3  # E3 means: "times ten to the third power"
32154E-1  # negative exponents are allowed
```

Some examples of floating-point expressions are presented in Listing 28-20.

Listing 28-20. Examples of Floating-Point Expressions.

```
(( a = r * r * 3.1415926535 ))            # Constants are easy as pi

if (( speed > 2.9E10 ))                    # Scientific notation
then
          print "You're going faster than light, nice trick!"
fi

(( newx = x*radius*cos(theta) ))           # Trig functions supported
```

The arithmetic command evaluates the expression and then returns zero if the expression evaluates to nonzero, and returns one otherwise. This may sound a little confusing, but it's what you want to happen because success in Shell is zero. So, using the arithmetic evaulation command inside an `if` statement does what you would expect—the `then` part is executed if the *expression* evaluates to nonzero. An example of using arithmetic evaluation in an if statement is shown in Listing 28-21.

Listing 28-21. Using Arithmetic with the if Statement.

```
if (( a > b ))                  # Does what you expect
then maximizefunc
elif (( a = b - 4 ))            # Note the assignment within the test
then minimizefunc
elif (( a++ < ball.height ))    # Compound names work too
then return
fi
```

The Test Command [[ ]]

The test command is useful for many kinds of nonarithmetic conditional statements. It takes the form:

```
[[ condition ]]
```

and returns success (zero) if the given condition evaluates to true. It can perform many powerful tests on strings, files, and devices. For historic reasons, it can also perform some arithmetic comparison tests as well.

Here is a list of all the conditions you can check using the test command:

`"string"`	True if *string* is not null.
`-b filename`	True if *filename* exists and is a block special file.
`-c filename`	True if *filename* exists and is a character special file.
`-d filename`	True if *filename* exists and is a directory.
`-e filename`	True if *filename* exists.
`-f filename`	True if *filename* exists and is an ordinary file, i.e., not a directory, device, named pipe, etc.
`-g filename`	True if *filename* exists and has its set group id permission bit set. See the UNIX system chmod(1) manual page.
`-k filename`	True if *filename* exists and has its sticky bit set. See chmod(1).
`-n "string"`	True if *string* is not zero length.
`-o option`	True if KornShell was invoked with the named *option*. For a list of options and their meanings see the explanation for *set* on page 618.
`-p filename`	True if *filename* exists and is a fifo special file (named pipe). See the mknod(1) manual page for more information.
`-r filename`	True if *filename* exists and the current KornShell process has permission to read its contents.
`-s filename`	True if *filename* exists and has a size greater than zero.
`-t filedescriptor`	True if the *filedescriptor* (an integer) is open and is associated with a terminal device. For example, in an interactive KornShell session *filedescriptor* number 0 (`stdin`) is associated with a terminal device, but in a noninteractive session the `stdin` might have been redirected to a file or some other device.

-u *filename*	True if *filename* exists and has its set user id bit set. See chmod(1) for details.
-w *filename*	True if *filename* exists and the current KornShell process has permission to write the file.
-x *filename*	True if *filename* exists and the current KornShell process has permission to execute it (if it's a regular file) or search it (if it's a directory).
-z "*string*"	True if *string* is zero length.
-L *filename*	True if *filename* exists and is a symbolic link. See ln(1) for details.
-O *filename*	True if *filename* exists and the current KornShell process' effective user id is the file's owner.
-G *filename*	True if *filename* exists and the current KornShell process' effective group id is the file's group.
-S *filename*	True if *filename* exists and is a socket device.
file1 -nt *file2*	True if both *file1* and *file2* exist and *file1* is newer than *file2*. This means the last modification time of *file1* is greater than the last modification time of *file2*.
file1 -ot *file2*	Similar to -nt, but *file1* must be older than *file2*.
file1 -ef *file2*	True if *file1* and *file2* both exist and refer to the same file, either because they are linked files or symbolically linked files.
KSH93⟩ *string* == *pattern*	True if *string* matches *pattern*. The syntax for patterns is explained later. You can quote any part of *pattern* if you want an exact string match instead of a pattern match. The use of the C style double equal sign is new in KornShell-93.
string != *pattern*	True if *string* does not match *pattern*.
string1 < *string2*	True if *string1* comes before *string2* when compared on the basis of the ASCII character set values.

string1 > *string2*   True if *string1* comes after *string2* when compared on the basis of the ASCII character set values.

Obsolete Arguments to the Test Command. Because the KornShell strives to maintain compatibility with previous versions of the Shell, certain obsolete constructs are also permitted in the test command. You should not use these constructs in new programs, they are provided here as a reference in case you need to work on an older program. The items below that are numerical in nature should be done using the arithmetic evaluation command: ((*expression*))

-a *filename*   Same as -e option, true if *filename* exists.

string = *pattern*   Same as *string* == *pattern*, true if *string* matches *pattern*.

expression1 -eq *expression2*   True if the mathematical expressions are equal.

expression1 -ne *expression2*   True if the mathematical expressions are not equal.

expression1 -lt *expression2*   True if *expression1* is less than *expression2*.

expression1 -gt *expression2*   True if *expression1* is greater than *expression2*.

expression1 -le *expression2*   True if *expression1* is less than or equal to *expression2*.

expression1 -ge *expression2*   True if *expression1* is greater than or equal to *expression2*.

Combining Test Operators. In addition to these basic operators, you can combine several tests using these notations:

(*operation*)   True if *operation* is true. Used to group operations.

! *operation*   True if *operation* is false. Used to negate an operation.

operation1 && *operation2*   True if both *operation1* and *operation2* are true.

operation1 || *operation2*   True if either *operation1* or *operation2* are true.

Combining Arithmetic and Test Commands

Because arithmetic comparisons are now considered obsolete in the test command, you might be wondering what to do if you want to use both an arithmetic and a string test in the same `if` statement. The solution to this problem is simple once you realize that both the arithmetic and the test statements behave just like any other KornShell command: they can be combined using the command list notations `&&` and `||`.

Listing 28-22. Combining Arithmetic and Test Commands.

```
if [[ -f $DB_LOCKFILE ]] && (( tries++ > 10 ))
then
        print "Sorry, too many attempts to get lock file."
        return
fi


if [[ $status == RETIRED ]] && (( age < 65 ))
then
        print "Employee $name retired early."
fi
```

28.8 The Case Statement

The case statement is used to match a string against one or more patterns. It does not handle arithmetic type conditions. Nonetheless, it is one of the most useful KornShell commands because of the rich pattern matching syntax allowed. First I'll cover the basic case statement, and in the next section we'll look at the subject of pattern matching. The case statement has the following syntax:

```
case string in
pattern[|pattern...])  command-list [ ;; | ;& ]
...
esac
```

Note that `esac` is `case` spelled backwards, and ends the case statement. Also, each *pattern*'s *command-list* is terminated by either a double semicolon (`;;`) or a semi-colon ampersand (`;&`). The double semicolon is the most common way to end the *pattern* clause, and it causes termination of the case statement. The semicolon ampersand is used when you wish to "fall through" so that further patterns are tested.

In its simplest form, the case statement is used to match a string against a number of other strings, executing a *command-list* for the first match. Used in this way, the string must exactly match one of the cases.

Listing 28-23. Simple Use of the Case Statement. The simplest use of the case statement is to exactly match one of several fixed strings.

```
read answer

case "$anser" in
yes)
        print "You have chosen wisely, my child."
        ;;
no)
        print "This could be a problem."
        ;;
esac
```

The case statement allows several patterns to be specified separated by pipe symbols: |. The following modification of the above program will accept more than just "yes" or "no".

Listing 28-24. Multiple Matches with the Case Command.

```
read answer

case "$answer" in
yes|ok|yep)
        print "You have chosen wisely."
        ;;
no|nope|"no way")                          # Note the quotes
        print "This could be a problem."
        ;;
esac
```

In these examples, I've only shown the simplest kind of patterns: those made of a string of alphabetic characters. In this case there must be an exact match of precisely the strings specified. Patterns are much more powerful, however, as you will see in the next section.

Patterns

Three special characters can be used to specify wild-card style matches within a pattern.

*   An asterisk matches any string of any length (including length zero).

?   A question mark matches any single character.

[*string*]   A string enclosed in brackets matches any character within the
                        brackets. In addition, you may match ranges of characters by put-
                        ting a dash between two other characters. For example: [A-Z]
                        matches any capital alphabetic character. You can match any char-
                        acter not listed by making the first character an exclamation mark.
                        For example: [!abc] matches any characters other than a, b, or c .

Also, using the [*string*] form, you can match certain classes of characters by
using the notation [[:*class*:]]. The allowed character class names are listed in
the following table.

Table 28-1. **Character Class Patterns**

Class	Explanation
[[:alnum:]]	Alphabetic or numeric, same as [A-Za-z0-9]
[[:alpha:]]	Aphabetic, same as [A-Za-z]
[[:cntrl:]]	Control characters
[[:digit:]]	Decimal digits, same as [0-9]
[[:graph:]]	Graphic characters
[[:lower:]]	Lower case characters, same as [a-z]
[[:print:]]	Printable characters: alphabetic, numeric, punctuation marks, etc. Does not include space, tab, or newline.
[[:punct:]]	Punctuation marks
[[:space:]]	Space, tab, and newlines
[[:upper:[]	Upper case characters, same as [A-Z]
[[:xdigit:]]	Hexidecimal digit, same as [0-9a-fA-F]

KSH93

Listing 28-25 shows some typical uses of these pattern sequences in a case statement. Patterns can be used in other places besides case statements, such as in filename matching.

Listing 28-25. **Using Patterns With the Case Statement.**

```
read answer

case "$answer" in
[Yy]*)                  # This would match any string beginning with
```

```
              A=YES       # an uppercase or lowercase y
              ;;
   [Nn]*)                 # Similary, any string beginning with N or n
              A=NO
              ;;
   [Ww][Hh]?)             # This matches things like who, why, Who, etc.
              A=QUESTION
              ;;
   [[:digit:]]*)          # Matches a digit followed by any other characters
              A=NUMBER
              ;;
esac
```

These basic patterns, built using the *, ?, and [...] notations, can be combined by using one of the following special pattern grouping statements. In the following explanations a *pattern-list* is one or more patterns separated by pipe symbols:

?(*pattern-list*)   Matches zero or one of the patterns.

@(*pattern-list*)   Matches exactly one of the given patterns. This is very similar to the previous pattern notation, but that one allows the empty string to match while this one does not.

*(*pattern-list*)   Matches zero or more of the patterns.

+(*pattern-list*)   Matches one or more of the patterns.

!(*pattern-list*)   Matches anything other than one of the patterns.

Table 28-2 gives examples of these kinds of pattern matches to give you a feel for how they can be used effectively.

Table 28-2. Examples of Pattern Matching

Pattern	Matches	Does Not Match
file?(.c|.o|.a)	file, file.c, file.o, file.a	Anything else.
file@(.c|.o|.a)	file.c, file.o, file.a	file, or anything else.

Table 28-2. Examples of Pattern Matching (continued)

Pattern	Matches	Does Not Match
`*(a|b)`	The empty string, `a,aa,aaa, etc.` `b,bb,bbb, etc.` `ab,ba,abb,aba, aab,baa,` etc.	Anything other than a string composed of any number of a's and b's.
`+([[:digit:]])`	any integer (a string composed only of the characters 0 through 9)	The empty string, or any string containing a non-numeric character.
`+([[:digit:]])?(.+([[:digit:]]))`	`1, 2, 33, 99, 456,` etc. `1.9, 12.7, 18.12, 3.14159,` etc. A number with optional decimal point and digits.	If there is a decimal point there must be one or more digits, so something like "1." would not match. Also, the empty string won't match.
`*(cat??|dog??)`	the empty string, `cater, catic, catcc,` etc. `dog, dog99, dogey,` etc. `caterdogme, catXX-catYY, dog99dog87, doggydoggycatty,` etc.	The string must be composed of sequences of the word `cat` or `dog` followed by any two arbitrary characters.
`!(*intro*|*index*)`	Any string that contains neither the string "intro" nor "index" anywhere within it.	Any string containing "intro" or "index".

Table 28-2. Examples of Pattern Matching (continued)

Pattern	Matches	Does Not Match
`+(*([[:print:]]):)`	Any string composed of fields of printable characters separated by colons, like: alpha:beta:gamma:delta: Note that there can be zero print able characters in a field.	As written, the match would fail if there was no trailing colon, so this would not match: alpha:beta:gamma:delta Also note that "print-able character" does not include spaces or tabs.

28.9 Looping Statements

This section discusses the shell looping constructs `for`, `while`, and `until`. There is another looping statement in KornShell called `select`, but that statement is useless in graphical programming so it is not covered here.

There is no `goto` statement in shell language, you must use one of the looping constructs shown here.

The `for` Statement (List Type)

The `for` statement takes two different forms in KornShell-93. The type that is discussed in this section is the traditional list processing form; the next section discusses the new arithmetic `for` loop. The list processing `for` loop has the following syntax:

```
for variable [in string-list]
do
        statement-list
done
```

Where *string-list* is a set of zero or more strings, *variable* is the name of a shell variable, and *statement-list* is a set of one or more KornShell commands. The *statement-list* is executed once for every item in the *string-list*, and *variable* takes on the given string value on each iteration. If the *string-list* is omitted, then the positional parameter list is used (i.e., omitting the *string-list* is equivalent to using "`$@`" to generate the string-list).

The `for` Statement (C-Style)

The arithmetic, or C style, `for` loop is new in KornShell-93. It takes the form:

```
for (( init-expr ; condition-expr; increment-expr ))
do
        command-list
done
```

Note the use of double parentheses instead of a single parenthesis as in the C language. This statement first evaluates the *init-expression*. Then, as long as the *condition-expression* evaluates to a nonzero value, the *command-list* is executed. After each execution of the *command-list*, the *increment-expression* is evaluated. In effect, the arithmetic for loop is roughly equivalent to the following while loop and arithmetic evaluation statements:

> Actually, the while loop shown is not quite equivalent if the *command-list* contains a continue statement, because in the case of the for loop a continue would execute the *increment-statement* again.

```
(( init-expr ))
while (( condition-expr ))
do
        command-list
        (( increment-expr ))
done
```

Listing 28-26. A C-Style for Statement. This example will print the numbers 0 through 9. Note the double parentheses.

```
for (( i = 0; i < 10; i++ ))
do
        print "$i"
done
```

28.10 Redirection After Compound Commands

The compound commands (if, case, for, while, and select) are just like any other commands. As such, they return a value (zero for success, nonzero for failure) and their file descriptors can be redirected. Any redirections should typically be placed after the terminating keyword of the compound command (after the fi, esac, or done).

Listing 28-27. Redirection of Compound Commands. When file redirection commands are placed after the closing part of a looping or conditional command (i.e., after the fi, esac, or done) they apply to the output of all commands within the compound command.

```
if (( A > B ))
then
        print "A is greater than B"
```

```
              sed -e "s/$A/$B/" $inputfile
fi > $outputfile

# In the next example, the output of a for loop is piped into an if

for file in receivable payable
do
              sort $file
done  |       if [[ "$DEBUGMODE ]]
              then tee tracefile
              fi
```

28.11 Functions

Functions are used to create reusable routines. They may include their own positional parameters, and it is also possible to create local variables in functions that
do not overwrite global variables with the same names. Functions can return values by any of several methods. It is also possible to set up reusable files of functions
that get pulled into your script automatically the first time they are referenced.

Defining Functions

For historical reasons, there are two different ways to define functions in Korn-
Shell:

```
function func-name {
          command-list
}
```

and

```
func-name() {
          command-list
}
```

These two ways of defining functions are equivalent except for one important point:
the first form (using the function keyword) allows you to declare local variables
using the typeset command, while the second form (using parentheses after the
function name) does not. The second form is the strict POSIX conforming style of
function declaration.

KSH93

Local variables are declared in the function using the typeset command. Any
variable declared using typeset in a function defined using the function keyword
will not modify a global variable that uses the same name. This is important for
writing robust programs, so I highly recommend using the function keyword method of defining functions.

KornShell variables are dynamically scoped. This is quite different from the scoping rules of the C language, which uses lexical scoping. This means that if you create a local variable in one function, then that variable is local to both the current function and all functions called from the first function. Listing 28-28 illustrates dynamic scoping.

Listing 28-28. Dynamic Variable Scope. A global version of X is initialized to 15. The function outer defines a local version of X and sets it to 0. The call to inner from there will pick up the version of X that is local to function outer. If function inner is called directly, the global version of X is accessed. This is different from languages like C in which function inner would have picked up the global version of X in both cases.

```
X=15

function outer {
        typeset X=0          # X is local to function outer

        inner
}

function inner {
        print $X
}

outer                   # Prints: 0

inner                   # Prints: 15
```

Returning Values from Functions

Functions can return an integer value from 0 to 255. This is accomplished using the return statement:

```
return [ number ]
```

If the optional number is not given, then the return code from the last statement that executed is returned. Because of the limited range of values available with the return statement, it is really only useful for communicating error conditions, or perhaps a boolean (true or false) value. Recall that in shell programming zero is the success or true return code, while any nonzero value is failure or false.

If you want to create a function that returns a more complex value, there are two alternatives:

1. Print the value to the function's standard output, and call the function using command substitution: $(funcname). This method is good for situations

where the function returns a single value. An example is shown in Listing 28-29.

2. Use name reference variables, making one or more of the function's parameters the name of a variable that will receive the output by reference. This is similar to passing a pointer to a variable in the C language, then allowing the function to modify the passed-in variable. An example of this method is shown in Listing 28-30.

Listing 28-29. Returning Values by Printing. When there is a single value to return from a function, an effective strategy is to print the value to the standard output and call the function using command substitution.

```
function cube {        # Print the cube of $1 to the standard output
        print $(( $1 * $1 * $1 ))
}

Result=$(cube 20)      # Result will be set to 8000
```

Listing 28-30. Returning Values in `nameref` Variables. When there are multiple return values from a function, the most effective strategy is to return them by passing variable names to the function and using the `nameref` feature. This is similar to passing pointers to variables in the C language.

```
# This function takes 4 arguments: a number and 3 variable names.
# Successive powers of the number are computed and returned by storing
# them in the variables.
function powers {
        float n=$1          # this is done for readability
        nameref p2=$2 p3=$3 p4=$4

        (( p2 = n * n ))
        (( p3 = p2 * n ))
        (( p4 = p3 * n ))
}

powers 3 A B C

print "$A $B $C"       # Prints: 9 27 243
```

Keeping Functions in Separate Files

Functions are often used to create reusable pieces of code that perform general-purpose operations. If you create a number of functions that are general-purpose, you don't necessarily want to copy the same function text into each program. It would be better to keep the general-purpose functions in common files that are referenced by all your other programs. There are two ways to accomplish this in Korn-Shell:

1. Use the "dot" command to pull in your files with general-purpose functions.

2. Use the "autoload" feature. The environment variable FPATH can be set to a colon (:) separated list of directory names. Whenever an unknown function is referenced in your KornShell script, this path will be searched for a file with the same name as the unknown function. If such a file is found, then it is read (in its entirety). The file should include a definition of the function, and thus the function will be defined after the file is read. Then, the function is executed.

Use of Typeset with Functions

The typeset command has several features that apply to function names:

typeset -f *funcname*	Print the definition of *funcname*. If *funcname* is not given, print the names and definitions of all functions.
typeset -ft *funcname*	Turn on debugging mode for the named function. This prints a trace to standard error of all lines in the named function as they execute (with values expanded). Using +ft instead of -ft turns off debugging again.
typeset -fx *funcname*	Exports the named function to child processes of the shell.
typeset -fu *funcname*	Causes the shell to search through the FPATH variable for the function name.

28.12 Aliases

Aliases give the programmer a simple way to create shorthand names for commonly needed commands. Aliases are defined using the alias command:

```
alias name=substitution ...
```

This defines *name* as an alias that will expand to *substitution* if it is detected as the first word of a command. If the substitution string ends in a blank, then the following word of the command will also be scanned to see if it matches any alias name.

A common mistake made by novice KornShell programmers is to think that an alias can be used to process arguments. This is not possible; an alias is purely a way to make a simple substitution at the beginning of a command string. If you need to do some kind of argument processing, you need to use a function.

There are two main reasons to define aliases: a shorthand to save typing in interactive shell use, and for readability in programs.

Listing 28-31. Typical Uses of Aliases.

```
alias ll="ls -l"
alias m=mailx
alias rightjust10="typeset -R10"

ll /tmp                          # does a long listing of /tmp
rightjust10 MESSAGE              # declares MESSAGE to be right justified

alias ll2='ls -l $1 $2'          # Common mistake!  Can't reference
                                 # parameters or do arg processing.
```

You can remove a previously defined alias using the `unalias` command:

```
unalias name ...
```

KornShell defines a number of aliases automatically. You've seen some of these in this chapter already: `integer`, `float`, `nameref` and `readonly` are all aliases for various options on the `typeset` command. They are examples of aliases being used to improve readability. You are allowed to `unalias` these automatically provided aliases, but I strongly recommend you don't do it, because it might confuse someone trying to understand your code (maybe even you!).

28.13 Other Built-in Commands

In this section, I cover some built-in commands that were not mentioned in previous sections. I'm not going to discuss every built-in command, just some that are a little tricky to use and are commonly found in KornShell programs. I also do not necessarily detail every last option of the built-in commands discussed here, just the most commonly used ones. There is a complete list of built-in commands with information on their options and usage in Chapter 31, *KornShell Command Reference*.

eval

The `eval` command takes its arguments, expands them, and runs the KornShell interpreter on the resulting string. In other words, you can create a command line and then execute it using the KornShell interpreter. In effect, you can write code that writes and executes code. This can be used in some situations to perform complex tasks in only a few lines of code. One thing you have to be careful about is quoting the string carefully. You often have to quote your quotation marks to make things work.

read

The `read` command can be used in line-oriented shell scripts to get input from the user. It can also be used to read lines from files, and can do some rudimentary parsing of lines of text. The most typical use of `read` has the following usage (this is not a complete usage for `read`, see Chapter 31, *KornShell Command Reference* for exhaustive details):

```
read [ -t timeout ] variable [ variable ... ]
```

With this usage, `read` gets one line from its standard input and breaks it into fields based on the characters in the `IFS` (internal field separator) variable. The `IFS` variable defaults to space and tab characters. Each field delimited by one of those characters is placed in the given environment variable names. The last variable name gets all remaining fields.

KSH93⟩

The `-t` option can be used to set a timeout value, in seconds (decimals allowed) for the `read` to complete.

In addition, `read` can be made to store each field in an array variable by using this form of the command:

```
read -A arrayname
```

By redefining the `IFS` variable, it is possible to do some simple parsing of files that consist of lines of text delimited by some character. If you use this technique be very sure you restore `IFS` to its orginal value after you're finished! A good way to do this is to perform the parsing inside a function and declare IFS as a local variable using the `typeset` command. An example is shown in Listing 28-32.

Listing 28-32. Parsing Files Using Read. This example shows how you can efficiently parse files whose lines are delimited by a certain character by redefining IFS and using the read command. It redefines IFS to be the colon character, which is used by the password file to delimit fields. It also illustrates using the -A option of read to parse fields into an array.

```
function PrintUserList {
        typeset IFS              # Make IFS local (avoids problems)
        typeset fields
        IFS=:
        while read -A fields  # Break up line into array
        do
                print "LOGIN=${fields[0]}"
                print "USERID=${fileds[1]}"
                print "GROUP=${fields[2]}"
        done < /etc/passwd
}
```

28.14 Summary

KornShell-93 provides a powerful command language. It is backward compatible with the Bourne Shell but has many useful extensions such as floating-point math, array variables, associative arrays, hierarchical variable names, many new built-in commands, and expanded pattern matching.

29 *KornShell Style Guide*

29.1 Introduction

This chapter outlines a set of recommended coding practices for KornShell and Desktop KornShell programs. Consistent coding style improves readability and reduces errors.

This chapter is included as a set of recommendations, and if you don't like some of them then by all means change whatever you see fit, or add more guidelines if that is appropriate. But whatever you decide for your coding style, be sure to write it down, especially for large projects involving multiple programmers. You will reap many benefits in terms of readability and avoiding errors by following a consistent style.

29.2 Comment Conventions

There are two styles of comments: block comments and in-line comments. Block comments are used to describe extensive information; in-line comments are for short pieces of information.

Block comments are indented to the same level as the code they comment. They begin with a sharp symbol (#) on a line by itself, followed by lines beginning with pound symbols containing commentary text, and end with another pound symbol on a line by itself.

Listing 29-1. Block Comment Format.

```
#
# Simulate a non-elastic bounce by subtracting the friction
# factor from the rebound velocity on each iteration
#
```

In-line comments only apply to a single line of code, and they appear following that code on the same line. There should be at least one tab between the end of the code and the sharp symbol associated with the in-line comment. If several in-line comments appear on successive lines, they should be aligned using additional tab characters.

Listing 29-2. In-Line Comment Format.

```
Velocity=Velocity*Friction                  # Reduce velocity
if (( Velocity < MinVelocity ))             # Too slow, game over
then
            return $GAMEOVER
fi
```

29.3 Sections of the Program

A program should be divided into the following sections, in this order:

- Copyright comment
- Source code control comment
- File contents comment
- Included files
- Global variables
- Functions
- Main line code

These sections are explained in more detail in the following sections.

Copyright Comment (Optional)

If applicable to your project, a copyright notice should appear in block comment style as the first section of the program.

Listing 29-3. Copyright Comment Format.

```
# Copyright (C) 1995 Addison-Wesley, Inc.
# All rights reserved in the United States and other countries.
```

Source Control Comment (Optional)

If applicable to your project, an identifier string used by your project's source code control system should appear next. For example, this is an SCCS style comment:

```
#ident "%W%"
```

File Contents Description Comment

A block comment describing the content of this source file. May also describe usage and option information, notable constraints on the use of the program, etc.

Listing 29-4. File Contents Comment Format.

```
# ammort.sh - a loan ammortization program
# usage:  ammort [principle interest-rate months]
#
# Brings up a screen to calculate loan payments.  The optional
# command arguments set defaults for the fields.  If not given,
# the file $HOME/.ammortdefs is used to set defaults, if it
# exists, otherwise the fields are left blank.
```

Included Files

All files that are included via the dot (.) operator come next. Such files should not usually be included using absolute hard-coded paths, but rather should be relative to a project-defined directory. A short in-line comment explaining the contents of the included file may be added if appropriate.

Listing 29-5. The Included Files Section.

```
. $(PROJECTDIR)/$LANG/strings.sh        # message catalog
. $(PROJECTDIR)/genfuncs.sh             # general functions
. $(PROJECTDIR)/dbfuncts.sh             # database functions
```

Global Variables

All global variables used in the file should be defined here using `typeset` (or its aliases, `integer`, `float`, etc.). Variables should be initialized if that makes sense. Short comments explaining the use of the global should be present. Globals should be kept to a minimum.

Listing 29-6. Global Variable Definitions.

```
float Velocity=0.0            # Velocity in pixels/second
integer Numtries=0           # Number of times player has crashed
typeset Username=$LOGNAME     # Name of the player
```

Functions

Functions used in the file should be defined next. Function formatting is discussed later.

Main Line Code (Optional)

The main body of code comes last. A block comment should precede the main line. Shell files that contain only function definitions to be used by other shell files may not have a main line section.

29.4 Function Layout

A function is laid out in well-defined sections, in the following order:
- Function purpose comment
- Function definition
- Local variable declarations
- Function body

Function Purpose Comment

Before the function definition, there should be a block comment describing the purpose of the function, arguments expected and usage, global variables modified and side effects (if any), and return codes.

Listing 29-7. Function Purpose Comment Format.

```
#
# Usage: tower numrings source dest using
#
# Compute a solution to the towers of Hanoi problem.   Arguments:
#          numrings: the number of rings to transfer
#          source:   the index of the source tower (1 to 3)
#          dest:     the index of the destination tower (1 to 3)
#          using:    the index of the tower to use for intermediate
#                    transfers (1 to 3)
# Output:
#          prints the solution to standard output
# Side effects:
#          sets the global NumMoves to the number of moves
#          required for the solution.
# Return Codes:
#          0 for success, 1 if arguments are of wrong type
```

This comment is more important for functions that are used as library routines for projects. For small, single-use subroutines used as a subpart of another function, a less elaborate comment is allowable, which simply lists the usage parameters following the function's definition after a comment mark. (See Listing 29-8.)

Listing 29-8. Simplified Function Usage Comment. For simple functions or those used only within a source file, it is allowable to use a simplified comment following the `func-tion` declaration that lists arguments.

```
function showmessage {  #  widget string
    XUset $1 labelString:"$2"
    XUbell
}
```

Function Definition

The function definition comes next. There are two ways to define a function in KornShell. One way is to use the keyword `function` followed by the function name, and the other is to follow the name of the function by parentheses: `name()`. In both cases the function body follows the declaration enclosed in curly braces.

Almost without exception it is better to use the `function name` format rather than the `name()` format for declaring a function. This is because the latter does not allow local variables as defined by the POSIX shell standard.

Listing 29-9. Alternate Function Definition Syntaxes. The first form, using the `function` keyword, is preferable because it allows local variables.

```
function first {
        print "first style of function declaration"
}

second() {
        print "second style of function declaration"
}
```

The opening curly brace should be on the same line as the function definition. The keyword `function` should be in column zero. Local variables used in the function should appear next, with in-line comments explaining the variable usage. The closing curly brace of the function should be on a line by itself in column zero. Arguments to the function that are of a fixed-position nature should be given meaningful names using `typeset` as the first local variables. This does not apply to variable arguments that are processed using shift, however. Variables should always be typeset to the appropriate type according to their intended use. Aliases provided for common `typeset` commands should be used for readability: `integer`, `float`.

The body of the code within the function should be indented one tab.

Listing 29-10. Function Format and Indentation.

```
function tower {
        integer num=$1
        typeset source=$2 dest=$3 using=$3
```

```
          if (( $1 == 1 ))
          then
                  print "$source $dest"
          else
                  tower $((num-1)) $source $using $dest
                  print "$source $dest"
                  tower $((num-1)) $using $dest $source
          fi
  }
```

29.5 Variable Naming Conventions

Variable names should be carefully chosen to aid in readability. Choose descriptive names that show the use of the variable. Short, cryptic variable names are discouraged. Exception: simple loop counters may be named with the traditional single-letter values: i, j, k, n, etc.

Global variables should begin with an uppercase letter. Local variables should be all lowercase. All global variables in a program should start with one of several unique prefixes defined by the application. All global variables should be declared near the start of the application using the typeset command or its aliases: float and integer. Some people follow the convention that exported variables should be all uppercase, while global unexported variables should be initial upper case followed by lower case letters, I leave that as an optional convention.

Whenever possible, variables used inside of functions should be made local by using the typeset command. Whenever possible, the variable should be declared using typeset to an appropriate type such as integer, float, etc.

Listing 29-11. Variable Names.

```
  float Xvelocity Yvelocity        # Global, begins with uppercase

  function accelerate {
          nameref x=$1 y=$2    # Local, lowercase
  etc....
```

Function Naming Conventions

Function names should be all lowercase. Exception: functions used as callbacks to widgets in graphical programs should end in the letters CB to indicate they are callbacks. Also, if your project has other specific naming conventions, document them as an addendum to this style guide and use them consistently.

Alternate convention: For graphical programs, the X Window convention of using mixed case with capital letters on the beginning of each "word" and using no underlines is acceptable.

For project-wide general-purpose functions, a unique prefix should start function names to minimize name space pollution.

29.6 Indentation

Indentation should, with few exceptions, be carried out using only the tab character, never spaces. Features of certain editors to redefine the number of blanks used to display a tab may be used—a common convention is to use 4 character tabs. If a tab stop is something other than 8 characters, a comment should appear near the beginning of the source file indicating the preferred tab settings.

If Statements

The then, else, elif, and fi components should be on lines by themselves, indented to the same level as the if. The code contained in the conditional should be indented one additional tab level. Exception: if the then and else clauses have exactly one statement associated with them, it is permissible to put that statement on the same line as the then or else..

Listing 29-12. The if Statement Format.

```
if (( a > b ))
then
		c=a-b
		(( a++ ))
else
		c=b-a
		(( a-- ))
fi

if [[ -d $Tmpdir ]]
then mv $file $Tmpdir
else mv $file /tmp
fi
```

For and while Loops

The do and done keywords should be on lines by themselves, indented to the same level as the for or while keywords. The body of the loop should be indented on additional level. In C-style for loops, there should be one space after each semicolon separator and no space before the semicolons.

Listing 29-13. The for and while Statement Format.

```
for name in $Allnames
do
		let count++
```

```
done

for (( i=0; i < Numentries; i++ ))
do
            addtodatabase "${Entry[i]}"
done

while (( maxtries-- > 0 ))
do
            sendmessage && break
done
```

Case Statement

The esac and patterns should be indented to the same level as the case keyword. The actions associated with each pattern, and the closing double semicolon (;;), should be indented one additional TAB level. The esac keyword and each pattern should be on a line by themselves.

Exception: if there is only one simple command for each pattern, it is acceptable to put the commands and double semicolons on the same line as the pattern, indented so they line up.

Listing 29-14. The case Statement Formats.

```
case "$animal" in
horse)
            let Count[horse]++
            print "neigh"
            ;;
cow)
            let Count[cow]++
            print "moo"
            ;;
esac

case "$file" in
*.sh)       print "Shell Script" ;;
*.c)        print "C Source File" ;;
*.o)        print "Object File" ;;
*.s)        print "Assembler File" ;;
*.a)        print "Archive File" ;;
esac
```

Indentation of Long Pipelines or Lists

Long pipelines or command lists can be indented by breaking the line after one of the pipe symbols and indenting the next item in the pipe one tab. This applies to the || and && operators as well as the regular pipe. This also applies to pipeline elements that are looping constructs such as for or while loops.

Listing 29-15. Long Pipeline Format.

```
getdata "$file" "$options" |
        sed -e "s/$string1/$replacement/" |
        while read field1 field2 rest
        do
                print "$field2"
        done
```

A command list which includes a set of commands grouped using the curly brace ({}) statement should place the open curly brace after the command list symbol with a newline after it. The close curly brace should be on a line by itself indented to the same level as the beginning of the command list.

Listing 29-16. Command List Followed by Grouped Commands.

```
initialize || {
        XUwarning "Could not Initialize"
        FailureFlag=true
        return 1
}
```

29.7 Quoting Conventions

Quoting is very important in shell programming. Many subtle errors are often caused by quoting problems.

Always quote any string in your program that is used as a command line argument, whether it strictly needs quotes or not. Use single quotes whenever you need to turn off the special meaning of all characters. Use double quotes when you need variable or command expansion, or by default if there are no special characters. In some cases you explicitly need to avoid using quotes. In this case, make sure there is a block or in-line comment indicating that this was not an oversight.

Listing 29-17. Quoting Command Arguments. It is best to quote command line arguments even if they contain no whitespace or metacharacters, because you might later edit the string and introduce metacharacters but forget to add the quotation marks, leading to subtle errors. Use single quotes to turn off special meaning of the $ character.

```
addrecord "$(getfirstname)" "(getlastname)" "$(getoccupation)"
addrecord "John" "Doe" "Dtksh Programmer"
addrecord "Jane" "Van Decamp" 'Currancy Analyst ($)'
```

```
recordnames $Allnames              # Leaving off quotes on purpose!
```

Exceptions: it is not necessary to quote simple variable renaming assignments, or such assignments in the typeset command, and it is not necessary to quote simple expansions in the test operator ([[ ]]).

Listing 29-18. Exceptions to Quoting Arguments. Some commands like typeset (and its aliases) and the test operator work faster if expansions are not quoted.

```
typeset firstname=$1 lastname=$2
integer age=$3
nameref returnvar=$4
if [[ $firstname == 'John' -a $lastname == 'Doe' ]]
then
            middlename=$(getmiddle "$firstname" "$lastname")
            print "Found $firstname $middlename $lastname"
fi
```

X Conventions

Because of long command names and commands that can take many arguments, some special formatting situations occur frequently in dtksh scripts.

Widget Creation Commands

The widget creation commands (XmCreate*, XtCreateManagedWidget, XtCreatePopupShell, the XU creation functions, etc.) should be formatted by placing all trailing resource setting arguments on lines by themselves, using back-slash characters as appropriate to break the command across lines. Each resource setting argument should be indented one tab level more than the creation command keyword's indentation level.

By convention, the widget name parameter should be the same as the variable name that will receive the widget handle, unless the programmer has a reason for a different name (such as convenience in resource file definitions). If the widget handle is not needed, use a variable name like tmp defined as a local variable.

Listing 29-19. Breaking Widget Creation Command Lines.

```
XUlabel LAB2 $FORM \
            labelString:"Enter Age:" \
            alignment:ALIGNMENT_BEGINNING \
            $(XUunder $LAB1)

typeset tmp              # local variable used for "don't care" widgets
```

```
XmCreatePushButton tmp $MENUBAR tmp \
            labelString:"Push Me"
```

29.8 Summary

A complete set of suggested KornShell and dtksh programming style conventions were outlined in this chapter.

- Consistent programming style aids readability and reduces errors, especially when multiple programmers are involved in a project.

- You can pick and choose which of these suggestions you wish to use, but be sure to write down your conventions and stick to them.

- The most important conventions are the ones concerning variable and function naming, using care when quoting strings, and use of descriptive comments.

30 *KornShell Editing Reference*

30.1 Introduction

This chapter contains a summary of KornShell editing features. These features are exclusively for interactive shell use.

Two editing modes are available: emacs and vi. These modes are selected by setting the VISUAL or EDITOR variables to strings ending in either gmacs, emacs, or vi. There are also options on the set command that will select the editing mode.

The editing modes assume the terminal line is 80 characters wide, unless the variable COLUMNS is defined. If a command is too long to fit in the allotted space, markers appear at the beginning and/or end of the line to show that there is more text. The beginning of line marker is the close angle bracket (<), the end line marker is open angle bracket (>). If there is unseen text at both the beginning and end of the line, an asterisk (*) appears in both places.

30.2 Emacs Editing Commands

This mode simulates commands of the emacs or gmacs editors. It is entered by either using the set command:

```
set -o emacs
```

or

```
set -o gmacs
```

or by setting the VISUAL or EDITOR variables to the string emacs or gmacs.

There is only one difference between emacs and gmacs mode: how they handle the CTL-T command (see below). In the remainder of this section, the word emacs will be used to mean emacs or gmacs mode unless otherwise noted.

In `emacs` mode editing the user is always in insert mode. All commands are either control characters or characters preceded by the ESCAPE key. Editing is completed and the command is executed when the ENTER (or RETURN) key is pressed.

In the descriptions below, the notation `CTL-X` means depress the CONTROL key and the character X at the same time. The notation `ESC-X` means depress the ESCAPE key, release it, and then depress the character X. Note that the SHIFT key is not used in these operations, the commands given are written in uppercase for readability.

Repeat Count

ESC-*digits*	Define a numeric parameter. The *digits* are interpreted as a decimal number, and the following nondecimal character or command is repeated that many times. The numeric parameter is honored on most commands. For example, to delete 11 words use: ESC-11 ESC-D. To move forward 7 words use ESC-7 ESC-F. In some cases this count is used for purposes other than repetition, which will be noted below.
CTL-U	Multiply the repeat count of the next command by a factor of 4. For example, to move forward 4 words use CTL-U ESC-F. To delete 16 words use CTL-U CTL-U ESC-D. This is a handy way to operate on a larger unit of text without typing multiple characters as is necessary with ESC-digits.

Command Execution

CTL-J	(NEWLINE) Execute current line.
CTL-M	(ENTER or RETURN) Execute the current line.

Motion

CTL-F	Forward one character.
ESC-F	Forward one word.
CTL-B	Backward one character.
ESC-B	Backward 1 word.
CTL-A	Start of line.
CTL-E	End of line.
CTL-] *char*	Forward to character *char* on current line, if it exists.

ESC-] *char*   Backward to character *char* on current line, if it exists.

Deletion

CTL-H	Delete previous character. Note: this assumes the user's erase character (as set by stty) is CTL-H. Otherwise, whatever character is defined as the erase character will delete the previous character.
CTL-D	Delete current character.
ESC-D	Delete current word.
ESC-CTL-H	Delete previous word.
ESC-DEL	Delete previous word. NOTE: if the user's interrupt character (as set by stty) is CTL-? or DEL, then this command is not available.
CTL-K	Delete from cursor to end of line. This may be preceded by a numerical parameter (see below), in which case the deletion occurs between the cursor and the character position specified by the number. The position may be either before or after the current cursor position.
CTL-W	Delete from the cursor to the mark (see Mark Commands below).
@	Delete the whole line. NOTE: this assumes the user's kill character (as set by stty) is @. Otherwise, whatever character is defined as the kill character will delete the line.
CTL-Y	Restore (yank) the last item deleted from the line.
CTL-R string	Search backward in the history file for the *string*. The string is terminated by an ENTER (RETURN, or NEWLINE) character. If it begins with a caret (^) then the string must match the leading part of a command. If the string is omitted, then the last string from a previous invocation of this command is used. A numeric parameter of 0 may be used to search forward instead of backward. For example, to search forward for a command beginning with the letter "c" use: ESC-0 CTL-R ^c ENTER.
CTL-T	Character transposition. In emacs mode: transpose the current character and the following character. In gmacs mode, transpose the two characters before the cursor.

Mark

`CTL-@`	Set the mark. The mark is used by some other commands as a second position in the text besides the cursor. Note: some terminals cannot transmit this character (the NULL character), so you must use ESC-SPACE instead.
`ESC-SPACE`	Set the mark.
`ESC-P`	Put the region from the cursor to the mark in the deletion buffer.
`CTL-X CTL-X`	Exchange the cursor and the mark.

Command History

`CTL-P`	Move back one command in the history file.
`CTL-N`	Move forward one command in the history file.
`ESC-<`	Move to the oldest command in the history file.
`ESC->`	Move to the most recent command in the history file.
`CTL-O`	(Operate) Execute the current line and fetch the line after the current line in the history file. This is useful for quickly executing a sequence of commands from the history file.

Expansion and Completion

`ESC-.`	(ESC-period) The last word of the previous command is inserted at the cursor position. This is often useful if you are operating on a certain file and the filename is the last word on a command. A numeric parameter can be used to specify a particular word to insert (where the number 1 represents the first word of the line, 2 the second, etc.)
`ESC-_`	Same as ESC-. (ESC-period).
`ESC-*`	Filename generation is attempted on the current word. This will take the current word, which can contain pattern metacharacters such as asterisk (*), and expands it into all filename matches. If there is no match and the word does not contain any pattern characters, this just appends an asterisk (*) to the word.

ESC-=   Command or filename completion is attempted on the current word. If the current word is the first word on a line, or the first word following a command metacharacter (semi-colon, pipe, ampersand, or open parenthesis), then this searches for a command, function, or alias whose leading characters match the current word. If a unique match exists, it is expanded. If the cursor is not on a word that could be a command name, the current word is used as a partial match for a filename, and if a unique match exists, the full filename is substituted.

Aliases

ESC-*letter*   The *letter* must not conflict with any of the other commands described here. The user's alias list is searched for an alias named *_letter* (an underscore followed by the *letter*). The definition string of that alias is inserted on the input queue. In other words, the alias definition can contain any emacs commands, or plain characters, and they will be interpreted as if typed from the keyboard.

ESC-[*letter*   Like ESC-letter above, but more handy for programming function keys since many terminals will transmit ESC-[as the beginning sequence of a function key.

30.3 Miscellaneous

CTL-L   Issue a linefeed and repaint the current line. Useful when line noise corrupts the output stream.

CTL-V   Print the version number of the shell.

\   (backslash) Escape the next character from special meaning to emacs editing mode.

ESC-#   If the current line does not begin with a pound sign (#), then insert a pound sign in front of each line of the command and execute it. In effect, this places the command in the history file as a comment. If the line begins with a pound sign, delete all pound signs from the beginning of each line of the command.

CTL-C   Capitalize the current character and move to the next character.

ESC-C	Capitalize the current word and move to the next word.
ESC-L	Lowercase the current word and move to the next word.

30.4 Vi Editing Commands

This mode simulates commands of the vi editor. It is entered by either using the set command:

```
set -o vi
```

or by setting the VISUAL or EDITOR variables to the string vi.

Unlike emacs, vi has two modes: insert and control. When you first enter a command, the insert mode is active. In this mode, characters are inserted as they are typed at the current cursor position. To edit the line, control mode must be entered by typing ESCAPE. When in control mode, the edit mode commands described below can be used to move and edit the line. Insert mode can be entered again by typing ESCAPE a second time. A few commands are also available in input mode, as noted later.

Some terminals require the viraw option to function properly. If you are having trouble editing in vi mode, try executing:

```
set -o viraw
```

In the following discussion, the notation CTL-X denotes depressing the CONTROL key simultaneously with key X. Case does not matter when using the CONTROL key. However, most commands in vi mode do not require the CONTROL key, and case is significant in those commands.

Input Mode Commands

CTL-H	Delete the previous character. Note: this assumes the user's erase character (as set by the stty command) is BACKSPACE. Otherwise, delete is performed by whatever character is defined as the erase character.
CTL-W	Delete the previous word. A word is defined as a sequence of characters that does not contain a SPACE, TAB, or NEWLINE.
CTL-D	Terminate the shell (unless ignoreeof mode is enabled).
CTL-V	Escape the next character. Allows the user to enter editing characters, erase, and kill characters during input mode or when entering a search string.
ESC	Exit input mode, start edit mode.

CTL-M   (ENTER or RETURN) Execute the command.
The rest of the vi editing commands are only available in edit mode.

Repeat Count

digits	In command mode, any *digits* that are typed form a repeat count that will apply to the following command. Most vi commands accept this repeat count. For example, typing 4dw will delete four words.

Motion

l	Forward one character.
w	Forward one word (a sequence of letters or digits, not counting blanks or punctuation).
W	Forward to the first word that follows a blank.
e	Forward to the end of the current word.
E	Forward to the end of the next word that is delimited by blanks.
h	Backward one character.
b	Backward one word.
B	Backward to preceding blank-separated word.
|	The current repeat count is interpreted as a column number, and the cursor is placed at that position on the line.
f *char*	Move forward to the character *char* in the current line.
F *char*	Move backward to the character *char* in the current line.
t *char*	Same as f *char* followed by h.
T *char*	Same as F *char* followed by l.
;	Repeats the last character find command, f, F, t, or T.
,	Reverses the direction of the last character find command, f, F, t, or T, and repeats it.
0	(zero) Move to the beginning of the line.
^	Move to the first nonblank character of the line.
$	Move to the end of the line.

%   Move to a matching brace character: parentheses, curly braces ({}), or brackets ([]). If the cursor is not on one of those characters, the line is scanned for the first occurrence of any of them. Failure to find a matching character rings the terminal bell. The match is not smart enough to ignore brace characters that appear in quoted strings or comments.

Deletion and Text Modification

x   Delete the current character.

X   Delete the previous character.

c *motion*   (Change) Delete text from the current character up through the character that the *motion* character would place the cursor on (see *Motion* above). Insert mode is entered following this command. For example, to delete the next word and enter input mode type cw. The *motion* character may be preceded by digits to indicate a repeat count. Also, the c command itself may be preceded by a repeat count. The motion can also be the character c, in which case the entire line is deleted.

C   (Change to end of line.) Delete text from the current character through the end of the line and enter insert mode. Equivalent to c$.

S   Delete the entire line and enter input mode. Equivalent to cc.

d *motion*   Delete text from the current character through the character that the *motion* character would place the cursor on (see *Motion* above). Like c, but does not enter input mode following the deletion. For example, to delete the next word type dw. The *motion* may also be the character d, in which case the entire line is deleted.

D   Delete the current character through the end of the line. Equivalent to d$. Unlike C, does not enter input mode following the deletion.

P   Place the previously deleted or modified text before the cursor.

p   Place the previously deleted or modified text after the cursor.

y *motion*   Yank text from the current character through the character that the *motion* command character would place the cursor on into the delete buffer. If the *motion* character is another letter y, then the entire line is yanked. No characters are actually deleted, but the P or p commands can be used to retrieve the yanked text later. This is a convenient way to copy text.

Y	Yank text into the delete buffer from the cursor to the end of the line. Equivalent to y$.
r *char*	Replace the current character with the letter *char*. The repeat count can be used to replace multiple characters.
.	(Period) Repeat the last text deletion or modification command.
u	Undo the last deletion or text modification command.
U	Undo all deletions or text modifications performed on the current line since it was last entered.

Entering Input Mode

Note that several of the deletion commands explained above also enter insert mode after deleting text.

a	(Append) Enter input mode following the cursor.
A	Append text to the end of the line. Equivalent to $a.
i	(Insert) Enter input mode before the cursor.
I	Enter input mode before the current line. Equivalent to 0i.
R	(Replace) Enter input mode, but replace characters by typing over them instead of inserting characters.

Transposing Characters

xp	This is a vi idiom composed of the x (delete character) and p (put character) commands. It has the effect of transposing the character the cursor is on with the next character. It's cute because "x" is often used in computer science as a shorthand for the word "trans," thus this naturally stands for "transpose." It is also useful because transposing characters is a common typing mistake.

Command History

_	(Underscore) Retrieves the last word of the previous command and inserts it in the current command at the cursor

	position, then enters input mode. If a repeat count is specified, then it is used as the word number (starting at 1) from the previous command string to insert.
k	Move back one command in the history file.
-	(dash) Same as k.
j	Move forward one command in the history file.
+	Same as j.
G	With no repeat count, goes to the last command in the history file. A count is taken as a command number, which is fetched.
/string	Search backward through the history file for a command that matches string. The string is terminated by an ENTER (RETURN or NEWLINE). If string begins with a caret (^), it must match starting at the beginning of the command. If string is omitted, the previous string from a / or ? command is used.
? string	Same as /, but searches forward rather than backward in the history file.
n	Search for the next occurrence of the previous pattern given in a / or ? command. Searches in the same direction as the last / or ? command.
N	Same as n, but reverses the search direction.

Expansion and Completion

*	An asterisk (*) is appended to the current word (unless there already is an asterisk there) and filename expansion is attempted. If successful, the word is replaced by all the matching filenames and input mode is entered. Otherwise, the bell rings.
\	(Backslash) Command or filename completion. If the current word is the first word on a line, or the first word following a command metacharacter (semicolon, pipe, ampersand, or open parenthesis), then this searches for a command, function, or alias whose leading characters match the current word. If a unique match exists, it is expanded. If the cursor is not on a word that could be a command name, the current word is used as a partial match for a filename, and if a unique match exists, the full filename is substituted.

=	Command or filename listing. Similar to the * command above, but instead of replacing the matched command or filename with all matches, simply prints a list of names that match.

Aliases

@ *letter*	The user's alias list is searched for an alias whose name is the given letter prefixed by an underscore, *_letter*. If such an alias exists, its value is inserted in the input queue. In other words, any vi commands, text insertions, etc., will be processed as if they were typed from the keyboard.

Miscellaneous

#	If the first character of the current command is not a pound sign (#), then insert a pound sign at the beginning of each line of the command and execute it. In effect, the command is inserted as a comment in the history file. If the first character of the command is a pound sign, then leading pound signs on all lines of the command are stripped.
CTL-L	Output a line feed and repaint the current line. This is useful when the output has been corrupted.
~	Invert the case of the current character, and advance the cursor.

31 *KornShell Command Reference*

31.1 Introduction

This chapter provides a reference style summary of all KornShell-93 built-in commands. Because dtksh is based on KornShell-93, it contains all the commands and features described here.

 This chapter does not include information on the dtksh extensions to KornShell. The KSH93 marker (shown here) is used to denote commands that are not available in older versions of the KornShell, or commands that have new options or features in KornShell-93. The commands are covered in alphabetical order.

31.2 Command Summary

In the following list of commands, several different markers may appear in the margin to indicate notes on a command, which are explained in the following sections.

Special Built-ins

SBI   This margin marker denotes a *special built-in*. Special built-in commands have the following properties:

1. If you assign variables on the same line as the command, the variable assignments remain in effect after the command completes.

2. If you redirect input or output file descriptors, the redirections are processed after variable assignments.

3. If an error occurs while processing a special built-in, your script will exit.

4. You cannot use a special built-in name as a function name.

Special Built-ins That Treat Assignment Differently

<u>SBI =</u>   This margin marker also denotes a special built-in, and such a command follows all
                   the rules outlined above for special built-ins, but in addition if a string that looks
                   like a variable assignment appears after the special built-in command, it is
                   expanded the same way as a variable assignment. For example, tilde substitution is
                   performed on the part of the string following the equal (=), and filename generation
                   does not occur.

Operating System-Dependent Built-ins

<u>OS</u>   The OS marker (shown to the left) indicates a command that may not be available
                   on every version of KornShell-93 because it depends on an operating system feature
                   that may not be available on some platforms. When this symbol appears, key letters
                   will follow it that indicate the kind of operating system feature required for this
                   command. The variations are:

<u>OS JC</u>   •   The OS JC marker (shown to the left) indicates that a command is only
                       available on operating systems that support job control.

<u>OS DSL</u>   •   The OS DSL marker (shown to the left) indicates that a command is only
                       available on operating systems that support dynamic shared libraries.

Command Line Options

                   All built-in commands accept the option -? as a help request and will print a usage
                   message on their standard error. Most built-in commands accept a double dash (--)
                   to indicate argument processing should stop (exceptions: `true`, `false`, `echo`, `com-
                   mand`, `newgrp`, and `login`).

31.3 Alphabetical List of Commands

`:` [arg ...]

<u>SBI</u>   The : (colon) command expands arguments and returns success. It is useful as a no-
                   operation command. Sometimes it is useful as a way to obtain side effects from
                   argument expansion without doing anything else.

`.` *name* [*arg* ...]

                   If *name* is the name of a function defined using the function name syntax then it is
                   executed in the current environment. Thus, local variables are not available, all ref-
                   erences are to global variables. In effect, it is as if the function had been defined
                   using the *name*() syntax.

                      If *name* is not the name of a function, then a file called *name* is searched for in
                   directories listed in the PATH variable. If such a file is found, it is read in its entirety
                   and then executed as a KornShell script.

If any positional parameters [*arg* ...] are given, they become the positional parameters during the execution of the dot command, otherwise the current parameters are used.

alias [-p]
alias [-p] *name* ...
alias *name=value* ...

SBI=

With no arguments prints a list of all aliases currently defined in the format *name=value*. With just the -p argument, inserts the string alias in front of each line printed so they could be re-input to the shell.

With arguments of the form *name* ... alias checks to see if there is an alias defined for all the given names, and returns a nonzero (false) exit value if there is not. The alias value, if there is on, for each *name* is printed. The -p option works as described above.

With arguments of the form *name=value*, new aliases are created. Aliased names are substituted if they are the first word of a command. If the *value* ends in a blank, then alias substitution is also carried out on the next word of the command.

There are two obsolete options -x and -t, that you might see in old KornShell scripts.

See also: unalias.

bg [*job* ...]

OS JC

Puts each *job* in the background. If no *jobs* are specified, the current job is put in the background.

break [*number*]

SBI

Breaks out of an enclosing for, while, until, or select loop. If *number* is specified, breaks out of that number of levels of loop command.

builtin [-s]
builtin -d *name* ...
builtin -f *library-path*
builtin *name* ...

OS DSL

KSH93

In the first form, builtin prints a list of built-in commands to the standard output. In the second form, builtin deletes a built-in command. In the third form, builtin attaches a shared library to the KornShell process. The symbols from this shared library become available for registration as new built-in commands.

In the fourth form, the *names* are registered as built-in commands. Shared libraries that have been attached to the KornShell process using the second form of are searched for an entry point named b_*name*. The entry point should be a function that takes `argc`, `argv` style **arguments** (like `main`) and returns an integer value. It should return zero for success and nonzero for failure, just as other Korn-Shell built-in commands do. Note that it is allowable to combine the second and third forms on a single invocation of `builtin`. Also note that libraries are searched in the reverse of the order in which they were attached.

---

cd [-LP] [*directory*]
cd [-LP] *old new*

> In the first form, `cd` changes the current working directory to *directory*. The *directory* argument may also be the dash character (-), in which case the previous directory is used. If the directory argument is not a full path and the CDPATH variable is set, then CDPATH is searched much like the PATH variable to find the named directory. CDPATH should be a colon separated list of directories. If it starts with a colon (:), then the current directory is searched first. If CDPATH is not set or set to the empty string the default is to search the current directory. The -L option causes `cd` to follow symbolic links. Note that the -L option continues to take effect on subsequent `cd` invocations even if not specified. It continues to do so until a -P option is given to a `cd` command, at which point symbolic links are no longer followed.
>
> The second form of `cd` is obsolete. It substitutes the string *new* for the first occurence of the string *old* in the current directory name, then changes to the resulting directory.
>
> In all cases, the PWD variable is updated to reflect the current working directory.

---

command [-p] *name* [*argument* ...]
command -v *name*
command -V *name*

> In its first form, `command` executes *name* with the given *arguments*. Function names are not searched, and if the *name* refers to a special built-in then the special properties are not honored (for example, a failure won't cause the shell to exit). With the -p option, a default path is searched instead of the one specified in PATH. This can be used as a security feature in scripts running with privilaged permissions.
>
> In the second form, `command` is equivalent to the `whence` built-in. In the third form `command` is equivalent to the `whence` command with the -v option.

---

continue [*number*]

> Branches to the next iteration of the enclosing `for`, `while`, `until`, or `select` loop. If *number* is given, the branch skips that many levels of enclosing loop.

disown [*job* ...]

<u>OS JC</u>   Causes KornShell not to send a hangup signal to the named jobs when a login shell exits. If no jobs are specified, then all currently active jobs are affected.

echo [*arg* ...]

The echo command prints its arguments separated by a space character and terminated by a newline. This command's behavior is operating system dependent, so it should not be used. It is better to use print, see below.

eval [*arg* ...]

<u>SBI</u>   The *args* are evaluated and the resulting string is executed by the shell interpreter. This allows you to build shell command lines and excute them.

exec [-c] [-a *arg*] *command* [*arg*...]
exec

<u>SBI</u>   In its first form, exec is used to overlay the KornShell process with another *command*. There is no return from a successful overlay, the KornShell process becomes the new command process. The -c option causes the environment to be cleared before any variable assignments associated with the exec invocation occur. The -a option causes *arg* to become the command name (i.e., argv[0]) for the new command instead of the default of *command*.

In the second form, where no *command* name is specified, exec can be used to redirect file descriptors in the current KornShell process.

exit [*expression*]

<u>SBI</u>   Causes KornShell to exit with a return code of *expression*. The *expression* should evaluate to a number be between 0 and 255, otherwise only the lower 8 bits will be used. The default if *expression* is not specified is zero (success).

The shell also exits when it receives an EOF character, unless the ignoreeof option has been set.

export [-p]
export *name*[=*value*] ...

<u>SBI=</u>   In its first form (with no *name*[=*value*] arguments), prints a list of all exported variables and their values. The values are quoted appropriately so that the output from export could be used as input to the shell interpreter. With the -p option, the word export is inserted before each variable name.

In its second form, the given *names* are marked for export. The optional *value* is assigned as well. Exported variables are available in the environment of all executed commands.

false

This command does nothing, then exits with status 1 (false or failure).

fg *[job ...]*

<u>OS JC</u>   The named *jobs* are brought into the foreground. They are waited for in the order specified. If no *jobs* are given, the current job is brought into the foreground.

getconf
getconf *name [path]*

In the first form, prints the current value of all POSIX configuration parameters. In the second form, prints the configuration parameter *name*. The optional *path* argument can be provided when the parameter *name* depends on a path.

getopts *spec variable [arg ...]*

The *getopts* command is used to parse options from the given *args*. If no *args* are given, then the current positional parameters are used. An option is an argument that begins with a dash (-) or plus (+) followed by a keyletter. An option may also have an argument following the keyletter. There may be whitespace between the keyletter and such an argument. The special double dash (--) option ends argument processing.

The *spec* specifies the allowed keyletters. If a keyletter in *spec* is followed by a colon (:), then that keyletter requires an argument.

The getopts command places the next option keyletter it finds in the *variable*. If the option began with plus (+), then the variable will contain a plus (+) followed by the keyletter. The index of the next *arg* is stored in the variable OPTIND. If the given option keyletter requires an argument, then it is stored in OPTARG. If the *spec* begins with a colon (:) then getopt will store the keyletter of an invalid option in OPTARG, and will set variable to a question mark (?) character if an unknown keyletter was encountered or to a colon (:) if a required argument is missing. If the *spec* does not begin with a colon, then errors in the option list causes a message to be printed to standard error.

The getopts command returns false (nonzero) when there are no more options.

Note that there is no way to use the following characters as keyletters: colon (:), plus (+), dash (-), question mark (?), brackets ([]). The pound sign (#) can only be used as a keyletter if it appears first in the spec.

hist -l [-nr] [*first* [*last*]]
hist [-e *editor*] [-r] [*first* [*last*]]
hist -s [*old=new*] [*command*]

When KornShell is invoked interactively, it keeps a history of commands entered at the terminal. Up to the last HISTSIZE commands are stored. Each command entered is assigned a sequence number, which can be used to reference it.

In its first form, hist lists commands to its standard output. The arguments *first* and last are used to selected the commands to list.

If neither is given, then the last 16 commands are listed. If *first* is specified but not *last*, then only the named command is listed. If both *first* and *last* are given, then they specify an inclusive range of commands to list. The *first* and *last* arguments may specify sequence numbers of commands, or they may be strings in which case the first command that begins with the string is selected. If they are negative numbers, then they are taken as offsets relative to the current command sequence number. The -n option suppresses printing of sequence numbers on the listed commands, the -r option reverses the order in which the commands are listed.

In its second form, hist can be used to edit previously entered commands. Range selection using the *first* and *last* arguments is the same as above, except that the default if neither *first* nor *last* is specified is the last command instead of the last 16 commands. If the -e *editor* option is given, then the named *editor* is invoked on the selected command range. Otherwise, if the variable HISTEDIT is set, then it is used as the editor command. If HISTEDIT is not set then FCEDIT is used, otherwise /bin/ed is used as the default editor.

KSH93⟩   In the third form, the given command is reexecuted after the substitution of the string *old* for the *string* is made.

jobs [-lnp] [*job* ...]

OS JC   The jobs command lists information about the named *jobs*, or all jobs if none is specified. The -l option lists process identifiers along with other information. The -n option limits the display to jobs that have stopped or exited since last notified. The -p option causes only the process group to be listed.

kill [-s *signalname*] *job* ...
kill [-n *signalnum*] *job* ...
kill -*signal job*...
kill -l [*signal* ...]

Sends signals to the named *jobs*. By default, sends the TERM signal. Signals may be specified by their number using the -n option, or by symbolic name using the -s option. The signal name is the same as that given in signal.h, but with the leading "SIG" string stripped off (one exception: SIGCHD becomes CHLD). It is also allowable to place either the signal number or signal name on the command line following a dash (-) as shown in the third form (this is for backward compatibility).

On systems that have job control, if the signal is TERM or HUP then the job will be sent a CONT signal if it is stopped.

In the fourth form, signal numbers and names are listed. If no *signal* arg is given, then all signal numbers and names are listed.

---

let [*arg* ...]

Each *arg* is evaluated as a mathematical expression. The exit status is true (zero) if the result of the expression is nonzero, and false otherwise.

---

newgrp [*arg* ...]

SBI   The same as exec /bin/newgrp *arg* .... See the UNIX manual page entry for newgrp(1).

---

print [-] [--] [*arg* ...]
print -f *fmt* [-ps] [-u *fd*] [*arg* ...]
print [-Rnprs] [-u *fd*] [*arg*...]

In the first form, with no options (or with options - or --), each *arg* is printed on the standard output, with a newline after the last one.

The second form, with the -f option, allows a format specifier, *fmt*, as described below under the printf command. In this case, without the -r or -R options the following escape conventions are used:

\a   The alert character (bell, ASCII 07)

\b   The backspace character (ASCII 010)

\c   The print ends without processing further args and without terminating with a NEWLINE.

\f   The formfeed character (ASCII 014)

\n   The newline character (ASCII 012)

\r   The carriage return character (ASCII 015)

\t   The TAB character (ASCII 011)

\v   The VERTICAL TAB character (ASCII 013)

\E   The ESCAPE character (ASCII 033)

\\   The backslash character (\)

The -R option will cause all further options and arguments to be printed, other than the -n option. The -p option sends output to the coprocess (process started using |&). The -u option sends output to the single digit file descriptor *fd* (the default is standard output, or file descriptor 1). The -n option suppresses the terminating newline (equivalent to ending the last arg with \c). The -s option causes output to be printed to the history file. The -r option turns off the escape processing described above.

---

printf *fmt* [*arg* ...]

Prints formatted output. This works similarly to the C language printf(3) subroutine, although there are numerous extensions to the available conversion characters. The fmt string contains a specification of the format used to output the remaining *arg* values. Within the fmt argument, a percent (%) starts a format specification. Following the percent there may be optional flags, an optional minimum field width specifier, an optional precision specifier, an optional numeric base, and a single character that specifies the type of conversion. For example, in the following command,

```
printf "%-10.20s" "$MYVAR"
```

In the fmt argument (the first argument), the percent starts the format specifier, the dash (-) is a flag indicating that left-justification is desired, the number 10 specifies the minimum field width, the .20 specifies the maximum field width, and the s character is the conversion character and specifies that a string is being printed. If the expansion of $MYVAR results in a string less than 10 characters wide, then it will be padded on the right with blanks. If the expansion is more than 20 characters wide, it will be truncated from the right.

The legal set of flags are:

-        Causes the corresponding *arg* to be left-justified within the field.

+   Prefix all numbers with their sign, + or -.

For octal conversions, prefix the output number with 0. For hexadecimal conversions, prefix the output number with 0x. For floating-point conversions, print the radix point. For the g or G conversions (described later), print trailing zeros.

SPACE   For numeric conversions, print - before negative numbers and print a SPACE character before positive numbers. This allows signed numbers to line up nicely in columnar output without printing plus (+) in front of positive numbers.

0   For floating-point conversions, pad the output with leading zeros.

The legal conversion characters are:

b   A string with special characters printed using the same escape conventions shown in the previous section for the print command. For example, a literal NEWLINE would be output as \n.

d, i   A signed decimal integer is printed.

n   The *arg* corresponding to this conversion character must be a legal KornShell variable name; the number of characters printed by the printf command up to this point in the string is stored in that variable.

o   An unsigned octal integer is printed.

P   The *arg* is a regular expression as defined by the regex(3). It is converted to a Shell-style pattern. For example,

            printf '%P' '[A-Z]*Hello'

results in: *([A-Z])Hello.

u   An unsigned decimal number is printed.

x   An unsigned hexadecimal number is printed using lowercase letters.

X   An unsigned hexadecimal number is printed using uppercase letters

f   A floating-point number is printed.

e   A floating-point number is printed using scientific notation with a lowercase letter e printed before the exponent.

E   A floating-point number is printed using scientific notation with a uppercase letter E printed before the exponent.

g, G   A floating-point number is printed using scientific notation. The number is printed only to the precision specified by the precision part of the fmt specifier. The g conversion character causes a lowercase e to be used before the exponent, and the G conversion character causes an uppercase E to be printed.

c   An unsigned character is printed.

s   A string is printed.

q   A string is printed, but all characters that are special to the Shell such
         as quotation marks and spaces are quoted.

%   The percent (%) character is printed.

Unlike the C language version of printf(3), the KornShell command will reuse
extra arguments with the same fmt specifier until all arguments are consumed.
Also, if you do not give enough arguments to satisfy all the conversion specifications, KornShell will use empty strings for string-type conversions and zero for
numeric conversions.

---

pwd [-LP]

Prints the current working directory to standard output. The -P option causes all
symbolic links to be followed to resolve the name. The -L option suppresses resolution of linked paths and is the default. The last of the options -L or -P becomes the
new default for subsequent pwd command execution.

---

read [*options*] *variable* ...
read -A [*options*] *array-variable*

Options:
    [-prs]
    [-d *delimiter*]
    [-t *seconds*]
    [-u *fd*]

The read command is used to receive input and break it into fields. In the first
form, a line is read from the standard input and is broken into fields according the
value of the IFS variable. Each successive field is assigned to the named *variables*. All leftover fields are placed in the final *variable*. If no *variables* are
specified, the line of input is placed in the variable REPLY. During input, the backslash (\) character is used for line continuation. If the first *variable* specified contains a question mark (?) character, then the string following the question mark is
printed to standard error as a prompt in interactive mode, and the string before the
question mark is used as the *variable* name.
    In the second form, each field of the input line is stored in successive elements of
the named *array*. The *array* is unset first, unless +A is used instead of -A.

The following options are supported in both forms of the `read` command:

-p	Read from the coprocess instead of standard input.
-r	Raw mode, backslash is not treated specially.
-s	The input is saved in the history file
-d *delimiter*	Instead of reading up to the first newline, read up to the single character *delimiter*.
-t *seconds*	Set a timeout on the read. Wait at most the named number of *seconds* (a floating-point number) for input, exit with a failure (nonzero) exit code if the input has not completed within that time.
-u *fd*	Read input from the single digit file descriptor *fd* instead of the standard input.

readonly [-p]
readonly *variable*[=*value*] ...

SBI=   In the first form, prints a list of `readonly` variables and their values. The values are quoted appropriately for reinput to the shell. With the -p option, inserts the string `readonly` in front of the printed variables.

In the second form, marks variables as read-only. The optional *value* is stored into each *variable* first. Once a variable is marked read-only, its *value* cannot be changed again.

The `readonly` command is like `typeset -r`, except that using `readonly` inside a function definition does not create a local variable.

return [*number*]

SBI   When used inside a function or a dot (.) command, causes a return to the previous invocation level. If *number* is given, it becomes the return code from the function or dot command, otherwise the return code of the last executed command is returned.

If `return` is executed outside a function or dot command, it behaves the same as the `exit` command.

set
set [-A *array*] [*arg* ...]
set [*options*]
set [+/-o *keyword*] [*arg* ...]
set [--] *arg* ...

In its first form, `set` prints to its standard output a list of the names and values of all variables.

In its second form, set can be used to conveniently set multiple items in an *array*. The named *array* is unset first, then each arg is stored in successive array positions starting at 0. If +A is used instead of -A, then the *array* is not unset first.

In its third form, set is used to turn on or off various KornShell *options*. Supported *options* are shown below. Any of these invoked with a plus (+) instead of a dash (-) turns off the named option.

-C   Stops redirection by the > notation from truncating existing files. To override this, you can use >| instead of >. Also, files created are opened with the O_EXCL flag, see creat(3) for more information.

-P   Makes the default mode for pwd and cd physical mode.

-a   All variables created after this are automatically exported.

-b   Job control completion messages are printed immediately instead of after the next interactive command.

-e   Causes any command that returns a false (nonzero) exit status to invoke the ERR trap then exit. This is automatically disabled during the reading of .profile scripts.

-f   Disables all filename generation.

-h   Commands become tracked aliases when first encountered.

-k   (Obsolete) Variable assignments may be placed either before or after a command word. This is for compatibility with old Bourne shell scripts.

-m   Background jobs are run in a separate process group and a message is printed when they complete. On systems with job control this is turned on automatically in interactive sessions.

-n   Read commands and check syntax, but don't execute them.

-p   Don't process $HOME/.profile, and use the file /etc/suid_profile instead of the ENV file. This is turned on automatically whenever the effective user id or group id is not equal to the real user id or group id. Turning this off sets the effective user and group id to be set back to the real user or group id.

-s   Sort the positional parameters lexicographically.

-t   (Obsolete) Read and execute one command and exit.

-u   When making substitutions, treat unset parameters as an error.

-v   Verbose, print shell input lines as they are read.

-x   Trace execution. Print commands and their expanded arguments as they execute.

In its fourth form, with the -o or +o options, set offers an alternate notation for setting most shell options that is more readable. A -o turns on an option, while a +o turns an option off. The options are specified by the following keywords:

allexport	Same as -a above.
bgnice	Run background jobs at a lower priority (this is the default).
errexit	Same as -e above.
emacs	Use emacs style editing for interactive sessions.
gmacs	Use gmacs style editing for interactive sessions.
ignoreeof	The shell will not exit on receiving end of file.
keyword	Same as -k.
markdirs	Appends a trailing slash (/) to filename-generated directories.
monitor	Same as -m.
noclobber	Same as -C.
noexec	Same as -n.
noglob	Same as -f.
nolog	Do not save function definitions in history files.
notify	Same as -b.
nounset	Same as -u.
physical	Same as -P.
privileged	Same as -p.

trackall	Same as -h.
verbose	Same as -v.
vi	Use vi style editing for interactive sessions. You are in insert mode until you hit the escape character (ASCII 033), which puts you in control mode. A carriage return sends the line.
viraw	In vi editing mode, each character is processed as it is typed. This is required on some terminals and some versions of the UNIX operating system. If you are having trouble editing in vi mode, try setting this option.
xtrace	Same as -x.

In its fifth form, set can be used to change the positional parameters to the given *args*. The double dash (--) option is useful to turn off option processing in case any of the given args starts with a dash (-) or plus (+). The *args* are assigned to the positional parameters $1, $2, etc.

---

shift [*expression*]

SBI   The positional parameters are shifted by removing *expression* leading parameters. If *expression* is not given, it defaults to 1. The *expression* can be any arithmetic expression that evaluates to a non-negative number less than the number of current parameters, $#.

---

sleep *seconds*

Suspends execution for the named number of *seconds*. *Seconds* can be a floating point number or an integer.

---

trap -p [*signal*]
trap *command* [*signal* ...]
trap - [*signal* ...]

SBI   In its first form, the trap command prints a list of actions registered with each *signal*, appropriately quoted. The *signal* may be specified by number or symbolic name (see kill above). In addition, the special signal number 0 or name EXIT sets an action that will occur when the shell exits. The special name ERR can be used to set a trap that is triggered when any command evaluates to false (nonzero), and the special name KEYBD can be used to set an action that is triggered whenever a key is read in emacs, gmacs, or vi editing mode. The DEBUG trap can be used to execute a command after each simple command is executed. DEBUG is not inherited by functions.

In its second form, trap is used to set a KornShell *command* to execute when the specified *signals* occur.

In its third form, any previous action that was registered on the named signals is cleared.

true

This command does nothing, then exits with a zero (true or success) exit code.

typeset [-p]
typeset [*options*] [*variable*[=*value*]]

In its first form, typeset prints a list of all variables and their attributes. With the -p option, the word typeset is printed before each line, thus allowing the output of this command to be re-input to the Shell.

In its second form, the typeset command is used to set attributes on variables or functions. In addition, when used inside a function, any *variables* created are local to that function; their values are restored on function exit. The following *options* are supported:

-A   Declares each *variable* to be an associative array. The subscripts may be arbitrary strings instead of being limited to integers. Whitespace in such subscripts is significant.

-E[*n*]   Declares each *variable* to be a double precision floating-point number. If the *n* option is given and is nonzero it defines the number of significant figures generated when expanding *name*, otherwise ten significant digits are generated.

-F[*n*]   Declares each *variable* to be a double precision floating-point number. If *n* is present and nonzero, it defines the number of digits to appear after the decimal point when *name* is expanded, otherwise ten digits appear.

-H   Provides file mapping of UNIX style files on non-UNIX machines.

-L[*n*]   Declares each *variable* as a left-justified string with leading blanks removed. If *n* is supplied and is nonzero it specifies the number of characters in the string. At the time of variable assignment, it is truncated or filled with blanks as needed at the end to enforce this width. If the -z option is also specified then leading zeros are also removed.

-R[n]	Declares each `variable` as right justified, filled with leading blanks. If n is supplied and nonzero it specifies the number of characters in the string. At the time of variable assignment, it is left-filled with blanks or truncated from the end to enforce this width.
-Z[n]	If the first non-blank character is a digit and the -L option is not present, right justify and fill name with leading zeros. If n is specified and nonzero it defines the width of the field, otherwise the width is set to that of the first assignment.
-f[tu]	The -f option can be used to display and change function attributes. If there are no further arguments, all functions are displayed. If function name arguments are provided, those functions are displayed along with their definitions. If +f is used instead of -f, then only the function names are displayed, not the definitions. Note that KornShell stores function definitions in your history file; if you don't have a history file or have set the `nolog` Shell option, then you can't display function definitions using this comand.

With the -ft suboption, run-time tracing is enabled on all named functions. Tracing may be turned off by using +ft.

With the -fu suboption, the named functions are undefined. The FPATH variable will be used to find the function again when it is referenced.

The -fx suboption allows the named functions to remain available across shell procedures invoked by name.

-i[n]	Declares each `variable` to be an integer. All assignments to the variables will be evaluated as arithmetic expressions. If n is specified and nonzero it defines the output arithmetic base, otherwise the default is base 10.
-l	On assignment, each `variable` will convert uppercase letters to lowercase.
-n	Declares each `variable` to be indirect references to another variable. In other words, the value of these variables is assumed to be other variable names, which are expanded when the named variable is referenced.
-r	The named `variables` are marked read-only and cannot be assigned subsequently.

-t   Places a tag on the variable. Tags are user defined and have no special meaning to the shell.

-u   On assignment, all lowercase letters are converted to uppercase.

-x   The given *variable* names are exported to the environment of future commands. Only simple variables may be exported (no periods).

---

ulimit [-HSacdfmnpstv]
ulimit [-HScdfmnpstv] *limit*

In its first form, ulimit prints the current value of the limit implied by its other arguments. The -a option prints all limits. See below for other options.

In its second form, ulimit can be used to change limits. The limit may be either a number or the string unlimited. The -H and -S options specify whether a hard or soft limit is set. Once set, a hard limit may not be increased. A soft limit may be increased up to the hard limit. If neither -H or -S is specified, both limits are set.

Other options are:

-c   The maximum number of 512-byte blocks that can be written to a core file.

-d   The maximum number of kilobytes of a data area.

-f   The maximum number of 512-byte blocks that can be written by child processes. There is no limit on reads.

-m   The maximum kilobytes of physical memory.

-n   The maximum number of file descriptors plus 1.

-p   The number of 512-byte blocks used for pipe buffering.

-s   The number of kilobytes in the stack area.

-t   The maximum number of seconds used by each process.

-v   The number of kilobytes of virtual memory.

Not all options are supported on all operating systems. If no options are specified, then -f is assumed.

---

umask [-S]
umask *mask*

In its first form, umask prints the current value of the umask as an octal value. If the -S option is specified, then a symbolic value is printed instead.

In its second form, the umask command is used to set the user file creation mask. See umask(2). The *mask* is specified the same way as described in chmod(1), which is either an octal number of a symbolic value. If a symbolic value is specified, the new value is the complement of the result of applying the symbolic value to the complement of the previous umask.

---

unalias *name* ...
unalias -a

SBI   In the first form, unalias removes the given names from the alias list. In the second form, all aliases are removed.

---

unset [-fnv] *variable* ...

The *variables* specified are unset, their values and attributes are erased. If the option -f is present, then the *variable* arguments refer to functions rather than variables. The -v option is the default and unsets variables. Variables marked read-only cannot be unset. The -n option causes any *variable* names which are name reference variables to be unset themselves rather than the variables to which they refer.

Unsetting the following variables removes their special meaning: ERRNO, LINENO, MAILCHECK, OPTARG, OPTIND, RANDOM, SECONDS, TMOUT, and _.

---

wait
wait *job* ...

OS JC   In its first form, waits for all outstanding background *jobs* to terminate.

In its second form, waits for the named *jobs* to terminate. The termination status of each job is reported to the standard output.

The exit status of wait is the same as the status of the last job waited for.

---

whence [-apfv] *name* ...

Prints how each *name* is interpreted if used as a command. The -v option produces more information. The -a option is similar to -v but also prints all possible interpretations of the given names (function, alias, each directory found in PATH, etc.) The -p option searches PATH for each name even if it is an alias, function, or reserved word. The -f option stops whence from checking for functions while searching for each *name*.

32 *Desktop KornShell Built-in Commands*

32.1 Introduction

This chapter presents a summary of all Desktop KornShell built-in command extensions beyond the base KornShell-93 language. KornShell-93 base built-in commands are summarized in Chapter 31. This list is meant as a terse reference only, and cannot give complete details on every command. The tutorial sections of this book give more detailed information and examples of typical usage for most of these commands—you can use the index to find references elsewhere in this book. You may also wish to consult X Window System C language reference materials for more detailed information, since these commands map directly to the C language subroutines.

The commands are presented in alphabetical order to facilitate lookup; they are alphabetized without regard to upper- or lowercase letters. When two or more closely related commands fall alphabetically next to each other, they are grouped and explained as a unit. Alphabetical ordering does have drawbacks—some commands that are related are split up. An example of this is the Text... commands, which are split in the middle by the TextField* commands.

32.2 Obtaining More Information

The commands are marked to indicate the C level interface to which they correspond. For example, some commands come from the Xlib layer of the X Window System, some come from Motif, some are Common Desktop Environment (CDE) specific, and some are unique to dtksh. These markings allow you to easily determine which other reference materials you might want to consult to get more detailed reference information. Table 32-1 lists suggested sources of information for each category of command.

Table 32-1. Command Types and Sources of More Information

Mark	Where to look for more detailed information
XLIB	Xlib layer commands for low-level drawing. In this book, see Chapter 18, *Xlib: Low-Level Graphics*. C language references include: [Nye (1) 1992] and [Nye (2) 1992]
XT	Xt Intrinsics toolkit commands for manipulating widgets. In this book, an overview of Xt concepts is contained in Chapter 2, *X Window Basics*, but more information is scattered throughout Part I. C language references include: [Nye and O'Reilly 1993] and [Flanagan 1992].
MOT	Motif Toolkit specific commands. In this book, commands are explained through XU library equivalents throughout Part I. C language references include: [Heller and Ferguson 1994], [Ferguson and Brennen 1993], and [McMinds 1992].
CDE	Common Desktop Environment interface commands. In this book, see Chapter 20, *The Workspace Manager*, Chapter 21, *The Session Manager*, Chapter 22, *Message Catalogs*, and Chapter 24, *Nongraphical Interfaces*. C language references include: [CDE Dtksh Guide 1995], [CDE Internationalization 1995], and [CDE ToolTalk 1995].
DTK	These commands are specific to dtksh. In this book information on these commands is scattered throughout, so use the index for more information. There are no C language equivalents to these commands, but there is some information in [CDE Dtksh Guide 1995].
CF	(Convenience function) This is a shell function that is provided for your convenience. These convenience functions are a standard part of CDE, and are contained in the file `/usr/dt/lib/scripts/DtFuncs.sh`. Most of these commands are not directly explained in this book, since the XU library provides (in general) a more powerful, complete, and internally consistent set of conveniences. The XU library is summarized in Chapter 33, *XU Library Reference*. There are no equivalent C language subroutines. Some information is contained in [CDE Dtksh Guide 1995].

32.3 Symbolic Parameters

Some symbolic names commonly appear in the usage section of the explanations:

widget   A widget handle, as returned from `XtCreateManagedWidget`, `XtCreateWidget`, `XtCreatePopupShell`, `XtInitialize`, or one of the `XmCreateWidget` commands.

variable   Many commands store their results in a *variable* name passed in on the command line. Whenever you see *variable* in the usage it will represent such a case. Also, some commands return multiple values, in this case there will be a suffix on *variable*, such as: *variable-width*, *variable-x*, or *variable-y*.

index   List widget commands often reference list items by their index number in the list. List item indexes start at 1. Most of these commands also allow the special index 0 to indicate the last item in the list.

position   Text and TextField widget commands often refer to the character position of the text stored in the widget. These character positions start at 0 and indicate an offset measured in characters (not bytes, as there could be multibyte characters in some languages) from the start of the text buffer.

window   A *window* is an X data structure. Every widget has a window associated with it. It is necessary to provide this as an argument to certain Xlib commands; it can be obtained using the XtWindow command, giving a widget handle as the argument.

drawable   A *drawable* is either a *window* or a pixmap. It is necessary for most Xlib commands. Typically in a dtksh script it will be the window of a DrawnButton or DrawingArea command as obtained by using the XtWindow command.

screen   A *screen* is an X data structure that is required for certain Xlib commands. It is usually obtained by using the XtScreen command on the top-level widget of your application.

display   Like a *screen*, a *display* is another X data structure that specifies the physical device on which a window resides. It is necessary for certain Xlib commands, and can be obtained using the XtDisplay command.

Other usage parameters are described in each command's explanation.

32.4 Alphabetical List of Commands

catclose *catalog-id*

DTK   Close an internationalization catalog. The *catalog-id* must have been returned from a previous call to catopen.

catgets `variable catalog-id set-number message-number default-message`

DTK   Get a message string from an international message catalog. The string is stored in `variable`. The `catalog-id` must have been returned from a previous call to catopen, and the combination of `set-number` and `message-number` must reference a valid message in that catalog. In case they are not, `default-message` is returned in `variable`.

catopen `variable catalog-file`

DTK   Open a message `catalog-file` for retrieving internationalized messages. A catalog identifier is stored in `variable`, and can be used on a later call to catclose or catgets.

DtActionDescription `variable action-name`

CDE   Retrieve the description associated with `action-name` from the action database, and store the result in `variable`.

DtActionExists `action-name`

CDE   Returns a boolean value indicating whether `action-name` exists in the action database. Thus, this command can be used in conjunction with the KornShell `if` statement.

DtActionInvoke `widget action-name term-options execution-host context-host \`
                        `context-directory use [file-name type host ...]`

CDE   Execute `action-name` on `execution-host`, taking context from `context-host`, and making the current working directory `context-directory`. Arguments to the action are specified by triplets that specify the `file-name`, the `type` of file, and the `host` on which the file resides. If members of this triplet are to be left out, use an empty string such as `""`.

DtActionLabel `variable action-name`

CDE   Retrieve the label associated with `action-name` from the action database, and store the result in `variable`.

DtCreateHelpDialog `variable parent name [resource:value ...]`
DtCreateHelpQuickDialog `variable parent name [resource:value ...]`

CDE   Create a CDE help dialog (or help quick dialog), storing its handle in `variable`.

DtDbLoad
DtDbReloadNotify *command*

CDE   The `DtDbLoad` command takes no arguments, and loads the action database. The `DtDbReloadNotify` command arranges for a dtksh *command* to be executed when the action database needs to be reloaded. The *command* normally would call `DtDbLoad`, and perhaps take other actions.

DtDtsDataTypeIsAction *data-type*

CDE   Returns a boolean value that indicates whether the *data-type* is an action.

DtDtsDataTypeNames *variable*

CDE   Returns a space-separated list of all data type names in the *variable*.

DtDtsDataTypeToAttributeList *variable data-type option*
DtDtsDataTypeToAttributeValue *variable data-type attribute option*

CDE   The `DtDtsDataTypeToAttributeList` command returns a comma-separated list of attributes associated with *data-type* in *variable*. The `DtDtsDataTypeToAttributeValue` command returns a specific *attribute* in *variable*.

DtDtsFileToAttributeList *variable path*
DtDtsFileToAttributeValue *variable path attribute*
DtDtsFileToDataType *variable path*

CDE   These commands are all used to retrieve information about a file. The first stores the a comma-separated list of attribute associated with *path* in the *variable*. The second stores a particular *attribute* value associated with *path* in the *variable*. The third stores the data type associated with *path* in the *variable*.

DtDtsFindAttribute *variable attribute-name attribute-value*

CDE   The `DtDtsFindAttribute` command stores a space separated list of data type names in *variable*; only data types that have an attribute called *attribute-name,* which is set to *attribute-value*, are returned.

DtDtsLoadDataTypes

CDE   This command takes no arguments, and loads the CDE data typing databases. It should be called before any other data typing command.

DtDtsSetDataType *variable path data-type override*

CDE   The named *path* is set to *data-type* if it does not currently have a type. If it does
             currently have a type, then the type is changed to *data-type* only if the *override*
             argument is the value true. The data type name associated with the *file* follow-
             ing execution of this command is stored in *variable*.

DtGetHourGlassCursor *variable display*

CDE   Return the X cursor identifier representing the hourglass (please wait); the cursor
             identifier is stored in the named *variable*.

DtHelpQuickDialogGetChild *variable widget child-type*

CDE   Get the handle of a child of the desktop help dialog widget. The child's handle is
             stored in *variable*. The child-type argument specifies which child:

HELP_QUICK_OK_BUTTON	The OK ToggleButton Gadget.
HELP_QUICK_PRINT_BUTTON	The Print ToggleButton Gadget.
HELP_QUICK_HELP_BUTTON	The Help ToggleButton Gadget.
HELP_QUICK_SEPARATOR	The SeparatorGadget.
HELP_QUICK_MORE_BUTTON	The More ToggleButton Gadget.
HELP_QUICK_BACK_BUTTON	The Back ToggleButton Gadget.

DtHelpReturnSelectedWidgetId *variable-status widget variable-selected*

CDE   Get the handle of the selected widget from a desktop help dialog referenced by *wid-
             get*. The selected widget handle is stored in *variable-selected*. A return code
             string is stored in *variable-status*:

HELP_SELECT_VALID	There was a valid selection, and the handle of the selected widget is stored in *variable-selected*.
HELP_SELECT_INVALID	No selection was available.
HELP_SELECT_ABORT	The selection was aborted.
HELP_SELECT_ERROR	An error occurred while trying to access the HelpDialog's selected widget.

DtHelpSetCatalogName *catalog*

<u>CDE</u>   Set the locale for the desktop help system to the *catalog* number.

DtkshAddButtons *parent widget-class* [*label callback* ...]
DtkshAddButtons -w *parent class* [*variable label callback* ...]

<u>CF</u>   This convenience function allows you to add multiple buttons to a parent widget in one simple function call. In the first form (without the -w option), *parent* specifies the parent widget to which the buttons are being added, and *widget-class* is the type of button to add (XmPushButton, XmPushButtonGadget, XmToggleButton, XmToggleButtonGadget, XmCascadeButton, or XmCascadeButtonGadget). The rest of the arguments are pairs representing the *label* and *callback* command of successive buttons. For every pair, one button is created.

         In the second form (with the -w option), instead of pairs of arguments, triplets of arguments are specified, where the first of each triplet is the name of a *variable* that will be set to the widget handle of the newly created button, and the second and third argument in each triplet specify the *label* and *callback* command as before.

         The first form is more convenient in the common case where the handles of the buttons are not needed for later use in the program. The second form is typically used when under some circumstances one or more buttons will be made insensitive by the application or otherwise require modification after creation.

DtkshAnchorBottom [*offset*]
DtkshAnchorLeft [*offset*]
DtkshAnchorRight [*offset*]
DtkshAnchorTop [*offset*]

<u>CF</u>   These convenience functions simplify the task of setting constraint resources on the children of Form widgets. They print out constraint resource settings that anchor a certain part of the child (the bottom, left, right, and top, respectively) to the Form. The optional *offset* argument can be used to specify that the attachment should occur offset pixels from the edge of the Form. These commands are typically used inside command substitution on the creation call to a child of the Form. For example:

```
XmCreateLabel LAB $FORM lab \
     $(DtkshAnchorRight 5; DtkshAnchorBottom 10)
```

This would anchor the right side of the newly created label widget to the right side of the Form, offset by 5 pixels, and would anchor the bottom of the label to the bottom of the Form offset by 10 pixels.

DtkshDisplayErrorDialog *title message* [*ok-cmd close-cmd help-cmd style*]

CF   This convenience function creates and displays an error dialog in one simple step. Only one error dialog will be created no matter how many times this is called; the same widget gets reused on each call. The handle of the error dialog widget is stored in the *variable* _DTKSH_ERROR_DIALOG_HANDLE. You should never destroy this widget, but rather unmanage it when it is not needed. The arguments specify the title of the dialog, the message string displayed in the message area, and optionally a set of callback commands (*ok-cmd, close-cmd, help-cmd*) to register for the dialog buttons. If no callbacks are given, the default is that only the OK button is managed and it causes the dialog to be popped down. Only buttons for which callbacks are specified will be managed (and only if the callback is not the empty string). The *style* argument, if specified, sets a value for the dialogStyle resource of the BulletinBoard widget.

DtkshDisplayHelpDialog *title help-type help-information* [*help-location*]

CF   These convenience functions create and display help dialogs (or quick help dialogs) in one convenient step. Only one help dialog will be created no matter how many times this is called, and the handle of the dialog will be stored in the *variable* _DTKSH_HELP_DIALOG_HANDLE (or _DTKSH_QUICK_HELP_DIALOG). You should not destroy the widget, but rather just unmanage it when it is no longer needed. The *title* argument specifies a string that will appear in the dialog's title bar. The remaining arguments are dependent on the value of the *help-type* parameter:

HELP_TYPE_TOPIC   In this case, *help-information* is the help volume name and *help-location* is the help topic location identifier.

HELP_TYPE_STRING   With this setting for *help-type*, *help-information* is the actual help string that is displayed, and *help-location* is not used and should be omitted.

HELP_TYPE_DYNAMIC_STRING   The dynamic string option for *help-type* causes the *help-string* parameter to be a dtksh command that is executed at run-time to produce the help text (to its standard output). The *help-location* argument is not used in this case and should be omitted.

HELP_TYPE_MAN_PAGE   With this setting for *help-type*, the *help-information* should be the name of a manual page, and the `help-location` parameter is not used.

HELP_TYPE_FILE   This causes the `help-information` to be interpreted as a filename that is read to obtain the help text; the `help-location` parameter is not used.

DtkshDisplayInformationDialog `title message [ok-cmd close-cmd help-cmd style]`

This convenience function creates and displays an information dialog in one simple step. The handle of the dialog is stoerd in _DTKSH_INFORMATION_DIALOG_HANDLE. See `DtkshDisplayErrorDialog` for details of the other arguments.

DtkshDisplayQuickHelpDialog `title help-type help-info [help-location]`

This creates a quick help dialog. The dialog's handle is stored in _DTKSH_QUICK_HELP_DIALOG_HANDLE. See `DtkshDisplayHelpDialog` for details of the other arguments.

DtkshDisplayQuestionDialog `title message [ok-cmd close-cmd help-cmd style]`

DtkshDisplayWarningDialog `title message [ok-cmd close-cmd help-cmd style]`

DtkshDisplayWorkingDialog `title message [ok-cmd close-cmd help-cmd style]`

CF   These convenience functions create and display different kinds of message dialogs in one simple step. Only one message dialog is created for each of these functions no matter how many times they are called; the same set of widgets is reused on subsequent invocations. The widget handle of each kind of dialog is stored in a *variable* for access by the programmer if necessary. These *variable*s are, respectively:

_DTKSH_QUICK_HELP_DIALOG_HANDLE

_DTKSH_WARNING_DIALOG_HANDLE

_DTKSH_WORKING_DIALOG_HANDLE

You should not destroy these dialog widgets, but rather just unmanage them when they are no longer needed. See `DtDisplayErrorDialog` for information on the other arguments.

DtkshFloatBottom [*offset*]
DtkshFloatLeft [*offset*]
DtkshFloatRight [*offset*]
DtkshFloatTop [*offset*]
DtkshLeftOf *widget* [*offset*]

CF   These convenience functions aid in specifying Form constraints when creating children of a Form widget. They print a set of Form constraints to standard output, and are typically used inside of command substitution on the creation call of a child of a Form widget. `DtkshFloatBottom` prints constraints that would cause a child of the Form to "float" attached to the bottom of the Form. If the Form is resized, the child remains fixed to the bottom. The optional *offset* argument can be used to specify a distance off the bottom of the Form (in pixels). The default is zero. Similarly, the other functions print constraints that would cause a child to float on the left, right, and top of the Form respectively. For example:

```
XmCreatePushButton PUSH $FORM push \
        $(DtFloatBottom 5)
```

This would cause the widget whose handle is $PUSH to be attached 5 pixels from the bottom of the Form. This is easier than trying to remember how to set the four resources required to accomplish the same thing.

    See also: `DtkshUnder`, `DtkshOver`, `DtkshLeftOf`, `DtkshRightOf`, `DtkshAnchorRight`, `DtkshAnchorLeft`, `DtkshAnchorTop`, `DtkshAnchorBottom`, `DtkshSpanWidth`, and `DtkshSpanHeight`, which work in similar fashion to these functions.

DtkshOver *widget* [*offset*]
DtkshRightOf *widget* [*offset*]

CF   These convenience functions aid in specifying Form constraints when creating children of a Form widget. They print a set of Form constraints to standard output, and are typically used inside of command substitution on the creation call of a child of a Form widget. `DtkshLeftOver` prints constraints that would cause a child of the Form to be placed above another widget (which must also be a child of the Form). The optional *offset* argument can be used to specify a distance from the reference widget (in pixels). The default is zero. Similarly, the `DtkshRightOf` command prints constraints that would cause a child to be placed to the right of another child of the Form. For example:

```
XmCreatePushButton PUSH2 $FORM push \
        $(DtkshRightOf $PUSH1 5)
```

This would cause the widget whose handle is $PUSH2 to be placed 5 pixels to the right of a widget whose handle is PUSH1 (which must also be a child of the widget FORM). This is easier than trying to remember how to set the four resources required to accomplish the same thing.

See also: DtkshUnder, DtkshAnchorRight, DtkshAnchorLeft, DtkshAnchorTop, DtkshAnchorBottom, DtkshSpanWidth, and DtkshSpanHeight, which work in similar fashion to these functions.

DtkshSetReturnKeyControls *widget1 widget2 form-widget button-widget*

CF   This convenience function sets up a Form widget so that the RETURN (or ENTER) key does not execute the default button, but rather traverses between two Text or TextField widgets. Multiple calls to this function can similarly configure multiple text widgets in this manner. The *form-widget* argument should be the parent of the other widget arguments. The *widget1* argument is the first text widget; the *widget2* argument is the text widget that should be traversed to from *widget1*. The *button-widget* argument should be the default button in the Form.

DtkshSpanHeight [*top-offset bottom-offset*]
DtkshSpanWidth [*left-offset right-offset*]

CF   These convenience functions aid in specifying Form constraints when creating children of a Form widget. They print a set of Form constraints to standard output, and are typically used inside of command substitution $( ) on the creation call of a child of a Form widget. DtkshSpanHeight prints constraints that would cause a child of the Form to be attached to the top and bottom of the Form, thus making it span the entire height of the Form. If the Form is resized, the child is resized such that it continues to span the entire height of the Form. The optional *top-offset* and *bottom-offset* arguments can be used to specify a distance from the top and bottom of the Form (in pixels). The defaults are zero. Similarly, the function DtSpanWidget prints constraints that cause a child to span the entire width of the Form by attaching its left and right sides. For example:

```
XmCreateTextField TEXT $FORM text \
     $(DtkshSpanWidth 5 5)
```

This would cause the widget whose handle is $TEXT to span the entire width of the Form widget $FORM. The left and right sides of $TEXT will be offset 5 pixels from the left and right. This is easier than trying to remember how to set the four resources required to accomplish the same thing.

DtkshUnder *widget* [*offset*]

<u>CF</u>   This convenience function prints to standard output appropriate Form widget constraint resources to place a sibling underneath *widget*. It is typically called from within command substitution when creating a sibling to the named *widget* inside a Form. The *offset*, if given, specifies a distance, in pixels, that the sibling should be placed under widget. For example:

```
XmCreateLabel LAB2 $FORM lab2 \
        $(DtkshUnder $LAB1 5)
```

In this case, the call to DtkshUnder would expand to Form constraints that would place the widget $LAB2 under the widget $LAB1. This is both more readable and easier to remember than trying to figure out the four resources that must be set to accomplish this directly using Motif.

DtLoadWidget *class-name class-record-symbol*

<u>DTK</u>   Load a new widget into dtksh's internal widget table. This is typically a widget whose class record and method functions have been loaded in a dynamic shared library that has previously been attached to the dtksh process using the KornShell builtin command with the -f option. The *class-name* argument is the name of the widget class that the dtksh programmer will use on calls to XtCreateWidget, XtCreateManagedWidget, etc. The *class-record-symbol* argument is the name of the C language symbol representing the class record of the widget (for example XmLabelWidgetClass). By convention, the *class-name* should be the same as the *class-record-symbol* with the WidgetClass suffix removed and initial uppercase, e.g. XmLabel.

DtSessionRestorePath *widget variable session-file*

<u>CDE</u>   Return a full path to a session file given the last component of a *session-file* and a *widget* handle. The full path is stored in the named *variable*.

DtSessionSavePath *widget variable-fullpath variable-filename*

<u>CDE</u>   Store the full path of a session file in the *variable-fullpath* argument, and the filename portion of the path is stored in the *variable-filename* argument.

DtSetIconifyHint *widget hint*

<u>CDE</u>   Set the initial iconified state for a shell *widget*. The *hint* argument is either true or false.

DtSetStartupCommand *widget command*

<u>CDE</u>   Tell the session manager how to restart this application by passing it a *command* string. The widget handle should be the top-level shell widget for the application.

DtShellIsIconified *widget*

<u>CDE</u>   Query the iconified state of a Shell-class *widget*. This command returns success (zero) if the shell is iconified, failure (nonzero) otherwise. Thus it can be used as the conditional command in an `if` or `while` statement.

DtTurnOffHourGlass *widget*

<u>CDE</u>   Removes the desktop hourglass (please wait) cursor in *widget*.

DtTurnOnHourGlass *widget*

<u>CDE</u>   Changes the cursor to the standard desktop hourglass (please wait) in *widget*.

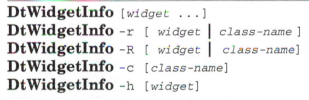

DtWidgetInfo [*widget* ...]
DtWidgetInfo -r [*widget* | *class-name*]
DtWidgetInfo -R [*widget* | *class-name*]
DtWidgetInfo -c [*class-name*]
DtWidgetInfo -h [*widget*]

<u>DTK</u>   The `DtWidgetInfo` command prints information about widgets and widget classes. With no arguments it prints a list of all widgets currently defined in the application, along with the name of the widget, the class, the parent, the environment *variable* in which the handle was originally stored, the widget handle, and the current state of the widget (mapped, managed, sensitive). By specifying one or more *widget* handles, information on the named *widgets* is printed. The information goes to standard out.

        Other information can be obtained by using one of the allowed options:

        -r   Print the list of resources available on the named widgets or widget class names.

        -R   Print constraint resources of the named widgets or widget classes.

        -c   With no other options, prints a list of all available widget classes. If one or more widget class names are supplied, prints out those that are defined and available, otherwise prints an error. Note that this also works for classes added via the `DtLoadWidget` command.

-h   With no other arguments, a list of all active widget handles will be displayed. With one or more arguments representing widget handles, the name of the associated widget is printed, or an error message if the given handle does not represent a valid widget (i.e., it has been destroyed or is not a valid format for a widget handle).

DtWsmAddCurrentWorkspaceCallback *variable widget command*

CDE   Register a *command* to be executed whenever the user changes workspaces. The *widget* should be a Shell-class widget. An identifier is stored in *variable* that can be used on a subsequent call to `DtWsmRemoveCurrentWorkspaceCallback`.

DtWsmAddWorkspaceFunctions *display window*

CDE   Forces the window manager menu to include workspace manager items to move the *window* to other workspaces. The *window* must be in the withdrawn state in order for this command to work.

DtWsmGetCurrentBackdropWindow *display root-window variable*

CDE   Returns a string composed of a comma-separated list of window identifiers. The window identifier list is stored in the *variable*, and represents the set of all root backdrop windows. The *root-window* argument is the window id of the root screen, which can be obtained using `XGetRootWindowOfScreen`.

DtWsmGetCurrentWorkspace *display root-window variable*

CDE   Store the X atom representing the current workspace in the named *variable*. To map this back into its string representation, use `XmGetAtomName`. The *root-window* argument is the window of the root screen, which can be obtained using `XGetRootWindowOfScreen`.

DtWsmGetWorkspaceList *display root-window variable*

CDE   Returns a string composed of comma-separated atoms representing the current set of all workspaces defined by the user. The atom list is stored in *variable*. The *root-window* argument is the window of the root screen.

DtWsmGetWorkspacesOccupied *display window variable*

CDE   Returns a string composed of comma-separated atoms representing the current set of all workspaces occupied by the application containing the given *window* and *display*. The atom list is stored in *variable*.

DtWsmOccupyAllWorkspaces *display window*

CDE   Sends a request to the window manager requesting that *window* be displayed on all workspaces. The application will also appear on new workspaces created after this command is issued.

DtWsmRemoveWorkspaceCallback *widget command callback-id*

CDE   Removes a workspace change handler callback. The *widget* handle and *command* must match those given on a previous call to DtWsmAddCurrentWorkspaceCallback, and the *callback-id* must match the identifier that was returned by such a call.

DtWsmRemoveWorkspaceFunctions *display window*

CDE   Removes workspace commands from the window manager menu associated with *window* on the given *display*. This command only works if the *window* is in the withdrawn state.

DtWsmSetCurrentWorkspace *widget workspace-atom*

CDE   Changes the current workspace to the one identified by the *workspace-atom*.

DtWsmSetWorkspacesOccupied *display window atom-list*

CDE   Changes the set of workspaces occupied by the Shell-class widget identified by *window* and *display* to those represented by *atom-list*. The *atom-list* is a comma-separated list of X atoms.

ttdt_close *status process-id new-process-id send-stopped*

CDE   Closes a ToolTalk communications session. If *send-stopped* is true, sends a Stopped notice.

ttdt_file_event *status operation patterns send*

CDE   Creates a ToolTalk notice announcing that an event has occurred that affects a file. If *send* is true, the notice is sent as well.

ttdt_file_join *variable status path scope join command*

<u>CDE</u>   Registers interest in Deleted, Modified, Reverted, Moved, and Saved messages. When such a message is received, the *command* is executed. In the scope of the command, *variables* are defined that contain information about the message: DD_TT_MSG, DD_TT_OP, DD_TT_PATHNAME, DD_TT_SAME_EUID_EGID, and DT_TT_SAME_PROCID.

ttdt_file_quit *status patterns quit*

<u>CDE</u>   Destroys message *patterns*. If *quit* is true, unregisters interest in the pathname passed to ttdt_file_join.

ttdt_Get_Modified *path scope timeout*

<u>CDE</u>   Sends a Get_Modified request in *scope* for *path*, waits for a reply (or a number of milliseconds indicated by *timeout* to elapse). Returns a boolean indicating whether a message came in before the *timeout* period elapsed.

ttdt_open *procid-variable status file-variable toolname vendor \\ version send-started*

<u>CDE</u>   Opens a ToolTalk communications endpoint. Returns the process id associated with the connection in *procid-variable* and the file descriptor in *file-variable*. If *send-started* is true, a Started message is sent.

ttdt_Revert *status path scope timeout*

<u>CDE</u>   Sends a Revert message within *scope* for *path* and waits for a reply (or for *timeout* milliseconds to elapse).

ttdt_Save *status path scope timeout*

<u>CDE</u>   Sends a Save message within *scope* for *path* and waits for a reply (or for *timeout* millseconds to elapse).

ttdt_session_join *variable sttus session-id shell-handle join*

<u>CDE</u>   Joins the session indicated by *session-id*. Registers patterns and default callbacks for standard interfaces. The *session-id* may be the empty string, in which case the default session is joined. Returns a pattern handle in *variable*.

ttdt_session_quit *status session-id session-patterns quit*

CDE   Destroys message patterns specified in *session-patterns*. If *quit* is true, quits the session indicated by *session-id*.

tttk_message_destroy *status message*

CDE   Destroys patterns stored in *message*.

tttk_message_fail *status message message-status status-string destroy*

CDE   Sets the *message-status* and *status-string* for a *message*, then fails the message. If *destroy* is true, destroys *message*.

tttk_message_reject *status message message-status status-string string destroy*

CDE   Sets the *message-status* and *status-string* for a *message*, then rejects the message. If *destroy* is true, destroys *message*.

tttk_Xt_input_handler *process-id input-source input-id*

CDE   Arrange for message receipt in X applications. This command should be registered as an input handler using XtAddInput with the -r (raw) option, using the file descriptor returned by the ttdt_open command. The process-id should be the process id returned from ttdt_open. The *input_source* should be $INPUT_SOURCE in the context of the input handler, and the *input-id* should be $INPUT_ID in the context of the input handler.

tt_error_pointer *variable status*

CDE   Returns ToolTalk's idea of an invalid pointer, depending on the *status*, which is the return from a Tt_status value.

tt_file_netfile *variable status file*

CDE   Converts a local *file* name to netfile name format, storing the result in *variable*.

tt_host_file_netfile *variable status host file*
tt_host_netfile_file *variable status host file*

CDE   The first command converts a *file* name (located on a specific *host*) to a corresponding netfile name that is then stored in *variable*. The second command does the opposite conversion.

---

tt_message_reply *status message*

<u>CDE</u>   Informs ToolTalk that a *message* has been handled.

---

tt_netfile_file *variable status netfile*

<u>CDE</u>   Converts a *netfile* name to a valid local filename, storing the result in *variable*.

XBell *display volume*

<u>XLIB</u>   Ring the X Window display's "bell." Normally you would use the display of $TOPLEVEL as the *display*. The *volume*, if given, must be between −100 and +100. Higher numbers are louder. The default volume is zero. Some devices do not support different volumes.

XClearArea *display window [GC-options] x y width height exposures*

<u>XLIB</u>   Clear a rectangular area on a *window*. The parameters *x* and *y* give the coordinates of the upper left corner of the rectangle to clear. The rectangle to clear will be *width* wide and *height* high. The *exposures* parameter is either the string true or false and indicates whether or not the clear should generate graphics exposure events.

XClearWindow *display window*

<u>XLIB</u>   Clear an entire *window*.

XCopyArea *display src dest srcx srcy width height dstx dsty [GC-options]*

<u>XLIB</u>   Copy graphics on the named *display* between windows specified by *src* and *dst*. The *srcx* and *srcy* arguments specify the upper left corner of the area to copy from the *src* window. The rectangle copied will be *width* wide and *height* high. Its upper left corner will be copied to position *dstx*, *dsty* on the *dst* window.

XDefineCursor *display window cursor*

<u>XLIB</u>   Define a new cursor. The *cursor* argument is a string that specifies a pathname to a cursor definition in X bitmap format.

XDrawArc *display window [GC-options] x y width height angle1 angle2*

<u>XLIB</u>   Draw a circular arc on *window*. The arc is defined by an enclosing rectangle with upper left corner specified by *x, y*. The enclosing rectangle is *width* wide and *height* high. The arc drawn is the part of a circle whose center is the center of the

rectangle, starting at `angle1`. The arc continues for a distance of `angle2` units. The angles are integers measured in 64ths of a degree. A value of zero for `angle1` specifies the "three o'clock" position. Positive values for `angle2` specify a counter-clockwise sweep, negative values go clockwise.

XDrawImageString `display window [GC-options] x y string`

XLIB   Draw a string on a `window` starting at position `x, y`, which is relative to the origin at the upper left corner of the window. The `x, y` coordinate specifies the baseline position of the string. The difference between `XDrawString` and `XDrawImage-String` is that the background color is opaquely drawn in the case of `XDrawImage-String`. For `XDrawString`, only the text itself is drawn on the existing background.

XDrawLine `display window [GC-options] x1 y1 x2 y2`
XDrawLines `display window [coord-mode-option] [GC-options] x1 y1 x2 y2 ...`

XLIB   These commands draw lines on a `window`. The first command draws a single line from `x1, y1` to `x2, y2` where a coordinate of 0,0 specifies the upper left corner of the `window`. Positive `x` values go to the right, positive `y` values go down the `window`. The second command, `XDrawLines`, can draw multiple lines. The arguments `x1, y1` specify the starting position of the lines, the rest of the values are interpreted according to the `coord-mode-option`, which is one of:

   -CoordModeOrigin   The `x, y` values after the first are absolute coordinate values relative to the origin in the upper left corner of the window. This is the default.

   -CoordModePrevious   The `x, y,` values after the first set are relative offsets from the previous `x, y` values.

XDrawPoint `display window [GC-options] x y`
XDrawPoints `display window [coord-mode-option] [GC-options] x1 y1 [ x2 y2 ...]`

XLIB   The first command draws a single point on a window. The `x, y` values specify the position of the point relative to the origin in the upper left corner of the window. In the second form, multiple points are draw. The `x1, y1` arguments specify the first point to draw relative to the origin, the rest of the `x, y` values are interpreted according to the `coord-mode-option`. See `XDrawLines` for an explanation of the allowed values for `coord-mode-option`.

XDrawRectangle *display window [GC-options] x y width height*

<u>XLIB</u>   Draw a rectangle on a window. The upper left corner of the rectangle is specified by *x, y.* The rectangle is *width* wide and *height* tall.

XDrawSegments *display window [GC-options] x1 y1 x2 y2 [x3 y3 x4 y4 ...]*

<u>XLIB</u>   Draw multiple unconnected line segments. Four-tuples of integer arguments specify the starting and ending coordinates of each line segment. All coordinates are relative to the origin at the upper left corner of the window.

XDrawString *display window [GC-options] x y string*

<u>XLIB</u>   Draw a string on a *window* starting at position *x, y* which is relative to the origin at the upper left corner of the window. The *x, y* coordinate specify the baseline position of the string. The difference between XDrawString and XDrawImageString is that the background color is opaquely drawn in the case of XDrawImageString. For XDrawString, only the text itself is drawn on the existing background.

XFillArc *display window [GC-options] x y width height angle1 angle2*

<u>XLIB</u>   Draw a filled arc. See XDrawArc for details of the other arguments.

XFillPolygon *display drawable [-shape-hint] [-coord-mode] [GC-options] x1 y1 ...*

<u>XLIB</u>   Draw a filled polygon. The *x1, y1* argument specifies the starting coordinate of the first line in the polygon. The remaining coordinates are interpreted according to the *coord-mode* (see XDrawLines). If the first and last points do not match, a final point is added automatically to connect the polygon. The *shape-hint* can give XFillPolygon information, which will allow it to choose faster algorithms for filling the polygon, and can be one of:

>   -Complex   The default. The polygon could have crossing lines, and can be any arbitrary shape. This is the slowest filling algorithm.
>
>   -NonConvex   The polygon could be concave, and has no crossing lines. This algorithm is of intermediate speed.
>
>   -Convex   The polygon is convex, and has no crossing lines. This is the fastest algorithm.

If you specify an incorrect value for the *shape-hint-option*, the results are undefined.

XFillRectangle *display window* [*GC-options*] *x y width height*

XLIB   Draw a filled rectangle. See `XDrawRectangle` for argument descriptions.

XFlush *display*

XLIB   Flush pending operations to the *display*.

XHeightOfScreen *variable screen*

XLIB   Store the *height* of a *screen* into *variable*.

XmAddWMProtocolCallback *widget protocol-atom command*

MOT   Add a command to be executed when a window manager protocol action occurs on
              widget. The *protocol-atom* would normally come from a call to `XmInternAtom`.

XmAddWMProtocols *widget protocol-atom . . .*

MOT   Add the named protocols to *widget*. The *widget* will be notified by the window
              manager whenever one of these protocol events occurs. The *protocol-atoms* nor-
              mally come from a call to `XmInternAtom`.

XmCommandAppendValue *widget string*

MOT   Append a *string* to a Command *widget*'s value resource.

XmCommandError *widget string*

MOT   Display an error message in a Command widget's history area.

XmCommandGetChild *variable widget child-type*

MOT   Get a child widget handle from a Command *widget* and store the child's handle in
              variable. The *child-type* argument specifies which child handle to get:

              DIALOG_COMMAND_TEXT   The Text widget used for prompting.

              DIALOG_PROMPT_LABEL   The Label widget next to the prompt.

              DIALOG_HISTORY_LIST   The List widget used for storing the history.

              DIALOG_WORK_AREA   The work area widget.

XmCommandSetValue *widget string*

MOT   Set the value resource of a Command *widget* to *string*.

XmCreateArrowButton *variable parent name* [*resource:value ...*]

MOT   Creates an ArrowButton widget, storing its handle in *variable*.

XmCreateArrowButtonGadget *variable parent name* [*resource:value ...*]

MOT   Creates a ArrowButtonGadget, storing its handle in *variable*.

XmCreateBulletinBoard *variable parent name* [*resource:value ...*]

MOT   Creates a BulletinBoard widget, storing its handle in *variable*.

XmCreateBulletinBoardDialog *variable parent name* [*resource:value ...*]

MOT   Creates a BulletinBoard widget inside a DialogShell widget. The handle of the Bul-
             letinBoard is stored in the named *variable*. The *resource:value* pairs apply to
             the BulletinBoard. To access the DialogShell widget, use XtParent on the returned
             variable.

XmCreateCascadeButton *variable parent name* [*resource:value ...*]

MOT   Creates a CascadeButton widget, storing its handle in *variable*.

XmCreateCascadeButtonGadget *variable parent name* [*resource:value ...*]

MOT   Creates a CascadeButton gadget, storing its handle in *variable*.

XmCreateCommand *variable parent name* [*resource:value ...*]

MOT   Creates a Command widget, storing its handle in *variable*.

XmCreateDialogShell *variable parent name* [*resource:value ...*]

MOT   Creates a Command widget, storing its handle in *variable*.

XmCreateDrawingArea *variable parent name* [*resource:value ...*]

MOT   Creates a DrawingArea widget, storing its handle in *variable*.

XmCreateDrawnButton *variable parent name* [*resource:value* ...]

MOT   Creates a DrawnButton widget, storing its handle in *variable*.

XmCreateErrorDialog *variable parent name* [*resource:value* ...]

MOT   Creates a DialogShell widget with a MessageBox widget child that displays the standard Motif symbol for an error. The MessageBox widget handle is stored in *variable*, and the *resource:value* pairs apply to it. To access the DialogShell widget, use XtParent on the returned *variable* to get its handle.

XmCreateFileSelectionBox *variable parent name* [*resource:value* ...]

MOT   Creates a FileSelectionBox widget, storing its handle in *variable*.

XmCreateFileSelectionDialog *variable parent name* [*resource:value* ...]

MOT   Creates a DialogShell widget with a FileSelectionBox widget as its child. The FileSelectionBox widget handle is stored in *variable*, and the *resource:value* pairs apply to it. To access the DialogShell widget, use XtParent on the returned *variable* to get its handle; to pop up (down) the dialog, use XtManageChild (XtUnmanageChild) on the returned *variable*.

XmCreateForm *variable parent name* [*resource:value* ...]

MOT   Creates a Form widget, storing its handle in *variable*.

XmCreateFormDialog *variable parent name* [*resource:value* ...]

MOT   Creates a DialogShell widget with a Form widget as its child. The Form widget handle is stored in *variable*, and the *resource:value* pairs apply to it. To access the DialogShell widget, use XtParent on the returned *variable* to get its handle; to pop up (down) the dialog, use XtManageChild (XtUnmanageChild) on the returned *variable*.

XmCreateFrame *variable parent name* [*resource:value* ...]

MOT   Creates a Frame widget, storing its handle in *variable*.

XmCreateInformationDialog *variable parent name* [*resource:value* ...]

MOT   Creates a DialogShell widget with a MessageBox widget child that displays the standard Motif symbol for an informational message. The MessageBox widget handle is stored in *variable*, and the *resource:value* pairs apply to it. To access the DialogShell widget, use `XtParent` on the returned *variable* to get its handle; to pop up (down) the dialog, use `XtManageChild` (`XtUnmanageChild`) on the returned *variable*.

XmCreateLabel *variable parent name* [*resource:value ...*]

MOT   Creates a Label widget, storing its handle in *variable*.

XmCreateLabelGadget *variable parent name* [*resource:value ...*]

MOT   Creates a Label gadget, storing its handle in *variable*.

XmCreateList *variable parent name* [*resource:value ...*]

MOT   Creates a List widget, storing its handle in *variable*.

XmCreateMainWindow *variable parent name* [*resource:value ...*]

MOT   Creates a MainWindow widget, storing its handle in *variable*.

XmCreateMenuBar *variable parent name* [*resource:value ...*]

MOT   Creates a MenuBar widget, storing its handle in *variable*.

XmCreateMenuShell *variable parent name* [*resource:value ...*]

MOT   Creates a MenuShell widget, storing its handle in *variable*.

XmCreateMessageBox *variable parent name* [*resource:value ...*]

MOT   Creates a MessageBox widget, storing its handle in *variable*.

XmCreateMessageDialog *variable parent name* [*resource:value ...*]

MOT   Creates a DialogShell widget with a MessageBox widget as its child. The Message-Box widget handle is stored in *variable*, and the resource:value pairs apply to it. To access the DialogShell widget, use `XtParent` on the returned *variable* to get its handle; to pop up (down) the dialog, use `XtManageChild` (`XtUnmanageChild`) on the returned *variable*.

XmCreateOptionMenu *variable parent name* [*resource:value ...*]

MOT   Creates a OptionMenu widget, storing its handle in *variable*.

XmCreatePanedWindow *variable parent name* [*resource:value* ...]

MOT   Creates a PanedWindow widget, storing its handle in *variable*.

XmCreatePopupMenu *variable parent name* [*resource:value* ...]

MOT   Creates a PopupMenu widget, storing its handle in *variable*.

XmCreatePromptDialog *variable parent name* [*resource:value* ...]

MOT   Creates a DialogShell widget with a MessageBox widget child that displays the standard Motif symbol for a prompt message. The MessageBox widget handle is stored in *variable*, and the *resource:value* pairs apply to it. To access the DialogShell widget, use XtParent on the returned *variable* to get its handle; to pop up (down) the dialog, use XtManageChild (XtUnmanageChild) on the returned *variable*.

XmCreatePulldownMenu *variable parent name* [*resource:value* ...]

MOT   Creates a PulldownMenu widget, storing its handle in *variable*.

XmCreatePushButton *variable parent name* [*resource:value* ...]

MOT   Creates a PushButton widget, storing its handle in *variable*.

XmCreatePushButtonGadget *variable parent name* [*resource:value* ...]

MOT   Creates a PushButton gadget, storing its handle in *variable*.

XmCreateQuestionDialog *variable parent name* [*resource:value* ...]

MOT   Creates a DialogShell widget with a MessageBox widget child that displays the standard Motif symbol for a question message. The MessageBox widget handle is stored in *variable*, and the *resource:value* pairs apply to it. To access the DialogShell widget, use XtParent on the returned *variable* to get its handle; to pop up (down) the dialog, use XtManageChild (XtUnmanageChild) on the returned *variable*.

XmCreateRadioBox *variable parent name* [*resource:value* ...]

MOT   Creates a RowColumn widget, storing its handle in *variable*. The RowColumn widget's resources are configured to make it appropriate for use as a radio box. This is equivalent to the following command:

```
XmCreateRowColumn variable parent name \
        rowColumnType:WORK_AREA \
        packing:PACK_COLUMN \
        radioBehavior:true \
        isHomogeneous:true \
        entryClass:ToggleButton Gadget
```

In this configuration, one or more ToggleButtonGadget children are added to the RowColumn with their `indicatorType` resources set to `ONE_OF_MANY` and the `visibleWhenOff` resources set to `true`. A setup like this allows at most one ToggleButtonGadget to be set at a time, simulating the way buttons work on a car radio.

XmCreateRowColumn *variable parent name* [*resource:value* ...]

MOT   Creates a RowColumn widget, storing its handle in *variable*.

XmCreateScale *variable parent name* [*resource:value* ...]

MOT   Creates a Scale widget, storing its handle in *variable*.

XmCreateScrollBar *variable parent name* [*resource:value* ...]

MOT   Creates a ScrollBar widget, storing its handle in *variable*.

XmCreateScrolledList *variable parent name* [*resource:value* ...]

MOT   Creates a ScrolledWindow widget with a List widget as its child. The handle of the XmList widget is stored in *variable*. The *resource:value* pairs apply to the List widget. To access the ScrolledWindow widget, use `XtParent` on the returned *variable* to get its handle.

XmCreateScrolledText *variable parent name* [*resource:value* ...]

MOT   Creates a ScrolledWindow widget with a Text widget as its child. The handle of the Text widget is stored in *variable*. The *resource:value* pairs apply to the Text widget. To access the ScrolledWindow widget, use `XtParent` on the returned *variable* to get its handle.

XmCreateScrolledWindow *variable parent name* [*resource:value* ...]

MOT   Creates a ScrolledWindow widget, storing its handle in *variable*.

XmCreateSelectionBox *variable parent name* [*resource:value ...*]

<u>MOT</u>   Creates a SelectionBox widget, storing its handle in *variable*.

XmCreateSelectionDialog *variable parent name* [*resource:value ...*]

<u>MOT</u>   Creates a DialogShell widget with a SelectionBox widget as its child. The Selection-Box widget handle is stored in *variable*, and the *resource:value* pairs apply to it. To access the DialogShell widget, use XtParent on the returned *variable* to get its handle; to pop up (down) the dialog, use XtManageChild (XtUnmanageChild) on the returned *variable*.

XmCreateSeparator *variable parent name* [*resource:value ...*]

<u>MOT</u>   Creates a Separator widget, storing its handle in *variable*.

XmCreateSeparatorGadget *variable parent name* [*resource:value ...*]

<u>MOT</u>   Creates a Separator gadget, storing its handle in *variable*.

XmCreateText *variable parent name* [*resource:value ...*]

<u>MOT</u>   Creates a Text widget, storing its handle in *variable*.

XmCreateTextField *variable parent name* [*resource:value ...*]

<u>MOT</u>   Creates a TextField widget, storing its handle in *variable*.

XmCreateToggleButton *variable parent name* [*resource:value ...*]

<u>MOT</u>   Creates a ToggleButton widget, storing its handle in *variable*.

XmCreateToggleButtonGadget *variable parent name* [*resource:value ...*]

<u>MOT</u>   Creates a Separator gadget, storing its handle in *variable*.

XmCreateWarningDialog *variable parent name* [*resource:value ...*]

<u>MOT</u>   Creates a DialogShell widget with a MessageBox widget child that displays the standard Motif symbol for a warning message. The MessageBox widget handle is stored in *variable*, and the *resource:value* pairs apply to it. To access the DialogShell widget, use XtParent on the returned *variable* to get its handle; to pop up (down) the dialog, use XtManageChild (XtUnmanageChild) on the returned *variable*.

XmCreateWorkArea *variable parent name* [*resource:value ...*]

<u>MOT</u>   Creates a RowColumn widget, storing its handle in *variable*. The `rowColumn-Type` resource is automatically set to `WORK_AREA` by this command.

XmCreateWorkingDialog *variable parent name* [*resource:value ...*]

<u>MOT</u>   Creates a DialogShell widget with a MessageBox widget child that displays the standard Motif symbol for a "working" message. The MessageBox widget handle is stored in *variable*, and the *resource:value* pairs apply to it. To access the DialogShell widget, use `XtParent` on the returned *variable* to get its handle; to pop up (down) the dialog, use `XtManageChild` (`XtUnmanageChild`) on the returned *variable*.

XmFileSelectionBoxGetChild *variable widget child-type*

<u>MOT</u>   Get a child widget handle from a FileSelectionBox widget, and store it in *variable*. The *child-type* argument specifies which child widget handle to get:

`DIALOG_APPLY_BUTTON`	The PushButtonGadget for the "Apply" button.
`DIALOG_CANCEL_BUTTON`	The PushButtonGadget for the "Cancel" button.
`DIALOG_DEFAULT_BUTTON`	The PushButtonGadget for the "Default" button.
`DIALOG_DIR_LIST`	The XmList widget holding the directory list.
`DIALOG_DIR_LIST_LABEL`	The Label widget next to the directory list.
`DIALOG_FILTER_LABEL`	The Label widget next to the filter text.
`DIALOG_FILTER_TEXT`	The TextField widget holding the filter value.
`DIALOG_HELP_BUTTON`	The PushButtonGadget for the Help button.
`DIALOG_LIST`	The XmList widget holding the filename list.
`DIALOG_LIST_LABEL`	The Label widget next to the filename list.
`DIALOG_OK_BUTTON`	The PushButtonGadget for the OK button.
`DIALOG_SEPARATOR`	The Separator widget.
`DIALOG_SELECTION_LABEL`	The Label widget next to the selected filename.
`DIALOG_TEXT`	The Text widget holding the selected filename.
`DIALOG_WORK_AREA`	The WorkArea widget.

XmFileSelectionDoSearch *widget directory-name*

This command allows you to programmatically force a reinitialization of a FileSelectionBox's lists. The `widget` argument is the handle of a FileSelectionBox widget, and the `directory-name` is the name of the directory to use as a starting point for the lists.

XmGetAtomName *variable* `display atom`

MOT

Get the string associated with an atom identifier, storing it in the named `variable`. The `display` argument normally comes from a call to XtDisplay `$TOPLEVEL`.

XmGetColors `widget background variable-fg variable-ts variable-bs variable-sel`

MOT

Takes a widget and a background color and returns foreground, top shadow, bottom shadow, and select pixel values in the respective `variable` names.

XmGetFocusWidget `variable widget`

MOT

Looks at the hierarchy starting at `widget` for the child that currently has keyboard focus, storing the result in the `variable`. If no widget has keyboard focus, the string NULL is stored in the `variable`.

XmGetPostedFromWidget `variable menu-widget`

MOT

Stores the handle of the widget from which a `menu-widget` was posted in the `variable`. This is typically used inside a callback for the `menu-widget`.

XmGetTabGroup `variable widget`

MOT

Given a `widget`, returns the handle of the widget which is the controlling tab group in the `variable`. If the widget itself is a tab group, its handle will be stored in the `variable`.

XmGetTearOffControl `variable menu-widget`

MOT

When a menu widget is a tear-off, it will contain an initial entry that is a button containing a dashed line. This button is called the tear-off control. The `XmGetTearOffControl` command returns the handle of the tear-off control for a `menu-widget` in the `variable`.

XmGetVisibility *variable widget*

This command returns information about whether the named *widget* is visible in the *variable*. Possible return values are:

VISIBILITY_UNOBSCURED   The widget is fully visible.

VISIBILITY_PARTIALLY_OBSCURED The widget is partially covered by some
                               other widget.

VISIBILITY_FULLY_OBSCURED   The widget is not at all visible on the
                               screen.

XmInternAtom *variable display atom-name existence-flag*

MOT   Store the atom corresponding to *atom-name* in *variable*. The *existence-flag* can be true or false, with true meaning the atom should be created if it does not exist. If *existence-flag* is false, and the *atom-name* does not exist, then None is stored in *variable*.

XmIsTraversable *widget*

MOT   Finds out if the named widget is traversable (i.e., eligible to receive focus via keyboard traversal) and returns success (zero) if it is, and failure (nonzero) otherwise. Thus, can be used as the conditional command of an if or while statement. Typically, a widget is eligible to receive focus if it is sensitive, is not in the process of being destroyed, has its traversalOn resource set to true, is realized, mapped, and managed, and is unobscured by other widgets. There are some exceptions. For example, a child of a ScrolledWindow widget is traversable only if the scrolling-Policy is AUTOMATIC and the traverseObscuredCallback is not NULL. Also, a DrawingArea widget is traversable only if it has no children whose traversalOn resource is true.

XmListAddItem *widget position string*
XmListAddItems *widget position string ...*
XmListAddItemUnselected *widget position string*
XmListAddItemsUnselected *widget position string ...*

MOT   Add items to a List widget. The *string* argument is the label that will appear in the list. The *position* argument specifies where to place the item. Item numbers start at 1, so making the position argument 1 would add the item at the head of the list. A position value of zero indicates that the item should be added to the end of the List. The pluralized commands, XmListAddItems and XmListAddItemsUn-

`selected`, allow multiple items to be added. The unselected commands add items such that they are not initially selected.

XmListDeleteAllItems *widget*

XmListDeleteItem *widget string*

XmListDeleteItems *widget string ...*

XmListDeleteItemsPos *widget number index*

XmListDeletePos *widget position*

XmListDeletePositions *widget index ...*

MOT   Delete items from a List widget. `XmListDeleteAllItems` removes all items from the list. `XmListDeleteItem` and `XmListDeleteItems` delete items based on their *string* labels. If the same label occurs on more than one item, the first is deleted. `XmListDeleteItemsPos` deletes multiple items. The *number* argument specifies the number of items starting at position *index*. `XmListDeletePos` and `XmList-DeletePositions` delete items based on their *index* number. Indexes start at 1.

XmListDeselectAllItems *widget*

XmListDeselectItem *widget string*

XmListDeselectPos *widget number*

MOT   Deselect items in a List widget. `XmListDeselectAll` deselects all items in the widget. `XmListDeselectItem` deselects items whose labels match the given *string*. `XmListDelselectPos` deselects items based on their *index* number in the list. Indexes start at 1, and an index of 0 indicates the last item in the list.

XmListGetKbdItemPos *variable widget*

MOT   Gets the index of the List widget item that currently has the mouseless focus, storing it in *variable*. Indexes start at 1. A returned index of 0 indicates that the list is empty.

XmListGetMatchPos *variable widget string*

XmListGetSelectedPos *variable widget*

MOT   `XmListGetMatchPos` returns a comma-separated list of indexes of items that match *string* in a List *widget*. The results are stored in the *variable*. This command can be used in a conditional statement to test if the *string* appears as any item. `XmListGetSelectedPos` returns a comma-separated list of the selected items in a List *widget*. The result is stored in the *variable*.

XmListItemExists *widget string*

MOT   Returns success (zero) if there is an item in the named List *widget* whose label matches *string*. Returns failure (nonzero) otherwise. Thus, this can be used as the conditional command to an `if` or `while` statement.

XmListItemPos *variable widget string*

MOT   Looks in the named List *widget* for an item whose label matches *string*. Puts the index of the item in *variable*. Indexes start at 1. If the item is not found, 0 is stored in the *variable*.

XmListPosSelected *widget number*

MOT   Returns success (zero) if the item at index *number* in the named List widget is currently selected, or failure (nonzero) otherwise. Thus, can be used as the conditional command to an `if` or `while` statement.

XmListPosToBounds *widget position variable-x variable-y *
variable-w variable-h

MOT   Returns the bounding rectangle of the List item at `position`. The x, y coordinates of the upper left corner are stored in *variable-x* and *variable-y*, and the width and height of the rectangle are stored in *variable-w* and *variable-h*.

XmListReplaceItemsPos *widget position string ...*
XmListReplaceItemsPosUnselected *widget position string ...*

MOT   Replace items in a List widget starting at *position*. The *strings* replace labels starting at the given index *position*. The `XmListReplaceItemsPosUnselected` function ensures that the items are not selected following the replacement.

XmListSelectItem *widget string notify-flag*
XmListSelectPos *widget number notify-flag*

MOT   Cause items in a List widget to become selected. The *notify-flag* is either `true` or `false` and indicates whether notification of the selection should be sent to the List widget by invoking the selection callback appropriate to the current list mode (i.e., `singleSelectionCallback` if the list is in single selection mode, and so on). The `XmListSelectItem` command finds the first item that matches *string* and selects it. The `XmListSelectPos` command selects the item at the given index *number*. Indexes start at 1, and an index of 0 indicates the last item in the list.

XmListSetAddMode *widget state*

MOT   Sets the add mode of the named List widget. The *state* is either `true` or `false` and indicates whether add mode should be active. Add mode allows items to be added in the extended selection input model.

XmListSetBottomItem *widget string*
XmListSetBottomPos *widget number*

MOT   Set which item appears at the bottom of a List widget. The `XmListSetBottomItem` command finds the first item whose label matches the given *string* and scrolls the list so that is the last item displayed. The `XmListSetBottomPos` command makes the item whose index is *number* the last displayed item.

XmListSetHorizPos *widget position*

MOT   Moves the horizontal Scrollbar of the named List widget to *position* (in pixels).

XmListSetItem *widget string*
XmListSetPos *widget number*

MOT   Sets the top item displayed in a List. The List is scrolled to make the specified item the first displayed. `XmListSetItem` finds the first item in the list whose label matches *string*, while `XmListSetItemPos` uses the item at index *number*.

XmListSetKBDItemPos *widget index*

MOT   Places the selection cursor in a List *widget* at the item with the given *index*. Indexes start at 1, and an index of 0 indicates the last item.

XmListUpdateSelectedList *widget*

MOT   Traverses all items in a List *widget*, finding those that are selected. The `selectedItems` resource of the List widget is updated to reflect the selected items.

XmMainWindowSep1 *variable widget*
XmMainWindowSep2 *variable widget*
XmMainWindowSep3 *variable widget*

MOT   Get widget handles for Separator children of a MainWindow widget.

XmMainWindowSetAreas *widget menu command hscroll vscroll work*

MOT   Set children on a MainWindow *widget*. The first argument is the MainWindow
widget itself; each other argument is a handle of a child of the MainWindow widget.
Any of the additional arguments may be the string NULL if that child is not present.

XmMenuPosition *widget event*

MOT   Positions the a PopupMenu widget appropriately given the *x*, *y* coordinates stored
in an event. The event typically comes from the EH_XEVENT or TRANSLATION_X-
EVENT variables (depending on whether this is called from an event handler or a
translation handler).

XmMessageBoxGetChild *variable widget child-type*

MOT   Get a child widget handle of a MessageBox widget. The child handle is stored in
variable. The *child-type* argument specifies which child to get:

DIALOG_CANCEL_BUTTON	The PushButtonGadget for the Cancel button.
DIALOG_DEFAULT_BUTTON	The PushButtonGadget for the Default button.
DIALOG_HELP_BUTTON	The PushButtonGadget for the Help button.
DIALOG_MESSAGE_LABEL	The Label widget used for the message.
DIALOG_OK_BUTTON	The PushButtonGadget for the OK button.
DIALOG_SEPARATOR	The Separator widget.
DIALOG_SYMBOL_LABEL	The Label widget that holds the graphic symbol for the message.

XmOptionButtonGadget *variable option-menu-widget*
XmOptionLabelGadget *variable option-menu-widget*

MOT   These commands return the button and label gadgets, respectively, of an Option-
Menu. The resulting handle is stored in the *variable*.

XmProcessTraversal *widget direction*

MOT   Move focus from one *widget* to another. The *direction* argument specifies where
to move the focus:

`TRAVERSE_CURRENT`	The *widget* gets focus.
`TRAVERSE_DOWN`	The widget below the specified *widget* gets focus.
`TRAVERSE_HOME`	The first widget in the specified *widget*'s tab group gets focus.
`TRAVERSE_LEFT`	The widget to the left of the specified *widget* gets focus.
`TRAVERSE_NEXT`	The next widget after the specified *widget* gets focus.
`TRAVERSE_NEXT_TAB_GROUP`	The next tab group after the tab group in which the specified *widget* is a member gets focus.
`TRAVERSE_PREV`	The previous widget before the specified *widget* gets focus.
`TRAVERSE_PREV_TAB_GROUP`	The previous tab group before the tab group that contains the specified *widget* gets focus.
`TRAVERSE_RIGHT`	The widget to the right of the specified *widget* gets focus.
`TRAVERSE_UP`	The widget above the specified *widget* gets focus.

In case there is no widget in the named direction, the command wraps. For example, if widget is the last in a row and `TRAVERSE_RIGHT` is specified, the command would cause the first item in the row to get focus.

XmRemoveWMProtocolCallback *widget protocol-atom command*

MOT   Remove a window manager protocol callback. The *widget, protocol-atom*, and *command* must match exactly to arguments previously specified on a call to the `XmAddWMProtocolCallback` command.

XmRemoveWMProtocols *widget protocol-atom command . . .*

MOT   Remove notification of the specified window manager protocols from *widget*. The *protocol-atom* and *command* must match those given on a previous call to `XmAddWMProtocols`.

XmScaleGetValue *widget variable*
XmScaleSetValue *widget value*

<u>MOT</u>   Convenience functions to get and set the `value` resource of a Scale widget.

XmScrollbarGetValues *widget variable-val variable-sz \
                          variable-inc variable-pg-inc*

<u>MOT</u>   A convenience function that returns several resource settings from a ScrollBar widget. Returns the associated slider's `value` (between its `minimum` and `maximum` resources), its size (the difference between `minimum` and `maximum`), its increment size, and the amount of a page increment and decrement in the various *variable* arguments.

XmScrollbarSetValues *widget value size increment page-increment notify-flag*

<u>MOT</u>   Sets several resources on a ScrollBar widget's slider. The *value* argument sets the current `value` of the slider (between its `minimum` and `maximum`), *size* sets the `sliderSize` resource, *increment* sets the `increment` resource, and *page-increment* sets the `pageIncrement` resource. If the *notify-flag* is true, then the `valueChangeCallback` is triggered to notify the ScrollBar widget of the change.

XmScrollVisible *widget child-widget left-right-margin top-bottom-margin*

<u>MOT</u>   Makes an invisible child of a ScrolledWindow widget visible by moving the scroll area. The *left-right-margin* specifies the amount of whitespace that should be maintained to the left and right of the child relative to the edges of the scroll area. Similarly the *top-bottom-margin* specifies whitespace to maintain between the child and the top and bottom edges of the scroll area. These margins are only enforced if scrolling is required to bring the child into view.

XmSelectionBoxGetChild *variable widget child-type*

<u>MOT</u>   Get a child widget handle from a SelectionBox widget. The child's handle is stored in the *variable*. The *child-type* argument specifies which child to get:

DIALOG_CANCEL_BUTTON   The PushButtonGadget used for the Cancel button.

DIALOG_DEFAULT_BUTTON   The PushButton gadget used for the default button.

DIALOG_HELP_BUTTON   The PushButton gadget used for the Help button.

DIALOG_APPLY_BUTTON	The PushButton gadget used for the Apply button.
DIALOG_LIST	The selection box List widget.
DIALOG_LIST_LABEL	The Label next to the List.
DIALOG_OK_BUTTON	The PushButton gadget used for the OK button.
DIALOG_SELECTION_LABEL	The Label next to the current selection TextField.
DIALOG_SEPARATOR	The Separator.
DIALOG_TEXT	The TextField widget used for the current selection.
DIALOG_WORK_AREA	The WorkArea widget.

XmTextClearSelection *widget time*

MOT   Clear the current selection in a Text widget. The time argument typically comes from the X event timestamp field, or from a call to XmLastTimeStampProcessed.

XmTextCopy *widget time*
XmTextCut *widget time*

MOT   Copy or cut selected text in a Text widget to the cut buffer. The time argument specifies an event timestamp and usually comes either from the TIMESTAMP field of a CB_CALL_DATA.EVENT structure or via a call to XtLastTimeStampProcessed.

XmTextDisableRedisplay *widget*

MOT   Stop redisplaying changes to the text in a Text *widget* until a call to TextEnable-Display. Typically used when there are several changes to make to the text and the programmer wishes to avoid intermediate screen updates.

XmTextEnableDisplay *widget*

MOT   Enable display of the text in a Text *widget*. Typically used after a previous call to XmTextDisableRedisplay.

XmTextFieldClearSelection *widget time*

MOT   Clear the selection in a TextField widget. The time argument is typically taken from an X event timestamp or obtained from the XtLastTimeStampProcessed command.

XmTextFieldCopy *widget time*
XmTextFieldCut *widget time*

<u>MOT</u>   Copy or cut selected text in a TextField widget to the cut buffer. The time argument
            specifies an event timestamp and usually comes either from the TIMESTAMP field of
            a CB_CALL_DATA.EVENT structure or via a call to XtLastTimeStampProcessed.

XmTextFieldGetBaseline *variable widget*

<u>MOT</u>   Stores the x position of the first baseline of the named TextField *widget* into the
            given *variable*. The position is relative to the top of the widget, and takes into
            account margins, shadows, highlights, and the font ascent of the first font in the
            font list.

XmTextFieldGetEditable *variable widget*
XmTextFieldGetInsertionPosition *variable widget*
XmTestFieldGetLastPosition *variable widget*
XmTextFieldGetMaxLength *variable widget*

<u>MOT</u>   These commands retrieve various attributes of a TextField *widget*, storing the
            attribute in the *variable*. The attributes are, respectively: the editable
            resource, the cursorPosition resource, the last text position, and the maxLength
            resource.

XmTextFieldGetSelection *variable widget*

<u>MOT</u>   Stores the selected text of the TextField *widget* into the named *variable*.

XmTextFieldGetSelectionPosition *variable widget variable-start variable-end*

<u>MOT</u>   The starting and ending positions of the primary selection in the TextField widget
            are stored in *variable-start* and *variable-end*. The string true is stored in
            variable if the widget owned the primary selection, otherwise false is stored
            there.

XmTextFieldGetString *variable widget*

<u>MOT</u>   Get the string resource of a TextField *widget*, storing it in *variable*.

XmTextFieldInsert *widget position string*

<u>MOT</u>   Insert a *string* at a given character *position* in a TextField *widget*.

XmTextFieldPaste *widget*

MOT   Paste the contents of the cut buffer into the insertion point of a Text *widget*.

XmTextFieldPosToXY *widget position variable-x variable-y*

MOT   Given a TextField *widget* and a character *position*, find the *x* and *y* offsets relative to the upper left corner of the widget to the given character position, storing the results in *variable-x* and *variable-y*.

XmTextFieldRemove *widget*

MOT   Deletes the primary selection text from a TextField *widget*. The widget's `valueChangedCallbacks`, `modifyVerifyCallback`, and/or `modifyVerifyCallbackWcs` are executed as appropriate. Returns zero (success) if there was a primary selection, nonzero (failure) otherwise. Thus can be used as the conditional command in an `if` or `while` statement.

XmTextFieldReplace *widget from to string*

MOT   Replace text in a TextField *widget*. The text starting at the *from* position going to the *to* position is replaced by the given *string*.

XmTextFieldSetAddMode *widget state*

Put the specified Textfield widget in add-mode. In this mode, mouseless movement operations can be used to add to the current selection.

XmTextFieldSetEditable *widget edit-flag*

MOT   Set the editable resource of a TextField *widget*. The *edit-flag* is either `true` or `false` indicating whether the widget should be editable or not.

XmTextFieldSetHighlight *widget left right mode*

MOT   Set the highlight mode of text in a TextField *widget*. The *left* and *right* parameters specify the starting and ending character positions within the text buffer. *Mode* specifies the type of highlighting, and must be one of:

`HIGHLIGHT_NORMAL`   Remove all special highlighting.

`HIGHLIGHT_SELECTED`   Highlight by reversing the foreground and background colors. Note: this does not change or set the selection.

HIGHLIGHT_SECONDARY_SELECTED   Highlight by underlining. Note: this does not change or set the secondary selection.

XmTextFieldSetInsertionPosition *widget position*

MOT   Set the insertion point in a TextField *widget* to *position*. The *position* argument is an offset into the TextField's text buffer.

XmTextFieldSetMaxLength *widget length*

Set the maxLength resource of a TextField *widget* to *length*.

XmTextFieldSetSelection *widget first last time*

MOT   Set the selected text in a TextField *widget*. The *first* and *last* parameters indicate offsets into the text buffer. The *time* parameter typically comes either from the timestamp field of an X event structure or from XtLastTimeStampProcessed.

XmTextFieldSetString *widget string*

MOT   Set the string resource of a TextField *widget* to the specified *string*.

XmTextFieldShowPosition *widget position*

MOT   Scroll text in a TextField *widget* so the character at *position* is visible.

XmTextFieldXYToPos *variable widget x y*

MOT   Given a TextField widget and *x*, *y* coordinates relative to the upper left corner of the *widget*, store the character position of the nearest character to the coordinates in the *variable*.

XmTextFindString *widget position string direction*

MOT   Find the given string in the Text *widget* starting at character *position*. The *direction* argument is either TEXT_FORWARD or TEXT_BACKWARD and specifies which way the search should proceed.

XmTextGetBaseline *variable widget*

MOT   Stores the x position of the first baseline of the named Text *widget* into the given *variable*. The position is relative to the top of the widget, and takes into account margins, shadows, highlights, and the font ascent of the first font in the font list.

XmTextGetEditable *widget*

MOT   Returns success (zero) if the given Text *widget* is editable, and failure (nonzero) otherwise. Thus, can be used as the condition command in an `if` or `while` statement.

XmTextGetInsertionPosition *variable widget*

MOT   Store the current insertion position (a character offset) in the named Text *widget* into *variable*.

XmTextGetLastPosition *variable widget*

MOT   Store the last position (the maximum character offset) in the named Text *widget* into *variable*.

XmTextGetMaxLength *variable widget*

MOT   Get the maximum allowed length of the given Text *widget* and store it into *variable*.

XmTextGetSelection *variable widget*

MOT   Store the currently selected text in a Text *widget* into *variable*.

XmTextGetSelectionPosition *widget variable-start variable-end*

MOT   Get the starting and ending character positions of the selected text in a Text *widget*. Store these results in the two *variable* arguments.

XmTextGetString *variable widget*

MOT   Get the entire string from a Text *widget* and store it in *variable*.

XmTextGetTopCharacter *variable widget*

MOT   Get the position of the topmost displayed character in a Text *widget*. The position is stored in *variable*.

XmTextInsert *widget position string*

MOT   Insert a *string* at the given character *position* in a Text *widget*.

XmTextPaste `widget`

MOT Paste the contents of the cut buffer into the insertion point of a Text `widget`.

XmTextPosToXY `widget position variable-x variable-y`

MOT Given a Text `widget` and a character `position`, find the x and y offsets relative to the upper left corner of the Text widget to the given character position, storing the results in `variable-x` and `variable-y`.

XmTextRemove `widget`

MOT Deletes the primary selection text from a Text `widget`. The Text widget's `valueChangedCallback`, `modifyVerifyCallback`, and/or `modifyVerifyCallbackWcs` are executed as appropriate. Returns zero (success) if there was a primary selection, nonzero (failure) otherwise. Thus, can be used as the conditional command in an `if` or `while` statement.

XmTextReplace `widget from to string`

MOT Replace text in a Text `widget`. The text starting at the `from` position going to the `to` position is replaced by `string`.

XmTextScroll `widget lines`

MOT Scroll a Text `widget` by the specified number of `lines` (which may be negative for backward scrolls).

XmTextSetAddMode `widget state`

MOT Set the add-mode `state` of a Text `widget`. The `state` argument is either `true` or `false`. When in add-mode, the insert cursor can be moved without changing the primary selection.

XmTextSetEditable `widget edit-flag`

MOT Set the `editable` resource of a Text `widget`. The `edit-flag` is either `true` or `false`.

XmTextSetHighlight `widget left right mode`

MOT Sets highlighting on text in a Text widget. The `left` and `right` arguments are character positions relative to the start of the text (starting at 0). The `mode` is one of:

HIGHLIGHT_NORMAL   Remove any special highlighting.

HIGHLIGHT_SELECTED   Make the text reverse video. Note that this does not change the selection, just the appearance of the text.

HIGHLIGHT_SECONDARY_SELECTED   Make the text underlined. Note that this does not actually change the secondary selection, just the appearance of the text.

XmTextSetInsertionPosition *widget position*

MOT   Set the `insertionPosition` resource of a Text *widget* to *position*.

XmTextSetMaxLength *widget length*

MOT   Set the `maxLength` resource of a Text *widget* to *length*.

XmTextSetSelection *widget first last time*

MOT   Set the selection in a Text widget. The selection spans from the *first* position to the *last* position. The *time* argument is a timestamp typically obtained either from the `CB_CALL_DATA.EVENT.TIMESTAMP` variable or from the `XtLastTimeStampProcessed` command.

XmTextSetString *widget string*

MOT   Set the `string` resource of a Text *widget* to the given *string*.

XmTextSetTopCharacter *widget position*

MOT   Scroll the display of a Text *widget* such that the given character *position* is the character at the top left of the viewing area.

XmTextShowPosition *widget position*

MOT   Force the text at the named character *position* to be displayed in a Text *widget*. The text is scrolled appropriately so the character at the named *position* is displayed.

XmTextXYToPos *variable widget x y*

<u>MOT</u>   Given a Text *widget* and *x, y* coordinates relative to the upper left corner of the widget, store the character position of the nearest character to the coordinates in the named *variable*.

XmToggleButtonGadgetGetState *toggle-button-gadget*

<u>MOT</u>   Gets the current state of the indicated ToggleButtonGadget, returning it as the exit status of the command. Thus, this command can be used conveniently in a conditional statement such as if.

XmToggleButtonGadgetSetState *widget state notify-flag*

<u>MOT</u>   Sets the state of the ToggleButton gadget. The *state* argument is true or false. If *notify-flag* is true, then the gadget's valueChangedCallback is called.

XmToggleButtonGetState *widget*

<u>MOT</u>   Get the state of the ToggleButton *widget*. This command returns success (zero) if the ToggleButton state is true, and failure (nonzero) otherwise. Thus, it can be used as the conditional command to an if or while statement.

XmToggleButtonSetState *widget state notify-flag*

<u>MOT</u>   Sets the state of the ToggleButton widget. The *state* argument is true or false. If *notify-flag* is true, then the widget's valueChangedCallback is called.

XmUpdateDisplay *widget*

<u>MOT</u>   All input events are processed immediately. Should be called at the beginning of any time consuming callback (more than a second or two), especially those called from a pulldown menu or triggered during the popdown of a transient dialog box. This is because otherwise underlying widgets below the menu or dialog won't update since they won't receive an expose event until after the time-consuming callback completes.

XRaiseWindow *display window*

<u>XLIB</u>   Bring *window* to the top of the stacking order on the given *display*.

XRootWindowOfScreen *variable screen*

<u>XLIB</u>   Store the root window id of the named *screen* into the given *variable*.

XSync *display discard*

<u>XLIB</u>   Synchronize output to a *display*. *Discard* is either the string `true` or `false`.

XtAddCallback *widget callback-name command*

<u>XT</u>   Add the given *command* (an arbitrary dtksh command string) to the callback list of the *callback-name* for widget. During the execution of the callback, the variable `CB_WIDGET` will be set to the handle of the widget on whose behalf the callback was registered. The variable `CB_CALL_DATA` will contain the address of the call data (if any). In addition, subfields of the variable `CB_CALL_DATA` may be set.

XtAddEventHandler *widget event-mask non-maskable-flag command*

<u>XT</u>   Register a *command* to be executed when an event triggers on a *widget*. The *event-mask* is a pipe-separated sequence of X event names: `ButtonPressMask`, `ButtonReleaseMask`, `Button[123]MotionMask`, `Button[123]PressMask`, `Button[123]ReleaseMask`, etc.

      The *non-maskable-flag* is a `true` or `false` value that specifies whether the named event can be masked. The *command* argument is any arbitrary dtksh command string.

      During the execution of the command, the variable `EH_WIDGET` is set to the handle of the widget on whose behalf the event handler was executed. The variable `EH_EVENT` is set to the address of the X event structure describing the event. In addition, subfields of the `EH_EVENT` variable are set to other fields of the event structure.

XtAddInput *variable* [-r] *file-descriptor command*

<u>XT</u>   Register a command to be executed when there is input available on the given *file-descriptor*. An identifier is returned in *variable* that can be used with `XtRemoveInput` later to remove the input event handler. The following variables are set in the context of the executing dtksh command:

    `INPUT_LINE`   If the -r option (raw mode) was not specified, then this *variable* holds the next available full line of input from the descriptor. Otherwise, it is empty.

INPUT_EOF   Set to the string `true` if an end-of-file condition occurred on the file descriptor.

INPUT_SOURCE   The file descriptor that was registered for this input source.

INPUT_ID   The input source id that was stored in *variable* on the original call to `XtAddInput`. Can be used as an argument to `XtRemoveInput` (typically when end of file has been reached).

If the `-r` option is not specified, the *command* is called whenever a full line (terminated by a non-escaped newline) is encountered on the input file descriptor, and the input source is removed automatically when end of file is reached. If `-r` (raw mode) is specified, then the command is called whenever there is any input available, and it is up to the command to read whatever data it needs from the file descriptor. In raw mode, it is also the responsibility of the command to remove the input source when end of file is reached.

XtAddTimeOut *variable milliseconds command*

XT   Register a command to be executed at a specified future time. The time is specified in the *milliseconds* argument. An identifier is stored in *variable* that can be used in a subsequent call to `XtRemoveTimeOut` to cancel the timed event.

XtAddWorkProc *variable command*

XT   Register a command to be executed whenever there is nothing else to do in the application. The command is registered when `XtMainLoop` has no other events pending. If the *command* returns zero (success) it remains registered for future executions. Any other return value causes the work procedure to be unregistered.

XtAugmentTranslations *widget translations*

XT   Add *translations* to a *widget*. The *translations* argument is a string formed in accordance with X translation syntax rules.

XtCallCallbacks *widget callback-name*

XT   Call all the callbacks associated with a *widget*'s callback list resource named *callback-name*.

XtClass *variable widget*

Retrieves the class name of the given *widget*, storing the result in the *variable*.

XtCreateApplicationShell *variable app-name widget-class* [*resource:value ...*]

XT   Create an ApplicationShell, storing its handle in *variable*. Its name is *app-name*, and the class is specified by *widget-class*. It must be a subclass of the Shell widget class. Any number of *resource:value* pairs may be specified to set creation time resources.

XtCreateManagedWidget *variable widget-name widget-class parent* \
                [*resource:value ...*]

XT   Create a new widget in the managed state, storing its handle in *variable*. The widget's name will be *widget-name*, and it will be of class *widget-class*. The widget will be a child of the widget handle specified in the *parent* argument. Any number of *resource:value* pairs can be specified to set initial resource values.

XtCreatePopupShell *variable widget-name widget-class parent* [*resource:value*]

XT   Create a Popup Shell widget. See XtCreateManagedWidget for argument explanations. The *widget-class* must be a subclass of Shell.

XtCreateWidget *variable widget-name widget-class parent* [*resource:value*]

XT   Create a widget in the unmanaged state (it will not appear on the display until a call to XtManageChildren is made). See XtCreateManagedWidget for argument explanations.

XtDestroyWidget *widget ...*

XT   Destroy one or more *widgets*.

XtDisplay *variable widget*
XtDisplayOfObject *variable widget*

XT   Get the *display* of the named *widget*, storing it in the named *variable*. The display is necessary for certain graphics operations. These commands are equivalent.

XTextWidth *variable font string*

XLIB   Store the width in pixels of *string* as rendered in *font* into *variable*.

XtGetValues *widget resource:variable ...*

XT   Get one or more resource values from a *widget*. Values of the *resources* are stored in the corresponding *variable* names.

XtHasCallbacks *variable widget callback-name*

XT   Check if a *widget* has any callbacks registered with the given *callback-name*.
            One of the following strings is stored in *variable*:

    CallbackNoList   There is no such callback list for the *widget*.

    CallbackHasNone   No callback procedures are registered.

    CallbackHasSome   One or more callback procedures are registered.

XtInitialize *variable app-name app-class arg ...*

XT   Initialize the toolkit. This should be the first graphics command executed. The top-
            level Shell widget handle for this application is stored in *variable*. The applica-
            tion's name and class are specified by *app-name* and *app-class*. Arguments (such
            as -iconic or -geometry) can be specified. Typically, you should put "$@" some-
            where in the *arg* section so the user can pass in standard X Window application
            arguments.
               Following execution of this command, the array variable DTKSH_ARGV will con-
            tain arguments from the arg list that were not recognized by the standard X appli-
            cation   argument   processing.   The   length   of   this   array   is   of   course
            ${#DTKSH_ARGV[@]}. The handle of the top level shell is copied to the variable
            DTKSH_TOPLEVEL, and the app-name argument is copied to the variable
            DTKSH_APPNAME. These variables are sometimes useful in library and convenience
            routines.

XtIsManaged *widget*
XtIsRealized *widget*
XtIsSensitive *widget*
XtIsShell *widget*
XtIsSubclass *widget class*

XT   Checks to determine whether the *widget* is managed, realized, sensitive, is a sub-
            class of Shell, or is a subclass of another widget *class*, respectively. All return suc-
            cess (zero) if the widget is realized, thus can be used as the condition on an if or
            while statement, or the antecedent of the && command list construct.

XtLastTimestampProcessed *variable display*

XT   Some graphics commands dealing with exposure events require an internal X
            parameter called the "timestamp." This command stores the last timestamp pro-
            cessed on the named *display* into the given *variable*.

XtMainLoop

XT   Go into a loop to process events. Typically the last statement of a dtksh graphical
              program.

XtManageChild *widget*
XtManageChildren *widget ...*

XT   Cause *widgets* to be managed. In the first form only a single widget is managed.
              In the second form, one or more widgets are managed. All the widgets must have a
              common parent.

XtMapWidget *widget*

XT   Cause *widget* to become mapped.

XtNameToWidget *variable ref-widget name*

XT   Given a widget *name* relative to a reference widget *ref-widget*, find its handle
              and store the handle in the named *variable*. Returns failure (nonzero) if there is
              no such widget. If there are multiple widgets with the same name, one of them is
              chosen in an unspecified manner.

XtOverrideTranslations *widget   translation-string*

XT   Override one or more translations in a *widget*. The *translation-string* argu-
              ment must be in valid X translation syntax.

XtParent *variable widget*

XT   Put the handle of *widget*'s parent in *variable*.

XtPopdown *widget*

XT   Cause the Shell-class *widget* to be popped down.

XtPopup *widget grab-type*

XT   Pop up a Shell-class widget. The *grab-type* argument is one of:

              GrabNone   Do not grab control of the application. This window will
                                          behave just like any other window on the screen, other

windows in the application can be made current and will respond to user input.

GrabExclusive   Grab exclusive control of the application. Other windows in the application cannot receive input until this window is popped down.

GrabNonExclusive   Like GrabNone.

XtRealizeWidget *widget*

XT   Realize the *widget*. Children of the widget are recursively realized.

XtRemoveAllCallbacks *widget callback-name*

XT   Remove all callback handlers from the callback list specified by *widget* and *callback-name*. The *callback-name* must be one of the callback list resource names supported by the given widget's class.

XtRemoveCallback *widget callback-name command*

XT   Remove the given dtksh command from the callback list specified by *widget* and *callback-name*. The *command* string must be identical character for character with the string that was originally registered as the callback (by XtAddCallback).

XtRemoveEventHandler *widget event-mask non-maskable-flag command*

XT   Remove the named dtksh *command* from the event handler list for the event specified by *widget*, *event-mask*, and *non-maskable-flag*. All the parameters must be identical with those given on a previous call to XtAddEventHandler.

XtRemoveInput *input-identifier*

XT   Remove an input source. The *input-identifier* is the string returned in the *variable* name parameter from a previous call to XtAddInput.

XtRemoveTimeOut *timeout-identifier*

XT   Remove a timer event. The *timeout-identifier* is the string returned in the *variable* parameter from a previous call to XtAddTimeOut.

XtRemoveWorkProc *workproc-identifier*

XT   Remove a work procedure. The *workproc-identifier* is the string returned in the *variable* parameter from a previous call to XtAddWorkProc.

XtScreen *variable widget*

XT   Get the screen data structure for *widget*. The screen identifier is placed in *variable*. This identifier is required by certain direct Xlib commands such as XRoot-WindowOfScreen.

XtSetSensitive *widget state*

XT   Set the sensitivity state of the named *widget*. The *state* argument is either true or false. Children of the named widget are also recursively set. If a widget's sensitivity is set to false, it will not respond to user input.

XtSetValues *widget resource:value ...*

XT   Set resource values for a *widget*. Any number of *resource:value* arguments can be specified.

XtUninstallTranslations *widget*

XT   Remove all translations from *widget*.

XtUnmanageChild *widget*
XtUnmanageChildren *widget ...*

XT   Unmanage widgets. The second form allows multiple *widgets*, which must all have a common parent.

XtUnmapWidget *widget*

XT   Unmap a *widget*.

XtUnrealizeWidget *widget*

XT   Unrealize a *widget*. Recursively unrealizes all the children of the widget.

XtWindow *variable widget*

XT   Put the window identifier of the *widget* into the given *variable*. The window identifier is required as an argument to certain direct Xlib commands.

XUndefineCursor *display window*

<u>XLIB</u>   Remove the cursor definition from a *window* on the named display.

XWidthOfScreen *variable screen*

<u>XLIB</u>   Store the width of the *screen* into *variable*.

33 *XU Library Reference*

33.1 Introduction

Part I of this book uses a simplified set of utilities to teach novice X programmers how to write applications. This set of functions is contained in the file `xutil.sh`, which is available without charge via the Internet (see *Obtaining the Example Programs* on page xxxii). This set of functions is referred to as the X Utility library (XU library for short). The library is used by bringing its code into your script using the KornShell dot command:

```
. $XUTILDIR/xutil.sh
```

where `XUTILDIR` is a variable set to the directory in which `xutil.sh` resides.

Many of the functions contained in this library are generally useful, even to the seasoned X programmer. This chapter presents a summary of all commands contained in this function library.

33.2 Simple Aliases

A number of the XU library commands are simply aliases for standard X commands. All standard Xlib, Xt, and Motif commands provided by dtksh have an alias in the XU library. One reason for providing these aliases is to make the name of the command easier to type by using the same prefix, XU, and reducing the number of case changes in the command name. For example, the Motif command `XmText-GetSelection` is aliased as `XUtextgetselection`.

A second, more important, reason for these aliases is so that in future versions of the XU library it will be possible to provide value-added functionality to these commands. So, if you are using the XU library, you should always use the XU library version of every command.

In the command reference below, any command that is a simple alias for a standard dtksh built-in command will be marked as such. The text will then refer you to the page number where more information on the base dtksh built-in can be found.

33.3 Widget Creation Commands

Many XU library commands are used to create widgets. These commands all take the same arguments:

```
XUwidgetname [-u] variable parent [resource:value ...]
```

Where *widgetname* is the name of the widget in question, in all lowercase letters, with no prefix such as Xm. The -u option causes the newly created widget to be unmanaged, the default is to manage the widget. The newly created widget's handle is stored in *variable*. The parent argument specifies the parent to which the newly created widget will be attached. Any number of resource:value pairs may be specified on the end of the command line to set initial resource values.

33.4 Alphabetical List of Functions

In this section, all XU library functions are listed, along with usage information and a terse explanation. Commands that are simple aliases for standard dtksh built-ins are listed here with only a usage message and the page number where the built-in is explained. Look in the index for examples of each command's use elsewhere in this book.

XUactionbuttons *form* [*variable label command*] ...

Create action area buttons attached to a *form* widget. Action buttons are defined by triples of arguments that specify a *variable* in which to store the button handle, a *label* that should appear on the button, and a *command* that should be executed when the button is pressed. The buttons are spaced evenly inside the form by setting the *form*'s fractionBase resource, so it is not advisable to place anything in the *form* besides the action buttons. Typically, such a *form* should be anchored to the bottom of a dialog window.

XUaddactionarea *variable form-widget under-widget*

This command creates a manager widget suitable for holding action area buttons (see XUactionbuttons). The newly created action area widget's handle is returned in *variable*. The action area is attached to a Form widget specified in the *form-widget* argument. The handle of the lowest widget that exists in the *form-widget* parent is provided in the *under-widget* resource; the action area will be created below that widget using Form constraints.

XUaddbuttons *parent* [*variable label command* ...]

Adds PushButton widgets to a *parent* widget. The buttons are defined by triplets of arguments that specify a *variable* in which the newly created button's handle is returned, a *label* that should appear on the button, and a *command* that should be executed when the button is pressed.

XUaddcallback *widget callback-name command*

This is a simple alias for XtAddCallback, which is explained on page 671.

XUadddatefields *parent* [*variable label* ...]

Creates one or more sets of controls useful for prompting for dates. The controls are added to the *parent* widget, which should stack its children horizontally (such as a row-wise stacking RowColumn widget). This command first creates a Label widget, which displays the label argument. Then, it creates a series of TextField and Label widgets that will hold a month, day, and year value. The handles of the components are stored in the hierarchical variables: *variable*.MM, *variable*.DD, and *variable*.YY (month, day, and year TextFields, respectively).

Validation functions are automatically added to the TextFields to ensure that a valid date is entered in the fields. A warning message is displayed if an invalid date is entered. The controls are also set up to move focus automatically when the user enters a two-digit number. In addition, the TextFields are put in autoselect mode (see XUtextautoselect).

XUaddeventhandler *widget event-mask non-maskable-flag*

This is a simple alias for XtAddEventHandler, which is explained on page 671.

XUaddfloatfields *parent* [*variable label columns* ...]

Creates captioned TextField widgets capable of prompting for floating-point values. The captions and TextFields are created as children of *parent*, which is assumed to be a manager widget that stacks its children horizontally (such as a row-wise stacking RowColumn widget). Triplets of arguments are used to define each control. The *label* argument is a string that is displayed on a Label widget, which is created first. The handle of each newly created TextField is stored in *variable*. The Text-Field will be created the specified number of *columns* wide.

Validation functions are automatically added to the TextField to ensure that it holds a valid floating-point number.

XUaddinput *variable* [-r] *file-descriptor command*

This is a simple alias for XtAddInput, which is explained on page 671.

XUaddintegerfields *parent* [*variable label columns* ...]

Creates captioned TextField widgets capable of prompting for integer values. The captions and TextFields are created as children of *parent*, which is assumed to be a manager widget that stacks its children horizontally (such as a row-wise stacking RowColumn widget). Triplets of arguments are used to define each control. The *label* argument is a string that is displayed on a Label widget, which is created first. The handle of each newly created TextField is stored in *variable*. The Text-Field will be created the specified number of *columns* wide.

Validation functions are automatically added to the TextField to ensure that it holds a valid integer.

XUaddmoneyfields *parent* [*variable label columns* ...]

Creates captioned TextField widgets capable of prompting for monetary values. The captions and TextFields are created as children of *parent*, which is assumed to be a manager widget that stacks its children horizontally (such as a row-wise stacking RowColumn widget). Triplets of arguments are used to define each control. The *label* argument is a string that is displayed on a Label widget, which is created first. The handle of each newly created TextField is stored in *variable*. The Text-Field will be created the specified number of *columns* wide.

Validation functions are automatically added to the TextField to ensure that it holds a monetary value (a number with two decimal places).

XUaddoptionmenu *variable parent caption* [*label* ...]

Creates an OptionMenu, storing its handle in *variable*. A Label widget is created first that displays the string specified by the *caption* argument. The Label is created as a child of the *parent* widget. Then, an OptionMenu is created as a child of *parent*. The items in the OptionMenu are initialized to the list of *labels* specified.

XUaddpixbuttons *parent* [*variable pixmap-file command* ...]

Adds PushButton widgets that display pixmaps. The buttons are attached to the *parent* widget. The buttons are defined by triplets of arguments that specify a *variable* in which the newly created button's handle is returned, a path to a *pixmap-file* that defines the graphic to appear on the button, and a *command* that should be executed when the button is pressed. The pixmap file should be in X11 Bitmap or X11 Pixmap format, as produced by the dticon utility.

XUaddtextfields *parent* [*variable caption verify-command columns* ...]

Creates captioned TextField widgets as children of a *parent* widget. Sets of four arguments define each captioned TextField. In each set of four arguments, a variable is specified that receives the handle of the newly created TextField widget. The *caption* argument is a string that is displayed in a Label widget that is created as a child of *parent* before the TextField itself. The *verify-command* argument is a dtksh command that is registered with the TextField's `activateCallback` (invoked if the user types ENTER to leave the TextField). The TextField's width, in characters, is defined by the *columns* argument.

XUaddtimeout *variable milliseconds command*

This is a simple alias for `XtAddTimeOut`, which is explained on page 672.

XUaddtogglefields *parent [variable caption label]* ...

Creates captioned ToggleButtons. The captions and ToggleButtons are created as a child of the parent widget. Sets of three arguments define each control. First, a Label widget is created as a child of the *parent* widget; this Label displays the string specified in the *caption* argument. The ToggleButton itself displays the *label* string. The handle of the newly created ToggleButton is stored in the *variable* argument.

XUaddwmprotocolcallback *widget protocol-atom command*

This is a simple alias for `XmAddWMProtocolCallback`, which is explained on page 647.

XUaddwmprotocols *widget protocol-atom*

This is a simple alias for `XmAddWMProtocols`, which is explained on page 647.

XUaddworkproc *variable command*

This is a simple alias for `XtAddWorkProc`, which is explained on page 672.

XUalign2col *widget*

This command sets the `numColumns` resource of the specified RowColumn *widget* such that the widget displays two columns. It does this by retrieving the `numChildren` resource, dividing by two, and then storing the result in the `numColumns` resource. This is necessary for horizontally stacking RowColumn widgets because the `numColumns` resource actually defines the number of rows for such a widget (which is quite confusing).

XUalignlabels *widget* ...

The arguments to this command are a set of Label *widgets*. This command scans the widths of all the *widgets*, finds the maximum, then sets the widths of all the widgets to this maximum value, thus aligning them.

XUarrowbutton [-u] *variable parent* [*resource:value* ...]

Creates an ArrowButton widget. For details see *Widget Creation Commands* on page 680.

XUarrowbuttongadget [-u] *variable parent* [*resource:value* ...]

Creates an ArrowButton gadget. For details see *Widget Creation Commands* on page 680.

XUattach [leftpos|rightpos|toppos|bottompos] [*offset*] ...
XUattach [left|right|top|bottom] [*offset*] ...
XUattach [under|over|leftof|rightof] *widget* [*offset*] ...

The XUattach command can be used to more easily specify Form children constraints. It prints to standard output a set of Form constraint specifications. It is typically used in command substitution on the creation command of a Form widget child. In its first form above, positional Form constraint resources are printed that sets the left, right, top, or bottom positions to the *offset* argument (the default if offset is not given is zero). In its second form above, constraints that are relative to the left, right, top, and bottom edges of the Form are specified. In its third form, constraints that are relative to other children in the Form are generated. These three forms of arguments can be mixed.

For example, the following code creates a Label whose top edge is 10 pixels from the top of the Form, placed to the left of another child (whose handle is in the variable LAB1), and whose bottom edge is attached to Form position 50:

```
XUlabel LAB2 $FORMPARENT \
        $(XUattach top 10 leftof $LAB1 bottompos 50)
```

This is clearly more readable and easier to specify than the 12 constraint resources you'd have to set if you were not using XUattach.

XUaugmenttranslations *widget translations*

This is a simple alias for XtAugmentTranslations, which is explained on page 672.

XUbell *display volume*

This is a simple alias for XBell, which is explained on page 644.

XUbulletinboard [-u] *variable parent* [*resource:value* ...]

Creates a BulletinBoard widget. For details see *Widget Creation Commands* on page 680.

XUbulletinboarddialog `[-u]` `variable parent` `[resource:value ...]`
Creates a BulletinBoardDialog, which is a BulletinBoard widget with a DialogShell parent. For details see *Widget Creation Commands* on page 680.

XUbusy `[widget]`
Turns the mouse pointer to a busy cursor in the specified `widget`, and arranges for the cursor to turn back to normal the next time the main event loop executes (i.e., which the callback returns). If `widget` is not specified then the root widget of the application is used. Note that you must call this separately for each Shell-class widget if you want a busy cursor in every window of your application.

XUcallcallbacks `widget callback-name`
This is a simple alias for `XtCallCallbacks`, which is explained on page 672.

XUcascadebutton `[-u]` `variable parent` `[resource:value ...]`
Creates a CascadeButton widget. For details see *Widget Creation Commands* on page 680.

XUcascadebuttongadget `[-u]` `variable parent` `[resource:value ...]`
Creates a CascadeButton gadget. For details see *Widget Creation Commands* on page 680.

XUcleararea `display window` `[GC-options]` `x y width height`
This is a simple alias for `XClearArea`, which is explained on page 644.

XUclearwindow `display window`
This is a simple alias for `XClearWindow`, which is explained on page 644.

XUcolumn `variable parent` `[resource:value ...]`
Creates a RowColumn widget with the `orientation` resource set to VERTICAL. Arguments are as in other widget creation commands.

XUcommand `[-u]` `variable parent` `[resource:value ...]`
Creates a Command widget. For details see *Widget Creation Commands* on page 680.

XUcommandappendvalue `widget string`
This is a simple alias for `XmCommandAppendValue`, which is explained on page 647.

XUcommanderror *widget string*

        This is a simple alias for `XmCommandError`, which is explained on page 647.

XUcommandgetchild *variable widget child-type*

        This is a simple alias for `XmCommandGetChild`, which is explained on page 647.

XUcommandsetvalue *widget string*

        This is a simple alias for `XmCommandSetValue`, which is explained on page 648.

XUcopyarea *display src dest src-x src-y width height*

        This is a simple alias for `XCopyArea`, which is explained on page 644.

XUcreateapplicationshell *variable app-name app-class [resource:value ...]*

        This is a simple alias for `XtCreateApplicationShell`, which is explained on page 673.

XUcreatemanagedwidget *variable widget-name widget-class \ [resource:value ...]*

        This is a simple alias for `XtCreateManagedWidget`, which is explained on page 673.

XUcreatepopupshell *varable widget-name widget-class [resource:value ...]*

        This is a simple alias for `XtCreatePopupShell`, which is explained on page 673.

XUcreatewidget *variable widget-name widget-class [resource:value ...]*

        This is a simple alias for `XtCreateWidget`, which is explained on page 673.

XUdbappend *db-variable record*

        Appends a *record* to a flat-file database that has previously been opened. The *db-variable* argument is an actual variable name (not an expanded variable name). The *db-variable* must have been initialized by a previous call to `XUdbopen`. Note that the record is appended to the in-core data; it is not written back to the physical file until a call to `XUdbsync` is made.

XUdbopen *variable file [delimiter]*

        Opens a flat-file database. Information about the data base is stored in a hierarchy starting at variable. The *file* is opened, and each line of it is read into a member of the array *variable.record*. The optional *delimiter* argument can be used to specify a preferred delimiter for data within each line [the default is pipe (|)]. The path is stored in *variable*.file. When other flat-file database commands have modified data in the file and it thus needs to be written back to disk to save changes, the variable *variable*.needsync will be set to the string true.

XUdbsort *db-variable [sort-options]*

Sorts a previously opened flat-file database whose information is stored in the variable named *db-variable* (this is an actual variable name, not an expanded variable). Any further options are passed to the sort(1) command to affect how the records are sorted. The XUdbsort command automatically adds arguments to tell sort what the delimiter is for the data. See the UNIX system manual page for sort for more information on options.

XUdbsplit *db-variable index array-variable*

Retrieves the record number *index* from a flat-file database defined by *db-variable* (a variable name previously initialized using XUdbopen). The record's fields are split up by the delimiter defined by the database. Each field is placed in a member of the *array-variable*.

XUdbsync *db-variable*

Writes the in-core data currently contained in the *db-variable* (a variable name previously initialized by a call to XUdbopen) back out to the database file.

XUdbwrite *db-variable*

Writes all data contained in the flat-file database specified in the *db-variable* argument to the standard output (*db-variable* is a variable name previously initialized by a call to XUdbopen).

XUdefer *command*

Defers execution of the given *command* (an arbitrary dtksh command string) until the next time the main event loop has nothing to do. Typically used inside a callback function to delay execution of some action until after the callback command returns.

XUdefinecursor *display window cursor*

This is a simple alias for XDefineCursor, which is explained on page 644.

XUdestroy *widget ...*
XUdestroywidget *widget ...*

This is a simple alias for XtDestroyWidget, which is explained on page 673.

XUdialogshell [-u] *variable parent* [*resource:value ...*]

Creates a DialogShell widget. For details see *Widget Creation Commands* on page 680.

XUdisplay *variable widget*

This is a simple alias for XtDisplay, which is explained on page 673.

XUdisplayofobject

This is a simple alias for XtDisplayOfObject.

XUdrawarc *window* [*GC-options*] *x y width height start-angle degrees*

This is a simple alias for XDrawArc, which is explained on page 644.

XUdrawimagestring *display window* [*GC-options*] *x y string*

This is a simple alias for XDrawImageString, which is explained on page 645.

XUdrawingarea [-u] *variable parent* [*resource:value ...*]

Creates a DrawingArea widget. For details see *Widget Creation Commands* on page 680.

XUdrawline *display window* [*GC-options*] *x1 y1 x2 y2*
XUdrawlines *display window* [*GC-options*] *x1 y1 x2 y2*

These are simple aliases for XDrawLine and XDrawLines, which are explained on page 645.

XUdrawnbutton [-u] *variable parent* [*resource:value ...*]

Creates a DrawnButton widget. For details see *Widget Creation Commands* on page 680.

XUdrawpoint *display window* [*GC-options*] *x y*
XUdrawpoints *display window* [*GC-options*] *x y ...*

These are simple aliases for XDrawPoint and XDrawPoints which are explained on page 645.

XUdrawrectangle *display window* [*GC-options*] *x y width height*

This is a simple alias for XDrawRectangle, which is explained on page 646.

XUdrawsegments *display window* [*GC-options*] *x1 y1 x2 y2 ...*

This is a simple alias for Xdrawsegments, which is explained on page 646.

XUdrawstring *display window* [*GC-options*] *x y string*
> This is a simple alias for Xdrawstring, which is explained on page 646.

XUerror [-m] *title message ok-cb quit-cb help-cb*
> Create an error dialog. The -m option makes the dialog full application modal. The *title* is displayed in the title bar. The *message* is displayed in the message area. Callbacks for the OK, Quit, and Help buttons may be specified by *ok-cb*, *quit-cb*, and *help-cb*. If one of those callback commands is the empty string ("") then the associated button will not appear.

XUerrordialog [-u] *variable parent* [*resource:value ...*]
> Creates an ErrorDialog, which is a MessageBox widget set to display an error icon with a DialogShell widget parent. For details see *Widget Creation Commands* on page 680.

XUfileselectionbox [-u] *variable parent* [*resource:value ...*]
> Creates a FileSelectionBox widget. For details see *Widget Creation Commands* on page 680.

XUfileselectionboxgetchild *variable widget child-type*
> This is a simple alias for XmFileSelectionBoxGetChild, which is explained on page 654.

XUfileselectiondialog [-u] *variable parent* [*resource:value ...*]
> Creates a FileSelectionDialog, which is a FileSelectionBox with a DialogShell parent. For details see *Widget Creation Commands* on page 680.

XUfillarc *display window* [*GC-options*] *x y width height angle1 angle2*
> This is a simple alias for XFillArc, which is explained on page 646.

XUfillpolygon *display drawable* [*shape-hint*] [*coord-mode*] [*GC-options*] *x1 y1 ...*
> This is a simple alias for XFillPolygon, which is explained on page 646.

XUfillrectangle *display window* [*GC-options*] *x y width height*
> This is a simple alias for XFillRectangle, which is explained on page 647.

XUflush *display*
> This is a simple alias for XFlush, which is explained on page 647.

XUform `[-u] variable parent [resource:value ...]`
> Creates a Form widget. For details see *Widget Creation Commands* on page 680.

XUformdialog `[-u] variable parent [resource:value ...]`
> Creates a FormDialog widget, which is a Form widget with a DialogShell parent.
> For details see *Widget Creation Commands* on page 680.

XUframe `[-u] variable parent [resource:value ...]`
> Creates a Frame widget. For details see *Widget Creation Commands* on page 680.

XUget `widget resource:variable ...`
> This is a simple alias for `XtGetValues`, which is explained on page 673.

XUgetatomname `variable display atom`
> This is a simple alias for `XmGetAtomName`, which is explained on page 655.

XUgetcolors `widget background variable-fg varaible-ts variable-bs variable-sel`
> This is a simple alias for `XmGetColors`, which is explained on page 655.

XUgetvalues `widget resource:variable ...`
> This is a simple alias for `XtGetValues`, which is explained on page 673. The pre-
> ferred XU command for this functionality is `XUget`.

XUhascallbacks `variable widget callback-name`
> This is a simple alias for `XtHasCallbacks`, which is explained on page 674.

XUheightofscreen `variable screen`
> This is a simple alias for `XHeightOfScreen`, which is explained on page 647.

XUhelpdialog `[-u] variable parent [resource:value ...]`
> Creates a HelpDialog widget. For details see *Widget Creation Commands* on page
> 680.

XUinformation `[-m] title message ok-cb quit-cb help-cb`
> Create and display an information dialog. The `-m` option makes the dialog full
> application modal. The `title` is displayed in the title bar. The `message` is dis-
> played in the message area. Callbacks for the OK, Quit, and Help buttons can be
> specified by `ok-cb`, `quit-cb`, and `help-cb`. If one of those callback commands is
> the empty string ("") then the associated button will not appear.

XUinformationdialog [-u] *variable parent* [*resource:value ...*]

Creates an InformationDialog. For details see *Widget Creation Commands* on page 680. Usually the preferred function for creating an InformationDialog is XUinformation, because it allows the message, button labels, and title to be set in a convenient way.

XUinitialize *variable application-class* [*other-args*]

Initializes the Motif toolkit and the XU library. The root widget of the application is returned in *variable*. The *application-class* argument is used as the application's class (which is the default string for the title bar as well as the default resource file named used for the application). The lowercase version of the *application-class* argument is used for the application's name (can be used inside of resource files). The other-args are any other aguments you wish to pass to XtInitialize. See Appendix B for a list of standard X options.

Any options not recognized by X will be placed in the array variable DTKSH_ARGS. The number of such arguments can be obtained using the dtksh notation for the number of items in an array: ${#DTKSH_ARGS[@]}.

The root widget handle is also stored in the global variable DTKSH_TOPLEVEL, and the application name is stored in DTKSH_APPNAME. This is useful when you need these values in a library routine, for example, to obtain a display address for an Xlib command, or if you wish to print the application name in an error message.

XUinsensitive *widget ...*

Makes the named *widgets* insensitive.

XUinternatom variable *display atom-name existence-flag*

This is a simple alias for XmInternAtom, which is explained on page 656.

XUisblank *string ...*
XUisdate *mm dd yy*
XUisfloat *string ...*
XUisinteger *string ...*

These commands validate whether their arguments are composed of whitespace, contain a valid date value, are a valid floating-point number, or a valid integer value, respectively. They return success if all arguments conform to the indicated format, and thus can be used inside of the KornShell if command:

```
if XUisdate 11 23 60
then print "yes, it is a valid date"
else print "no, it is not a valid date"
fi
```

XUismanaged *widget*
XUisrealized *widget*
XUissensitive *widget*
XUisshell *widget*
XUissubclass *widget*
XUistraversable *widget*

> These are simple aliases for `XtIsManaged`, `XtIsRealized`, `XtIsSensitive`, `XtIsShell`, `XtIsSubclass`, and `XtIsTraversable` which are explained on page 674.

XUlabel `[-u]` *variable parent* `[resource:value ...]`

> Creates a Label widget. For details see *Widget Creation Commands* on page 680.

XUlabelgadget `[-u]` *variable parent* `[resource:value ...]`

> Creates a Label gadget. For details see *Widget Creation Commands* on page 680.

XUlasttimestampprocessed *variable display*

> This is a simple alias for `XtLastTimeStampProcessed`, which is explained on page 674.

XUlist `[-u]` *variable parent* `[resource:value ...]`

> Creates a List widget. For details see *Widget Creation Commands* on page 680.

XUlistadd *widget position string ...*
XUlistadditem *widget position string*
XUlistadditems *widget position string ...*

> `XUlistadd` and `XUlistadditems` are simple aliases for `XmListAddItems`, which is explained on page 656.
>
> `XUlistadditem` is a simple alias for `XmListAddItem`, which is explained on page 656. There is no particular reason to use this command instead of `XUlistadd`, because this command is identical to `XUlistadd` except it only allows a single string argument.

XUlistadditemsunselected
XUlistadditemunselected

> These are simple aliases for `XmListAddItemsUnselected` and `XmListAddItem-Unselected`, which are explained on page 656.

XUlistappend *widget item ...*

> Append new *items* to a List *widget*.

XUlistbottom [-s] *widget item*

> Make the given *item* the bottom-most one displayed in a List *widget*. With the -s option, *item* is a string value that must match an item in the List, otherwise *item* is an index in the List.

XUlistdeleteall *widget*
XUlistdeleteallitems *widget*

> These are simple aliases for XmListDeleteAllItems, which is explained on page 657.

XUlistdeleteitems *widget string ...*
XUlistdeleteitemspos *widget number*
XUlistdeletepositions *widget number ...*

> These are simple aliases for XmListDeleteItems, XmListDeleteItemsPos, and XmListDeletePositions, which are explained on page 657. The preferred way to delete items from a list is by using XUlistdelete.

XUlistdeselect [-n] [-s] *widget item ...*

> Deselect items in a List *widget*. With the -s option the *items* are string values that should match items in the List, otherwise the *items* are indexes. With the -n option (notify), callbacks are triggered as if the user selected the items.

XUlistdeselectall *widget*
XUlistdeselectallitems *widget*

> These are simple aliases for XmListDeselectAll, which is explained on page 657.

XUlistdeselectitem *widget string*
XUlistdeselectpos *widget number*

> This is a simple alias for XtAddCallback, which is explained on page 657. The preferred method of deselecting list items is by using XUlistdeselect.

XUlistfind *variable widget search-string*

> Find the first item in a List *widget* that matches the given *search-string*, and store its string value in the *variable*. This command returns success if an item is actually found. The string must match exactly, including case.

XUlistget *variable widget index*

Get the string value of the List item at position *index*. Indexes for List widget items start at 1, the index 0 gets the last item. The string is stored in *variable*.

XUlistgetkbditempos *variable widget*

This is a simple alias for XmListGetKbdItemPos, which is explained on page 657.

XUlistgetselected *variable widget*

Get a list of selected List widget item indexes and store them in *variable*.

XUlistitemexists *widget string*
XUlistitempos *variable widget string*

These are simple aliases for XmListItemExists and XmListItemPos, which are explained beginning on page 658.

XUlistparse *array string*

Parse a *string* composed of comma-separated items into successive positions in an *array* variable. Correctly takes into account backslashed commas.

XUlistposselected *widget number*
XUlistpostobounds *widget position variable-x variable-y \
                       variable-width variable-height*

These are simple aliases for XmListPosSelected, and XmListPosToBounds which are explained beginning on page 658.

XUlistreplace *widget position string ...*
XUlistreplaceitemspos *widget position string ...*

These are simple aliases for XmListReplaceItemsPos, which is explained on page 658.

XUlistreplaceitemsposunselected *widget position string ...*

This is a simple alias for XmListReplaceItemsPosUnselected, which is explained on page 658.

XUlistselect [-n] [-s] *widget item ...*

Select items in a List *widget*. With the -s option the *items* are string values that should match items in the List, otherwise the *items* are indexes. With the -n option, (notify) callbacks are triggered as if the user selected the items.

XUlistselectall *widget*

Select all items in a List *widget*.

XUlistselectitem *widget string notify-flag*
XUlistselectpos *widget string notify-flag*

These are simple aliases for `XmListSelectItem` and `XmListSelectItemPos`, which is explained on page 658. The preferred function for selecting List items is `XUlistselect`.

XUlistsetaddmode

This is a simple alias for `XmListSetAddMode`, which is explained on page 659.

XUlistsetbottomitem *widget string*
XUlistsetbottompos *widget number*
XUlistsethorizpos *widget position*
XUlistsetitem *widget string*
XUlistsetkbditempos *widget index*
XUlistsetpos *widget number*

These are simple aliases for `XmListSetBottomItem`, `XmListSetBottomPos`, `XmListSetHorizPos`, `XmListSetItem`, `XmListSetPos`, and `XmListSetKbdItemPos` which are explained beginning on page 659.

XUlisttop [-s] *list item*

Make the given *item* the topmost one displayed in a List *widget*. With the -s option, *item* is a string value that must match an item in the List, otherwise *item* is an index in the List.

XUlistupdateselectedlist *widget*

This is a simple alias for `XmListUpdateSelectedList`, which is explained on page 659.

XUmainloop

This is a simple alias for `XtMainLoop`, which is explained on page 675.

XUmainwindow [-u] *variable parent* [*resource:value ...*]

Creates an ArrowButton. For details see *Widget Creation Commands* on page 680.

XUmainwindowsep1 *variable widget*
XUmainwindowsep2 *variable widget*
XUmainwindowsep3 *variable widget*
XUmainwindowsetareas

These are simple aliases for XmMainWindowSep1, XmMainWindowSep2, XmMainWindowSep3, and XmMainWindowSetAreas which are explained beginning on page 659.

XUmanage *widget ...*
XUmanagechildren *widget ...*

These are simple aliases for XtManageChildren, which is explained on page 675.

XUmap *widget*
XUmapwidget *widget*

These are simple aliases for XtMapWidget, which is explained on page 675.

XUmenubar [-u] *variable parent* [*resource:value ...*]

Creates a MenuBar, which is a RowColumn widget with certain resource defaults. For details see *Widget Creation Commands* on page 680.

XUmenuposition *widget event*

This is a simple alias for XmMenuPosition, which is explained on page 660.

XUmenushell [-u] *variable parent* [*resource:value ...*]

Creates an ArrowButton. For details see *Widget Creation Commands* on page 680.

XUmenusystem *parent* [[*options*] *variable label mnemonic action ...*]

Creates a PullDown menu system attached to a *parent* widget. Usually the *parent* is a MenuBar. Menu buttons and menu items are defined by sets of four arguments: a *variable*, which recieves the widget handle; a *label*, which appears on the button; a *mnemonic* character for the item; and an action. The *action* is either a dtksh command to be executed when the button is selected, or an open curly brace. If it is an open curly brace, then further sets of four arguments can be enclosed up to a matching close curly brace, and another level of cascading menu is thus created. Any number of levels of cascade can be created in this manner.

A set of four dash characters may be used to create a Separator at any given point in the menu.

The options argument can precede any given set of four arguments. It can either be -t, in which case a ToggleButton is created, or -e *variable*, in which case a ToggleButton in radio button mode is created, which is exclusive among any other such items in the menu which use the same *variable*.

XUmessagebox [-u] *variable parent* [*resource:value ...*]
> Creates an ArrowButton. For details see *Widget Creation Commands* on page 680.

XUmessageboxgetchild *variable widget child*
> This is a simple alias for XmMessageBoxGetChild, which is explained on page 660.

XUmessagedialog [-u] *variable parent* [*resource:value ...*]
> Creates an ArrowButton. For details see *Widget Creation Commands* on page 680.

XUnametowidget *variable ref-widget name*
> This is a simple alias for XtNameToWidget, which is explained on page 675.

XUoptionmenu [-u] *variable parent* [*resource:value ...*]
> Creates an OptionMenu, which is a RowColumn widget configured with certain resource defaults. For details on command arguments see *Widget Creation Commands* on page 680.

XUoverridetranslations *widget translation-string*
> This is a simple alias for XtOverrideTranslations, which is explained on page 675.

XUpanedwindow [-u] *variable parent* [*resource:value ...*]
> Creates a PanedWindow widget. For details see *Widget Creation Commands* on page 680.

XUparent *variable widget*
> This is a simple alias for XtParent, which is explained on page 675.

XUpopdown *widget*
> This is a simple alias for XtPopdown, which is explained on page 675.

XUpopup *widget* [*grab-type*]
> Causes the named *widget* to be popped up. The *widget* must be a shell-class widget. The *grab-type* argument may be one of:

GrabNone   Do not grab control of the application. This window will
                            behave just like any other window on the screen. Other
                            windows in the application may be made current and will
                            respond to user input.

GrabExclusive   Grab exclusive control of the application. Other windows
                            in the application cannot receive input until this window is
                            popped down.

GrabNonExclusive   Like GrabNone.

This command is just like XtPopup, but you may leave out the *grab-type* in which
case it defaults to GrabNone.

XUpopupmenu [-u] *variable parent* [*resource:value ...*]
Creates a PopupMenu widget. For details see *Widget Creation Commands* on page
680.

XUpromptdialog [-u] *variable parent* [*resource:value ...*]
Creates a PromptDialog, which is a MessageBox widget configured with a prompt
icon with a DialogShell parent. For details see *Widget Creation Commands* on page
680.

XUprocesstraversal *widget direction*
This is a simple alias for XmProcessTraversal, which is explained on page 660.

XUpulldownmenu [-u] *variable parent* [*resource:value ...*]
Creates a PulldownMenu widget. For details see *Widget Creation Commands* on
page 680.

XUpushbutton [-u] *variable parent* [*resource:value ...*]
Creates a PushButton widget. For details see *Widget Creation Commands* on page
680.

XUpushbuttongadget [-u] *variable parent* [*resource:value ...*]
Creates a PushButton gadget. For details see *Widget Creation Commands* on page
680.

XUquestion [-m] *title message ok-cb quit-cb help-cb*
> Create a QuestionDialog. See XUerror for argument details.

XUquestiondialog [-u] *variable parent* [*resource:value ...*]
> Creates a QuestionDialog, which is a MessageBox widget configured with a question icon with a DialogShell parent. For details see *Widget Creation Commands* on page 680.

XUquickhelpdialog [-u] *variable parent* [*resource:value ...*]
> Creates a QuickHelpDialog, which is a QuickHelp widget with a DialogShell parent. For details see *Widget Creation Commands* on page 680.

XUradiobox [-u] *variable parent* [*resource:value ...*]
> Creates a RadioBox, which is a RowColumn widget configured with certain resource settings so that ToggleButton widgets added to it later will only have one set item at a time. For details of the options see *Widget Creation Commands* on page 680.

XUraisewindow *display window*
> This is a simple alias for XRaiseWindow, which is explained on page 670.

XUrealize *widget*

XUrealizewidget *widget*
> These are simple aliases for XtRealizeWidget, which is explained on page 676.

XUregisterpopup *widget popupmenu-widget*
> Register a *popupmenu-widget* to appear when the user presses mouse button two while in *widget*. This command takes care of positioning the menu.

XUregisterwindowclose *command*
> Register a *command* to be executed if the user closes the application using the window manager. This also arranges for the application to avoid being killed when the user tries to close it using the window manager (thus, the *command* would have to exit explicitly if the application should really be closed).

XUremoveallcallbacks *widget callback-name*
XUremovecallback *widget callback-name command*
XUremoveeventhandler *widget event-mask non-maskable-flag command*
XUremoveinput *input-identifier*
XUremovetimeout *timeout-identifier*

> These are simple aliases for XtRemoveAllCallbacks, XtRemoveCallback, XtRemoveEventHandler, XtRemoveInput, and XtRemoveTimeOut, which are explained starting on page 676.

XUremovewmprotocolcallback *widget protocol-atom command*
XUremovewmprotocols *widget protocol-atom command*

> These are simple aliases for XmRemoveWMProtocolCallback and XmRemoveWM-Protocols, which are explained beginning on page 661.

XUremoveworkproc *workproc-identifier*

> This is a simple alias for XtRemoveWorkProc, which is explained on page 677.

XUrootwindowofscreen *variable screen*

> This is a simple alias for XRootWindowOfScreen, which is explained on page 671.

XUrow *variable parent [resource:value ...]*

> Create a RowColumn widget with the orientation resource set to HORIZONTAL. Arguments are as in any other widget creation command.

XUrowcolumn *[-u] variable parent [resource:value ...]*

> Creates a RowColumn widget. For details see *Widget Creation Commands* on page 680.

XUscale *[-u] variable parent [resource:value ...]*

> Creates a Scale widget. For details see *Widget Creation Commands* on page 680.

XUscalegetvalue *widget variable*
XUscalesetvalue *widget variable*

> These are simple aliases for XmScaleGetValue and XmScaleSetValue, which are explained beginning on page 662.

XUscreen

> This is a simple alias for XtAddCallback, which is explained on page 671.

XUscrollbar [-u] *variable parent* [*resource:value ...*]

Creates a ScrollBar widget. For details see *Widget Creation Commands* on page 680.

XUscrollbargetvalues *widget variable-val variable-sz variable-inc* \
variable-pg-inc

XUscrollbarsetvalues *widget value size increment page-increment notify-flag*

These are simple aliases for `XmScrollBarGetValues` and `XmScroll-BarSetValues` which are explained beginning on page 662.

XUscrolledlist [-u] *variable parent* [*resource:value ...*]

Creates a ScrolledList widget, which is a List widget with a ScrolledWindow parent. For details see *Widget Creation Commands* on page 680.

XUscrolledtext [-u] *variable parent* [*resource:value ...*]

Creates a ScrolledText widget, which is a Text widget with a ScrolledWindow parent. For details see *Widget Creation Commands* on page 680.

XUscrolledwindow [-u] *variable parent* [*resource:value ...*]

Creates an ArrowButton. For details see *Widget Creation Commands* on page 680.

XUscrollvisible *widget child-widget left-right-margin top-bottom-margin*

This is a simple alias for `XmScrollVisible`, which is explained on page 662.

XUselectionbox [-u] *variable parent* [*resource:value ...*]

Creates a SelectionBox widget. For details see *Widget Creation Commands* on page 680.

XUselectionboxgetchild *variable widget child-type*

This is a simple alias for `XmSelectionBoxGetChild`, which is explained on page 662.

XUselectionchildren *variable*

Break out children widgets of a SelectionDialog (or SelectionBox) into a hierarchy starting at *variable*.

XUselectiondialog [-u] *variable parent* [*resource:value ...*]

Creates a SelectionDialog, which is a SelectionBox widget with a DialogShell widget parent. For details see *Widget Creation Commands* on page 680.

XUsensitive *widget ...*
> Makes the specified *widgets* sensitive.

XUseparator [*-u*] *variable parent* [*resource:value ...*]
> Creates a Separator widget. For details of the arguments see *Widget Creation Commands* on page 680.

XUseparatorgadget [*-u*] *variable parent* [*resource:value ...*]
> Creates a Separator gadget. For details see *Widget Creation Commands* on page 680.

XUset *widget resource:value ...*
XUsetvalues *widget resource:value ...*
> These are simple aliases for XtSetValues, which is explained on page 677. The first form is preferred, because it is easier to type.

XUsetaccelerators [*widget accelerator accelerator-text*] *...*
> A convenient way to set *accelerators* and *accelerator-text* on multiple *widgets*. Any number of sets of three arguments can be specified.

XUsetfocus *widget* [*direction*]
> Sets focus to a *widget*. If the *direction* argument is specified, it can be one of the values allowable in XmProcessTraversal.

XUsethelp [*widget command*] *...*
> Conveniently set the helpCallback on multiple *widgets*. Any number of pairs of arguments may be specified.

XUsetsensitive *widget state*
> This is a simple alias for XtSetSensitive, which is explained on page 677. It is usually easier to use XUsensitive and XUinsensitive instead of this command.

XUsettraversalorder *form-widget default-widget widget ...*
> Arrange for the ENTER key to traverse to the next of a series of *widgets* instead of executing the default action in a Form, *form-widget*. The actual default button handle should be provided in *default-widget*.

XUsimpledialog [-u] `variable parent` [`resource:value ...`]
> Creates a simple dialog, which is a DialogShell widget with a RowColumn child. For details of the arguments see *Widget Creation Commands* on page 680.

XUsync `display discard`
> This is a simple alias for `XSync`, which is explained on page 671.

XUtext [-u] `variable parent` [`resource:value ...`]
> Creates a TextField widget. For details see *Widget Creation Commands* on page 680.

XUtextallowchars [`widget pattern`] `...`
> Sets up validation functions on Text or TextField `widgets` to only allow the user to type characters that match the specified KornShell `pattern`. For example, this command would cause the widget TEXT to only allow digits:
>
> ```
> XUtextallowchars $TEXT '[0-9]'
> ```
>
> The terminal bell rings if the user types an incorrect character, and the incorrect character is not inserted. Any number of pairs of arguments can be specified.

XUtextappend `widget string`
> Append a `string` to the text displayed in a Text or TextField `widget`.

XUtextautocursor `widget ...`
> Set up Text or TextField `widgets` so the cursor does not appear when the widget does not have focus.

XUtextautoselect `widget ...`
> Set up Text or TextField `widgets` so all text is automatically selected when the widget gains focus.

XUtextautotraverse [`widget position`] `...`
> Set up Text or TextField `widgets` so when the cursor exceeds the text `position` focus is moved to the following control. This is useful for fixed-width fields. Any number of pairs of arguments can be given.

XUtextclearselection `widget time`
> This is a simple alias for `XmTextClearSelection`, which is explained on page 663.

XUtextcopy *widget*
XUtextcut *widget*

> Copy or cut text from a Text or TextField *widget*. The copied or cut text goes to the cut buffer and can be retrieved using XUtextpaste.

XUtextdelete *widget string*

> Delete a *string* from a Text or TextField *widget*.

XUtextdeselect *widget*

> Deselect any selected text in a Text or TextField *widget*.

XUtextdisable *widget*
XUtextdisableredisplay *widget*

> This is a simple alias for XmTextDisableRedisplay, which is explained on page 663. The first form is preferred, because it is easier to type.

XUtextenable *widget*
XUtextenableredisplay *widget*

> These are simple aliases for XmTextEnableRedisplay, which is explained on page 663. The first form is preferred, because it is easier to type.

XUtextfield [-u] *variable parent* [*resource:value ...*]

> Creates a TextField widget. For details see *Widget Creation Commands* on page 680.

XUtextfind [-b] *variable widget start-position string*

> Find a *string* in a Text widget. The search starts at *start-position*. With the -b option, the search proceeds backward. If found, the position is stored in *variable* and the command returns success, otherwise the command returns failure.

XUtextfindstring *widget position string direction*

> This is a simple alias for XmTextFindString, which is explained on page 666. XUtextfind is usually easier to use.

XUtextforcecase [-u|-l] *widget*

> Arrange for a Text or TextField widget to convert case automatically while the user types values. With the -u option, text is converted to uppercase, with the -l option lowercase.

XUtextgetbaseline *variable widget*
> This is a simple alias for `XmTextGetBaseline`, which is explained on page 666.

XUtextgeteditable *widget*
> This is a simple alias for `XmTextGetEditable`, which is explained on page 667.

XUtextgetinsertionposition *variable widget*
> This is a simple alias for `XmTextGetInsertionPosition`, which is explained on page 667.

XUtextgetlast *variable widget*
XUtextgetlastposition *variable widget*
> These are simple aliases for `XmTextGetLastPosition`, which is explained on page 667.

XUtextgetmaxlength *variable widget*
> This is a simple alias for `XmTextGetMaxLength`, which is explained on page 667.

XUtextgetselection *variable widget*
> This is a simple alias for `XmTextGetSelection`, which is explained on page 667.

XUtextgetselectionposition *widget variable-from variable-to*
> This is a simple alias for `XmTextGetSelectionPosition`, which is explained on page 667.

XUtextgetstring *variable widget*
> This is a simple alias for `XmTextGetString`, which is explained on page 667.

XUtextgettopcharacter *variable widget*
> This is a simple alias for `XmTextGetTopCharacter`, which is explained on page 667.

XUtextinsert *widget position string*
> This is a simple alias for `XmTextInsert`, which is explained on page 667.

XUtextpaste *widget*
> Paste text from the cut buffer into a Text or TextField *widget*.

XUtextpostoxy *widget position variable-x variable-y*

This is a simple alias for XmTextPosToXY, which is explained on page 668.

XUtextremove *widget*

This is a simple alias for XmTextRemove, which is explained on page 668.

XUtextreplace *widget from to string*

This is a simple alias for XmTextReplace, which is explained on page 668.

XUtextscroll *widget lines*

This is a simple alias for XmTextScroll, which is explained on page 668.

XUtextselect *widget start-pos end-pos*

Select text between *start-pos* and *end-pos* in a Text or TextField *widget*.

XUtextsetaddmode *widget state*

This is a simple alias for XmTextSetAddMode, which is explained on page 668.

XUtextseteditable *widget edit-flag*

This is a simple alias for XmTextSetEditable, which is explained on page 668.

XUtextsethighlight *widget start-pos end-pos [type]*

Like XmTextSetHighlight, except the *type* argument is optional and defaults to HIGHLIGHT_PRIMARY_SELECTION. See page page 668 for more details.

XUtextsetinsertionposition *widget position*

This is a simple alias for XmTextSetInsertionPosition, which is explained on page 669.

XUtextsetmaxlength *widget length*

This is a simple alias for XmTextSetMaxLength, which is explained on page 669.

XUtextsetselection *widget first last time*

This is a simple alias for XmTextSetSelection, which is explained on page 669.

XUtextsetstring *widget string*

This is a simple alias for XmTextSetString, which is explained on page 669.

XUtextsettopcharacter *widget position*
>This is a simple alias for `XmTextSetTopPosition`, which is explained on page 669.

XUtextshow *widget position*
XUtextshowposition *widget position*
>These are simple aliases for `XmTextShowPosition`, which is explained on page 669.

XUtextwidth *variable font string*
>This is a simple alias for `XTextWidth`, which is explained on page 673.

XUtextxytopos *variable widget x y*
>This is a simple alias for `XmTextXYToPos`, which is explained on page 670.

XUtogglebutton `[-u]` *variable parent* `[resource:value ...]`
>Creates a ToggleButton widget. For details see *Widget Creation Commands* on page 680.

XUtogglebuttongadget `[-u]` *variable parent* `[resource:value ...]`
>Creates a ToggleButton gadget. For details see *Widget Creation Commands* on page 680.

XUtogglebuttongadgetgetstate
>This is a simple alias for `XmToggleButtonGadgetGetState`, which is explained on page 670.

XUtogglebuttongadgetsetstate *widget state*
>This is a simple alias for `XmToggleButtonGadgetSetState`, which is explained on page 670.

XUtogglebuttongetstate *widget*
>This is a simple alias for `XmToggleButtonGetState`, which is explained on page 670.

XUtogglebuttonsetstate *widget* `[true|false]`
XUtoggleselect *widget*
>The first command sets the state of a ToggleButton widget to either `true` or `false` and triggers any callbacks registered for the `valueChangedCallback`. The second command simulates a user selection of a ToggleButton: it sets the state to `TRUE` and

triggers any callbacks associated with the ToggleButton that would normally trigger on selection.

XUundefinecursor *display window*
> This is a simple alias for `XUndefineCursor`, which is explained on page 678.

XUuninstalltranslations *widget*
> This is a simple alias for `XtUninstallTranslations`, which is explained on page 677.

XUunmanage *widget ...*
XUunmanagechildren *widget ...*
> These are simple aliases for `XtUnmanageChildren`, which is explained on page 677.

XUunmap *widget*
XUunmapwidget *widget*
> This is a simple alias for `XtUnmapWidget`, which is explained on page 677.

XUunrealize *widget*
XUunrealizewidget *widget*
> These are simple aliases for `XtUnrealizeWidget`, which is explained on page 677.

XUupdatedisplay *widget*
> This is a simple alias for `XtAddCallback`, which is explained on page 670.

XUwarning [-m] *title message ok-cb quit-cb help-cb*
> Display a WorkingDialog. See `XUerror` for details of the arguments.

XUwarningdialog [-u] *variable parent* [*resource:value ...*]
> Creates a WarningDialog. For details see *Widget Creation Commands* on page 680.

XUwidgethelp *parent*
> Turns the mouse cursor into a question mark icon, waits for the user to select a widget, then calls the `helpCallback` of the selected widget. If the widget does not have a `helpCallback`, then the widget hierarchy is searched upward for the closest parent with a `helpCallback`. If the user does not select a widget under the given *parent*, no callback is invoked.

XUwidthofscreen *variable screen*
> This is a simple alias for XWidthOfScreen, which is explained on page 678.

XUwindow *variable widget*
> This is a simple alias for XtWindow, which is explained on page 677.

XUworkarea [-u] *variable parent* [*resource:value ...*]
> Creates a WorkArea, which is a RowColumn widget with certain resource settings. For details see *Widget Creation Commands* on page 680.

XUworking [-m] *title message ok-cb quit-cb help-cb*
> Display a WorkingDialog. See XUerror for details of the arguments.

XUworkingdialog [-u] *variable parent* [*resource:value ...*]
> Creates an ArrowButton. For details see *Widget Creation Commands* on page 680.

34 *Motif Widget Reference*

34.1 Introduction

This chapter presents Motif widget information. It is meant as a terse reference; full information on the use of every resource of every widget is better obtained by referring to [Ferguson and Brennen 1993].

The information presented here differs from traditional (C language) widget references in several respects, which makes it far more convenient for the dtksh programmer. First, traditional resource references include information that is rarely required by the dtksh programmer, such as the resource class. Because of long names, this causes the tables to require the use of an eye-straining typeface. Second, the traditional resource table includes the "type" of the resource, which is a C language definition. Because dtksh does not require you to declare types, this information is not necessary. Third, some resources have limitations when used from dtksh, as noted in the following text.

34.2 Standard Sections

The reference material for each widget is divided into the following sections:

Resources

A resource table describes the name, default value, and other legal values of the unique resources for this widget. Resources that are inherited from the widget's superclass are not usually listed here. In addition to normal resources, manager widgets that give constraint resources to their children will contain a table labeled **Constraint Resources**.

Resource Descriptions

This section presents short explanations of the resources described in the resource tables. The intent of these descriptions is to provide a terse reminder of what information a resource contains; this is useful for day-to-day programming tasks. Due to space limitations, it is not possible to provide complete information on every resource, you should consult the index to find more information on resources and widgets that you do not understand, or consult [Ferguson and Brennen 1993].

Other Resources

A simple list is provided of other resource names that are inherited by the widget (or gadget). Each of these resources is inherited from some other widget described in this chapter, and more information about them can be obtained by looking under the appropriate widget description. In addition to this section, widgets that have a gadget form will have a section called **Other Gadget Resources**.

Callbacks

A table is given that lists available callbacks with information on what actions trigger them and what CB_CALL_DATA fields are available within the context of the callback function execution.

Every Motif callback receives the X event that triggered the callback in the variable CB_CALL_DATA.EVENT. This variable contains the hexadecimal value of the actual C language pointer that holds the X event structure associated with the call data. There are many subfields of the X event available that use this variable as their parent (for example, the type of event is held in CB_CALL_DATA.EVENT.XANY.TYPE). Because there are sometimes dozens of such fields, they are not described individually below; instead you can find a complete list of available subfields in Appendix C.

The Resource Table

There are three columns in each widget's resource table:

Resource Name

The name of the resource, in the format that the dtksh programmer would use (i.e., the C language XmN prefix is stripped). This is the same name that would be used in a resource file.

Default Value

The default value of the resource. If this value is enclosed in brackets, then it is a symbolic rather than an actual value. For example, the notation *[dynamic]* in this column means that the default value of this resource is computed at run-time and depends on other factors. Resources such as width and height often fall into this category because the widget will attempt to size itself appropriately. For example, by default the Label widget sizes itself to fit the string text it contains. Also, the notation [*NULL*] means the resource is not set initially to any value.

Other Values

Other legal values are listed here. This can be a list of all other possible values (if there are a relatively small number), or if enclosed in brackets it represents a description of what types of values are legal. Some of the more common descriptions include:

[*integer*]	Integer values.
[*short integer*]	Integer limited to the range −32,767 to +32,768.
[*string*]	Any text string.
[*color*]	A color name or a numeric color value. See the section *Colors*, on page 155.
[*path to a pixmap file*]	A full path to a file in X Pixmap format. See the section *Pixmaps and Bitmaps*, on page 163.
[*requires C code*]	This resource is difficult or impossible to set from dtksh due to its nature, and would require the programmer to use the C code attach features of dtksh. You will have to consult C language Motif references to use this resource effectively. See Chapter 23, *Attaching C Code*.

There are more elaborate descriptions in some cases, such as:

> [*positive integer*]

These are self-explanatory.

The Callback Table

Callbacks are triggered when some event occurs. In the context of a callback function's execution, variables are set that provide further information specific to the callback and widget.

The variable CB_WIDGET is always set to the handle of the widget on whose behalf the callback is executing.

The variable CB_CALL_DATA is set to the address of a C structure that provides further information specific to the callback. This address is in hexadecimal, and can be passed to C functions attached to the dtksh script. However, there is no need to attach C code to take advantage of the call data information in most cases, because

CB_CALL_DATA is also the root of a hierarchy of variables that contain the most generally useful call data parameters.

For example, all callbacks provide the variable CB_CALL_DATA.REASON. That variable holds a string that names the reason for the callback execution. It is useful in cases when a single function is registered for several different callbacks. In addition, all callbacks provide the variable CB_CALL_DATA.EVENT. This variable contains the address an X event structure describing the event that triggered the callback. Again, that can be passed to a C function attached to the dtksh script. Subfields are also available that can be used directly in the dtksh script without attaching C code. These are always the same for every widget and callback. Refer to Appendix C for a list of X event subfields.

34.3 The ApplicationShell Widget

An ApplicationShell is returned from XtInitialize to be used for the application's main shell widget.

Table 34-1. ApplicationShell Widget Resources

Resource Name	Default	Other Values
argc	0	[integer]
argv	[NULL]	[requires C code]

Resource Descriptions

argc   A count of the command line arguments passed to the shell script.

argv   The command line arguments passed to the shell script.

Other Widget Resources

From ToplevelShell:
        iconic, iconName, iconNameEncoding.

From VendorShell:
        audibleWarning, buttonFontList, defaultFontList, deleteResponse, inputMethod, keyboardFocusPolicy, labelFontList, mwmDecorations, mwmFunctions, mwmInputMode, mwmMenu, preeditType, shellUnitType, textFontList, useAsyncGeometry.

From WMShell:
        baseHeight, baseWidth, heightInc, iconMask, iconPixmap, iconWindow, iconX, iconY, initialState, input, maxAspectX, maxAspectY, maxHeight, maxWidth, minAspectX, minAspectY, minHeight, minWidth, title, titleEncoding, transient, waitForWm, widthInc, windowGroup, winGravity, wmTimeout.

From Shell:
>   allowShellResize, createPopupChildProc, geometry, over-
>   rideRedirect, popdownCallback, popupCallback, saveUnder,
>   visual.

From Composite:
>   children, insertPosition, numChildren.

From Core:
>   accelerators, ancestorSensitive, background, background-
>   Pixmap, borderColor, borderPixmap, borderWidth, colormap,
>   depth, destroyCallback, height, initialResourcesPer-
>   sistent, mappedWhenManaged, screen, sensitive, transla-
>   tions, width, x, y.

34.4 The Composite Class

The Composite class is never instantiated by itself; it is only used as a superclass
for other widgets. It provides the ability to manage other widget children.

Table 34-2. Composite Class Resources

Resource Name	Default	Other Values
children	[NULL]	[requires C code]
insertPosition	[NULL]	[requires C code]
numChildren	0	[integer, read-only value]

Resource Descriptions

children
>   A list of all the composite widget's children.

insertPosition
>   Specifies a procedure that determines the order in which the children are
>   inserted into the children array.

numChildren
>   The number of children attached to the Composite widget.

Other Widget Resources

From Core:
>   accelerators, ancestorSensitive, background, background-
>   Pixmap, borderColor, borderPixmap, borderWidth, colormap,
>   depth, destroyCallback, height, initialResourcesPer-

```
sistent, mappedWhenManaged, screen, sensitive, transla-
tions, width, x, y.
```

34.5 The Constraint Class

The Constraint class gives the ability for a Composite widget to size and position its children based on resources set on the children themselves. These special resources are called constraint resources because they communicate the geometry constraints of a child to the parent Composite widget. There are no additional resources for the Constraint class.

Other Widget Resources

From Composite:

```
children, insertPosition, numChildren.
```

From Core:

```
accelerators, ancestorSensitive, background, background-
Pixmap, borderColor, borderPixmap, borderWidth, colormap,
depth,   destroyCallback,   height,   initialResourcesPer-
sistent, mappedWhenManaged, screen, sensitive, transla-
tions, width, x, y.
```

34.6 The Core Class

The Core class is the base class for all other widget classes. It is never instantiated by itself. Its sole use is as a superclass to all widgets. It provides common widget features such as background and geometry.

Table 34-3. Core Class Resources

Resource Name	Default	Other Values
accelerators	[dynamic]	[requires C code]
ancestorSensitive	[dynamic]	true, false
background	[dynamic]	[color]
backgroundPixmap	UNSPECIFIED_PIXMAP	[path to a pixmap file]
borderColor	[default foreground color]	[color]
borderPixmap	UNSPECIFIED_PIXMAP	[path to a pixmap file]
borderWidth	1	[integer]
colormap	[dynamic]	[requires C code]
depth	[dynamic]	[integer]
height	[dynamic]	[integer]

Table 34-3. Core Class Resources (continued)

Resource Name	Default	Other Values
initialResources- Persistent	true	false
mappedWhenManaged	true	false
screen	*[dynamic]*	*[screen pointer, read-only]*
sensitive	true	false
translations	*[dynamic]*	*[translation string, set-only]*
width	*[dynamic]*	*[integer]*
x	0	*[integer]*
y	0	*[integer]*

Resource Descriptions

accelerators
> A translation table string that specifies shortcuts for a widget's actions.

ancestorSensitive
> A read-only resource that determines if the widget's parent can receive input.

background
> The pixel used to color the widget's background.

backgroundPixmap
> The pixmap used to tile the widget's background.

borderColor
> The pixel used to color the border.

borderPixmap
> The pixmap used to tile the border.

borderWidth
> The width of the widget's border.

colormap
> The colormap used to determine the value of pixels.

depth
> The number of bits in each pixel.

height
> The height of the widget (not including the border.)

initialResourcesPersistent

Determines if the resources of this widget should be referenced counted. When `true`, resources will not be referenced counted, which may improve performance if the widget is never going to be destroyed. Set this resource to `false` if the widget could be destroyed.

mappedWhenManaged

Controls when the widget is mapped, i.e., appears on the screen. When `true`, the widget is mapped when it is realized. When `false`, the application controls the mapping.

screen

The screen on which the widget was created.

sensitive

Use the `XtSetSensitive` command to set the sensitivity of a widget and all of its children. Setting this resource determines if the widget responds to input.

translations

A translation table string for the widget.

width

The width of the widget (not including the border.)

x

The x position of the upper left corner of the widget.

y

The y position of the upper left corner of the widget.

Callbacks

destroyCallback

Invoked when the widget is destroyed. Call data:
`CB_CALL_DATA.EVENT=X` *event*

34.7 The ArrowButton Widget and Gadget

The ArrowButton widget (and gadget) provides a button that displays a picture of an arrow. The arrow can point up, down, left, or right. It is used when there is a directional meaning to selecting a button..

Table 34-4. ArrowButton Widget and Gadget Resources

Resource Name	Default	Other Values
arrowDirection	ARROW_UP	ARROW_DOWN, ARROW_LEFT, ARROW_RIGHT

Table 34-4. ArrowButton Widget and Gadget Resources (continued)

Resource Name	Default	Other Values (continued)
multiClick	MULTICLICK_DISCARD when in a menu system, MULTICLICK_KEEP otherwise	There are no other legal values.

Resource Descriptions

arrowDirection   Specifies the direction in which the arrow points: ARROW_UP, ARROW_DOWN, ARROW_LEFT, ARROW_RIGHT.

multiClick   If set to MULTICLICK_KEEP, then the activateCallback is invoked once per selection, otherwise multiple clicks that occur close together in time will only invoke the activateCallback once with the CB_CALL_DATA.CLICK_COUNT variable set to the number of selections.

Other Widget Resources

From Primitive:

bottomShadowColor, highlightPixmap, highlightThickness, navigationType, shadowThickness, bottomShadowPixmap, foreground, helpCallback, highlightColor, highlightOnEnter, topShadowColor, topShadowPixmap, traversalOn, unitType, userData.

From Core:

accelerators, ancestorSensitive, background, backgroundPixmap, borderColor, borderPixmap, borderWidth, colormap, depth, destroyCallback, height, initialResourcesPersistent, mappedWhenManaged, screen, sensitive, translations, width, x, y.

Other Gadget Resources

From Gadget:

helpCallback, highlightOnEnter, highlightThickness, navigationType, shadowThickness, traversalOn, unitType, userData.

From RectObj (see information on equivalent resources under Core):

```
ancestorSensitive, borderWidth, height, sensitive, width,
x, y.
```

From Object:

```
destroyCallback.
```

Callbacks

activateCallback
> Invoked whenever the button is selected. Call data:
> CB_CALL_DATA.REASON=CR_ACTIVATE
> CB_CALL_DATA.EVENT=X event
> CB_CALL_DATA.CLICK_COUNT=*number of clicks*

armCallback
> Invoked when the user presses the mouse button. Call data:
> CB_CALL_DATA.REASON=CR_ARM
> CB_CALL_DATA.EVENT=*X event*

disarmCallback
> Invoked when the user releases the mouse button. Call data:
> CB_CALL_DATA.REASON=CR_DISARM
> CB_CALL_DATA.EVENT=*X event*

34.8 The BulletinBoard Widget

A manager widget that can position children by x, y coordinates. It has some features that only take effect when the BulletinBoard is an immediate child of a DialogShell widget.

Table 34-5. BulletinBoard Widget Resources

Resource Name	Default	Other Values
allowOverlap	true	false
autoUnmanage	true	false
buttonFontList	*[dynamic]*	*[font name]*
cancelButton	NULL	*[widget handle]*
defaultButton	NULL	*[widget handle]*
defaultPosition	true	false

Table 34-5. BulletinBoard Widget Resources

Resource Name	Default	Other Values (continued)
dialogStyle	DIALOG_MODELESS when parent is a Dia-logShell, else DIALOG_WORK_AREA	DIALOG_PRIMARY_APPLICATION_MODAL, DIALOG_FULL_APPLICATION_MODAL, DIALOG_SYSTEM_MODAL
dialogTitle	NULL	[string]
labelFontList	[dynamic]	[font name]
marginHeight	10	[positive integer]
marginWidth	10	[positive integer]
noResize	false	true
resizePolicy	RESIZE_ANY	RESIZE_NONE, RESIZE_GROW_ONLY
shadowType	SHADOW_OUT	SHADOW_OUT, SHADOW_ETCHED_IN, SHADOW_ETCHED_OUT
textFontList	[dynamic]	[font name]
textTransla-tions	[NULL]	[translations]

Resource Descriptions

allowOverlap
> Specifies whether children are allowed to overlap or not.

autoUnmanage
> If true, any button press inside the BulletinBoard other than Apply or OK causes the BulletinBoard to become unmanaged.

buttonFontList
> The font used for button children that do not specify a font.

cancelButton
> The widget handle for the automatically created cancel button.

defaultButton
> Specifies the button widget handle that is the default button for the Bullet-inBoard.

defaultPosition
> If true and if its parent is a DialogShell, the BulletinBoard is centered in relationship with the DialogShell's parent.

dialogStyle
> Can be set on an unmanaged BulletinBoard widget to deter-
> mine the style of the dialog.

dialogTitle
> The title of the BulletinBoard dialog that is passed to the WMShell ances-
> tor.

labelFontList
> The font used for label children that do not specify a font.

marginHeight (marginWidth)
> The minimum spacing from the top or bottom (left or right) edge of the Bul-
> letinBoard and any of its children.

noResize
> If true, no resize corners are provided by the window manager. Default is
> false.

resizePolicy
> If RESIZE_NONE, the BulletinBoard remains a fixed size. If RESIZE_GROW,
> the BulletinBoard can only grow, never shrink. If RESIZE_ANY, the Bullet-
> inBoard can grow and shrink as needed to fit its children.

shadowType
> The style of the border shadow.

textFontList
> The font used for text children that do not specify a font.

textTranslations
> Translations that are added to all Text children of the BulletinBoard
> widget.

Other Widget Resources

From Manager:
> bottomShadowColor, bottomShadowPixmap, foreground, help-
> Callback, highlightColor, highlightPixmap, navigationType,
> shadowThickness, stringDirection topShadowColor, topShad-
> owPixmap, traversalOn, unitType, userData

From Composite:
> children, insertPosition, numChildren.

From Core:
> accelerators, ancestorSensitive, background, background-
> Pixmap, borderColor, borderPixmap, borderWidth, colormap,
> depth, destroyCallback, height, initialResourcesPer-

sistent, mappedWhenManaged, screen, sensitive, translations, width, x, y.

Callbacks

focusCallback
> Invoked when the BulletinBoard gains focus. Call data:
> CB_CALL_DATA.REASON=CR_FOCUS
> CB_CALL_DATA.EVENT=*X event*

mapCallback
> Invoked whenever the BulletinBoard is mapped. Call data:
> CB_CALL_DATA.REASON=CR_MAP
> CB_CALL_DATA.EVENT=*X event*

unmapCallback
> Invoked when the BulletinBoard is unmapped. Call data:
> CB_CALL_DATA.REASON=CR_UNMAP
> CB_CALL_DATA.EVENT=*X event*

34.9 The BulletinBoardDialog

This is simply a DialogShell widget with a BulletinBoard widget as a child. It can
be used to create highly customized dialogs.

34.10 The CascadeButton Widget and Gadget

This is a specialized button that is used to pop up menus. It can be used to create
nested menus (cascades).

Table 34-6. CascadeButton Widget and Gadget Resources

Resource Name	Default	Other Values
cascadePixmap	*[dynamic]*	*[path to a pixmap file]*
labelString	the name of the widget	*[string]*
mappingDelay	180 (milliseconds)	*[positive integer]*
subMenuId	*[NULL]*	*[widget handle]*

Resource Descriptions

cascadePixmap
> A pixmap that indicates that the CascadeButton has a submenu.

mappingDelay
> Specifies a time delay, in milliseconds, between the time the widget is
> armed and the time the menu is displayed.

subMenuId
> The CascadeButton and a PulldownMenu must both be children of a common parent. After both are created, you set the subMenuId to the widget handle of the PulldownMenu.

Other Widget Resources

From Label:
> accelerator, acceleratorText, alignment, fontList, labelInsensitivePixmap, labelPixmap, labelString, labelType, marginBottom, marginHeight, marginLeft, marginRight, marginTop, marginWidth, mnemonic, mnemonicCharSet, stringDirection.

From Primitive:
> bottomShadowColor, bottomShadowPixmap, foreground, highlightColor, highlightOnEnter, highlightPixmap, highlightThickness, navigationType, shadowThickness, topShadowColor, topShadowPixmap, traversalOn, unitType, userData.

From Core:
> accelerators, ancestorSensitive, background, backgroundPixmap, borderColor, borderPixmap, borderWidth, colormap, depth, destroyCallback, height, initialResourcesPersistent, mappedWhenManaged, screen, sensitive, translations, width, x, y.

Other Gadget Resources

From LabelGadget:
> accelerator, acceleratorText, alignment, fontList, labelInsensitivePixmap, labelPixmap, labelString, labelType, marginBottom, marginHeight, marginLeft, marginRight, marginTop, marginWidth, mnemonic, mnemonicCharSet, stringDirection.

From Gadget:
> helpCallback, highlightOnEnter, highlightThickness, navigationType, shadowThickness, traversalOn, unitType, userData.

From RectObj (see information on equivalent resources under Core):
> ancestorSensitive, borderWidth, height, sensitive, width, x, y.

From Object:
        destroyCallback.

Callbacks

activateCallback
        Invoked when the CascadeButton is selected using a click-move-click style
        selection. Call data:
        CB_CALL_DATA.REASON=CR_ACTIVATE
        CB_CALL_DATA.EVENT=*X event*

cascadingCallback
        Invoked when the CascadeButton is in the process of displaying a menu
        during a drag-select (i.e., the user pressed the mouse button and held it
        down to drag through the menu). Call data:
        CB_CALL_DATA.REASON=CR_CASCADING
        CB_CALL_DATA.EVENT=*X event*

34.11 The CheckBox Widget

This is simply a RowColumn widget with rowColumnType set to WORK_AREA and
radioAlwaysOne set to false. It is meant to hold one or more ToggleButtons, any
number of which can be set at a time.

34.12 The Command Widget

The command widget allows the user to type in commands to be executed by the
application, and it automatically maintains a history list of previous commands.

Table 34-7. Command Widget Resources

Resource Name	Default	Other Values
command	" "	*[string]*
historyItems	*[NULL]*	*[comma-separated list of strings]*
historyItemCount	0	*[positive integer]*
historyMaxItems	100	*[positive integer]*
historyVisibleItem-Count	8	*[positive integer]*
promptString	">" (in English)	*[string]*

Resource Descriptions

command
>The current command string contained in the command input field.

historyItems (historyItemCount)
>The list of items (number of items) contained in the history area. When retrieved using XtGetValues (or XUget) or changed using XtSetValues (or XUset), the form is a comma-separated list of items.

historyVisibleItemCount
>The number of initial items displayed in the history area.

historyMaxItems
>The maximum number of items kept in the history area. The Command widget removes the first item in the list when this number is exceeded to make room for a new item.

promptString
>The string displayed as the command line prompt.

Other Resources

From SelectionBox:
>applyCallback, applyLabelString, cancelCallback, cancelLabelString, childPlacement, dialogType, helpLabelString, listItemCount, listItems, listLabelString, listVisibleItemCount, minimizeButtons, mustMatch, noMatchCallback, okCallback, okLabelString, selectionLabelString, textAccelerators, textColumns, textString.

From BulletinBoard:
>allowOverlap, autoUnmanage, buttonFontList, cancelButton, defaultButton, defaultPosition, dialogStyle, dialogTitle, focusCallback, labelFontList, mapCallback, marginHeight, marginWidth, noResize, resizePolicy, shadowType, textFontList, textTranslations, unmapCallback.

From Manager:
>bottomShadowColor, bottomShadowPixmap, foreground, helpCallback, highlightColor, highlightPixmap, navigationType, shadowThickness, stringDirection topShadowColor, topShadowPixmap, traversalOn, unitType, userData.

From Composite:
>children, insertPosition, numChildren.

From Core:
>accelerators, ancestorSensitive, background, background-

Pixmap, borderColor, borderPixmap, borderWidth, colormap, depth, destroyCallback, height, initialResourcesPersistent, mappedWhenManaged, screen, sensitive, translations, width, x, y.

Callbacks

commandChangedCallback

Invoked whenever the command area changes. Call data:
CB_CALL_DATA.REASON=CR_COMMAND_CHANGED
CB_CALL_DATA.EVENT=*X event*
CB_CALL_DATA.VALUE=*Command String*
CB_CALL_DATA.LENGTH=*Length of Command String*

commandEnteredCallback

Invoked when the users presses ENTER in the command area. Call data:
CB_CALL_DATA.REASON=CR_COMMAND_ENTERED
CB_CALL_DATA.EVENT=*X event*
CB_CALL_DATA.VALUE=*Command String*
CB_CALL_DATA.LENGTH=*Length of Command String*

34.13 The DialogShell Widget

The DialogShell widget provides a separate window for its children. A DialogShell widget cannot be iconified separately from its ApplicationShell parent. The one child of the DialogShell should be a class derived from BulletinBoard such as a MessageBox or Form widget.

Other Widget Resources

From TransientShell:

transientFor.

From VendorShell:

audibleWarning, buttonFontList, defaultFontList, deleteResponse, inputMethod, keyboardFocusPolicy, labelFontList, mwmDecorations, mwmFunctions, mwmInputMode, mwmMenu, preeditType, shellUnitType, textFontList, useAsyncGeometry.

From WMShell:

baseHeight, baseWidth, heightInc, iconMask, iconPixmap, iconWindow, iconX, iconY, initialState, input, maxAspectX, maxAspectY, maxHeight, maxWidth, minAspectX, minAspectY, minHeight, minWidth, title, titleEncoding, transient, waitForWM, widthInc, windowGroup, winGravity, wmTimeout.

From Shell:

allowShellResize, createPopupChildProc, geometry, over-

```
rideRedirect, popdownCallback, popupCallback, saveUnder,
visual.
```

From Composite:

```
children, insertPosition, numChildren.
```

From Core:

```
accelerators, ancestorSensitive, background, background-
Pixmap, borderColor, borderPixmap, borderWidth, colormap,
depth, destroyCallback, height, initialResourcesPer-
sistent, mappedWhenManaged, screen, sensitive, transla-
tions, width, x, y.
```

34.14 The DrawingArea Widget

The DrawingArea provides an empty area for programmer-defined graphics. Callbacks are used to notify the application when areas of the widget need to be redrawn. The DrawingArea is a manager widget, and it is possible to place children inside it with some minimal geometry management.

Table 34-8. DrawingArea Widget Resources

Resource Name	Default	Other Values
`marginHeight`	10	`[integer >= 0]`
`maginWidth`	10	`[integer >= 0]`
`resizePolicy`	`RESIZE_ANY`	`RESIZE_NONE`, `RESIZE_GROW`

Resource Descriptions

`marginHeight`(`marginWidth`)

The minimum spacing between the top and bottom (left or right edge) of children of the DrawingArea.

`resizePolicy`

If set to `RESIZE_NONE`, the DrawingArea stays a fixed size. If `RESIZE_ANY`, the DrawingArea attempts to resize to accommodate children (both larger and smaller). If set to `RESIZE_GROW`, the DrawingArea is allowed to grow larger to accommodate children, but never shrinks even if children shrink or become unmanaged.

Other Widget Resources

From Manager:

```
bottomShadowColor, bottomShadowPixmap, foreground, help-
Callback, highlightColor, highlightPixmap, navigationType,
```

shadowThickness, stringDirection topShadowColor, topShadowPixmap, traversalOn, unitType, userData.

From Composite:
children, insertPosition, numChildren.

From Core:
accelerators, ancestorSensitive, background, background-
Pixmap, borderColor, borderPixmap, borderWidth, colormap,
depth, destroyCallback, height, initialResourcesPersistent, mappedWhenManaged, screen, sensitive, translations, width, x, y.

Callbacks

exposeCallback
Invoked when a portion of the widget is exposed. The application must re-
draw the exposed area. Call data:
CB_CALL_DATA.REASON=CR_EXPOSE
CB_CALL_DATA.EVENT=*X event*
CB_CALL_DATA.WINDOW=*DrawingArea's Window ID*

inputCallback
Invoked when keyboard or mouse input is available for the DrawingArea.
The EVENT subfield contains the X input event. Call data:
CB_CALL_DATA.REASON=CR_INPUT
CB_CALL_DATA.EVENT=*X event*
CB_CALL_DATA.WINDOW=*DrawingArea's Window ID*

resizeCallback
Invoked when the DrawingArea is resized. Call data:
CB_CALL_DATA.REASON=CR_RESIZE
CB_CALL_DATA.EVENT=*X event*
CB_CALL_DATA.WINDOW=*DrawingArea's Window ID*

34.15 The DrawnButton Widget

Similar to a PushButton, this widget provides a blank button area on which arbitrary graphics can be displayed by the application. Callbacks are used to inform
the application when the button is exposed or resized so redrawing can occur..

Table 34-9. DrawnButton Widget Resources

Resource Name	Default	Other Values
multiClick	When in a menu: MULTICLICK_DISCARD, otherwise: MULTICLICK_KEEP.	There are no other legal values.

Table 34-9. DrawnButton Widget Resources (continued)

Resource Name	Default	Other Values
pushButtonEnabled	false	true
shadowType	SHADOW_ETCHED_IN	SHADOW_IN, SHADOW_OUT, SHADOW_ETCHED_OUT

Resource Descriptions

multiClick

If set to MULTICLICK_KEEP, then the activateCallback is invoked once per selection, otherwise multiple clicks that occur close together in time will only invoke the activateCallback once with the CB_CALL_DA-TA.CLICK_COUNT variable set to the number of selections.

pushButtonEnabled

When this resources is set to true, the DrawnButton has the appearance of a PushButton widget, i.e., the 3D shadow is drawn. When false, the shadow is not drawn.

shadowType

Specifies the appearance of the border shadow.

Other Widget Resources

From Label:

accelerator, acceleratorText, alignment, fontList, labelInsensitivePixmap, labelPixmap, labelString, labelType, marginBottom, marginHeight, marginLeft, marginRight, marginTop, marginWidth, mnemonic, mnemonicCharSet, stringDirection.

From Primitive:

bottomShadowColor, bottomShadowPixmap, foreground, highlightColor, highlightOnEnter, highlightPixmap, highlightThickness, navigationType, shadowThickness, topShadowColor, topShadowPixmap, traversalOn, unitType, userData.

From Core:

accelerators, ancestorSensitive, background, backgroundPixmap, borderColor, borderPixmap, borderWidth, colormap, depth, destroyCallback, height, initialResourcesPersistent, mappedWhenManaged, screen, sensitive, translations, width, x, y.

Callbacks

activateCallback
>   Invoked when the button is selected. Call data:
>   CB_CALL_DATA.REASON=CR_ACTIVATE
>   CB_CALL_DATA.EVENT=*X event*
>   CB_CALL_DATA.WINDOW=*DrawnButton's Window ID*
>   CB_CALL_DATA.CLICK_COUNT=*Number of Clicks*

armCallback
>   Invoked when the mouse button is pressed while the pointer is over the widget. Call data:
>   CB_CALL_DATA.REASON=CR_VALUE_CHANGED
>   CB_CALL_DATA.EVENT=*X event*
>   CB_CALL_DATA.WINDOW=*DrawnButton's Window ID*

disarmCallback
>   Invoked when the mouse button is released while the pointer is over the widget. Call data:
>   CB_CALL_DATA.REASON=CR_VALUE_CHANGED
>   CB_CALL_DATA.EVENT=*X event*
>   CB_CALL_DATA.WINDOW=*DrawnButton's Window ID*

exposeCallback
>   Invoked when any part of the DrawnButton is exposed. Call data:
>   CB_CALL_DATA.REASON = CR_EXPOSE
>   CB_CALL_DATA.EVENT = *X event*
>   CB_CALL_DATA.WINDOW = *DrawnButton's Window*

resizeCallback
>   Invoked when the widget is resized. Call data:
>   CB_CALL_DATA.REASON = CR_EXPOSE
>   CB_CALL_DATA.EVENT = *X event*
>   CB_CALL_DATA.WINDOW = *DrawnButton's Window*

34.16 The FileSelectionBox Widget

The FileSelectionBox widget is used to present the user with an interface to the files and directories on the system. The widget contains two lists: the directories and the files. The user can enter a selection directly or select it from the lists.

.

Table 34-10. FileSelectionBox Widget Resources

Resource Name	Default	Other Values
directory	*[dynamic]*	*[string]*

Table 34-10. FileSelectionBox Widget Resources (continued)

Resource Name	Default	Other Values
directoryValid	[dynamic]	true, false
dirListItems	[dynamic]	[comma-separated list of strings]
dirListItemCount	[dynamic]	[integer]
dirListLabelString	[dynamic]	[string]
dirMask	[dynamic]	[string]
dirSearchProc	default procedure	[requires C code]
dirSpec	[dynamic] .	[string]
fileListItems	[dynamic]	[comma-separated list of strings]
fileListItemCount	[dynamic]	[integer]
fileListLabel-String	[dynamic]	[string]
fileSearchProc	[default search procedure]	[requires C code]
fileTypeMask	FILE_REGULAR	FILE_DIRECTORY, FILE_REGULAR, or FILE_ANY_TYPE
filterLabelString	[dynamic]	[string]
listUpdated	[dynamic]	true, false
noMatchString	"[ ]"	[string]
pattern	[dynamic]	[string]
qualifySearch-DataProc	[default search procedure]	[requires C code]

Resource Descriptions

directory
> The path to the directory that the widget displays.

directoryValid
> This resource is used only by the dirSearchProc to indicate if the directory is valid or not.

dirListItems
> This resource is set only by the dirSearchProc to the list of valid directories. The list returned is not a copy, so do not free it.

dirListItemCount

> This resource is set only by the dirSearchProc to the number of items in the list of valid directories.

dirListLabelString

> This resource specifies the label for the list of directories.

dirMask

> The concatenation of directory and pattern that determines which files the FileSelectionBox will display.

dirSearchProc

> Specifies a procedure that searches a given directory for valid directories and populates the directory List.

dirSpec

> Specifies the full path to the selected file.

fileListItems

> This resource is set only by the fileSearchProc to the list of valid files. The list returned is not a copy, so do not free it.

fileListItemCount

> This resource is set only by the fileSearchProc to the number of items in the list of valid files.

fileListLabelString

> This resource specifies the label for the list of files.

fileSearchProc

> Specifies a procedure that searches a given directory for valid files and populates the file List.

fileTypeMask

> This resource does simple filtering of the files to be displayed in the file list. FILE_DIRECTORY means display only directories, FILE_REGULAR means only regular files, and FILE_ANY_TYPE means both regular and directory files will be displayed.

filterLabelString

> This resource specifies the label for the directory mask input field.

listUpdated

> This resource is set only by the dirSearchProc or fileSearchProc to indicate whether the list was updated by the search procedure.

noMatchString

> Specifies a string that is placed in the file List when there are no filenames to display.

pattern
>   A pattern-matching string that determines which files will be displayed.

qualifySearchDataProc
>   This procedure calculates the input to the dirSearchProc and file-
>   SearchProc callback data: mask, dir, pattern.

Other Widget Resources

From SelectionBox:
>   applyCallback, applyLabelString, cancelCallback, cancelLa-
>   belString, childPlacement, dialogType, helpLabelString,
>   listItemCount, listItems, listLabelString, listVisible-
>   ItemCount, minimizeButtons, mustMatch, noMatchCallback,
>   okCallback, okLabelString, selectionLabelString, textAc-
>   celerators, textColumns, textString.

From BulletinBoard:
>   allowOverlap, autoUnmanage, buttonFontList, cancelButton,
>   defaultButton, defaultPosition, dialogStyle, dialogTitle,
>   focusCallback, labelFontList, mapCallback, marginHeight,
>   marginWidth, noResize, resizePolicy, shadowType, text-
>   FontList, textTranslations, unmapCallback.

From Manager:
>   bottomShadowColor, bottomShadowPixmap, foreground, help-
>   Callback, highlightColor, highlightPixmap, navigationType,
>   shadowThickness, stringDirection topShadowColor, topShad-
>   owPixmap, traversalOn, unitType, userData.

From Composite:
>   children, insertPosition, numChildren.

From Core:
>   accelerators, ancestorSensitive, background, background-
>   Pixmap, borderColor, borderPixmap, borderWidth, colormap,
>   depth, destroyCallback, height, initialResourcesPer-
>   sistent, mappedWhenManaged, screen, sensitive, transla-
>   tions, width, x, y.

34.17 The FileSelectionDialog Widget

This is simply a FileSelectionBox widget with a DialogShell parent.

34.18 The Form Widget

The Form widget is a manager widget that provides constraint resources to position
its children. The position is based on what the widget is attached to and the offset
between the widget and the attachment.

Table 34-11. Form Widget Resources

Resource Name	Default	Other Values
fractionBase	100	*[integer]*
horizontalSpacing	0	*[positive integer]*
rubberPositioning	false	true
verticalSpacing	0	*[positive integer]*

Table 34-12. Form Widget Constraint Resources

Resource Name	Default	Other Values
bottomAttachment	ATTACH_NONE	ATTACH_NONE, ATTACH_FORM, ATTACH_OPPOSITE_FORM, ATTACH_WIDGET, ATTACH_OPPOSITE_WIDGET, ATTACH_POSITION, ATTACH_SELF
bottomOffset	0	*[integer]*
bottomPosition	0	*[integer]*
bottomWidget	*[NULL]*	*[widget handle]*
leftAttachment	ATTACH_NONE	see bottomAttachment
leftOffset	0	*[integer]*
leftPosition	0	*[integer]*
leftWidget	*[NULL]*	*[widget handle]*
resizable	true	false
rightAttachment	ATTACH_NONE	see bottomAttachment
rightOffset	0	*[integer]*
rightPosition	0	*[integer]*
rightWidget	*[NULL]*	*[widget handle]*
topAttachment	ATTACH_NONE	see bottomAttachment
topOffset	0	*[integer]*
topPosition	0	*[integer]*
topWidget	*[NULL]*	*[widget handle]*

Resource Descriptions

fractionBase

> Used in conjunction with the attachPosition constraint resources to determine a position for the child that is relative to the size of the form. The default is 100 so that the positions can be thought of as a percentage of the form's total size.

horizontalSpacing, verticalSpacing

> The offset for the right and left attachments (horizontalSpacing) or the offset for the top and bottom attachments (verticalSpacing).

rubberPositioning

> When true the default positioning of children is relative to the size of the form. When false, children are positioned absolutely.

Constraint Resources

bottomAttachment

> Determines how the bottom of the child widget will be attached. The possible values are ATTACH_NONE to remain unattached, ATTACH_FORM to attach to the corresponding edge of the Form, ATTACH_OPPOSITE_FORM to attach to the opposite edge of the form, ATTACH_WIDGET to attach to the given widget, ATTACH_OPPOSITE_WIDGET to attach to the opposite edge of the given widget, ATTACH_POSITION to position relative to the size of the Form, ATTACH_SELF to position relative to the widget's current position and to the Form.

bottomOffset

> The space between the bottom of the child widget and the object to which it is attached.

bottomPosition

> Used with the fractionBase resource to determine a position relative to the size of the Form. The bottomAttachment must be set to ATTACH_POSITION for this layout to be used.

bottomWidget

> Attach the bottom of this child to the object given in this resource. The bottomAttachment must be set to ATTACH_WIDGET or ATTACH_OPPOSITE_WIDGET.

leftAttachment

> Determines how the left side of the child widget will be attached. The possible values are: ATTACH_NONE to remain unattached, ATTACH_FORM to attach to the corresponding edge of the Form, ATTACH_OPPOSITE_FORM to attach to the opposite edge of the form, ATTACH_WIDGET to attach to the given widget, ATTACH_OPPOSITE_WIDGET to attach to the opposite edge of

the given widget, `ATTACH_POSITION` to position relative to the size of the Form, `ATTACH_SELF` to position relative to the widget's current position and to the Form.

`leftOffset`

The space between the left side of the child widget and the object to which it is attached.

`leftPosition`

Used with the `fractionBase` resource to determine a position relative to the size of the Form. The `leftAttachment` must be set to `ATTACH_POSI-TION` for this layout to be used.

`leftWidget`

Attach the left side of this child to the object given in this resource. The `leftAttachment` must be set to `ATTACH_WIDGET` or `ATTACH_OPPO-SITE_WIDGET`.

`resizable`

When this resource it `true`, a child's resize request will be attempted based on the constraints. When it is `false`, all resize requests are denied.

`rightAttachment`

Determines how the right side of the child widget will be attached. The possible values are `ATTACH_NONE` to remain unattached, `ATTACH_FORM` to attach to the corresponding edge of the Form, `ATTACH_OPPOSITE_FORM` to attach to the opposite edge of the form, `ATTACH_WIDGET` to attach to the given widget, `ATTACH_OPPOSITE_WIDGET` to attach to the opposite edge of the given widget, `ATTACH_POSITION` to position relative to the size of the Form, `ATTACH_SELF` to position relative to the widget's current position and to the Form.

`rightOffset`

The space between the right side of the child widget and the object to which it is attached.

`rightPosition`

Used with the `fractionBase` resource to determine a position relative to the size of the Form. The `rightAttachment` must be set to `ATTACH_POSI-TION` for this layout to be used.

`rightWidget`

Attach the right side of this child to the object give in this resource. The `rightAttachment` must be set to `ATTACH_WIDGET` or `ATTACH_OPPO-SITE_WIDGET`.

`topAttachment`

Determines how the top of the child widget will be attached. The possible values are ATTACH_NONE to remain unattached, ATTACH_FORM to attach to the corresponding edge of the Form, ATTACH_OPPOSITE_FORM to attach to the opposite edge of the form, ATTACH_WIDGET to attach to the given widget, ATTACH_OPPOSITE_WIDGET to attach to the opposite edge of the given widget, ATTACH_POSITION to position relative to the size of the Form, ATTACH_SELF to position relative to the widget's current position and to the Form.

topOffset
> The space between the top of the child widget and the object to which it is attached.

topPosition
> Used with the fractionBase resource to determine a position relative to the size of the Form. The topAttachment must be set to ATTACH_POSITION for this layout to be used.

topWidget
> Attach the bottom of this child to the object given in this resource. The topAttachment must be set to ATTACH_WIDGET or ATTACH_OPPOSITE_WIDGET.

Other Widget Resources

From BulletinBoard:
> allowOverlap, autoUnmanage, buttonFontList, cancelButton, defaultButton, defaultPosition, dialogStyle, dialogTitle, focusCallback, labelFontList, mapCallback, marginHeight, marginWidth, noResize, resizePolicy, shadowType, textFontList, textTranslations, unmapCallback.

From Manager:
> bottomShadowColor, bottomShadowPixmap, foreground, helpCallback, highlightColor, highlightPixmap, navigationType, shadowThickness, stringDirection topShadowColor, topShadowPixmap, traversalOn, unitType, userData.

From Composite:
> children, insertPosition, numChildren.

From Core:
> accelerators, ancestorSensitive, background, backgroundPixmap, borderColor, borderPixmap, borderWidth, colormap, depth, destroyCallback, height, initialResourcesPersistent, mappedWhenManaged, screen, sensitive, translations, width, x, y.

34.19 The Frame Widget

The Frame widget manages a border around its child. It can also display a title for the frame in many positions.

Table 34-13. Frame Widget Resources

Resource Name	Default	Other Values
marginHeight	0	*[positive integer]*
marginWidth	0	*[positive integer]*
shadowType	[dynamic]	SHADOW_IN, SHADOW_OUT, SHADOW_ETCHED_IN, SHADOW_ETCHED_OUT,

Table 34-14. Frame Widget Constraint Resources

Resource Name	Default	Other Values
childType	FRAME_WORKAREA_CHILD	FRAME_TITLE_CHILD, FRAME_GENERIC_CHILD
childHorizontal-Alignment	ALIGNMENT_BEGINNING	ALIGNMENT_CENTER, ALIGNMENT_END
childHorizontal-Spacing	*[dynamic]*	*[positive integer]*
childVertical-Alignment	ALIGNMENT_CENTER	ALIGNMENT_BASELINE_BOTTOM, ALIGNMENT_BASELINE_TOP, ALIGNMENT_WIDGET_TOP, ALIGNMENT_WIDGET_BOTTOM

Resource Descriptions

marginHeight
> The vertical spacing between the Frame's child and the shadow border.

marginWidth
> The horizontal spacing between the Frame's child and the shadow border.

shadowType
> This resource specifies the style of the border shadow: SHADOW_IN, SHADOW_OUT, SHADOW_ETCHED_IN, SHADOW_ETCHED_OUT.

Constraint Resources

childType
> A FRAME_TITLE_CHILD is used as the title for the Frame. A FRAME_WORK-

AREA_CHILD is the widget that the Frame surrounds. A FRAME_GEN-ERIC_CHILD is ignored.

childHorizontalAlignment
Specifies the horizontal alignment of the Frame's title child.

childHorizontalSpacing
The space between the Frame's shadow and the title.

childVerticalAlignment
Specifies the vertical alignment of the Frame's title child in relation to the frame's top shadow.

Other Widget Resources

From Manager:
bottomShadowColor, bottomShadowPixmap, foreground, help-Callback, highlightColor, highlightPixmap, navigationType, shadowThickness, stringDirection topShadowColor, topShadowPixmap, traversalOn, unitType, userData.

From Composite:
children, insertPosition, numChildren.

From Core:
accelerators, ancestorSensitive, background, background-Pixmap, borderColor, borderPixmap, borderWidth, colormap, depth, destroyCallback, height, initialResourcesPersistent, mappedWhenManaged, screen, sensitive, translations, width, x, y.

34.20 The Gadget Class

The Gadget class is never instantiated on its own. It provides all Gadgets with keyboard traversal functionality and consistent border resources.

Table 34-15. Gadget Class Resources

Resource Name	Default	Other Values
bottomShadowColor	*[dynamic]*	*[color]*
highlightColor	*[dynamic]*	*[color]*
highlightOnEnter	false	true
highlightThickness	2	*[positive integer]*

Table 34-15. Gadget Class Resources (continued)

Resource Name	Default	Other Values
navigationType	NONE	TAB_GROUP, STICK_TAB_GROUP, EXCLUSIVE_TAB_GROUP
shadowThickness	2	[positive integer]
topShadowColor	[dynamic]	[color]
traversalOn	true	false
unitType	[dynamic]	PIXELS, 100TH_MILLIMETERS, 100TH_INCHES, 100TH_POINTS, 100TH_FONT_UNITS
userData	[NULL]	[requires C code]

Resource Descriptions

bottomShadowColor
> The color that is used on the bottom and right in drawing the border.

highlightColor
> The color that is used to draw the solid border that indicates that the object has input focus.

highlightOnEnter
> This resource applies only when the object's shell has the keyboardFocus-Policy of POINTER. When the mouse pointer moves into the object and this resource is true, then the input focus highlight is drawn. Otherwise, the highlighting is not drawn unless focus is explicitly moved to the object.

highlightThickness
> Specifies the thickness of the input focus highlight.

navigationType
> Specifies the way navigation works with this object. NONE means that the object is not traversable. TAB_GROUP means that it is traversable and is part of a tab group. STICKY_TAB_GROUP includes an object in traversal even if it is its own tab group. EXCLUSIVE_TAB_GROUP is used to make the object a separate tab group.

shadowThickness
> Specifies the thickness of the border shadow.

topShadowColor
> The color that is used on the top and left in drawing the border.

traversalOn
> Traversal to this object is allowed when this resource is true. When set to false, it is not possible to traverse to this object.

unitType
> Defines the unit type for all resources that specify a Dimension, e.g., margins.

userData
> This resource is reserved for the application. It is a pointer to whatever data an application may want to associate with this object.

Callbacks

helpCallback
> Invoked when help is requested. Call data:
> CB_CALL_DATA.REASON=CR_HELP
> CB_CALL_DATA.EVENT=X event

Other Gadget Resources

> From RectObj (see information on equivalent resources under Core):
> ancestorSensitive, borderWidth, height, sensitive, width, x, y.

> From Object:
> destroyCallback.

34.21 The Label Widget and Gadget

The Label displays a text or pixmap label. It is used as the superclass for other button classes. This widget is used to display text or pixmaps that do not need to be activated.

.

Table 34-16. Label Widget and Gadget Resources

Resource Name	Default	Other Values
accelerator	[NULL]	[string]
acceleratorText	[NULL]	[string]
alignment	[dynamic]	ALIGNMENT_BEGINNING, ALIGNMENT_CENTER, ALIGNMENT_END
fontList	[dynamic]	[font name]

Table 34-16. Label Widget and Gadget Resources (continued)

Resource Name	Default	Other Values
labelInsensitive-Pixmap	UNSPECIFIED_PIXMAP	[path to a pixmap file]
labelPixmap	UNSPECIFIED_PIXMAP	[path to a pixmap file]
labelString	[dynamic]	[string]
labelType	STRING	PIXMAP
marginBottom	0	[positive integer]
marginHeight	2	[positive integer]
marginLeft	0	[positive integer]
marginRight	2	[positive integer]
marginTop	0	[positive integer]
marginWidth	2	[positive integer]
mnemonic	[NULL}	[single letter]
mnemonicCharSet	FONTLIST_DEFAULT_TAG	[string]
recomputeSize	true	false
stringDirection	[dynamic]	STRING_DIRECTION_L_TO_R, STRING_DIRECTION_R_TO_L

Resource Descriptions

accelerator
> The key press event that is the button's accelerator. Pressing this modifier and key causes the button to be activated.

acceleratorText
> The string that is appended to the label to describe the accelerator.

alignment
> The alignment of the label or pixmap in the horizontal direction. It can be set to ALIGNMENT_BEGINNING, ALIGNMENT_CENTER, or ALIGNMENT_END.

fontList
> The font that is used to draw the labelString.

labelInsensitivePixmap
> The pixmap that is displayed when the Label is insensitive.

labelPixmap
> The pixmap that is displayed when labelType is PIXMAP.

labelString
> The string that is displayed when labelType is STRING.

labelType
> The labelType can be either STRING or PIXMAP.

marginBottom
> The space from the bottom of the label to the bottom of the widget.

marginHeight
> The space above and below the label.

marginLeft
> The space from the left side of the label to the left side of the widget.

marginRight
> The space from the right side of the label to the right side of the widget.

marginTop
> The space from the top of the label to the top of the widget.

marginWidth
> The space to the right and left of the label.

mnemonic
> A character that can be used to select the button. It appears underlined in the labelString.

mnemonicCharSet
> The character set for the mnemonic.

recomputeSize
> The Label recomputes its size when the labelString or labelPixmap is changed and this resource is true. When false, the Label may clip or align the contents.

stringDirection
> The direction in which the labelString is drawn.

Other Widget Resources

From Primitive:
> bottomShadowColor, bottomShadowPixmap, foreground, high-lightColor, highlightOnEnter, highlightPixmap, highlight-Thickness, navigationType, shadowThickness, topShadowColor, topShadowPixmap, traversalOn, unitType, userData.

From Core:
> accelerators, ancestorSensitive, background, background-

Pixmap, borderColor, borderPixmap, borderWidth, colormap, depth, destroyCallback, height, initialResourcesPersistent, mappedWhenManaged, screen, sensitive, translations, width, x, y.

Other Gadget Resources

From Gadget:

helpCallback, highlightOnEnter, highlightThickness, navigationType, shadowThickness, traversalOn, unitType, userData.

From RectObj (see information on equivalent resources under Core):

ancestorSensitive, borderWidth, height, sensitive, width, x, y.

From Object:

destroyCallback.

34.22 The List Widget

The List widget displays a list of items from which the user can select. It is used to present the user with a set of fixed choices. The List has four different selection policies that determine how the List operates: single selection, multiple selection, browse selection, or extended selection.

Table 34-17. List Widget Resources

Resource Name	Default	Other Values
automaticSelection	false	true
doubleClickInterval	[dynamic]	[integer]
fontList	[dynamic]	[font]
itemCount	0	[positive integer]
items	[NULL]	[list of strings]
listMarginHeight	0	[positive integer]
listMarginWidth	0	[positive integer]
listSizePolicy	VARIABLE	CONSTANT, RESIZE_IF_POSSIBLE
listSpacing	0	[positive integer]
scrollBarDisplayPolicy	AS_NEEDED	STATIC

Table 34-17. List Widget Resources (continued)

Resource Name	Default	Other Values
selectedItemCount	0	*[positive integer]*
selectedItems	*[NULL]*	*[list of strings]*
selectionPolicy	BROWSE_SELECT	SINGLE_SELECT, MULTIPLE_SELECT, EXTENDED_SELECT
stringDirection	*[dynamic]*	STRING_DIRECTION_L_TO_R, STRING_DIRECTION_R_TO_L
topItemPosition	1	*[positive integer]*
visibleItemCount	*[dynamic]*	*[positive integer]*

Resource Descriptions

automaticSelection

This resource is useful for selectionPolicy BROWSE_SELECT and EXTENDED_SELECT. When it is set to true, the singleSelectionCallback is invoked when the user moves into another item. Otherwise, the mouse button must be released before the callback is invoked.

doubleClickInterval

The time in milliseconds that distinguishes two single clicks from one double-click sequence.

fontList

The font that is used to draw the list items.

itemCount

The number of items.

items

A list of strings that are used as the items in the List.

listMarginHeight

The space between the top and bottom of the items and the list border.

listMarginWidth

The space between the right and left sides of the items and the list border.

listSizePolicy

This resource handles the horizontal sizing of the List. When set to VARIABLE, the List will be resized to fit the widest item. When it is CONSTANT, the width remains the same and a ScrollBar is added. If set to RESIZE_IF_POSSIBLE, the List will grow and shrink based on the widest item, and if the List cannot grow, then a ScrollBar will be added.

`listSpacing`
>   The interitem spacing.

`scrollBarDisplayPolicy`
>   When set to STATIC the vertical ScrollBar is always displayed. When this resource is set to AS_NEEDED, the ScrollBar is automatically added when all the items in the list cannot be displayed.

`selectedItemCount`
>   The number of selected items.

`selectedItems`
>   A list of strings corresponding to the strings in `items` that are selected.

`selectionPolicy`
>   Specifies the style of the List. SINGLE_SELECT allows only a single item to be selected and automatically deselects the previous selection. MULTI-PLE_SELECT allows any number of items to be selected, and selecting an item that is already selected causes it to be deselected. BROWSE_SELECT allows only a single selection and has the ability to browse by dragging the selection along with the mouse pointer. EXTENDED_SELECT allows multiple items to be selected and has actions that allow the user to select discontiguous groups of items.

`stringDirection`
>   The direction in which the list item strings are drawn.

`topItemPosition`
>   The position of the item displayed at the top of the list. The last position is 0.

`visibleItemCount`
>   The number of items displayed in the List.

Other Widget Resources

From Primitive:
>   bottomShadowColor, bottomShadowPixmap, foreground, highlightColor, highlightOnEnter, highlightPixmap, highlightThickness, navigationType, shadowThickness, topShadowColor, topShadowPixmap, traversalOn, unitType, userData.

From Core:
>   accelerators, ancestorSensitive, background, backgroundPixmap, borderColor, borderPixmap, borderWidth, colormap, depth, destroyCallback, height, initialResourcesPersistent, mappedWhenManaged, screen, sensitive, translations, width, x, y.

Callbacks

browseSelectionCallback

Invoked when the List's selectionPolicy is BROWSE_SELECT and a list item is selected. Call data:
CB_CALL_DATA.REASON=CR_DRAG
CB_CALL_DATA.EVENT=*X event*
CB_CALL_DATA.ITEM=*item selected by the event*
CB_CALL_DATA.ITEM_LENGTH=*size of the item*
CB_CALL_DATA.ITEM_POSITION=*item's position in item array*

defaultActionCallback

Invoked when the user double clicks an item or the KActivate key is pressed. Call data:
CB_CALL_DATA.REASON=CR_DEFAULT_ACTION
CB_CALL_DATA.EVENT=*X event*
CB_CALL_DATA.ITEM=*item selected as a result of the event*
CB_CALL_DATA.ITEM_LENGTH=*size of the item*
CB_CALL_DATA.ITEM_POSITION=*item's position in item array*

extendedSelectionCallback

Invoked when the List's selectionPolicy is EXTENDED_SELECT and a list item is selected. Call data:
CB_CALL_DATA.REASON=CR_DEFAULT_ACTION
CB_CALL_DATA.EVENT=*X event*
CB_CALL_DATA.ITEM=*item selected as a result of the event*
CB_CALL_DATA.ITEM_LENGTH=*size of the item*
CB_CALL_DATA.ITEM_POSITION=*The item's position in the item array*
CB_CALL_DATA.SELECTED_ITEMS=*list of all selected items*
CB_CALL_DATA.SELECTED_ITEM_COUNT=*number of* selected items
CB_CALL_DATA.SELECTED_ITEM_POSITIONS=*indexes of selected items*
CB_CALL_DATA.SELECTION_TYPE =one of INITIAL, MODIFICATION, or ADDITION

multipleSelectionCallback

Invoked when the List's selectionPolicy is MULTIPLE_SELECT and a list item is selected. Call data:
CB_CALL_DATA.REASON=CR_DEFAULT_ACTION
CB_CALL_DATA.EVENT=*X event*
CB_CALL_DATA.ITEM=*item selected as a result of the event*
CB_CALL_DATA.ITEM_LENGTH=*size of* the item
CB_CALL_DATA.ITEM_POSITION=the item's *index*
CB_CALL_DATA.SELECTED_ITEMS=*list of all items selected in*

the List
CB_CALL_DATA.SELECTED_ITEM_COUNT=*size of* SELECTED_ITEMS
CB_CALL_DATA.SELECTED_ITEM_POSITIONS = *positions of corre-*
sponding items in SELECTED_ITEMS

singleSelectionCallback
    Invoked when the List's selectionPolicy is SINGLE_SELECT and a list item
is selected. Call data:
CB_CALL_DATA.REASON=CR_DEFAULT_ACTION
CB_CALL_DATA.EVENT=*X event*
CB_CALL_DATA.ITEM=*item selected as a result of the event*
CB_CALL_DATA.ITEM_LENGTH=*size of* the item
CB_CALL_DATA.ITEM_POSITION=the item*'s position in array of*
items

34.23 The MainWindow Widget

The MainWindow widget is used as the application's primary window. It positions
the standard elements of the application: the menu bar, command window, work
area, message window, and scroll bars.

Table 34-18. MainWindow Widget Resources

Resource Name	Default	Other Values
commandWindow	*[NULL]*	*[widget handle]*
commandWindowLoca-tion	COMMAND_ABOVE_-WORKSPACE	COMMAND_BELOW_WORKSPACE
mainWindowMargin-Height	0	*[positive integer]*
mainWindowMargin-Width	0	*[positive integer]*
menuBar	*[NULL]*	*[widget handle]*
messageWindow	*[NULL]*	*[widget handle]*
showSeparator	false	true

Resource Descriptions

commandWindow
    The widget handle of the command window.

commandWindowLocation
    The position of the command window relative to the other MainWindow
components. COMMAND_ABOVE_WORKSPACE places the command window

just below the menu bar. COMMAND_BELOW_WORKSPACE places the command window below the work area and above the message area.

mainWindowMarginHeight
> The top and bottom margin of the MainWindow.

mainWindowMarginWidth
> The right and left margin of the MainWindow.

menuBar
> The widget handle of the menu bar.

messageWindow
> The widget handle of the message window.

showSeparator
> Setting this resource to true adds Separator between each of the MainWindow components. When false, no Separators are displayed.

Other Widget Resources

From ScrolledWindow:
> clipWindow, horizontalScrollBar, scrollBarDisplayPolicy, scrollBarPlacement, scrolledWindowMarginHeight, scrolledWindowMarginWidth, scrollingPolicy, spacing, verticalScrollBar, visualPolicy, workWindow.

From Manager:
> bottomShadowColor, bottomShadowPixmap, foreground, helpCallback, highlightColor, highlightPixmap, navigationType, shadowThickness, stringDirection topShadowColor, topShadowPixmap, traversalOn, unitType, userData.

From Composite:
> children, insertPosition, numChildren.

From Core:
> accelerators, ancestorSensitive, background, backgroundPixmap, borderColor, borderPixmap, borderWidth, colormap, depth, destroyCallback, height, initialResourcesPersistent, mappedWhenManaged, screen, sensitive, translations, width, x, y.

34.24 The Manager Class

The Manager class is never instantiated on its own. It is the superclass for all Motif composite widgets. The Manager class provides keyboard traversal and consistent border resources.

Table 34-19. Manager Class Resources

Resource Name	Default	Other Values
bottomShadowColor	[dynamic]	[color]
bottomShadowPixmap	UNSPECIFIED_PIXMAP	[path to a pixmap file]
foreground	[dynamic]	[color]
highlightColor	[dynamic]	[color]
highlightPixmap	[dynamic]	[path to a pixmap file]
initialFocus	[NULL]	[widget handle]
navigationType	TAB_GROUP	NONE, STICKY_TAB_GROUP, EXCLUSIVE_TAB_GROUP
shadowThickness	[dynamic]	[positive integer]
stringDirection	[dynamic]	STRING_DIRECTION_L_TO_R, STRING_DIRECTION_R_TO_L
topShadowColor	[dynamic]	[color]
topShadowPixmap	[dynamic]	[path to a pixmap file]
traversalOn	true	false
unitType	[dynamic]	PIXELS, 100TH_MILLIMETERS, 1000TH_INCHES, 100TH_POINTS, 100TH_FONT_UNITS
userData	[NULL]	[requires C code]

Resource Descriptions

bottomShadowColor
> The color that is used on the bottom and right in drawing the border.

bottomShadowPixmap
> The pixmap that is used on the bottom and right in drawing the border.

foreground
> The color that is used to draw the foreground.

highlightColor
> The color that is used to draw the solid border that indicates that the object has input focus.

highlightPixmap
> The pixmap that is used to draw the border that indicates that the object has input focus.

highlightThickness
> Specifies the thickness of the input focus highlight.

initialFocus
> The widget that receives focus the first time the Manager's shell receives focus.

navigationType
> Specifies the way navigation works with this object. NONE means that the object is not traversable. TAB_GROUP means that it is traversable and is part of a tab group. STICKY_TAB_GROUP includes an object in traversal even if it is its own tab group. EXCLUSIVE_TAB_GROUP is used to make the object a separate tab group.

shadowThickness
> Specifies the thickness of the border shadow.

stringDirection
> The direction in which to draw strings.

topShadowColor
> The color that is used on the top and left in drawing the border.

topShadowPixmap
> The pixmap that is used on the top and left in drawing the border.

traversalOn
> Traversal to this object is allowed when this resource is true. When set to false, it is not possible to traverse to this object.

unitType
> Defines the unit type for all resources that specify a Dimension, e.g., margins.

userData
> This resource is reserved for the application. It is a pointer to whatever data an application may want to associate with this object.

Other Widget Resources

From Composite:
> children, insertPosition, numChildren.

From Core:
> accelerators, ancestorSensitive, background, background-Pixmap, borderColor, borderPixmap, borderWidth, colormap,

```
depth,    destroyCallback,    height,    initialResourcesPer-
sistent,  mappedWhenManaged,   screen,   sensitive,  transla-
tions, width, x, y.
```

Callbacks

helpCallback
> Invoked when help is requested by the user, typically by selecting the F1
> function key or some special keyboard key. Call data:
> CB_CALL_DATA.REASON=CR_HELP
> CB_CALL_DATA.EVENT=X *event*

34.25 The MenuShell Widget

The MenuShell widget is used to create pop-up and pull-down menus. Most application writers use the convenience routines to create menu hierarchies, such as XUmenusystem.

.

Table 34-20. MenuShell Widget Resources

Resource Name	Default	Other Values
buttonFontList	*[dynamic]*	*[font]*
defaultFontList	*[dynamic]*	*[font]*
labelFontList	*[dynamic]*	*[font]*

Resource Descriptions

buttonFontlist
> The font that is used to draw button children that do not specify a font.

defaultFontList
> The font that is used to draw children that do not specify a font.

labelFontList
> The font that is used to draw label children that do not specify a font.

Other Widget Resources

From Shell:
> allowShellResize, createPopupChildProc, geometry, overrideRedirect, popdownCallback, popupCallback, saveUnder, visual.

From Composite:
> children, insertPosition, numChildren.

From Core:

```
accelerators, ancestorSensitive, background, background-
Pixmap, borderColor, borderPixmap, borderWidth, colormap,
depth, destroyCallback, height, initialResourcesPersis-
tent, mappedWhenManaged, screen, sensitive, translations,
width, x, y.
```

34.26 The MessageBox Widget

The MessageBox widget is a manager widget that presents a consistent style for short modal messages. It is used to display warnings, errors, questions, information, or working messages. The MessageBox can automatically create and place OK, Cancel, and Help buttons.

Table 34-21. MessageBox Widget Resources

Resource Name	Default	Other Values
cancelLabelString	[dynami]c	[string]
defaultButtonType	DIALOG_OK_BUTTON	DIALOG_CANCEL_BUTTON, DIALOG_HELP_BUTTON
dialogType	DIALOG_MESSAGE	DIALOG_ERROR, DIALOG_INFORMATION, DIALOG_QUESTION, DIALOG_TEMPLATE, DIALOG_WARNING, DIALOG_WORKING
helpLabelString	[dynamic]	[string]
messageAlignment	ALIGNMENT_BEGINNING	ALIGNMENT_CENTER, ALIGNMENT_END
messageString	" "	[string]
minimizeButtons	false	true
okLabelString	[dynamic]	[string]
symbolPixmap	[dynamic]	[path to a pixmap file]

Resource Descriptions

cancelLabelString
> The label string for the Cancel button.

defaultButtonType
> Specifies which button is the default action of the MessageBox: DIA-LOG_CANCEL_BUTTON, DIALOG_OK_BUTTON, or DIALOG_HELP_BUTTON.

`dialogType`
> The style of the MessageBox. The only difference between these types is the `symbolPixmap` that is used: DIALOG_ERROR, DIALOG_INFORMATION, DIALOG_MESSAGE, DIALOG_QUESTION, DIALOG_WARNING, or DIALOG_WORKING. The DIALOG_TEMPLATE type is used to create a new dialog style. The application can set the `messageString`, `symbolPixmap`, and callbacks to create the dialog.

`helpLabelString`
> The label string for the Help button.

`messageAlignment`
> The horizontal alignment of the message.

`messageString`
> The string that is the contents of the MessageBox.

`minimizeButtons`
> Determines the size of the MessageBox's button children. When this resource is `true`, the buttons are their smallest preferred size. When `false`, the buttons are all set to be as wide as the widest button.

`okLabelString`
> The label string for the OK button.

`symbolPixmap`
> The pixmap to use as the message symbol.

Other Widget Resources

From BulletinBoard:
> `allowOverlap`, `autoUnmanage`, `buttonFontList`, `cancelButton`, `defaultButton`, `defaultPosition`, `dialogStyle`, `dialogTitle`, `focusCallback`, `labelFontList`, `mapCallback`, `marginHeight`, `marginWidth`, `noResize`, `resizePolicy`, `shadowType`, `textFontList`, `textTranslations`, `unmapCallback`.

From Manager:
> `bottomShadowColor`, `bottomShadowPixmap`, `foreground`, `helpCallback`, `highlightColor`, `highlightPixmap`, `navigationType`, `shadowThickness`, `stringDirection topShadowColor`, `topShadowPixmap`, `traversalOn`, `unitType`, `userData`.

From Composite:
> `children`, `insertPosition`, `numChildren`.

From Core:
> `accelerators`, `ancestorSensitive`, `background`, `backgroundPixmap`, `borderColor`, `borderPixmap`, `borderWidth`, `colormap`, `depth`, `destroyCallback`, `height`, `initialResourcesPersis-`

```
tent, mappedWhenManaged, screen, sensitive, translations,
width, x, y.
```

Callbacks

cancelCallback
Invoked when the Cancel button is pressed. Call data:
CB_CALL_DATA.REASON=CR_CANCEL
CB_CALL_DATA.EVENT=*X event*

okCallback
Invoked when the OK button is pressed. Call data:
CB_CALL_DATA.REASON=CR_OK
CB_CALL_DATA.EVENT=*X event*

34.27 The PanedWindow Widget

The PanedWindow is a manager widget that positions its children in a single vertical column. Between each child is a sash that the user can move to change the size of each pane...

Table 34-22. PanedWindow Widget Resources

Resource Name	Default	Other Values
marginHeight	3	*[positive integer]*
marginWidth	3	*[positive integer]*
refigureMode	true	false
sashHeight	10	*[positive integer]*
sashIndent	-10	*[integer]*
sashShadowThick-ness	*[dynamic]*	*[positive integer]*
sashWidth	10	*[integer]*
separatorOn	true	false
spacing	8	*[positive integer]*

Table 34-23. PanedWindow Widget Constraint Resources

Resource Name	Default	Other Values
allowResize	false	true
paneMaximum	1000	*[positive integer]*
paneMinimum	1	*[positive integer]*
positionIndex	LAST_POSITION	0

Table 34-23. PanedWindow Widget Constraint Resources (continued)

Resource Name	Default	Other Values
skipAdjust	false	true

Resource Descriptions

marginHeight
> The space between the top and bottom edges of the PanedWindow and the top and bottom children.

marginWidth
> The space between the right and left edges of the PanedWindow and the right and left sides of the children.

refigureMode
> When refigureMode is true, the children are repositioned after a change to the PanedWindow. If refigureMode is false, then the children are not reconfigured.

sashHeight
> The height of the sash.

sashWidth
> The width of the sash.

sashIndent
> The indentation of the sash from the edge of the widget. A positive indentation is relative to the left edge, and a negative indentation is relative to the right edge.

sashShadowThickness
> The thickness of the sash's border shadow.

separatorOn
> When this resource is true, a Separator is added between each child of the PanedWindow.

spacing
> The space between each child.

Constraint Resources

allowResize
> When true, the PanedWindow tries to honor a child's request to change size. Otherwise, the child remains a fixed size.

paneMaximum, paneMinimum
> The pane's maximum and minimum size. These are used to determine how much the child can be resized.

positionIndex
> The position of the child in the list of PanedWindow children. 0 is the first pane and LAST_POSITION is the last pane.

skipAdjust
> When set to true, the PanedWindow may skip the adjustment of this child when the PanedWindow is resized. Otherwise, this child is automatically resized.

Other Widget Resources

From Manager:
> bottomShadowColor, bottomShadowPixmap, foreground, help-Callback, highlightColor, highlightPixmap, navigationType, shadowThickness, stringDirection topShadowColor, topShadowPixmap, traversalOn, unitType, userData.

From Composite:
> children, insertPosition, numChildren.

From Core:
> accelerators, ancestorSensitive, background, backgroundPixmap, borderColor, borderPixmap, borderWidth, colormap, depth, destroyCallback, height, initialResourcesPersistent, mappedWhenManaged, screen, sensitive, translations, width, x, y.

34.28 The Primitive Class

The Primitive class is never instantiated on its own. It provides consistent resources for keyboard traversal and drawing the widget borders.

Table 34-24. Primitive Class Resources

Resource Name	Default	Other Values
bottomShadowColor	[dynamic]	[color]
bottomShadowPixmap	UNSPECIFIED_PIXMAP	[path to a pixmap file]
foreground	[dynamic]	[color]
highlightColor	[dynamic]	[color]
highlightOnEnter	false	true

Table 34-24. Primitive Class Resources (continued)

Resource Name	Default	Other Values
highlightPixmap	[dynamic]	[path to a pixmap file]
highlightThickness	2	[positive integer]
navigationType	NONE	TAB_GROUP, STICKY_TAB_GROUP, EXCLUSIVE_TAB_GROUP
shadowThickness	2	[positive integer]
topShadowColor	[dynamic]	[color]
topShadowPixmap	[dynamic]	[path to a pixmap file]
traversalOn	true	false
unitType	[dynamic]	PIXELS, 100TH_MILLIMETERS, 1000TH_INCHES, 100TH_POINTS, 100TH_FONT_UNITS
userData	[NULL]	[requires C code]

Resource Descriptions

bottomShadowColor
> The color that is used on the bottom and right in drawing the border.

bottomShadowPixmap
> The pixmap that is used on the bottom and right in drawing the border.

foreground
> The color that is used to draw the foreground.

highlightColor
> The color that is used to draw the solid border that indicates that the object has input focus.

highlightOnEnter
> This resource applies only when the object's shell has the keyboardFocus-Policy of POINTER. When the mouse pointer moves into the object and this resource is true, then the input focus highlight is drawn. Otherwise, the highlighting is not drawn unless focus is explicitly moved to the object.

highlightPixmap
> The pixmap that is used to draw the border that indicates that the object has input focus.

highlightThickness
> Specifies the thickness of the input focus highlight.

navigationType
> Specifies the way navigation works with this object. NONE means that the object is not traversable. TAB_GROUP means that it is traversable and is part of a tab group. STICKY_TAB_GROUP includes an object in traversal even if it is its own tab group. EXCLUSIVE_TAB_GROUP is used to make the object a separate tab group.

shadowThickness
> Specifies the thickness of the border shadow.

topShadowColor
> The color that is used on the top and left in drawing the border.

topShadowPixmap
> The pixmap that is used on the top and left in drawing the border.

traversalOn
> Traversal to this object is allowed when this resource is true. When set to false, it is not possible to traverse to this object.

unitType
> Defines the unit type for all resources that specify a Dimension, e.g., margins.

userData
> This resource is reserved for the application. It is a pointer to whatever data that an application may want to associate with this object.

Other Widget Resources

From Core:
> accelerators, ancestorSensitive, background, background-Pixmap, borderColor, borderPixmap, borderWidth, colormap, depth, destroyCallback, height, initialResourcesPersistent, mappedWhenManaged, screen, sensitive, translations, width, x, y.

Callbacks

helpCallback
> Invoked when help is requested. Call data:
> CB_CALL_DATA.REASON=CR_HELP
> CB_CALL_DATA.EVENT=X event

34.29 The PushButton Widget and Gadget

The PushButton is a button that activates a command, e.g., an OK button. The PushButton has both a widget and gadget class.

Table 34-25. PushButton Widget and Gadget Resources

Resource Name	Default	Other Values
armColor	[dynamic]	[color]
armPixmap	UNSPECIFIED_PIXMAP	[path to a pixmap file]
defaultButtonShad-owThickness	[dynamic]	[positive integer]
fillOnArm	true	false
multiClick	[dynamic]	MULTICLICK_DISCARD, MULTICLICK_KEEP
showAsDefault	0	[positive integer]

Resource Descriptions

armColor
> The color used when fillOnArm is true and the PushButton is armed.

armPixmap
> The pixmap that is displayed in the armed PushButton when the label-Type resource is PIXMAP.

defaultButtonShadowThickness
> The width of the additional shadow border used on default buttons.

fillOnArm
> If true, the PushButton is filled with the armColor when it is in the armed state. If this resource is false, the PushButton only changes the border shadows when the PushButton is armed.

multiClick
> This resource determines how multiple clicks are handled. When set to MULTICLICK_DISCARD, multiple clicks are discarded. When set to MULTICLICK_KEEP, multiple clicks are counted and passed to the application in the callback data.

showAsDefault
> When 1 or greater, this button is displayed with another shadow surrounding the button to indicate that it is the default action. The value of the re-

source is used as the thickness of the additional border shadow. When this resource is `0`, the button is not the default.

Other Widget Resources

From Primitive:
> `bottomShadowColor`, `highlightPixmap`, `highlightThickness`, `navigationType`, `shadowThickness`, `bottomShadowPixmap`, `foreground`, `helpCallback`, `highlightColor`, `highlightOnEnter`, `topShadowColor`, `topShadowPixmap`, `traversalOn`, `unitType`, `userData`.

From Core:
> `accelerators`, `ancestorSensitive`, `background`, `backgroundPixmap`, `borderColor`, `borderPixmap`, `borderWidth`, `colormap`, `depth`, `destroyCallback`, `height`, `initialResourcesPersistent`, `mappedWhenManaged`, `screen`, `sensitive`, `translations`, `width`, `x`, `y`.

Other Gadget Resources

From Gadget:
> `helpCallback`, `highlightOnEnter`, `highlightThickness`, `navigationType`, `shadowThickness`, `traversalOn`, `unitType`, `userData`.

From RectObj (see information on equivalent resources under Core):
> `ancestorSensitive`, `borderWidth`, `height`, `sensitive`, `width`, `x`, `y`.

From Object:
> `destroyCallback`.

Callbacks

`activateCallback`
> Invoked when the button is activated. Call data:
> `CB_CALL_DATA.REASON=CR_ACTIVATE`
> `CB_CALL_DATA.EVENT=`*X event*
> `CB_CALL_DATA.CLICK_COUNT=` *number of multiple clicks*

`armCallback`
> Invoked when the user presses the `BSelect` button (usually the leftmost mouse button) in the PushButton. Call data:
> `CB_CALL_DATA.REASON=CR_ARM`
> `CB_CALL_DATA.EVENT=`*X event*

disarmCallback
> Invoked when the user releases the BSelectbutton (usually the leftmost mouse button). Call data:
> CB_CALL_DATA.REASON=CR_DISARM
> CB_CALL_DATA.EVENT=X event

34.30 The RowColumn Widget

The RowColumn widget is used to position widgets in grid-like layouts. This is one of the most feature-rich widgets in Motif. The RowColumn has some unlikely resources that do things such as determining the type of menu, setting the exclusivity of radio buttons, and even determining what mouse button pops up a menu.

Table 34-26. RowColumn Widget Resources

Resource Name	Default	Other Values
adjustLast	true	false
adjustMargin	true	false
entryAlignment	ALIGNMENT_BEGINNING	ALIGNMENT_CENTER, ALIGNMENT_END
entryBorder	0	[positive integer]
entryClass	[dynamic]	[widget handle]
entryVertical-ALignment	ALIGNMENT_CENTER	ALIGNMENT_BASELINE_BOTTOM, ALIGNMENT_BASELINE_TOP, ALIGNNET_CONTENTS_BOTTOM, ALIGNMENT_CONTENTS_TOP
isAligned	true	false
isHomogeneous	[dynamic]	true, false
labelString	[NULL]	[string]
marginHeight	[dynamic]	[positive integer]
marginWidth	[dynamic]	[positive integer]
menuAccelerator	[dynamic]	[string]
menuHelpWidget	[NULL]	[widget handle]
menuHistory	[NULL]	[widget handle]
menuPost	[NULL]	[string]
mnemonic	[NULL]	[single letter]
mnemonicCharSet	FONTLIST_DEFAULT_TAG	[string]

Table 34-26. RowColumn Widget Resources (continued)

Resource Name	Default	Other Values
numColumns	1	*[short integer]*
orientation	*[dynamic]*	VERTICAL, HORIZONTAL
packing	*[dynamic]*	PACK_TIGHT, PACK_COLUMN, PACK_NONE
popupEnabled	true	false
radioAlwaysOne	true	false
radioBehavior	false	true
resizeHeight	true	false
resizeWidth	true	false
rowColumnType	WORK_AREA	MENU_BAR, MENU_POPUP, MENU_PULLDOWN, MENU_OPTION
spacing	*[dynamic]*	*[positive integer]*
subMenuId	*[NULL]*	*[widget handle]*
tearOffModel	TEAR_OFF_DISABLED	TEAR_OFF_ENABLED

Table 34-27. RowColumn Widget Constraint Resources

Resource Name	Default	Other Values
positionIndex	LAST_POSITION	*[short integer]*

Resource Descriptions

adjustLast

> When true the last row or column of the RowColumn is expanded to fill to the edge of the widget.

adjustMargin

> When true, the margin resources for children will be adjusted to have the same value so that text will align. For a RowColumn with orientation set to VERTICAL, this means that the marginLeft and marginRight resource will be adjusted. For a HORIZONTAL orientation, the marginTop and marginBottom resources will be adjusted. When this resource is false, the margins are not modified by the RowColumn widget.

entryAlignment

> The resource applies when isAligned is true. It specifies how to align children that are subclasses of the Label widget or gadget. It allows the wid-

gets to have the following alignments: `ALIGNMENT_BEGINNING`, `ALIGNMENT_CENTER`, or `ALIGNMENT_END`.

`entryBorder`

> The border width of the children.

`entryClass`

> This resource applies when `isHomogeneous` is `true`. It specifies the class to which all of the RowColumn children must belong.

`entryVerticalAlignment`

> This resource applies when `orientation` is `HORIZONTAL` and `packing` is `PACK_COLUMN` or `PACK_NONE`. It specifies how Label, Text, and TextField children can be aligned vertically.

`isAligned`

> When this resource is `true`, the alignment of the children is done according to the value of the `entryAlignment` resource.

`isHomogeneous`

> When true, the RowColumn only accepts children of the same class. When false, any class can be added to the RowColumn.

`labelString`

> This resource applies when `rowColumnType` is `MENU_OPTION`. It specifies the label used in the option menu button.

`marginHeight`, `marginWidth`

> The space between the edges of the RowColumn and the border children.

`menuAccelerator`

> This resource applies when `rowColumnType` is `MENU_POPUP` or `MENU_BAR`. It specifies a single key press event that posts the menu.

`menuHelpWidget`

> This resource applies when the `rowColumnType` is `MENU_BAR`. It specifies the widget handle of the CascadeButton that is the Help menu for the menu bar.

`menuHistory`

> The widget handle of the last activated item.

`menuPost`

> A string that specifies a button event that posts the menu. The default for `MENU_POPUP` is `BMenu` (by default the rightmost mouse button). The default for `MENU_OPTION`, `MENU_BAR` and `WORK_AREA` is `BSelect` (by default the leftmost mouse button).

mnemonic

> This resource applies when `rowColumnType` is `MENU_OPTION`. It can be set to a character that combined with the ALT modifier will post the option menu. The first character in the `labelString` that matches the character will be underlined.

mnemonicCharSet

> This resource applies when `rowColumnType` is `MENU_OPTION`.

numColumns

> This resource depends on the setting of `orientation` and only applies to widget with `packing` set to `PACK_COLUMN`. When the RowColumn is vertically oriented, `numColumns` specifies the number of columns in the widget. When the RowColumn is horizontally oriented, the `numColumns` resource actually specifies the number of rows in the widget.

orientation

> The direction for filling in the RowColumn widget with its children. When `VERTICAL`, the children are placed in columns from top to bottom. When `HORIZONTAL`, the children are placed in rows from left to right.

packing

> Determines the layout of items in the RowColumn. `PACK_TIGHT` makes each item as small as possible. `PACK_COLUMN` pads the size of the items so that they will align. `PACK_NONE` does not change the size of the widget.

popupEnabled

> Controls the ability to use mnemonics and accelerators on popup menus. When set to `false`, mnemonics and accelerators are active for popup menus. Otherwise, they are disabled.

radioAlwaysOne

> This resource applies when `radioBehavior` is `true`. When this resource is set to `true`, one of the ToggleButtons will always be set, i.e., clicking on a set button will not unset it. When `radioAlwaysOne` is `false`, it is possible for none of the ToggleButtons to be set.

radioBehavior

> When set to `true`, the RowColumn acts like a radio box for its ToggleButton children. It sets `indicatorType` to `ONE_OF_MANY` and `visibleWhenOff` to `true`.

resizeHeight, resizeWidth

> When these resources are `true` the RowColumn will try to resize in the given direction when some change in the RowColumn requires it to grow or shrink. When these resources are `false`, the RowColumn will remain a fixed size.

`rowColumnType`

> The style of the RowColumn set only at initialization time.

`spacing`

> The horizontal and vertical space between all children in the RowColumn.

`subMenuId`

> This resource applies when `rowColumnType` is `MENU_OPTION`. It specifies the widget handle for the pull-down menu attached to a OptionMenu.

`tearOffModel`

> This resource applies when `rowColumnType` is `MENU_PULLDOWN` or `MENU_POPUP`. When set to `TEAR_OFF_ENABLED`, the menu will have an additional tear off button added that enables the tear-off menu behavior. When set to `TEAR_OFF_DISABLED`, the menu does not have the tear-off behavior.

Other Widget Resources

From Manager:

> `bottomShadowColor`, `bottomShadowPixmap`, `foreground`, `help-Callback`, `highlightColor`, `highlightPixmap`, `navigationType`, `shadowThickness`, `stringDirection topShadowColor`, `topShadowPixmap`, `traversalOn`, `unitType`, `userData`.

From Composite:

> `children`, `insertPosition`, `numChildren`.

From Core:

> `accelerators`, `ancestorSensitive`, `background`, `backgroundPixmap`, `borderColor`, `borderPixmap`, `borderWidth`, `colormap`, `depth`, `destroyCallback`, `height`, `initialResourcesPersistent`, `mappedWhenManaged`, `screen`, `sensitive`, `translations`, `width`, `x`, `y`.

Callbacks

`entryCallback`

> Must be registered when RowColumn is created. It is called instead of `activateCallback` and `valueChangedCallback` for all CascadeButtons, PushButtons, DrawnButtons, and ToggleButtons. Call data:
> `CB_CALL_DATA.REASON=CR_ACTIVATE`
> `CB_CALL_DATA.EVENT=X event`
> `CB_CALL_DATA.WIDGET=the activated item`
> `CB_CALL_DATA.DATA=the WIDGET's userData`
> `CB_CALL_DATA.CALLBACKSTRUCT =callback structure for WIDGET's CR_ACTIVATE`

mapCallback
> Invoked when the RowColumn widget is about to be mapped. Call data:
> CB_CALL_DATA.REASON=CR_MAP
> CB_CALL_DATA.EVENT=*X event*

tearOffMenuActivateCallback
> Invoked when the tear-off menu is about to be torn off. Call data:
> CB_CALL_DATA.REASON=CR_TEAR_OFF_ACTIVATE
> CB_CALL_DATA.EVENT=*X event*

tearOffMenuDeactivateCallback
> Invoked when the tear-off menu is deactivated. Call data:
> CB_CALL_DATA.REASON = CR_TEAR_OFF_DEACTIVATE
> CB_CALL_DATA.EVENT=*X event*

unmapCallback
> Invoked when the RowColumn is about to be unmapped. Call data:
> CB_CALL_DATA.REASON=CR_UMMAP
> CB_CALL_DATA.EVENT=*X event*

34.31 The Scale Widget

The Scale widget is used to display and prompt for integer values. The user can modify the value by dragging the grip area of the widget. Children can be added to the Scale widget to decorate the axis (for example, Label children can provide tick marks).

Table 34-28. Scale Widget Resources

Resource Name	Default	Other Values
decimalPoints	0	*[integer]*
fontList	*[dynamic]*	*[font]*
highlightOnEnter	false	true
highlightThickness	2	*[positive integer]*
maximum	100	*[integer]*
minimum	0	*[integer]*
orientation	VERTICAL	HORIZONTAL
processingDirec-tion	MAX_ON_TOP for vertical Scales, MAX_ON_RIGHT for horizontal Scales.	MAX_ON_BOTTOM, MAX_ON_LEFT
scaleHeight	*[dynamic]*	*[integer]*

Table 34-28. Scale Widget Resources (continued)

Resource Name	Default	Other Values
scaleMultiple	[10% of max − min]	[integer]
scaleWidth	[dynamic]	[integer]
showValue	false	true
titleString	[NULL]	[string]
value	0	[integer between minimum and maximum]

Other Resources

From Manager:

> bottomShadowColor, bottomShadowPixmap, foreground, helpCallback, highlightColor, highlightPixmap, navigationType, shadowThickness, stringDirection topShadowColor, topShadowPixmap, traversalOn, unitType, userData.

From Composite:

> children, insertPosition, numChildren.

From Core:

> accelerators, ancestorSensitive, background, backgroundPixmap, borderColor, borderPixmap, borderWidth, colormap, depth, destroyCallback, height, initialResourcesPersistent, mappedWhenManaged, screen, sensitive, translations, width, x, y.

Resource Descriptions

decimalPoints
> The number of decimal digits to display. The value resource is still an integer, so 4350 would be displayed as 43.50. You need to multiply the maximum and minimum by ten raised to the power of this resource.

fontList
> The font that is used to draw the title of the Scale.

highlightOnEnter
> This resource applies only when the Scale's shell has the keyboardFocusPolicy of POINTER. When the mouse pointer moves into the Scale and this resource is true, then the input focus highlight is drawn. Otherwise, the highlighting is not drawn unless focus is explicitly moved to the Scale.

highlightThickness
> Specifies the thickness of the input focus highlight.

maximum
> The maximum value of the Slider.

minimum
> The minimum value of the Slider.

orientation
> The direction of the Slider is either HORIZONTAL or VERTICAL.

processingDirection
> Determines whether the maximum value is on the left or right for horizontal Scales, or on the top or bottom for vertical Scales.

scaleHeight
> The height of the Scale's slider.

scaleMultiple
> Determines how far the Scale moves when the user clicks to the left or right of the grab area. The default is 10% of the maximum – minimum value.

scaleWidth
> The width of the Scale's slider.

showValue
> When this resource is true, the value is displayed next to the slider. When it is false, the value is not displayed.

titleString
> The string used as the Scale's title.

value
> The position of the slider in the Scale in the range between maximum and minimum.

Scale Widget Callbacks

dragCallback
> Invoked whenever the scale moves. Call data:
> CB_CALL_DATA.REASON=CR_DRAG
> CB_CALL_DATA.VALUE=*current scale value*
> CB_CALL_DATA.EVENT=*X event*

valueChangedCallback
> Invoked when the user releases the scale, thus choosing a final value. Call data:
> CB_CALL_DATA.REASON=CR_VALUE_CHANGED
> CB_CALL_DATA.VALUE=*current scale value*
> CB_CALL_DATA.EVENT=*X event*

34.32 The ScrollBar Widget

The ScrollBar widget is used to move the view of another widget. It is most frequently used in the ScrolledWindow widget, but can be used on its own. The controls can move directly to the top or bottom, or move an increment or page at a time.

Table 34-29. ScrollBar Widget Resources

Resource Name	Default	Other Values
increment	1	[integer]
initialDelay	250	[integer]
maximum	[dynamic]	[integer]
minimum	0	[integer]
orientation	VERTICAL	HORIZONTAL
pageIncrement	10	[integer]
processingDirection	[dynamic]	MAX_ON_TOP, MAX_ON_BOTTOM, MAX_ON_LEFT, MAX_ON_RIGHT
repeatDelay	50	[integer]
showArrows	true	false
sliderSize	[dynamic]	[integer between 1 and max - min]
troughColor	[dynamic]	[color]
value	[dynamic]	[integer between minimum and maximum - sliderSize]

Resource Descriptions

increment
> Defines the amount by which the value changes when the slider is moved one increment.

initialDelay
> The number of milliseconds for which the mouse button must be pressed before the action is considered a drag.

maximum
> The maximum value of the Slider.

minimum
> The minimum value of the Slider.

orientation
>   The direction of the ScrollBar is either HORIZONTAL or VERTICAL.

pageIncrement
>   Defines the amount by which the value changes when the slider is moved one page increment.

processingDirection
>   Determines which end of the ScrollBar is maximum and which is minimum.

repeatDelay
>   The time in milliseconds for which the mouse button must be pressed before the action is repeated. The initialDelay is used for the first trigger.

showArrows
>   When set to false, the arrows are not displayed. The default value for this resource is true, which means that the arrows are displayed.

sliderSize
>   The length of the slider in the range between 1 and maximum − minimum.

troughColor
>   The color inside of the ScrollBar excluding the slider itself.

value
>   The position of the slider in the Scrollbar in the range between minimum and maximum − sliderSize.

Other Widget Resources

From Primitive:
>   bottomShadowColor, bottomShadowPixmap, foreground, high-lightColor, highlightOnEnter, highlightPixmap, highlight-Thickness, navigationType, shadowThickness, topShadow-Color, topShadowPixmap, traversalOn, unitType, userData.

From Core:
>   accelerators, ancestorSensitive, background, background-Pixmap, borderColor, borderPixmap, borderWidth, colormap, depth, destroyCallback, height, initialResourcesPer-sistent, mappedWhenManaged, screen, sensitive, transla-tions, width, x, y.

Callbacks

decrementCallback
>   Invoked when the ScrollBar value is decremented by one increment. Call data:

```
CB_CALL_DATA.REASON=CR_DECREMENT
CB_CALL_DATA.EVENT=X event
CB_CALL_DATA.VALUE = slider's new location
```

dragCallback
> Invoked when the slider changes position as the user drags it. Call data:
```
CB_CALL_DATA.REASON=CR_DRAG
CB_CALL_DATA.EVENT=X event
CB_CALL_DATA.VALUE = slider's new location
```

incrementCallback
> Invoked when the ScrollBar value is incremented by one increment. Call data:
```
CB_CALL_DATA.REASON=CR_INCREMENT
CB_CALL_DATA.EVENT=X event
CB_CALL_DATA.VALUE = slider's new location
```

pageDecrementCallback
> Invoked when the ScrollBar value is decremented by one page increment. Call data:
```
CB_CALL_DATA.REASON=CR_PAGE_DECREMENT
CB_CALL_DATA.EVENT=X event
CB_CALL_DATA.VALUE = slider's new location
```

pageIncrementCallback
> Invoked when the ScrollBar value is incremented by one page increment. Call data:
```
CB_CALL_DATA.REASON=CR_PAGE_INCREMENT
CB_CALL_DATA.EVENT=X event
CB_CALL_DATA.VALUE = slider's new location
```

toBottomCallback
> Invoked when the ScrollBar's slider is moved to the bottom (maximum) value. Call data:
```
CB_CALL_DATA.REASON=CR_TO_BOTTOM
CB_CALL_DATA.EVENT=X event
CB_CALL_DATA.VALUE = slider's new location
CB_CALL_DATA.PIXEL = coordinate of selection - x for hori-
zontal and y for vertical.
```

toTopCallback
> Invoked when the ScrollBar's slider is moved to the top (minimum) value. Call data:
```
CB_CALL_DATA.REASON=CR_TO_TOP
CB_CALL_DATA.EVENT=X event
CB_CALL_DATA.VALUE = slider's new location
```

CB_CALL_DATA.PIXEL = *coordinate of selection - x for horizontal and y for vertical.*

valueChangedCallback
Invoked at the end of a user's drag of the slider. Call data:
CB_CALL_DATA.REASON=CR_VALUE_CHANGED
CB_CALL_DATA.EVENT=*X event*
CB_CALL_DATA.VALUE = *slider's new location*

34.33 The ScrolledWindow Widget

The ScrolledWindow widget is a Manager widget that displays a view of its child. When the widget is too small to show the entire child, it automatically creates and positions ScrollBars to allow the user to move the view on the child.

Table 34-30. ScrolledWindow Widget Resources

Resource Name	Default	Other Values
clipWindow	*[dynamic]*	*[window]*
horizontalScrollBar	*[dynamic]*	*[widget handle]*
scrollBarDisplay-Policy	*[dynamic]*	STATIC, AS_NEEDED
scrollBarPlacement	BOTTOM_RIGHT	TOP_LEFT, BOTTOM_LEFT, TOP_RIGHT
scrolledWindowMargin-Height	0	*[positive integer]*
scrolledWindowMargin-Width	0	*[positive integer]*
scrollingPolicy	APPLICATION_DEFINED	AUTOMATIC
spacing	4	*[positive integer]*
verticalScrollBar	*[dynamic]*	*[widget handle]*
visualPolicy	*[dynamic]*	CONSTANT, VARIABLE
workWindow	*[NULL]*	*[widget handle]*

Resource Descriptions

clipWindow
This resource only applies when visualPolicy is CONSTANT. This resource can be initialized to a widget that will act as the clipping area.

`horizontalScrollBar, verticalScrollBar`
> Give access to the automatically created ScrollBars or allow the application to add ScrollBars when the `scrollingPolicy` is APPLICATION_DEFINED.

`scrollBarDisplayPolicy`
> Determines if the ScrollBars should always be displayed, or if they should be displayed only when they are needed. When set to STATIC, the Scroll-Bars are always displayed. When set to AS_NEEDED, the ScrollBars are displayed when the contents of the work window grow larger than the view.

`scrollBarPlacement`
> Determines the placement of the ScrollBars around the work window. The values define the position of the horizontal ScrollBar and then the vertical ScrollBar, e.g. TOP_LEFT positions the horizontal ScrollBar on the top and the vertical on the left.

`scrolledWindowMarginHeight`
> The space between the top and bottom of the work window and the top and bottom edges of the ScrolledWindow.

`scrolledWindowMarginWidth`
> The space between the right and left sides of the work window and the top and bottom edges of the ScrolledWindow.

`scrollingPolicy`
> When this resource is set to AUTOMATIC, the ScrolledWindow automatically does the scrolling. When it is set to APPLICATION_DEFINED, it is up to the application to change the contents of the work window when it receives scrolling callbacks.

`spacing`
> The space between the ScrollBars and the work window.

`visualPolicy`
> When the `visualPolicy` is CONSTANT the viewing area size remains constant and is clipped when necessary. When this resource is set to VARIABLE, the layout can get larger or smaller.

`workWindow`
> The widget ID of the work window.

Other Widget Resources

From Manager:
> `bottomShadowColor, bottomShadowPixmap, foreground, help-Callback, highlightColor, highlightPixmap, navigationType, shadowThickness, stringDirection topShadowColor, topShad-owPixmap, traversalOn, unitType, userData.`

From Composite:
>   children, insertPosition, numChildren.

From Core:
>   accelerators, ancestorSensitive, background, background-
>   Pixmap, borderColor, borderPixmap, borderWidth, colormap,
>   depth, destroyCallback, height, initialResourcesPer-
>   sistent, mappedWhenManaged, screen, sensitive, transla-
>   tions, width, x, y.

From Object:
>   destroyCallback.

Callbacks

traverseObscuredCallback
>   Invoked when traversal moves focus to a widget that is obscured. Call data:
>   CB_CALL_DATA.REASON=CR_OBSCURED_TRAVERSAL
>   CB_CALL_DATA.EVENT=X event
>   CD_CALL_DATA.TRAVERSAL_DESTINATION = next   widget   to
>   traverse to
>   CB_CALL_DATA.DIRECTION=direction of traversal

34.34 The SelectionBox Widget

The SelectionBox widget presents the user with a list of choices to choose from and a text field to enter a selection not in the list. It can automatically create OK, Apply, Cancel, and Help buttons and position them at the bottom of the box.

Table 34-31. SelectionBox Widget Resources

Resource Name	Default	Other Values
applyLabelString	[dynamic]	[string]
cancelLabelString	[dynamic]	[string]
childPlacement	PLACE_ABOVE_SELECTION	PLACE_BELOW_SELECTION, PLACE_TOP
dialogType	[dynamic]	DIALOG_WORK_AREA, DIALOG_PROMPT, DIALOG_SELECTION, DIALOG_COMAND, DIALOG_FILE_SELECTION
helpLabelString	[dynamic]	[string]
listItemCount	0	[integer]

Table 34-31. SelectionBox Widget Resources (continued)

Resource Name	Default	Other Values
listItems	[NULL]	[string table]
listLabelString	[dynamic]	[string]
listVisibleItem-Count	[dynamic]	[integer]
minimizeButtons	false	true
mustMatch	false	true
okLabelString	[dynamic]	[string]
selectionLabel-String	[dynamic]	[string]
textAccelerators	[default]	[requires C code]
textColumns	[dynamic]	[short integer]
textString	[dynamic]	[string]

Resource Descriptions

applyLabelString
> The label for the Apply button.

cancelLabelString
> The label for the Cancel button.

childPlacement
> Sets the position of the work area child. PLACE_ABOVE_SELECTION puts the work area above the TextField. PLACE_BELOW_SELECTION puts the work area below the TextField. PLACE_TOP puts the work area above the List.

dialogType
> Sets the SelectionBox style. DIALOG_WORK_AREA is the default style that is used when the SelectionBox is not a child of the DialogShell. DIALOG_PROMPT does not create a List. DIALOG_SELECTION is the default style when the SelectionBox is a child of a DialogShell. DIALOG_COMMAND and DIALOG_FILE_SELECTION should not be set directly; create these styles by creating the Command and FileSelectionBox classes, respectively.

helpLabelString
> The label for the Help button.

listItemCount
> The number of items in listItems.

`listItems`
> The items in the SelectionBox's List.

`listLabelString`
> The label for the SelectionBox's List.

`listVisibleItemCount`
> The height of the SelectionBox's List in items.

`minimizeButtons`
> Determines the size of the SelectionBox's button children. When this resource is `true`, the buttons are their smallest preferred size. When `false`, the buttons are all set to be as wide as the widest button.

`mustMatch`
> When this resource is `true`, the user's selection must match one of the items in the SelectionBox's List. If it doesn't, then the `noMatchCallback` is called. When `mustMatch` is `false`, the user can enter any value, and the `okCallback` is always called.

`okLabelString`
> The label for the OK button.

`selectionLabelString`
> The label for the selection TextField.

`textAccelerators`
> This resource is only valid when the `accelerators` resource uses the default value. It specifies a translation string to add to the SelectionBox's TextField widget.

`textColumns`
> The number of columns for the SelectionBox's TextField.

`textString`
> The string value for the SelectionBox's TextField.

Other Widget Resources

From BulletinBoard:
> `allowOverlap`, `autoUnmanage`, `buttonFontList`, `cancelButton`, `defaultButton`, `defaultPosition`, `dialogStyle`, `dialogTitle`, `focusCallback`, `labelFontList`, `mapCallback`, `marginHeight`, `marginWidth`, `noResize`, `resizePolicy`, `shadowType`, `textFontList`, `textTranslations`, `unmapCallback`.

From Manager:
> `bottomShadowColor`, `bottomShadowPixmap`, `foreground`, `helpCallback`, `highlightColor`, `highlightPixmap`, `navigationType`,

shadowThickness, stringDirection topShadowColor, topShadowPixmap, traversalOn, unitType, userData.

From Composite:

children, insertPosition, numChildren.

From Core:

accelerators, ancestorSensitive, background, background-
Pixmap, borderColor, borderPixmap, borderWidth, colormap,
depth, destroyCallback, height, initialResourcesPersistent, mappedWhenManaged, screen, sensitive, translations, width, x, y.

Callbacks

applyCallback
> Invoked when the Apply button is activated. Call data:
> CB_CALL_DATA.REASON=CR_APPLY
> CB_CALL_DATA.EVENT=*X event*
> CB_CALL_DATA.VALUE = *selection string*
> CB_CALL_DATA.LENGTH = *size of* VALUE

cancelCallback
> Invoked when the Cancel button is activated. Call data:
> CB_CALL_DATA.REASON=CR_CANCEL
> CB_CALL_DATA.EVENT=*X event*
> CB_CALL_DATA.VALUE = *selection string*
> CB_CALL_DATA.LENGTH = *size of* VALUE

noMatchCallback
> Invoked when the selection that is typed in does not match an item in the
> list. Call data:
> CB_CALL_DATA.REASON=CR_NO_MATCH
> CB_CALL_DATA.EVENT=*X event*
> CB_CALL_DATA.VALUE = *selection string*
> CB_CALL_DATA.LENGTH = *size of* VALUE

okCallback
> Invoked when the OK button is activated. Call data:
> CB_CALL_DATA.REASON=CR_OK
> CB_CALL_DATA.EVENT=*X event*
> CB_CALL_DATA.VALUE = *selection string*
> CB_CALL_DATA.LENGTH = *size of* VALUE

34.35 The Separator Widget and Gadget

The Separator draws lines in various styles: etched, single, double, single dashed, or double dashed.

Table 34-32. Separator Widget Resources

Resource Name	Default	Other Values
margin	0	*[positive integer]*
orientation	HORIZONTAL	VERTICAL
separatorType	SHADOW_ETCHED_IN	NO_LINE, SINGLE_LINE, DOUBLE_LINE, SINGLE_DASHED_LINE, DOUBLE_DASHED_LINE, SHADOW_ETCHED_OUT

Resource Descriptions

margin
> Specifies the right and left margin for a HORIZONTAL Separator, and the top and bottom margin for a VERTICAL Separator.

orientation
> The direction of the Separator line.

separatorType
> The style of the Separator line.

Other Widget Resources

From Primitive:
> bottomShadowColor, bottomShadowPixmap, foreground, high-lightColor, highlightOnEnter, highlightPixmap, highlight-Thickness, navigationType, shadowThickness, topShadow-Color, topShadowPixmap, traversalOn, unitType, userData.

From Core:
> accelerators, ancestorSensitive, background, background-Pixmap, borderColor, borderPixmap, borderWidth, colormap, depth, destroyCallback, height, initialResourcesPer-sistent, mappedWhenManaged, screen, sensitive, transla-tions, width, x, y.

Other Gadget Resources

From Gadget:

helpCallback, highlightOnEnter, highlightThickness, navigationType, shadowThickness, traversalOn, unitType, user-
Data.

From RectObj (see information on equivalent resources under Core):

ancestorSensitive, borderWidth, height, sensitive, width,
x, y.

From Object:

destroyCallback.

34.36 The TextField Widget

The TextField widget is a single-line text editor. The widget supports common text
editing capabilities like drag and drop, selection, and word wrap.

Table 34-33. TextField Widget Resources

Resource Name	Default	Other Values
blinkRate	500	[integer]
columns	[dynamic]	[short integer]
cursorPosition	0	[integer greater than or equal to 0]
cursorPositionVisible	true	false
editable	true	false
fontList	[dynamic]	[font]
marginHeight	5	[positive integer]
marginWidth	5	[positive integer]
maxLength	largest integer	[integer]
pendingDelete	true	false
resizeWidth	false	true
selectionArray	SELECT_POSITION, SELECT_WORD, SELECT_LINE	[requires C code]
selectionArrayCount	3	[requires C code]

Table 34-33. TextField Widget Resources (continued)

Resource Name	Default	Other Values
selectThreshold	5	*[integer]*
value	" "	*[string]*
valueWcs	" " (wide character)	*[requires C code]*
verifyBell	*[dynamic]*	true, false

Resource Descriptions

blinkRate
>   The number of milliseconds for which the cursor is shown on and then shown off. Setting blinkRate to 0 stops the cursor from blinking.

columns
>   The initial width of the TextField widget in character spaces. It is only used if width is not set.

cursorPosition
>   The location of the input cursor relative to the beginning of the text. The position before the first character is 0.

cursorPositionVisible
>   Specifies whether the input cursor is visible.

editable
>   Specifies whether the TextField is read-write or read-only.

fontList
>   The font used to draw the text.

marginHeight
>   The space between the top and bottom of the text and the edges of the Text-Field widget.

marginWidth
>   The space between the right and left sides of the text and the edges of the TextField widget.

maxLength
>   Can be set if the TextField has a fixed length, so that the TextField widget can optimize its performance. It can be set to the maximum length string that the user can enter.

pendingDelete
>   Controls pending delete mode. When true, selected text is deleted when

text is inserted. When `false`, the selected text is not deleted on the next text insertion.

`resizeWidth`
Determines how the TextField widget resizes as text is entered. When `false`, the widget will not grow as text is entered. When this resource is `true`, the TextField widget grows as text is entered.

`selectionArray`
Specifies an array of actions triggered by multiple clicks from a single click to *n* clicks.

`selectionArrayCount`
The size of the `selectionArray`.

`selectThreshold`
The number of pixels the mouse pointer must be dragged before the next character is selected.

`value`
The contents of the TextField widget represented as a string.

`valueWcs`
The contents of the TextField widget represented as a wide character string.

`verifyBell`
When this resource is `true`, a bell will ring when the verify callback rejects a modification. Otherwise, the bell will not ring.

Other Widget Resources

From Primitive:
`bottomShadowColor`, `bottomShadowPixmap`, `foreground`, `highlightColor`, `highlightOnEnter`, `highlightPixmap`, `highlightThickness`, `navigationType`, `shadowThickness`, `topShadowColor`, `topShadowPixmap`, `traversalOn`, `unitType`, `userData`.

From Core:
`accelerators`, `ancestorSensitive`, `background`, `backgroundPixmap`, `borderColor`, `borderPixmap`, `borderWidth`, `colormap`, `depth`, `destroyCallback`, `height`, `initialResourcesPersistent`, `mappedWhenManaged`, `screen`, `sensitive`, `translations`, `width`, `x`, `y`.

Callbacks

The TextField widget provides the exact same callbacks as the Text widget. Refer to the Text widget for these callbacks.

34.37 The Text Widget

The Text widget is a multiline text editor. It can operate as a read-only text or editable text. The Text widget supports common editing functionality such as selection, drag and drop, and word wrap. The callbacks it provides allow the application notification before and after the user changes the text.

Table 34-34. Text Widget Resources

Resource Name	Default	Other Values
autoShowCursor-Position	true	false
blinkRate	500	[integer]
columns	[dynamic]	[short integer]
cursorPosition	0	[positive integer]
cursorPositionVis-ible	true	false
editable	true	false
editMode	MULTI_LINE_EDIT	SINGLE_LINE_EDIT
fontList	[dynamic]	[font]
marginHeight	5	[positive integer]
marginWidth	5	[positive integer]
maxLength	largest integer	[integer]
pendingDelete	true	false
resizeHeight	false	true
resizeWidth	false	true
rows	[dynamic]	[short integer]
selectionArray	SELECT_POSITION, SELECT_WORD, SELECT_LINE, SELECT_ALL	[requires C code] Array of actions triggered by multiple clicks from a single click to n clicks.
selectionArray-Count	4	[requires C code] size of selectionArray

Table 34-34. Text Widget Resources (continued)

Resource Name	Default	Other Values
selectThreshold	5	[integer]
source	[default source]	[requires C code]
topCharacter	0	[positive integer]
value	" "	[string]
valueWcs	NULL	[requires C code]
verifyBell	true	false
wordWrap	false	true

Resource Descriptions

autoShowCursorPosition

When true, the insert cursor will always be positioned in the visible text. The text will scroll if necessary.

blinkRate

The number of milliseconds that the cursor is shown on and then shown off. Setting blinkRate to 0 stops the cursor from blinking.

columns

The initial width of the Text widget in character spaces. It is only used if width is not set.

cursorPosition

The location of the cursor relative to the beginning of the text source. The position before the first character is 0.

cursorPositionVisible

Specifies whether the input cursor is visible.

editable

Specifies whether the Text is read-write or read-only.

editMode

Specifies if the Text displays one or many lines of text: SINGLE_LIST_EDIT, MULTI_LINE_EDIT.

fontList

The font used to draw the text.

marginHeight

The space between the top and bottom of the text and the edges of the Text-Field widget.

marginWidth
> The space between the right and left sides of the text and the edges of the TextField widget.

maxLength
> Can be set if the Text has a fixed length, so that the Text widget can optimize its performance. It can be set to the maximum length string that the user can enter.

pendingDelete
> Controls pending delete mode. When `true`, selected text is deleted when text is inserted. When `false`, the selected text is not deleted on the next text insertion.

resizeHeight, resizeWidth
> Determines how the Text widget resizes as text is entered. When `false`, the widget will not grow as text is entered, and the application will have to use ScrollBars to allow the user to view the entire Text. When these resources are `true`, the Text widget grows as text is entered.

rows
> The initial height of the Text widget in character spaces. It is only used if `height` is not set.

selectionArray
> Specifies an array of actions triggered by multiple clicks from a single click to *n* clicks.

selectionArrayCount
> The size of the `selectionArray`.

selectThreshold
> The number of pixels that the mouse pointer must be dragged before the next character is selected.

source
> Specifies the source of the Text widget's text data. Retrieving the `source` from one Text and setting it on another allows two widgets to share the same data.

topCharacter
> Setting this resource to a character position will cause the line that contains that character to be displayed as the first line in the Text widget. The position of a character is relative to the first character in the source.

value
> The contents of the Text widget represented as a string.

valueWcs

> The contents of the Text widget represented as a wide character string.

verifyBell

> When this resource is true, a bell will ring when the verify callback rejects a modification. Otherwise, the bell will not ring.

wordWrap

> This resource applies when editMode is set to MULTI_LINE_EDIT. If this resource is true, the text wraps to a new line at a space or tab when the line is too long to fit in the Text's width. If wordWrap is false, text only wraps to a new line when the user enters a newline explicitly.

Other Widget Resources

From Primitive:

> bottomShadowColor, bottomShadowPixmap, foreground, highlightColor, highlightOnEnter, highlightPixmap, highlightThickness, navigationType, shadowThickness, topShadowColor, topShadowPixmap, traversalOn, unitType, userData.

From Core:

> accelerators, ancestorSensitive, background, backgroundPixmap, borderColor, borderPixmap, borderWidth, colormap, depth, destroyCallback, height, initialResourcesPersistent, mappedWhenManaged, screen, sensitive, translations, width, x, y.

Callbacks

activateCallback

> Invoked when Text is activated. Call data:
> CB_CALL_DATA.REASON=CR_ACTIVATE
> CB_CALL_DATA.EVENT=*X event*
> CB_CALL_DATA.DOIT=*verify the action:* true, false
> CB_CALL_DATA.CURRENT_INSERT=*insert cursor position*
> CB_CALL_DATA.NEW_INSERT = *position where the insert cursor will be moved*
> CB_CALL_DATA.START_POS=*start position of the text change*
> CB_CALL_DATA.END_POS =*end position of the text change*
> CB_CALL_DATA.TEXT.PTR=*text to be inserted*
> CB_CALL_DATA.TEXT.LENGTH=*length of text to be inserted*
> CB_CALL_DATA.TEXT.FORMAT=*text format:* FMT8BIT, FMT16BIT

focusCallback

> Invoked when Text gains input focus. Call data:

```
CB_CALL_DATA.REASON=CR_FOCUS
CB_CALL_DATA.EVENT=X event
CB_CALL_DATA.DOIT=verify the action: true, false
CB_CALL_DATA.CURRENT_INSERT=insert cursor position
CB_CALL_DATA.NEW_INSERT = position where the insert cursor
will be moved
CB_CALL_DATA.START_POS=start position of the text change
CB_CALL_DATA.END_POS =end position of the text change
CB_CALL_DATA.TEXT.PTR=text to be inserted
CB_CALL_DATA.TEXT.LENGTH=length of text to be inserted
CB_CALL_DATA.TEXT.FORMAT=text format: FMT8BIT, FMT16BIT
```

gainPrimaryCallback

Invoked when Text gains ownership of the Primary selection. Call data:

```
CB_CALL_DATA.REASON=CR_GAIN_PRIMARY
CB_CALL_DATA.EVENT=X event
CB_CALL_DATA.DOIT=verify the action: true, false
CB_CALL_DATA.CURRENT_INSERT=insert cursor position
B_CALL_DATA.NEW_INSERT = position where the insert cursor
will be moved
CB_CALL_DATA.START_POS=start position of the text change
B_CALL_DATA.END_POS =end position of the text change
CB_CALL_DATA.TEXT.PTR=text to be inserted
B_CALL_DATA.TEXT.LENGTH=length of text to be inserted
B_CALL_DATA.TEXT.FORMAT=text format: FMT8BIT, FMT16BIT
```

losePrimaryCallback

Invoked when Text loses ownership of the primary selection. Call data:

```
CB_CALL_DATA.REASON=CR_LOSE_PRIMARY
CB_CALL_DATA.EVENT=X event
CB_CALL_DATA.DOIT=verify the action: true, false
CB_CALL_DATA.CURRENT_INSERT=insert cursor position
CB_CALL_DATA.NEW_INSERT = position where the insert cursor
will be moved
CB_CALL_DATA.START_POS=start position of the text change
CB_CALL_DATA.END_POS =end position of the text change
CB_CALL_DATA.TEXT.PTR=text to be inserted
CB_CALL_DATA.TEXT.LENGTH=length of text to be inserted
CB_CALL_DATA.TEXT.FORMAT=text format: FMT8BIT, FMT16BIT
```

losingFocusCallback

Invoked when Text loses input focus. Call data:

```
CB_CALL_DATA.REASON=CR_LOSING_FOCUS
CB_CALL_DATA.EVENT=X event
CB_CALL_DATA.DOIT=verify the action: true, false
```

```
        CB_CALL_DATA.CURRENT_INSERT=insert cursor position
        CB_CALL_DATA.NEW_INSERT = position where the insert cursor
        will be moved
        CB_CALL_DATA.START_POS=start position of the text change
        CB_CALL_DATA.END_POS =end position of the text change
        CB_CALL_DATA.TEXT.PTR=text to be inserted
        CB_CALL_DATA.TEXT.LENGTH=length of text to be inserted
        CB_CALL_DATA.TEXT.FORMAT=text format: FMT8BIT, FMT16BIT
```

modifyVerifyCallback
        Invoked before the value of the Text widget is actually changed. Call data:
```
        CB_CALL_DATA.REASON= CR_MODIFYING_TEXT_VALUE
        CB_CALL_DATA.EVENT=X event
        CB_CALL_DATA.DOIT=verify the action: true, false
        CB_CALL_DATA.CURRENT_INSERT=insert cursor position
        CB_CALL_DATA.NEW_INSERT = position where the insert cursor
        will be moved
        CB_CALL_DATA.START_POS=start position of the text change
        CB_CALL_DATA.END_POS =end position of the text change
        CB_CALL_DATA.TEXT.PTR=text to be inserted
        CB_CALL_DATA.TEXT.LENGTH=length of text to be inserted
        CB_CALL_DATA.TEXT.FORMAT=text format: FMT8BIT, FMT16BIT
```

modifyVerifyCallbackWcs
        Invoked before the value of the Text widget is actually changed. Called af-
        ter modifyVerifyCallback if both are registered. Call data:
```
        CB_CALL_DATA.REASON= CR_MODIFYING_TEXT_VALUE
        CB_CALL_DATA.EVENT=X event
        CB_CALL_DATA.DOIT=verify the action: true, false
        CB_CALL_DATA.CURRENT_INSERT=insert cursor position
        CB_CALL_DATA.NEW_INSERT = position where the insert cursor
        will be moved
        B_CALL_DATA.START_POS=start position of the text change
        CB_CALL_DATA.END_POS =end position of the text change
        CB_CALL_DATA.TEXT.PTR=text to be inserted
        CB_CALL_DATA.TEXT.LENGTH=length of text to be inserted
```

motionVerifyCallback
        Invoked when the insert cursor is moved. Call data:
```
        CB_CALL_DATA.REASON= CR_MOVING_INSERT_CURSOR
        CB_CALL_DATA.EVENT=X event
        CB_CALL_DATA.DOIT=verify the action: true, false
        CB_CALL_DATA.CURRENT_INSERT=insert cursor position
        CB_CALL_DATA.NEW_INSERT = position where the insert cursor
```

> *will be moved*
> CB_CALL_DATA.START_POS=*start position of the text change*
> CB_CALL_DATA.END_POS =*end position of the text change*
> CB_CALL_DATA.TEXT.PTR=*text to be inserted*
> CB_CALL_DATA.TEXT.LENGTH=*length of text to be inserted*
> CB_CALL_DATA.TEXT.FORMAT=*text format:* FMT8BIT, FMT16BIT

valueChangedCallback
> Invoked after the value of the Text widget has been changed. Call data:
> CB_CALL_DATA.REASON=CR_VALUE_CHANGED
> CB_CALL_DATA.EVENT=*X event*
> CB_CALL_DATA.DOIT=*verify the action:* true, false
> CB_CALL_DATA.CURRENT_INSERT=*insert cursor position*
> CB_CALL_DATA.NEW_INSERT = *position where the insert cursor will be moved*
> CB_CALL_DATA.START_POS=*start position of the text change*
> CB_CALL_DATA.END_POS =*end position of the text change*
> CB_CALL_DATA.TEXT.PTR=*text to be inserted*
> CB_CALL_DATA.TEXT.LENGTH=*length of text to be inserted*
> CB_CALL_DATA.TEXT.FORMAT=*text format:* FMT8BIT, FMT16BIT

34.38 The ToggleButton Widget and Gadget

A ToggleButton is used as a button that is either set or unset, e.g., a checkbox. The ToggleButton has both a widget and gadget class.

Table 34-35. ToggleButton Widget and Gadget Resources

Resource Name	Default	Other Values
fillOnSelect	*[dynamic]*	true, false
indicatorOn	true	false
indicatorSize	*[dynamic]*	*[positive integer]*
indicatorType	*[dynamic]*	N_OF_MANY, ONE_OF_MANY
selectColor	*[dynamic]*	*[color]*
selectInsensitive-Pixmap	UNSPECIFIED_PIXMAP	*[path to a pixmap file]*
selectPixmap	UNSPECIFIED_PIXMAP	*[path to a pixmap file]*
set	false	true
spacing	4	*[positive integer]*
visibleWhenOff	*[dynamic]*	true, false

Resource Descriptions

fillOnSelect
> When this resource is `true`, the indicator is filled with the color given in the `selectColor` resource. Otherwise, the state of the ToggleButton is shown by the top and bottom shadow colors.

indicatorOn
> When `true`, the indicator is displayed and used to show the state of the ToggleButton. When `false`, the indicator is not used in the ToggleButton and the border shadow is used to show the state.

indicatorSize
> The size of the indicator.

indicatorType
> When set to `N_OF_MANY` the indicator is a square. When set to `ONE_OF_MANY` the indicator is a diamond.

selectColor
> This color is used to fill the interior of the indicator when the `fillOnSelect` resource is `true` and the ToggleButton is set.

selectInsensitivePixmap
> This is valid only when the `labelType` is `PIXMAP`. It specifies a pixmap label that is displayed when the ToggleButton is selected and insensitive.

selectPixmap
> This pixmap is used to fill the interior of the indicator when the `fillOnSelect` resource is `true` and the ToggleButton is set.

set
> The state of the ToggleButton.

spacing
> The space between the indicator and the label.

visibleWhenOff
> Determines if the indicator is visible when the ToggleButton is not set. When `visibleWhenOff` is `true`, the indicator is visible in both states; otherwise, the indicator is visible only when the ToggleButton is set.

Other Widget Resources

From Primitive:
> bottomShadowColor, highlightPixmap, highlightThickness, navigationType, shadowThickness, bottomShadowPixmap, foreground, helpCallback, highlightColor, highlightOnEnter,

```
        topShadowColor,  topShadowPixmap,  traversalOn,  unitType,
        userData.
```

From Core:
```
        accelerators,  ancestorSensitive,  background,  background-
        Pixmap,  borderColor,  borderPixmap,  borderWidth,  colormap,
        depth,   destroyCallback,   height,   initialResourcesPer-
        sistent,  mappedWhenManaged,  screen,  sensitive,  transla-
        tions, width, x, y.
```

Other Gadget Resources

From Gadget:
```
        helpCallback,  highlightOnEnter,  highlightThickness,  navi-
        gationType,  shadowThickness,  traversalOn,  unitType,  user-
        Data.
```

From RectObj (see information on equivalent resources under Core):
```
        ancestorSensitive,  borderWidth,  height,  sensitive,  width,
        x, y.
```

From Object:
```
        destroyCallback.
```

Callbacks

armCallback
>   Invoked when the BSelect button (usually the leftmost mouse button) is
>   pressed in the ToggleButton. Call data:
>   CB_CALL_DATA.REASON=CR_ARM
>   CB_CALL_DATA.EVENT=*X event*
>   CB_CALL_DATA.SET = *selection state of the button*

disarmCallback
>   Invoked when the BSelect button (usually the leftmost mouse button) is
>   released. Call data:
>   CB_CALL_DATA.REASON=CR_DISARM
>   CB_CALL_DATA.EVENT=*X event*
>   CB_CALL_DATA.SET = *selection state of the button*

valueChangedCallback
>   Invoked when the value of the ToggleButton is changed. Call data:
>   CB_CALL_DATA.REASON=CR_VALUE_CHANGED
>   CB_CALL_DATA.EVENT=*X event*
>   CB_CALL_DATA.SET = *selection state of the button*

A *KornShell Math Operators*

Expression Evaluation

Mathematical expressions can appear in several different places:

- Array subscripts: A[*expression*]
- Assignment to integer or floating-point variables: float x; x=3.2*4.5
- Assignment using the let statment: let result=x*32.4+y*12.7
- The arithmetic command: ((*expression*))
- Arithmetic substitution: print $((*expression*))

All mathematical expressions are evaluated using double-precision floating-point math. Constants can be expressed using ANSI standard floating-point format as in the C language, including the use of scientific notation exponents:

$$[+|-] digits [. digits] [E[+|-] digits]$$

Many of the C language math library functions are supported by KornShell arithmetic evaluation. Table A-1 summarizes these functions. For complete details see manual pages for the C language math library. It is important to note that these functions are only available within mathematical evaluation, they are not functions in the sense of a Shell function. Also, there is no way to create new built-in math functions in this release of KornShell.

Table A-2 summarizes all the operators allowed in an expression. In this table precedence is indicated by a number where lower numbers bind tighter than higher numbers. For example, for the expression:

```
(( x = 2 + 3 * 4 ))
```

x evaluates to 14 because the * operator has a precedence of 1 and the + operator has a precedence of 2, thus the * operator evaluates first.

Table A-1. KornShell Math Functions

Function	Operation
abs(*expr*)	Absolute value
acos(*expr*)	Arc cosine
asin(*expr*)	Arc sine
atan(*expr*)	Arc tangent
cos(*expr*)	Cosine
cosh(*expr*)	Hyperbolic cosine
exp(*expr*)	Exponentiation
int(*expr*)	Integer
log(*expr*)	Logarithm
sin(*expr*)	Sine
sinh(*expr*)	Hyperbolic sine
sqrt(*expr*)	Square root
tan(*expr*)	Tangent
tanh(*expr*)	Hyperbolic tangent

Table A-2. KornShell Math Operators

Operator	Explanation	Precedence
var++	Increment, return var	0
++*var*	Increment, return var+1	0
var--	Decrement, return var	0
--*var*	Decrement, return var−1	0
! *expr*	Logical not	0
~ *expr*	Bitwise not	0
expr * *expr*	Multiplication	1
expr / *expr*	Division	1
expr % *expr*	Modulo	1

Table A-2. KornShell Math Operators (continued)

Operator	Explanation	Precedence
expr + *expr*	Addition	2
expr - *expr*	Subtraction	2
expr << *expr*	Left shift	3
expr >> *expr*	Right shift	3
expr < *expr*	Less than	4
expr > *expr*	Greater than	4
expr >= *expr*	Greater than or equal	4
expr <= *expr*	Less than or equal	4
expr == *expr*	Equal	5
expr != *expr*	Not equal	5
expr & *expr*	Logical and	6
expr ^ *expr*	Bitwise exclusive or	7
expr | *expr*	Bitwise or	8
expr && *expr*	Logical and	9
expr || *expr*	Logical or	10
expr ? *expr* : *expr*	Ternary test	11
var = *expr*	Assignment	12
var += *expr*	Increment assignment	12
var -= *expr*	Decrement assignment	12
var *= *expr*	Multiplication assignment	12
var /= *expr*	Division assignment	12
var %= *expr*	Modulo assignment	12
var >>= *expr*	Right-shift assignment	12
var <<= *expr*	Left-shift assignment	12
var &= *expr*	Bitwise and assignment	12
var ^= *expr*	Bitwise exclusive or assignment	12
var |= *expr*	Bitwise or assignment	12
expr1 , *expr2*	Sequential evaluation, evaluates both expressions, returns *expr2*	13

B *Standard X Options*

XtInitialize (and XUinitialize) can interpret a number of standard command arguments. Normally, it is called as follows in a dtksh script:

```
XtInitialize variable app-name app-class "$@"
```

or, using the XU library:

```
XUinitialize variable app-class "$@"
```

The final argument expands to whatever options were passed to the script on the command line. These can consist of both standard X arguments or arguments to be interpreted by the application. X will interpret any arguments it recognizes, and will place any remaining arguments in the array variable DTKSH_ARGV so that the script can interpret its own arguments.

Table B-1 lists all the standard X options interpreted by XtInitialize (or XUintialize).

Table B-1. Standard X Options

Option	Effect
-bg *color* -background *color*	Sets the default background to *color*.
-bd *color*	Sets the default border color to *color*.
-bw *number* -borderwidth *number*	Sets the default border width to *number* pixels.

Table B-1. Standard X Options (continued)

Option	Effect
-display *server-address*	Sets the display device for the application to *server-address*. This can be a host name or IP address followed by a colon, display number, a period, and the screen number. For example mymachine:0.0 would display the application on a machine whose network name is mymachine on display number 0 and screen number 0.
-fg *color* -foreground *color*	Sets the default foreground color to *color*.
-fn *fontname* -font *fontname*	Sets the default font to *fontname*.
-geometry *geometry-spec*	Sets the initial size and placement of the application's main window. The *geometry-spec* is of the form: [*width* x *height*][[+-]*x-coord*[+-]*y-coord*]. For example 200x400+0+0 would make the initialize size of the application 200 pixels wide and 400 pixels high, and would place the window in the upper left corner of the display screen. For more examples, see *Geometry* on page 162.
-iconic	The application will initially appear as an icon.
-reverse -rv	The application will be reverse video.
+rv	The application will not be reverse video.
-selectionTimeout *timeout*	Set the timeout period for selection communications. You should not usually use this option.
-synchronous	Turn on synchronous debug mode. This is rarely useful for dtksh programs.

Table B-1. Standard X Options (continued)

Option	Effect
`+synchronous`	Turn off synchronous debug mode.
`-title` *title-string*	Set the title of the application. The *title-string* will appear in the title bar at the top of the main application window.
`-xrm` *resource-spec*	This allows you to set any arbitrary resource default for the application. The *resource-string* is a string that uses resource file notation to specify the widget or class and value. For example, this option is identical to setting the background color to blue using the `-bg` option: `-xrm '*background:blue'`

C *Event Data Structures*

X event structures are passed to dtksh functions in the following ways:

- The variable CB_CALL_DATA.EVENT in callback functions
- The variable TRANSLATION_EVENT in translation handler functions
- The variable EH_EVENT for event handler functions.

In each case, the variable in question is set to the hexadecimal address of the X event structure. (This is useful if you wish to pass the address to an attached C function.) Subfields are defined for various components of the event structure that are useful in dtksh applications. The names of the subfields are the same as they are in the C langauge XEvent structure, but all uppercase.

The CDE 1.0 version of dtksh does not provide every single union member of the event structure. It provides the following members: XANY, XBUTTON, XEXPOSE, XNOEXPOSE, XGRAPHICSEXPOSE, XKEY, XMOTION. Of the union members that dtksh does support, all data contained in the member are provided in subfields to the hierarchical variables. The fields provided by dtksh are listed in Tables C-1 through C-7. XANY fields are always available. Other subfields depend on the value of the XANY.TYPE subfield. For example, this code prints the type of event, and is legal in all cases:

```
print ${CB_CALL_DATA.EVENT.XANY.TYPE}
```

If the value of the TYPE field is XBUTTON, then the XBUTTON subfields are available, if it is XEXPOSE, then the XEXPOSE subfields are allowed, etc. This appendix provides one table for each setting of the TYPE subfield.

In these tables, the string *BASE* will be used to denote the X event base variable, which is one of CB_CALL_DATA.EVENT, TRANSLATION_EVENT, or EH_EVENT.

Table C-1. X Event Subfields Always Available

Variable	Use
BASE.XANY.TYPE	The type of event.
BASE.XANY.SERIAL	The serial number of the event (rarely useful in dtksh).
BASE.XANY.SEND_EVENT	This is a boolean value (true or false).
BASE.XANY.DISPLAY	A hexadecimal value, this is the address of the display structure with which the event is associated.
BASE.XANY.WINDOW	The window id associated with the event.

Table C-2. X Event Subfields When TYPE = XBUTTON

Variable	Use
BASE.XBUTTON.TYPE	The type of event.
BASE.XBUTTON.SERIAL	The serial number of the event (rarely useful in dtksh).
BASE.XBUTTON.SEND_EVENT	This is a boolean value (true or false).
BASE.XBUTTON.DISPLAY	A hexadecimal value, this is the address of the display structure with which the event is associated.
BASE.XBUTTON.WINDOW	The window id associated with the event.
BASE.XBUTTON.ROOT	The root window involved in the event.
BASE.XBUTTON.SUBWINDOW	The subwindow id involved in the event.
BASE.XBUTTON.TIME	The time of the button event.
BASE.XBUTTON.X *BASE*.XBUTTON.Y	The x and y of the mouse pointer relative to the widget in which the pointer was located when the event occurred.

Table C-2. X Event Subfields When TYPE = XBUTTON (continued)

Variable	Use
BASE.XBUTTON.XROOT *BASE*.XBUTTON.YROOT	The x and y coordinates of the mouse pointer relative to the root window when the event occurred.
BASE.XBUTTON.STATE	A list of modifier keys that was depressed at the time the button was clicked. The modifiers are separated by a pipe symbol, such as Ctrl|Shift.
BASE.XBUTTON.BUTTON	The button number: 1, 2, or 3.
BASE.XBUTTON.SAME_SCREEN	A boolean value.

Table C-3. X Event Subfields When TYPE = XEXPOSE

Variable	Use
BASE.XEXPOSE.TYPE	The type of event.
BASE.XEXPOSE.SERIAL	The serial number of the event (rarely useful in dtksh).
BASE.XEXPOSE.SEND_EVENT	This is a boolean value (true or false).
BASE.XANY.DISPLAY	A hexadecimal value, this is the address of the display structure with which the event is associated.
BASE.XANY.WINDOW	The window id associated with the event.
BASE.XEXPOSE.ROOT	The root window involved in the event.
BASE.XEXPOSE.SUBWINDOW	The subwindow id involved in the event.
BASE.XEXPOSE.TIME	The time of the button event.
BASE.XEXPOSE.X *BASE*.XEXPOSE.Y	The x and y coordinate of the upper left corner of the exposure.

Table C-3. X Event Subfields When TYPE = XEXPOSE (continued)

Variable	Use
BASE.XEXPOSE.WIDTH BASE.XEXPOSE.HEIGHT	The width and height of the exposed area.
BASE.XEXPOSE.COUNT	An integer, the number of exposures.

Table C-4. X Event Subfields When TYPE = XGRAPHICSEXPOSE

Variable	Use
BASE.XGRAPHICSEXPOSE.TYPE	The type of event.
BASE.XGRAPHICSEXPOSE.SERIAL	The serial number of the event (rarely useful in dtksh).
BASE.XGRAPHICSEXPOSE.SEND_EVENT	This is a boolean value (true or false).
BASE.XGRAPHICSEXPOSE.DISPLAY	A hexadecimal value, this is the address of the display structure with which the event is associated.
BASE.XGRAPHICSEXPOSE.DRAWABLE	The window id or pixmap id associated with the event.
BASE.XGRAPHICSEXPOSE.X BASE.XGRAPHICSEXPOSE.Y	The x and y coordinate of the upper left corner of the exposure.
BASE.XGRAPHICSEXPOSE.WIDTH BASE.XGRAPHICSEXPOSE.HEIGHT	The width and height of the exposed area.
BASE.XGRAPHICSEXPOSE.COUNT	An integer, the number of exposures.
BASE.XGRAPHICSEXPOSE.MAJOR	The x protocol major number of the event
BASE.XGRAPHICSEXPOSE.MINOR	The x protocol minor number of the event.

Table C-5. X Event Subfields When TYPE = XNOEXPOSE

Variable	Use
BASE.XNOEXPOSE.TYPE	The type of event.
BASE.XNOEXPOSE.SERIAL	The serial number of the event (rarely useful in dtksh).
BASE.XNOEXPOSE.SEND_EVENT	This is a boolean value (true or false).
BASE.XNOEXPOSE.DISPLAY	A hexadecimal value, this is the address of the display structure with which the event is associated.
BASE.XNOEXPOSE.DRAWABLE	The window id or pixmap id associated with the event.
BASE.XNOEXPOSE.MAJOR_CODE *BASE*.XNOEXPOSE.MINOR_CODE	The major and minor operation codes of the x protocol involved in the event.

Table C-6. X Event Subfields When TYPE = XKEY

Variable	Use
BASE.XKEY.TYPE	The type of event.
BASE.XKEY.SERIAL	The serial number of the event (rarely useful in dtksh).
BASE.XKEY.SEND_EVENT	This is a boolean value (true or false).
BASE.XKEY.DISPLAY	A hexadecimal value, this is the address of the display structure with which the event is associated.
BASE.XKEY.WINDOW	The window id associated with the event.
BASE.XKEY.ROOT	The root window involved in the event.
BASE.XKEY.SUBWINDOW	The subwindow id involved in the event.
BASE.XKEY.TIME	The time of the button event.

Table C-6. X Event Subfields When TYPE = XKEY (continued)

Variable	Use
BASE.XKEY.X *BASE*.XKEY.Y	The x and y coordinate of the mouse pointer relative to the widget during the event.
BASE.XKEY.XROOT *BASE*.XKEY.YROOT	The x and y coordinate of the mouse pointer relative to the root window.
BASE.XKEY.STATE	A pipe-separated list of modifier keys held down at the same time as the event occurred.
BASE.XKEY.KEYCODE	An integer, the key pressed (may be multibyte for international applications).
BASE.XKEY.SAME_SCREEN	A boolean value.

Table C-7. X Event Subfields When TYPE = XMOTION

Variable	Use
BASE.XMOTION.TYPE	The type of event.
BASE.XMOTION.SERIAL	The serial number of the event (rarely useful in dtksh).
BASE.XMOTION.SEND_EVENT	This is a boolean value (true or false).
BASE.XMOTION.DISPLAY	A hexadecimal value, this is the address of the display structure with which the event is associated.
BASE.XANY.WINDOW	The window id associated with the event.
BASE.XMOTION.ROOT	The root window involved in the event.
BASE.XMOTION.SUBWINDOW	The subwindow id involved in the event.
BASE.XMOTION.TIME	The time of the button event.

Table C-7. X Event Subfields When TYPE = XMOTION (continued)

Variable	Use
BASE.XMOTION.X *BASE*.XMOTION.Y	The x and y coordinate of the mouse pointer relative to the widget during the event.
BASE.XMOTION.XROOT *BASE*.XMOTION.YROOT	The x and y coordinate of the mouse pointer relative to the root window.
BASE.XMOTION.STATE	A pipe-separated list of modifier keys held down at the same time as the event occurred.
BASE.XMOTION.IS_HINT	A boolean value.
BASE.XMOTION.SAME_SCREEN	A boolean value.

D ToolTalk Defined Values

The ToolTalk programming interfaces use several sets of defined values. Various ToolTalk commands use or return these values. Table D-1 lists values of scope parameters, which are used to define the range of clients that could receive a message. Table D-2 is a list of all the possible return values stored in status variable arguments to ToolTalk commands. Table D-3 lists the possible values of the operation argument that several commands use to specify the operation that is being performed.

For more information on ToolTalk, see [CDE ToolTalk 1995].

Table D-1. ToolTalk Scope Values

TT_BOTH

TT_FILE

TT_FILE_IN_SESSION

TT_SESSION

TT_SCOPE_NONE

Table D-2. ToolTalk Status Codes

TT_DESKTOP	TT_DESKTOP_EACCES	TT_DESKTOP_EAGAIN
TT_DESKTOP_EALREADY	TT_DESKTOP_ECANCELED	TT_DESKTOP_EDEADLK
TT_DESKTOP_EEXIST	TT_DESKTOP_EFAULT	TT_DESKTOP_EFBIG
TT_DESKTOP_EINTR	TT_DESKTOP_EINVAL	TT_DESKTOP_EIO
TT_DESKTOP_EISDIR	TT_DESKTOP_EMFILE	TT_DESKTOP_EMLINK
TT_DESKTOP_ENFILE	TT_DESKTOP_ENODATA	TT_DESKTOP_ENODEV
TT_DESKTOP_ENOENT	TT_DESKTOP_ENOMEM	TT_DESKTOP_ENOMSG
TT_DESKTOP_ENOSPC	TT_DESKTOP_ENOTDIR	TT_DESKTOP_ENOTEMPTY
TT_DESKTOP_ENOTSUP	TT_DESKTOP_EPERM	TT_DESKTOP_EPIPE
TT_DESKTOP_EPROTO	TT_DESKTOP_EROFS	TT_DESKTOP_ETIMEDOUT
TT_DESKTOP_ETXTBSY	TT_DESKTOP_UNMODIFIED	TT_ERR_ACCESS
TT_ERR_ADDRESS	TT_ERR_APPFIRST	TT_ERR_CATEGORY
TT_ERR_CLASS	TT_ERR_DBAVAIL	TT_ERR_DBCONSIST
TT_ERR_DBEXIST	TT_ERR_DBFULL	TT_ERR_DBUPDATE
TT_ERR_DISPOSITION	TT_ERR_FILE	TT_ERR_INTERNAL
TT_ERR_INVALID	TT_ERR_LAST	TT_ERR_MODE
TT_ERR_NETFILE	TT_ERR_NOMEM	TT_ERR_NOMP
TT_ERR_NOTHANDLER	TT_ERR_NO_MATCH	TT_ERR_NO_VALUE
TT_ERR_NUM	TT_ERR_OBJID	TT_ERR_OP
TT_ERR_OTYPE	TT_ERR_OVERFLOW	TT_ERR_PATH
TT_ERR_POINTER	TT_ERR_PROCID	TT_ERR_PROPLEN
TT_ERR_PROPNAME	TT_ERR_PTYPE	TT_ERR_PTYPE_START
TT_ERR_READONLY	TT_ERR_SCOPE	TT_ERR_SESSION
TT_ERR_SLOTNAME	TT_ERR_STATE	TT_ERR_UNIMP
TT_ERR_VTYPE	TT_ERR_XDR	TT_MEDIA_ERR_FORMAT
TT_MEDIA_ERR_SIZE	TT_OK	TT_STATUS_LAST
TT_WRN_APPFIRST	TT_WRN_LAST	TT_WRN_NOTFOUND
TT_WRN_SAME_OBJID	TT_WRN_STALE_OBJID	TT_WRN_START_MESSAGE
TT_WRN_STOPPED		

Table D-3. ToolTalk Desktop Operation Codes

TTDT_CREATED	TTDT_DELETED	TTDT_DO_COMMAND
TTDT_GET_ENVIRONMENT	TTDT_GET_GEOMETRY	TTDT_GET_ICONIFIED
TTDT_GET_LOCALE	TTDT_GET_MAPPED	TTDT_GET_MODIFIED
TTDT_GET_SITUATION	TTDT_GET_STATUS	TTDT_GET_SYSINFO
TTDT_GET_XINFO	TTDT_LOWER	TTDT_MODIFIED
TTDT_MOVED	TTDT_OP_LAST	TTDT_OP_NONE
TTDT_PAUSE	TTDT_QUIT	TTDT_RAISE
TTDT_RESUME	TTDT_REVERT	TTDT_REVERTED
TTDT_SAVE	TTDT_SAVED	TTDT_SET_ENVIRONMENT
TTDT_SET_GEOMETRY	TTDT_SET_ICONIFIED	TTDT_SET_LOCALE
TTDT_SET_MAPPED	TTDT_SET_SITUATION	TTDT_SET_XINFO
TTDT_SIGNAL	TTDT_STARTED	TTDT_STATUS
TTDT_STOPPED	TTME_ABSTRACT	TTME_COMPOSE
TTME_DEPOSIT	TTME_DISPLAY	TTME_EDIT
TTME_INTERPRET	TTME_MAIL	TTME_PRINT
TTME_TRANSLATE		

Bibliography

Throughout this book, references to other works that are listed in this bibiography are composed of the authors' last names and the year of publication enclosed in brackets. In the case of CDE reference books, there are no authors (the authors are simply the CDE development companies), and all the CDE reference books were initially published in the same year (1994). Thus, I have taken the liberty of making up descriptive names for these, such as [CDE Help Guide 1994].

To avoid confusion, I include the bracket-enclosed reference titles used in the main text of this book for all works listed here, and have alphabetized the listings according to these reference titles.

[Bolsky and Korn 1995]   Bolsky, Morris I., and Korn, David G., 1995. *The New KornShell Command and Programming Language*. Prentice Hall, Englewood Cliffs, NJ. ISBN: 0-13-516972-0

[CDE Dtksh Guide 1995]   Hewlett-Packard Company, International Business Machines Corp., Novell, Inc., and Sun Microsystems, Inc., 1995. *Common Desktop Environment: Dtksh User's Guide*.

[CDE Help Guide 1995]   Hewlett-Packard Company, International Business Machines Corp., Novell, Inc., and Sun Microsystems, Inc., 1995. *The CDE Help System Author's and Programmer's Guide*.

[CDE Internationalization 1995]   Hewlett-Packard Company, International Business Machines Corp., Novell, Inc., and Sun Microsystems, Inc., 1995. *Common Desktop Environment: Internationalization Programmer's Guide*.

[CDE ToolTalk 1995]   Hewlett-Packard Company, International Business Machines Corp., Novell, Inc., and Sun Microsystems, Inc., 1995. *Common Desktop Environment: Getting Started Using ToolTalk Messaging*.

[Ferguson and Brennen 1993]   Ferguson, Paula M., and Brennen, David, 1993. *The Definitive Guides to the X Window System, Volume Six B, Motif Reference Manual for OSF/Motif Release 1.2*. O'Reilly & Associates, Sebastopol, CA. ISBN: 1-56592-038-4.

[Flanagan 1992]   Edited by Flanagan, David, 1992. *The Definitive Guides to the X Window System, Volume Five, X Toolkit Intrinsics Reference Manual*. O'Reilly & Associates, Sebastopol, CA. ISBN: 1-56592-007-4.

[Heller and Ferguson 1994]   Heller, Dan, and Ferguson, Paula M., 1994. *The Definitive Guides to the X Window System, Volume Six A, Motif Programming Manual for OSF/Motif Release 1.2*. O'Reilly & Associates, Sebastopol, CA. ISBN: 1-56592-016-3.

[McMinds 1992]   McMinds, Donald L., 1992. *Mastering OSF/Motif Widgets*. Addison-Wesley, Reading, MA. ISBN: 0-201-56342-8

[Nye and O'Reilly 1993]   Nye, Adrian, and O'Reilly, Tim, 1993 . *The Definitive Guides to the X Window System, Volume Four M, X Toolkit Intrinsics Programming Manual*. O'Reilly & Associates, Sebastopol, CA. ISBN: 1-56592-013-9.

[Nye (1) 1992]   Nye, Adrian, 1992. *The Definitive Guides to the X Window System, Volume One, Xlib Programming Manual*. O'Reilly & Associates, Sebastopol, CA. ISBN: 1-56592-002-3.

[Nye (2) 1992]   Nye, Adrian, 1992. *The Definitive Guides to the X Window System, Volume Two, Xlib Reference Manual*. O'Reilly & Associates, Sebastopol, CA. ISBN: 1-56592-006-6.

[Quercia and O'Reilly 1993]   Quercia, Valerie, and O'Reilly, Tim, 1993 . *The Definitive Guides to the X Window System, Volume Three M, X Window System User's Guide*. O'Reilly & Associates, Sebastopol, CA. ISBN: 1-56592-015-5.

Index

T